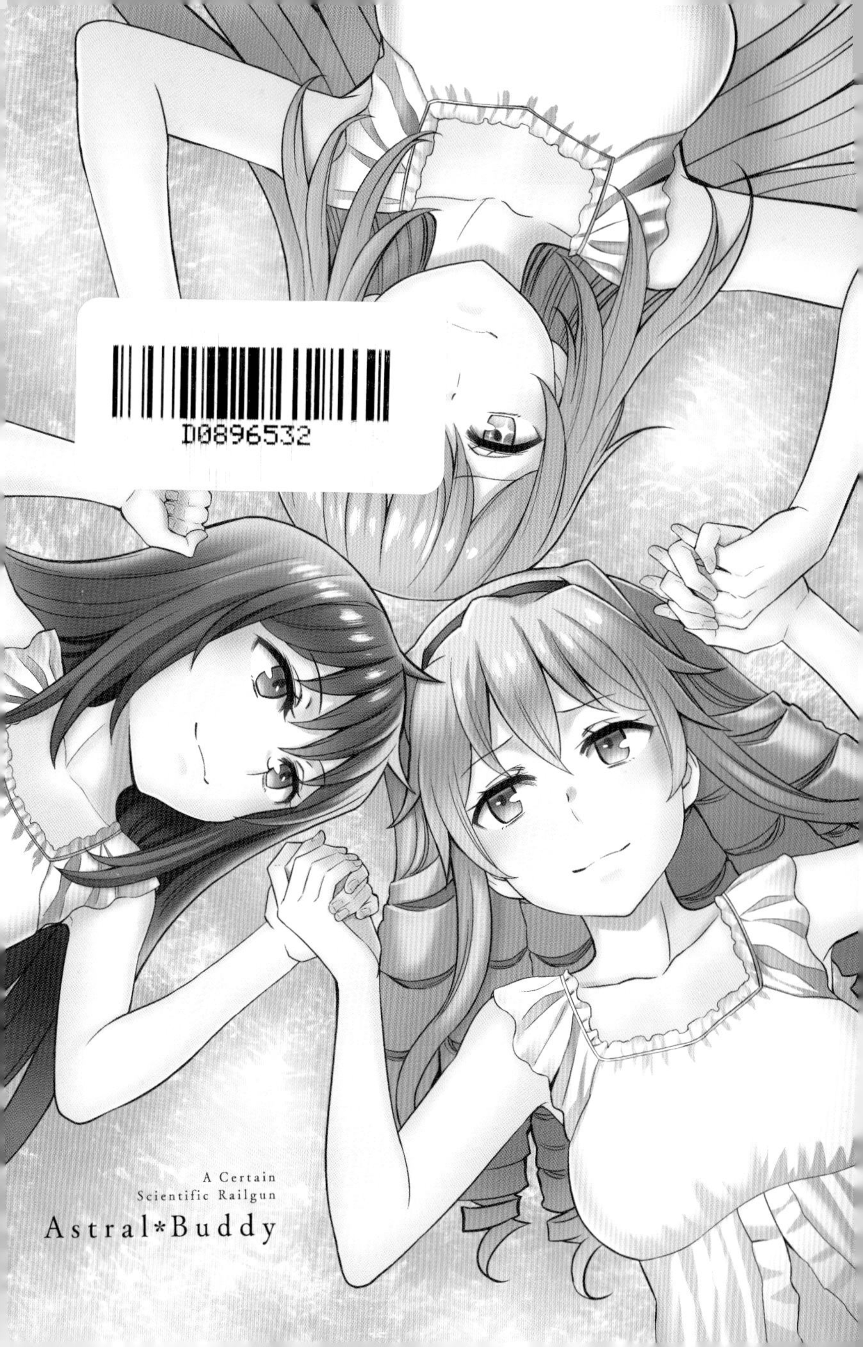
A Certain
Scientific Railgun
Astral*Buddy

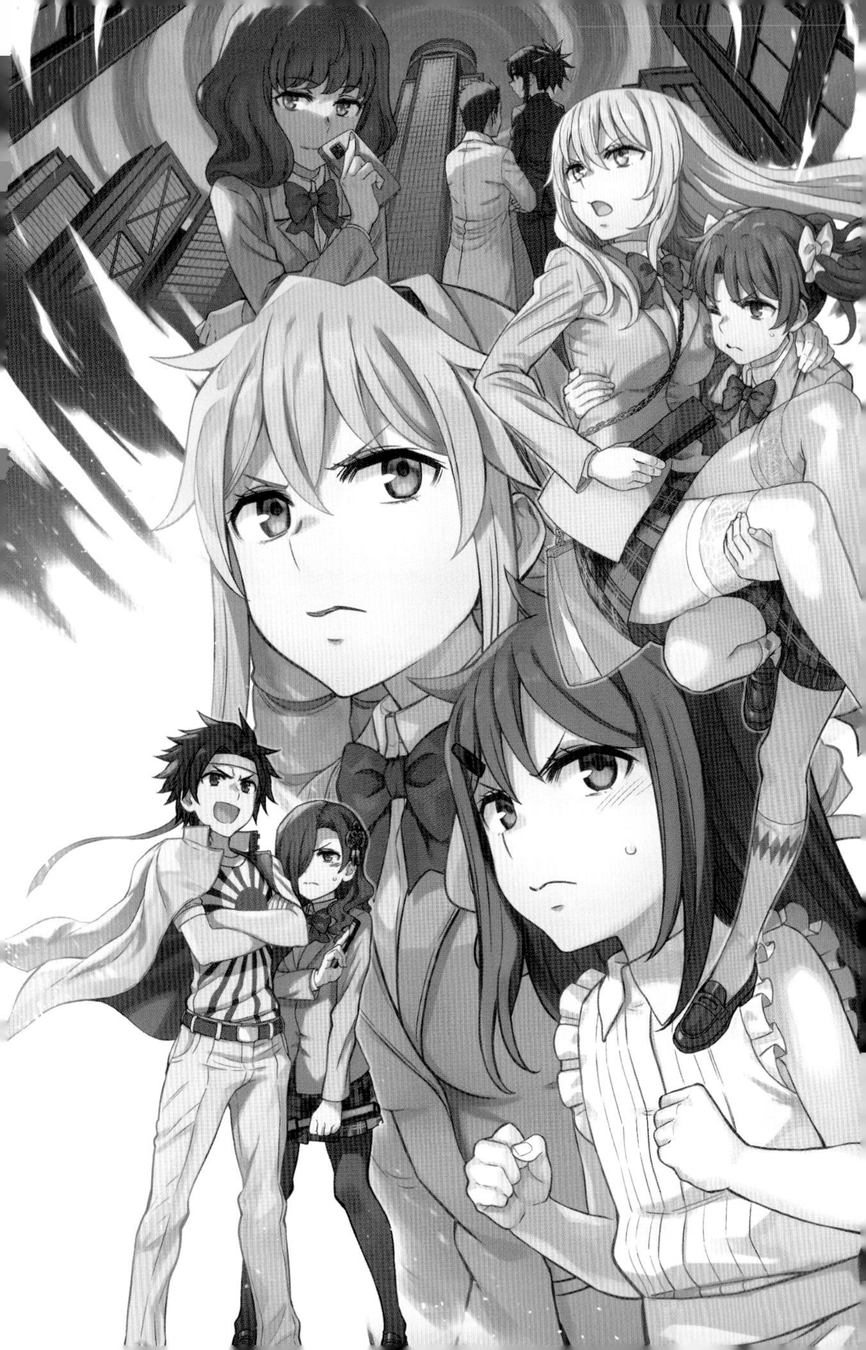

CHAPTER 20: Rarity

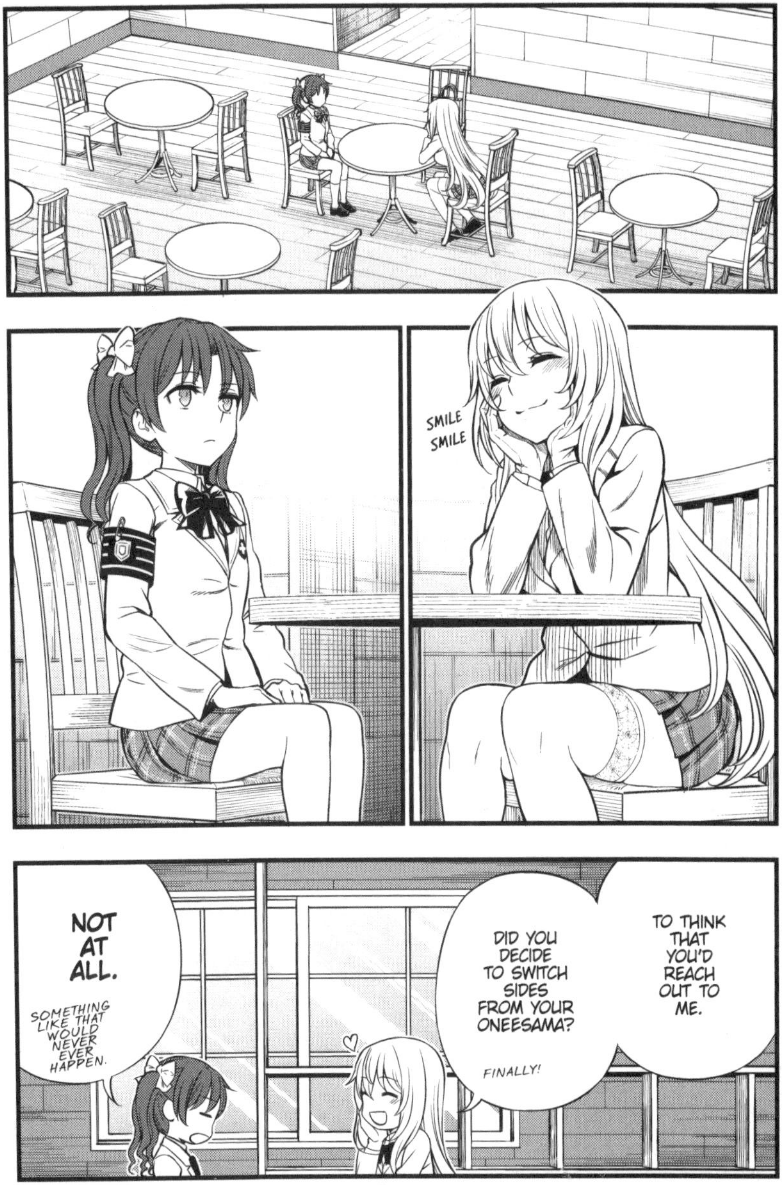
SMILE SMILE
TO THINK THAT YOU'D REACH OUT TO ME.
DID YOU DECIDE TO SWITCH SIDES FROM YOUR ONEESAMA?
FINALLY!
NOT AT ALL.
SOMETHING LIKE THAT WOULD NEVER EVER HAPPEN.

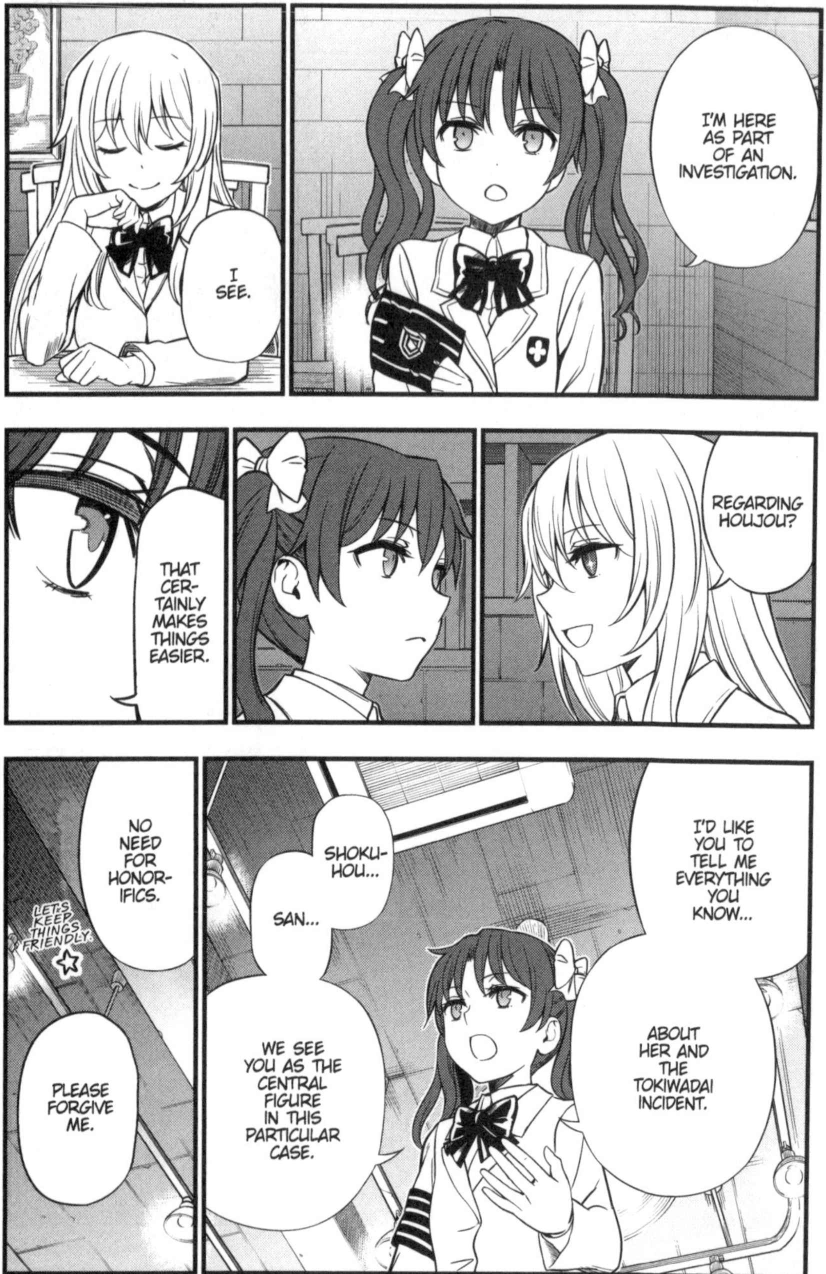
I'M HERE AS PART OF AN INVESTIGATION.
I SEE.
REGARDING HOUJOU?
THAT CER-TAINLY MAKES THINGS EASIER.
I'D LIKE YOU TO TELL ME EVERYTHING YOU KNOW...
ABOUT HER AND THE TOKIWADAI INCIDENT.
SHOKU-HOU...
SAN...
WE SEE YOU AS THE CENTRAL FIGURE IN THIS PARTICULAR CASE.
NO NEED FOR HONOR-IFICS.
LET'S KEEP THINGS FRIENDLY.
PLEASE FORGIVE ME.

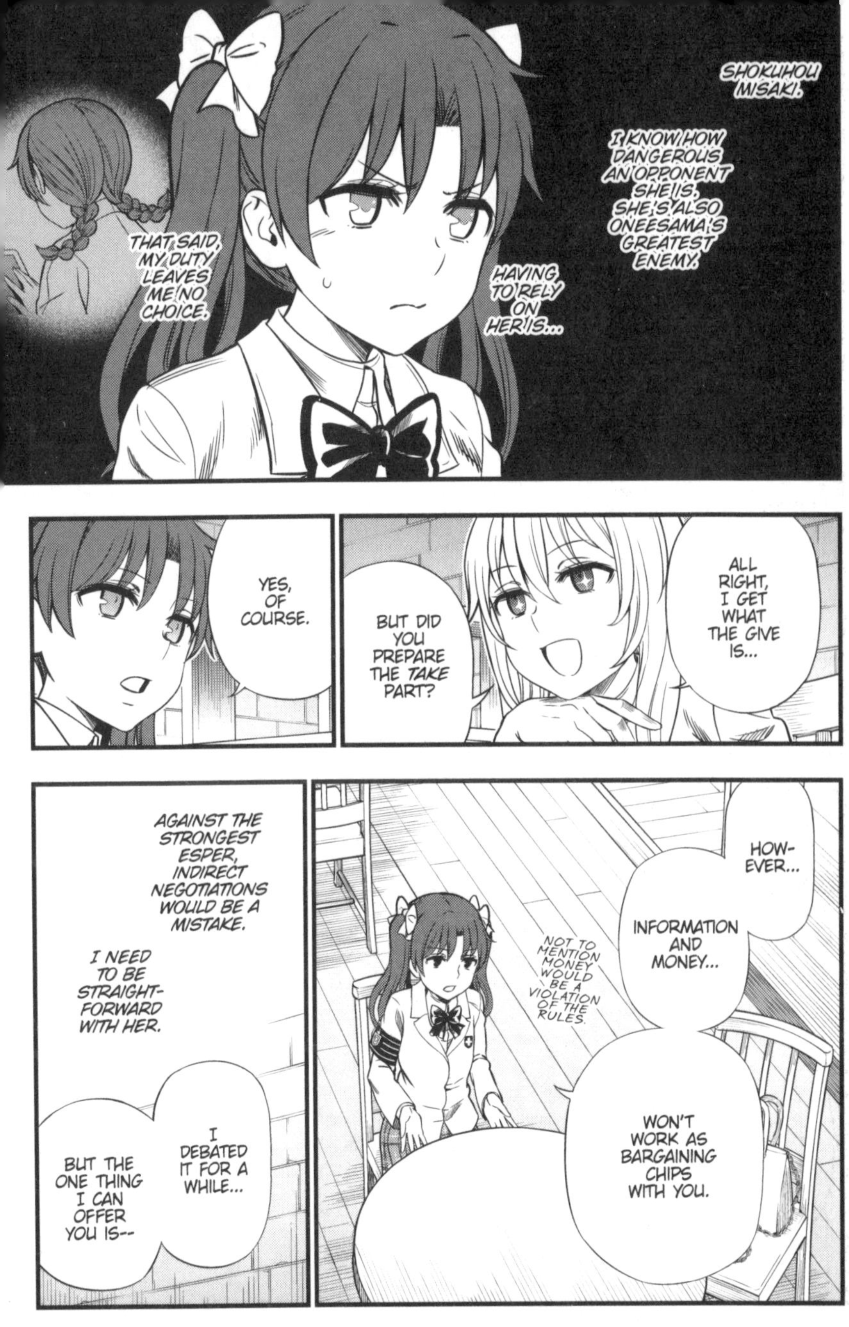
SHOKUHOU MISAKI.
I KNOW HOW DANGEROUS AN OPPONENT SHE IS. SHE'S ALSO ONEESAMA'S GREATEST ENEMY.
HAVING TO RELY ON HER IS...
THAT SAID, MY DUTY LEAVES ME NO CHOICE.
ALL RIGHT, I GET WHAT THE GIVE IS...
BUT DID YOU PREPARE THE *TAKE* PART?
YES, OF COURSE.
HOW-EVER...
INFORMATION AND MONEY...
NOT TO MENTION MONEY WOULD BE A VIOLATION OF THE RULES.
WON'T WORK AS BARGAINING CHIPS WITH YOU.
AGAINST THE STRONGEST ESPER, INDIRECT NEGOTIATIONS WOULD BE A MISTAKE.
I NEED TO BE STRAIGHT-FORWARD WITH HER.
I DEBATED IT FOR A WHILE...
BUT THE ONE THING I CAN OFFER YOU IS--

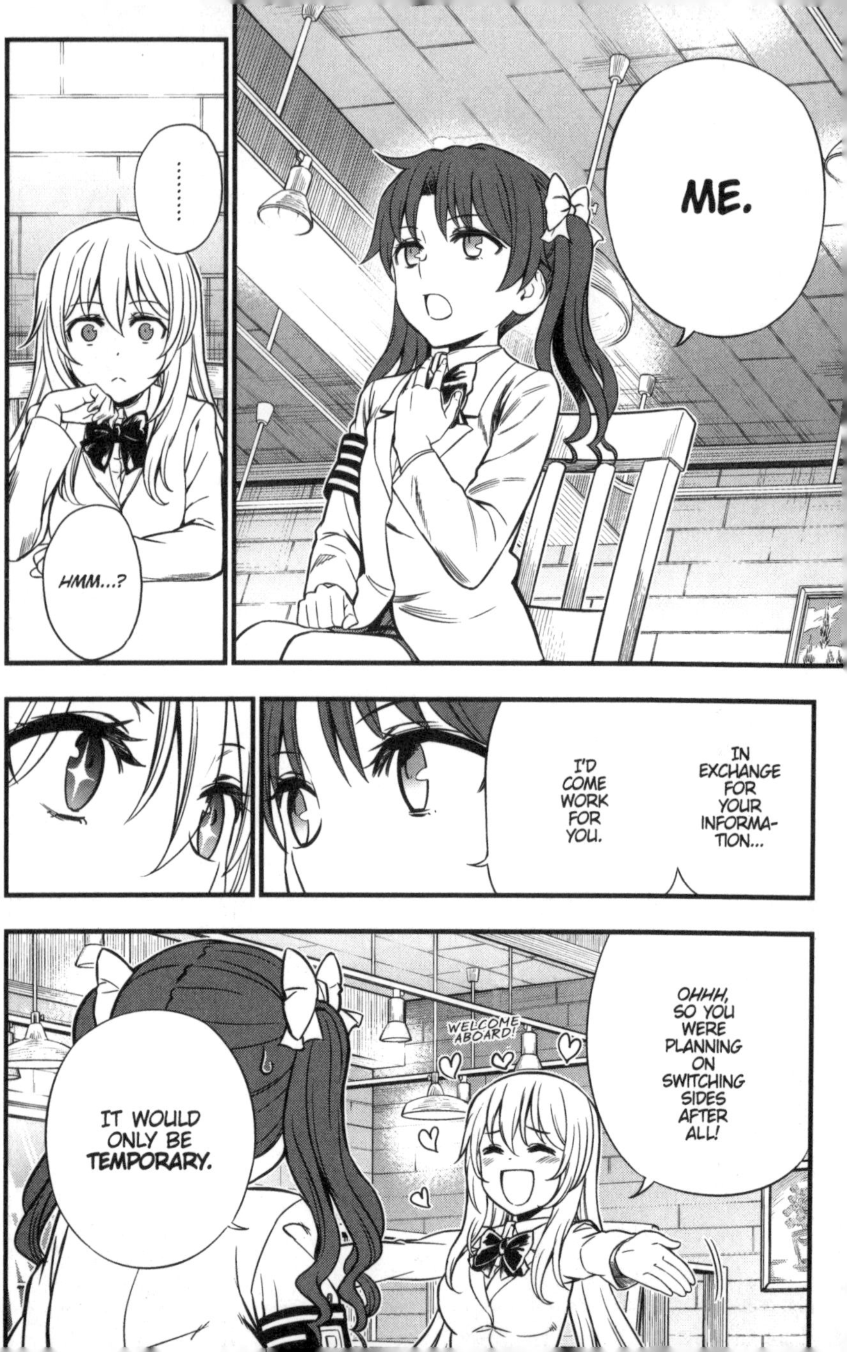
ME.
......
HMM...?
IN EXCHANGE FOR YOUR INFORMATION...
I'D COME WORK FOR YOU.
OHHH, SO YOU WERE PLANNING ON SWITCHING SIDES AFTER ALL!
WELCOME ABOARD!
IT WOULD ONLY BE TEMPORARY.

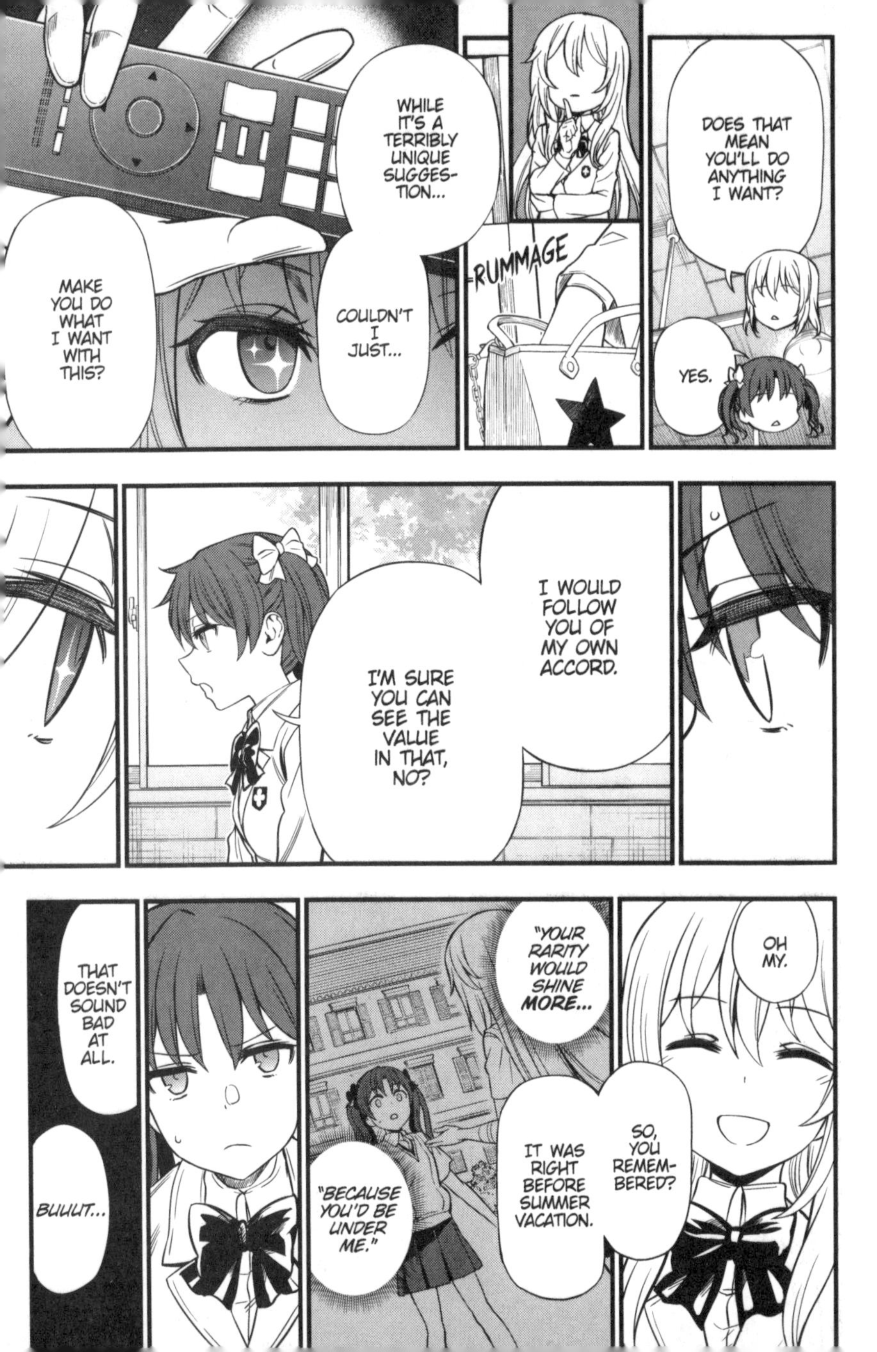
DOES THAT MEAN YOU'LL DO ANYTHING I WANT?
YES.
RUMMAGE
WHILE IT'S A TERRIBLY UNIQUE SUGGESTION...
COULDN'T I JUST...
MAKE YOU DO WHAT I WANT WITH THIS?
I WOULD FOLLOW YOU OF MY OWN ACCORD.
I'M SURE YOU CAN SEE THE VALUE IN THAT, NO?
OH MY.
SO, YOU REMEMBERED?
IT WAS RIGHT BEFORE SUMMER VACATION.
"YOUR RARITY WOULD SHINE MORE...
"BECAUSE YOU'D BE UNDER ME."
THAT DOESN'T SOUND BAD AT ALL.
BUUUT...

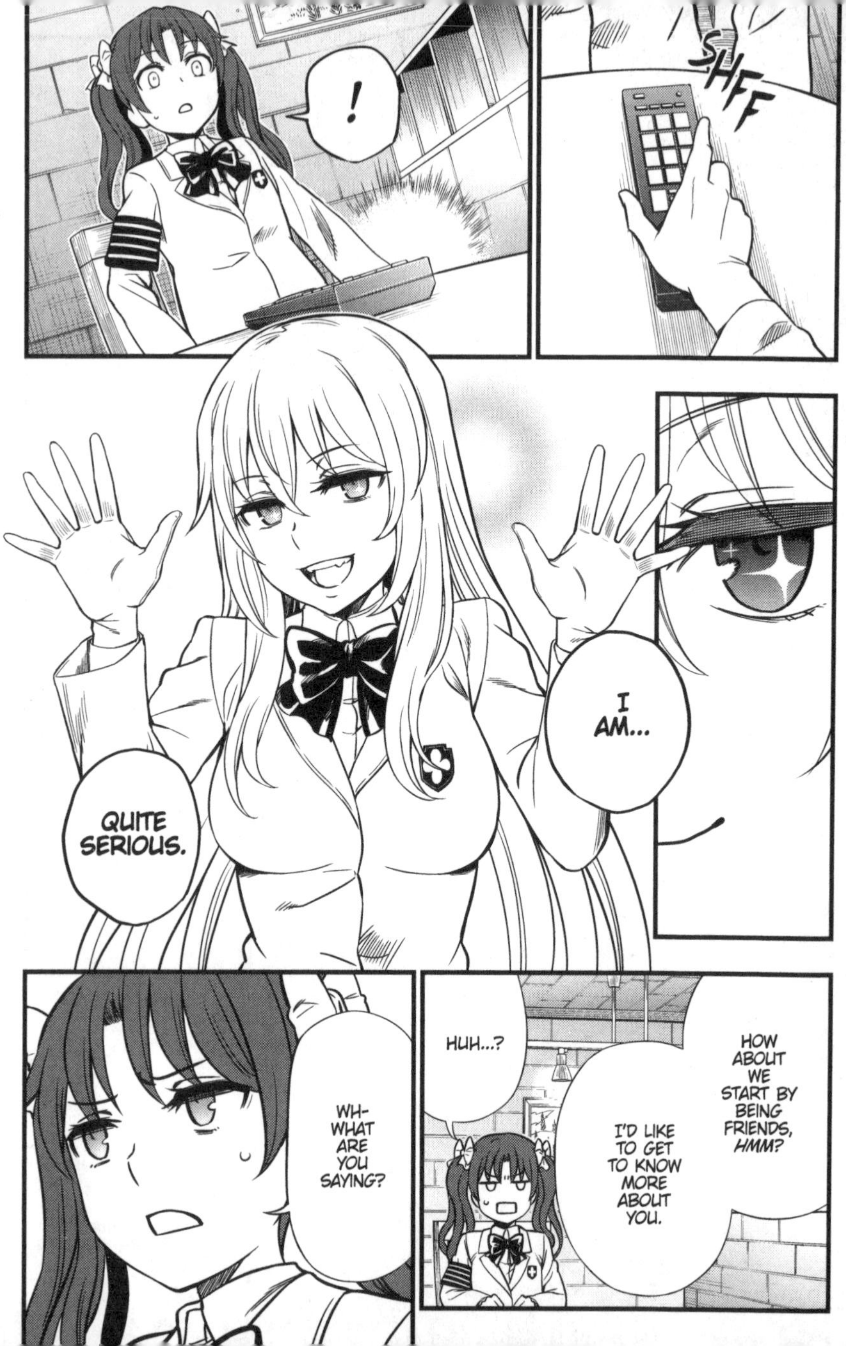
SHFF
!
I AM...
QUITE SERIOUS.
HOW ABOUT WE START BY BEING FRIENDS, *HMM?*
I'D LIKE TO GET TO KNOW MORE ABOUT YOU.
HUH...?
WH- WHAT ARE YOU SAYING?

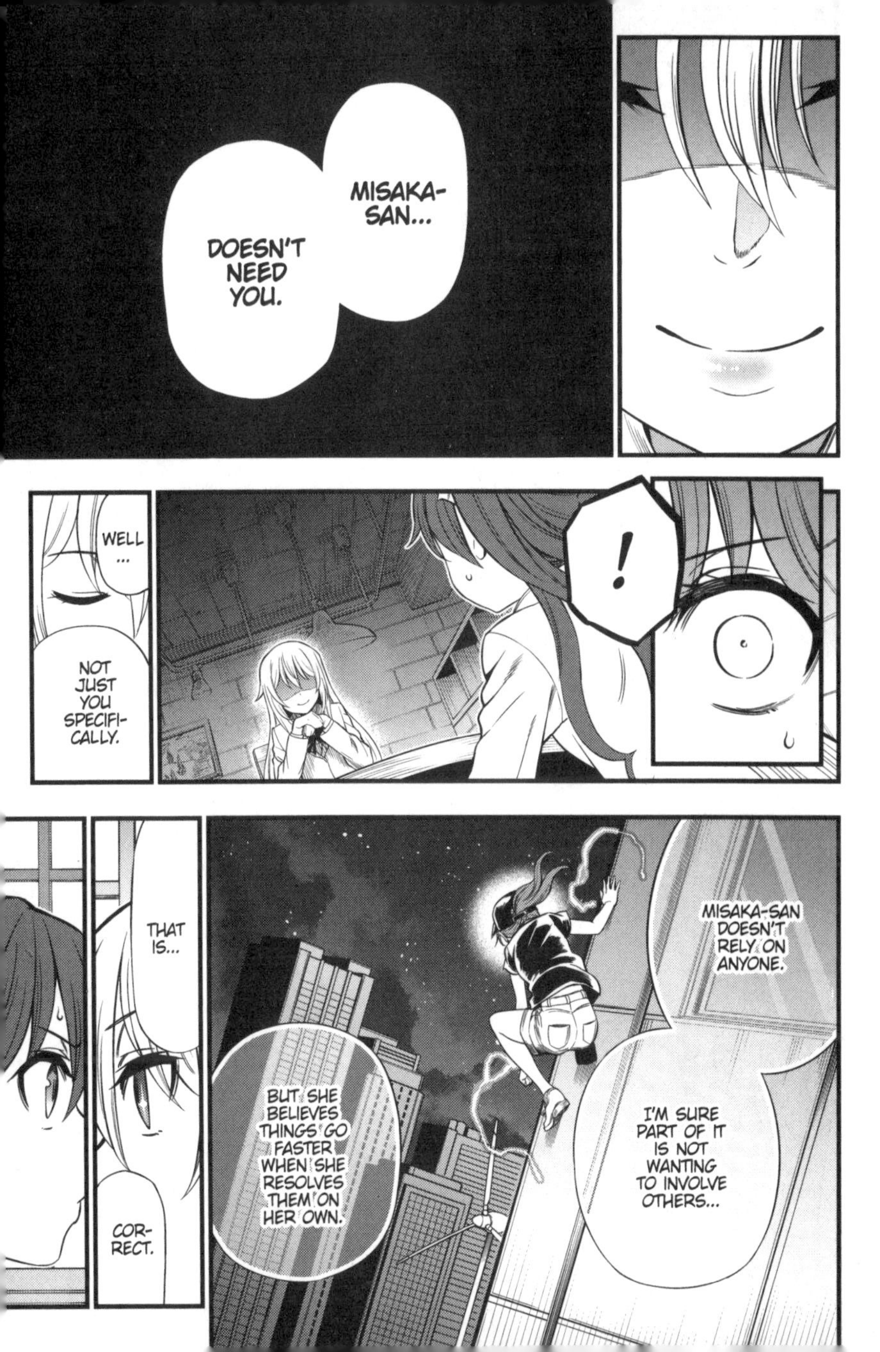
MISAKA-SAN...
DOESN'T NEED YOU.
!
WELL ...
NOT JUST YOU SPECIFI-CALLY.
MISAKA-SAN DOESN'T RELY ON ANYONE.
I'M SURE PART OF IT IS NOT WANTING TO INVOLVE OTHERS...
BUT SHE BELIEVES THINGS GO FASTER WHEN SHE RESOLVES THEM ON HER OWN.
THAT IS...
COR-RECT.

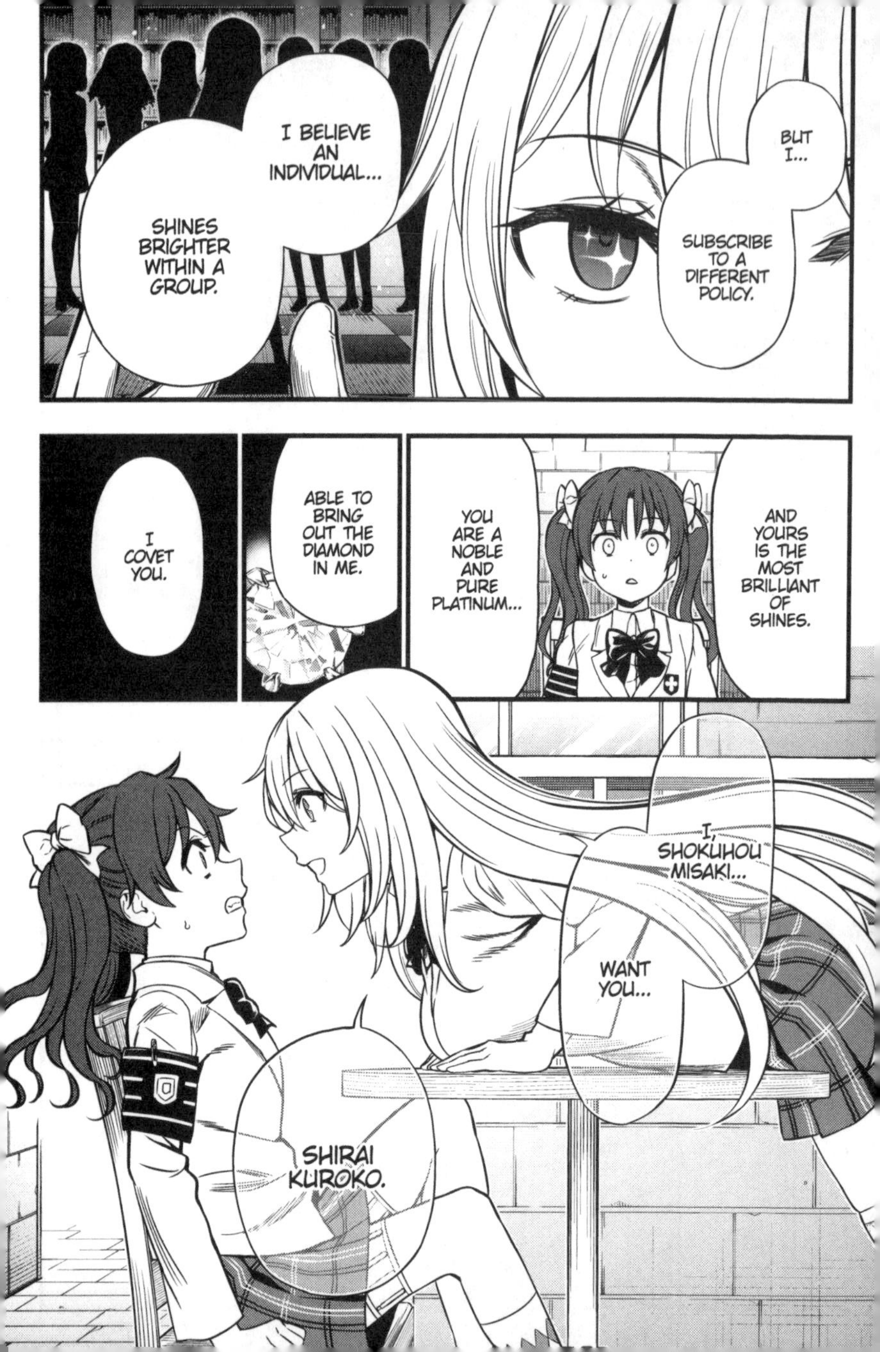
I BELIEVE AN INDIVIDUAL...
SHINES BRIGHTER WITHIN A GROUP.
BUT I...
SUBSCRIBE TO A DIFFERENT POLICY.
AND YOURS IS THE MOST BRILLIANT OF SHINES.
YOU ARE A NOBLE AND PURE PLATINUM...
ABLE TO BRING OUT THE DIAMOND IN ME.
I COVET YOU.
I, SHOKUHOU MISAKI...
WANT YOU...
SHIRAI KUROKO.

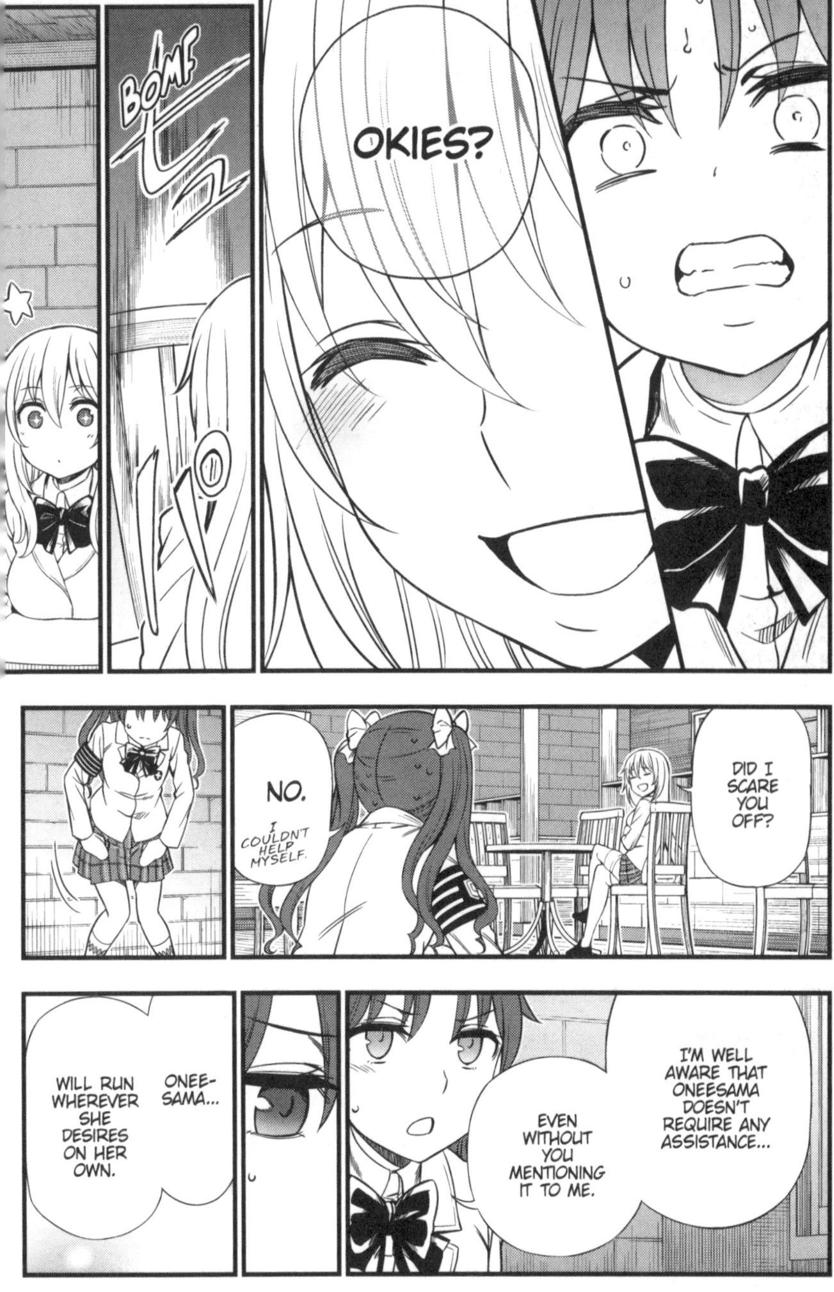
OKIES?
BOMF
DID I SCARE YOU OFF?
NO.
I COULDN'T HELP MYSELF.
I'M WELL AWARE THAT ONEESAMA DOESN'T REQUIRE ANY ASSISTANCE...
EVEN WITHOUT YOU MENTIONING IT TO ME.
ONEE-SAMA...
WILL RUN WHEREVER SHE DESIRES ON HER OWN.

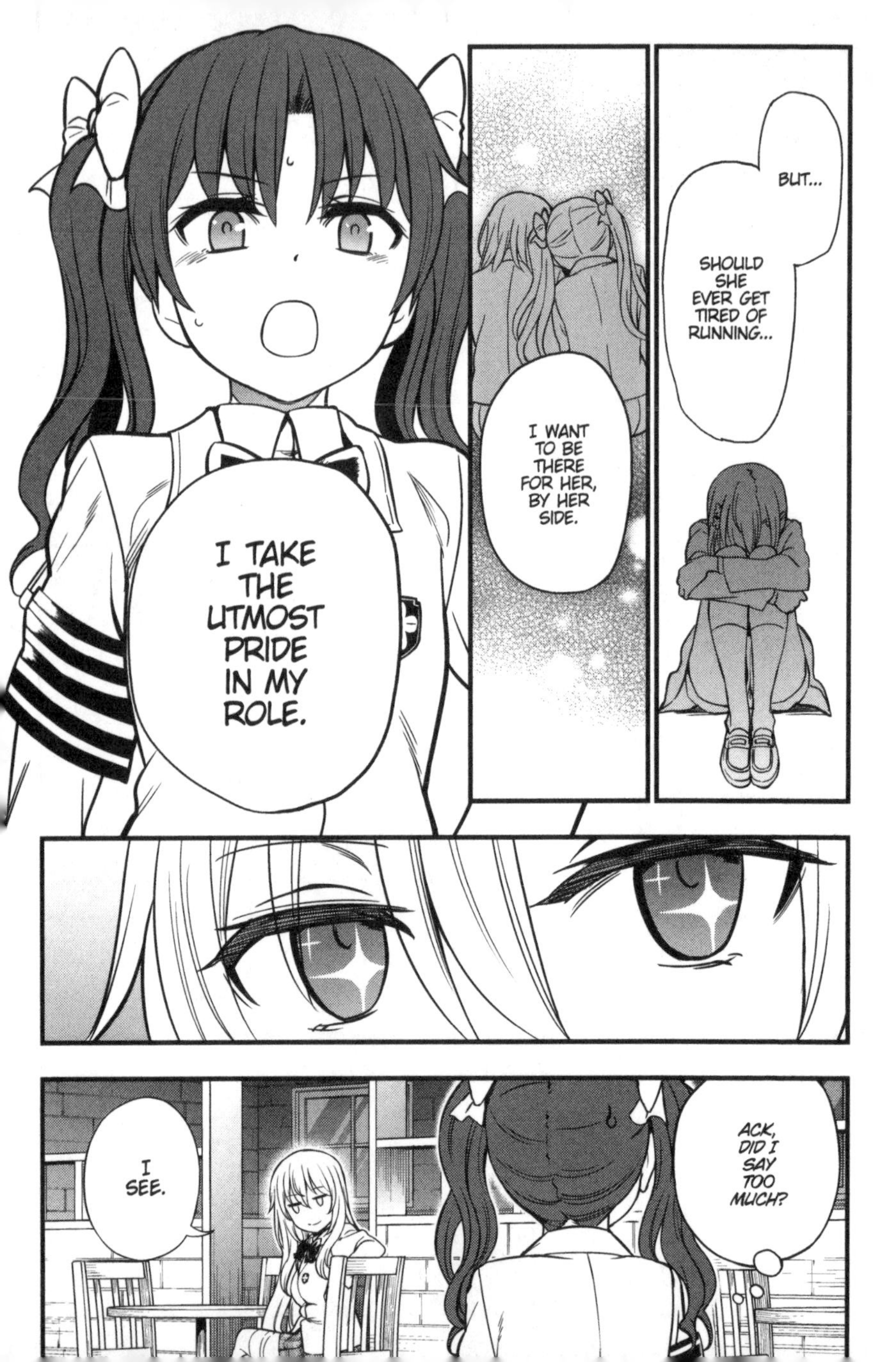
BUT...
SHOULD SHE EVER GET TIRED OF RUNNING...
I WANT TO BE THERE FOR HER, BY HER SIDE.
I TAKE THE UTMOST PRIDE IN MY ROLE.
ACK, DID I SAY TOO MUCH?
I SEE.

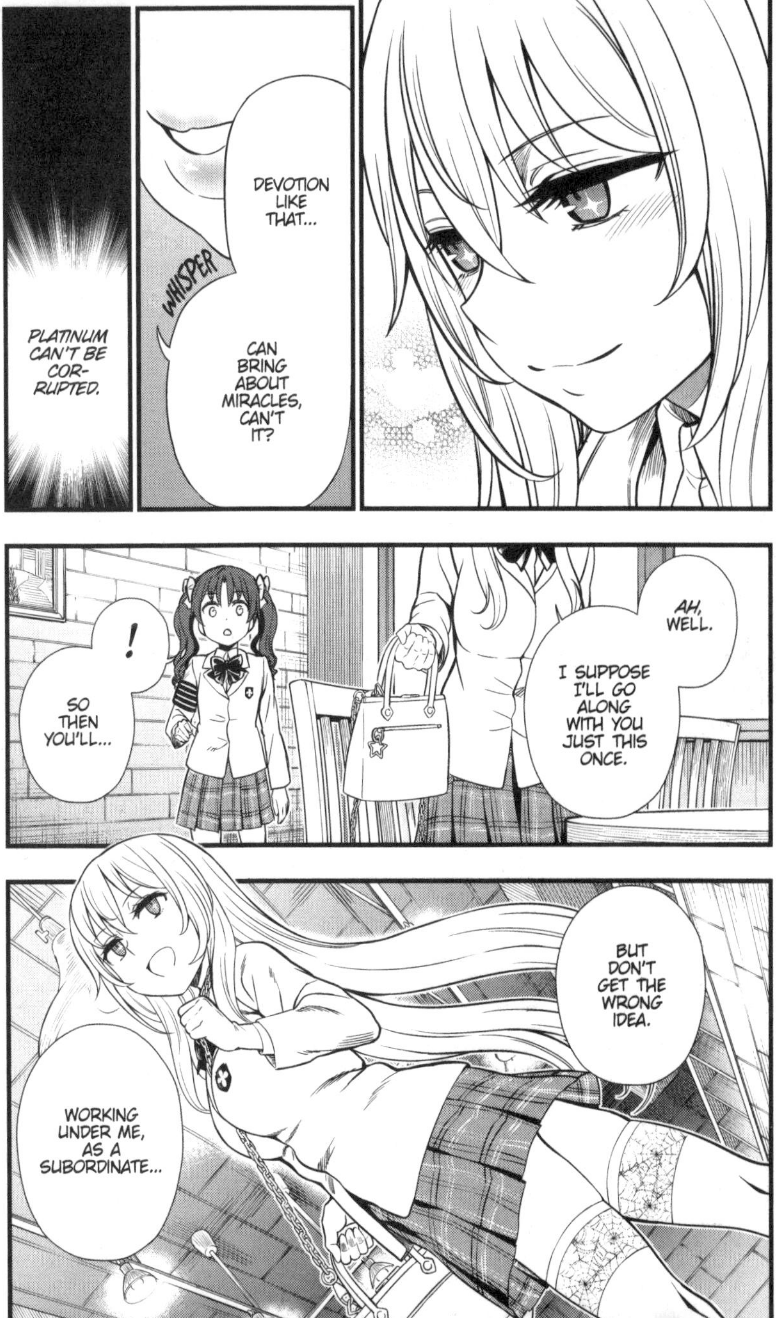
DEVOTION LIKE THAT...
WHISPER
CAN BRING ABOUT MIRACLES, CAN'T IT?
PLATINUM CAN'T BE COR-RUPTED.
AH, WELL.
I SUPPOSE I'LL GO ALONG WITH YOU JUST THIS ONCE.
!
SO THEN YOU'LL...
BUT DON'T GET THE WRONG IDEA.
WORKING UNDER ME, AS A SUBORDINATE...

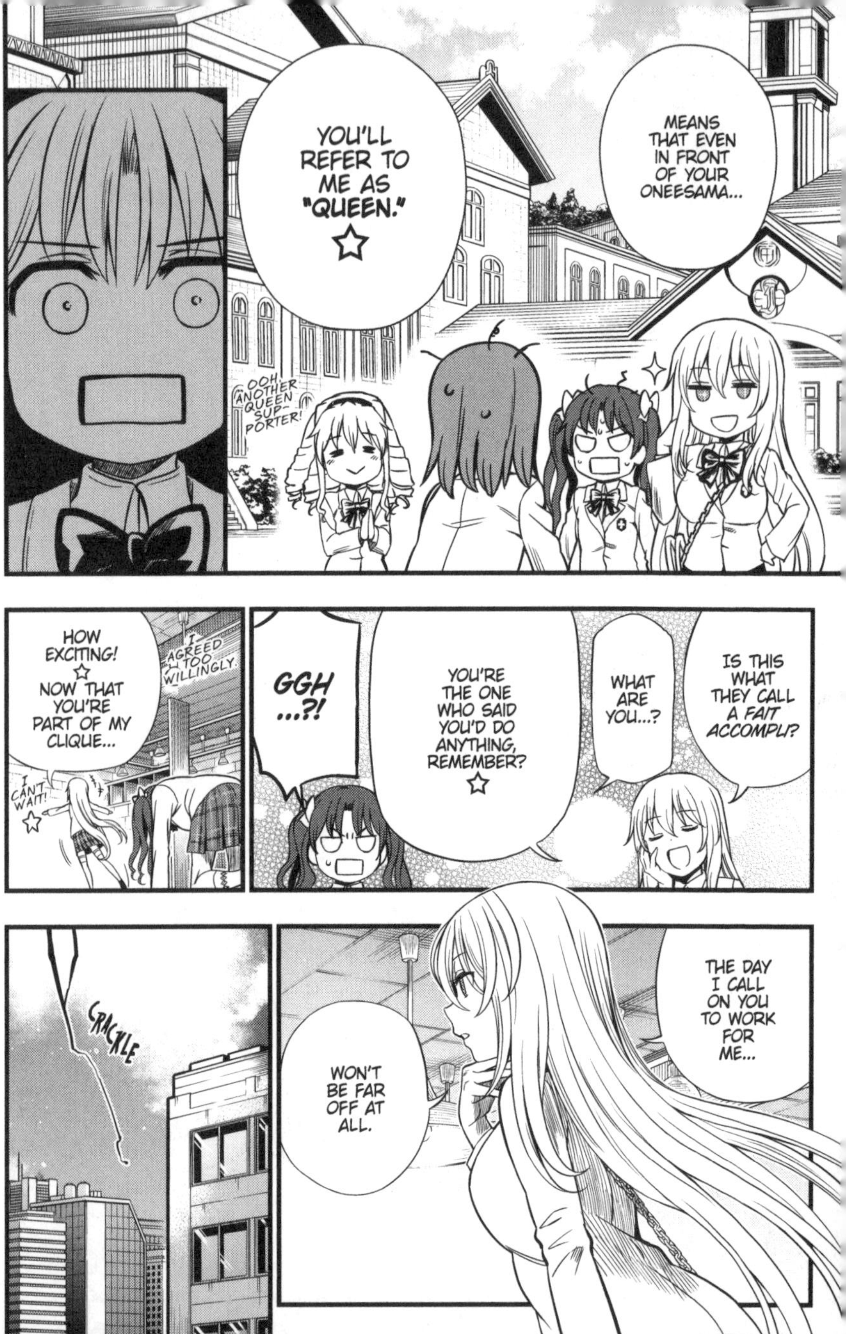
MEANS THAT EVEN IN FRONT OF YOUR ONEESAMA...
YOU'LL REFER TO ME AS "QUEEN." ☆
OOH, ANOTHER QUEEN SUP-PORTER!
IS THIS WHAT THEY CALL A *FAIT ACCOMPLI*?
WHAT ARE YOU...?
YOU'RE THE ONE WHO SAID YOU'D DO ANYTHING, REMEMBER? ☆
GGH ...?!
HOW EXCITING! ☆ NOW THAT YOU'RE PART OF MY CLIQUE...
I AGREED TOO WILLINGLY.
I CAN'T WAIT! ☆
THE DAY I CALL ON YOU TO WORK FOR ME...
WON'T BE FAR OFF AT ALL.
CRACKLE

CHAPTER 21: You're Making Me Slightly Angry

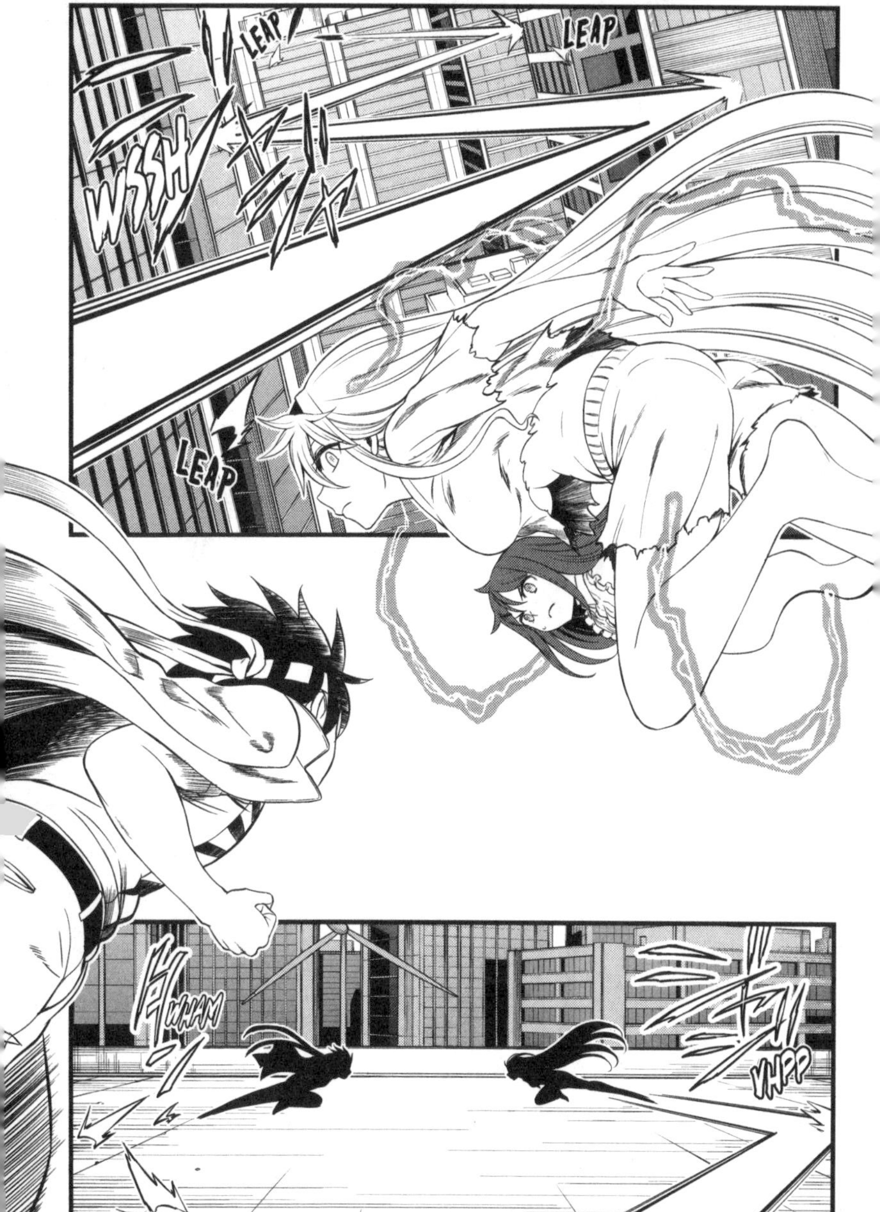
LEAP
LEAP
WSSH
LEAP
VHPP
WHAM

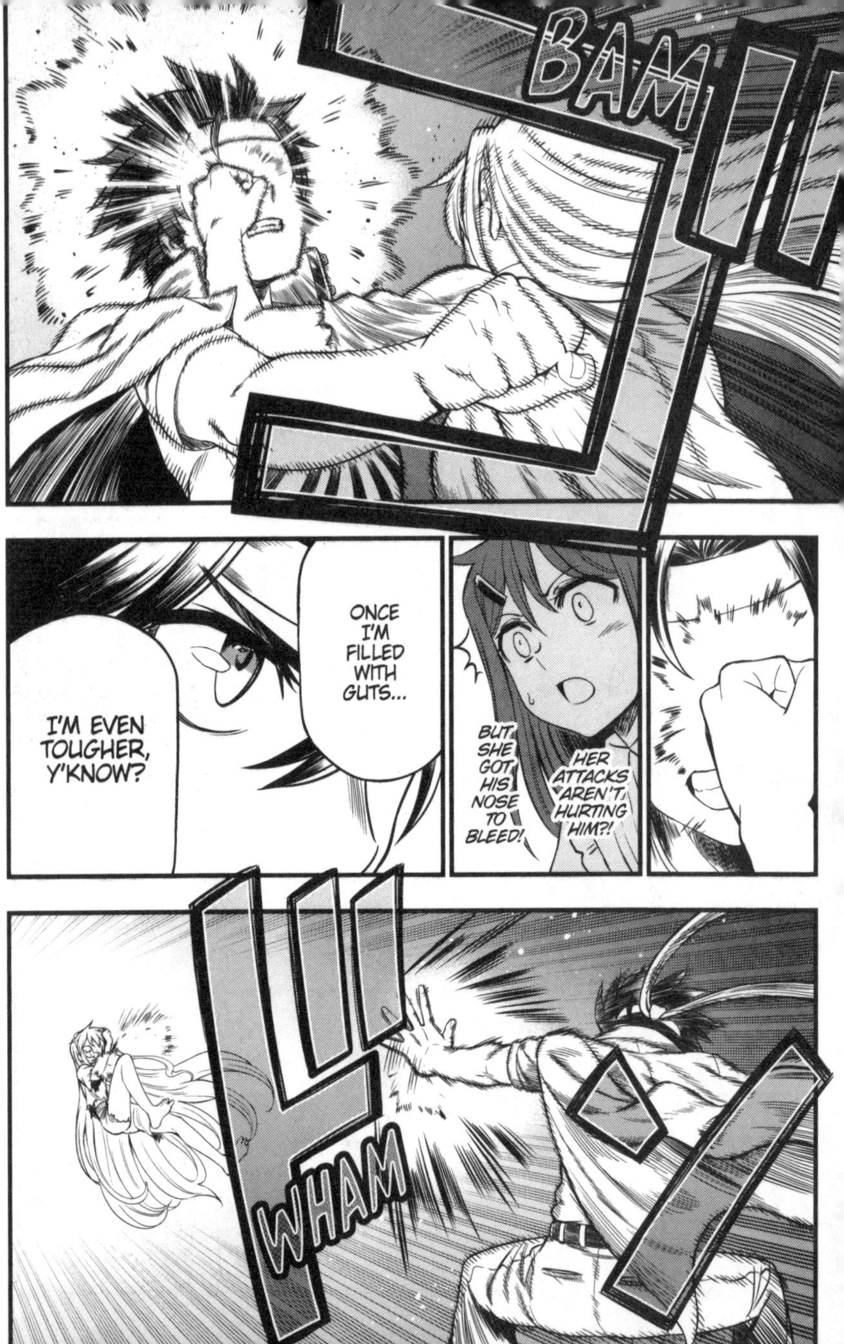
BAM
HER ATTACKS AREN'T HURTING HIM?!
BUT SHE GOT HIS NOSE TO BLEED!
ONCE I'M FILLED WITH GUTS...
I'M EVEN TOUGHER, Y'KNOW?
WHAM

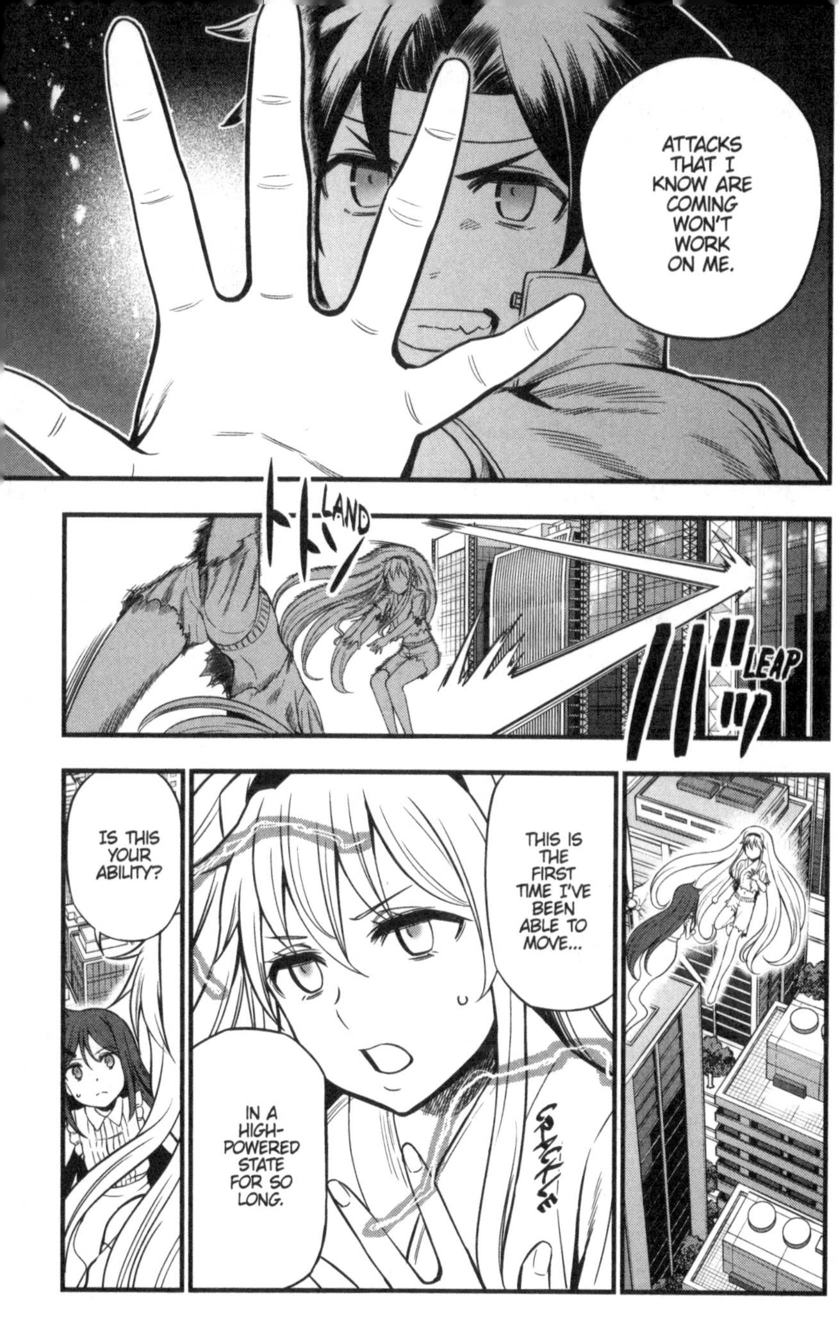
ATTACKS THAT I KNOW ARE COMING WON'T WORK ON ME.
LEAP
LAND
THIS IS THE FIRST TIME I'VE BEEN ABLE TO MOVE...
IN A HIGH-POWERED STATE FOR SO LONG.
CRACKLE
IS THIS YOUR ABILITY?

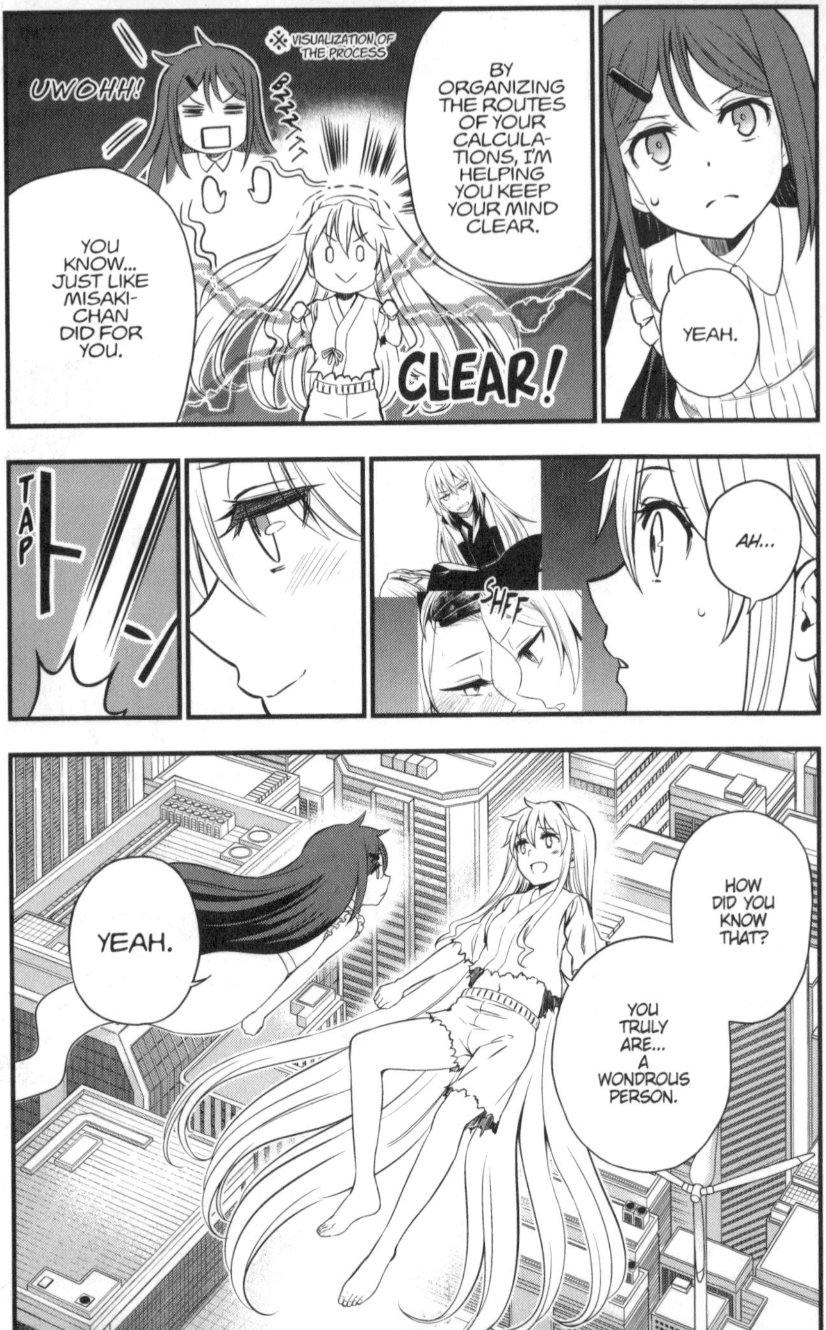
YEAH.
VISUALIZATION OF THE PROCESS
BY ORGANIZING THE ROUTES OF YOUR CALCULATIONS, I'M HELPING YOU KEEP YOUR MIND CLEAR.
UWOHH!
BZZZTT
CLEAR!
YOU KNOW... JUST LIKE MISAKI-CHAN DID FOR YOU.
AH...
SHFF
TAP
HOW DID YOU KNOW THAT?
YOU TRULY ARE... A WONDROUS PERSON.
YEAH.

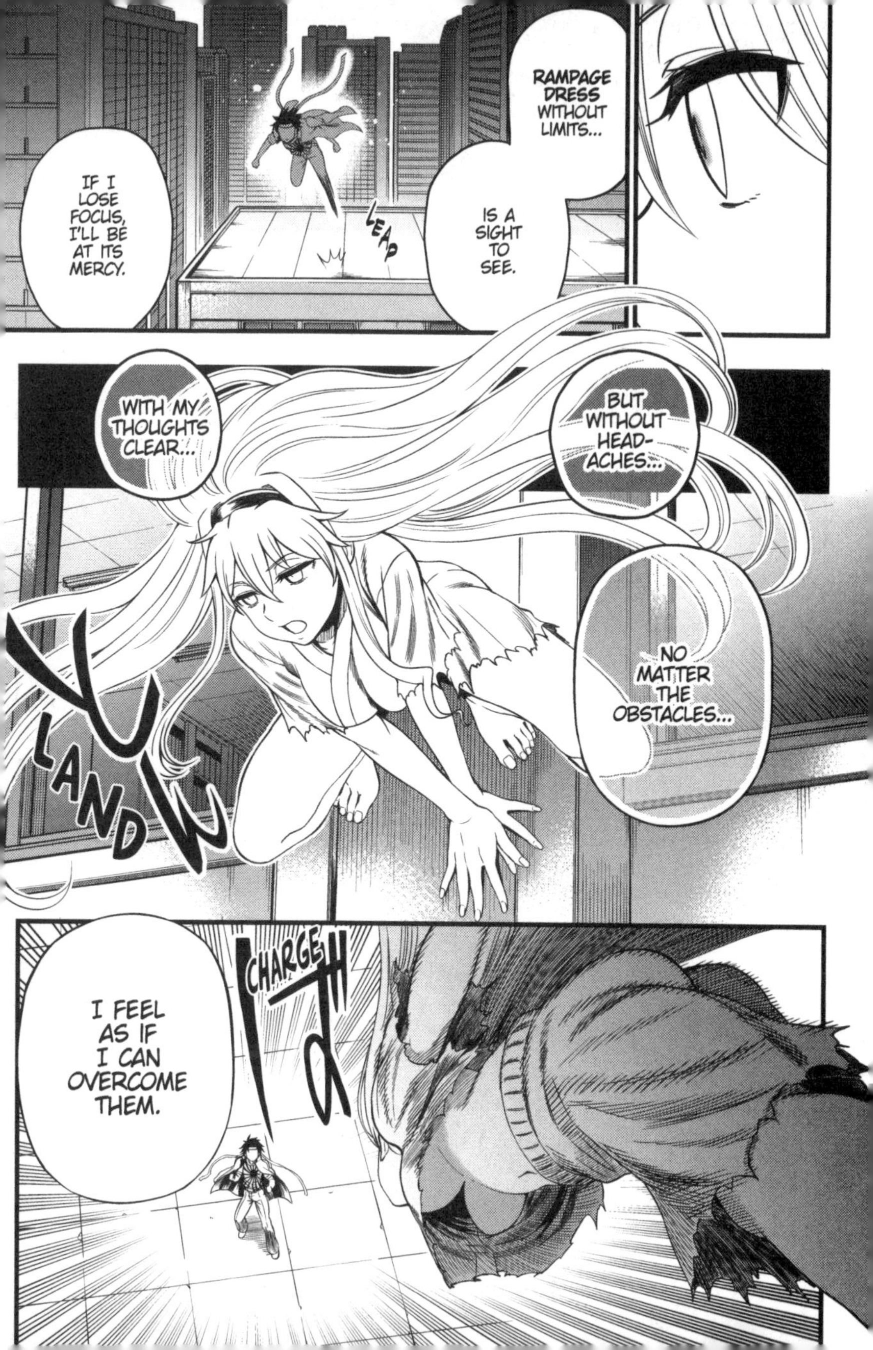
RAMPAGE DRESS WITHOUT LIMITS...
IS A SIGHT TO SEE.
LEAP
IF I LOSE FOCUS, I'LL BE AT ITS MERCY.
BUT WITHOUT HEAD-ACHES...
WITH MY THOUGHTS CLEAR...
NO MATTER THE OBSTACLES...
LAND
CHARGE
I FEEL AS IF I CAN OVERCOME THEM.

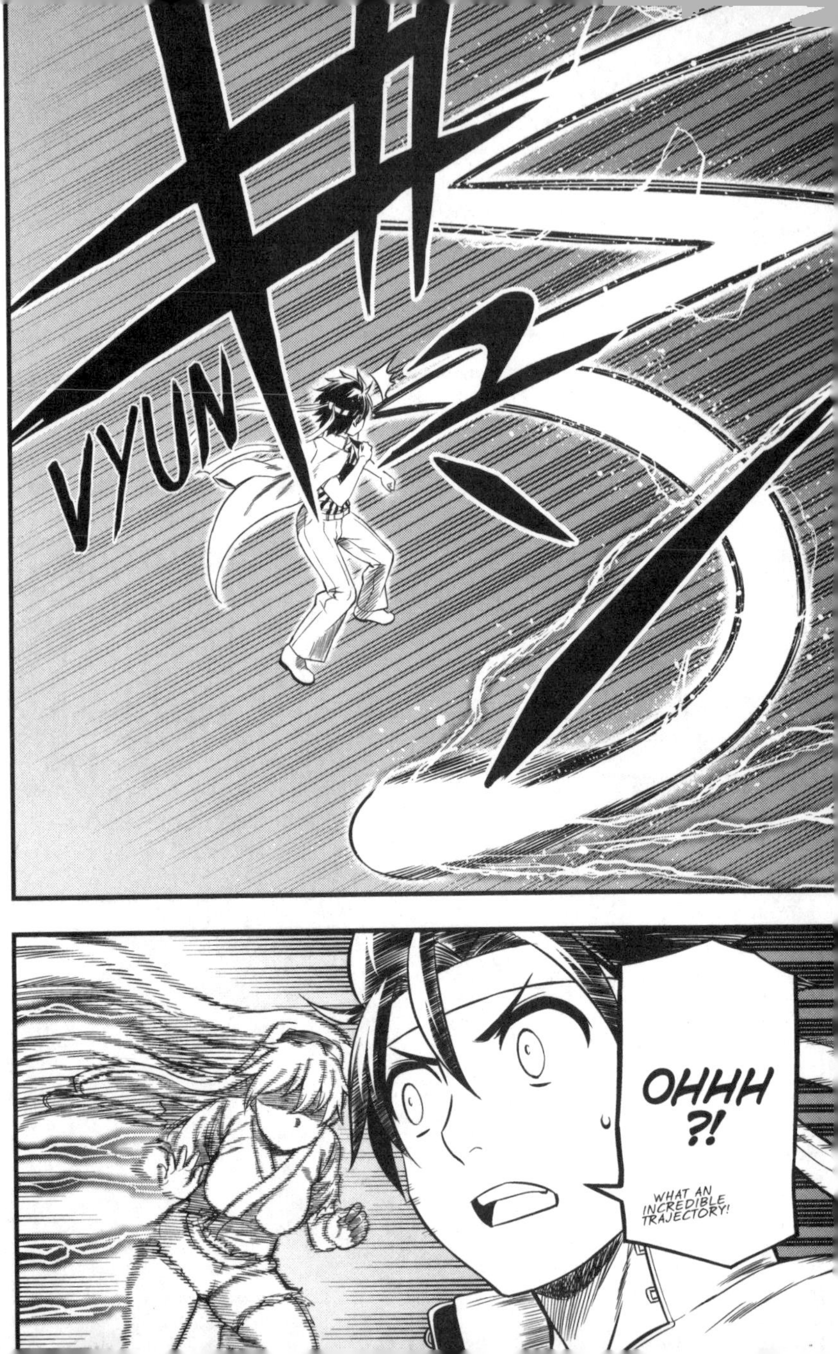
VYUN
OHHH ?!
WHAT AN INCREDIBLE TRAJECTORY!

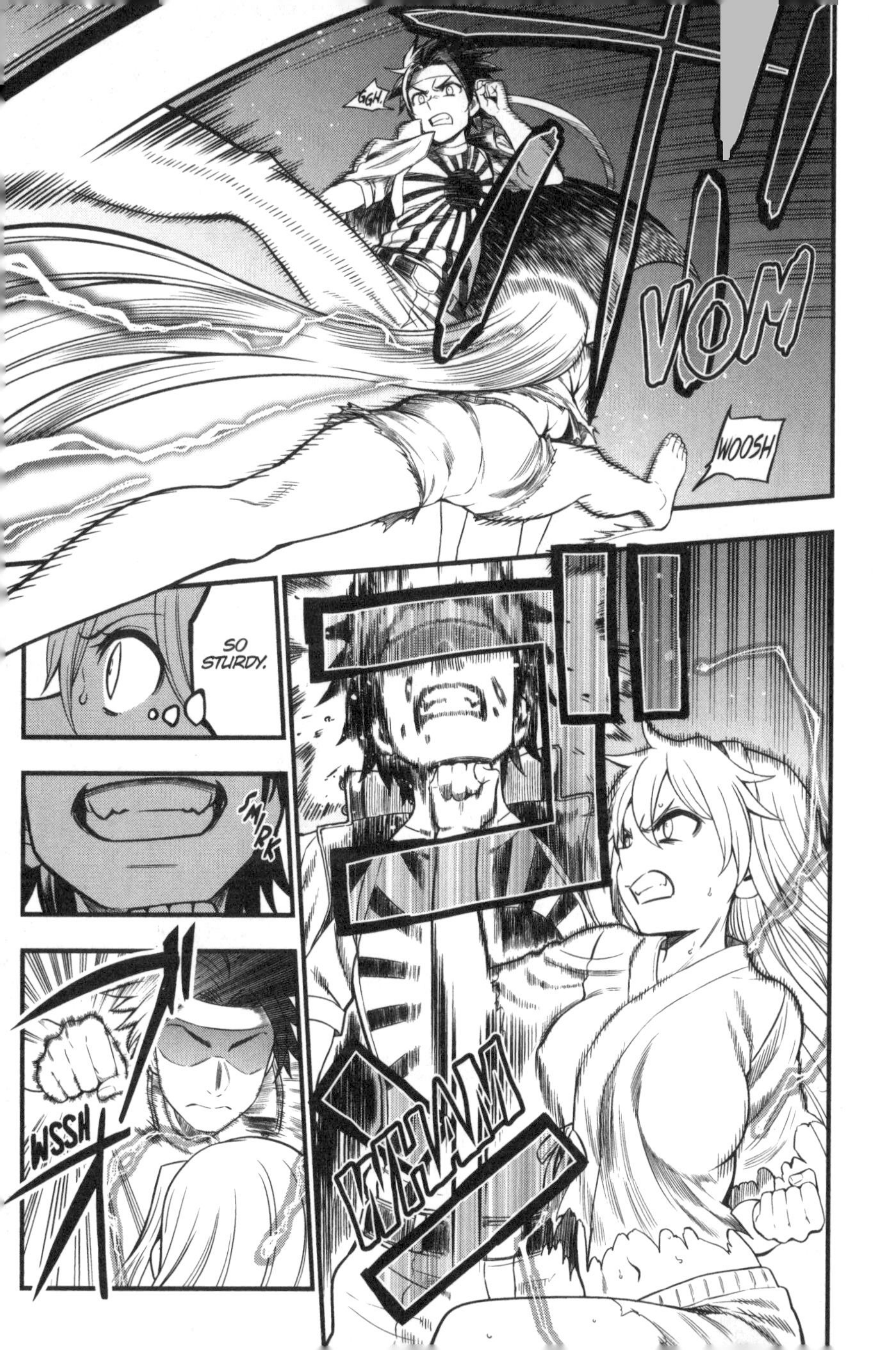
GGH.
VOM
WOOSH
SO STURDY.
SMIRK
WSSH
WHAM

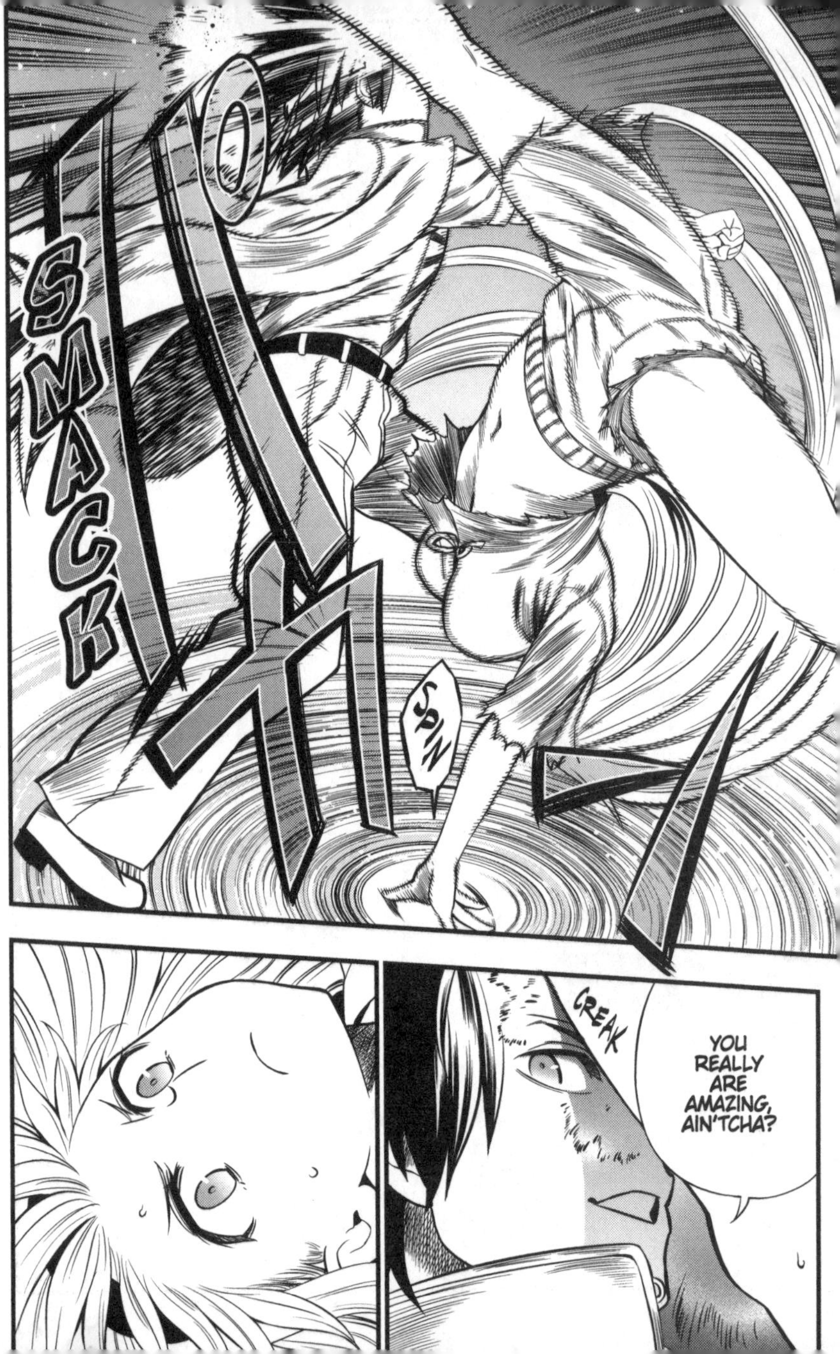
SMACK
SPIN
CREAK
YOU REALLY ARE AMAZING, AIN'TCHA?

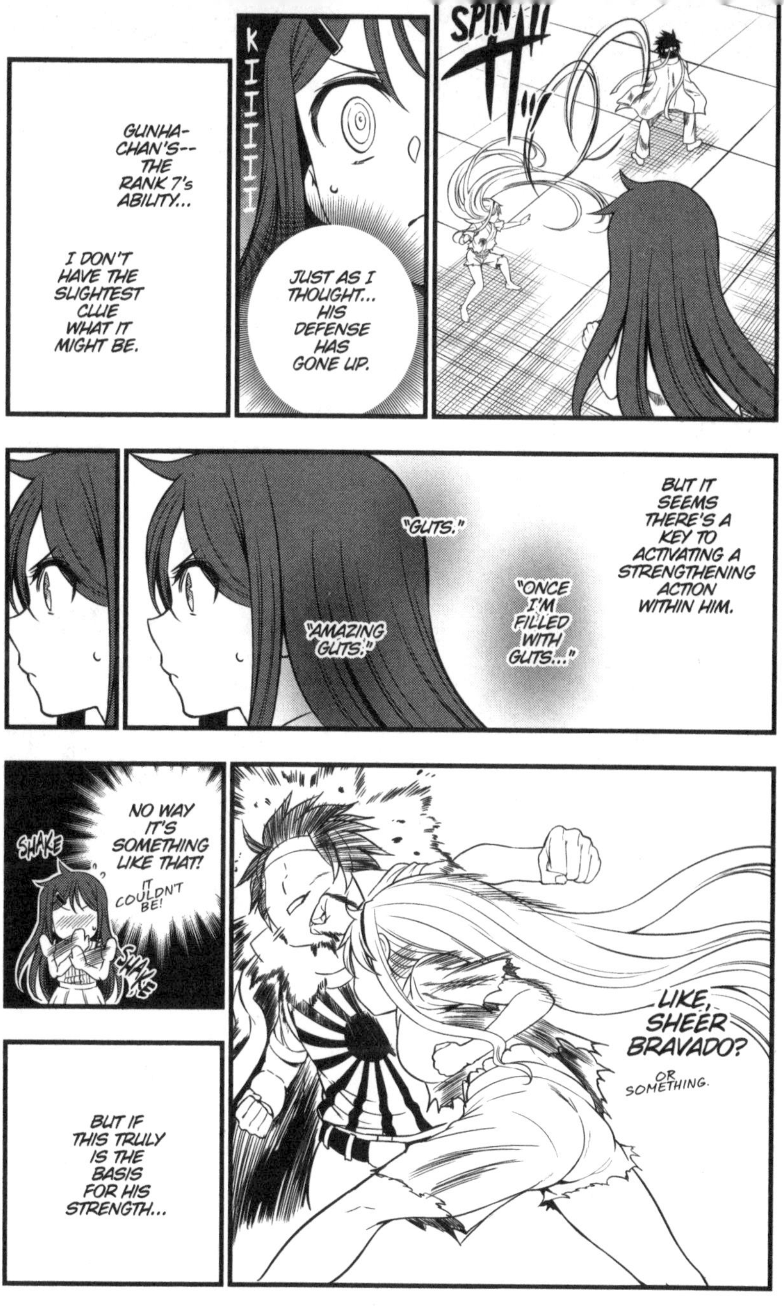
SPIN!!!
KIIIIIII
JUST AS I THOUGHT... HIS DEFENSE HAS GONE UP.
GUNHA-CHAN'S-- THE RANK 7's ABILITY...
I DON'T HAVE THE SLIGHTEST CLUE WHAT IT MIGHT BE.
BUT IT SEEMS THERE'S A KEY TO ACTIVATING A STRENGTHENING ACTION WITHIN HIM.
"ONCE I'M FILLED WITH GUTS..."
"GUTS."
"AMAZING GUTS."
LIKE, SHEER BRAVADO?
OR SOMETHING.
NO WAY IT'S SOMETHING LIKE THAT!
IT COULDN'T BE!
SHAKE
SHAKE
BUT IF THIS TRULY IS THE BASIS FOR HIS STRENGTH...

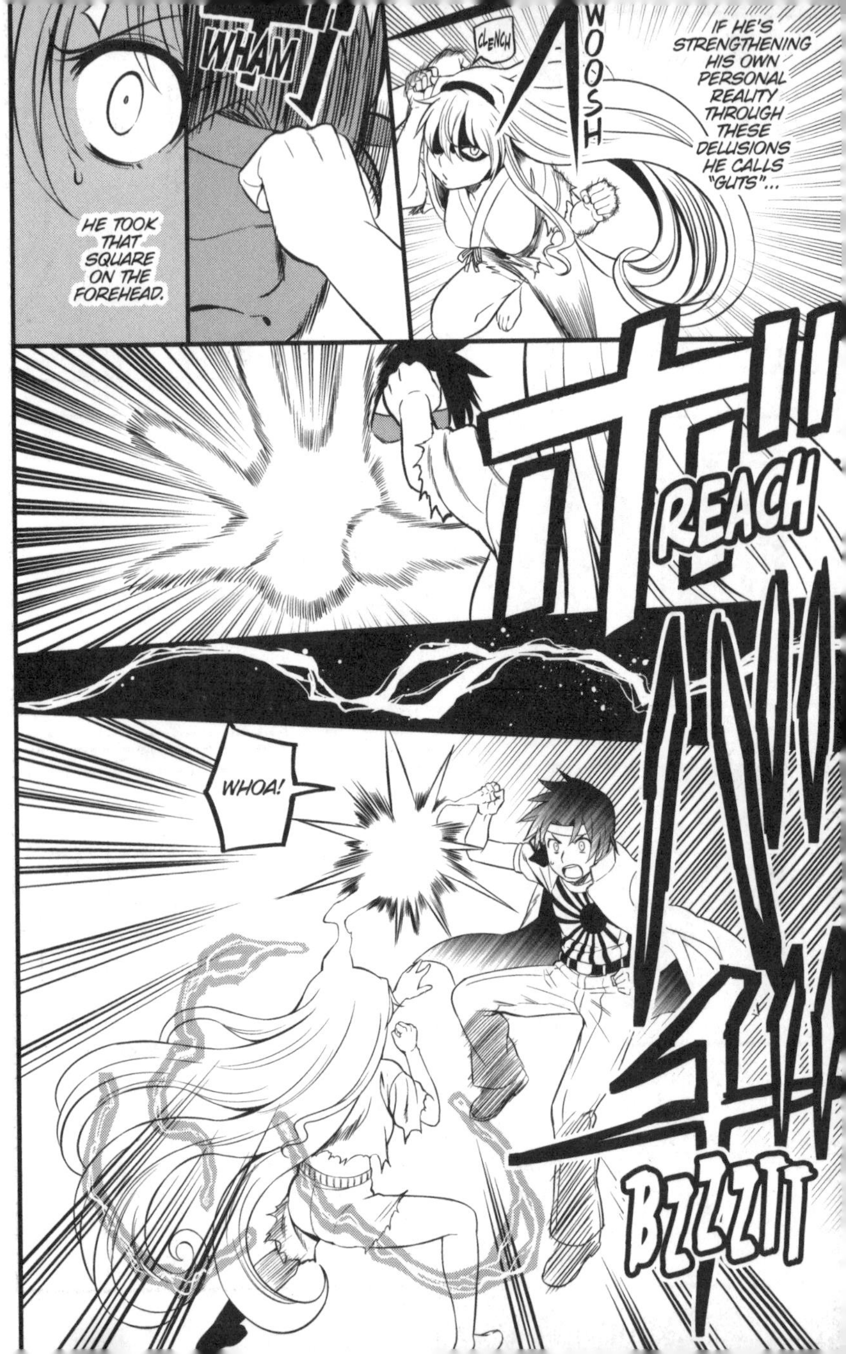
IF HE'S STRENGTHENING HIS OWN PERSONAL REALITY THROUGH THESE DELLUSIONS HE CALLS "GUTS"...
WOOSH
CLENCH
WHAM
HE TOOK THAT SQUARE ON THE FOREHEAD.
REACH
WHOA!
BZZZTT

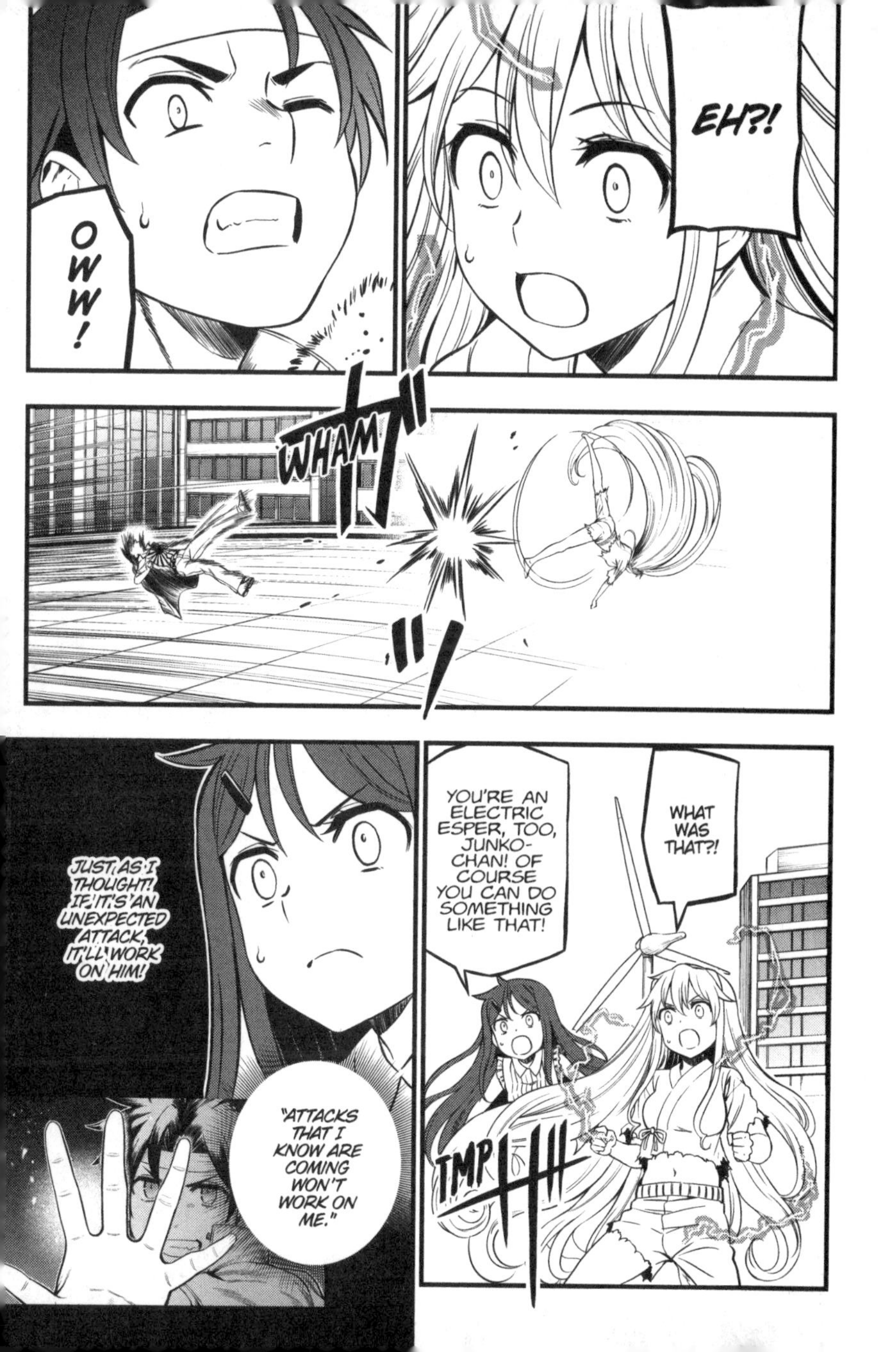
EH?!
OWW!
WHAM
WHAT WAS THAT?!
YOU'RE AN ELECTRIC ESPER, TOO, JUNKO-CHAN! OF COURSE YOU CAN DO SOMETHING LIKE THAT!
TMP
JUST AS I THOUGHT! IF IT'S AN UNEXPECTED ATTACK, IT'LL WORK ON HIM!
"ATTACKS THAT I KNOW ARE COMING WON'T WORK ON ME."

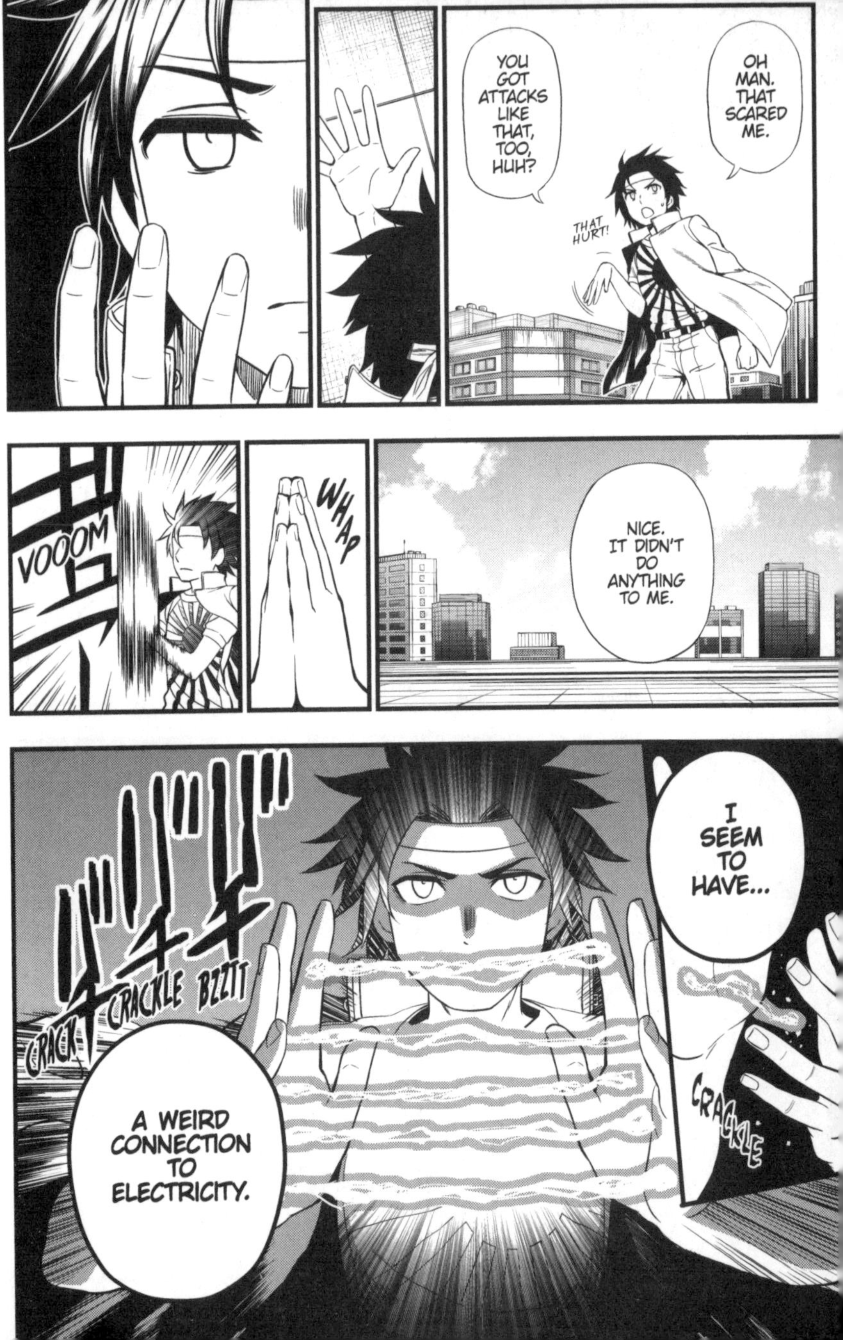
OH MAN. THAT SCARED ME.
THAT HURT!
YOU GOT ATTACKS LIKE THAT, TOO, HUH?
NICE. IT DIDN'T DO ANYTHING TO ME.
WHAP
VOOOM
I SEEM TO HAVE...
CRACKLE
CRACK CRACKLE BZZT
A WEIRD CONNECTION TO ELECTRICITY.

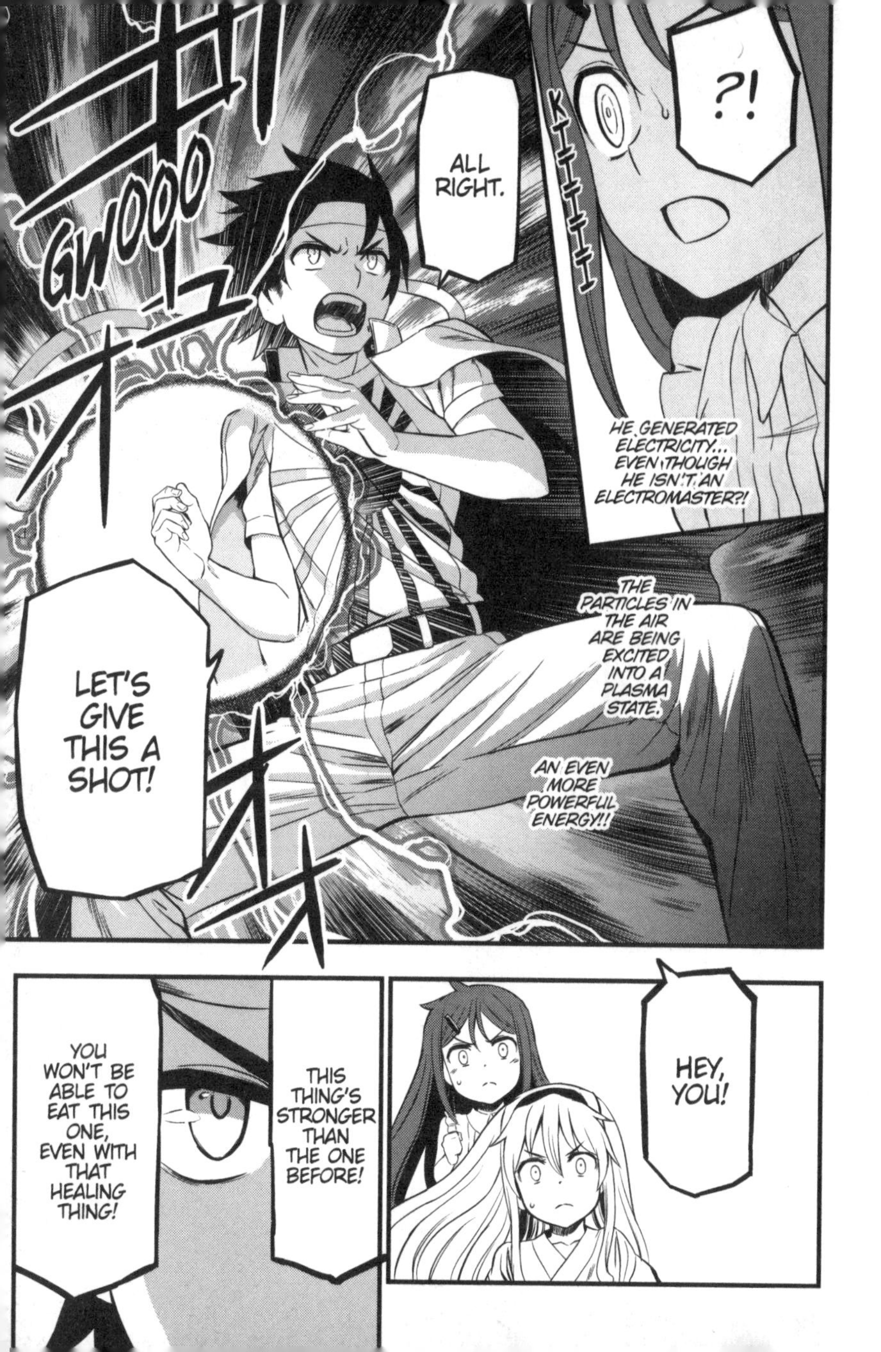
?!
HE GENERATED ELECTRICITY... EVEN THOUGH HE ISN'T AN ELECTROMASTER?!
ALL RIGHT.
GWOOO
THE PARTICLES IN THE AIR ARE BEING EXCITED INTO A PLASMA STATE.
AN EVEN MORE POWERFUL ENERGY!!
LET'S GIVE THIS A SHOT!
HEY, YOU!
THIS THING'S STRONGER THAN THE ONE BEFORE!
YOU WON'T BE ABLE TO EAT THIS ONE, EVEN WITH THAT HEALING THING!

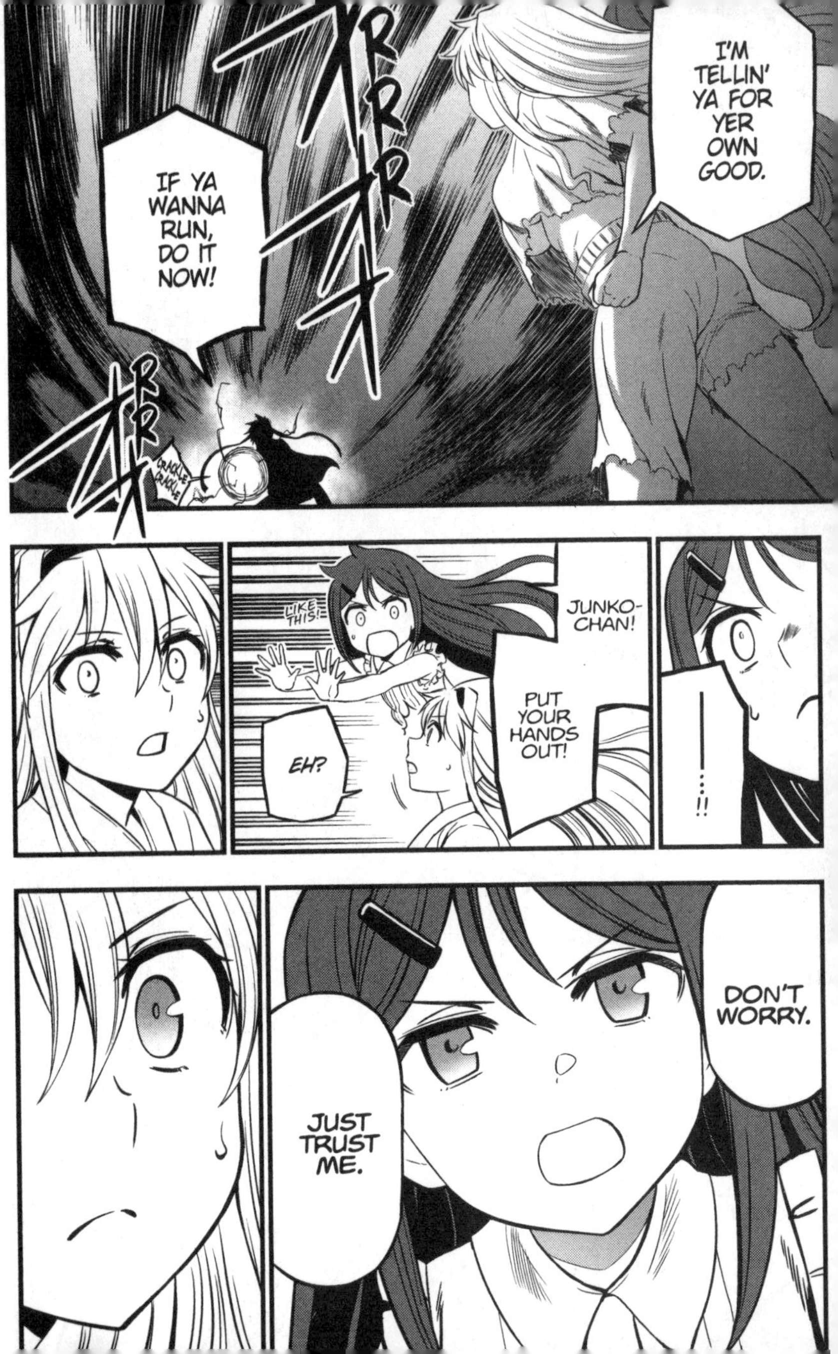

I'M TELLIN' YA FOR YER OWN GOOD.
IF YA WANNA RUN, DO IT NOW!
CRACKLE CRACKLE
JUNKO-CHAN!
PUT YOUR HANDS OUT!
LIKE THIS!
EH?
......!!
DON'T WORRY.
JUST TRUST ME.

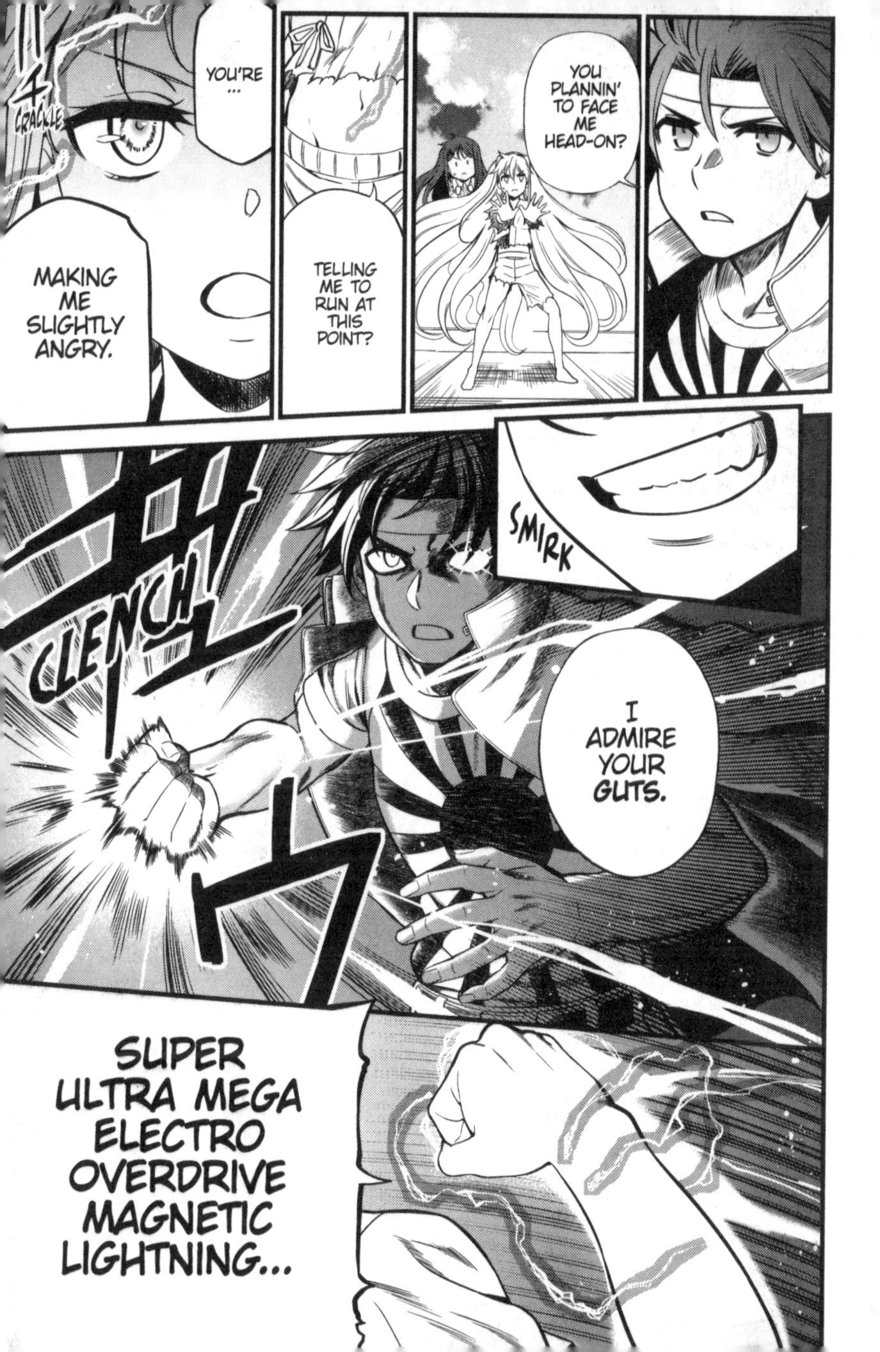
YOU PLANNIN' TO FACE ME HEAD-ON?
TELLING ME TO RUN AT THIS POINT?
YOU'RE ...
MAKING ME SLIGHTLY ANGRY.
CRACKLE
SMIRK
CLENCH
I ADMIRE YOUR GUTS.
SUPER ULTRA MEGA ELECTRO OVERDRIVE MAGNETIC LIGHTNING...

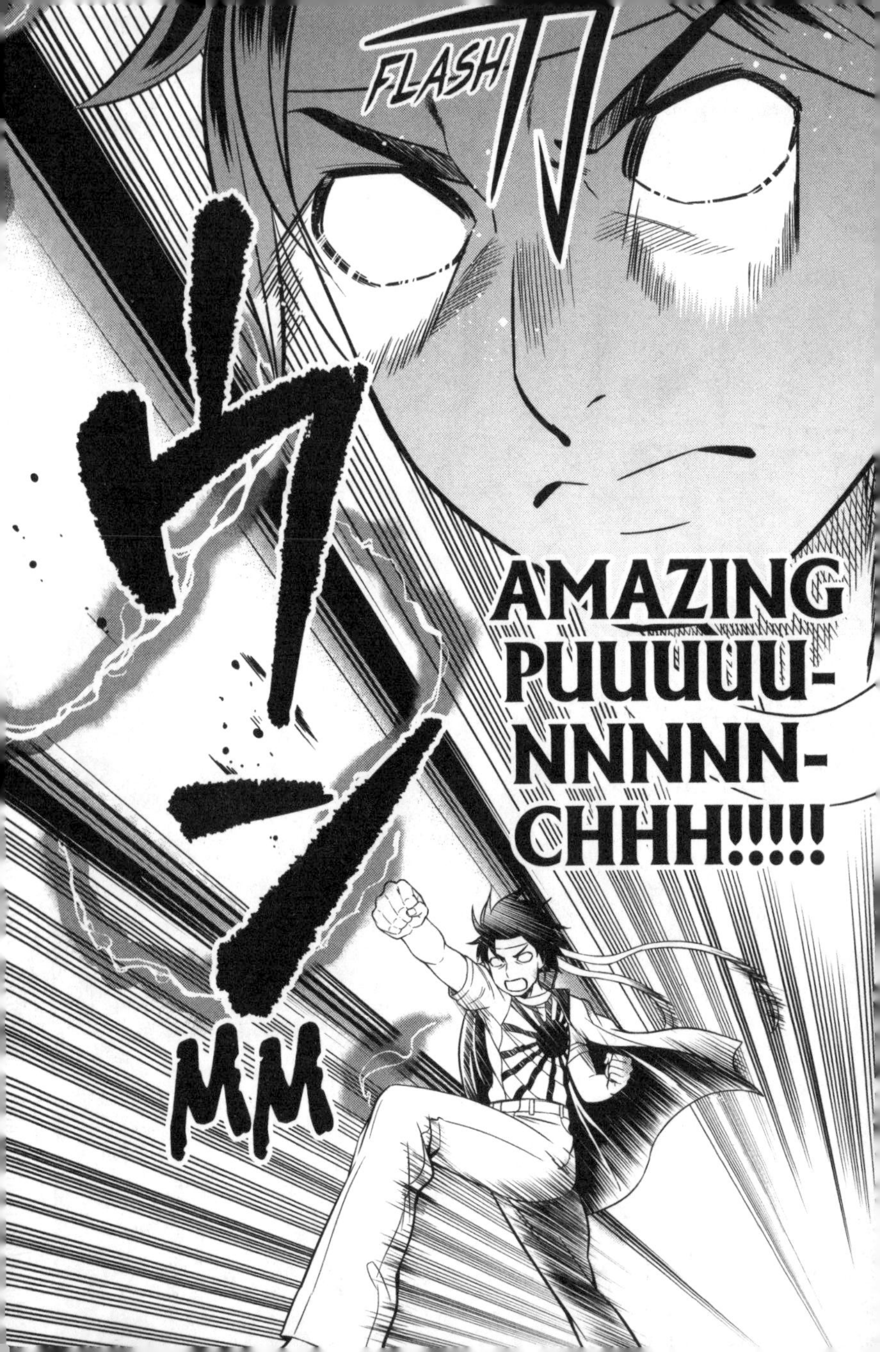

FLASH
AMAZING PUUUUU-NNNNN-CHHH!!!!!
MM

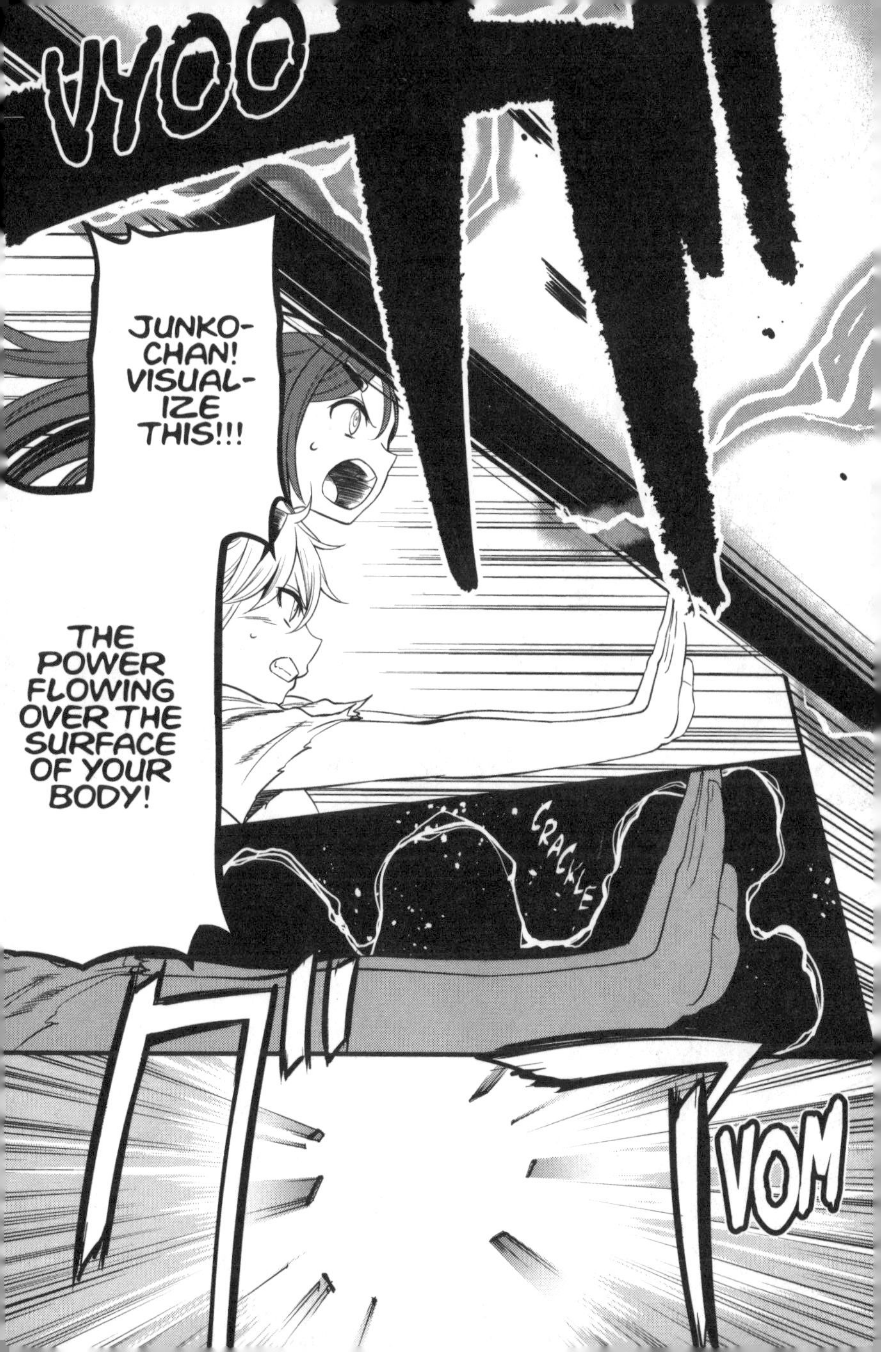
VYOO
JUNKO-CHAN! VISUAL-IZE THIS!!!
THE POWER FLOWING OVER THE SURFACE OF YOUR BODY!
CRACKLE
VOM

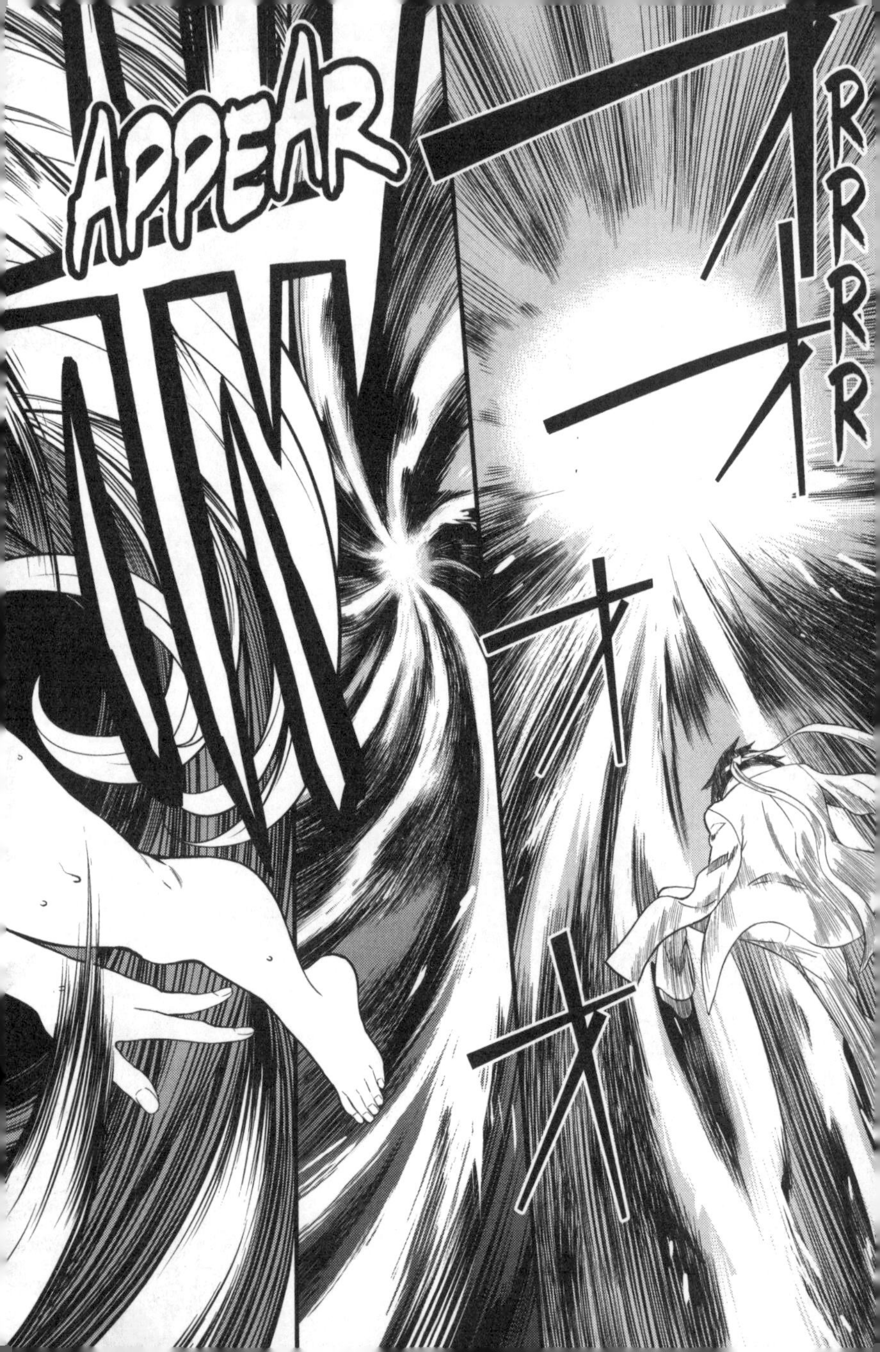
APPEAR
RRRR

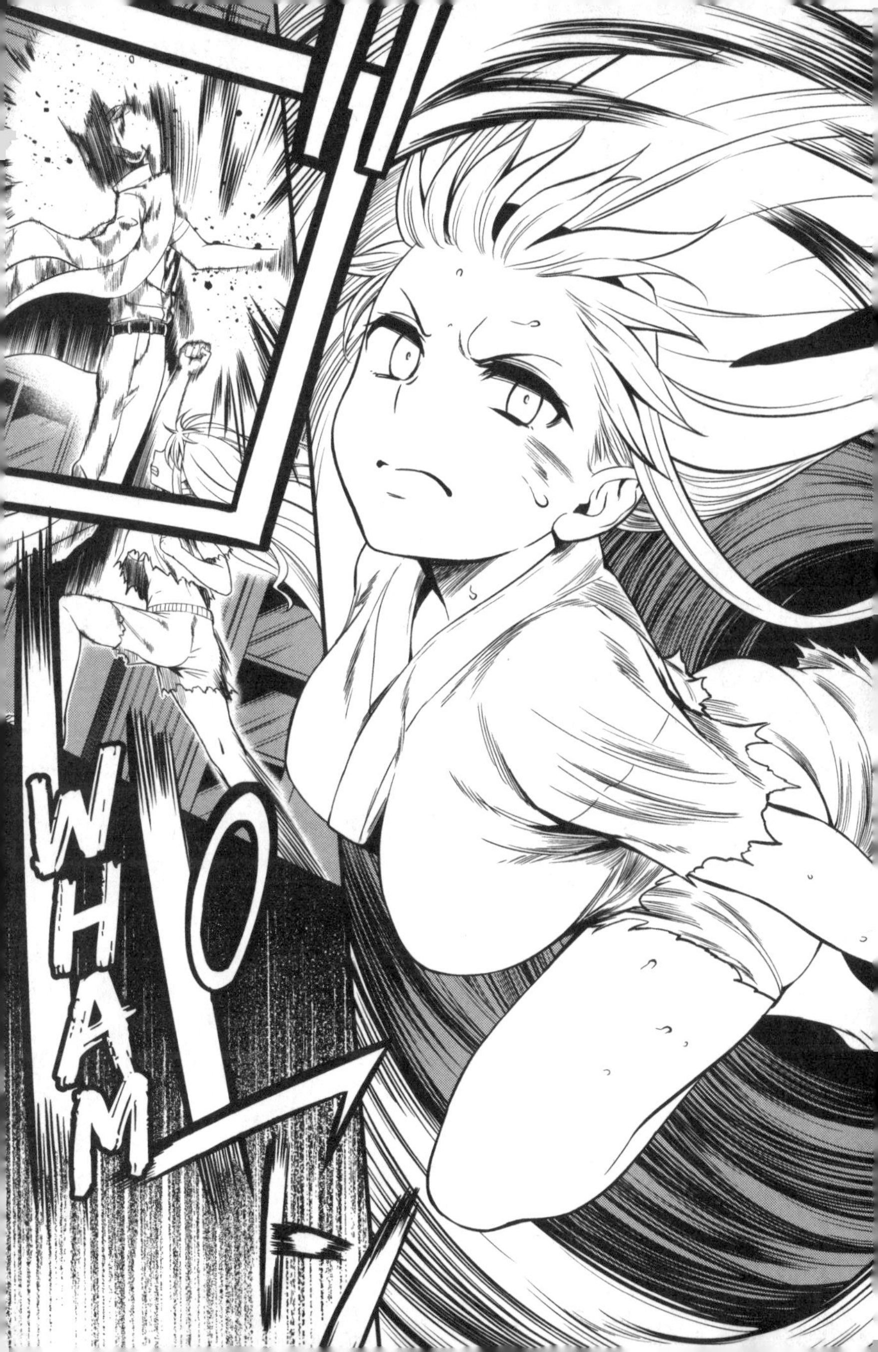
WHAM

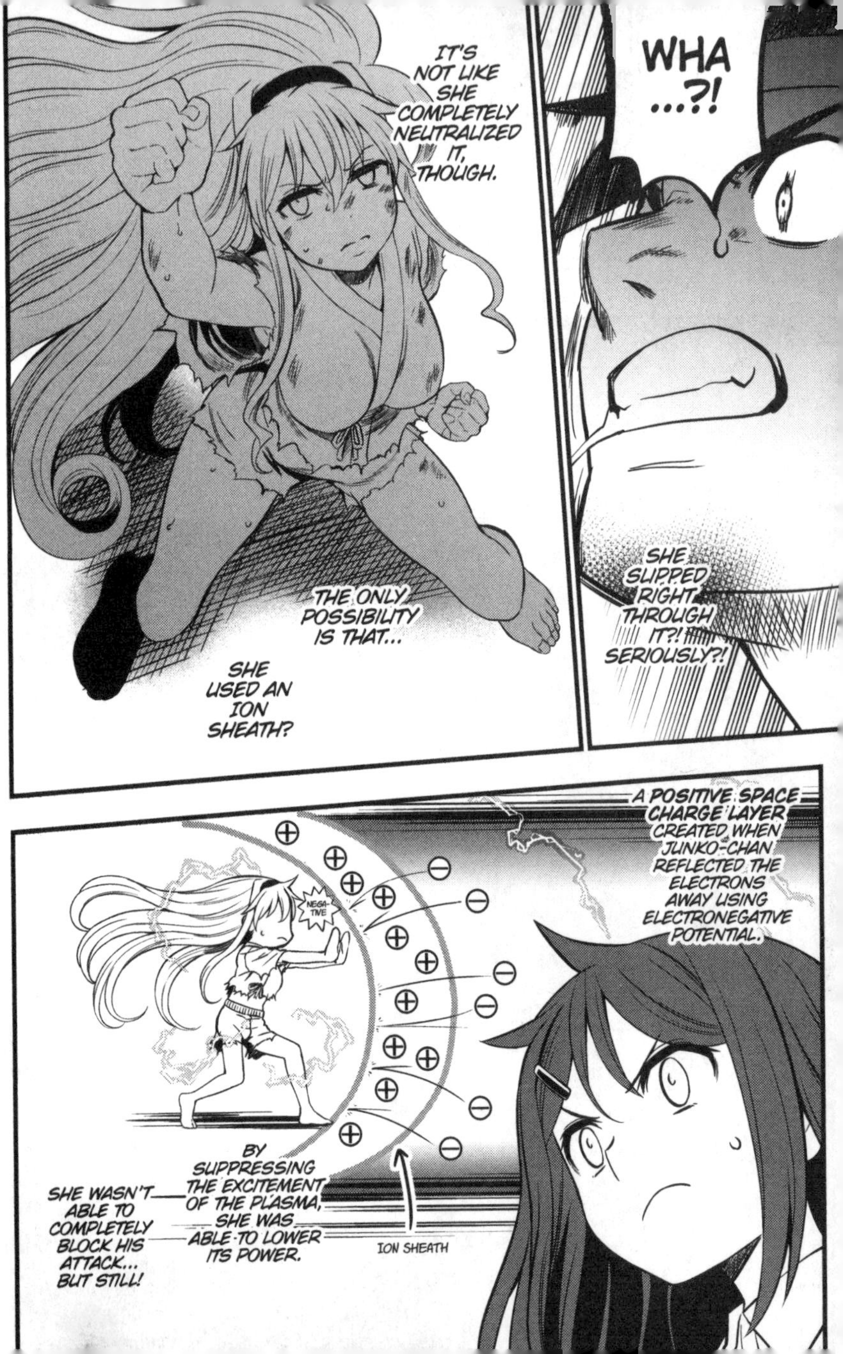
WHA ...?!
SHE SLIPPED RIGHT THROUGH IT?! SERIOUSLY?!
IT'S NOT LIKE SHE COMPLETELY NEUTRALIZED IT, THOUGH.
THE ONLY POSSIBILITY IS THAT...
SHE USED AN ION SHEATH?
A POSITIVE SPACE CHARGE LAYER CREATED WHEN JUNKO-CHAN REFLECTED THE ELECTRONS AWAY USING ELECTRONEGATIVE POTENTIAL.
NEGATIVE
ION SHEATH
BY SUPPRESSING THE EXCITEMENT OF THE PLASMA, SHE WAS ABLE TO LOWER ITS POWER.
SHE WASN'T ABLE TO COMPLETELY BLOCK HIS ATTACK... BUT STILL!

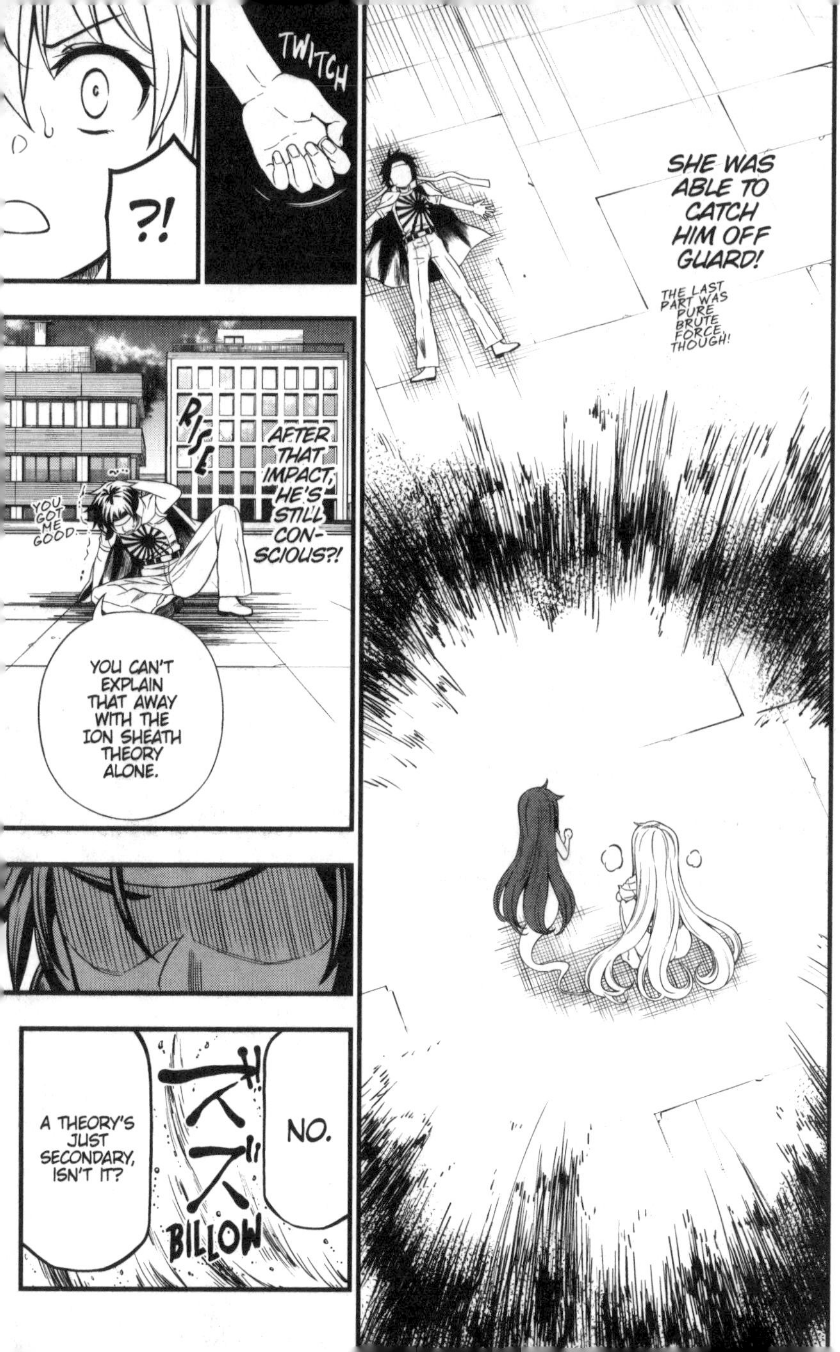

SHE WAS ABLE TO CATCH HIM OFF GUARD!
THE LAST PART WAS PURE BRUTE FORCE, THOUGH!
TWITCH
?!
RISE
AFTER THAT IMPACT, HE'S STILL CON-SCIOUS?!
YOU GOT ME GOOD...
YOU CAN'T EXPLAIN THAT AWAY WITH THE ION SHEATH THEORY ALONE.
NO.
A THEORY'S JUST SECONDARY, ISN'T IT?
BILLOW

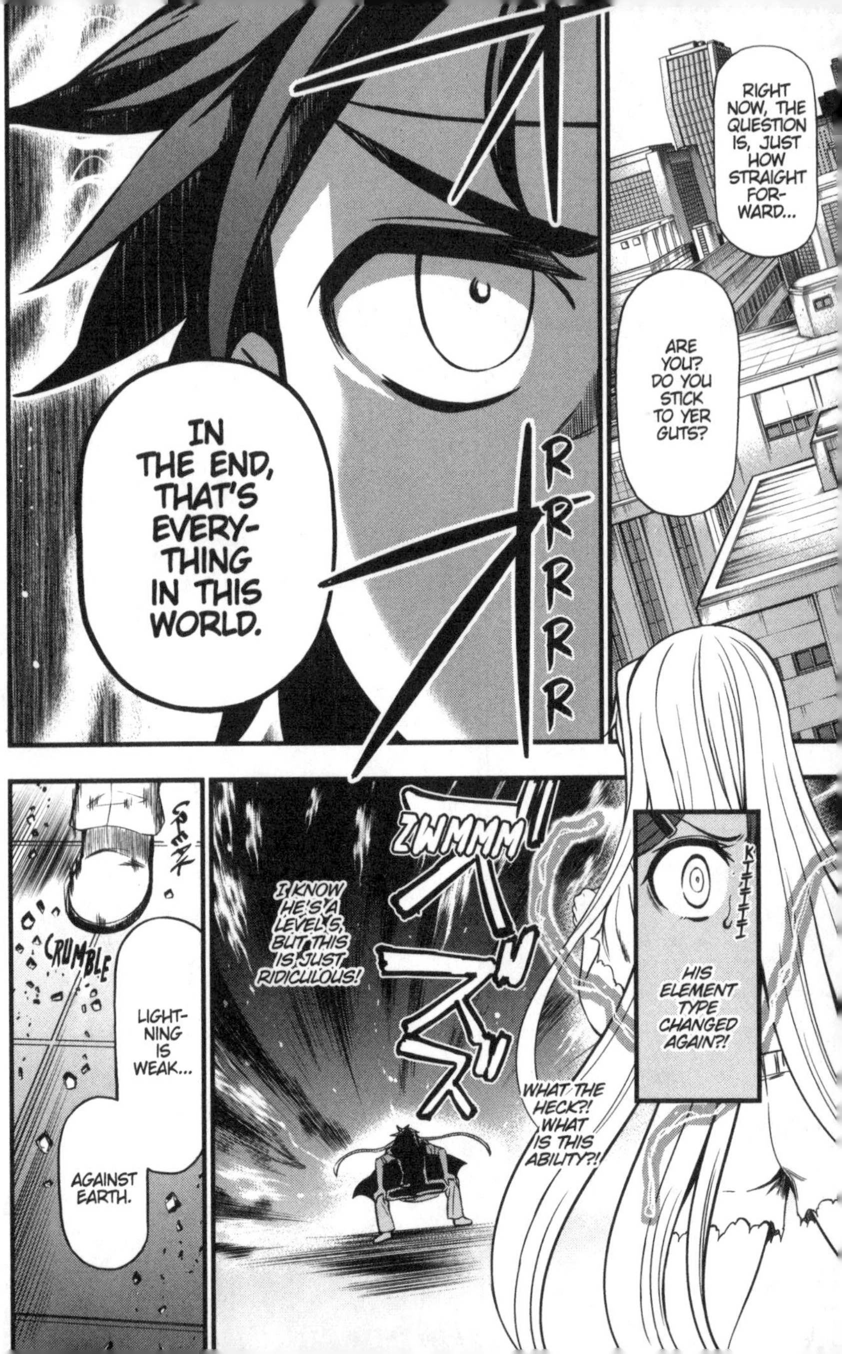
RIGHT NOW, THE QUESTION IS, JUST HOW STRAIGHTFORWARD...
ARE YOU? DO YOU STICK TO YER GUTS?
IN THE END, THAT'S EVERYTHING IN THIS WORLD.
RRRRR
KIIIII
HIS ELEMENT TYPE CHANGED AGAIN?!
WHAT THE HECK?! WHAT IS THIS ABILITY?!
ZWMMM
I KNOW HE'S A LEVEL 5, BUT THIS IS JUST RIDICULOUS!
CREAK
CRUMBLE
LIGHTNING IS WEAK...
AGAINST EARTH.

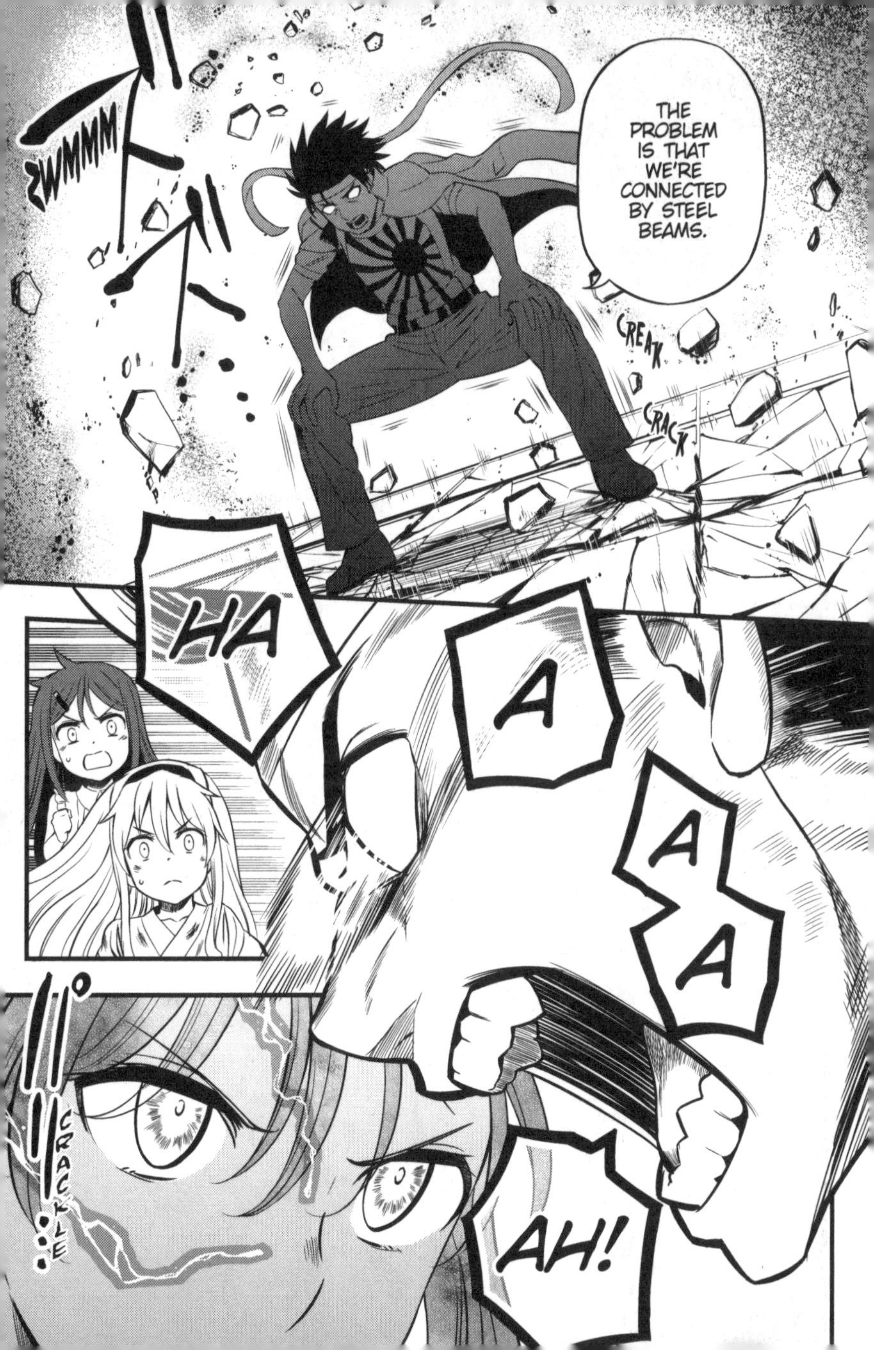
THE PROBLEM IS THAT WE'RE CONNECTED BY STEEL BEAMS.
ZWMMM
CREAK
CRACK
HA
A
A
A
AH!
CRACKLE...

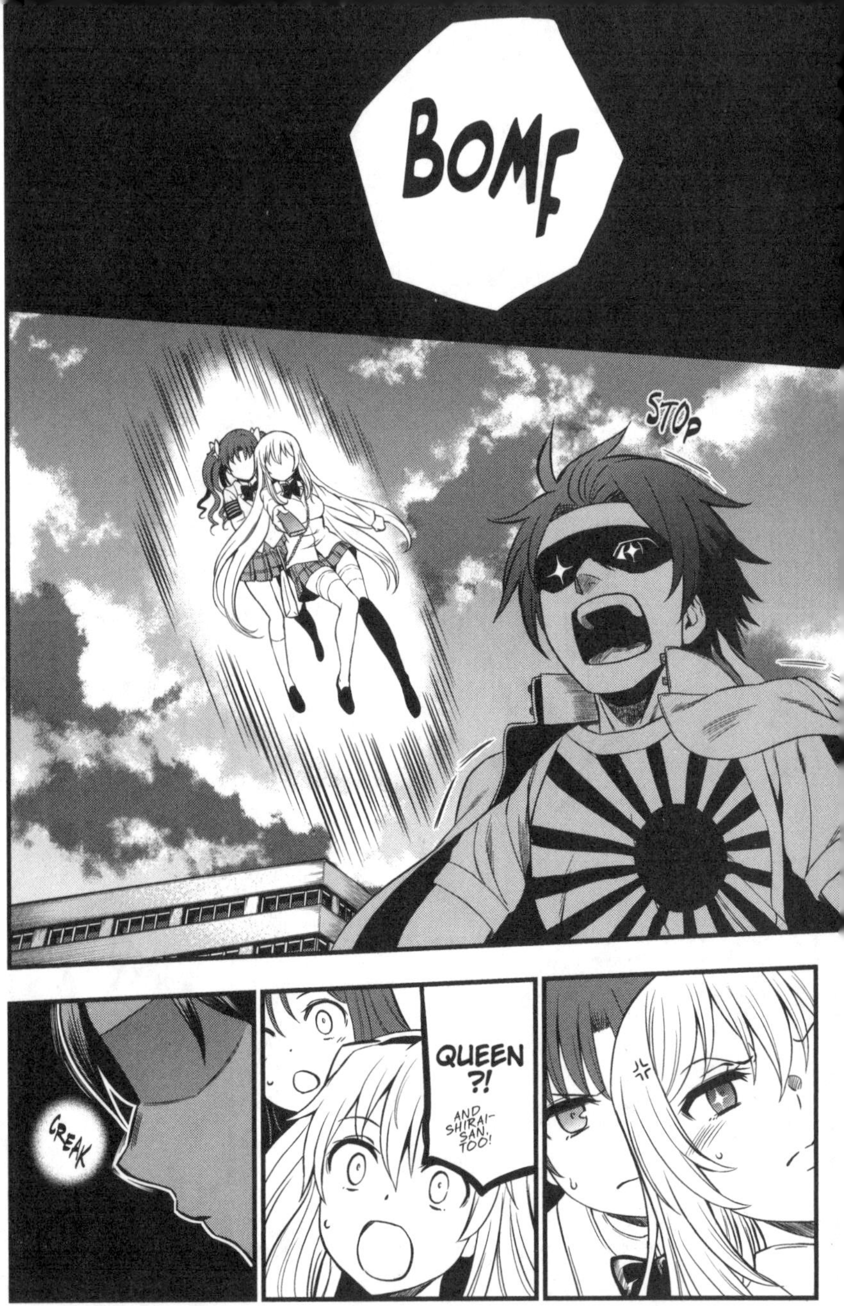
BOMF
STOP
QUEEN ?!
AND SHIRAI-SAN, TOO!
CREAK

CHAPTER 22: If I Had More Power

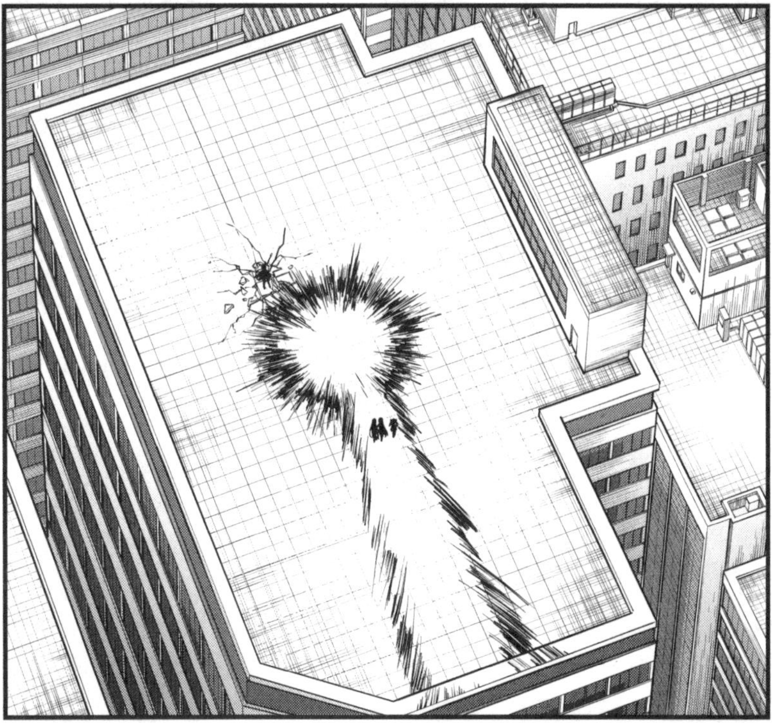

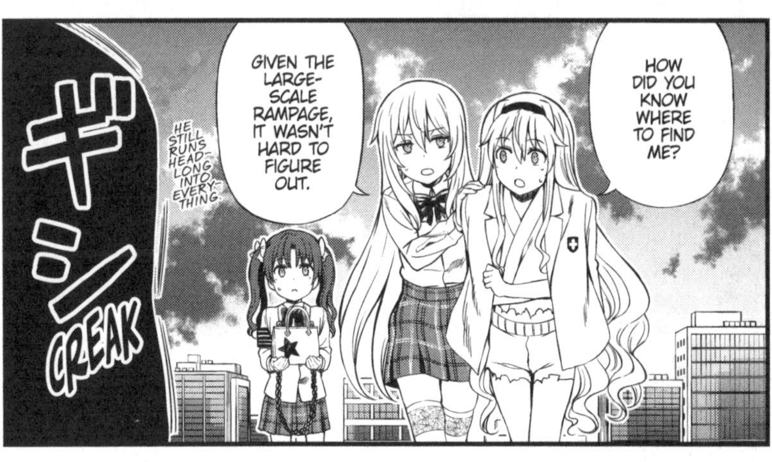
HOW DID YOU KNOW WHERE TO FIND ME?
GIVEN THE LARGE-SCALE RAMPAGE, IT WASN'T HARD TO FIGURE OUT.
HE STILL RUNS HEADLONG INTO EVERYTHING.
ギシ
CREAK

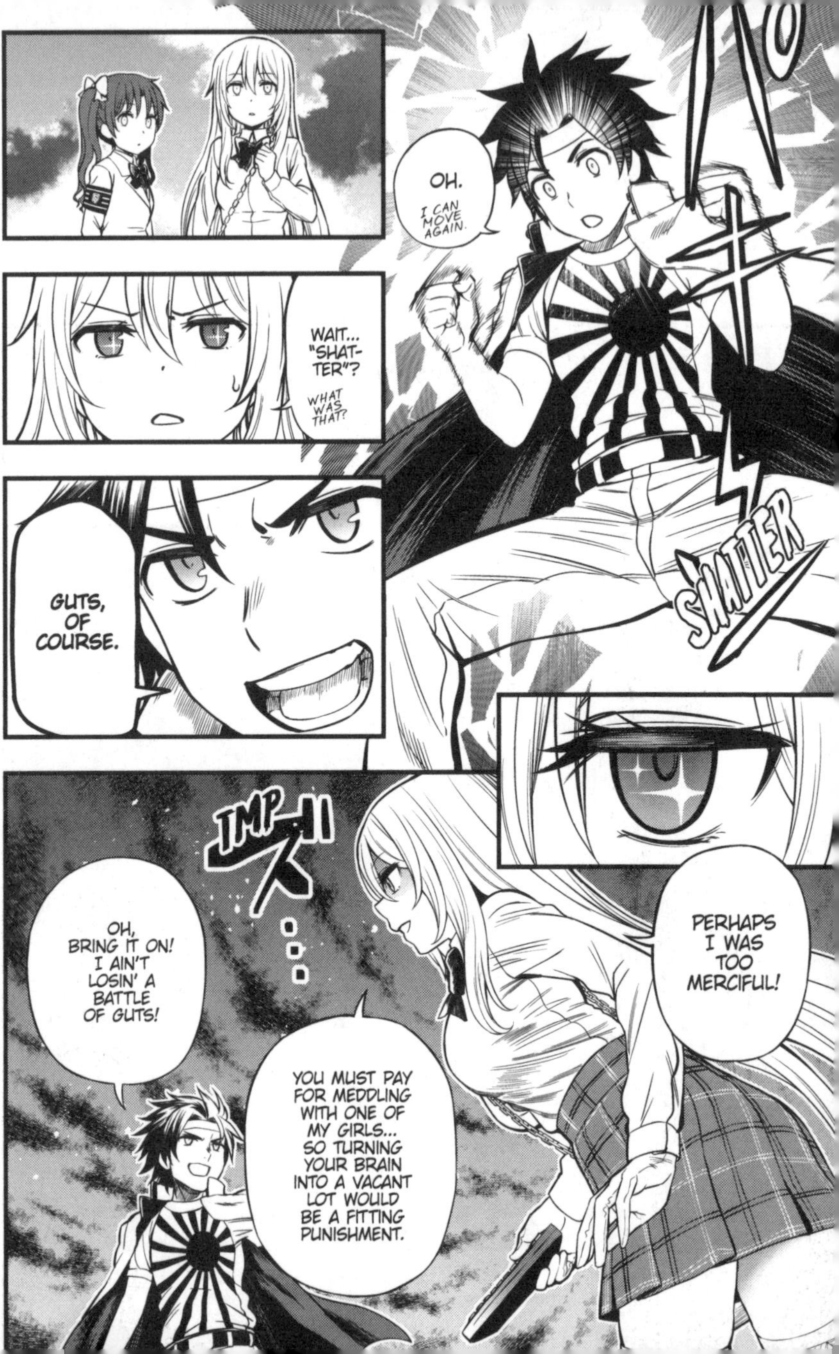

OH.
I CAN MOVE AGAIN.
WAIT... "SHAT-TER"?
WHAT WAS THAT?
SHATTER
GUTS, OF COURSE.
PERHAPS I WAS TOO MERCIFUL!
IMP-
YOU MUST PAY FOR MEDDLING WITH ONE OF MY GIRLS... SO TURNING YOUR BRAIN INTO A VACANT LOT WOULD BE A FITTING PUNISHMENT.
OH, BRING IT ON! I AIN'T LOSIN' A BATTLE OF GUTS!

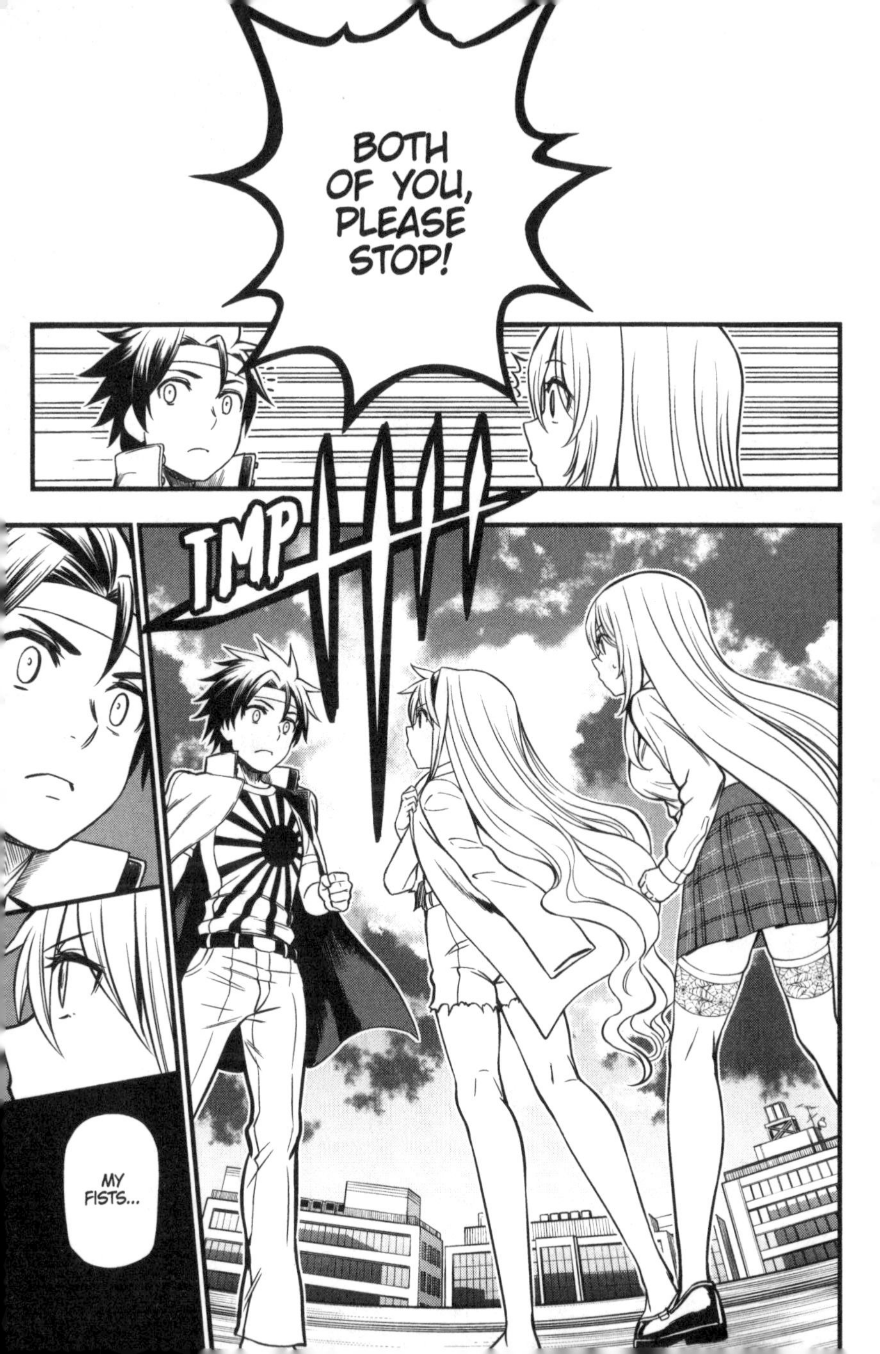
BOTH OF YOU, PLEASE STOP!
TMP
MY FISTS...

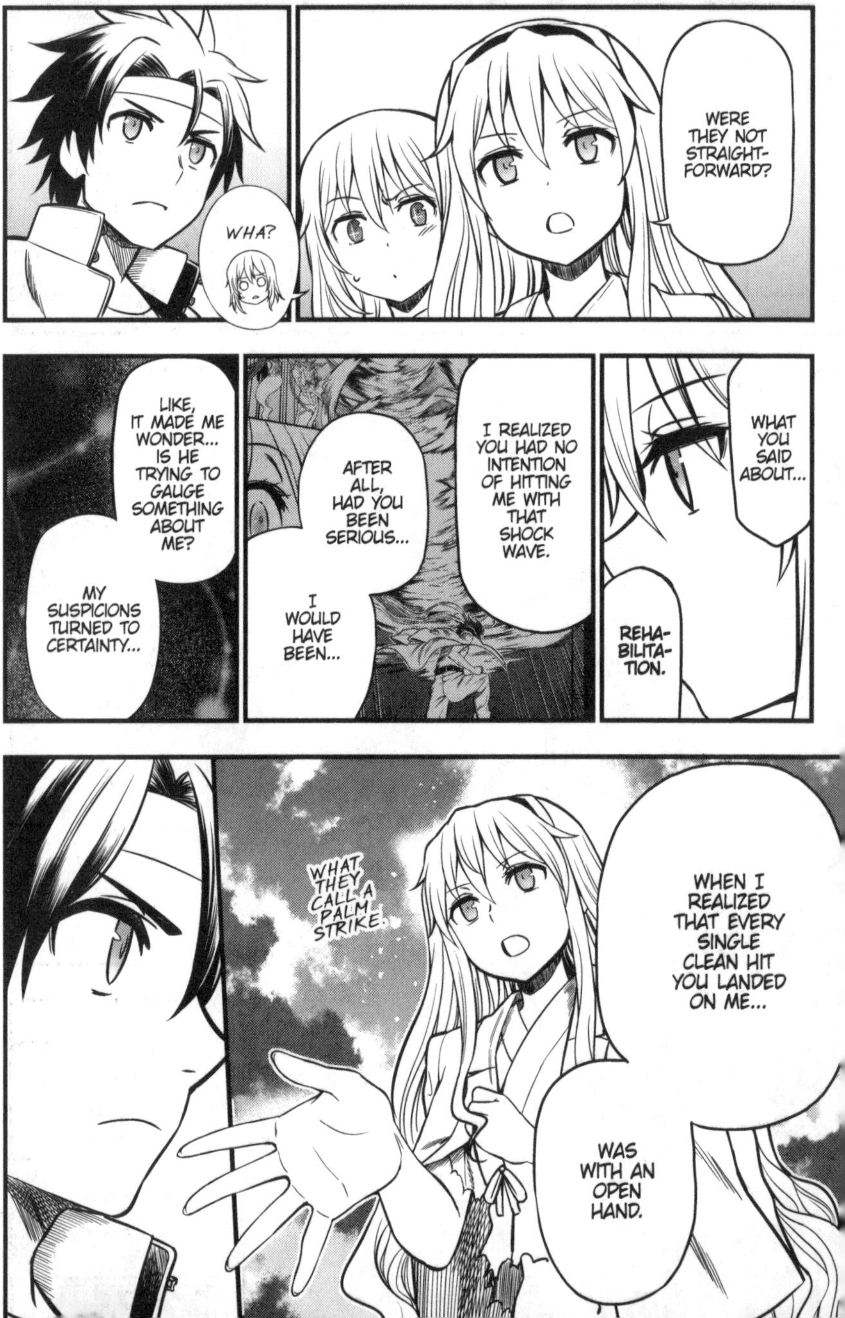
WERE THEY NOT STRAIGHT-FORWARD?
WHA?
WHAT YOU SAID ABOUT...
REHA-BILITA-TION.
I REALIZED YOU HAD NO INTENTION OF HITTING ME WITH THAT SHOCK WAVE.
AFTER ALL, HAD YOU BEEN SERIOUS...
I WOULD HAVE BEEN...
LIKE, IT MADE ME WONDER... IS HE TRYING TO GAUGE SOMETHING ABOUT ME?
MY SUSPICIONS TURNED TO CERTAINTY...
WHEN I REALIZED THAT EVERY SINGLE CLEAN HIT YOU LANDED ON ME...
WAS WITH AN OPEN HAND.
WHAT THEY CALL A PALM STRIKE.

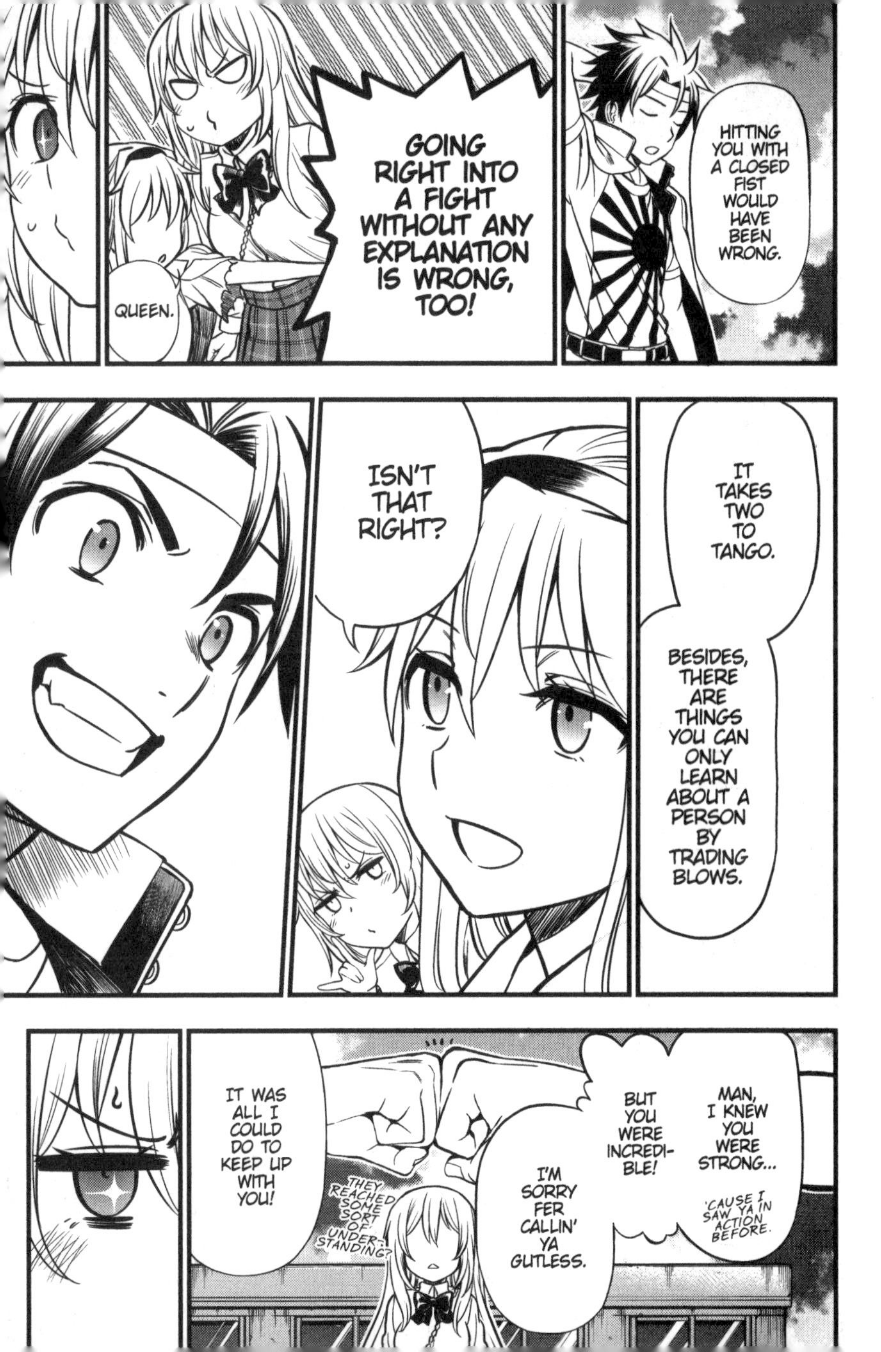
HITTING YOU WITH A CLOSED FIST WOULD HAVE BEEN WRONG.
GOING RIGHT INTO A FIGHT WITHOUT ANY EXPLANATION IS WRONG, TOO!
QUEEN.
IT TAKES TWO TO TANGO.
BESIDES, THERE ARE THINGS YOU CAN ONLY LEARN ABOUT A PERSON BY TRADING BLOWS.
ISN'T THAT RIGHT?
MAN, I KNEW YOU WERE STRONG...
'CAUSE I SAW YA IN ACTION BEFORE.
BUT YOU WERE INCREDIBLE!
I'M SORRY FER CALLIN' YA GUTLESS.
IT WAS ALL I COULD DO TO KEEP UP WITH YOU!
THEY REACHED SOME SORT OF UNDER-STANDING?

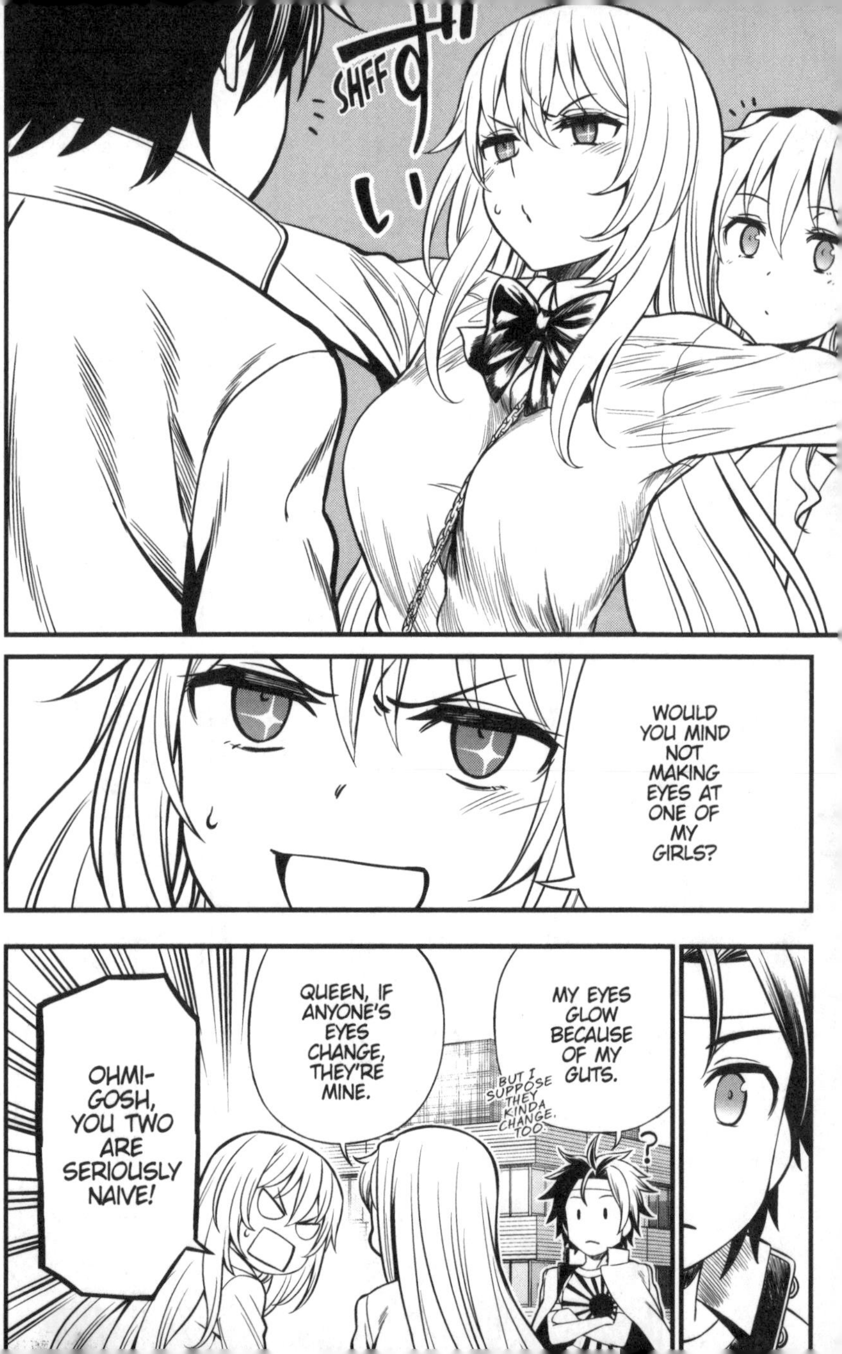
SHFF
WOULD YOU MIND NOT MAKING EYES AT ONE OF MY GIRLS?
MY EYES GLOW BECAUSE OF MY GUTS.
BUT I SUPPOSE THEY KINDA CHANGE, TOO.
?
QUEEN, IF ANYONE'S EYES CHANGE, THEY'RE MINE.
OHMI-GOSH, YOU TWO ARE SERIOUSLY NAIVE!

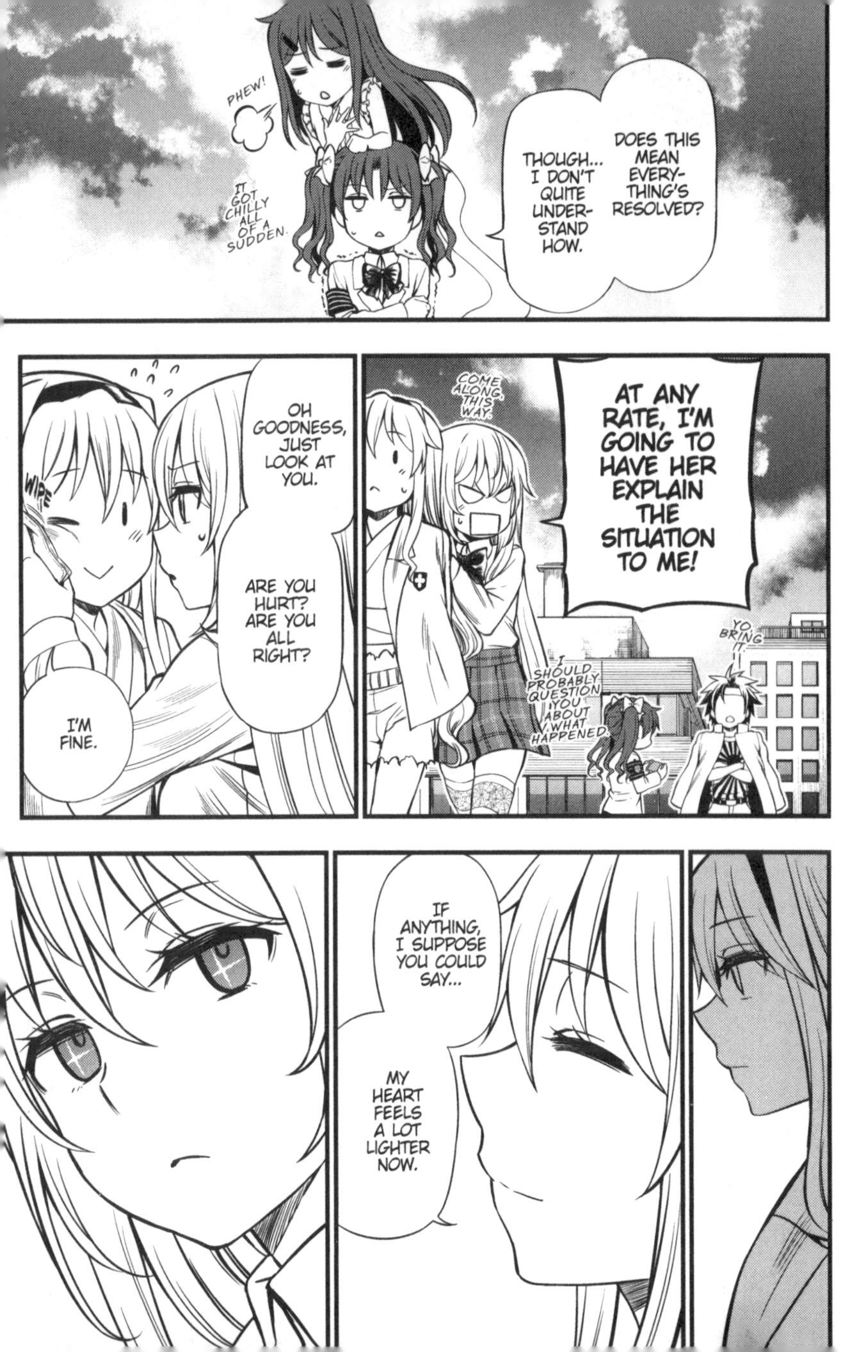
DOES THIS MEAN EVERYTHING'S RESOLVED?
THOUGH... I DON'T QUITE UNDERSTAND HOW.
PHEW!
IT GOT CHILLY ALL OF A SUDDEN.
AT ANY RATE, I'M GOING TO HAVE HER EXPLAIN THE SITUATION TO ME!
COME ALONG, THIS WAY.
YO BRING IT.
I SHOULD PROBABLY QUESTION YOU ABOUT WHAT HAPPENED.
OH GOODNESS, JUST LOOK AT YOU.
WIPE
ARE YOU HURT? ARE YOU ALL RIGHT?
I'M FINE.
IF ANYTHING, I SUPPOSE YOU COULD SAY...
MY HEART FEELS A LOT LIGHTER NOW.

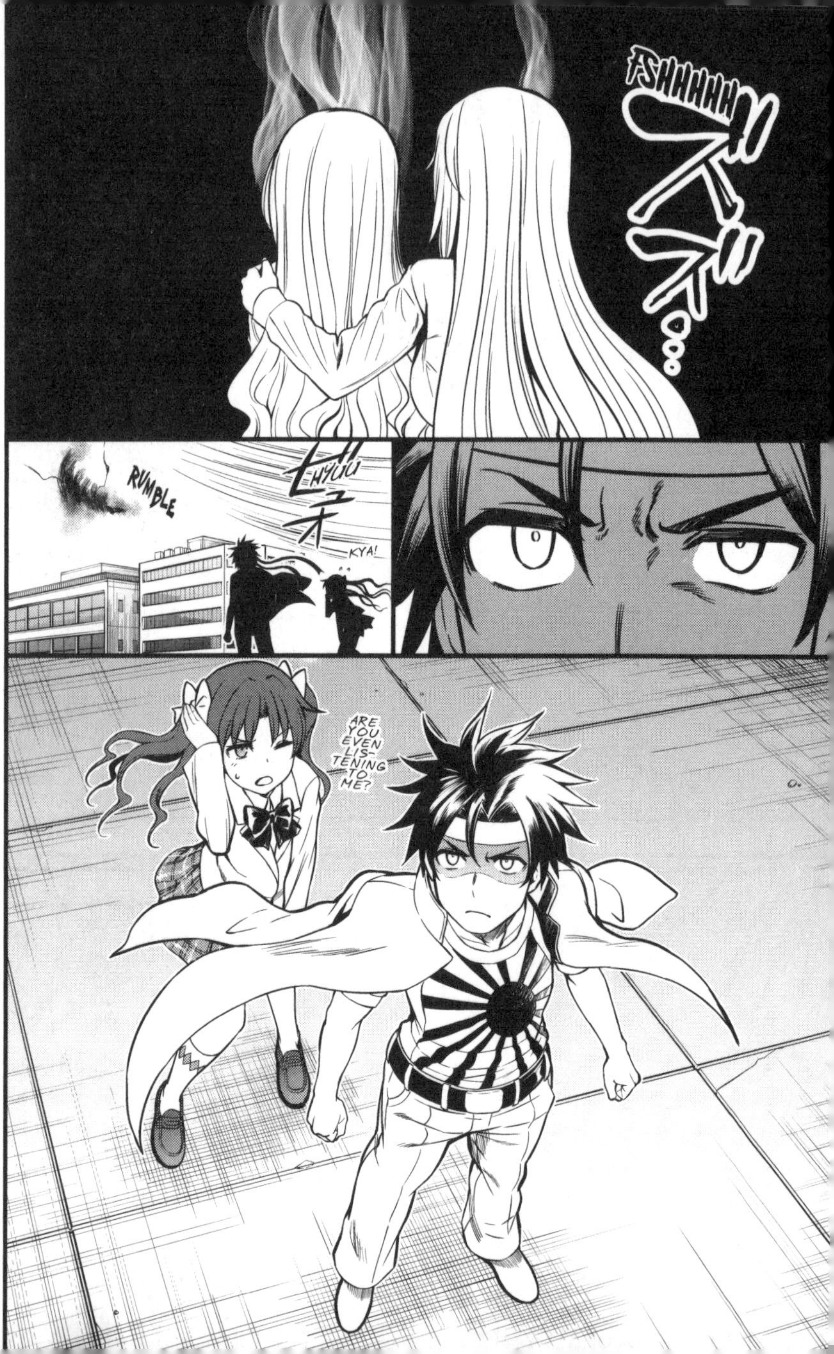
FSHHHHH
RUMBLE
HYUU
KYA!
ARE YOU EVEN LIS-TENING TO ME?

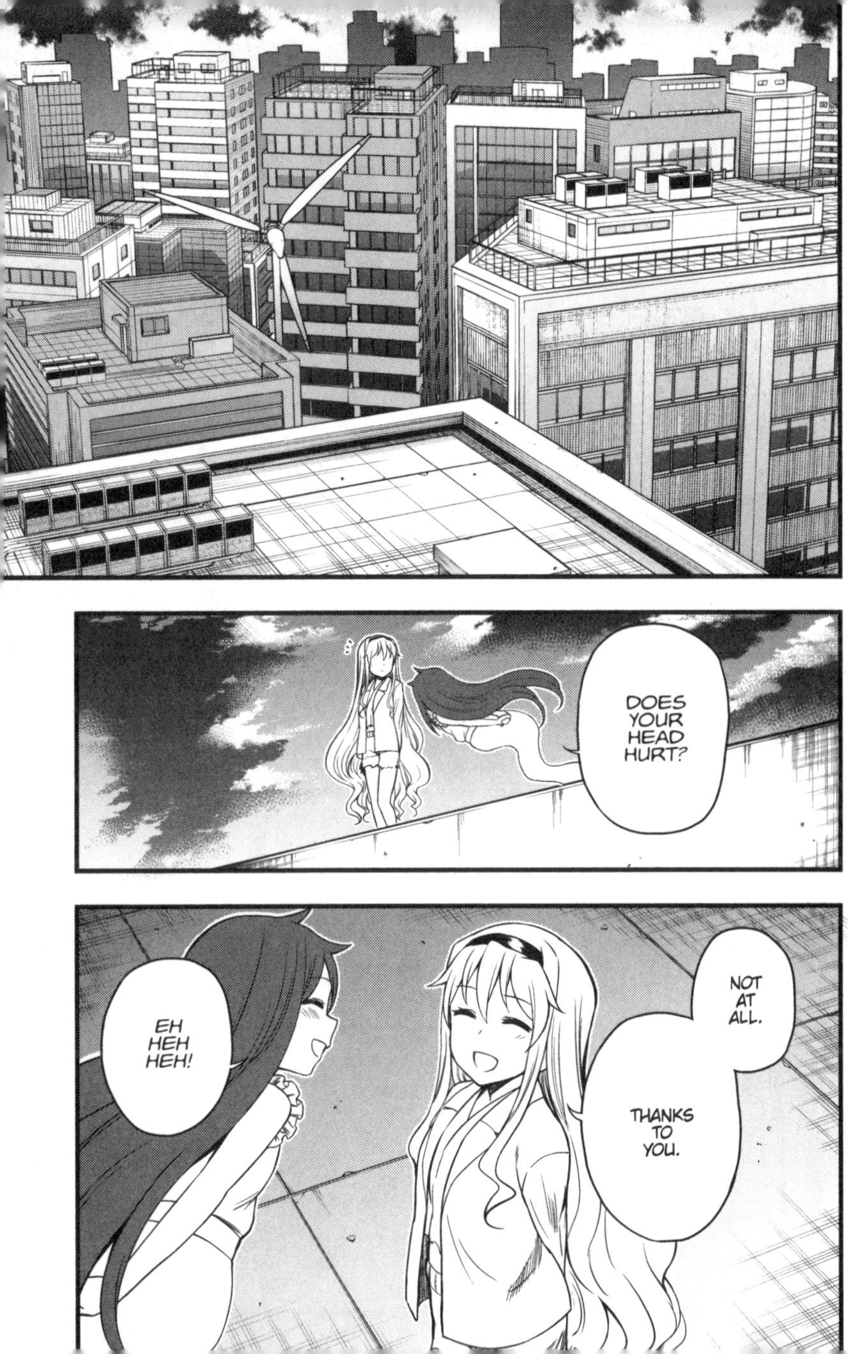
DOES YOUR HEAD HURT?
NOT AT ALL.
THANKS TO YOU.
EH HEH HEH!

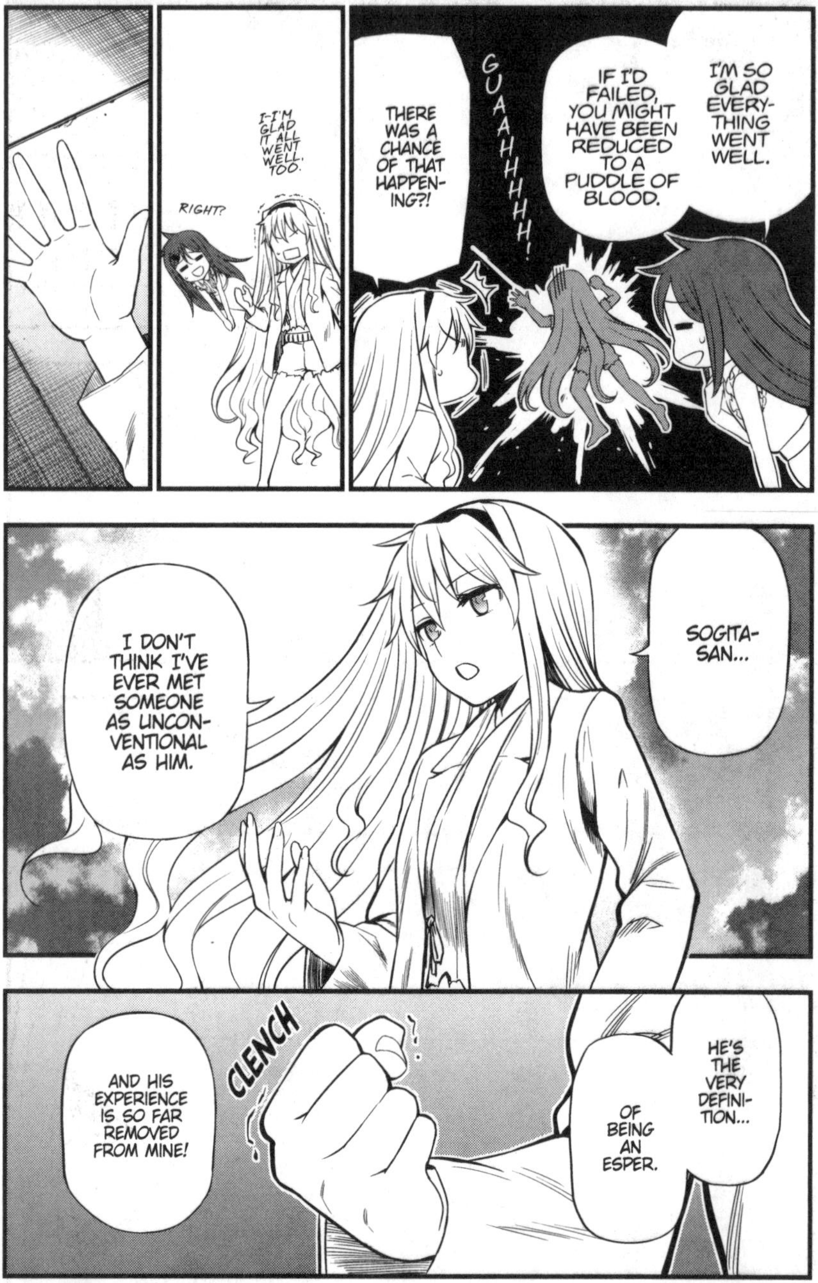
I'M SO GLAD EVERYTHING WENT WELL.
IF I'D FAILED, YOU MIGHT HAVE BEEN REDUCED TO A PUDDLE OF BLOOD.
GUAAHHHHH!
THERE WAS A CHANCE OF THAT HAPPENING?!
I-I'M GLAD IT ALL WENT WELL, TOO.
RIGHT?
SOGITA-SAN...
I DON'T THINK I'VE EVER MET SOMEONE AS UNCONVENTIONAL AS HIM.
HE'S THE VERY DEFINITION...
OF BEING AN ESPER.
CLENCH
AND HIS EXPERIENCE IS SO FAR REMOVED FROM MINE!

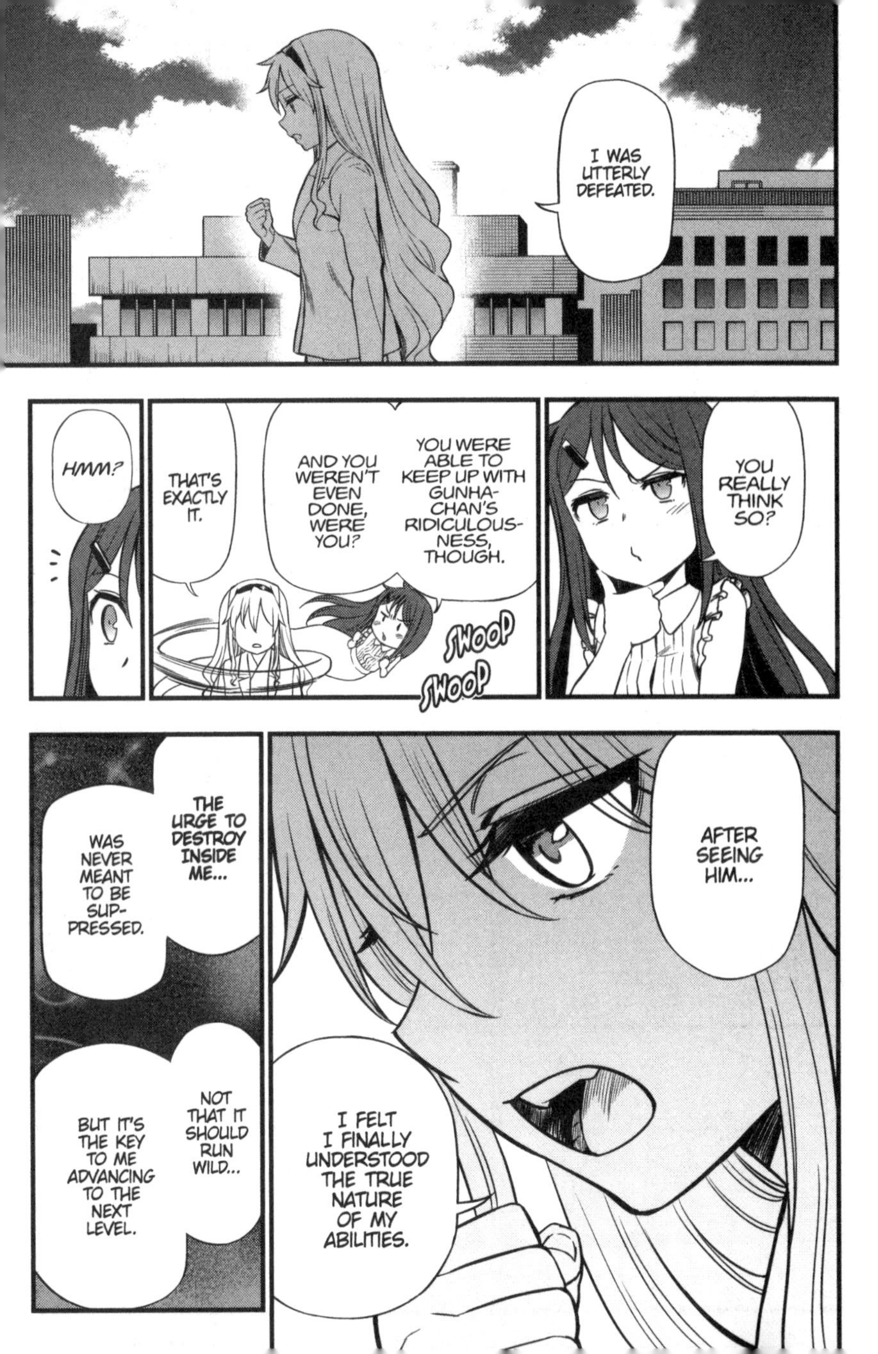
I WAS UTTERLY DEFEATED.
YOU REALLY THINK SO?
YOU WERE ABLE TO KEEP UP WITH GUNHA-CHAN'S RIDICULOUSNESS, THOUGH.
AND YOU WEREN'T EVEN DONE, WERE YOU?
THAT'S EXACTLY IT.
SWOOP
SWOOP
HMM?
AFTER SEEING HIM...
I FELT I FINALLY UNDERSTOOD THE TRUE NATURE OF MY ABILITIES.
THE URGE TO DESTROY INSIDE ME...
WAS NEVER MEANT TO BE SUPPRESSED.
NOT THAT IT SHOULD RUN WILD...
BUT IT'S THE KEY TO ME ADVANCING TO THE NEXT LEVEL.

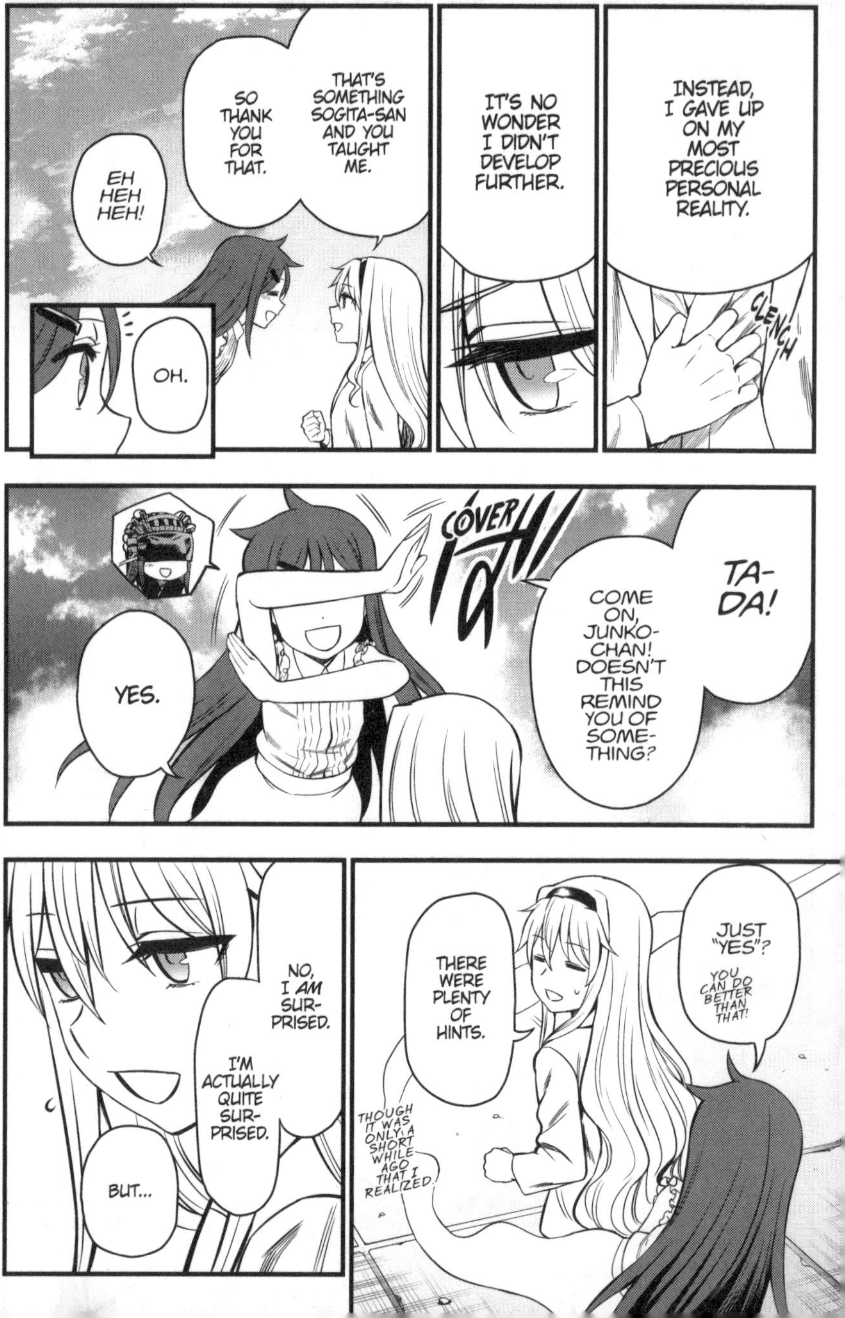
INSTEAD, I GAVE UP ON MY MOST PRECIOUS PERSONAL REALITY.
CLENCH
IT'S NO WONDER I DIDN'T DEVELOP FURTHER.
THAT'S SOMETHING SOGITA-SAN AND YOU TAUGHT ME.
SO THANK YOU FOR THAT.
EH HEH HEH!
OH.
TA-DA!
COME ON, JUNKO-CHAN! DOESN'T THIS REMIND YOU OF SOMETHING?
COVER
YES.
JUST "YES"?
YOU CAN DO BETTER THAN THAT!
THERE WERE PLENTY OF HINTS.
THOUGH IT WAS ONLY A SHORT WHILE AGO THAT I REALIZED.
NO, I *AM* SURPRISED.
I'M ACTUALLY QUITE SURPRISED.
BUT...

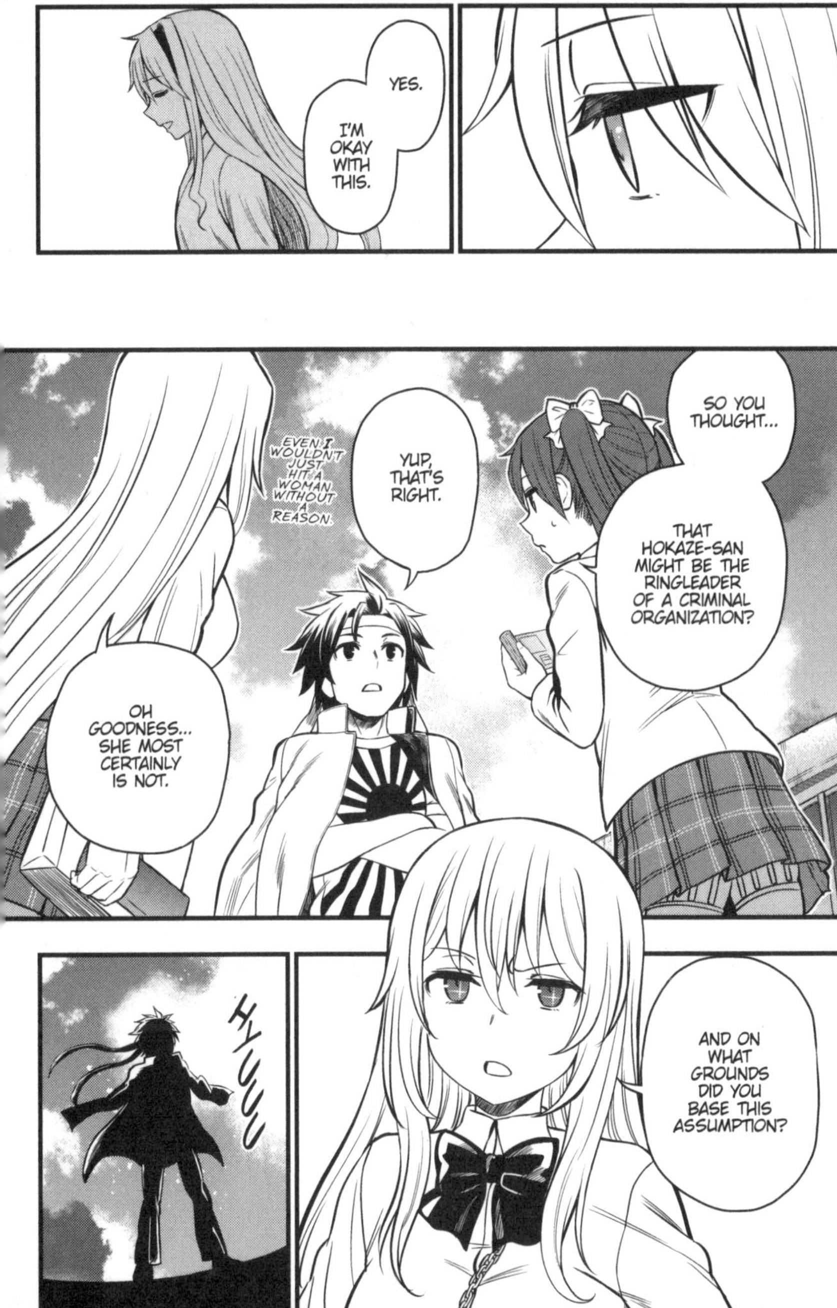
YES.
I'M OKAY WITH THIS.
SO YOU THOUGHT...
THAT HOKAZE-SAN MIGHT BE THE RINGLEADER OF A CRIMINAL ORGANIZATION?
YUP, THAT'S RIGHT.
EVEN I WOULDN'T JUST HIT A WOMAN WITHOUT A REASON.
OH GOODNESS... SHE MOST CERTAINLY IS NOT.
AND ON WHAT GROUNDS DID YOU BASE THIS ASSUMPTION?
HYUUU

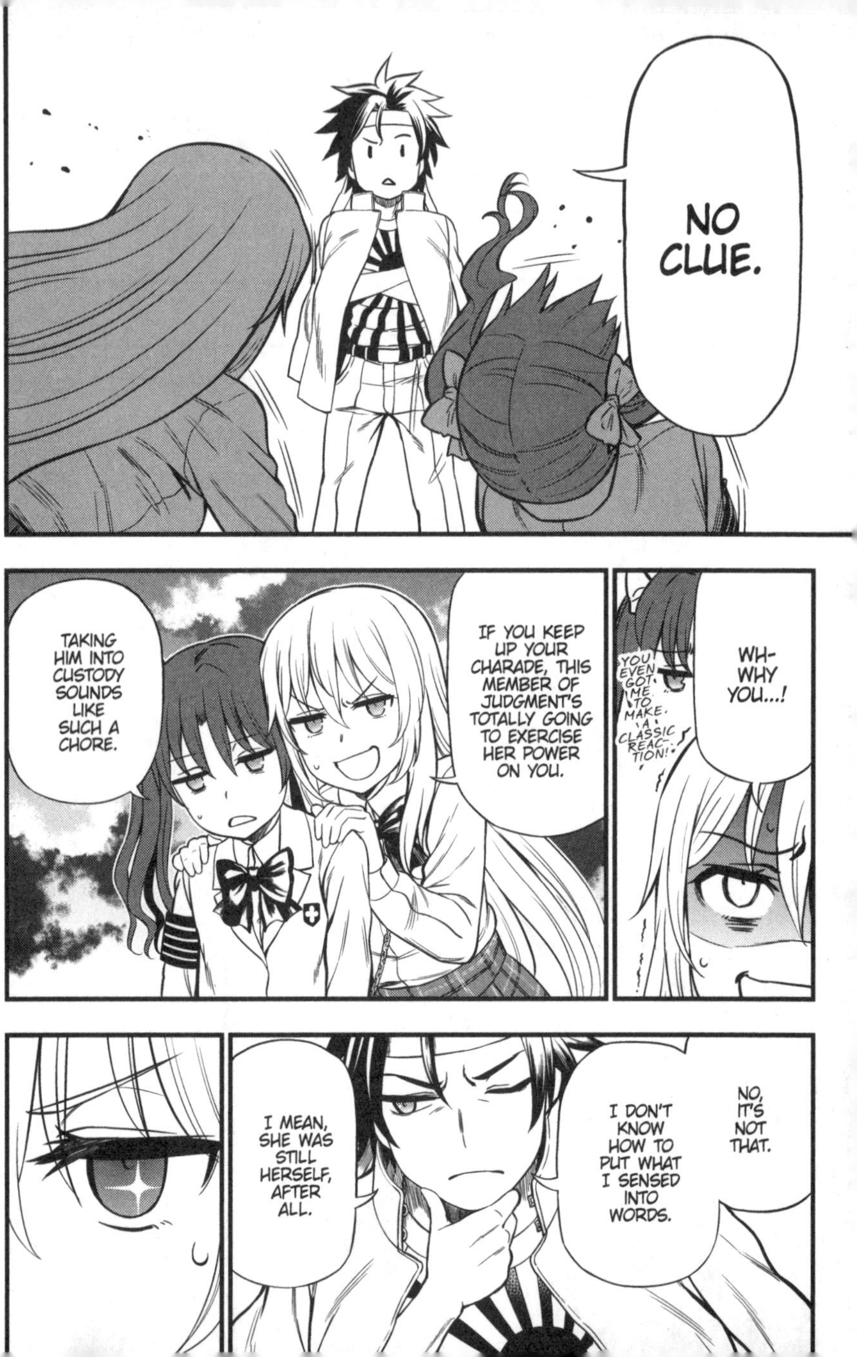
NO CLUE.
WH- WHY YOU...!
YOU EVEN GOT ME TO MAKE A CLASSIC REACTION!
IF YOU KEEP UP YOUR CHARADE, THIS MEMBER OF JUDGMENT'S TOTALLY GOING TO EXERCISE HER POWER ON YOU.
TAKING HIM INTO CUSTODY SOUNDS LIKE SUCH A CHORE.
NO, IT'S NOT THAT.
I DON'T KNOW HOW TO PUT WHAT I SENSED INTO WORDS.
I MEAN, SHE WAS STILL HERSELF, AFTER ALL.

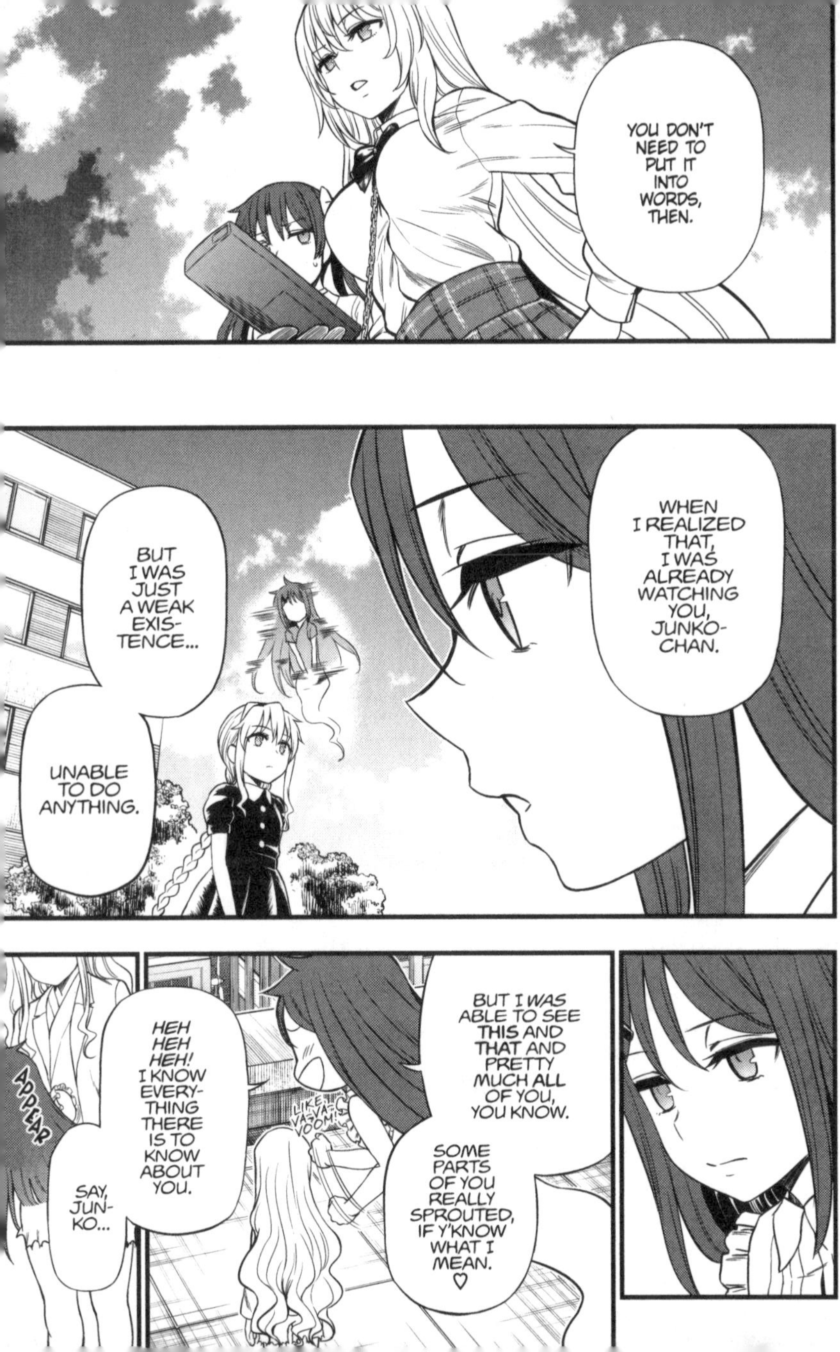
YOU DON'T NEED TO PUT IT INTO WORDS, THEN.
WHEN I REALIZED THAT, I WAS ALREADY WATCHING YOU, JUNKO-CHAN.
BUT I WAS JUST A WEAK EXIS-TENCE...
UNABLE TO DO ANYTHING.
BUT I WAS ABLE TO SEE THIS AND THAT AND PRETTY MUCH ALL OF YOU, YOU KNOW.
SOME PARTS OF YOU REALLY SPROUTED, IF Y'KNOW WHAT I MEAN. ♡
LIKE VA-VA-VOOM!
HEH HEH HEH! I KNOW EVERY-THING THERE IS TO KNOW ABOUT YOU.
APPEAR
SAY, JUN-KO...

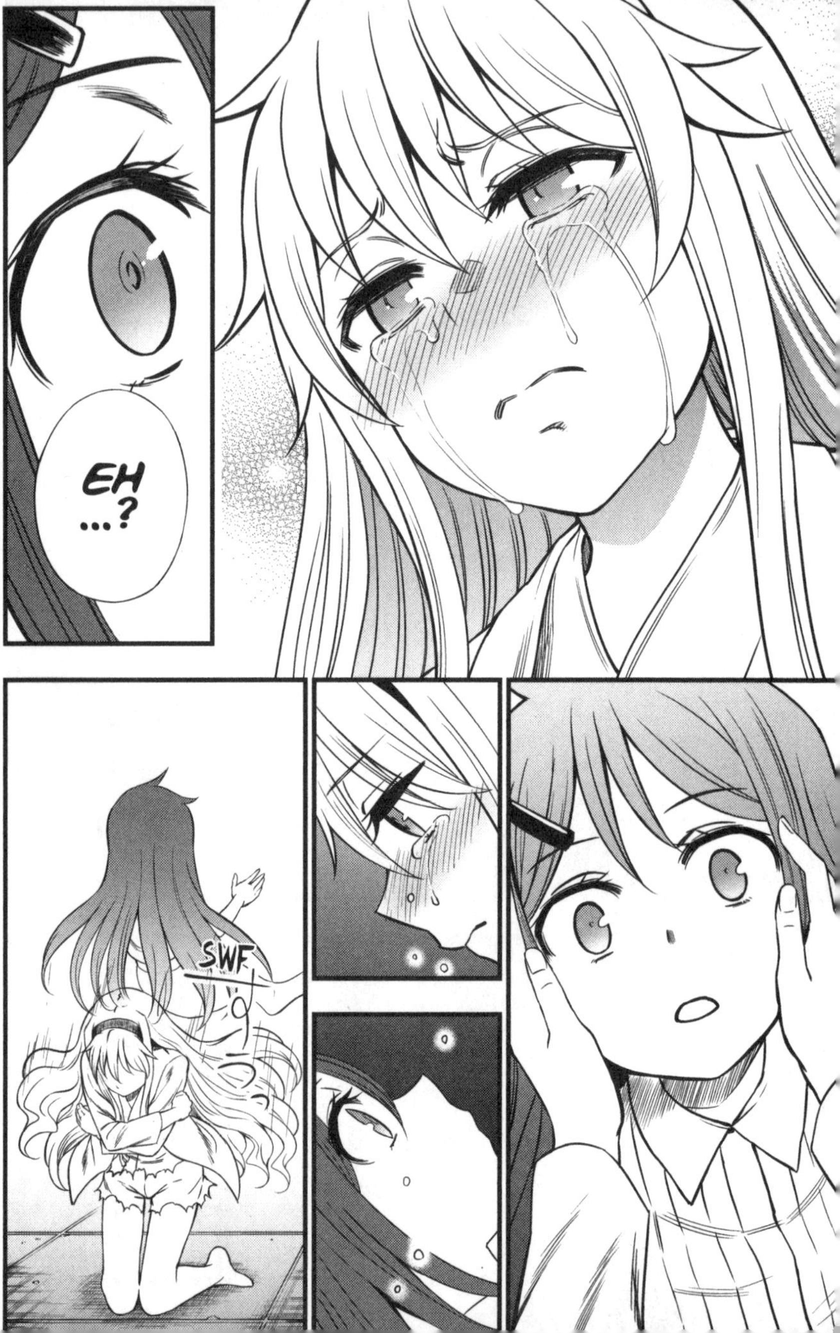
EH ...?
SWF

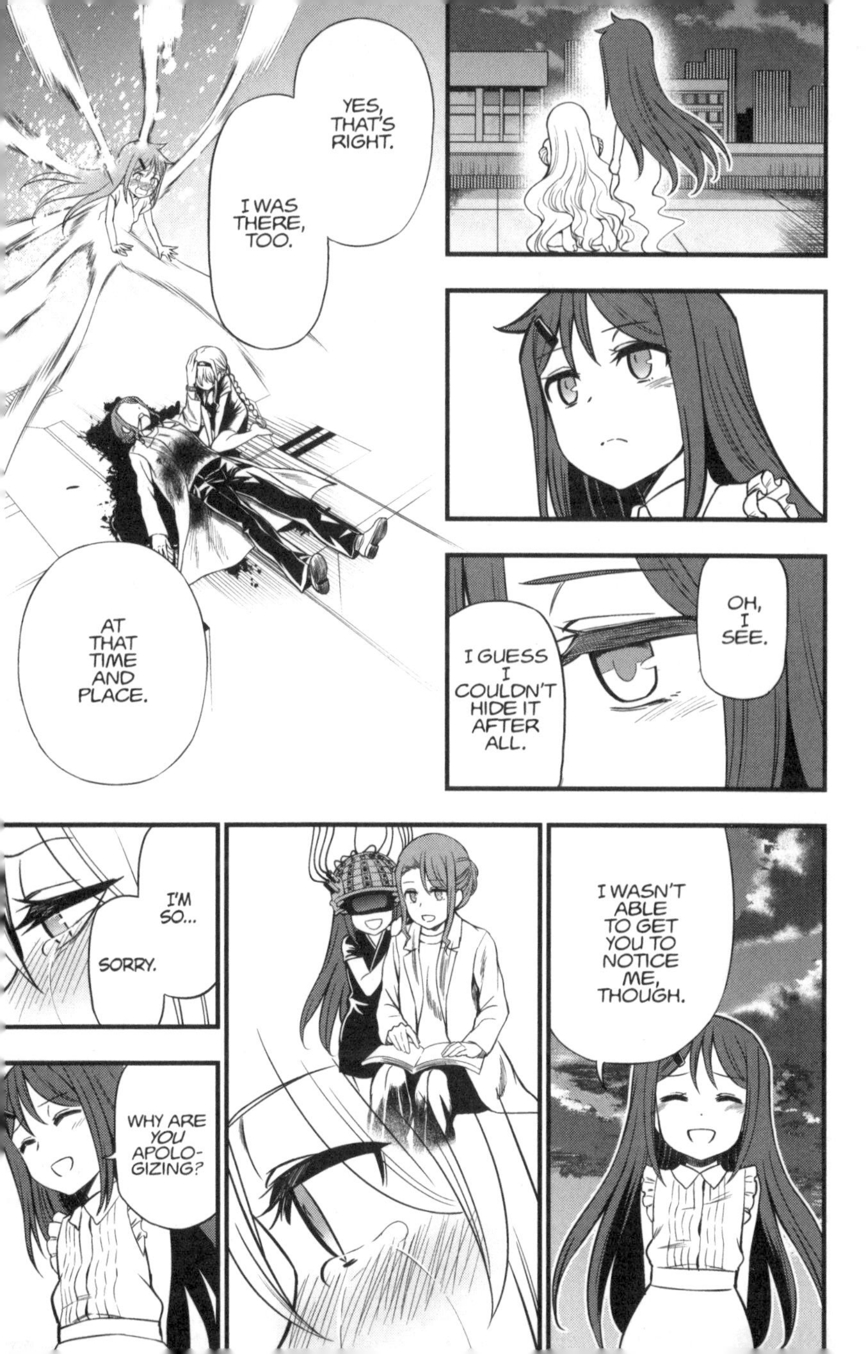
YES, THAT'S RIGHT.
I WAS THERE, TOO.
AT THAT TIME AND PLACE.
OH, I SEE.
I GUESS I COULDN'T HIDE IT AFTER ALL.
I WASN'T ABLE TO GET YOU TO NOTICE ME, THOUGH.
I'M SO...
SORRY.
WHY ARE *YOU* APOLOGIZING?

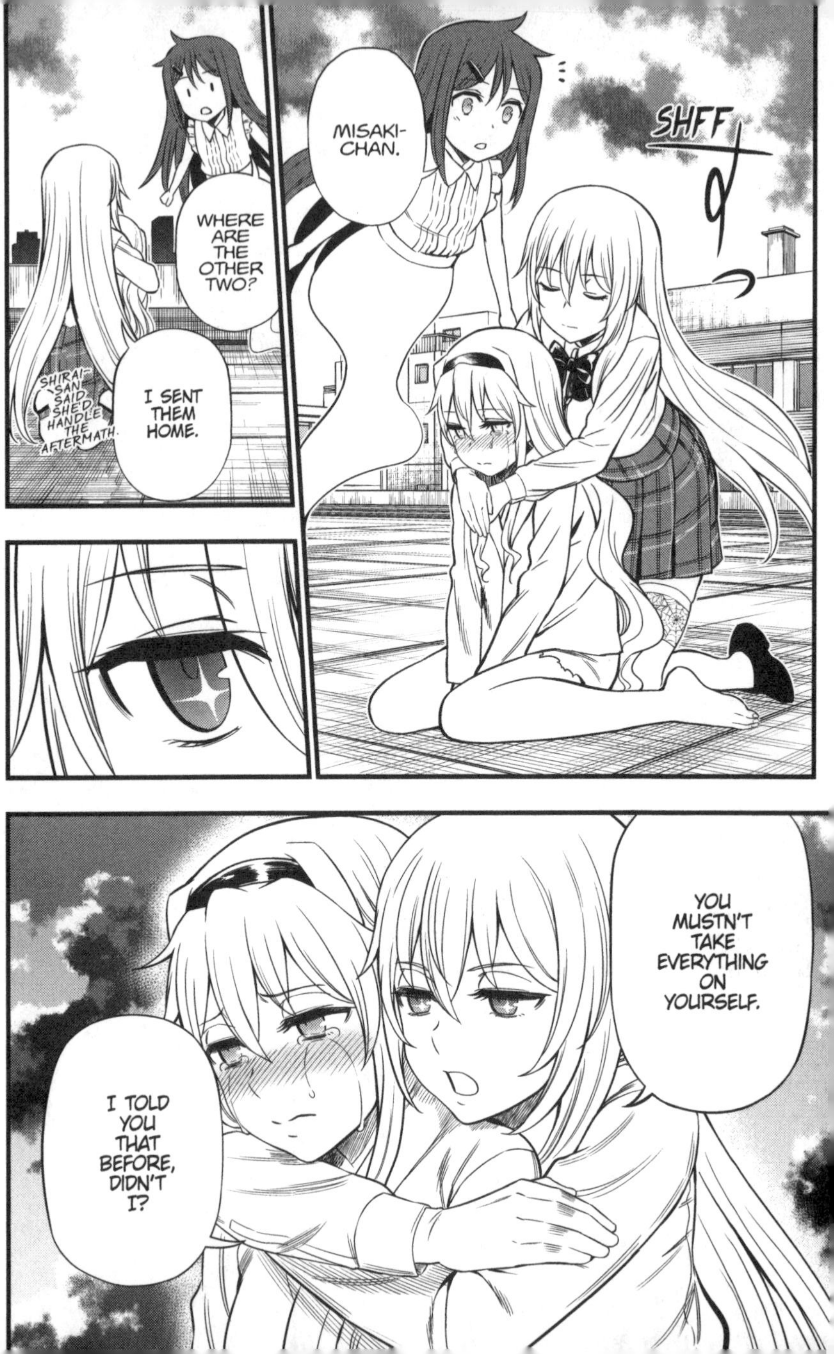
SHFF
MISAKI-CHAN.
WHERE ARE THE OTHER TWO?
I SENT THEM HOME.
SHIRAI-SAN SAID SHE'D HANDLE THE AFTERMATH.
YOU MUSTN'T TAKE EVERYTHING ON YOURSELF.
I TOLD YOU THAT BEFORE, DIDN'T I?

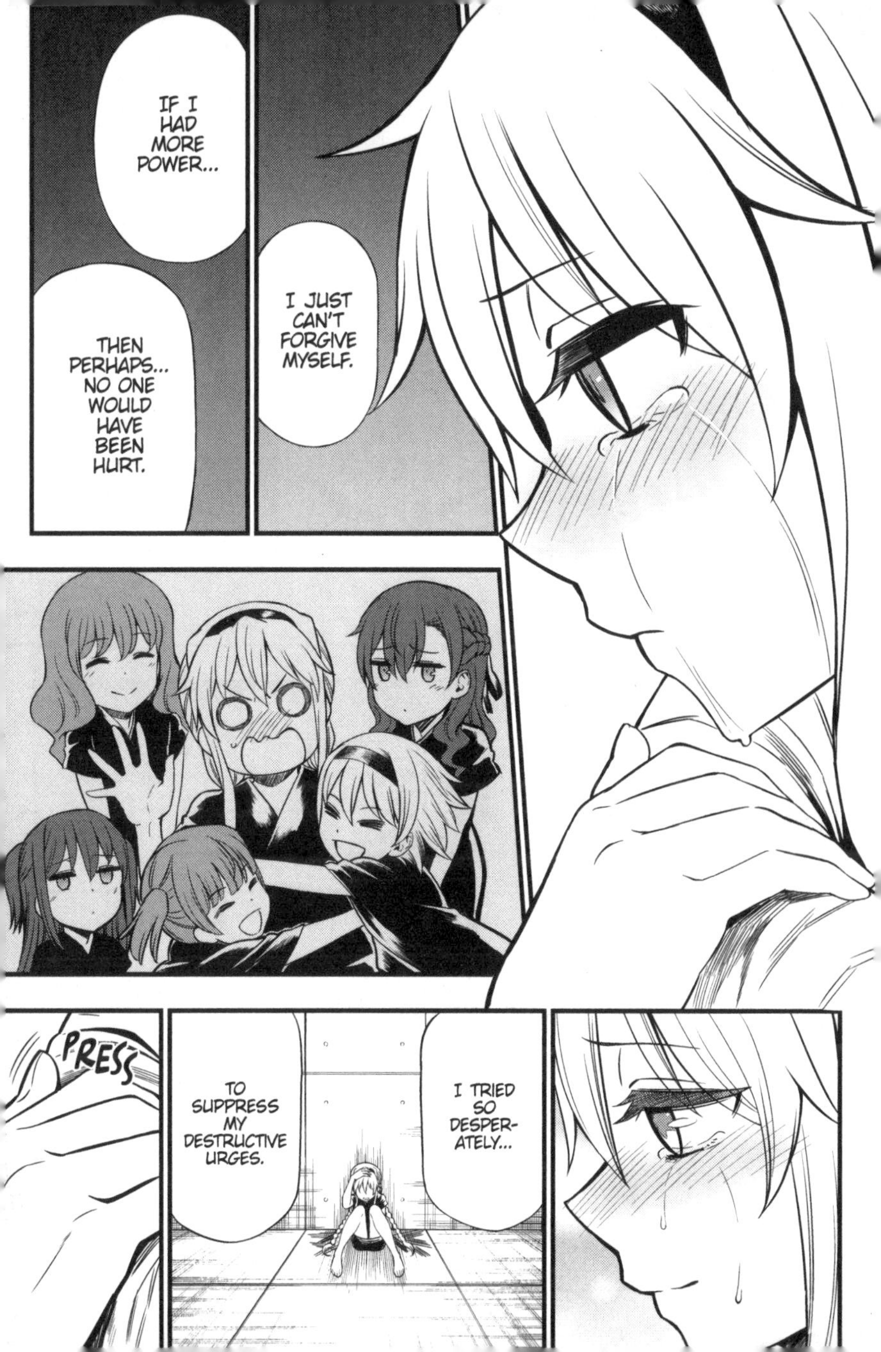
I JUST CAN'T FORGIVE MYSELF.
IF I HAD MORE POWER...
THEN PERHAPS... NO ONE WOULD HAVE BEEN HURT.
I TRIED SO DESPER-ATELY...
TO SUPPRESS MY DESTRUCTIVE URGES.
PRESS

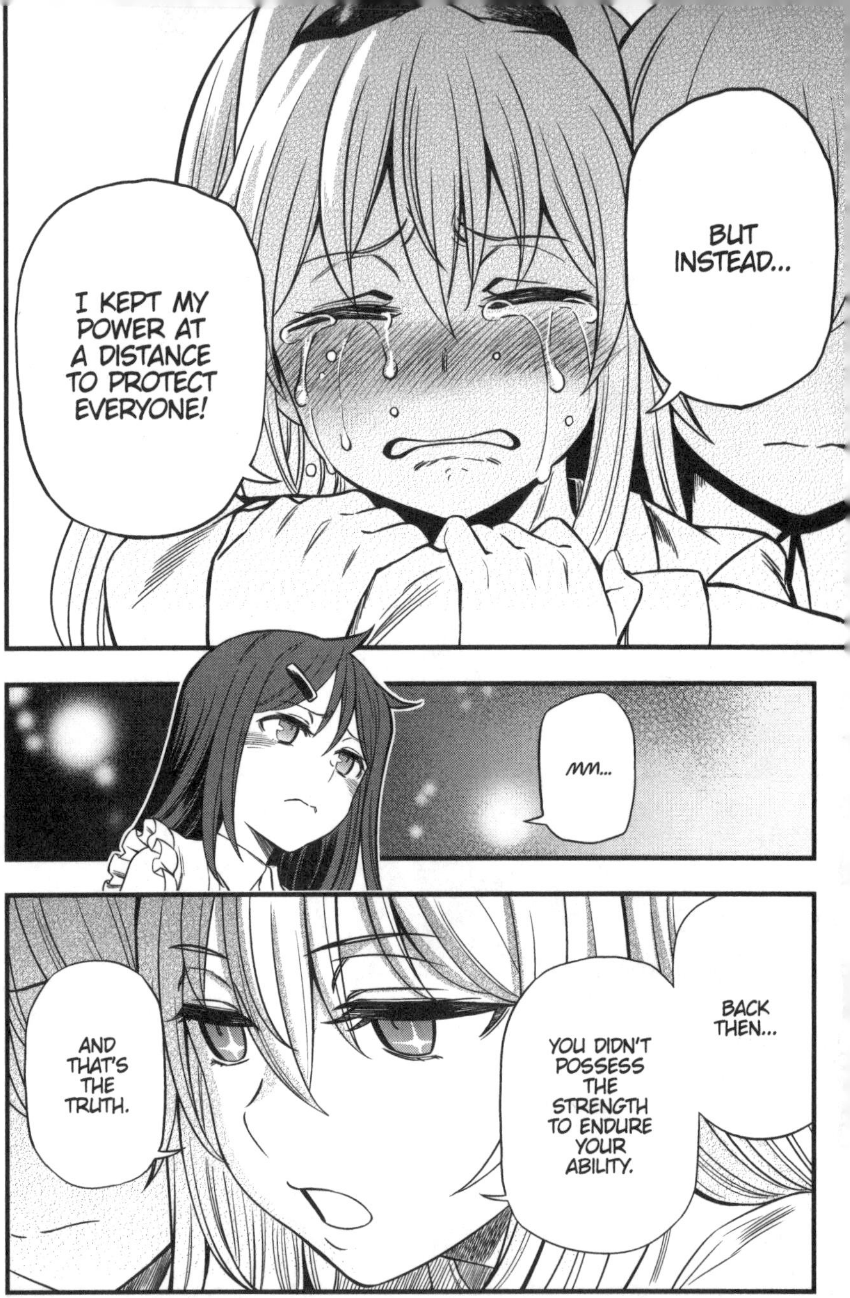
BUT INSTEAD...
I KEPT MY POWER AT A DISTANCE TO PROTECT EVERYONE!
MM...
BACK THEN...
YOU DIDN'T POSSESS THE STRENGTH TO ENDURE YOUR ABILITY.
AND THAT'S THE TRUTH.

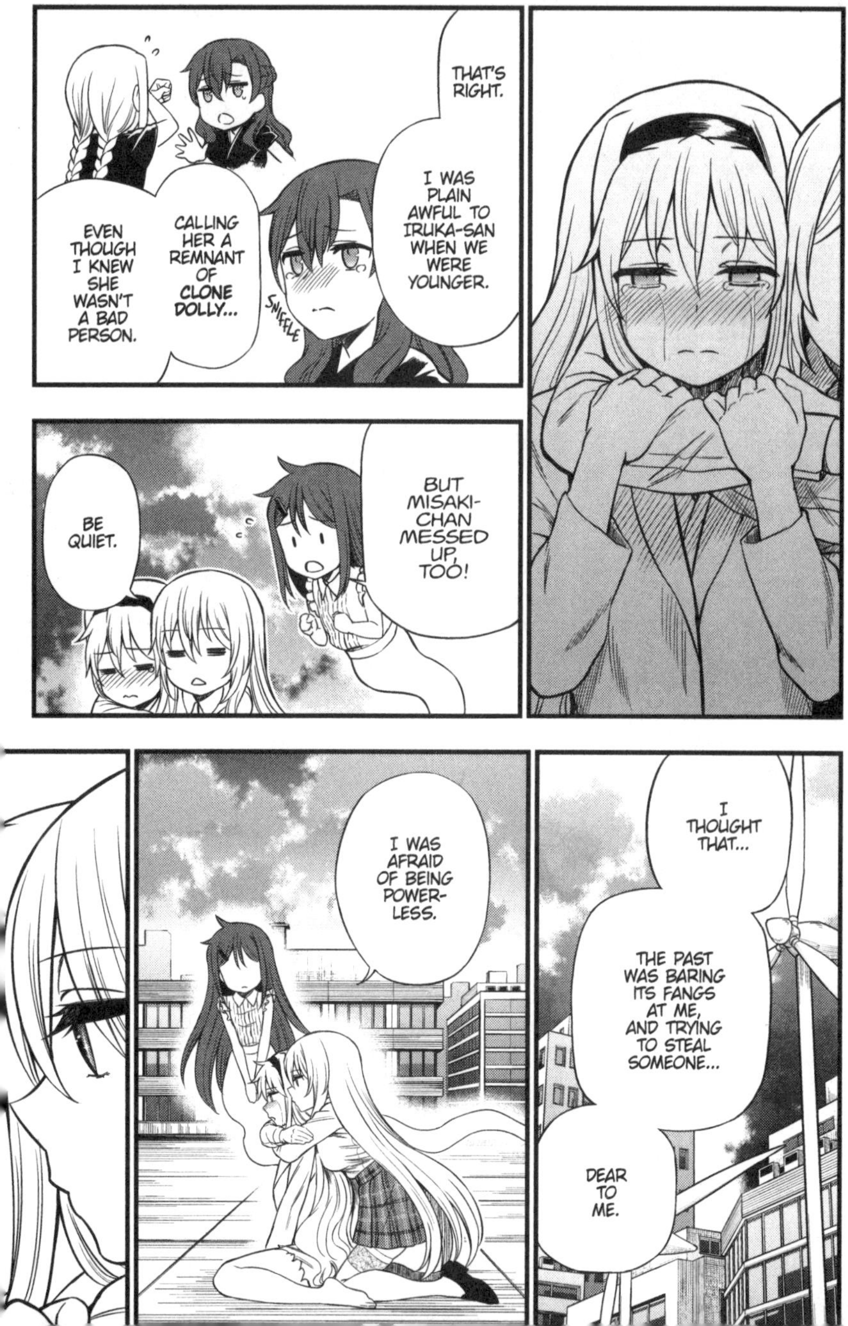
THAT'S RIGHT.
I WAS PLAIN AWFUL TO IRUKA-SAN WHEN WE WERE YOUNGER.
SNIFFLE
CALLING HER A REMNANT OF CLONE DOLLY...
EVEN THOUGH I KNEW SHE WASN'T A BAD PERSON.
BUT MISAKI-CHAN MESSED UP, TOO!
BE QUIET.
I THOUGHT THAT...
THE PAST WAS BARING ITS FANGS AT ME, AND TRYING TO STEAL SOMEONE...
DEAR TO ME.
I WAS AFRAID OF BEING POWER-LESS.

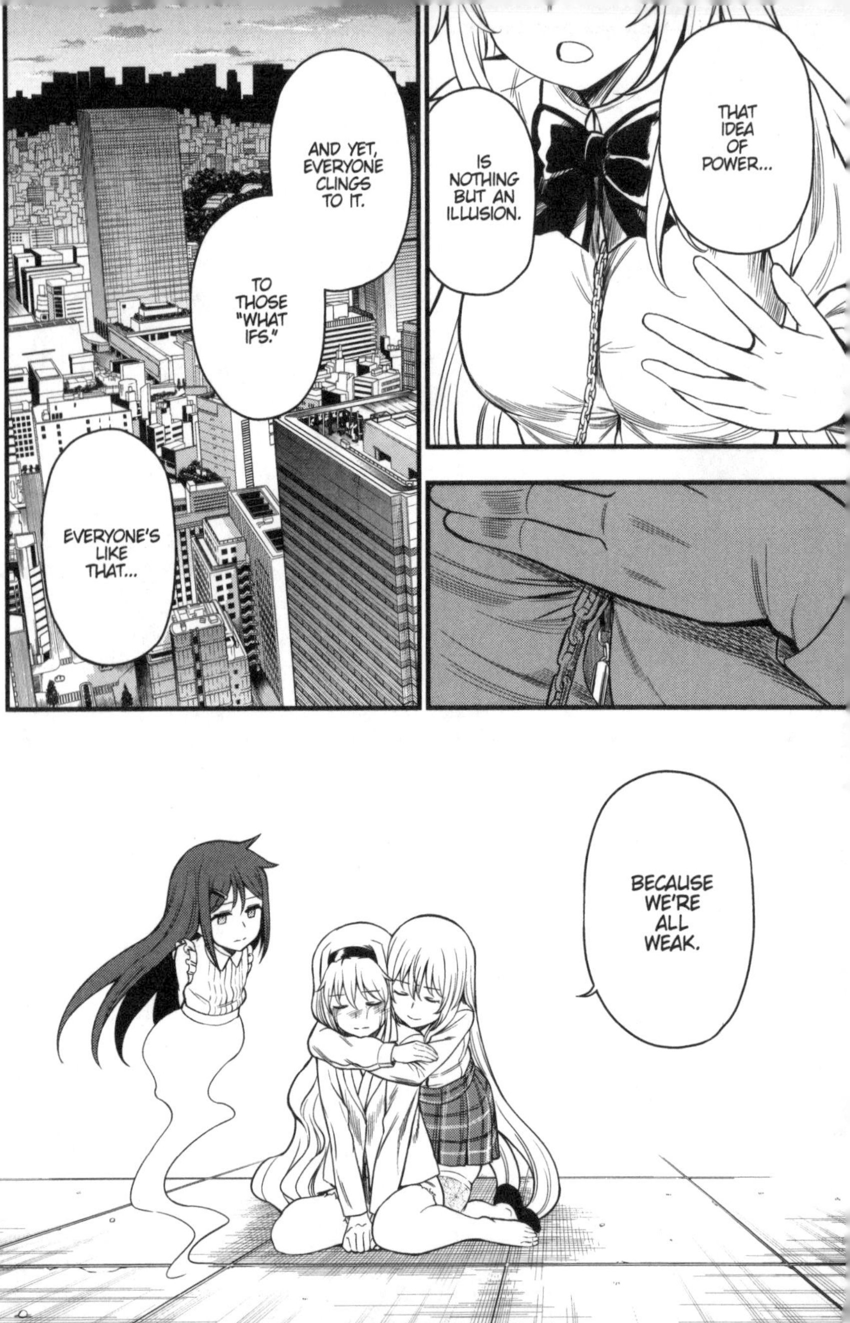
THAT IDEA OF POWER...
IS NOTHING BUT AN ILLUSION.
AND YET, EVERYONE CLINGS TO IT.
TO THOSE "WHAT IFS."
EVERYONE'S LIKE THAT...
BECAUSE WE'RE ALL WEAK.

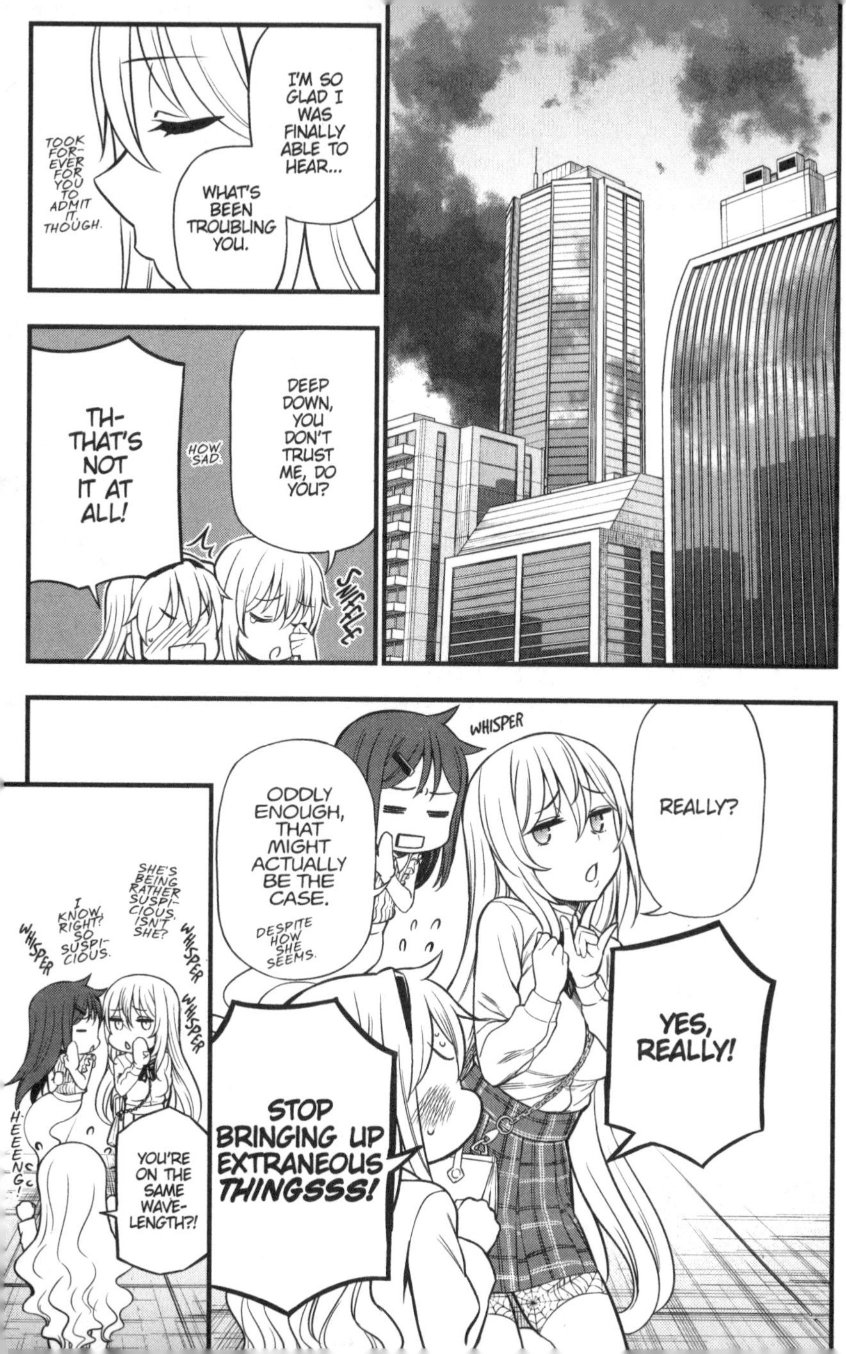
I'M SO GLAD I WAS FINALLY ABLE TO HEAR...
WHAT'S BEEN TROUBLING YOU.
TOOK FOR-EVER FOR YOU TO ADMIT IT, THOUGH.
DEEP DOWN, YOU DON'T TRUST ME, DO YOU?
HOW SAD.
TH- THAT'S NOT IT AT ALL!
SNIFFLE
WHISPER
REALLY?
ODDLY ENOUGH, THAT MIGHT ACTUALLY BE THE CASE.
DESPITE HOW SHE SEEMS.
YES, REALLY!
STOP BRINGING UP EXTRANEOUS THINGSSS!
SHE'S BEING RATHER SUSPI-CIOUS, ISN'T SHE?
I KNOW, RIGHT? SO SUSPI-CIOUS.
WHISPER
WHISPER
WHISPER
YOU'RE ON THE SAME WAVE-LENGTH?!
HEEEENG!

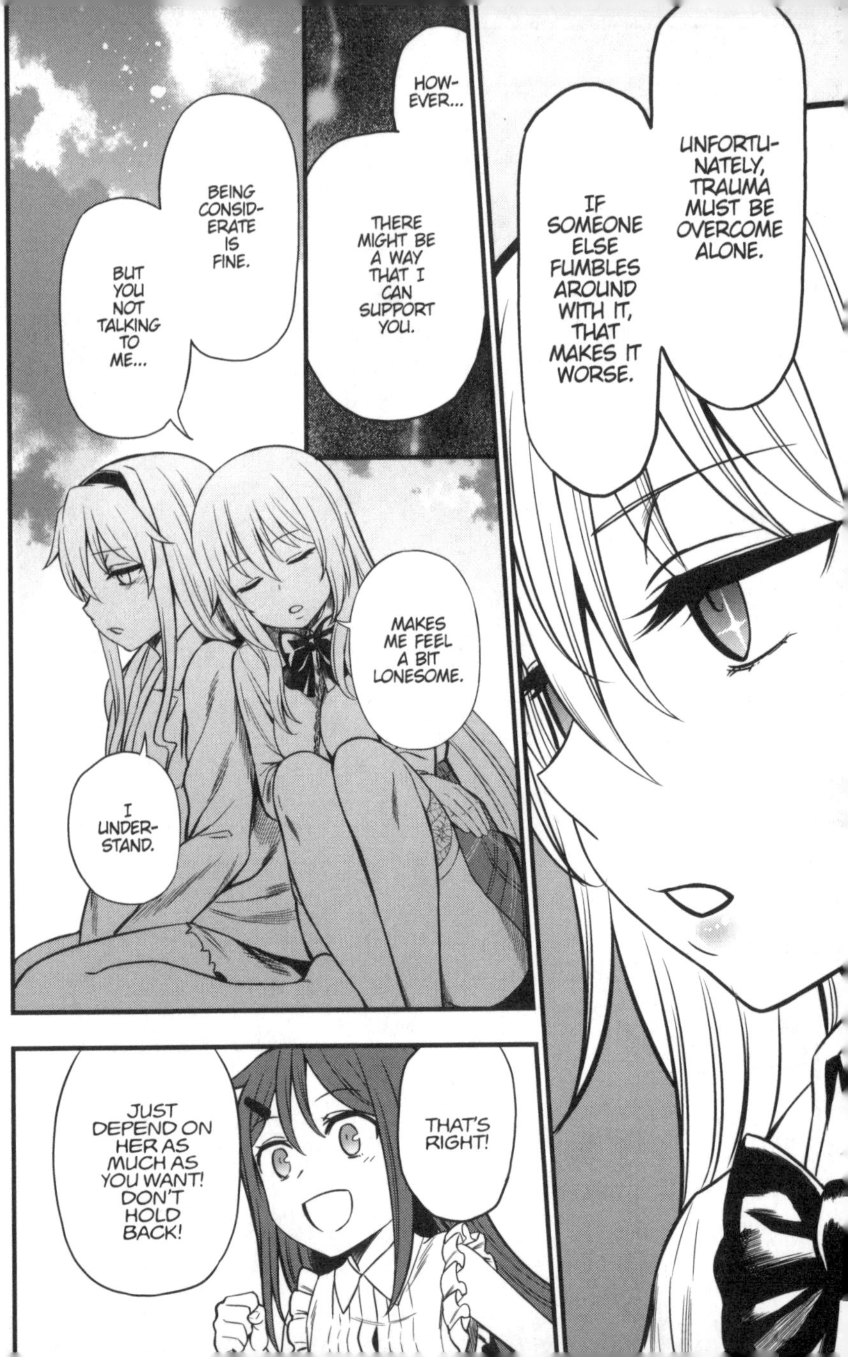
UNFORTUNATELY, TRAUMA MUST BE OVERCOME ALONE.
IF SOMEONE ELSE FUMBLES AROUND WITH IT, THAT MAKES IT WORSE.
HOWEVER...
THERE MIGHT BE A WAY THAT I CAN SUPPORT YOU.
BEING CONSIDERATE IS FINE.
BUT YOU NOT TALKING TO ME...
MAKES ME FEEL A BIT LONESOME.
I UNDERSTAND.
THAT'S RIGHT!
JUST DEPEND ON HER AS MUCH AS YOU WANT! DON'T HOLD BACK!

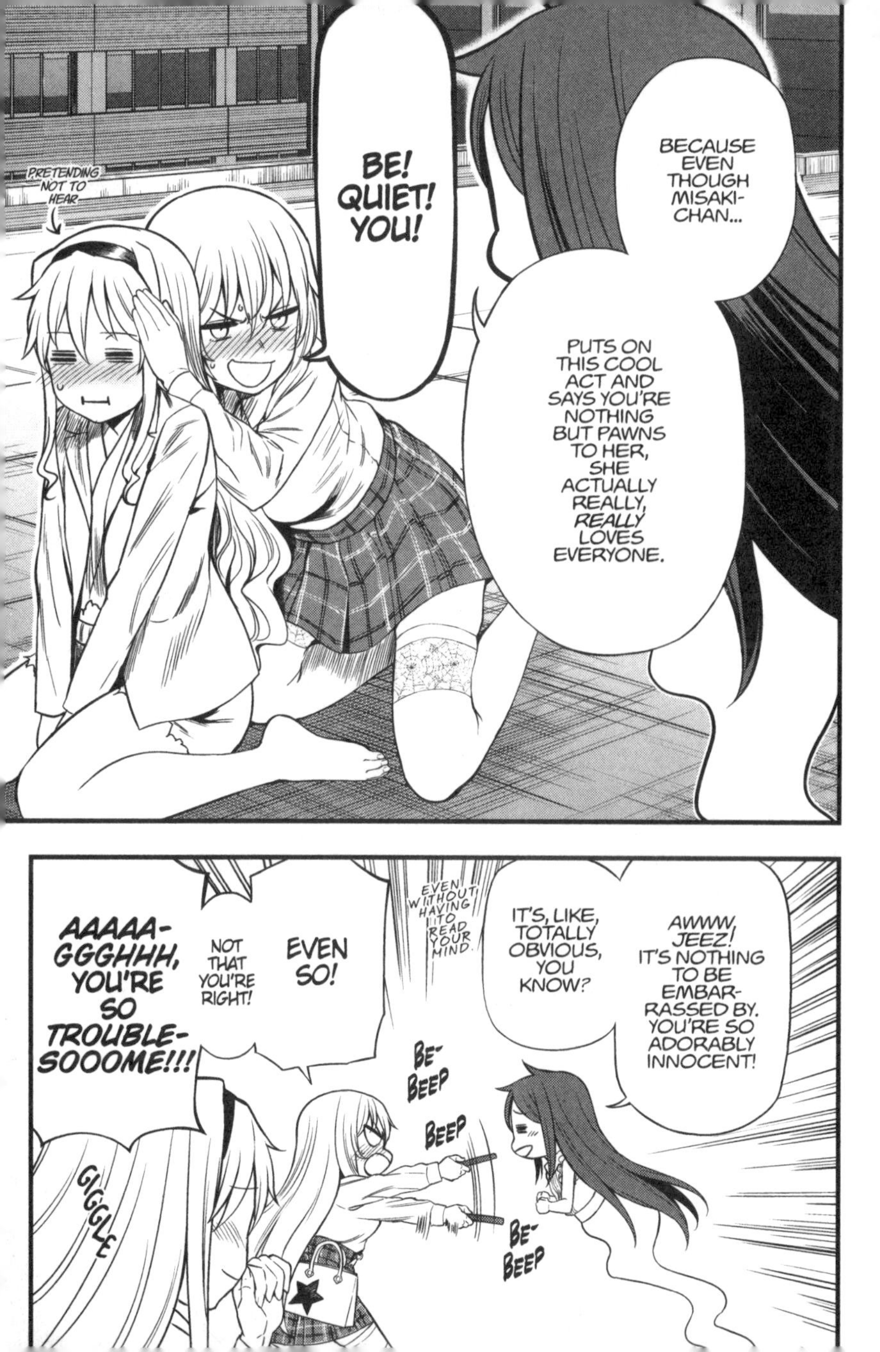
BECAUSE EVEN THOUGH MISAKI-CHAN...
PUTS ON THIS COOL ACT AND SAYS YOU'RE NOTHING BUT PAWNS TO HER, SHE ACTUALLY REALLY, *REALLY* LOVES EVERYONE.
BE! QUIET! YOU!
PRETENDING NOT TO HEAR
AWWW, JEEZ! IT'S NOTHING TO BE EMBARRASSED BY. YOU'RE SO ADORABLY INNOCENT!
IT'S, LIKE, TOTALLY OBVIOUS, YOU KNOW?
EVEN WITHOUT HAVING TO READ YOUR MIND.
EVEN SO!
NOT THAT YOU'RE RIGHT!
AAAAA-GGGHHH, YOU'RE SO TROUBLE-SOOOME!!!
BE-BEEP
BEEP
BE-BEEP
GIGGLE

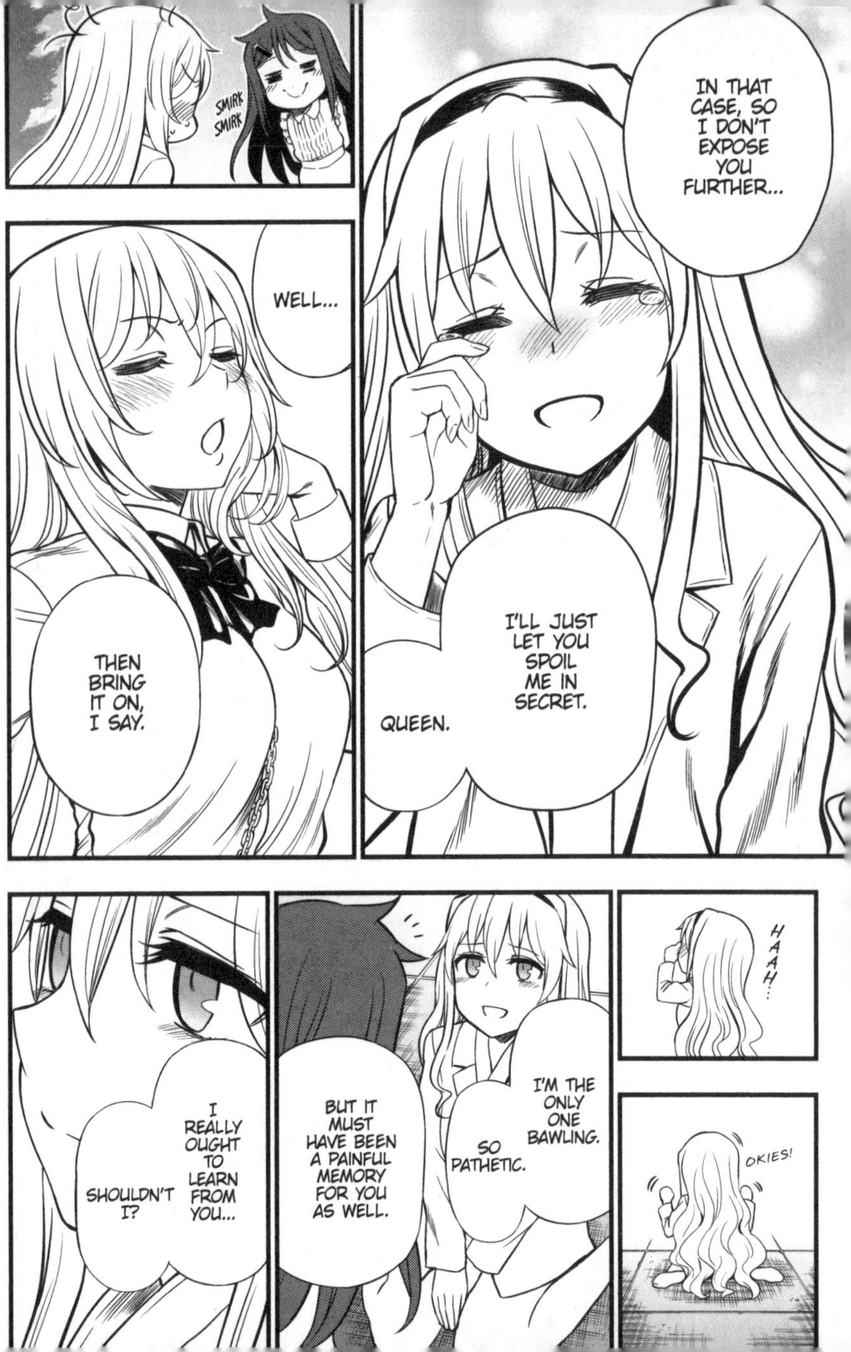
IN THAT CASE, SO I DON'T EXPOSE YOU FURTHER...
I'LL JUST LET YOU SPOIL ME IN SECRET.
QUEEN.
SMIRK SMIRK
WELL...
THEN BRING IT ON, I SAY.
HAAAH...
OKIES!
I'M THE ONLY ONE BAWLING.
SO PATHETIC.
BUT IT MUST HAVE BEEN A PAINFUL MEMORY FOR YOU AS WELL.
I REALLY OUGHT TO LEARN FROM YOU...
SHOULDN'T I?

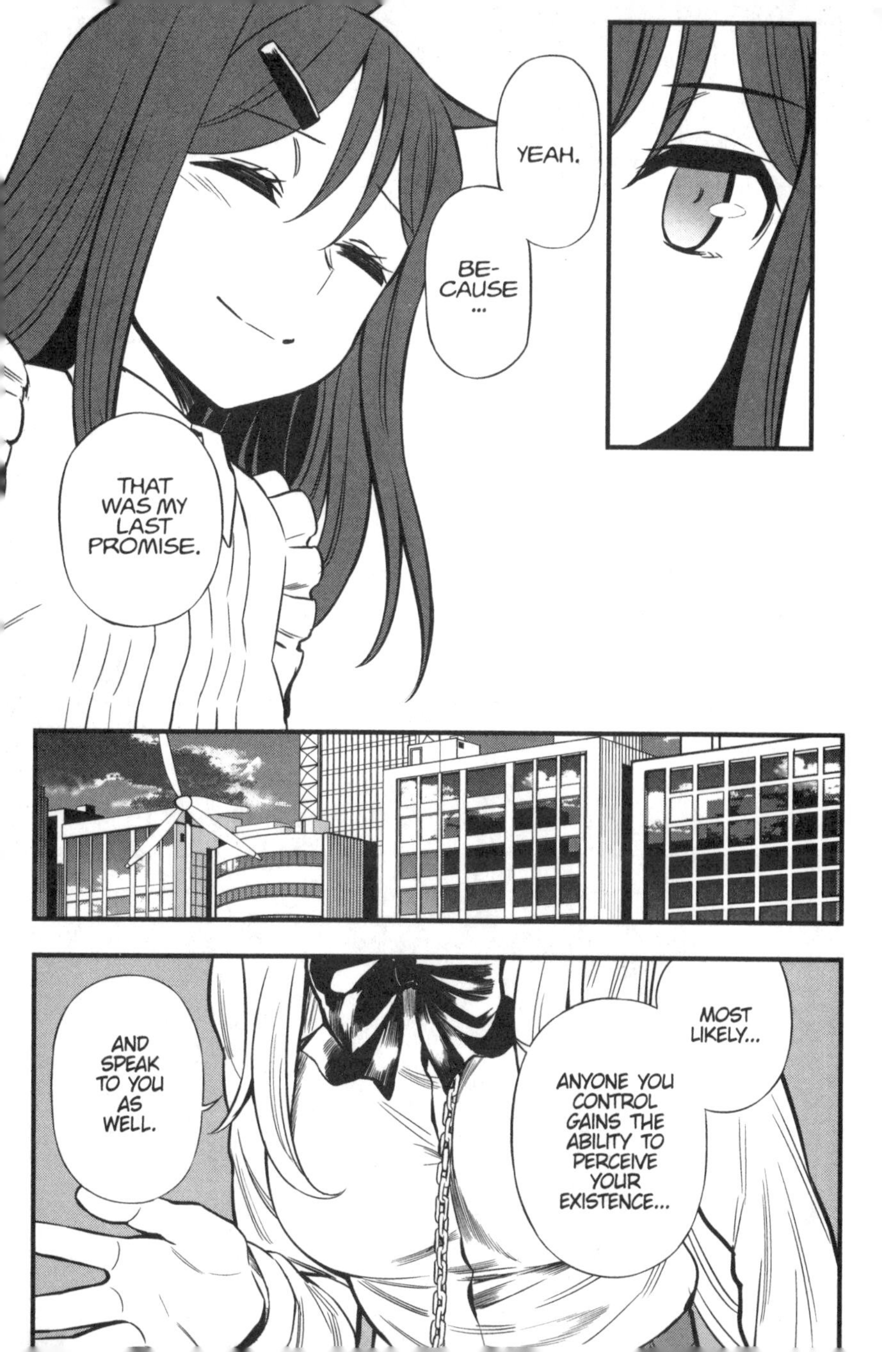
YEAH.
BE-CAUSE...
THAT WAS MY LAST PROMISE.
MOST LIKELY...
ANYONE YOU CONTROL GAINS THE ABILITY TO PERCEIVE YOUR EXISTENCE...
AND SPEAK TO YOU AS WELL.

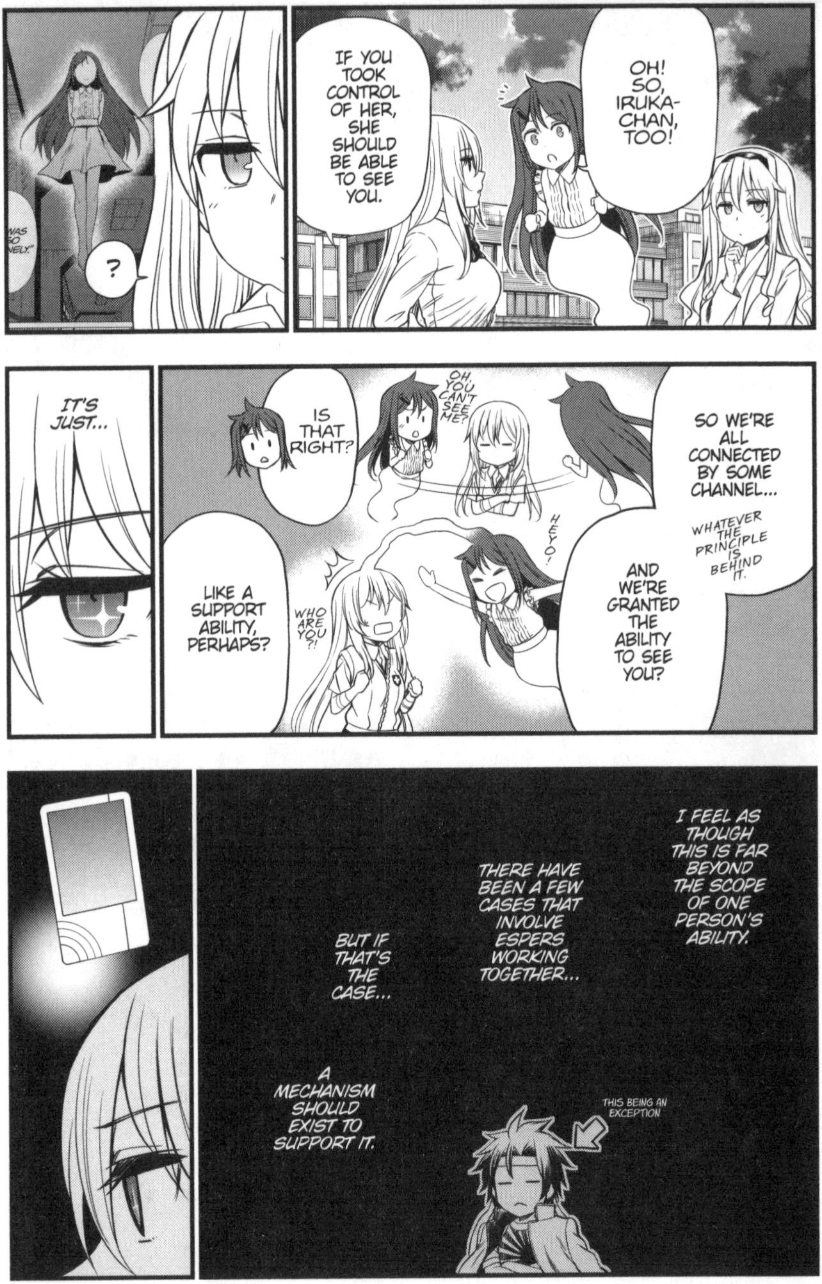
OH! SO, IRUKA-CHAN, TOO!
IF YOU TOOK CONTROL OF HER, SHE SHOULD BE ABLE TO SEE YOU.
?
SO WE'RE ALL CONNECTED BY SOME CHANNEL...
WHATEVER THE PRINCIPLE IS BEHIND IT.
AND WE'RE GRANTED THE ABILITY TO SEE YOU?
HEYO!
OH, YOU CAN'T SEE ME?
IS THAT RIGHT?
LIKE A SUPPORT ABILITY, PERHAPS?
WHO ARE YOU?!
IT'S JUST...
I FEEL AS THOUGH THIS IS FAR BEYOND THE SCOPE OF ONE PERSON'S ABILITY.
THERE HAVE BEEN A FEW CASES THAT INVOLVE ESPERS WORKING TOGETHER...
BUT IF THAT'S THE CASE...
A MECHANISM SHOULD EXIST TO SUPPORT IT.
THIS BEING AN EXCEPTION

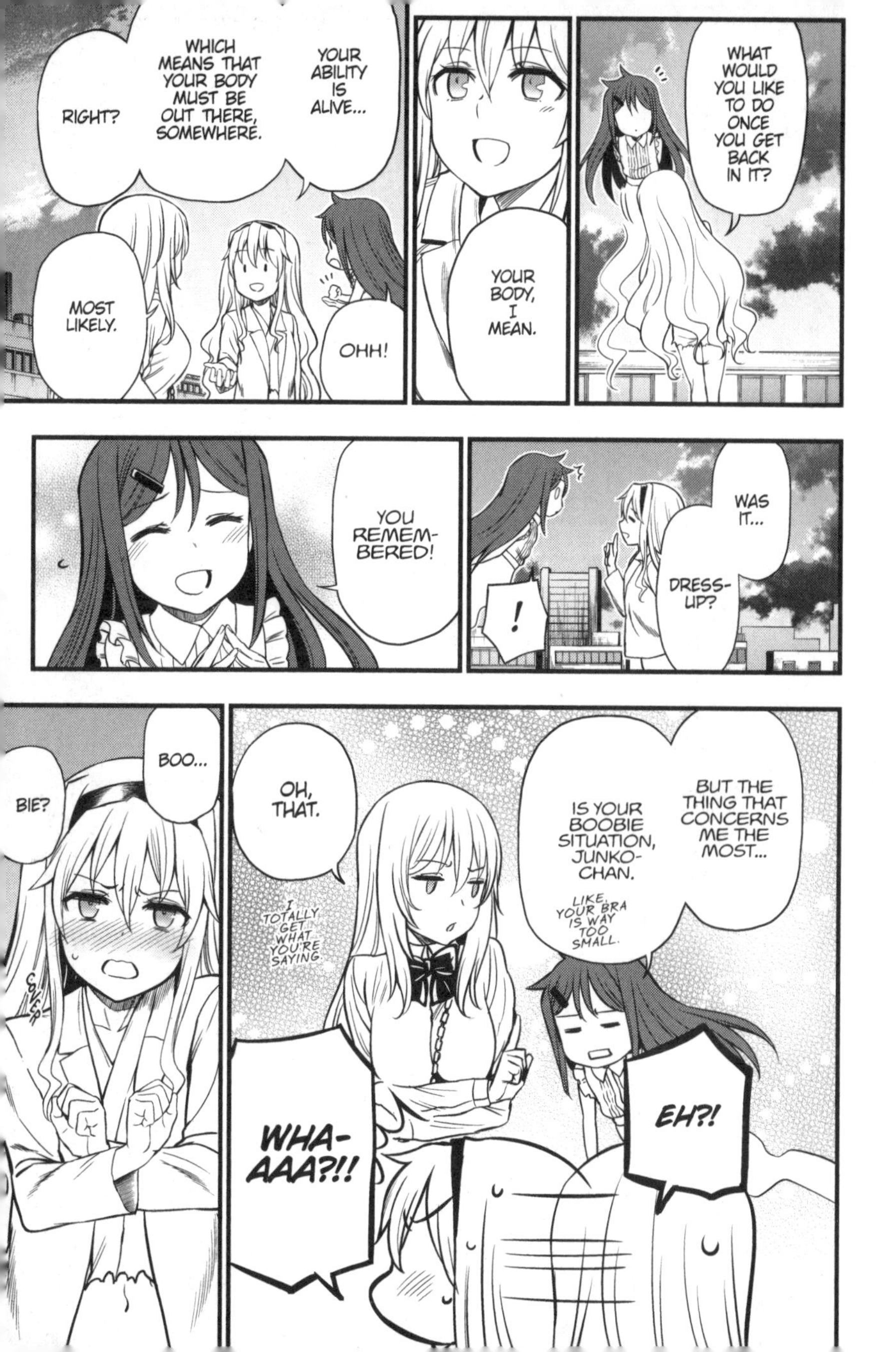
YOUR ABILITY IS ALIVE...
WHICH MEANS THAT YOUR BODY MUST BE OUT THERE, SOMEWHERE.
RIGHT?
MOST LIKELY.
OHH!
WHAT WOULD YOU LIKE TO DO ONCE YOU GET BACK IN IT?
YOUR BODY, I MEAN.
WAS IT...
DRESS-UP?
!
YOU REMEMBERED!
BUT THE THING THAT CONCERNS ME THE MOST...
IS YOUR BOOBIE SITUATION, JUNKO-CHAN.
LIKE, YOUR BRA IS WAY TOO SMALL.
OH, THAT.
I TOTALLY GET WHAT YOU'RE SAYING.
EH?!
WHA-AAA?!!
BOO...
BIE?
COVER

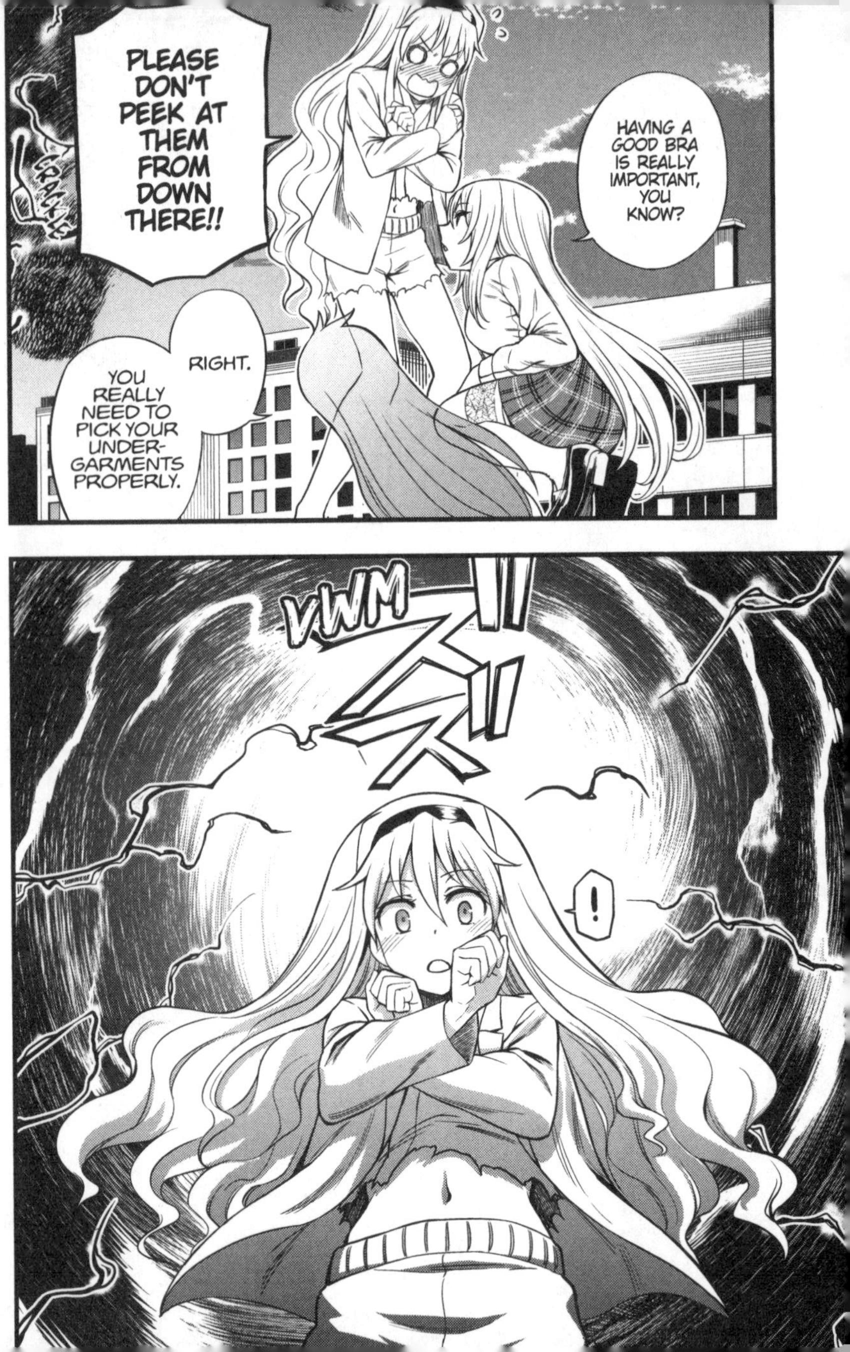
HAVING A GOOD BRA IS REALLY IMPORTANT, YOU KNOW?
PLEASE DON'T PEEK AT THEM FROM DOWN THERE!!
CRACKLE
RIGHT.
YOU REALLY NEED TO PICK YOUR UNDER-GARMENTS PROPERLY.
VWM
!

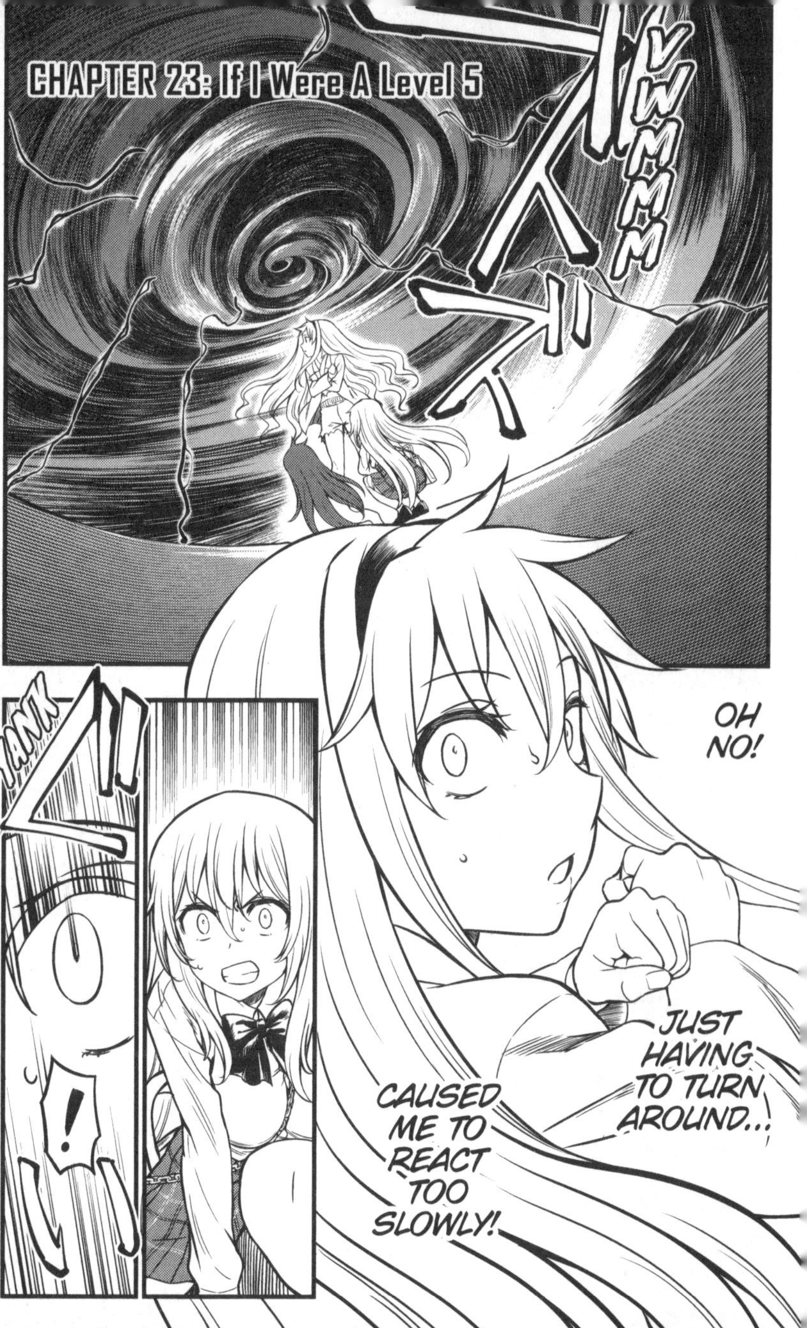
CHAPTER 23: If I Were A Level 5
VWMMM
OH NO!
YANK
!!
!
JUST HAVING TO TURN AROUND...
CAUSED ME TO REACT TOO SLOWLY!

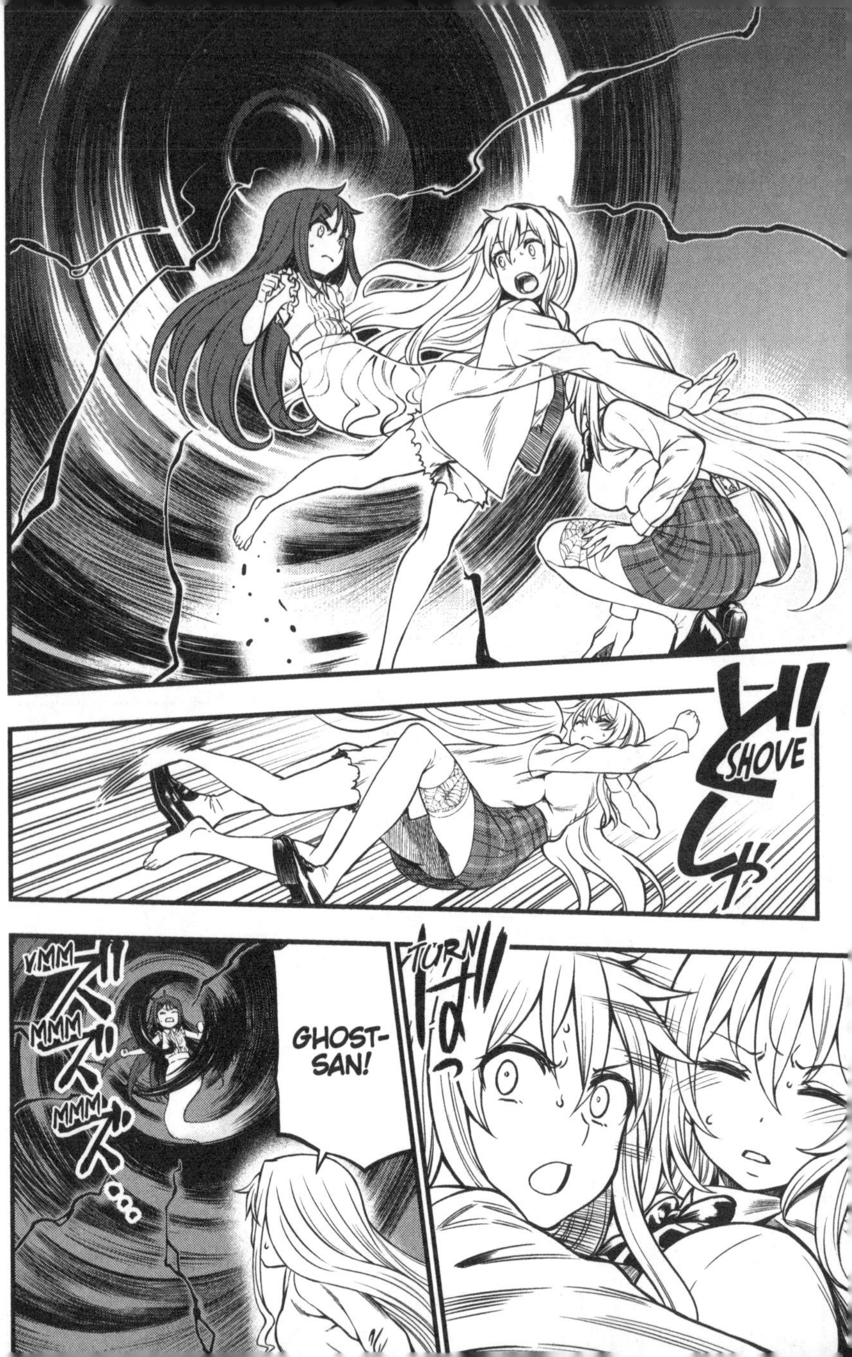

SHOVE
TURN
GHOST-SAN!
VMMM
MMM
MMM

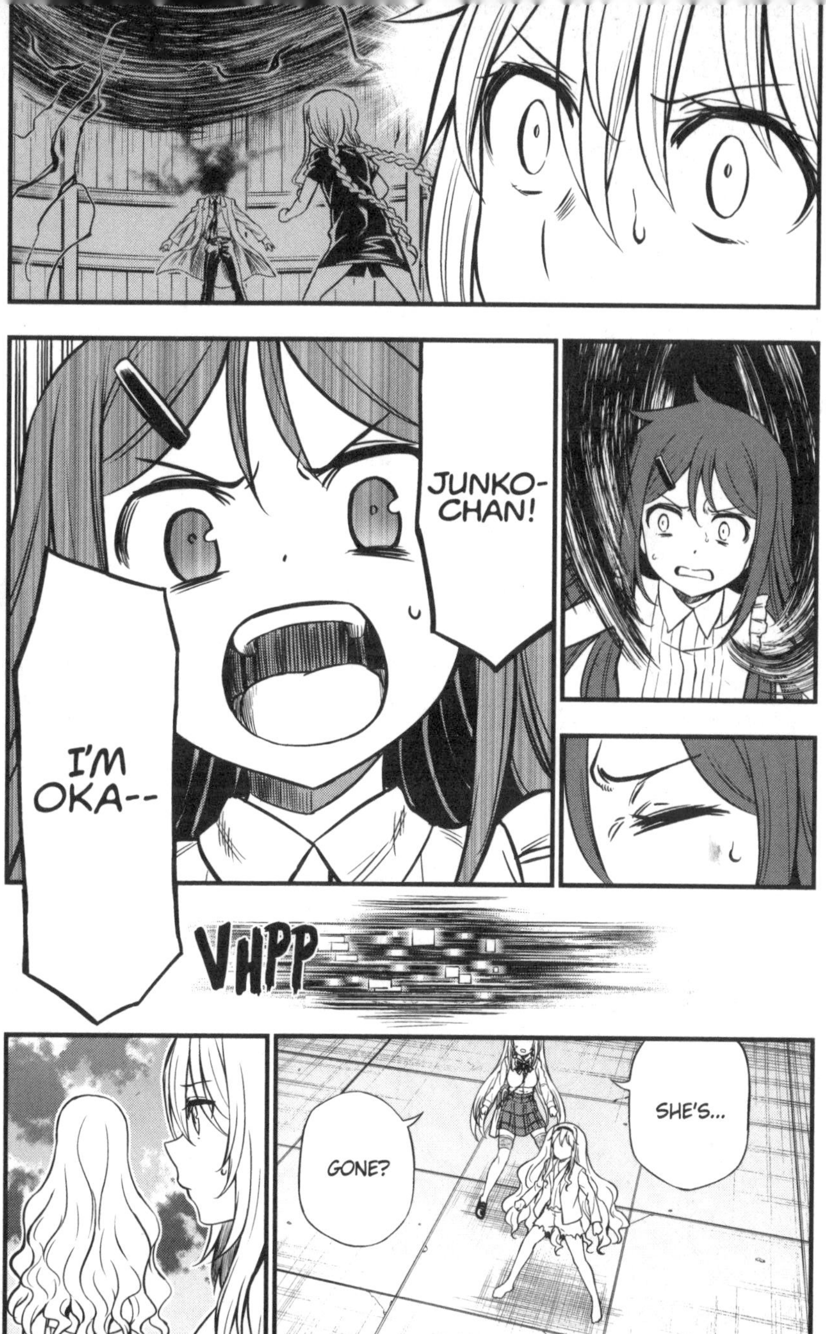
JUNKO-CHAN!
I'M OKA--
VHPP
SHE'S...
GONE?

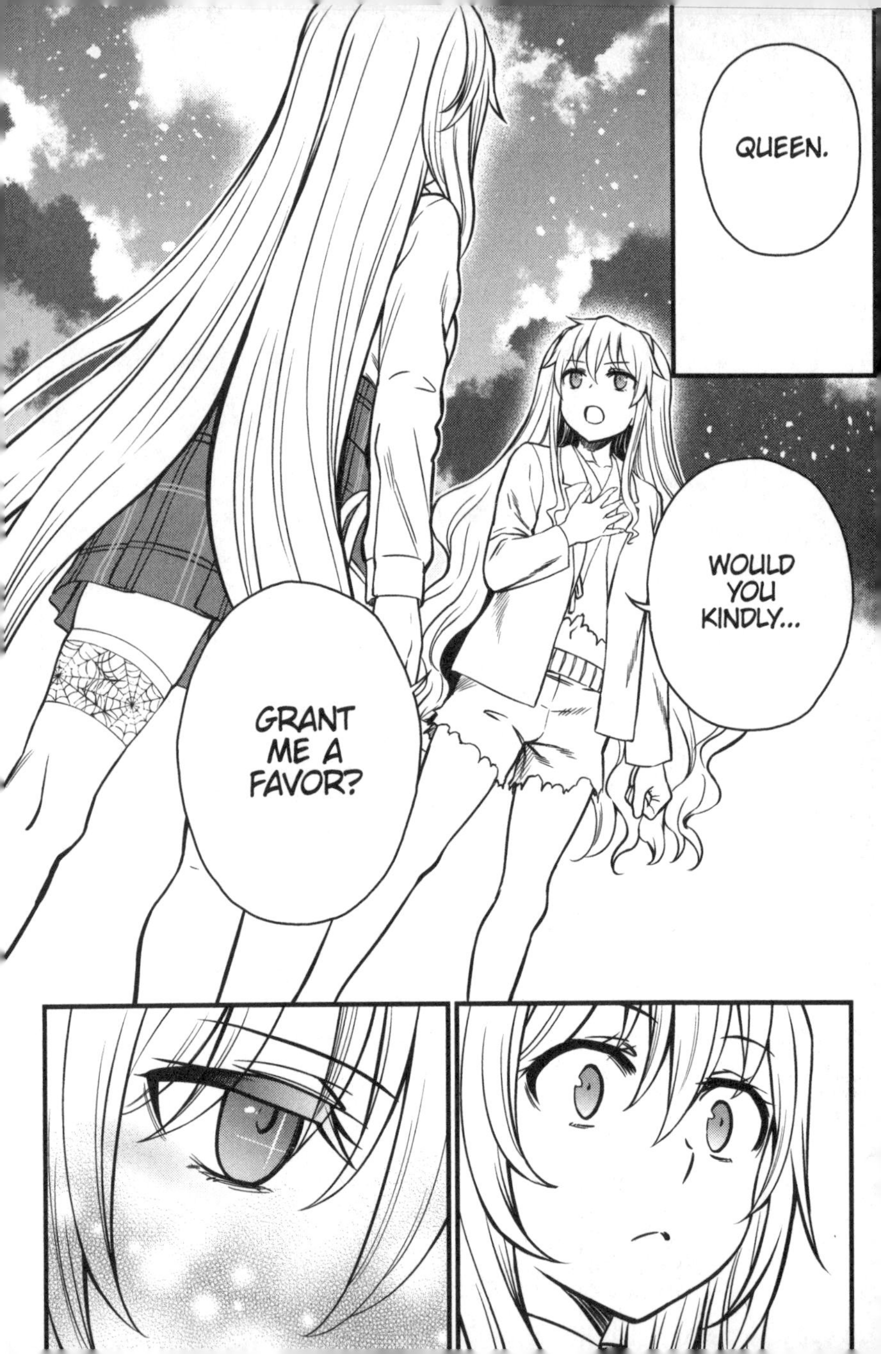
QUEEN.
WOULD YOU KINDLY...
GRANT ME A FAVOR?

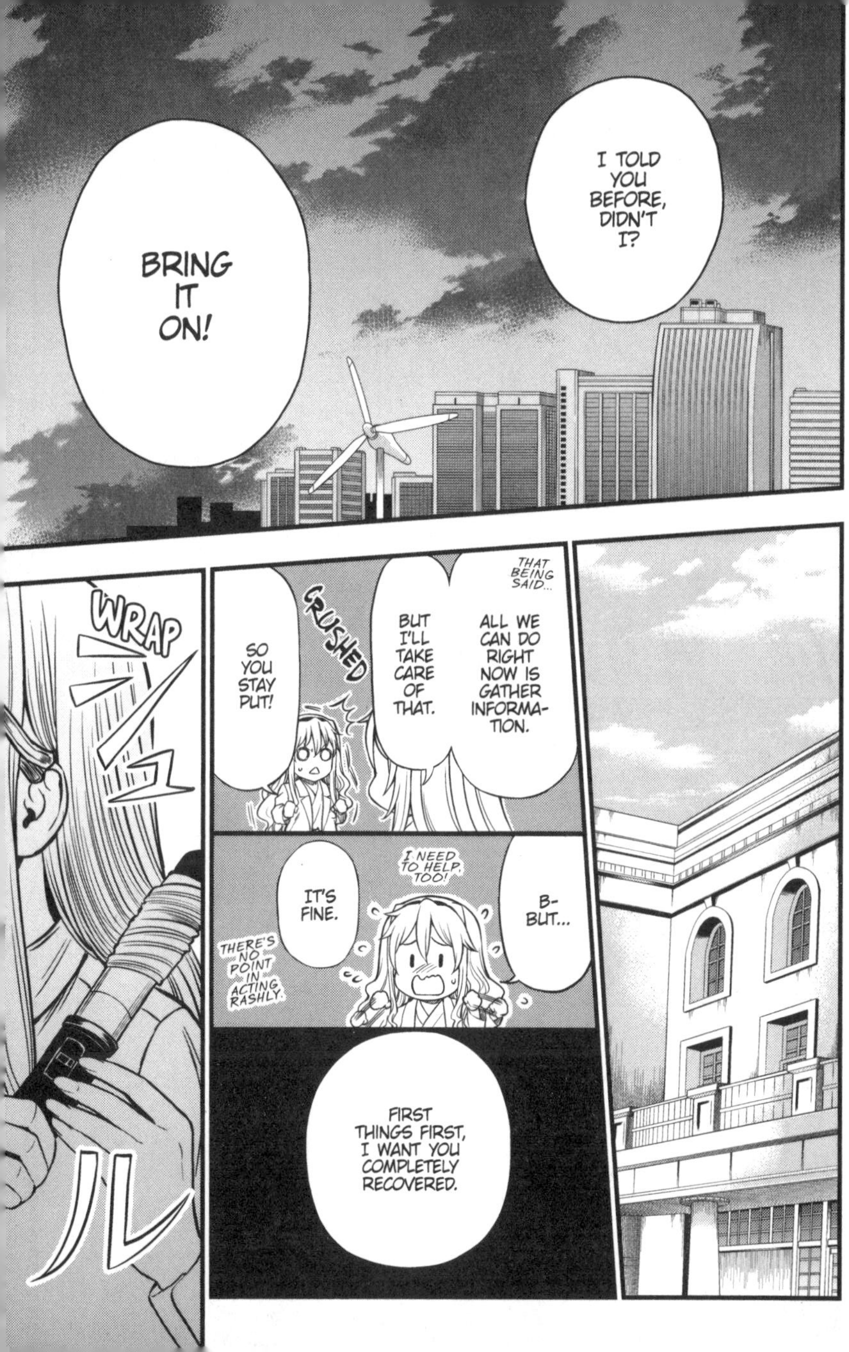

I TOLD YOU BEFORE, DIDN'T I?
BRING IT ON!
THAT BEING SAID...
ALL WE CAN DO RIGHT NOW IS GATHER INFORMATION.
BUT I'LL TAKE CARE OF THAT.
CRUSHED
SO YOU STAY PUT!
B-BUT...
I NEED TO HELP, TOO!
IT'S FINE.
THERE'S NO POINT IN ACTING RASHLY.
FIRST THINGS FIRST, I WANT YOU COMPLETELY RECOVERED.
WRAP
ル

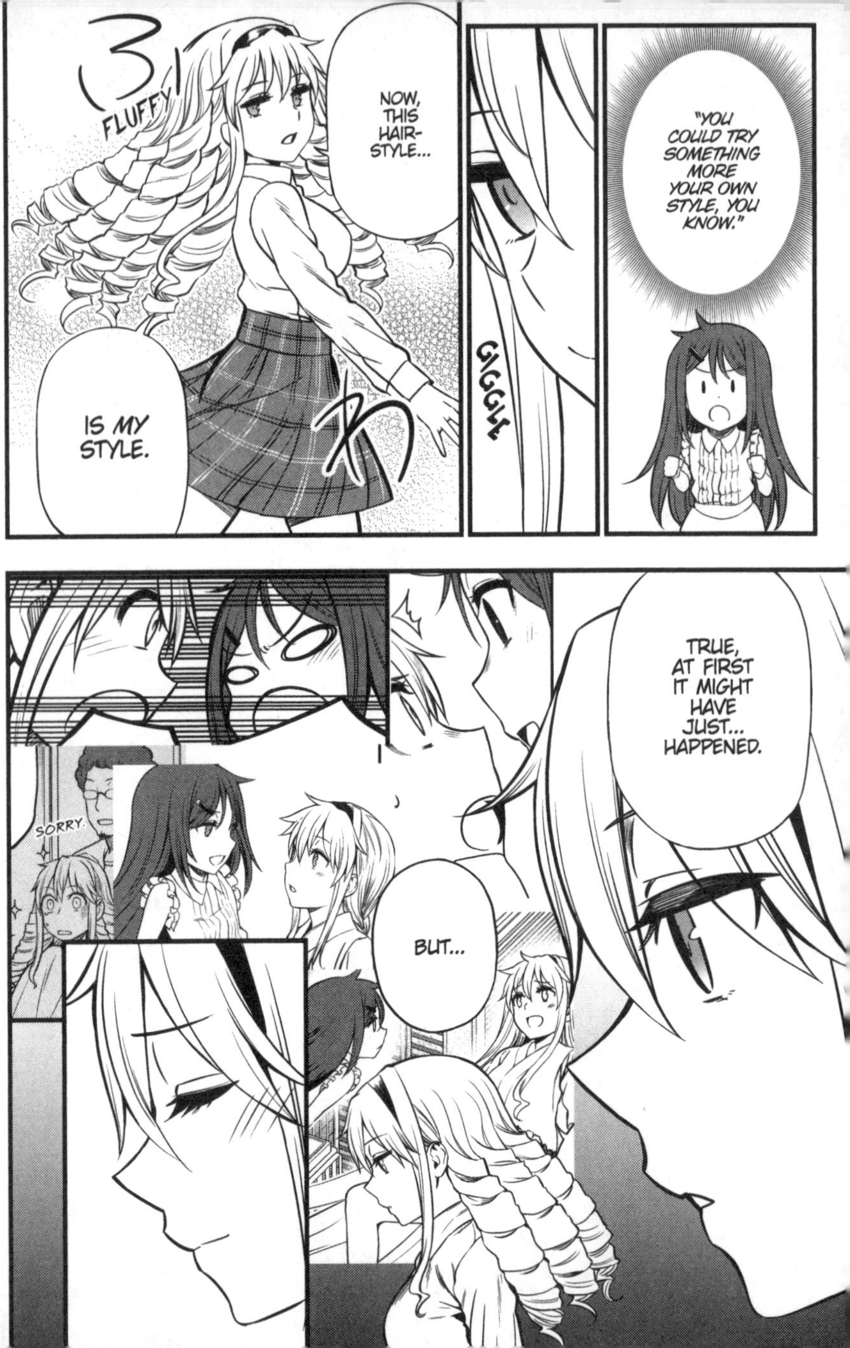
"YOU COULD TRY SOMETHING MORE YOUR OWN STYLE, YOU KNOW."
GIGGLE
NOW, THIS HAIR-STYLE...
FLUFFY
IS MY STYLE.
TRUE, AT FIRST IT MIGHT HAVE JUST... HAPPENED.
SORRY.
BUT...

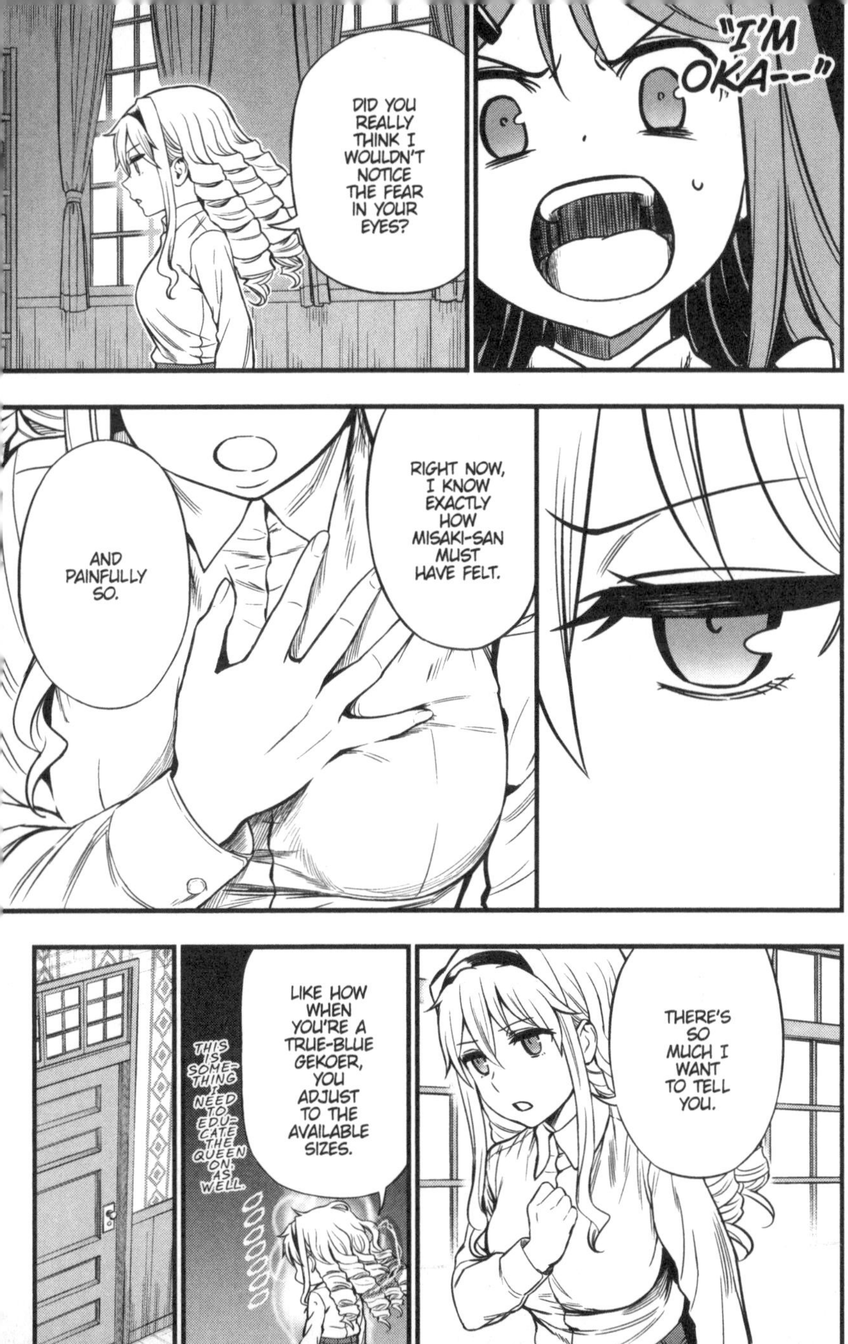
"I'M OKA--"
DID YOU REALLY THINK I WOULDN'T NOTICE THE FEAR IN YOUR EYES?
RIGHT NOW, I KNOW EXACTLY HOW MISAKI-SAN MUST HAVE FELT.
AND PAINFULLY SO.
THERE'S SO MUCH I WANT TO TELL YOU.
LIKE HOW WHEN YOU'RE A TRUE-BLUE GEKOER, YOU ADJUST TO THE AVAILABLE SIZES.
THIS IS SOMETHING I NEED TO EDUCATE THE QUEEN ON AS WELL.

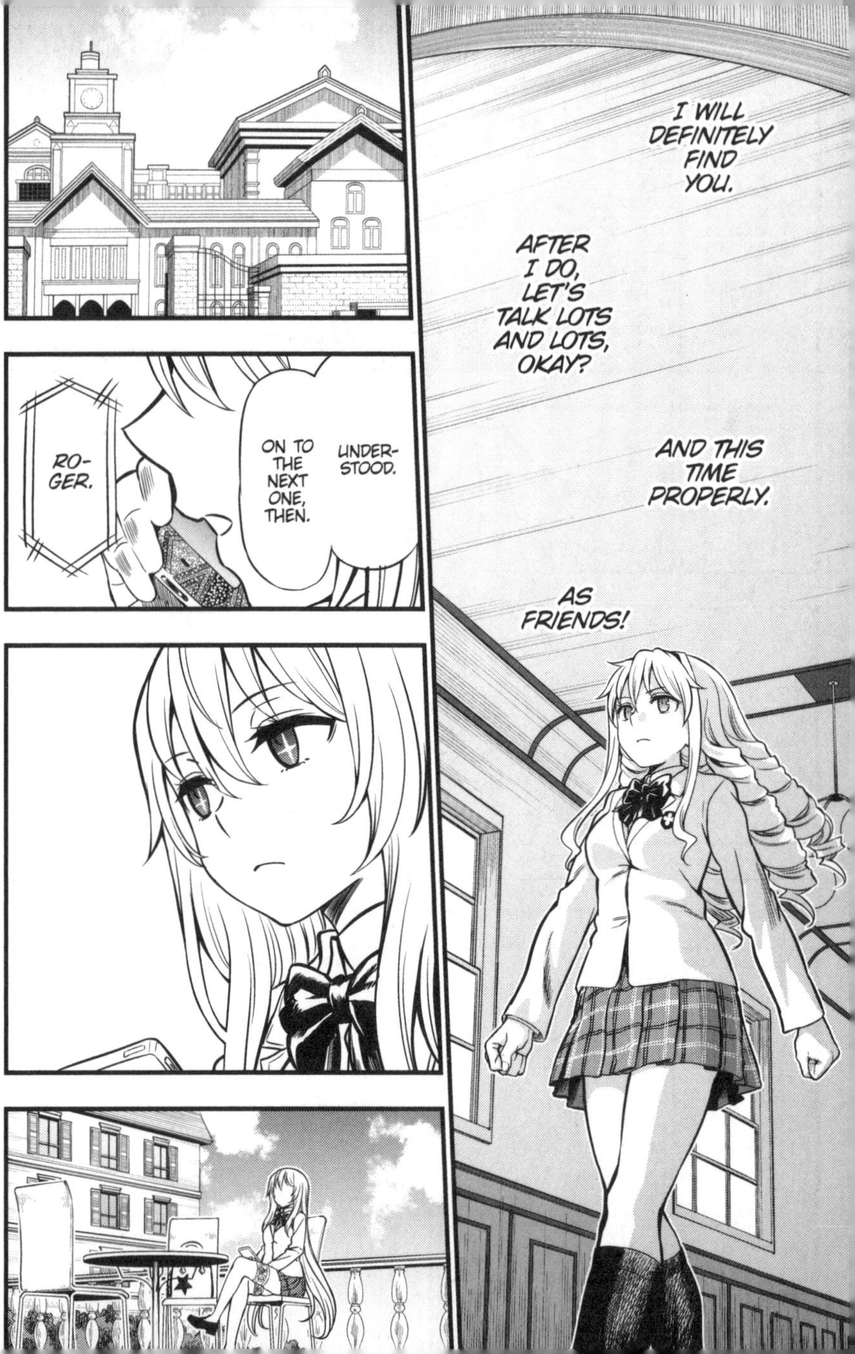

I WILL DEFINITELY FIND YOU.
AFTER I DO, LET'S TALK LOTS AND LOTS, OKAY?
AND THIS TIME PROPERLY.
AS FRIENDS!
UNDER-STOOD.
ON TO THE NEXT ONE, THEN.
RO-GER.

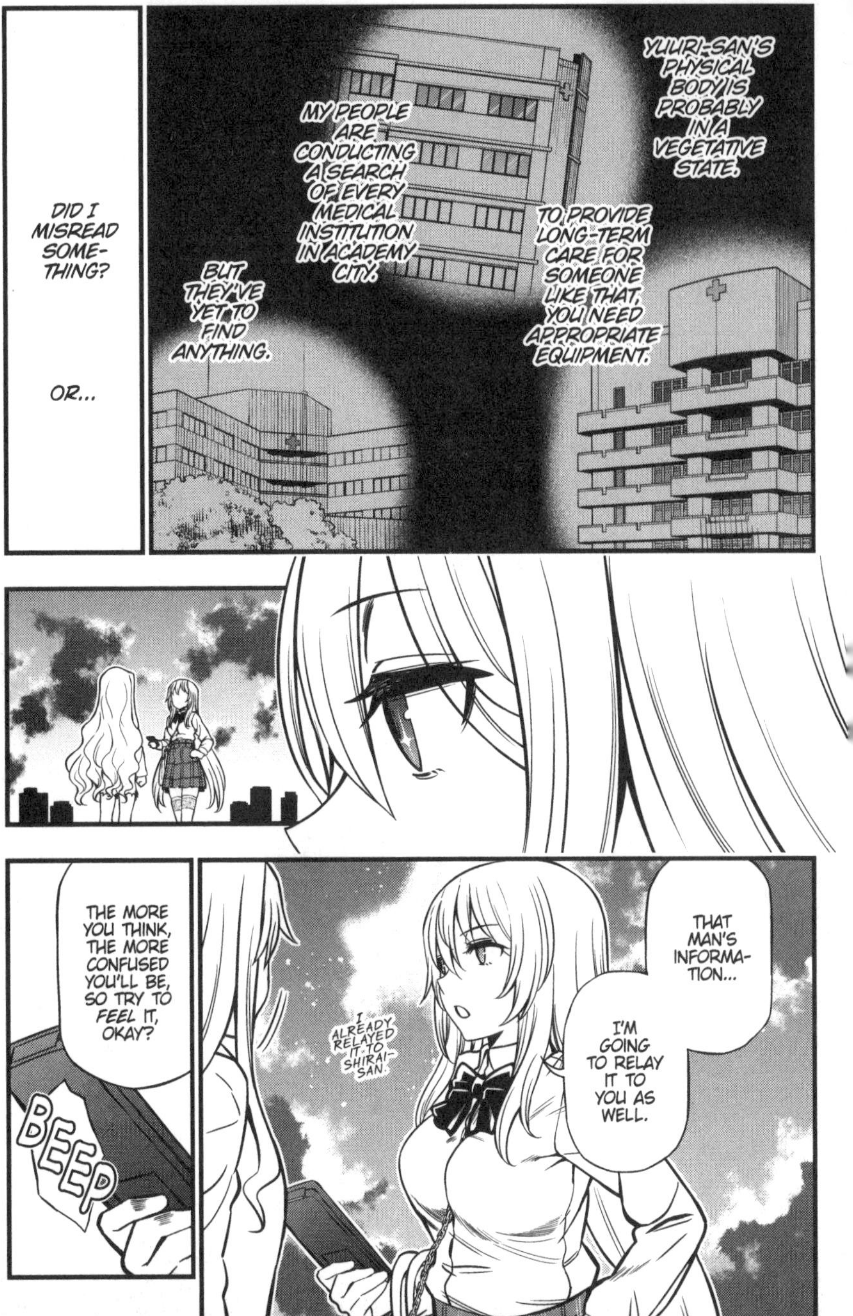
YUURI-SAN'S PHYSICAL BODY IS PROBABLY IN A VEGETATIVE STATE.
TO PROVIDE LONG-TERM CARE FOR SOMEONE LIKE THAT, YOU NEED APPROPRIATE EQUIPMENT.
MY PEOPLE ARE CONDUCTING A SEARCH OF EVERY MEDICAL INSTITUTION IN ACADEMY CITY.
BUT THEY'VE YET TO FIND ANYTHING.
DID I MISREAD SOME-THING?
OR...
THAT MAN'S INFORMA-TION...
I'M GOING TO RELAY IT TO YOU AS WELL.
I ALREADY RELAYED IT TO SHIRAI-SAN.
THE MORE YOU THINK, THE MORE CONFUSED YOU'LL BE, SO TRY TO FEEL IT, OKAY?
BEEP

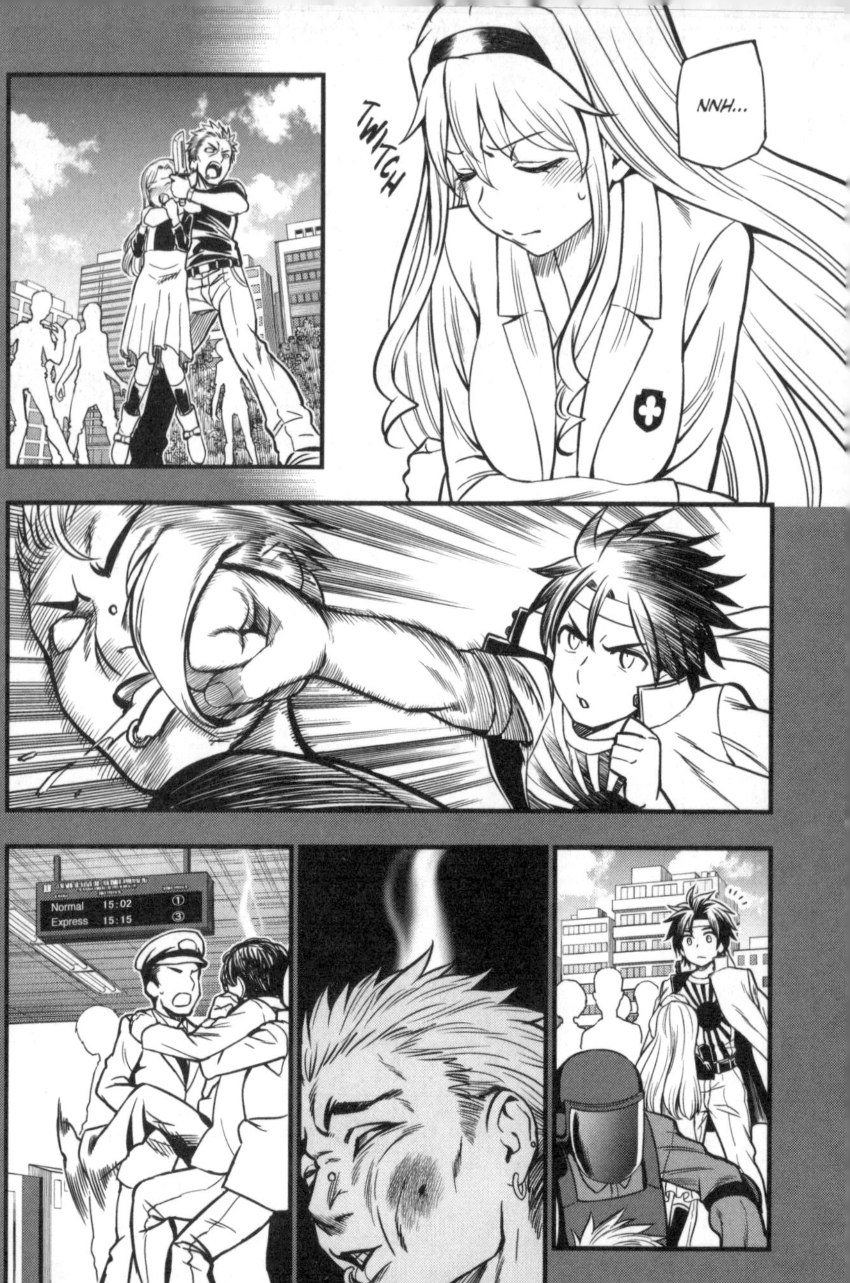
NNH...
TWITCH
Normal 15:02 ①
Express 15:15 ③

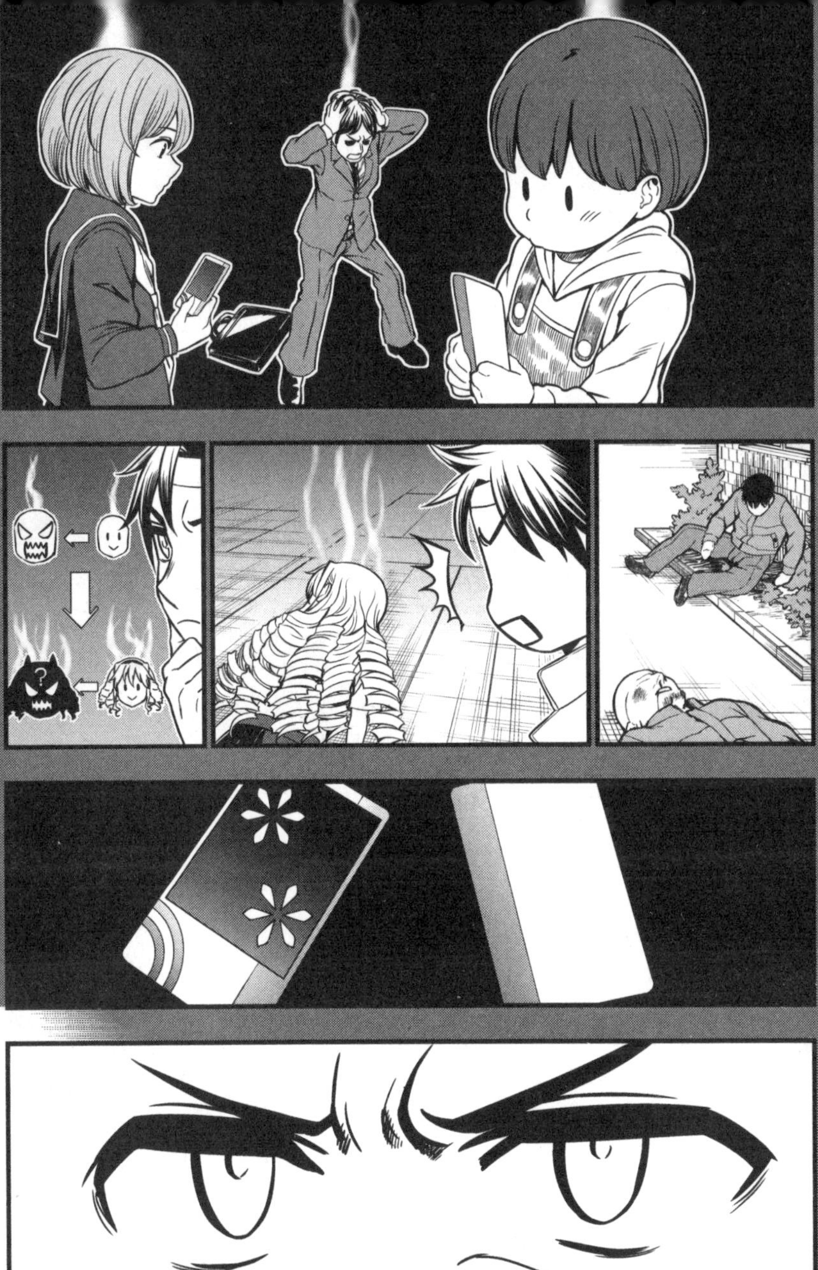

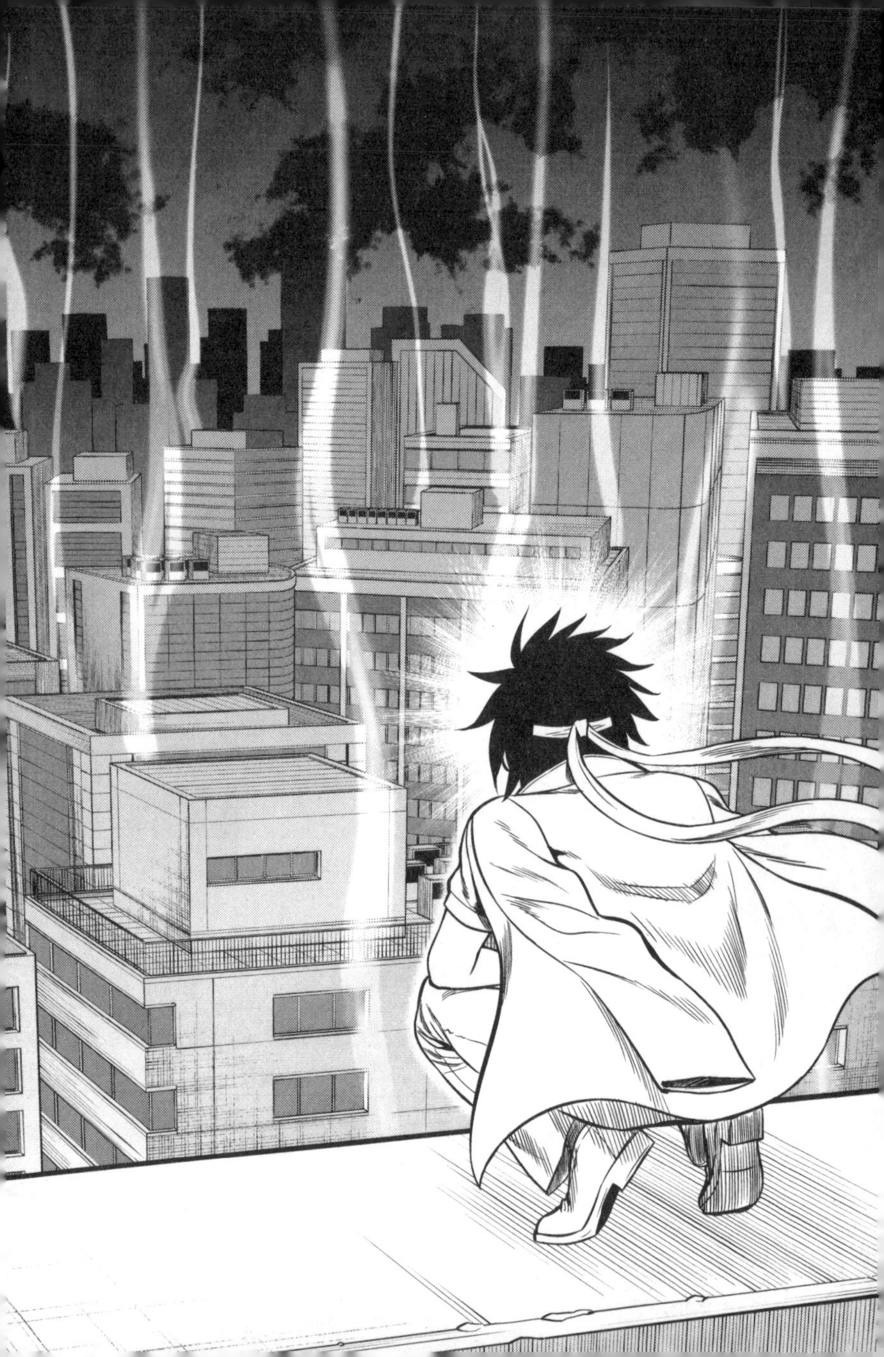

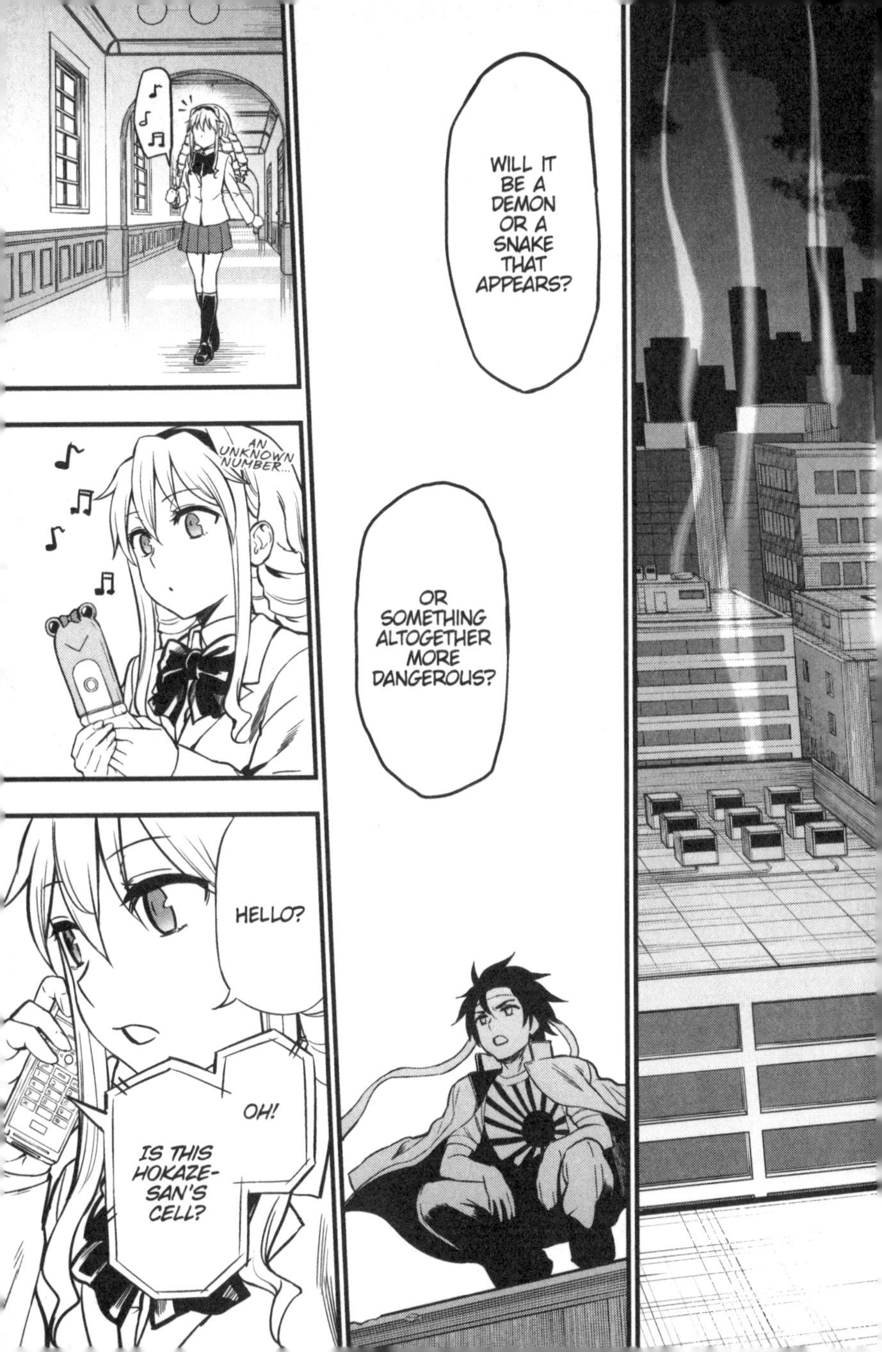
WILL IT BE A DEMON OR A SNAKE THAT APPEARS?
OR SOMETHING ALTOGETHER MORE DANGEROUS?
AN UNKNOWN NUMBER...
HELLO?
OH!
IS THIS HOKAZE-SAN'S CELL?

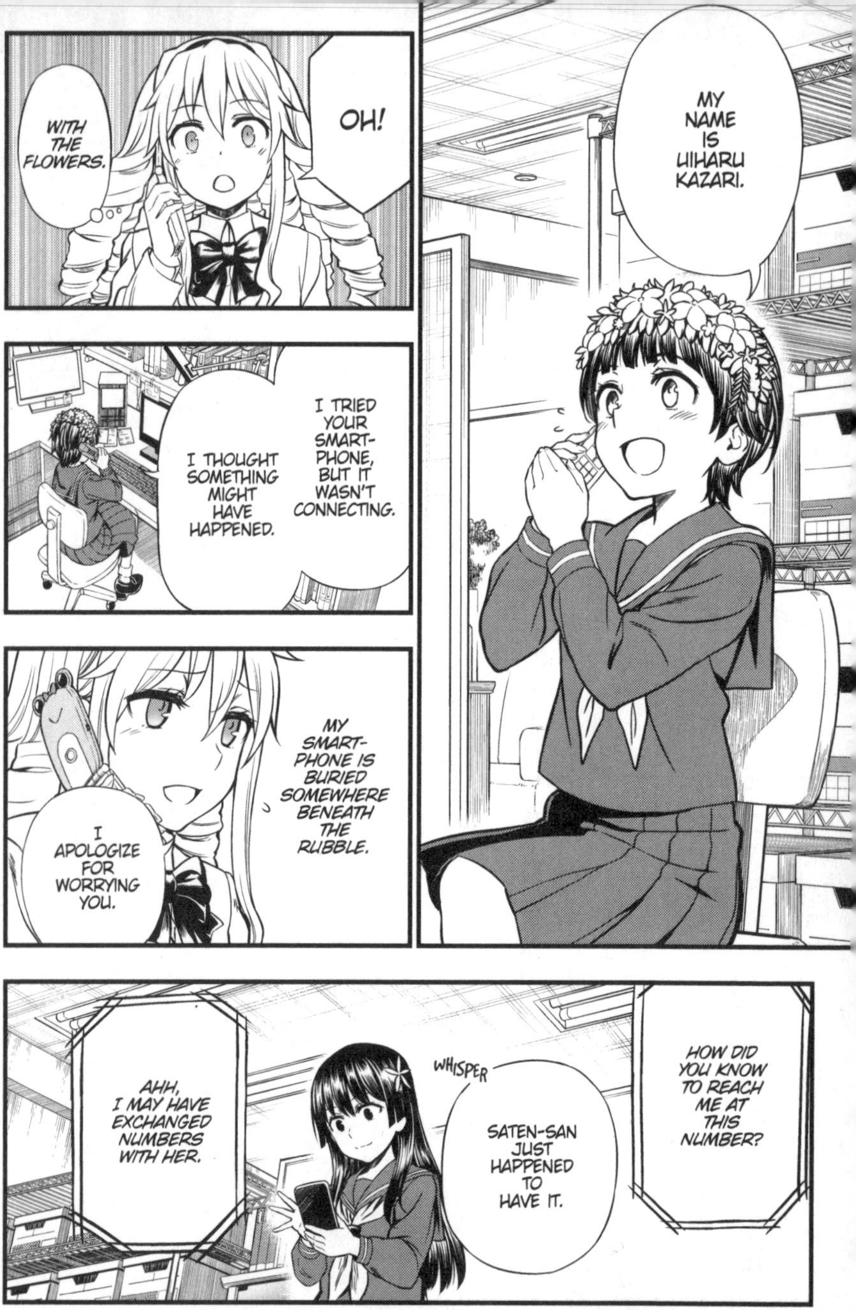
MY NAME IS UIHARU KAZARI.
OH!
WITH THE FLOWERS.
I TRIED YOUR SMARTPHONE, BUT IT WASN'T CONNECTING.
I THOUGHT SOMETHING MIGHT HAVE HAPPENED.
MY SMARTPHONE IS BURIED SOMEWHERE BENEATH THE RUBBLE.
I APOLOGIZE FOR WORRYING YOU.
HOW DID YOU KNOW TO REACH ME AT THIS NUMBER?
WHISPER
SATEN-SAN JUST HAPPENED TO HAVE IT.
AHH, I MAY HAVE EXCHANGED NUMBERS WITH HER.

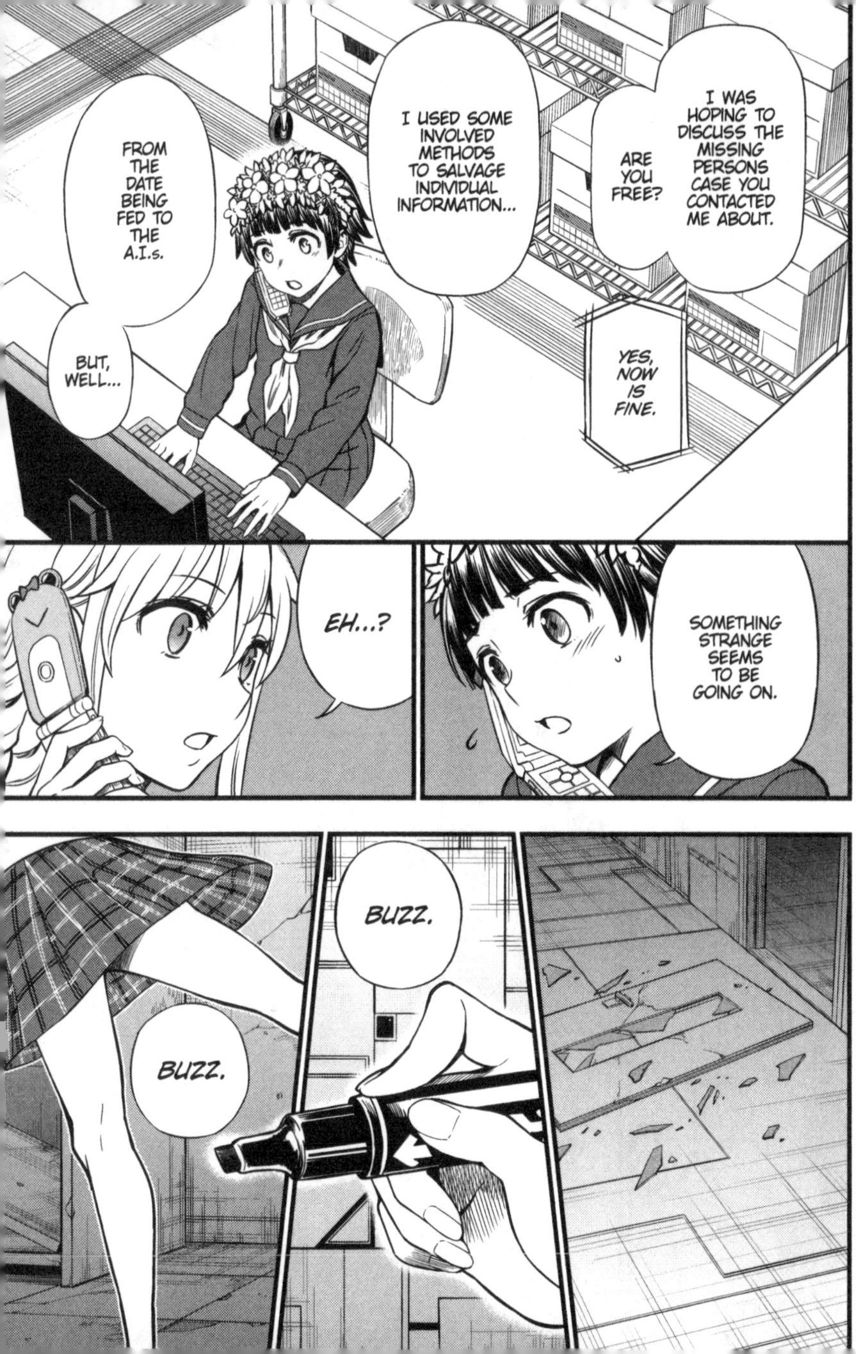
I WAS HOPING TO DISCUSS THE MISSING PERSONS CASE YOU CONTACTED ME ABOUT.
ARE YOU FREE?
YES, NOW IS FINE.
I USED SOME INVOLVED METHODS TO SALVAGE INDIVIDUAL INFORMATION...
FROM THE DATE BEING FED TO THE A.I.s.
BUT, WELL...
SOMETHING STRANGE SEEMS TO BE GOING ON.
EH...?
BUZZ.
BUZZ.

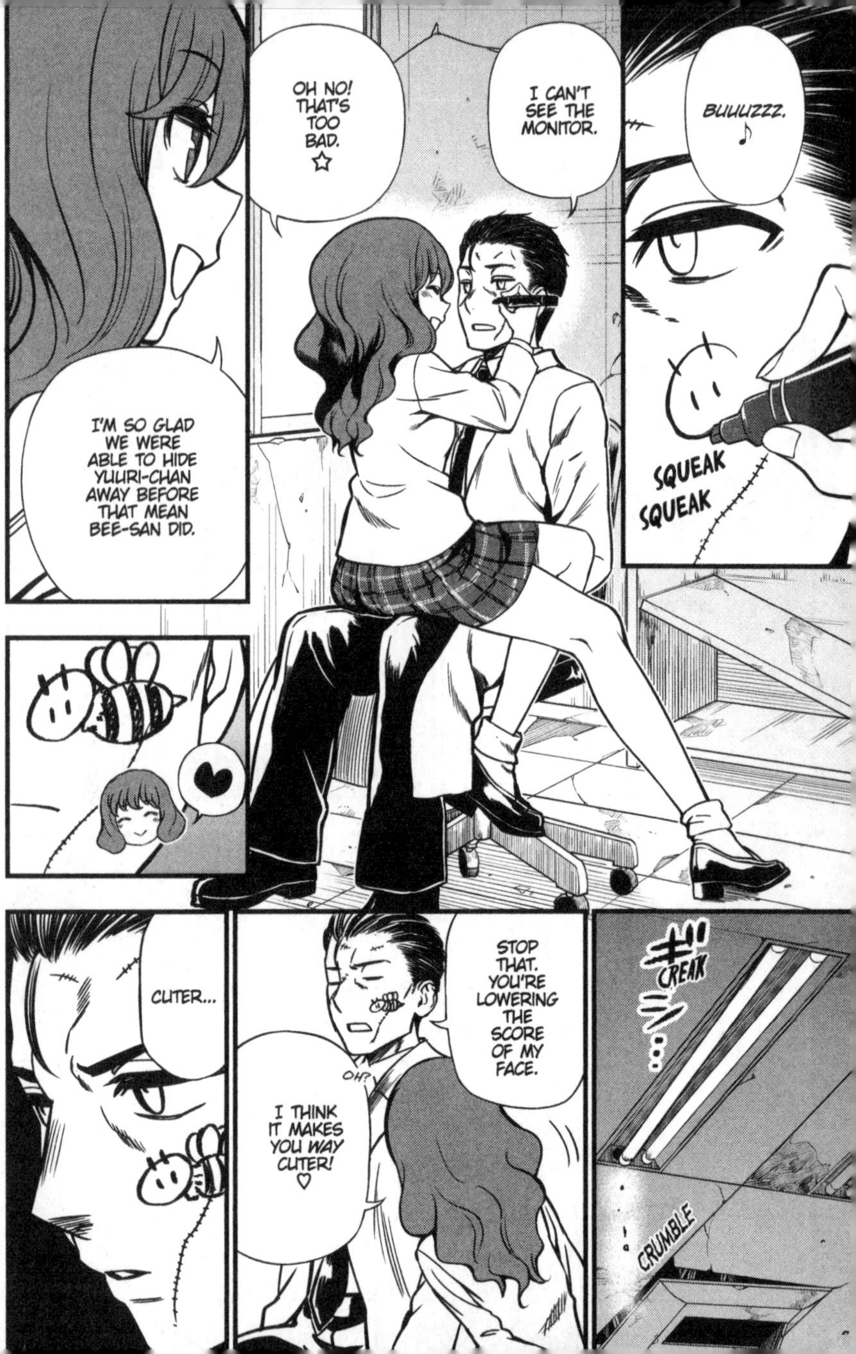
BUUUZZZ. ♪
SQUEAK SQUEAK
I CAN'T SEE THE MONITOR.
OH NO! THAT'S TOO BAD. ☆
I'M SO GLAD WE WERE ABLE TO HIDE YUURI-CHAN AWAY BEFORE THAT MEAN BEE-SAN DID.
CREAK
CRUMBLE
STOP THAT. YOU'RE LOWERING THE SCORE OF MY FACE.
OH?
I THINK IT MAKES YOU *WAY* CUTER! ♡
CUTER...

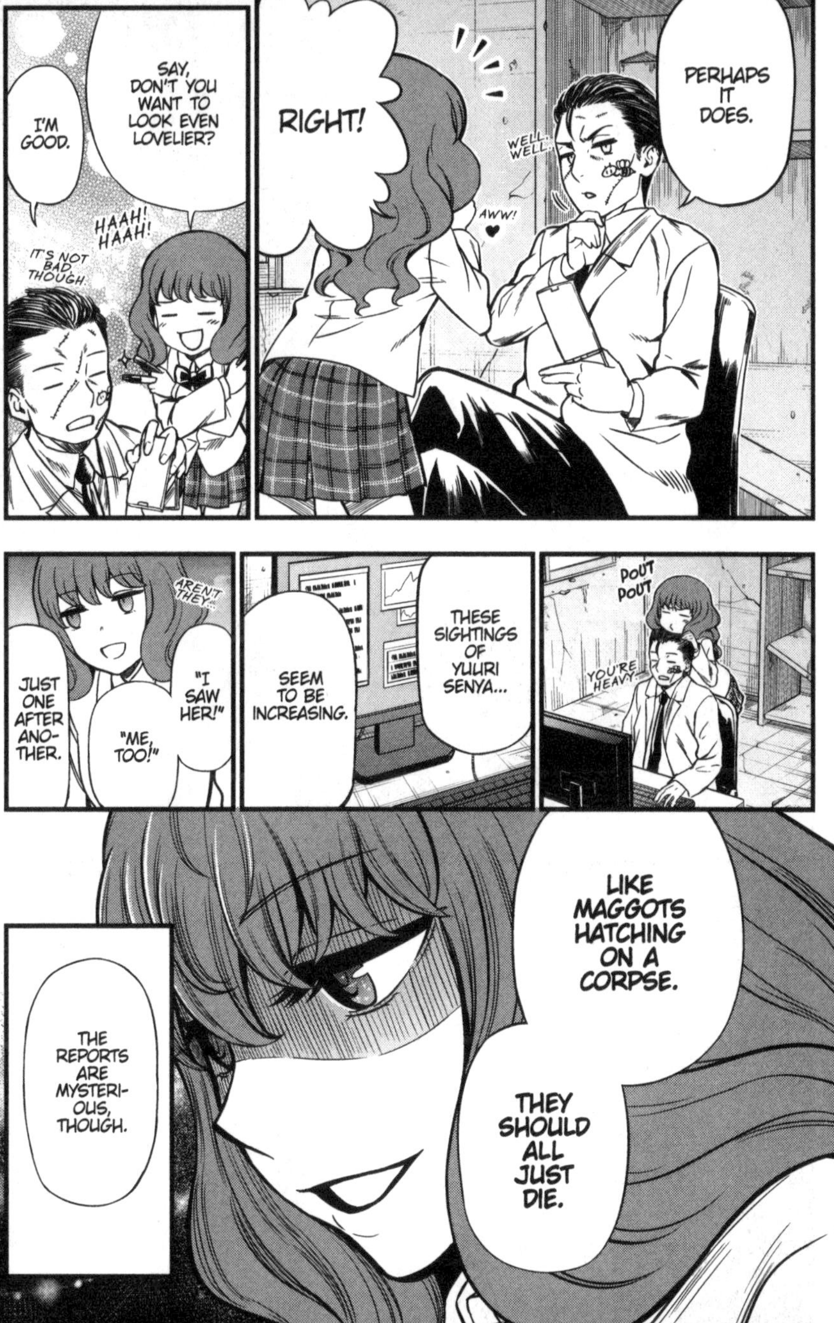
PERHAPS IT DOES.
WELL, WELL.
AWW!
RIGHT!
SAY, DON'T YOU WANT TO LOOK EVEN LOVELIER?
I'M GOOD.
HAAH! HAAH!
IT'S NOT BAD, THOUGH.
POUT POUT
YOU'RE HEAVY...
THESE SIGHTINGS OF YUURI SENYA...
SEEM TO BE INCREASING.
"I SAW HER!"
"ME, TOO!"
JUST ONE AFTER ANO-THER.
AREN'T THEY...
LIKE MAGGOTS HATCHING ON A CORPSE.
THEY SHOULD ALL JUST DIE.
THE REPORTS ARE MYSTERI-OUS, THOUGH.

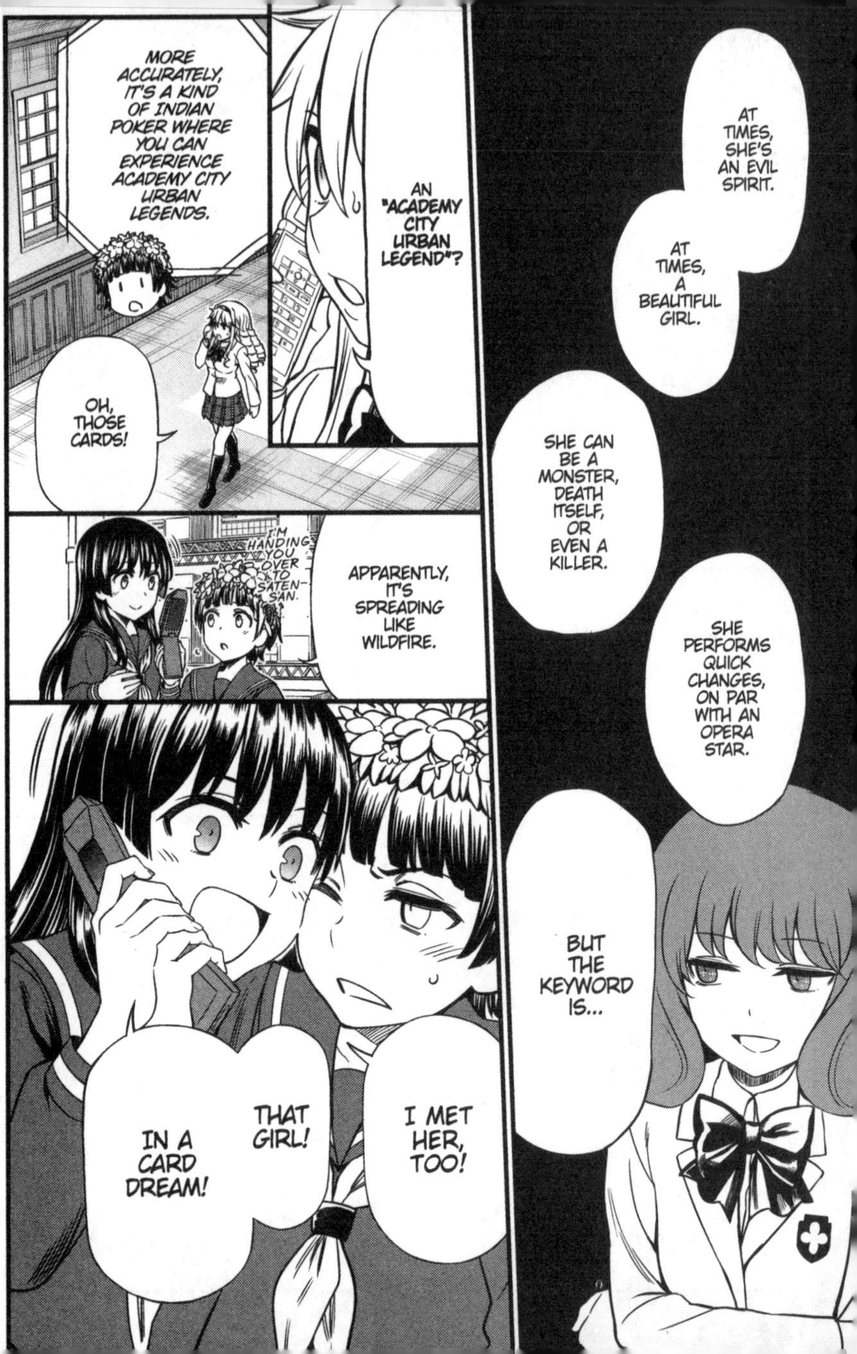
AT TIMES, SHE'S AN EVIL SPIRIT.
AT TIMES, A BEAUTIFUL GIRL.
SHE CAN BE A MONSTER, DEATH ITSELF, OR EVEN A KILLER.
SHE PERFORMS QUICK CHANGES, ON PAR WITH AN OPERA STAR.
BUT THE KEYWORD IS...
AN "ACADEMY CITY URBAN LEGEND"?
MORE ACCURATELY, IT'S A KIND OF INDIAN POKER WHERE YOU CAN EXPERIENCE ACADEMY CITY URBAN LEGENDS.
OH, THOSE CARDS!
APPARENTLY, IT'S SPREADING LIKE WILDFIRE.
I'M HANDING YOU OVER TO SATEN-SAN.
I MET HER, TOO!
THAT GIRL!
IN A CARD DREAM!

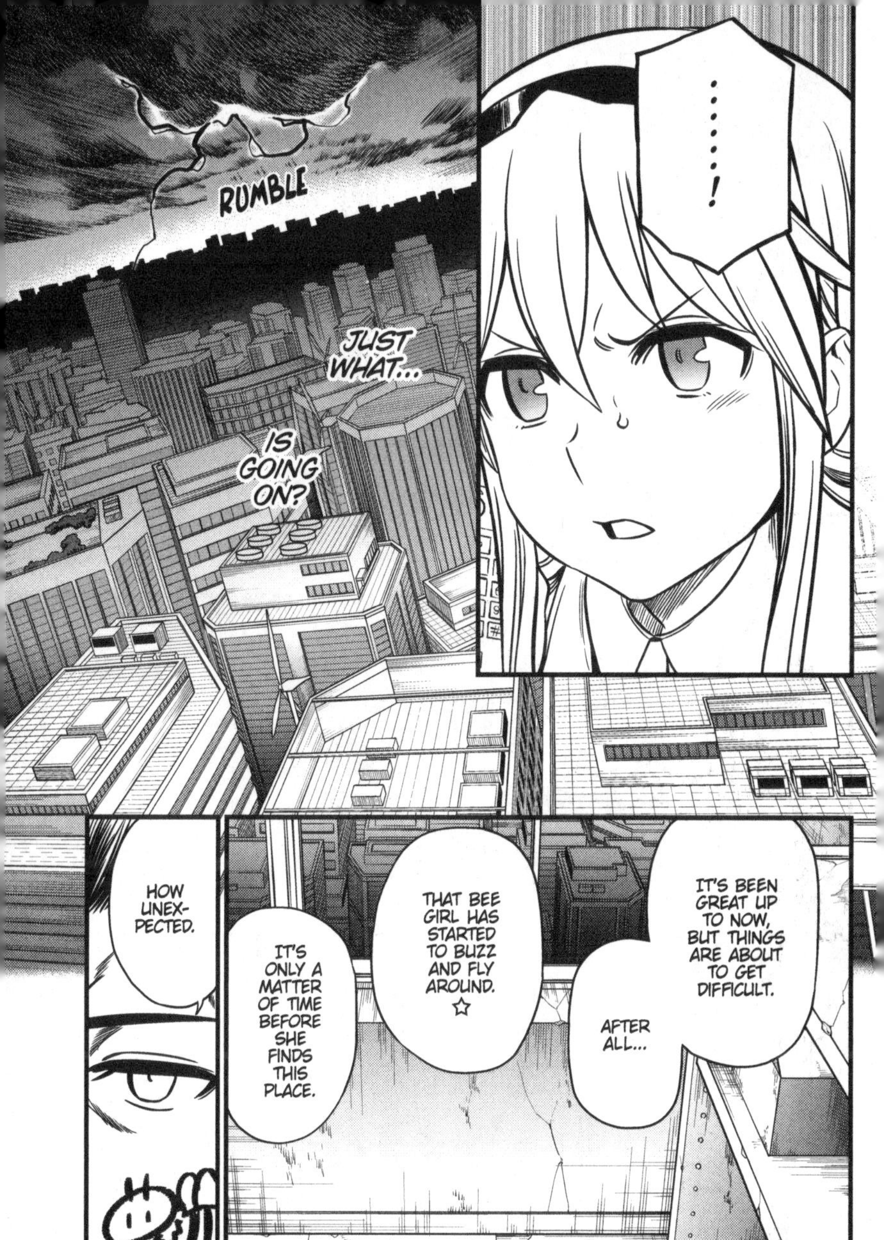

......!
RUMBLE
JUST WHAT...
IS GOING ON?
IT'S BEEN GREAT UP TO NOW, BUT THINGS ARE ABOUT TO GET DIFFICULT.
AFTER ALL...
THAT BEE GIRL HAS STARTED TO BUZZ AND FLY AROUND. ☆
IT'S ONLY A MATTER OF TIME BEFORE SHE FINDS THIS PLACE.
HOW UNEXPECTED.

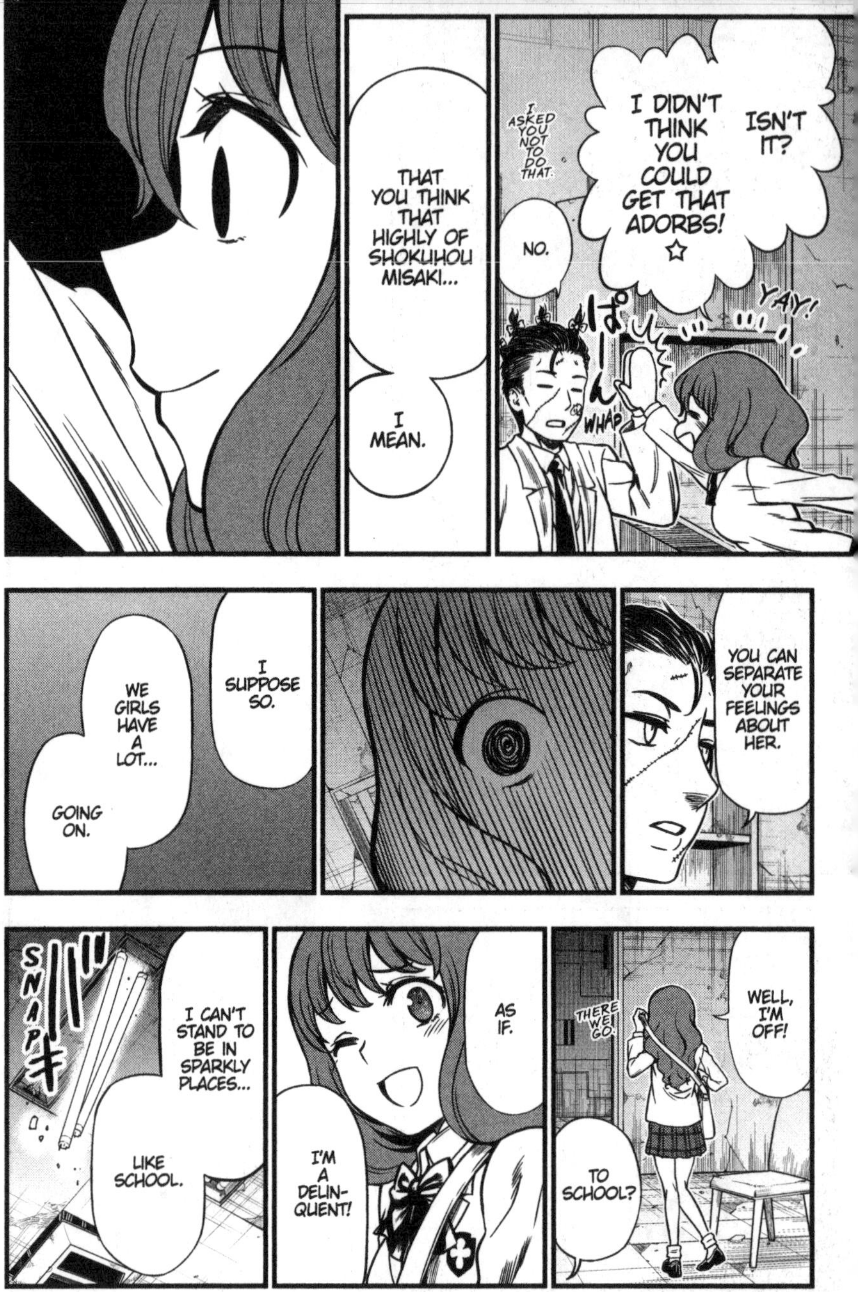
ISN'T IT?
I DIDN'T THINK YOU COULD GET THAT ADORBS! ☆
I ASKED YOU NOT TO DO THAT.
NO.
YAY!
ぱーん
WHAP
THAT YOU THINK THAT HIGHLY OF SHOKUHOU MISAKI...
I MEAN.
YOU CAN SEPARATE YOUR FEELINGS ABOUT HER.
I SUPPOSE SO.
WE GIRLS HAVE A LOT...
GOING ON.
WELL, I'M OFF!
THERE WE GO.
TO SCHOOL?
AS IF.
I'M A DELINQUENT!
I CAN'T STAND TO BE IN SPARKLY PLACES...
LIKE SCHOOL.
SNAP

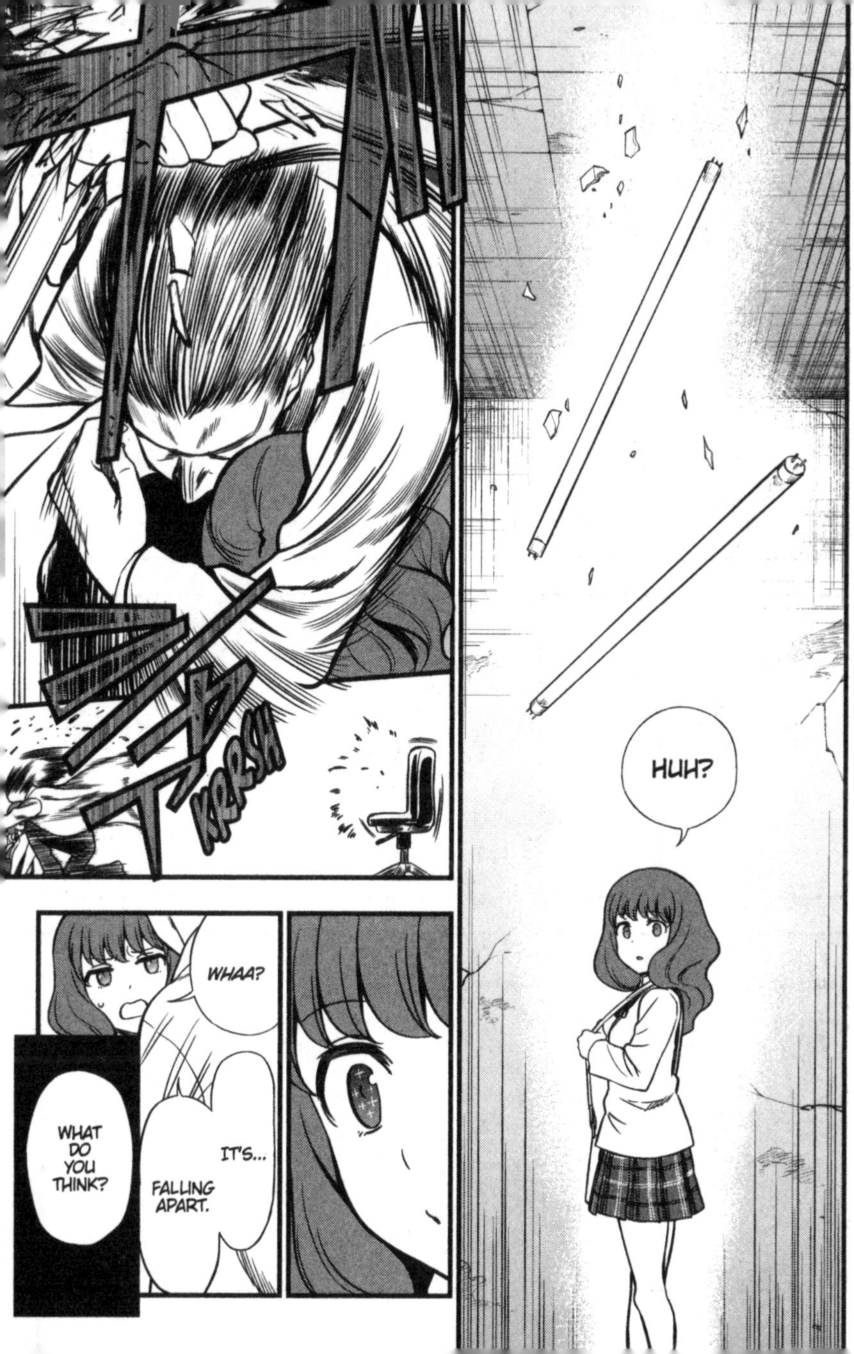
HUH?
KRRSH
WHAA?
IT'S... FALLING APART.
WHAT DO YOU THINK?

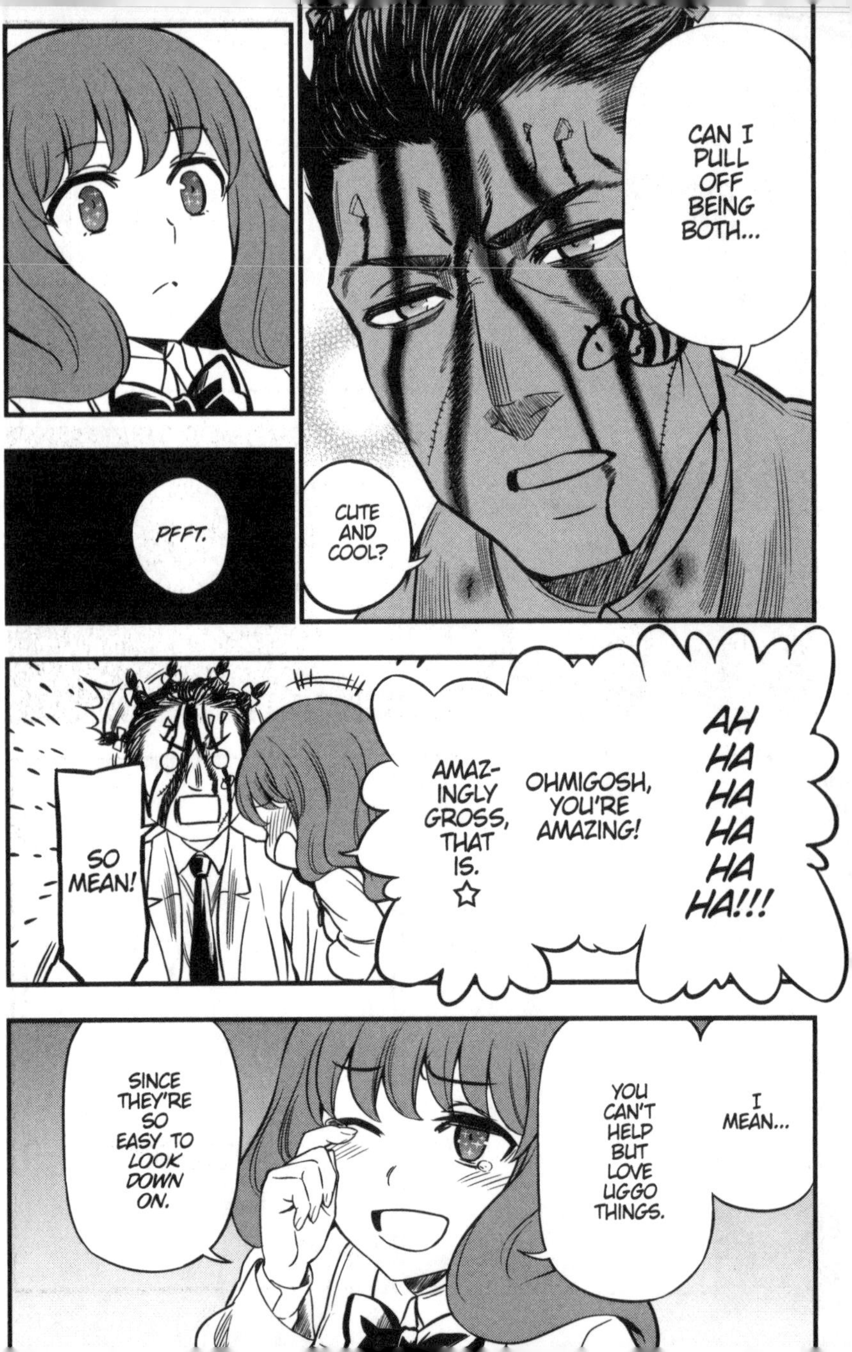
CAN I PULL OFF BEING BOTH...
CUTE AND COOL?
PFFT.
AH HA HA HA HA HA!!!
OHMIGOSH, YOU'RE AMAZING!
AMAZINGLY GROSS, THAT IS. ☆
SO MEAN!
I MEAN...
YOU CAN'T HELP BUT LOVE UGGO THINGS.
SINCE THEY'RE SO EASY TO LOOK DOWN ON.

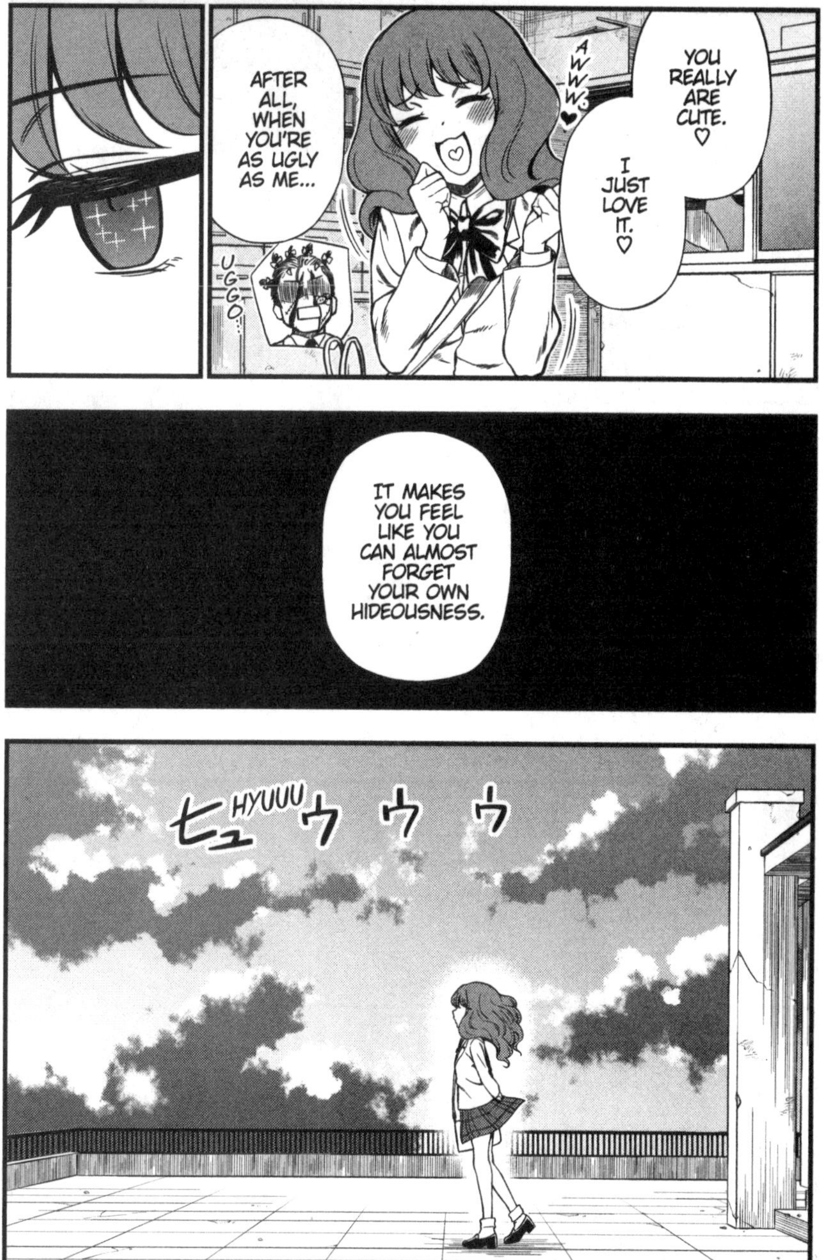

YOU REALLY ARE CUTE. ♡
AWWW. ♥
I JUST LOVE IT. ♡
AFTER ALL, WHEN YOU'RE AS UGLY AS ME...
UGGO...
IT MAKES YOU FEEL LIKE YOU CAN ALMOST FORGET YOUR OWN HIDEOUSNESS.
ヒュウウウ HYUUU

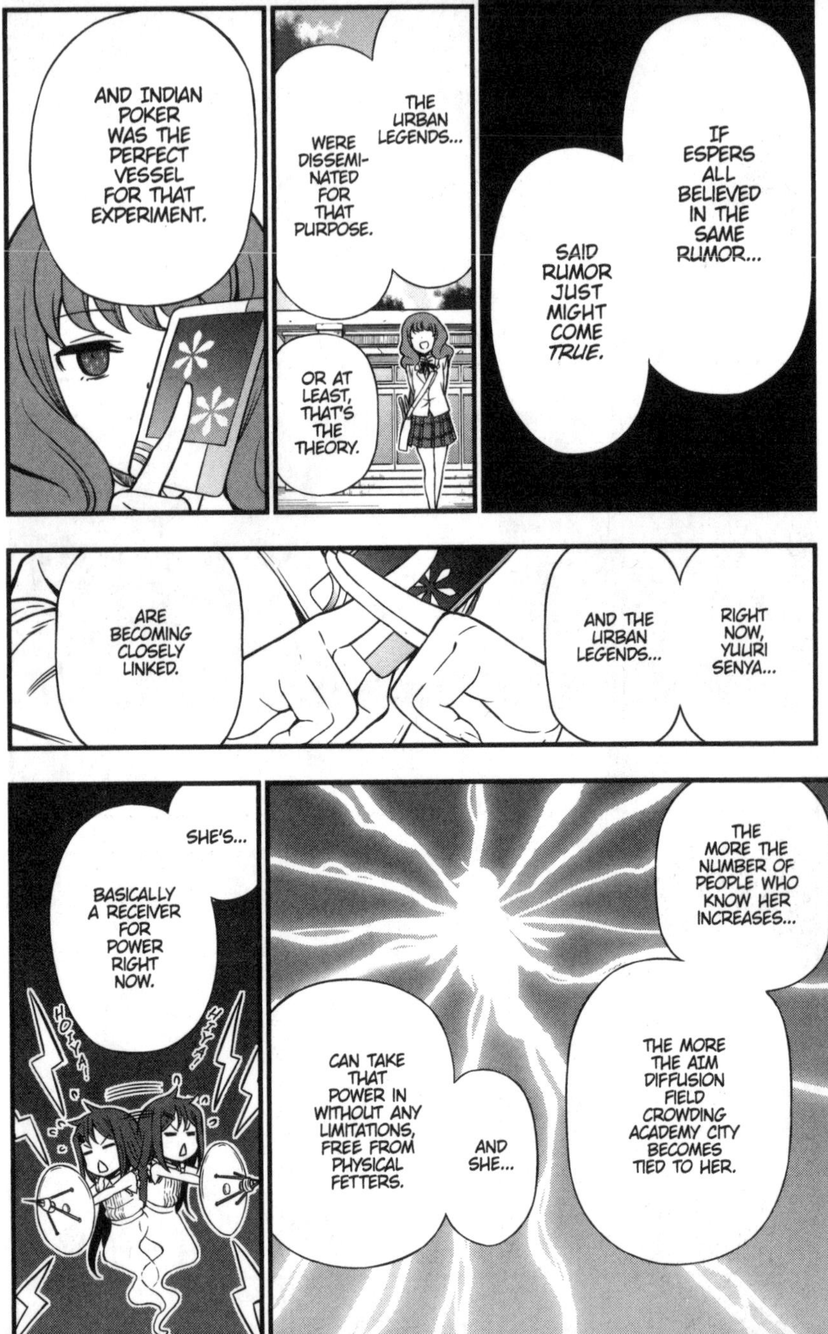
IF ESPERS ALL BELIEVED IN THE SAME RUMOR...
SAID RUMOR JUST MIGHT COME *TRUE*.
THE URBAN LEGENDS...
WERE DISSEMINATED FOR THAT PURPOSE.
OR AT LEAST, THAT'S THE THEORY.
AND INDIAN POKER WAS THE PERFECT VESSEL FOR THAT EXPERIMENT.
RIGHT NOW, YUURI SENYA...
AND THE URBAN LEGENDS...
ARE BECOMING CLOSELY LINKED.
THE MORE THE NUMBER OF PEOPLE WHO KNOW HER INCREASES...
THE MORE THE AIM DIFFUSION FIELD CROWDING ACADEMY CITY BECOMES TIED TO HER.
AND SHE...
CAN TAKE THAT POWER IN WITHOUT ANY LIMITATIONS, FREE FROM PHYSICAL FETTERS.
SHE'S...
BASICALLY A RECEIVER FOR POWER RIGHT NOW.
HOIYA!

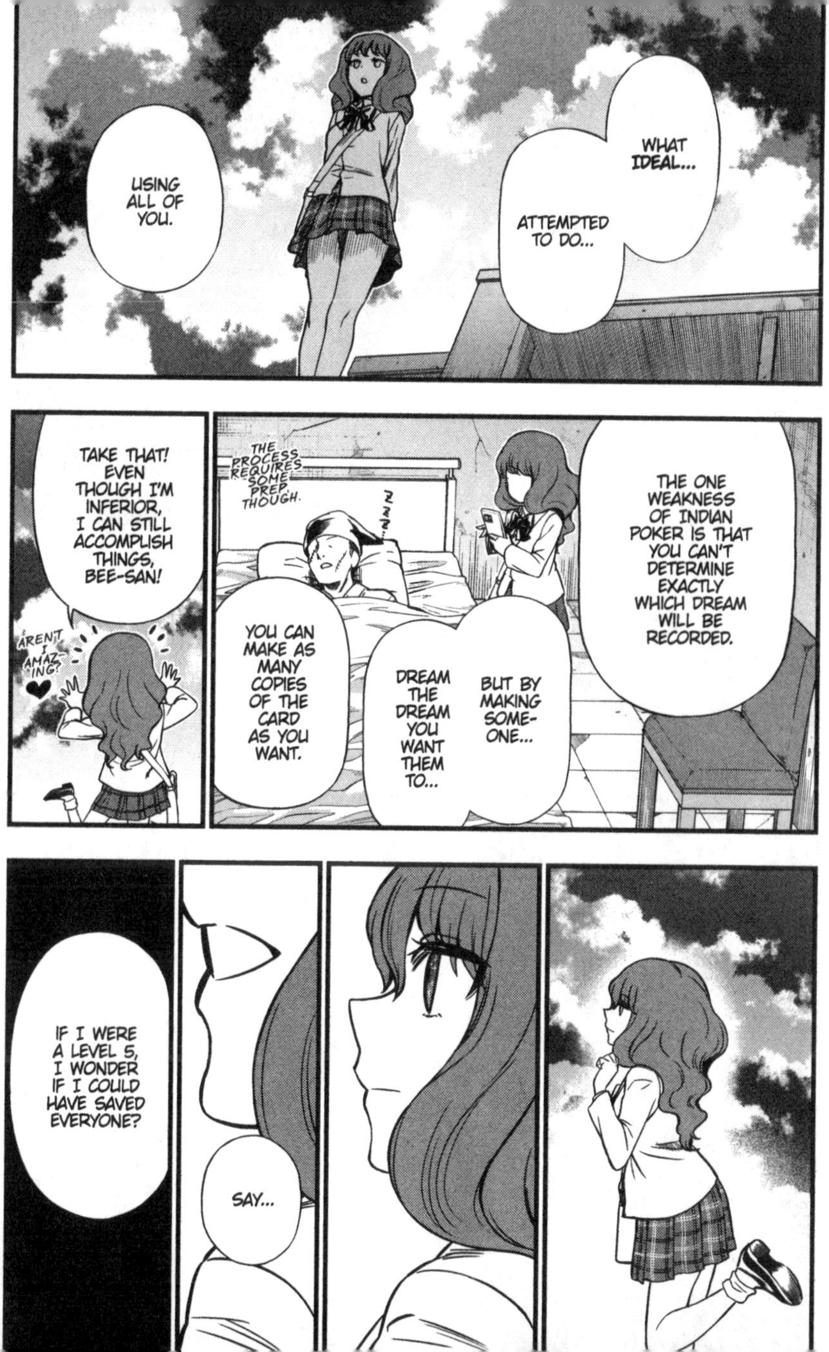
WHAT IDEAL...
ATTEMPTED TO DO...
USING ALL OF YOU.
THE ONE WEAKNESS OF INDIAN POKER IS THAT YOU CAN'T DETERMINE EXACTLY WHICH DREAM WILL BE RECORDED.
BUT BY MAKING SOME-ONE...
DREAM THE DREAM YOU WANT THEM TO...
YOU CAN MAKE AS MANY COPIES OF THE CARD AS YOU WANT.
THE PROCESS REQUIRES SOME PREP, THOUGH.
TAKE THAT! EVEN THOUGH I'M INFERIOR, I CAN STILL ACCOMPLISH THINGS, BEE-SAN!
AREN'T I AMAZ-ING?
SAY...
IF I WERE A LEVEL 5, I WONDER IF I COULD HAVE SAVED EVERYONE?

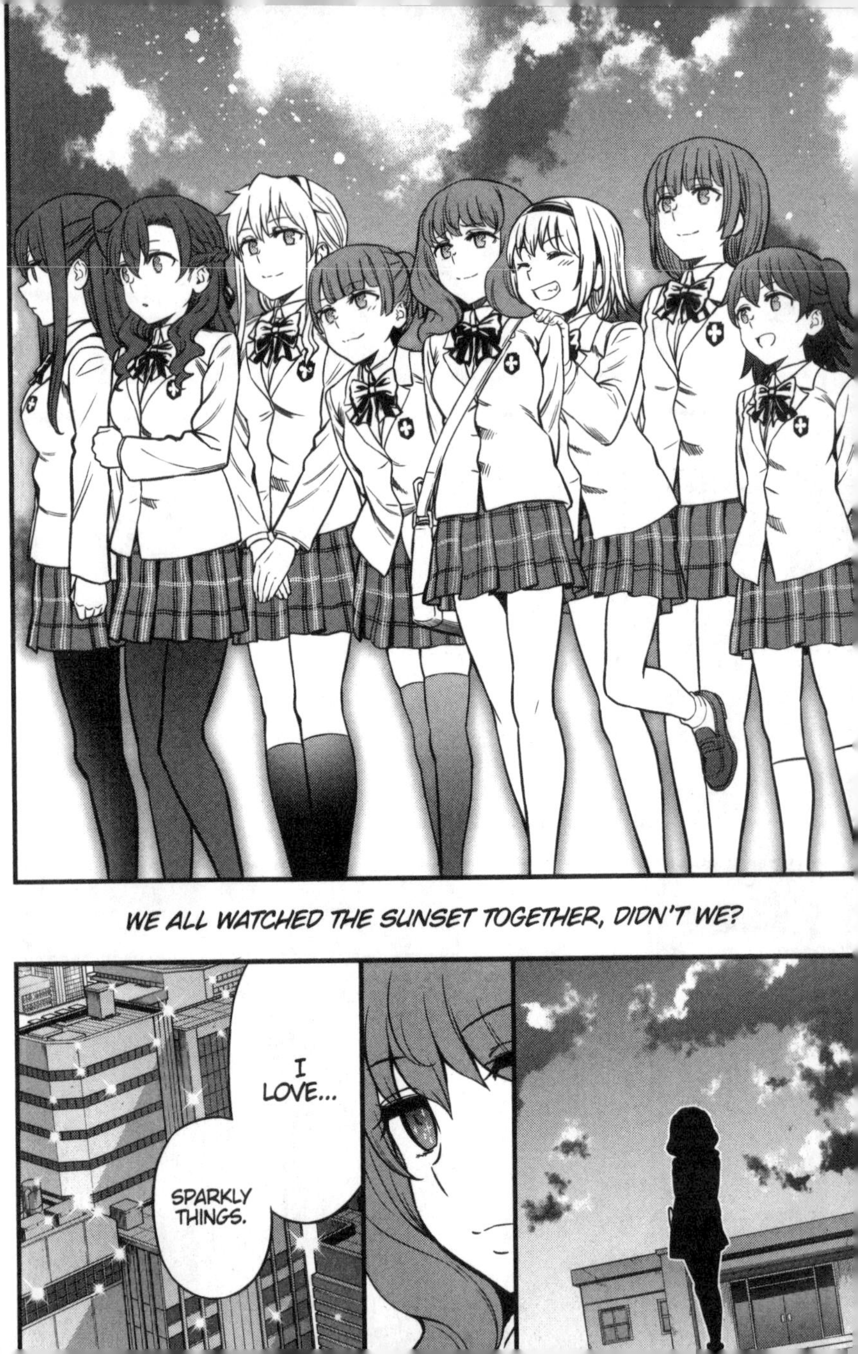
WE ALL WATCHED THE SUNSET TOGETHER, DIDN'T WE?
I LOVE...
SPARKLY THINGS.

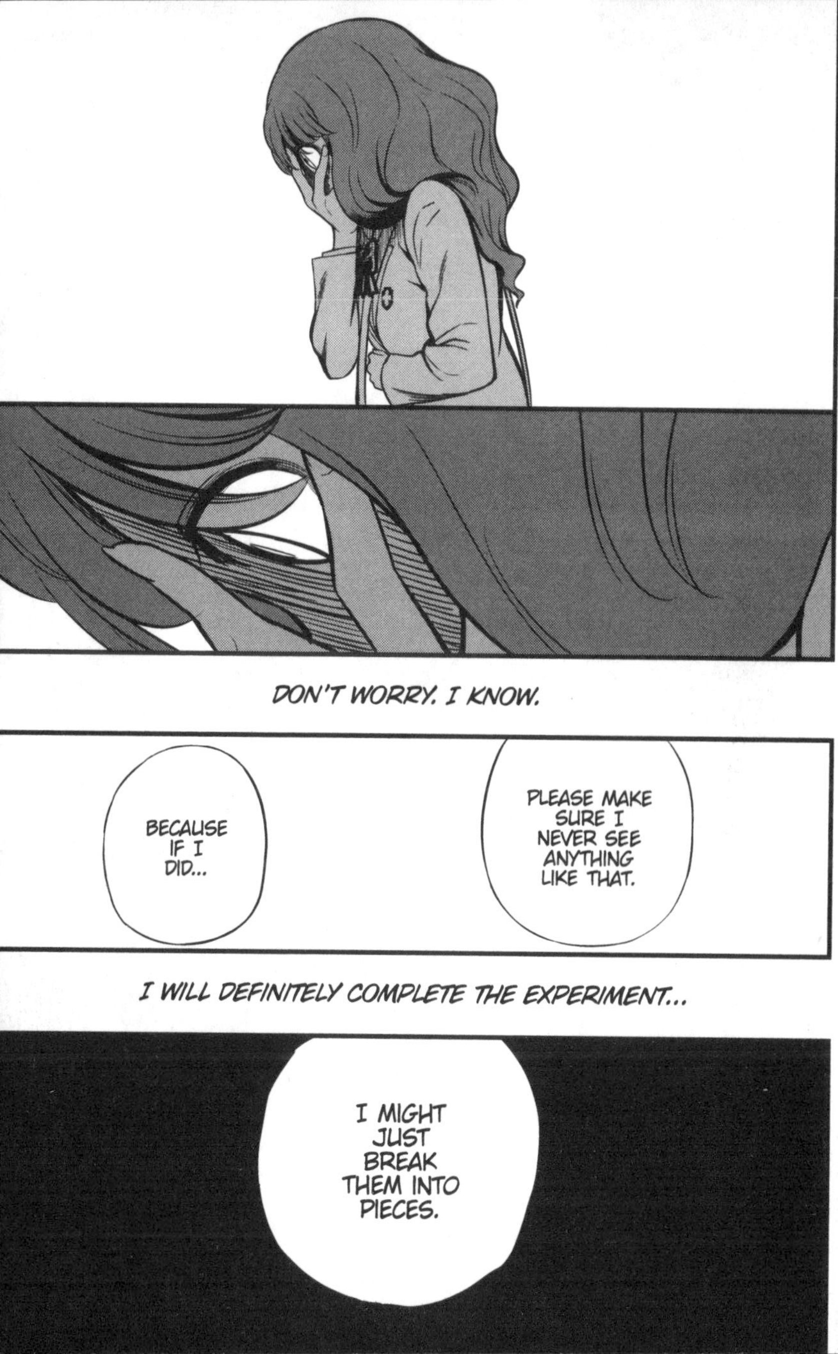
DON'T WORRY. I KNOW.
PLEASE MAKE SURE I NEVER SEE ANYTHING LIKE THAT.
BECAUSE IF I DID...
I WILL DEFINITELY COMPLETE THE EXPERIMENT...
I MIGHT JUST BREAK THEM INTO PIECES.

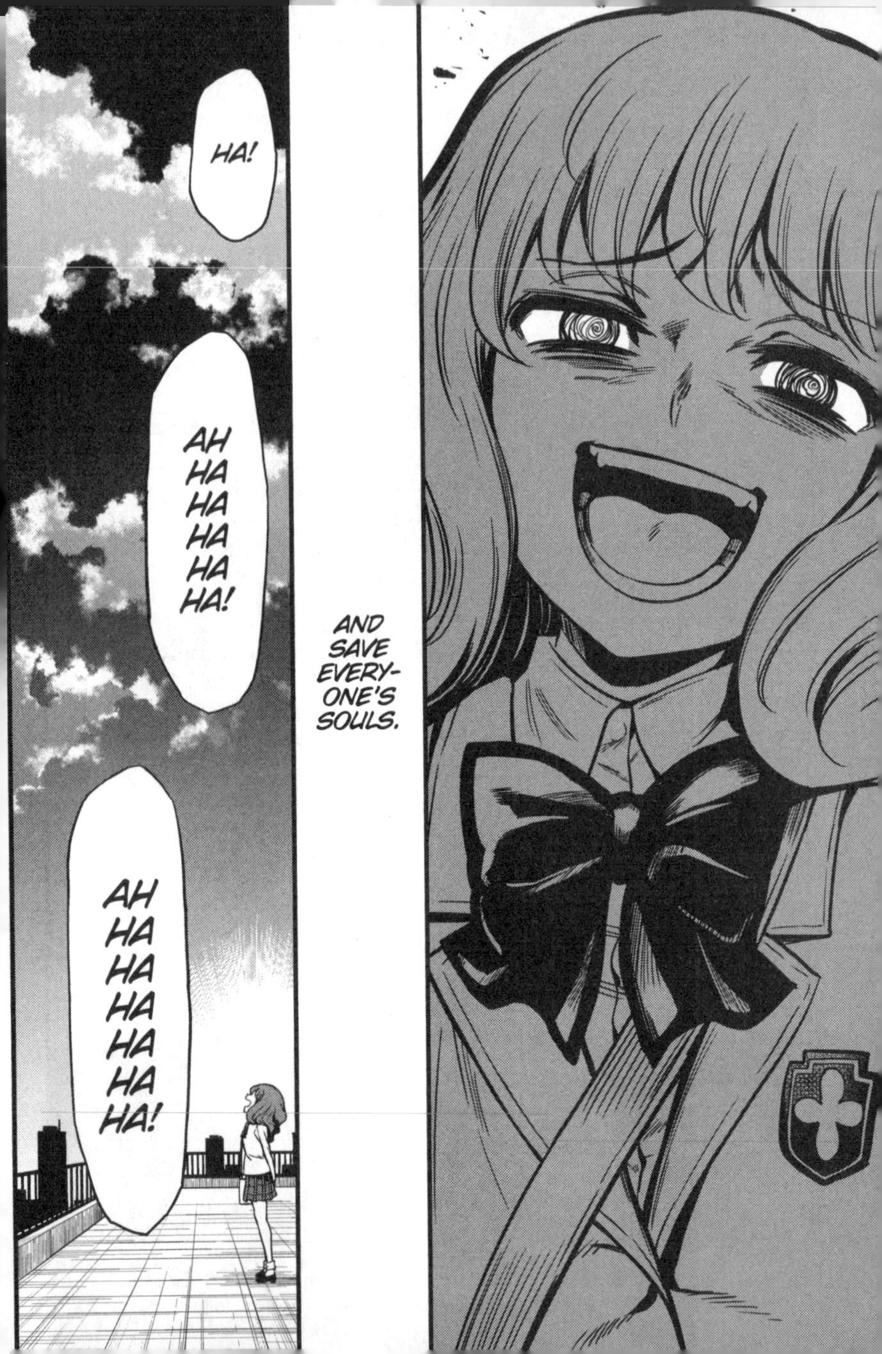
AND SAVE EVERY-ONE'S SOULS.
HA!
AH HA HA HA HA HA!
AH HA HA HA HA HA HA!

CHAPTER 24: I Have An Intellectual Side As Well

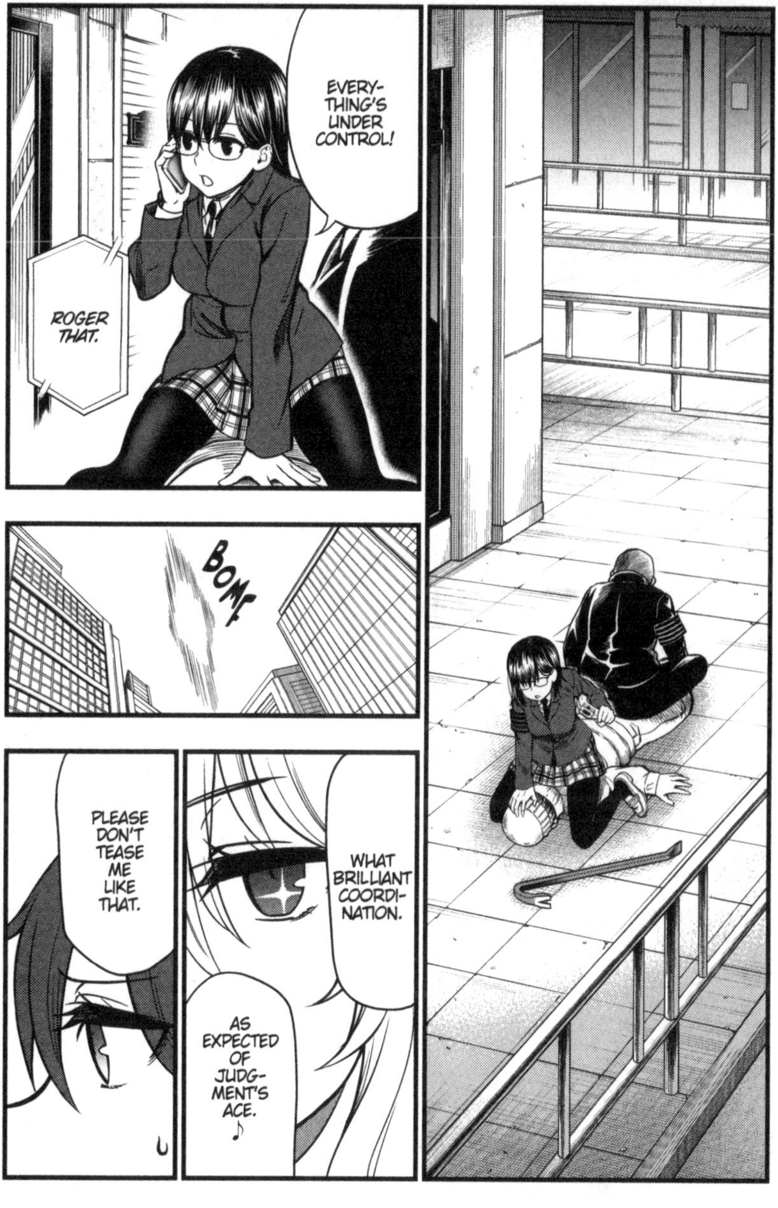
EVERY-THING'S UNDER CONTROL!
ROGER THAT.
BOMF
WHAT BRILLIANT COORDI-NATION.
AS EXPECTED OF JUDG-MENT'S ACE. ♪
PLEASE DON'T TEASE ME LIKE THAT.

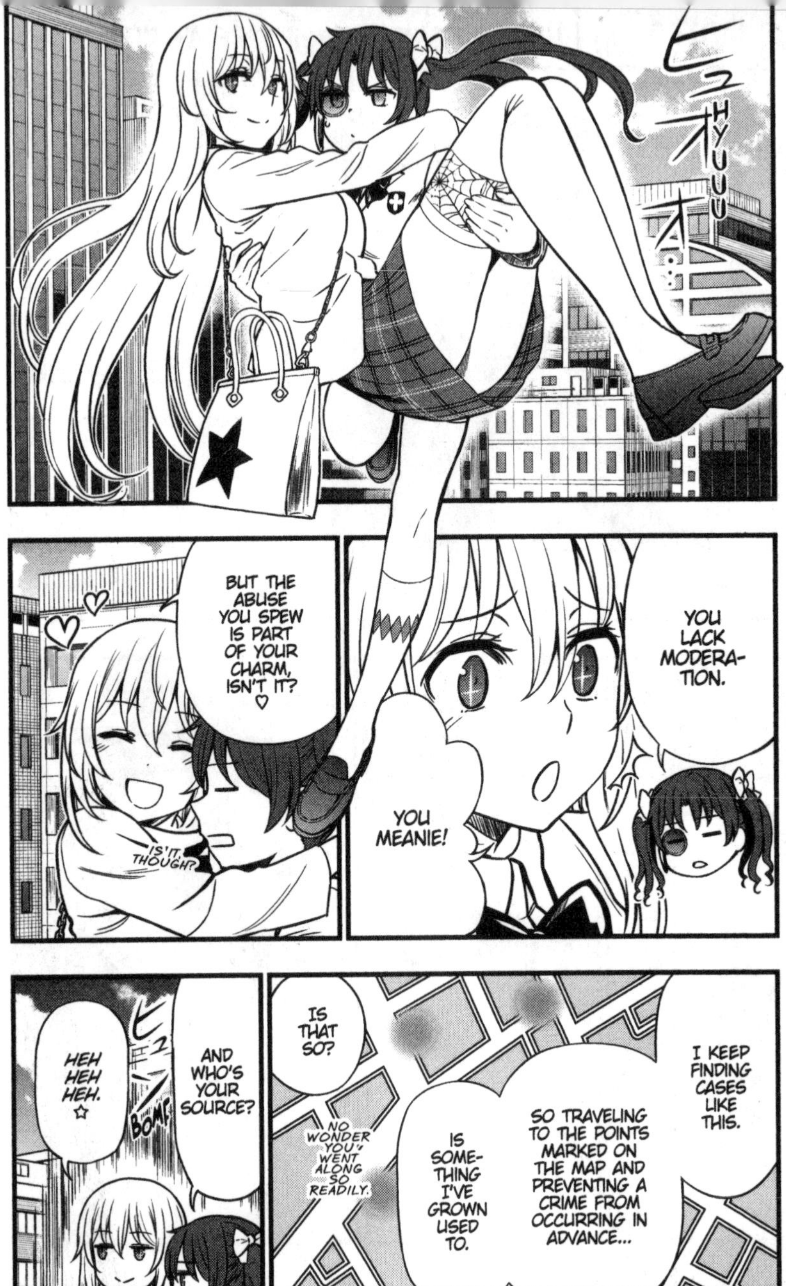
ヒュオオ…
HYUUUU
YOU LACK MODERATION.
YOU MEANIE!
BUT THE ABUSE YOU SPEW IS PART OF YOUR CHARM, ISN'T IT? ♡
IS IT, THOUGH?
I KEEP FINDING CASES LIKE THIS.
SO TRAVELING TO THE POINTS MARKED ON THE MAP AND PREVENTING A CRIME FROM OCCURRING IN ADVANCE...
IS SOMETHING I'VE GROWN USED TO.
IS THAT SO?
NO WONDER YOU WENT ALONG SO READILY.
AND WHO'S YOUR SOURCE?
HEH HEH HEH. ☆
ヒュ
BOMF

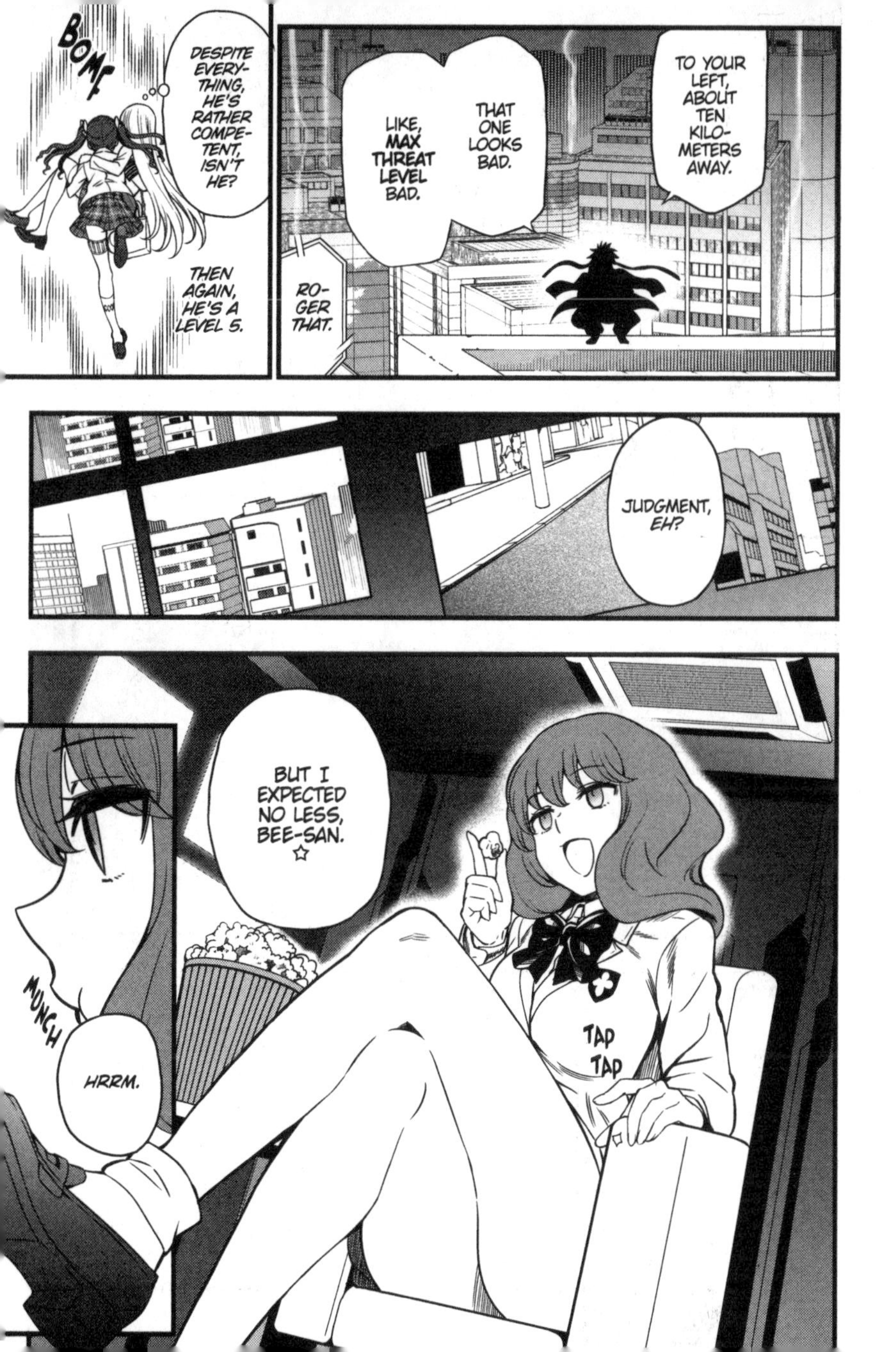

TO YOUR LEFT, ABOUT TEN KILO-METERS AWAY.
THAT ONE LOOKS BAD.
LIKE, MAX THREAT LEVEL BAD.
RO-GER THAT.
BOM!
DESPITE EVERY-THING, HE'S RATHER COMPE-TENT, ISN'T HE?
THEN AGAIN, HE'S A LEVEL 5.
JUDGMENT, EH?
BUT I EXPECTED NO LESS, BEE-SAN. ☆
TAP TAP
MUNCH
HRRM.

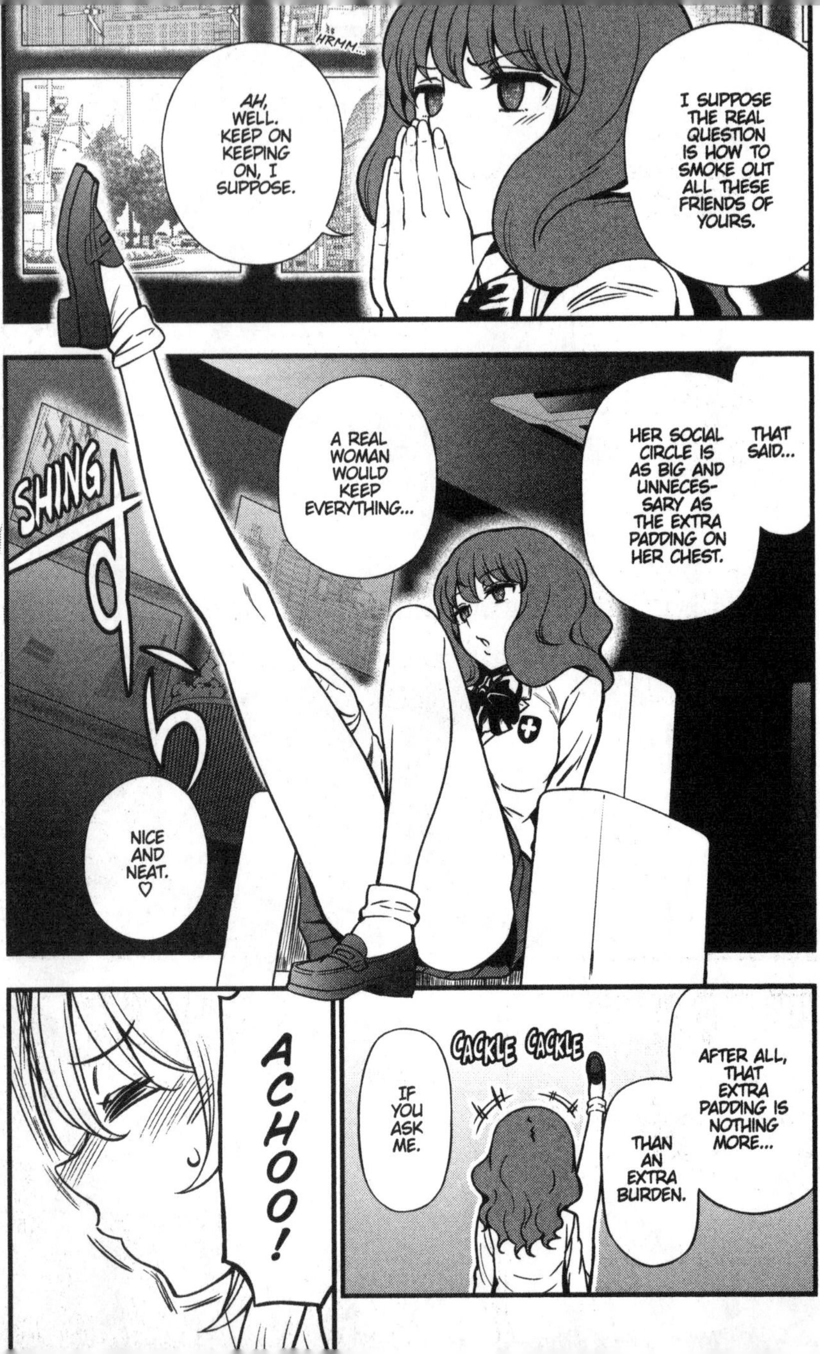
I SUPPOSE THE REAL QUESTION IS HOW TO SMOKE OUT ALL THESE FRIENDS OF YOURS.
HRMM...
AH, WELL. KEEP ON KEEPING ON, I SUPPOSE.
THAT SAID...
HER SOCIAL CIRCLE IS AS BIG AND UNNECES-SARY AS THE EXTRA PADDING ON HER CHEST.
A REAL WOMAN WOULD KEEP EVERYTHING...
SHING
NICE AND NEAT. ♡
AFTER ALL, THAT EXTRA PADDING IS NOTHING MORE...
THAN AN EXTRA BURDEN.
CACKLE CACKLE
IF YOU ASK ME.
ACHOO!

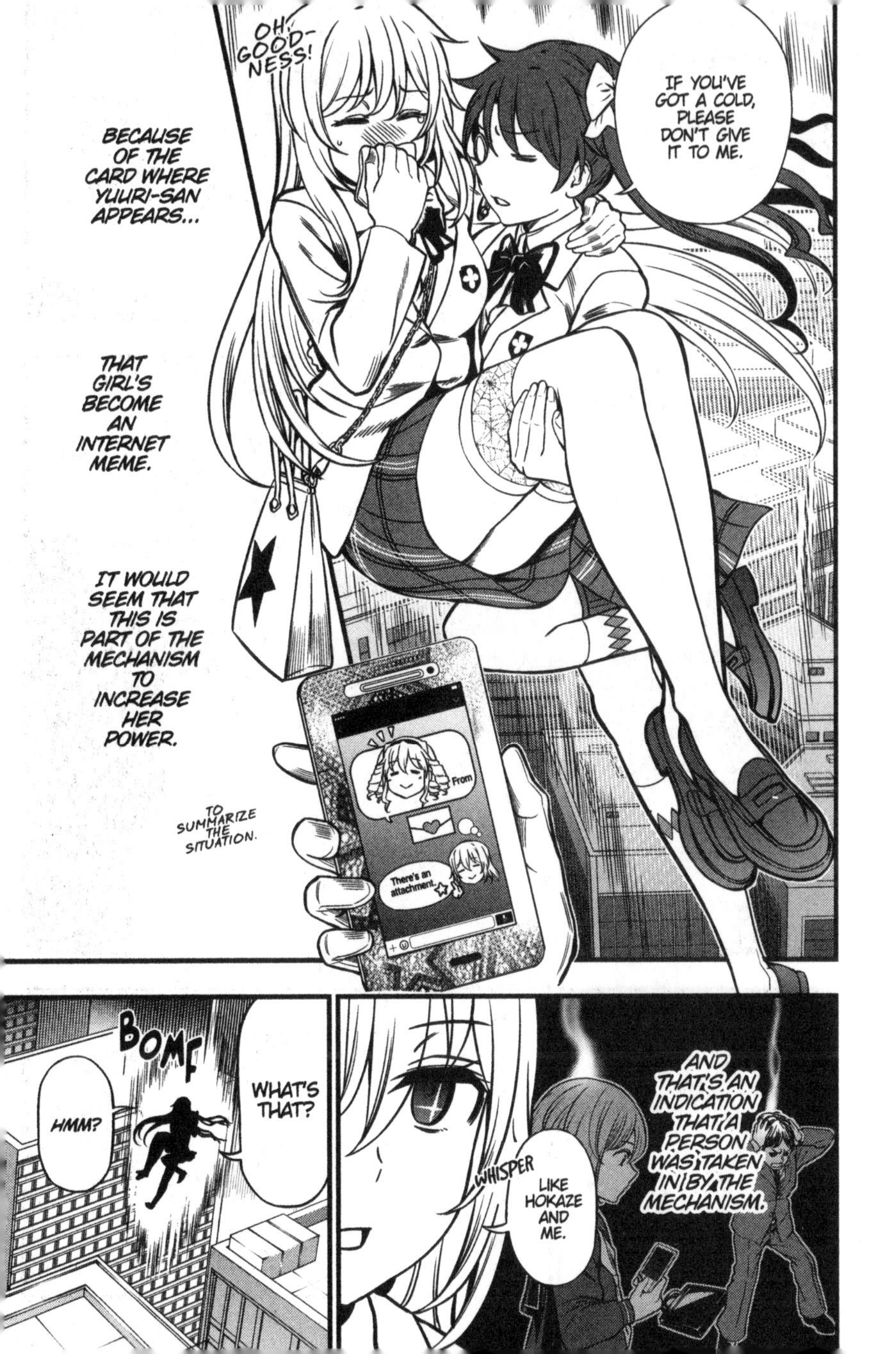
OH! GOOD-NESS!
IF YOU'VE GOT A COLD, PLEASE DON'T GIVE IT TO ME.
BECAUSE OF THE CARD WHERE YUURI-SAN APPEARS...
THAT GIRL'S BECOME AN INTERNET MEME.
IT WOULD SEEM THAT THIS IS PART OF THE MECHANISM TO INCREASE HER POWER.
TO SUMMARIZE THE SITUATION.
From
There's an attachment.
AND THAT'S AN INDICATION THAT A PERSON WAS TAKEN IN BY THE MECHANISM.
WHISPER
LIKE HOKAZE AND ME.
WHAT'S THAT?
BOMF
HMM?

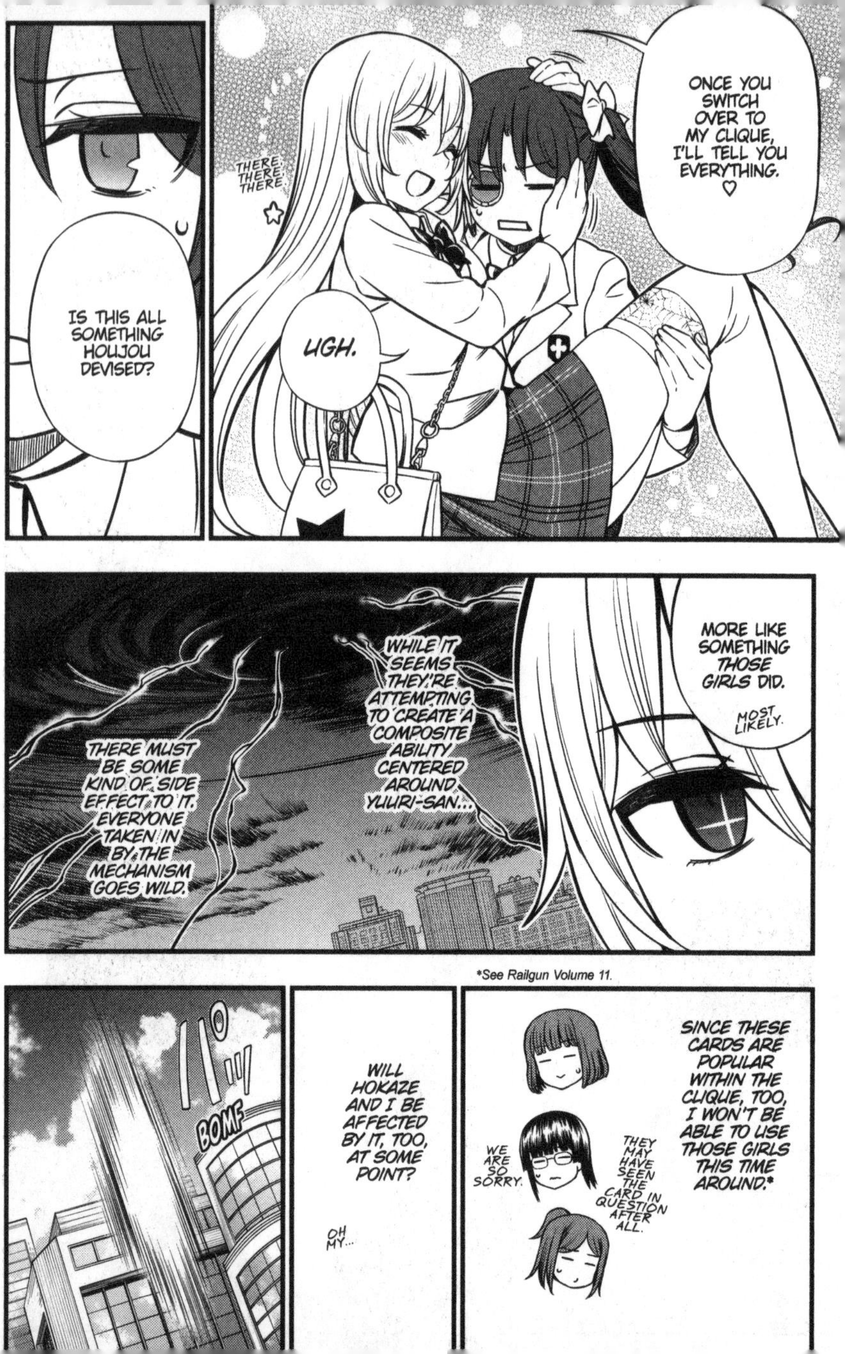
ONCE YOU SWITCH OVER TO MY CLIQUE, I'LL TELL YOU EVERYTHING. ♡
THERE, THERE, THERE.
UGH.
IS THIS ALL SOMETHING HOUJOU DEVISED?
MORE LIKE SOMETHING THOSE GIRLS DID.
MOST LIKELY.
WHILE IT SEEMS THEY'RE ATTEMPTING TO CREATE A COMPOSITE ABILITY CENTERED AROUND YUURI-SAN...
THERE MUST BE SOME KIND OF SIDE EFFECT TO IT. EVERYONE TAKEN IN BY THE MECHANISM GOES WILD.
SINCE THESE CARDS ARE POPULAR WITHIN THE CLIQUE, TOO, I WON'T BE ABLE TO USE THOSE GIRLS THIS TIME AROUND.*
THEY MAY HAVE SEEN THE CARD IN QUESTION AFTER ALL.
WE ARE SO SORRY.
WILL HOKAZE AND I BE AFFECTED BY IT, TOO, AT SOME POINT?
OH MY...
BOMF

*See Railgun Volume 11.

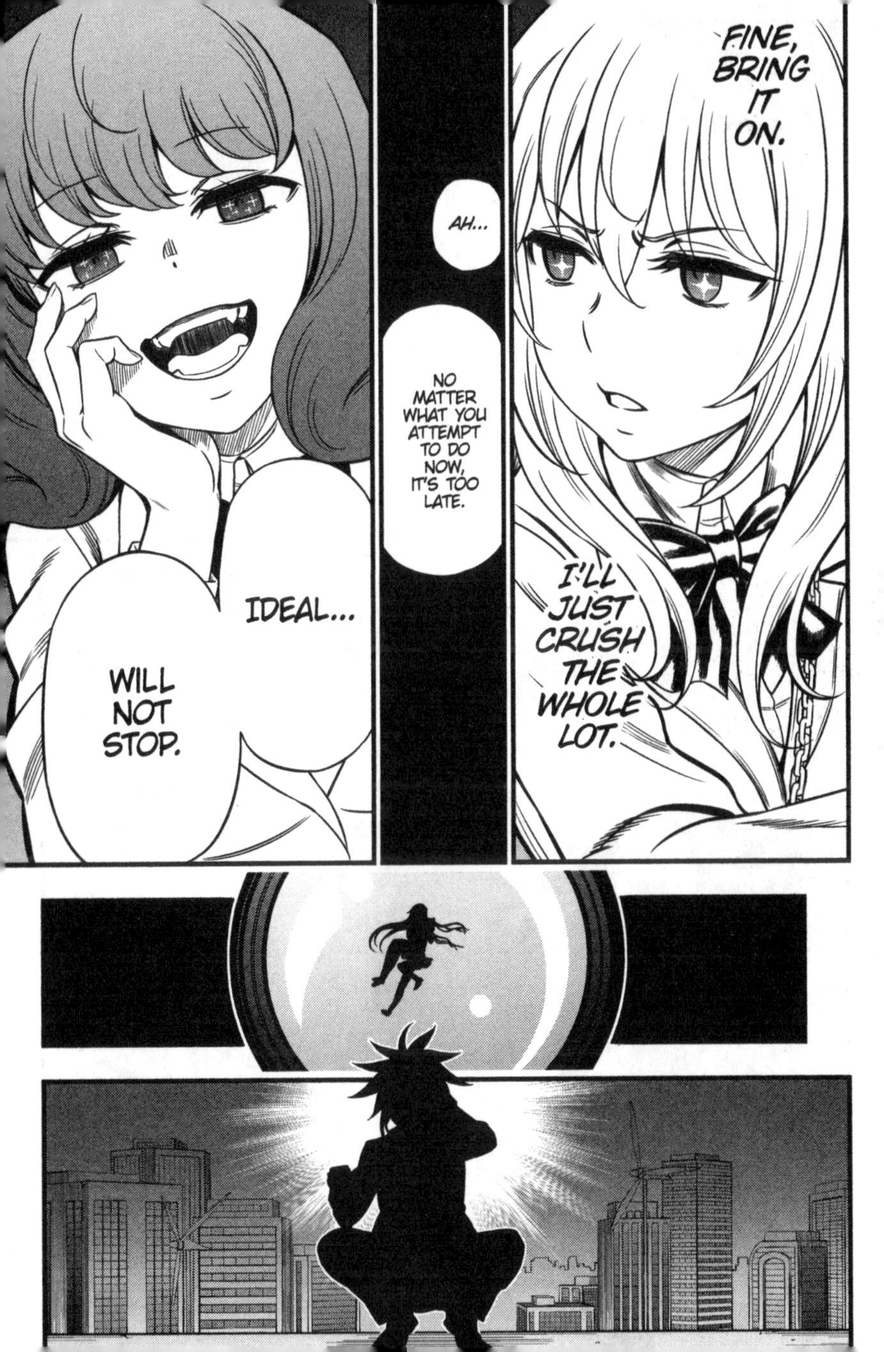
FINE, BRING IT ON.
AH...
NO MATTER WHAT YOU ATTEMPT TO DO NOW, IT'S TOO LATE.
I'LL JUST CRUSH THE WHOLE LOT.
IDEAL...
WILL NOT STOP.

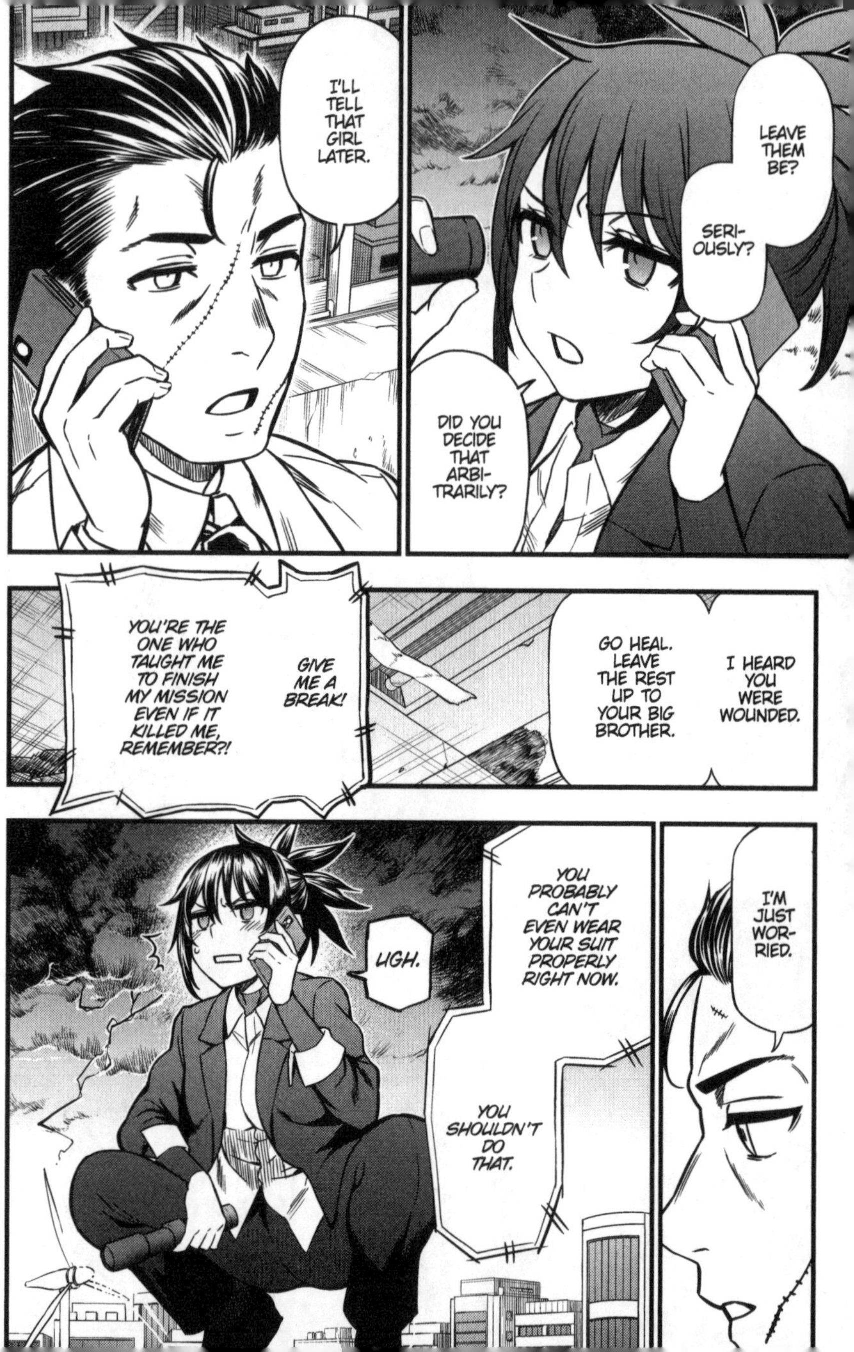
LEAVE THEM BE?
SERI-OUSLY?
DID YOU DECIDE THAT ARBI-TRARILY?
I'LL TELL THAT GIRL LATER.
I HEARD YOU WERE WOUNDED.
GO HEAL. LEAVE THE REST UP TO YOUR BIG BROTHER.
GIVE ME A BREAK!
YOU'RE THE ONE WHO TAUGHT ME TO FINISH MY MISSION EVEN IF IT KILLED ME, REMEMBER?!
I'M JUST WOR-RIED.
YOU PROBABLY CAN'T EVEN WEAR YOUR SUIT PROPERLY RIGHT NOW.
YOU SHOULDN'T DO THAT.
UGH.

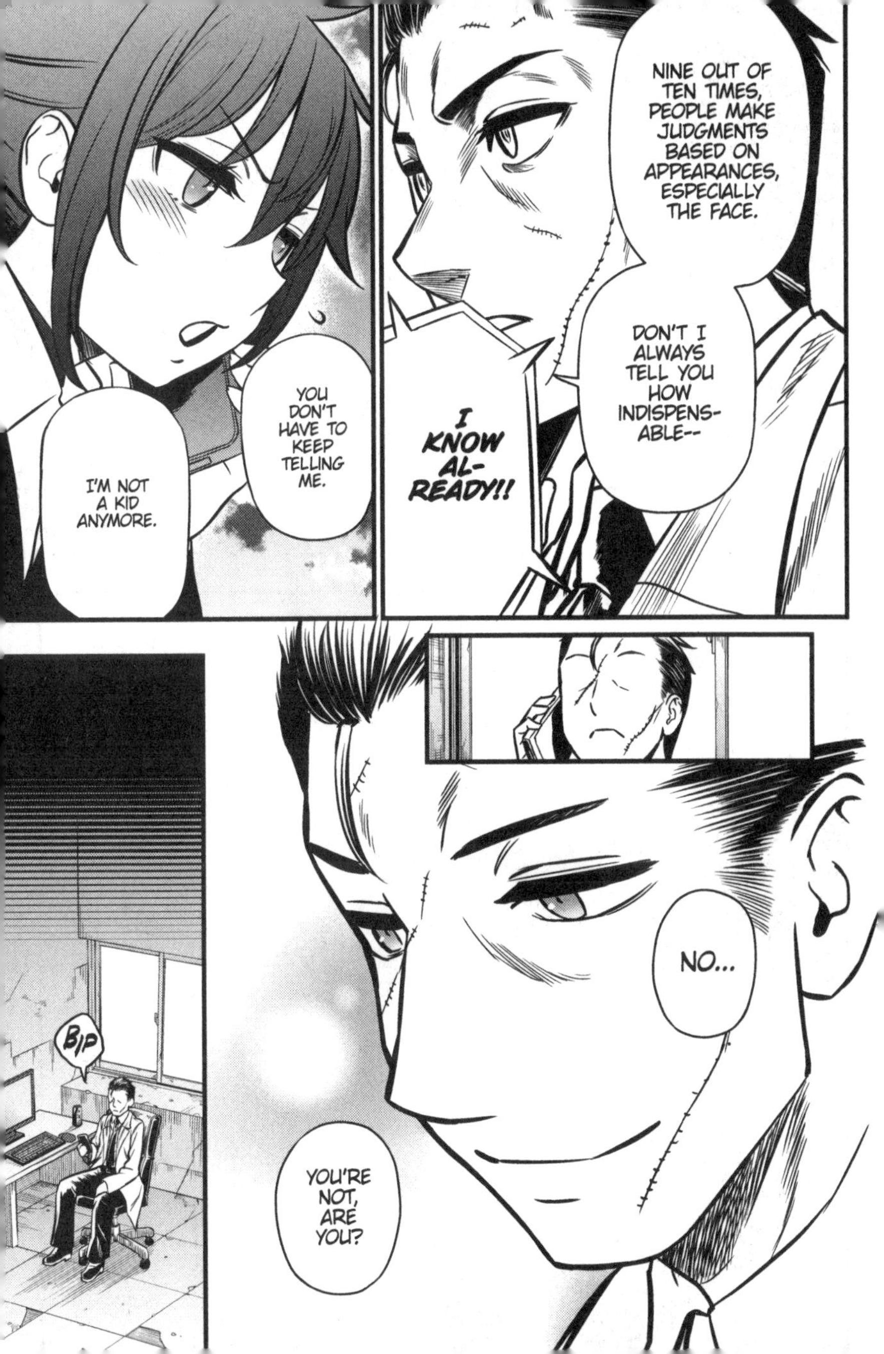
NINE OUT OF TEN TIMES, PEOPLE MAKE JUDGMENTS BASED ON APPEARANCES, ESPECIALLY THE FACE.
DON'T I ALWAYS TELL YOU HOW INDISPENS-ABLE--
I KNOW AL-READY!!
YOU DON'T HAVE TO KEEP TELLING ME.
I'M NOT A KID ANYMORE.
NO...
YOU'RE NOT, ARE YOU?
BIP

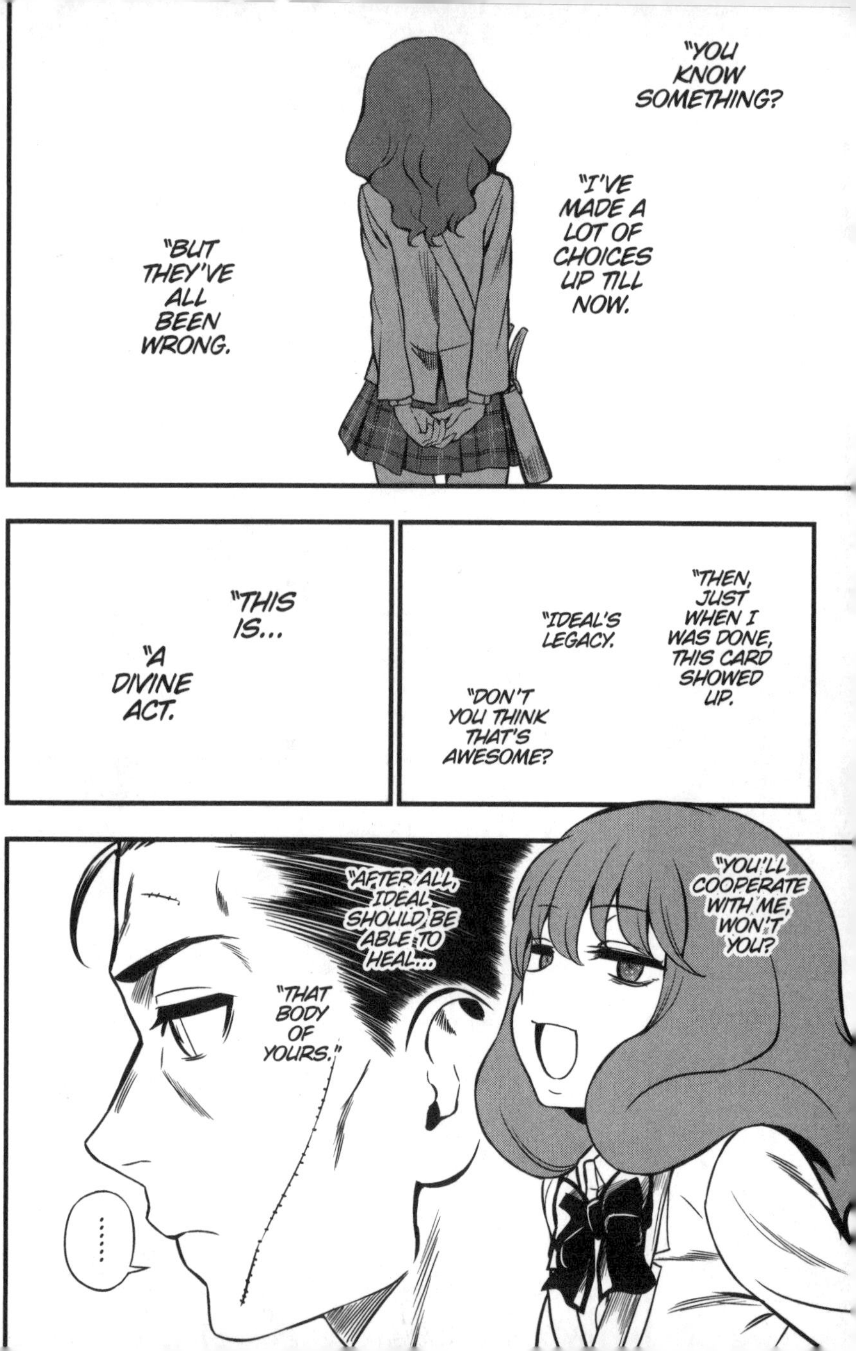
"YOU KNOW SOMETHING?
"I'VE MADE A LOT OF CHOICES UP TILL NOW.
"BUT THEY'VE ALL BEEN WRONG.
"THEN, JUST WHEN I WAS DONE, THIS CARD SHOWED UP.
"IDEAL'S LEGACY.
"DON'T YOU THINK THAT'S AWESOME?
"THIS IS...
"A DIVINE ACT.
"YOU'LL COOPERATE WITH ME, WON'T YOU?
"AFTER ALL, IDEAL SHOULD BE ABLE TO HEAL...
"THAT BODY OF YOURS."
......

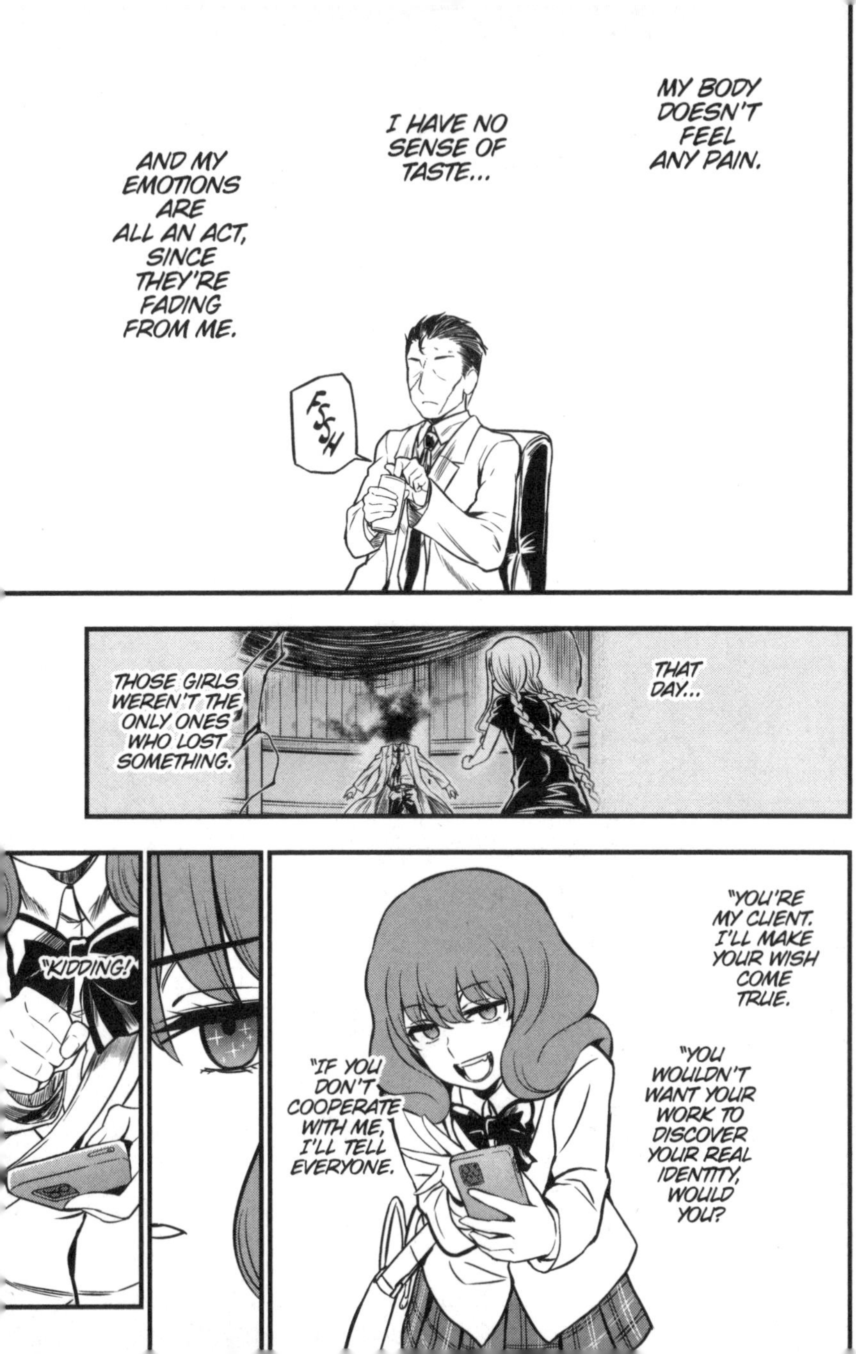
MY BODY DOESN'T FEEL ANY PAIN.
I HAVE NO SENSE OF TASTE...
AND MY EMOTIONS ARE ALL AN ACT, SINCE THEY'RE FADING FROM ME.
FSSH
THAT DAY...
THOSE GIRLS WEREN'T THE ONLY ONES WHO LOST SOMETHING.
"YOU'RE MY CLIENT. I'LL MAKE YOUR WISH COME TRUE.
"YOU WOULDN'T WANT YOUR WORK TO DISCOVER YOUR REAL IDENTITY, WOULD YOU?
"IF YOU DON'T COOPERATE WITH ME, I'LL TELL EVERYONE.
"KIDDING!

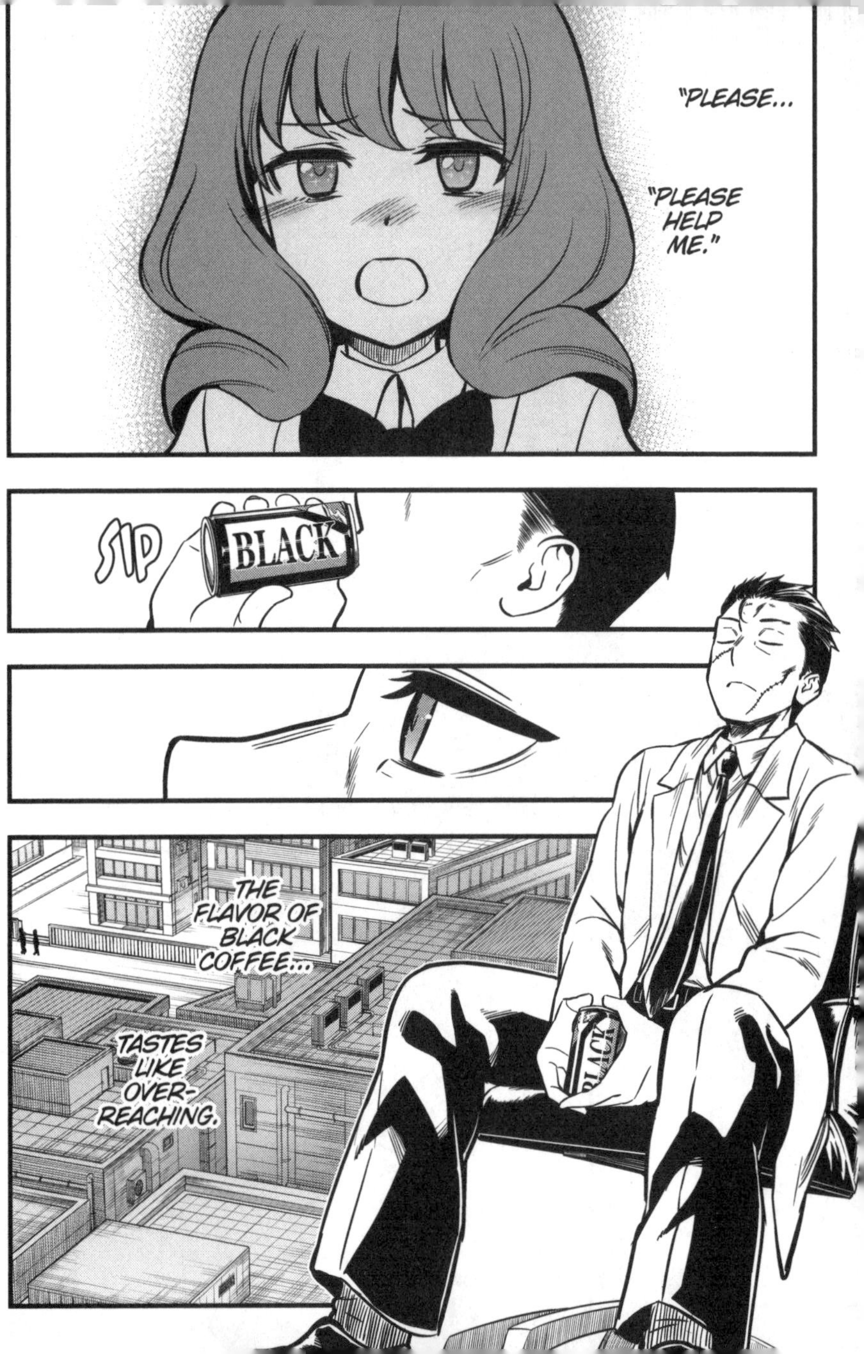
"PLEASE...
"PLEASE HELP ME."
SIP
BLACK
THE FLAVOR OF BLACK COFFEE...
TASTES LIKE OVER-REACHING.
BLACK

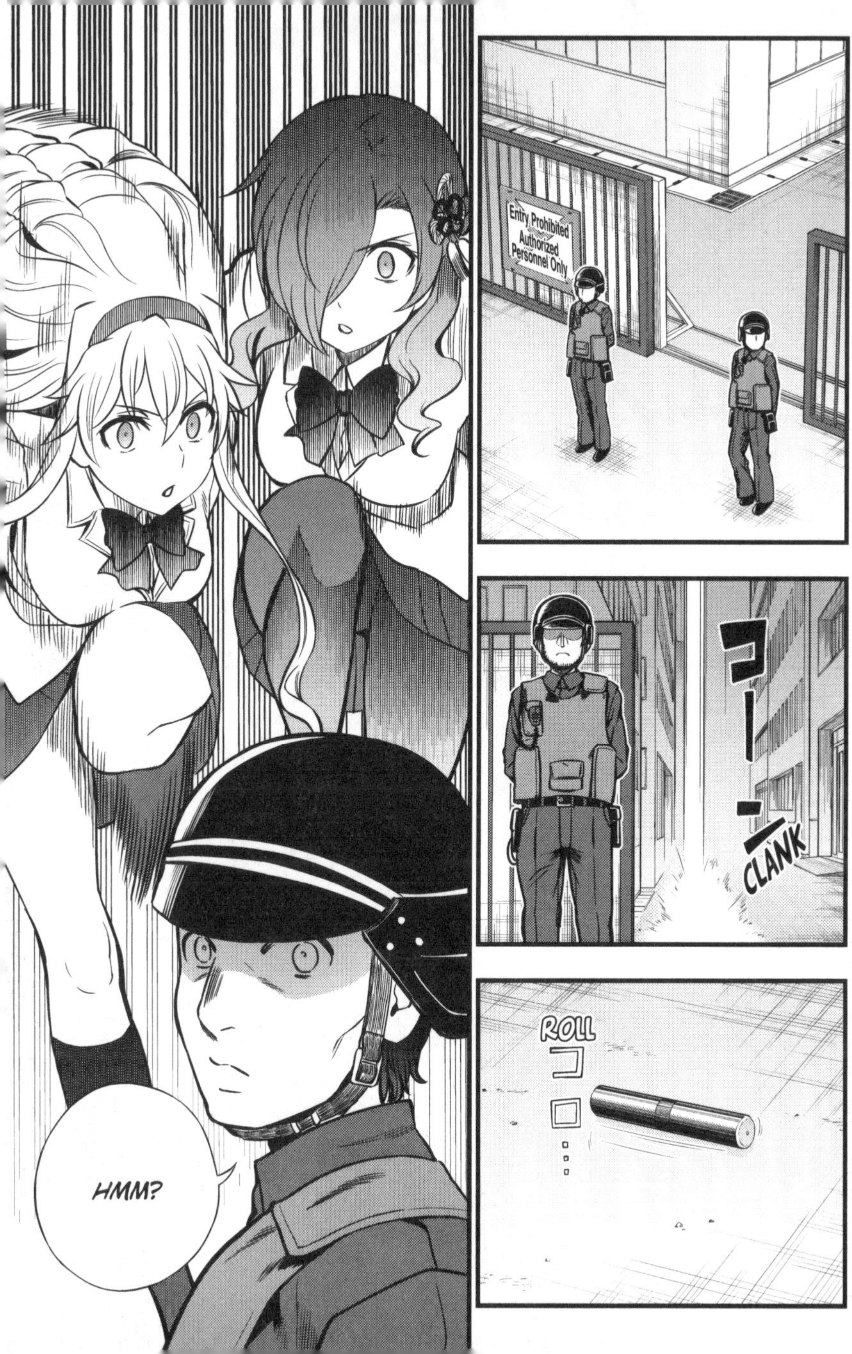
Entry Prohibited
Authorized
Personnel Only
CLANK
ROLL
コロ
HMM?

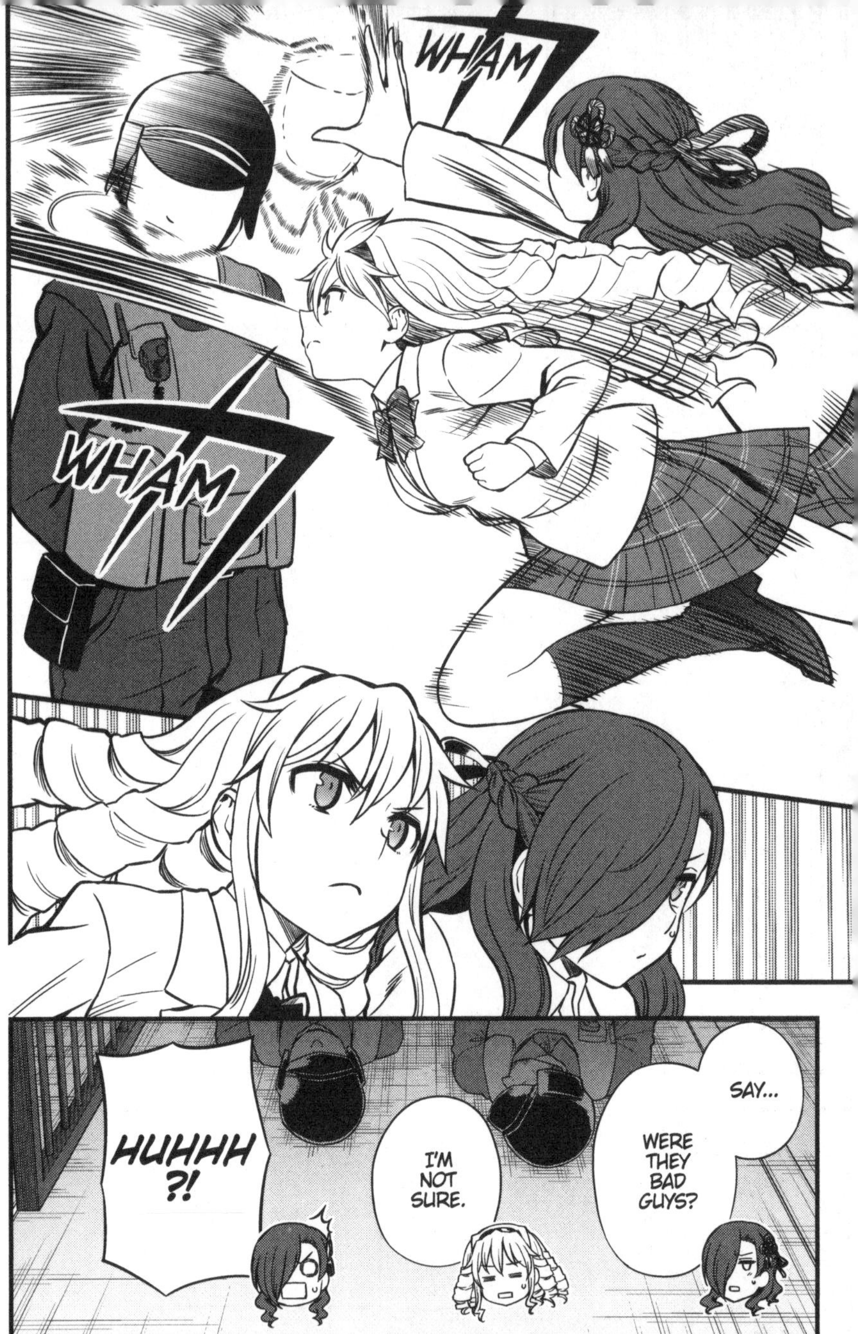
WHAM
WHAM
SAY...
WERE THEY BAD GUYS?
I'M NOT SURE.
HUHHH ?!

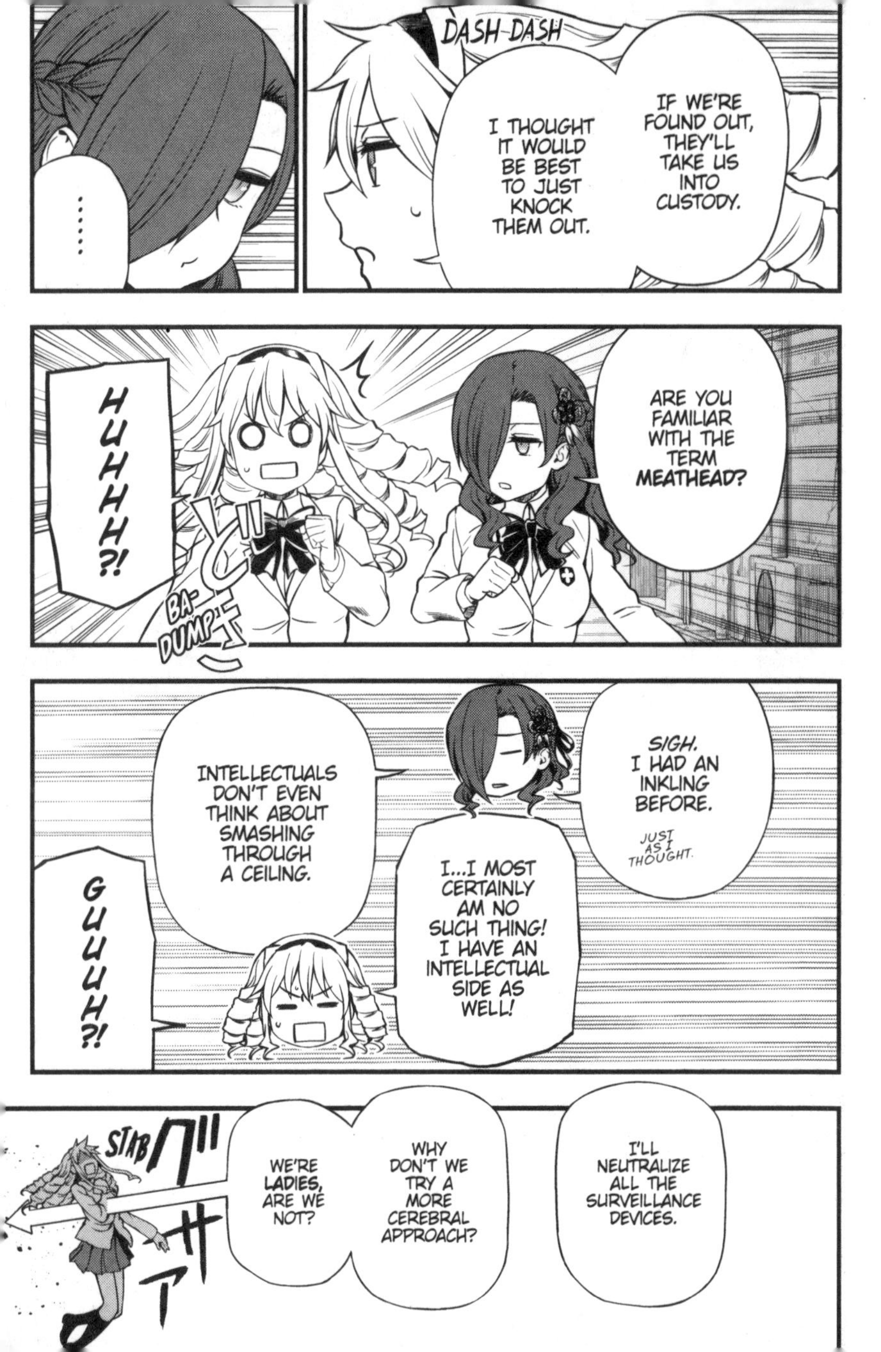
DASH-DASH
IF WE'RE FOUND OUT, THEY'LL TAKE US INTO CUSTODY.
I THOUGHT IT WOULD BE BEST TO JUST KNOCK THEM OUT.
......
ARE YOU FAMILIAR WITH THE TERM MEATHEAD?
HUHHHH?!
BA-DUMP
SIGH. I HAD AN INKLING BEFORE.
JUST AS I THOUGHT.
I...I MOST CERTAINLY AM NO SUCH THING! I HAVE AN INTELLECTUAL SIDE AS WELL!
INTELLECTUALS DON'T EVEN THINK ABOUT SMASHING THROUGH A CEILING.
GUUUH?!
I'LL NEUTRALIZE ALL THE SURVEILLANCE DEVICES.
WHY DON'T WE TRY A MORE CEREBRAL APPROACH?
WE'RE LADIES, ARE WE NOT?
STAB

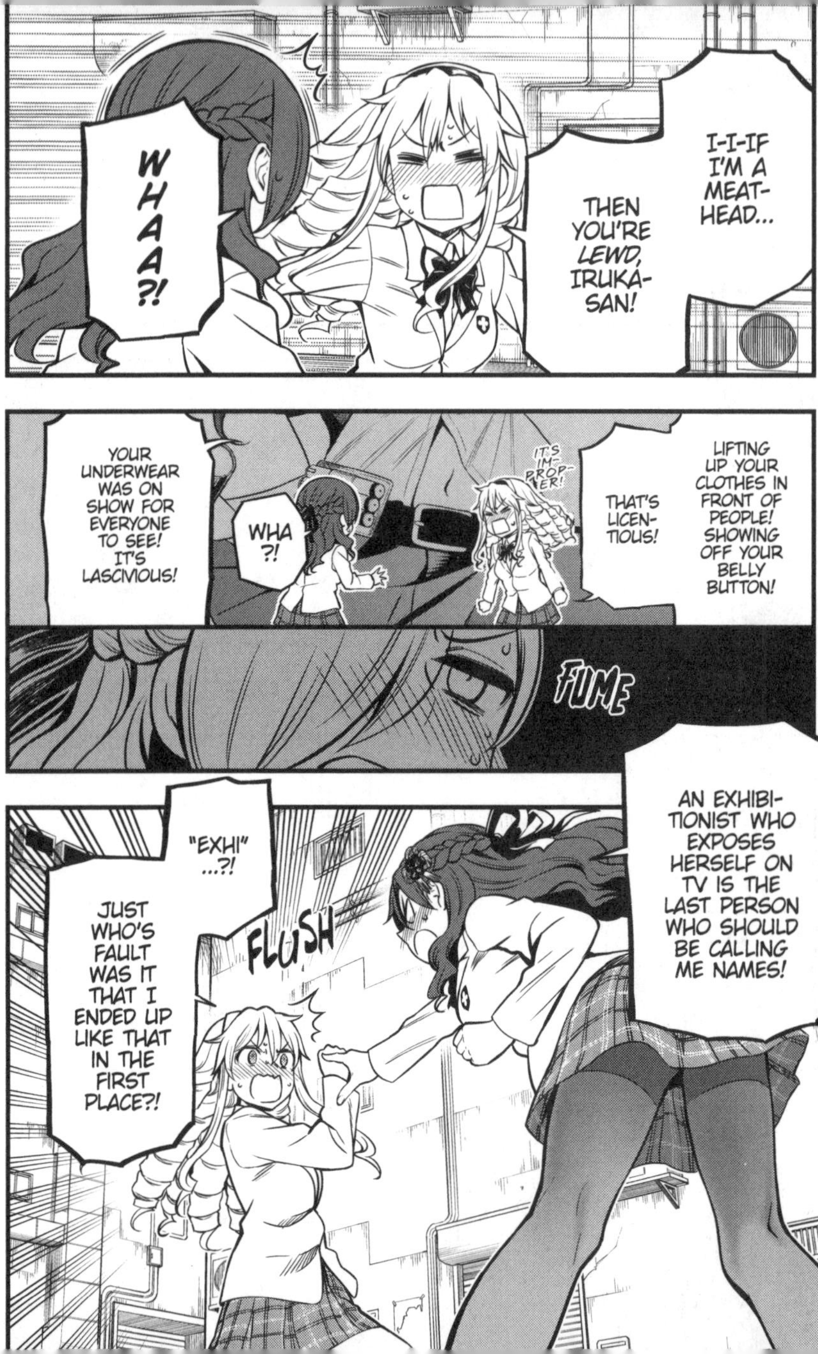
I-I-IF I'M A MEAT-HEAD...
THEN YOU'RE LEWD, IRUKA-SAN!
WHAAA?!
LIFTING UP YOUR CLOTHES IN FRONT OF PEOPLE! SHOWING OFF YOUR BELLY BUTTON!
THAT'S LICEN-TIOUS!
IT'S IM-PROP-ER!
WHA?!
YOUR UNDERWEAR WAS ON SHOW FOR EVERYONE TO SEE! IT'S LASCIVIOUS!
FUME
AN EXHIBI-TIONIST WHO EXPOSES HERSELF ON TV IS THE LAST PERSON WHO SHOULD BE CALLING ME NAMES!
FLUSH
"EXHI" ...?!
JUST WHO'S FAULT WAS IT THAT I ENDED UP LIKE THAT IN THE FIRST PLACE?!

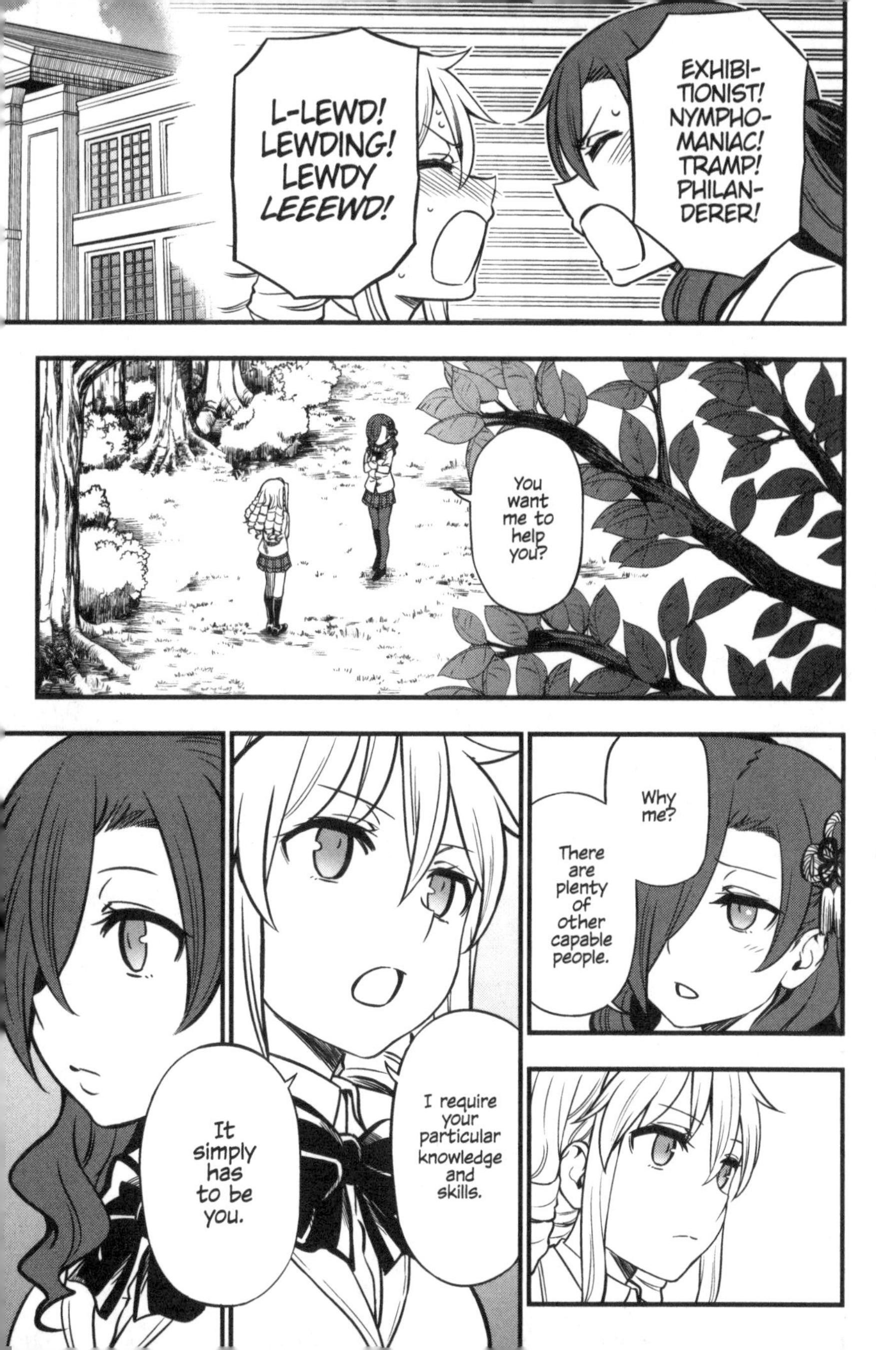
EXHIBITIONIST! NYMPHOMANIAC! TRAMP! PHILANDERER!
L-LEWD! LEWDING! LEWDY LEEEWD!
You want me to help you?
Why me?
There are plenty of other capable people.
I require your particular knowledge and skills.
It simply has to be you.

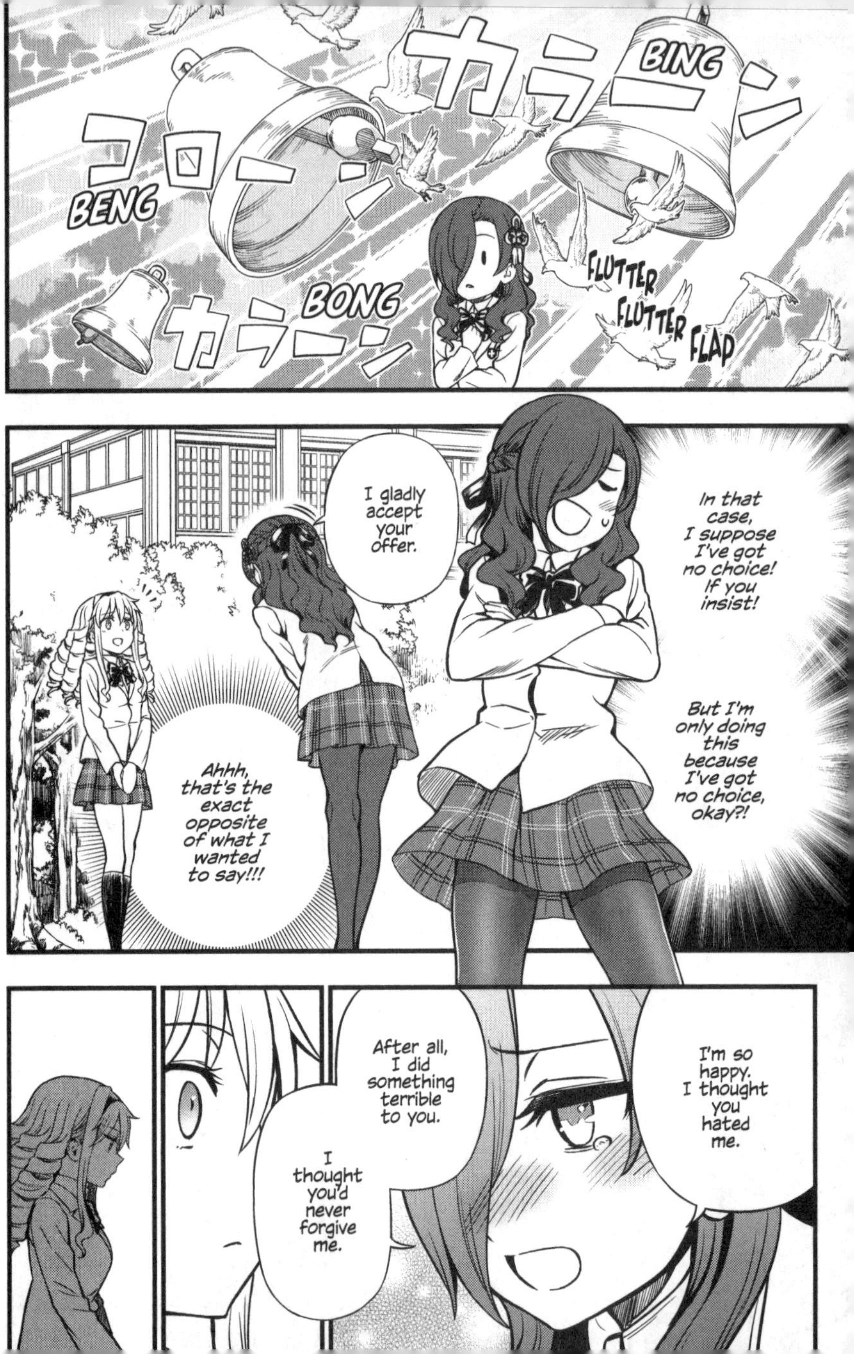
カラーン
BING
コローン
BENG
カラーン
BONG
FLUTTER
FLUTTER
FLAP
In that case, I suppose I've got no choice! If you insist!
But I'm only doing this because I've got no choice, okay?!
I gladly accept your offer.
Ahhh, that's the exact opposite of what I wanted to say!!!
I'm so happy. I thought you hated me.
After all, I did something terrible to you.
I thought you'd never forgive me.

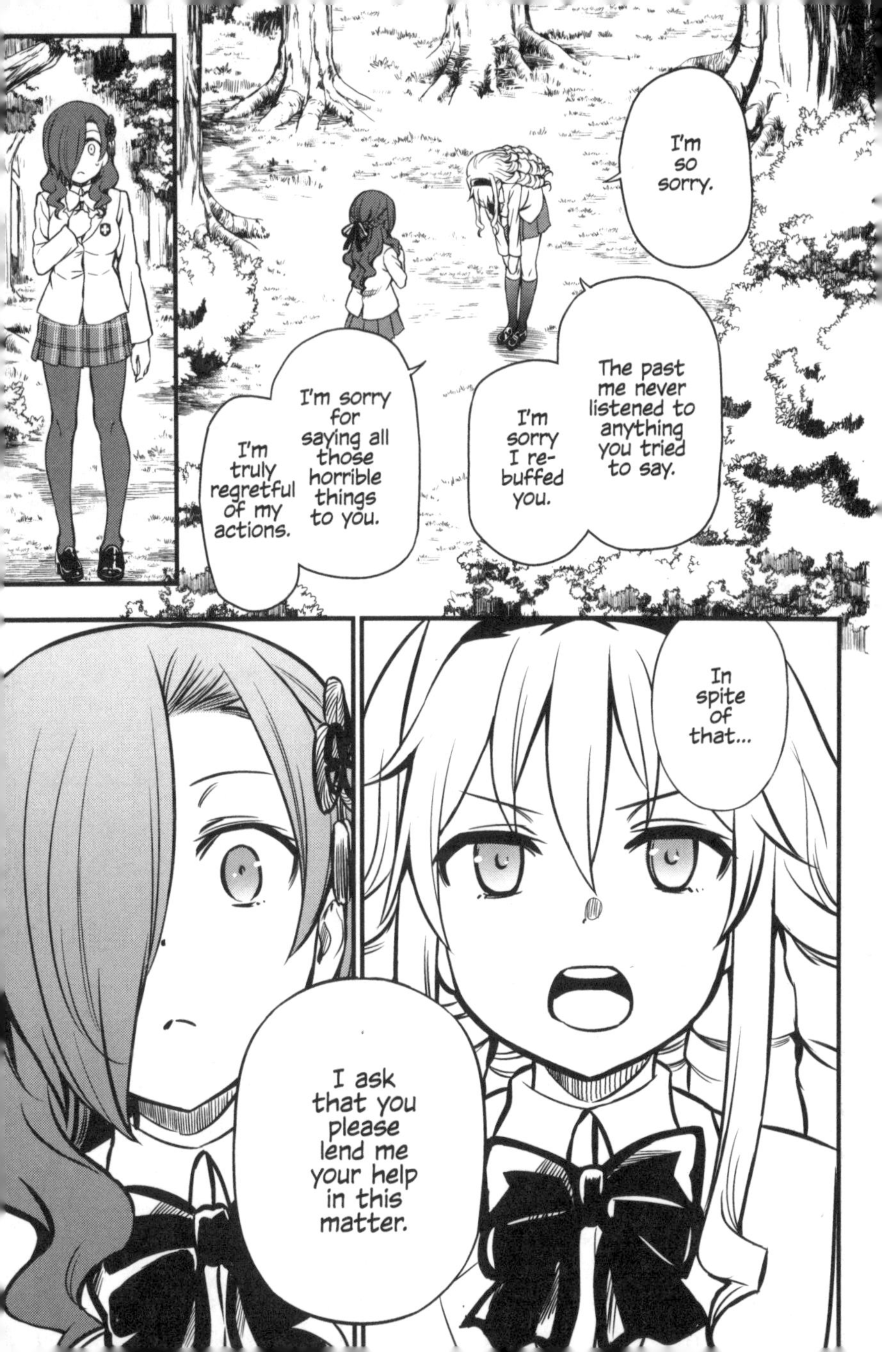
I'm so sorry.
The past me never listened to anything you tried to say.
I'm sorry I re-buffed you.
I'm sorry for saying all those horrible things to you.
I'm truly regretful of my actions.
In spite of that...
I ask that you please lend me your help in this matter.

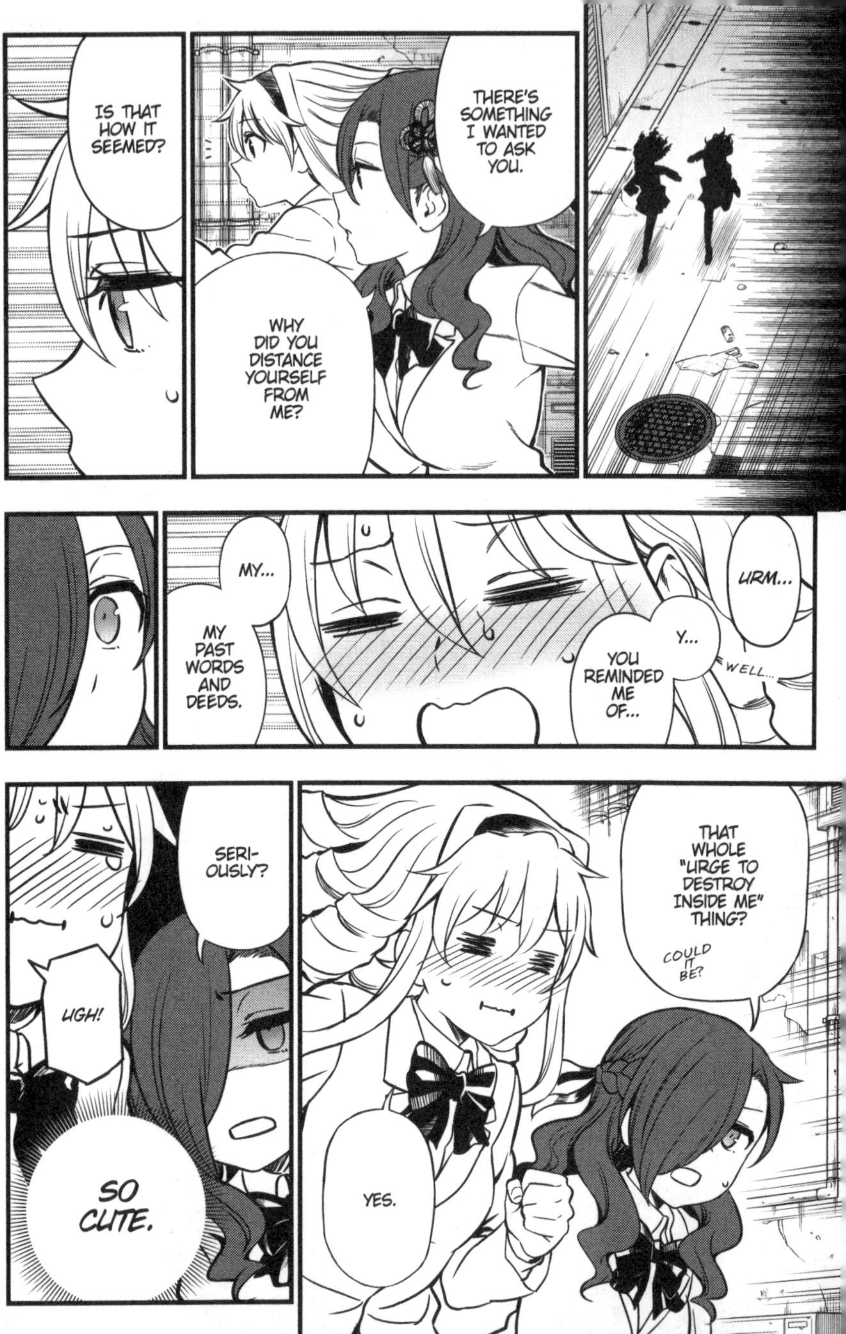
THERE'S SOMETHING I WANTED TO ASK YOU.
WHY DID YOU DISTANCE YOURSELF FROM ME?
IS THAT HOW IT SEEMED?
URM...
WELL...
Y...
YOU REMINDED ME OF...
MY...
MY PAST WORDS AND DEEDS.
THAT WHOLE "URGE TO DESTROY INSIDE ME" THING?
COULD IT BE?
YES.
SERI-OUSLY?
UGH!
SO CUTE.

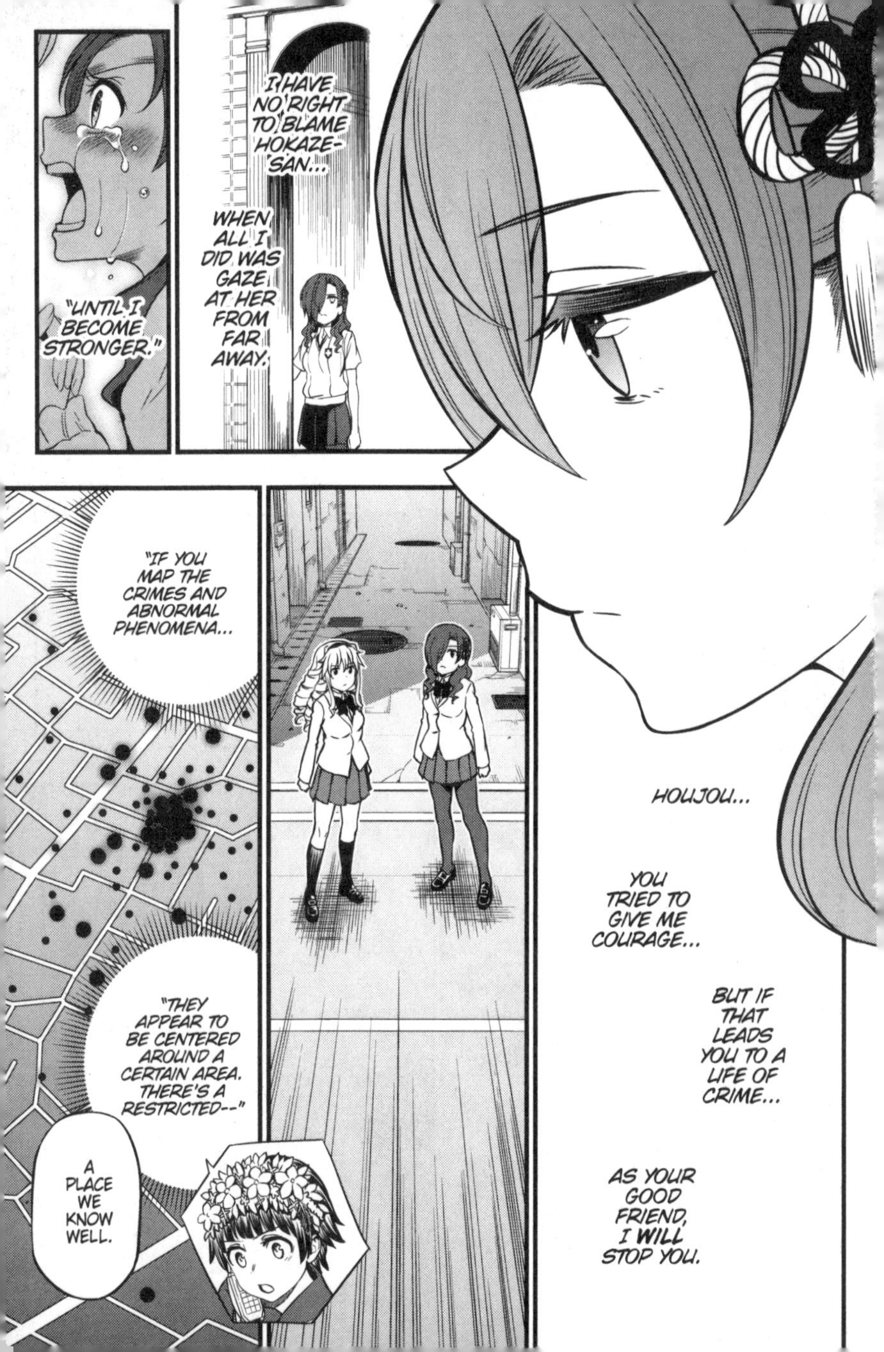

I HAVE NO RIGHT TO BLAME HOKAZE-SAN...
WHEN ALL I DID WAS GAZE AT HER FROM FAR AWAY.
"UNTIL I BECOME STRONGER."
"IF YOU MAP THE CRIMES AND ABNORMAL PHENOMENA...
"THEY APPEAR TO BE CENTERED AROUND A CERTAIN AREA. THERE'S A RESTRICTED--"
A PLACE WE KNOW WELL.
HOUJOU...
YOU TRIED TO GIVE ME COURAGE...
BUT IF THAT LEADS YOU TO A LIFE OF CRIME...
AS YOUR GOOD FRIEND, I **WILL** STOP YOU.

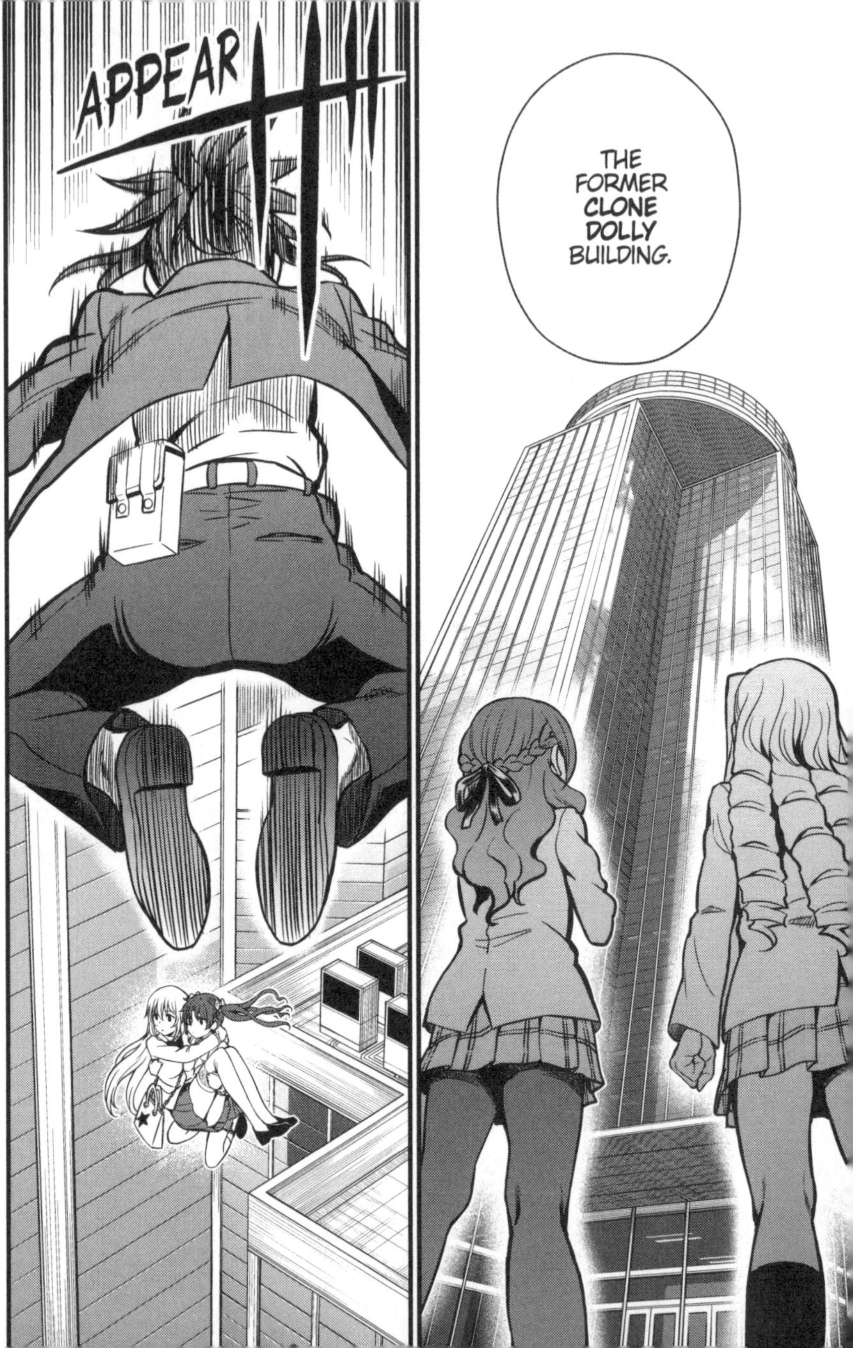
THE FORMER CLONE DOLLY BUILDING.
APPEAR

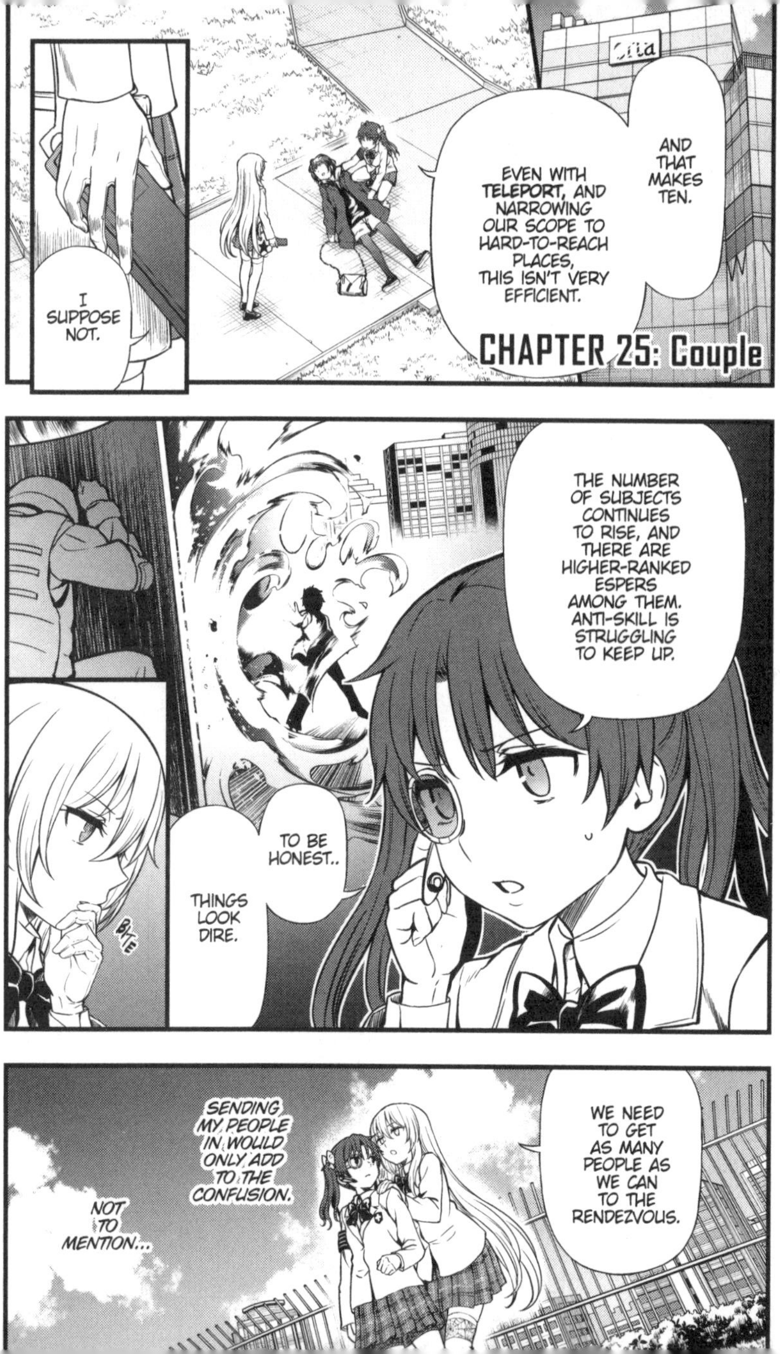

AND THAT MAKES TEN.
EVEN WITH TELEPORT, AND NARROWING OUR SCOPE TO HARD-TO-REACH PLACES, THIS ISN'T VERY EFFICIENT.
I SUPPOSE NOT.
CHAPTER 25: Couple
THE NUMBER OF SUBJECTS CONTINUES TO RISE, AND THERE ARE HIGHER-RANKED ESPERS AMONG THEM. ANTI-SKILL IS STRUGGLING TO KEEP UP.
TO BE HONEST..
THINGS LOOK DIRE.
BITE
WE NEED TO GET AS MANY PEOPLE AS WE CAN TO THE RENDEZVOUS.
SENDING MY PEOPLE IN WOULD ONLY ADD TO THE CONFUSION.
NOT TO MENTION...

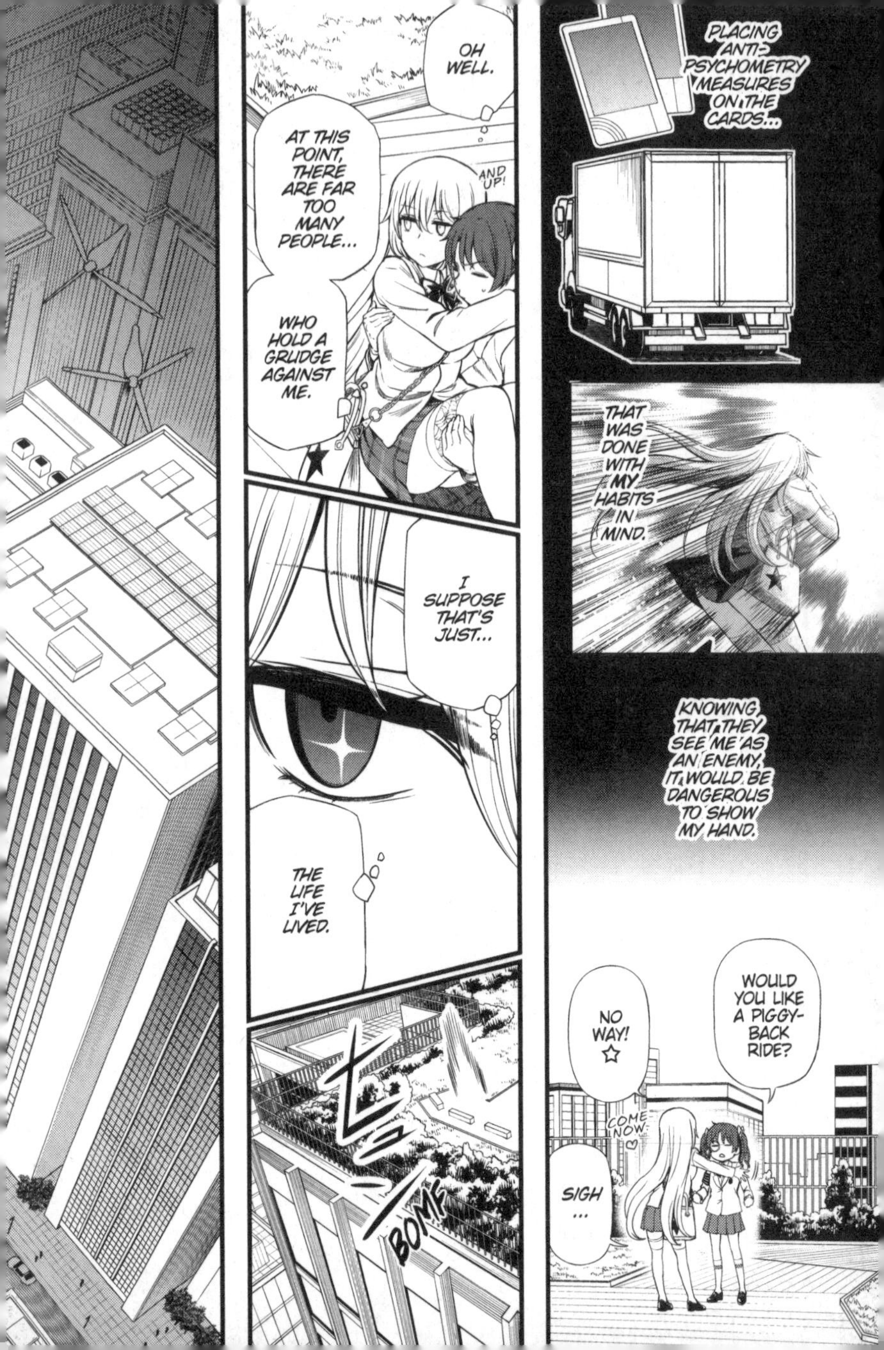
PLACING ANTI-PSYCHOMETRY MEASURES ON THE CARDS...
THAT WAS DONE WITH MY HABITS IN MIND.
KNOWING THAT THEY SEE ME AS AN ENEMY, IT WOULD BE DANGEROUS TO SHOW MY HAND.
WOULD YOU LIKE A PIGGY-BACK RIDE?
NO WAY! ☆
COME NOW ♡
SIGH ...
OH WELL.
AT THIS POINT, THERE ARE FAR TOO MANY PEOPLE...
AND UP!
WHO HOLD A GRUDGE AGAINST ME.
I SUPPOSE THAT'S JUST...
THE LIFE I'VE LIVED.
BOMF

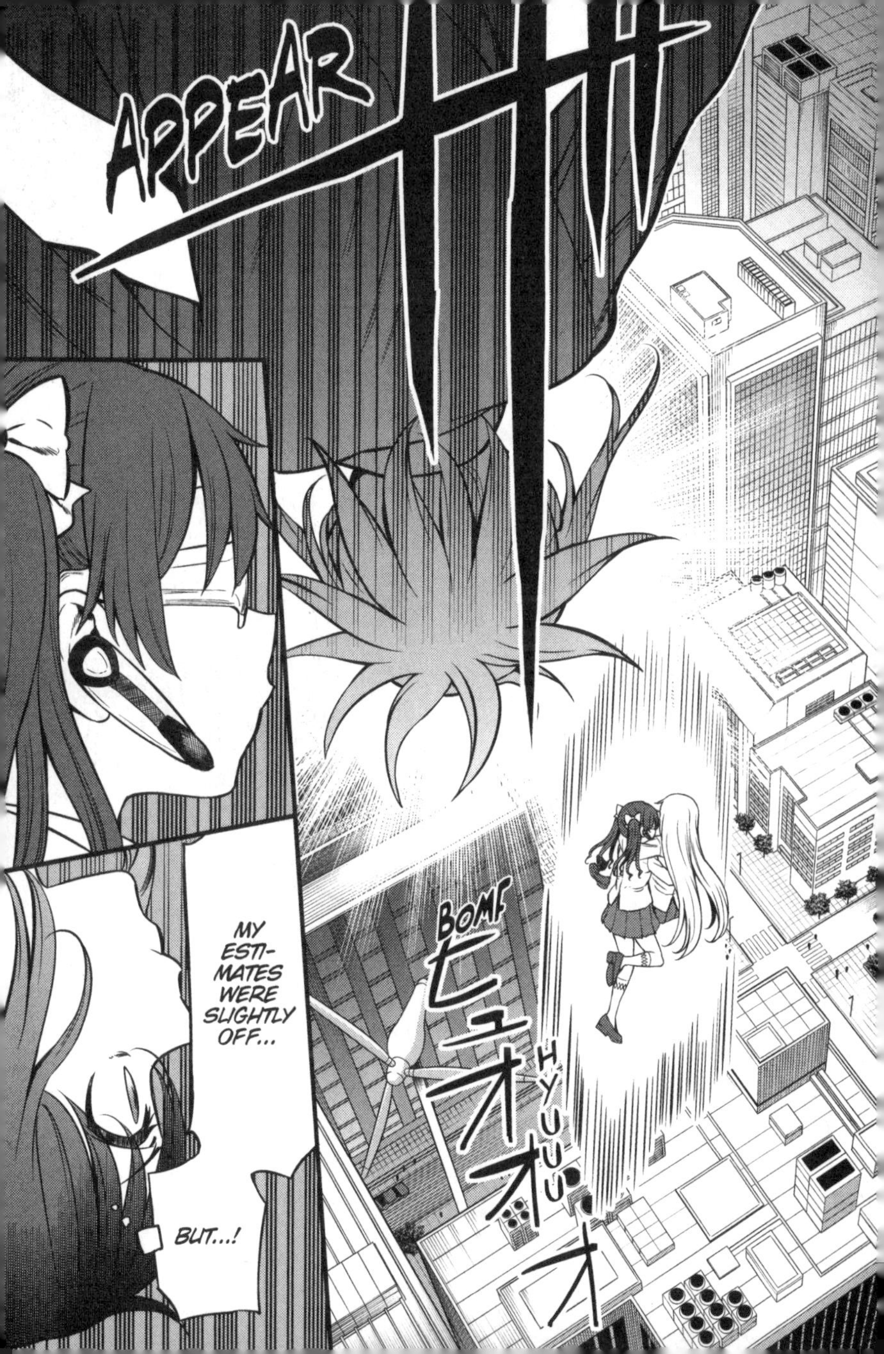
APPEAR
BOMF
HYUUUU
ヒュオオオ
MY ESTI-MATES WERE SLIGHTLY OFF...
BUT...!

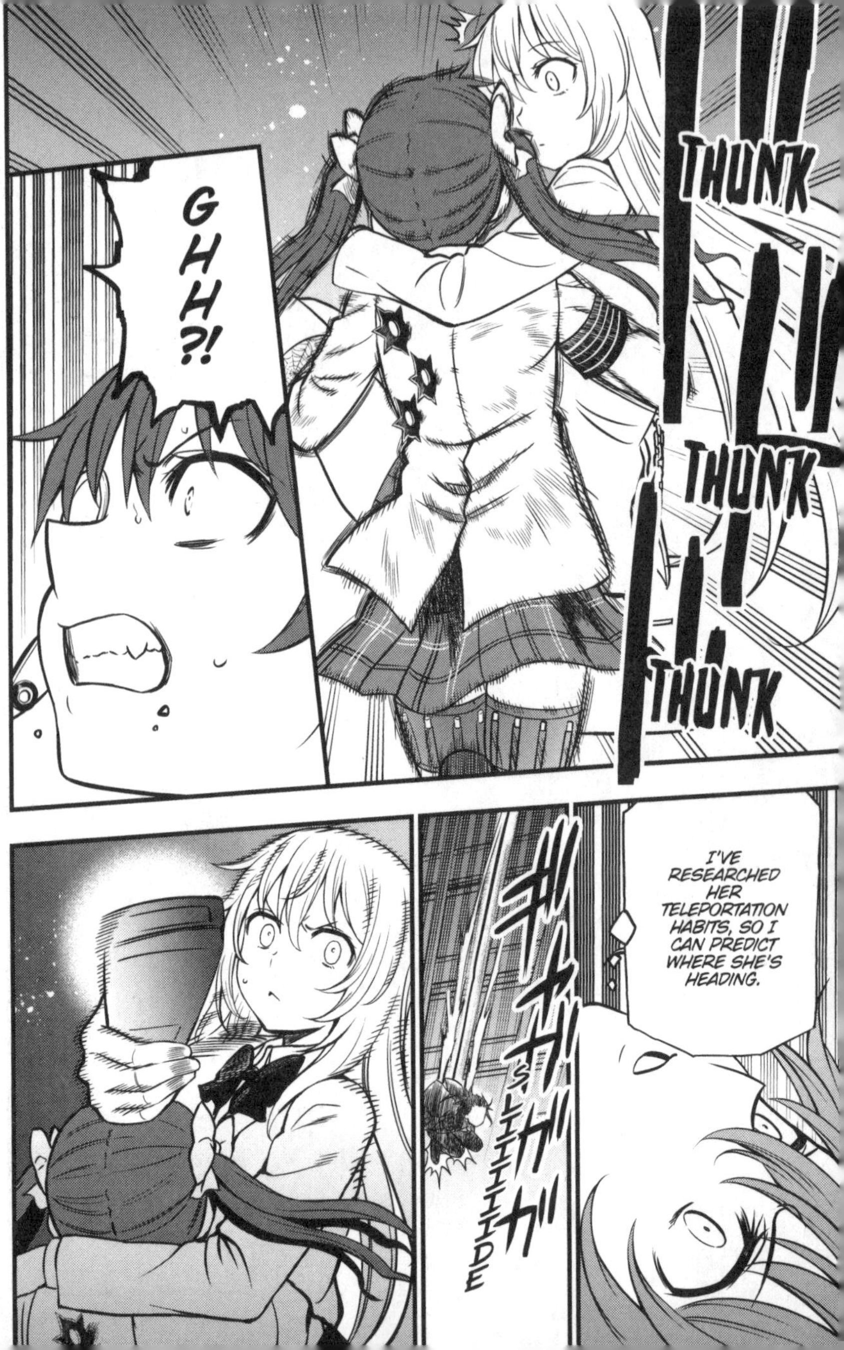
THUNK
THUNK
THUNK
GHHH?!
I'VE RESEARCHED HER TELEPORTATION HABITS, SO I CAN PREDICT WHERE SHE'S HEADING.
SLIIIIIDE

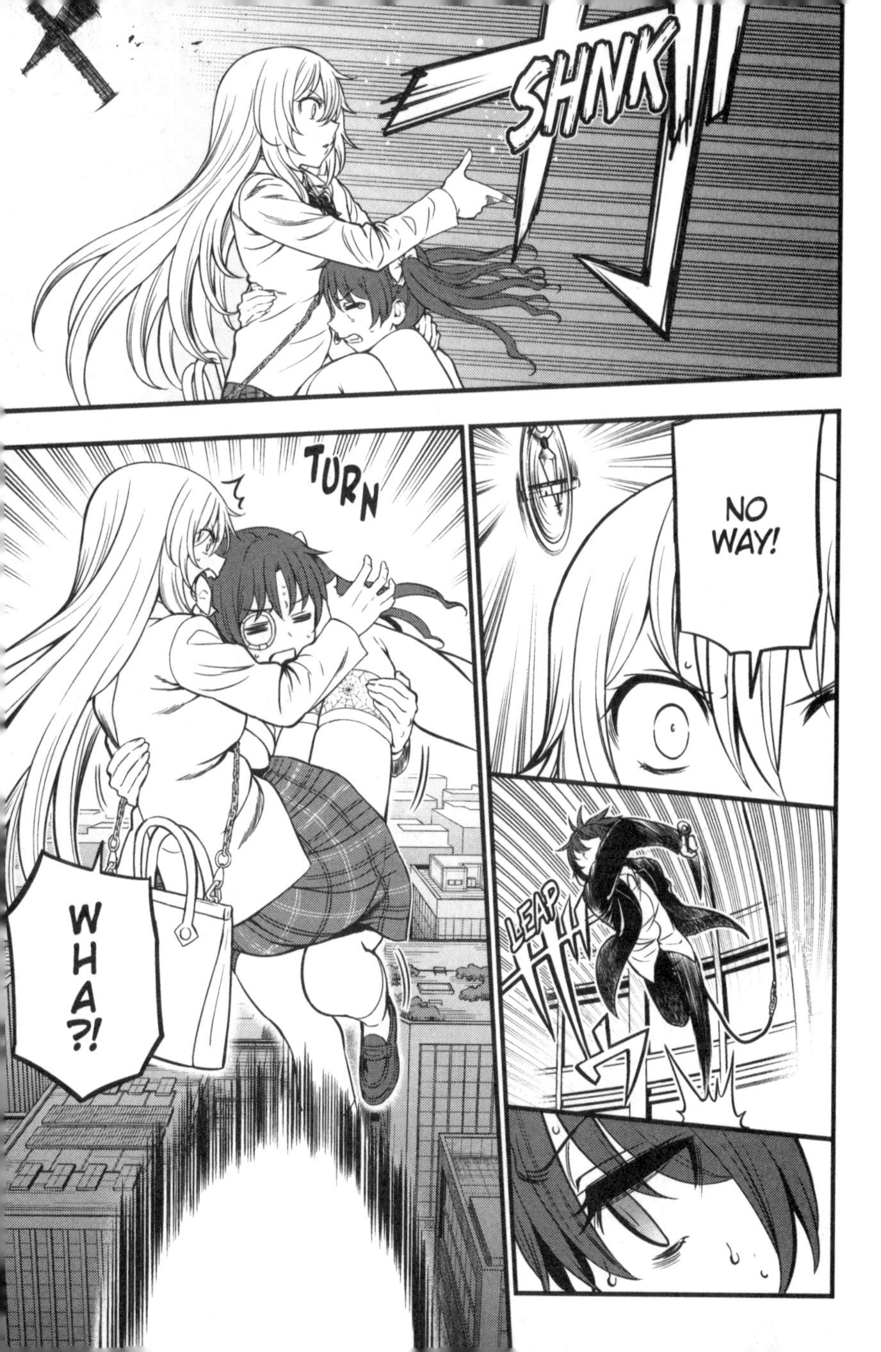
SHNK
NO WAY!
TURN
WHA?!
LEAP

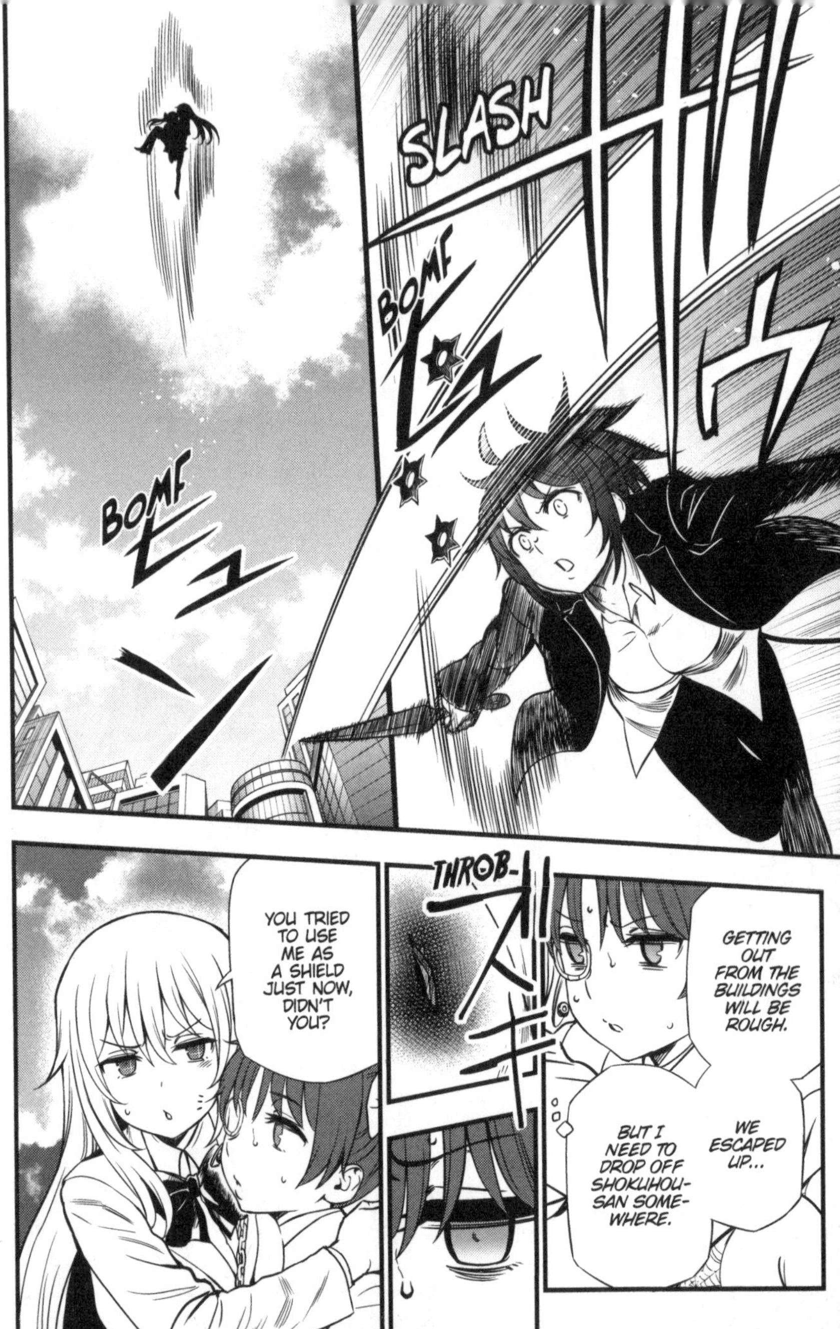
SLASH
BOMF
BOMF
BOMF
THROB-
GETTING OUT FROM THE BUILDINGS WILL BE ROUGH.
WE ESCAPED UP...
BUT I NEED TO DROP OFF SHOKUHOU-SAN SOMEWHERE.
YOU TRIED TO USE ME AS A SHIELD JUST NOW, DIDN'T YOU?

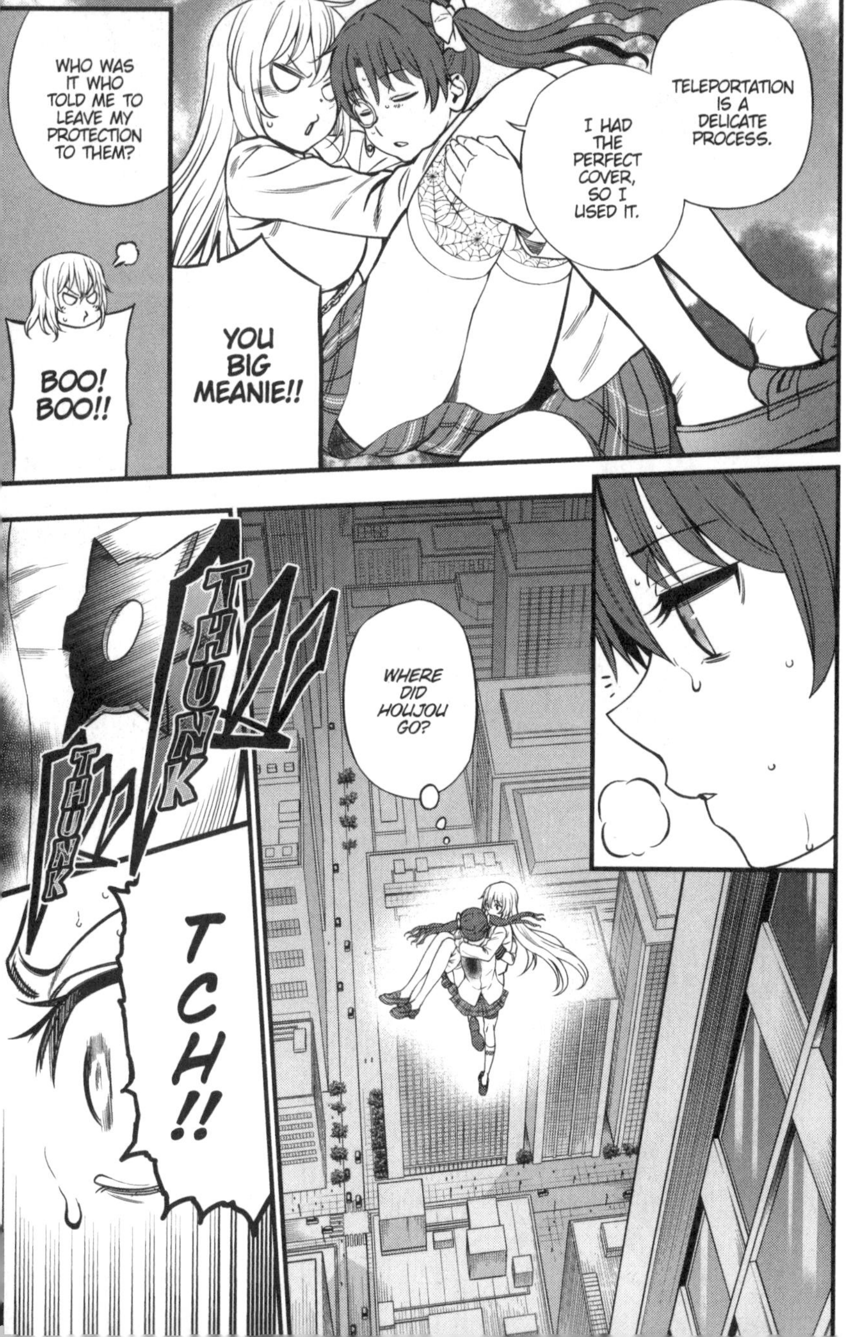
TELEPORTATION IS A DELICATE PROCESS.
I HAD THE PERFECT COVER, SO I USED IT.
WHO WAS IT WHO TOLD ME TO LEAVE MY PROTECTION TO THEM?
YOU BIG MEANIE!!
BOO! BOO!!
WHERE DID HOUJOU GO?
THUNK
THUNK
TCH!!

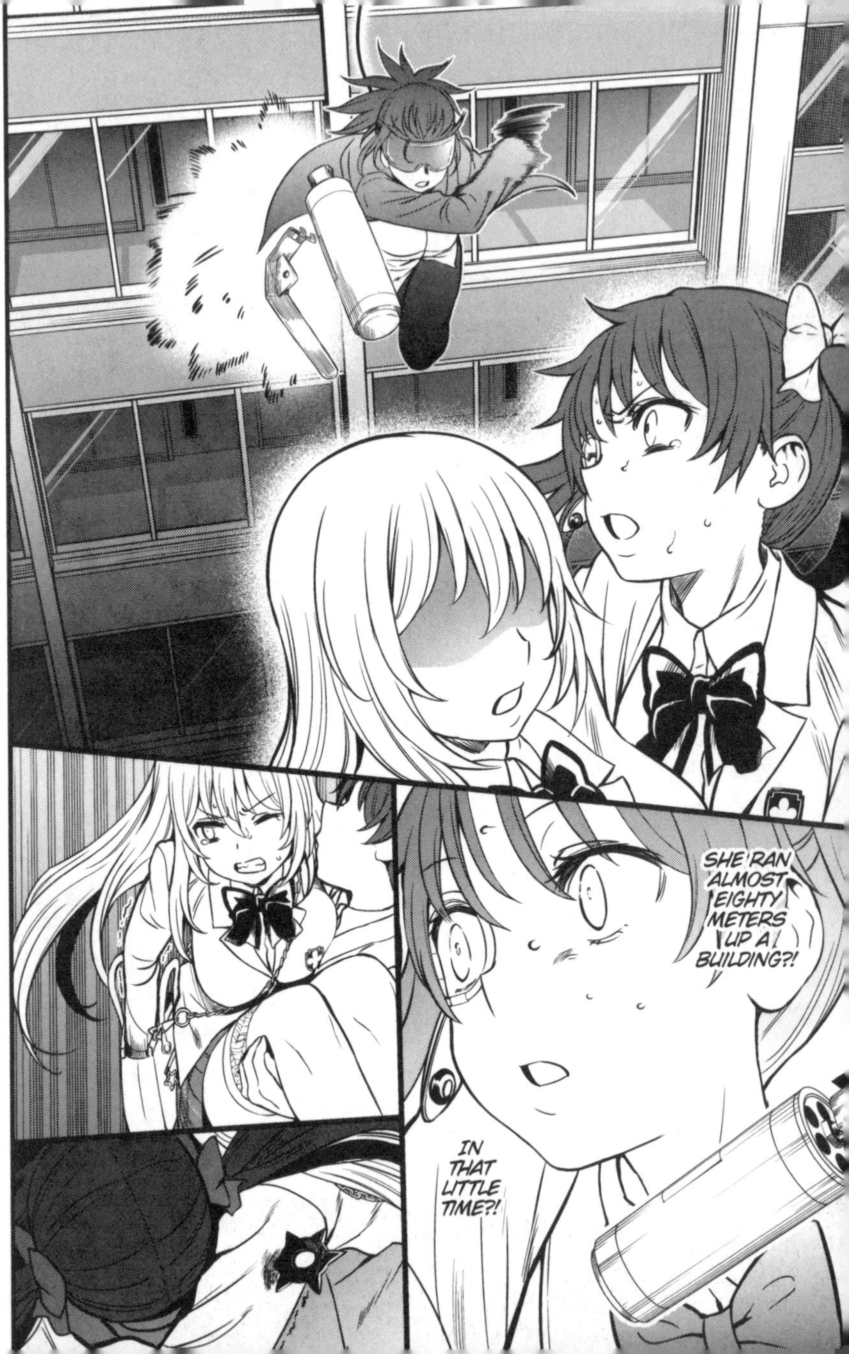
SHE RAN ALMOST EIGHTY METERS UP A BUILDING?!
IN THAT LITTLE TIME?!

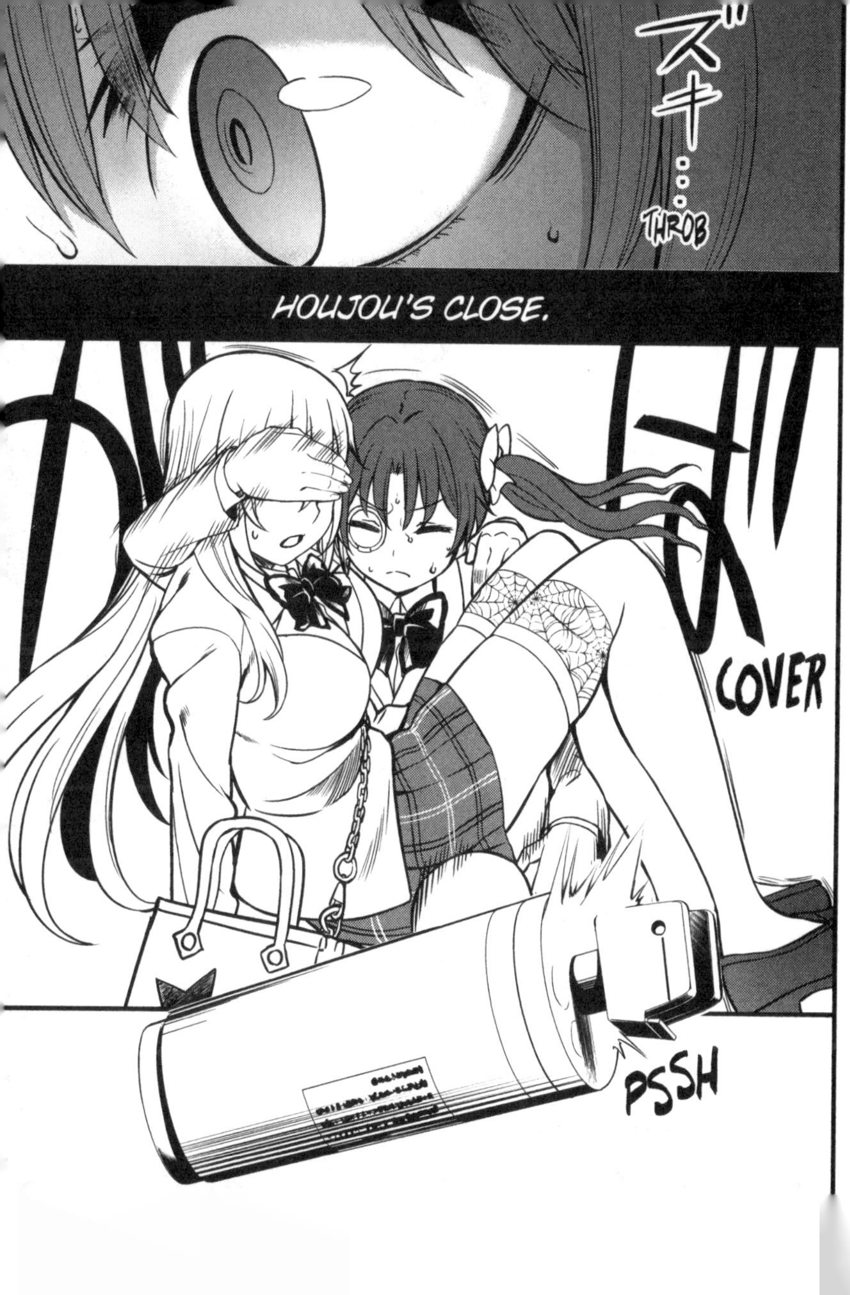
ズキ…
THROB
HOUJOU'S CLOSE.
COVER
PSSH

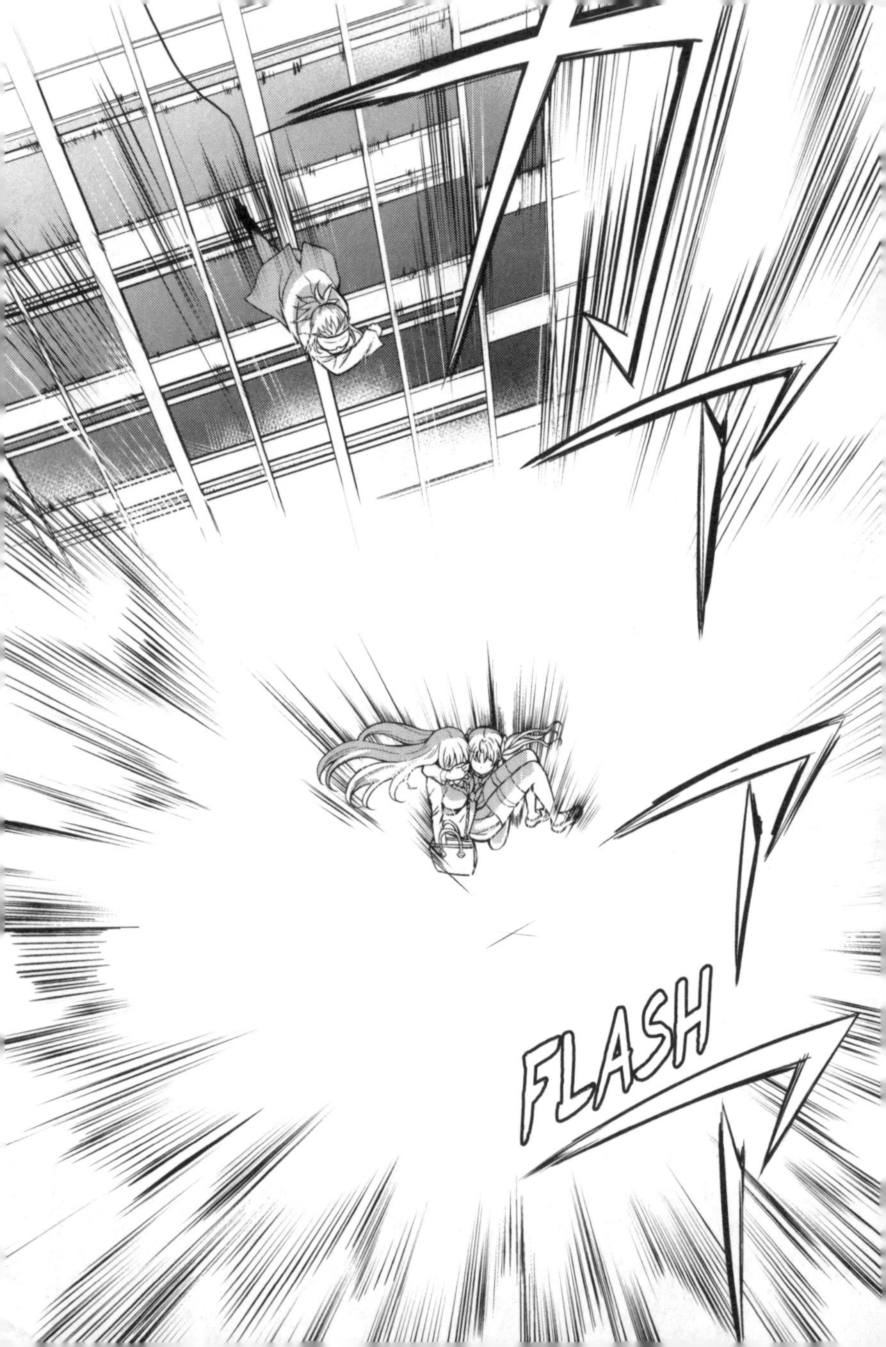
FLASH

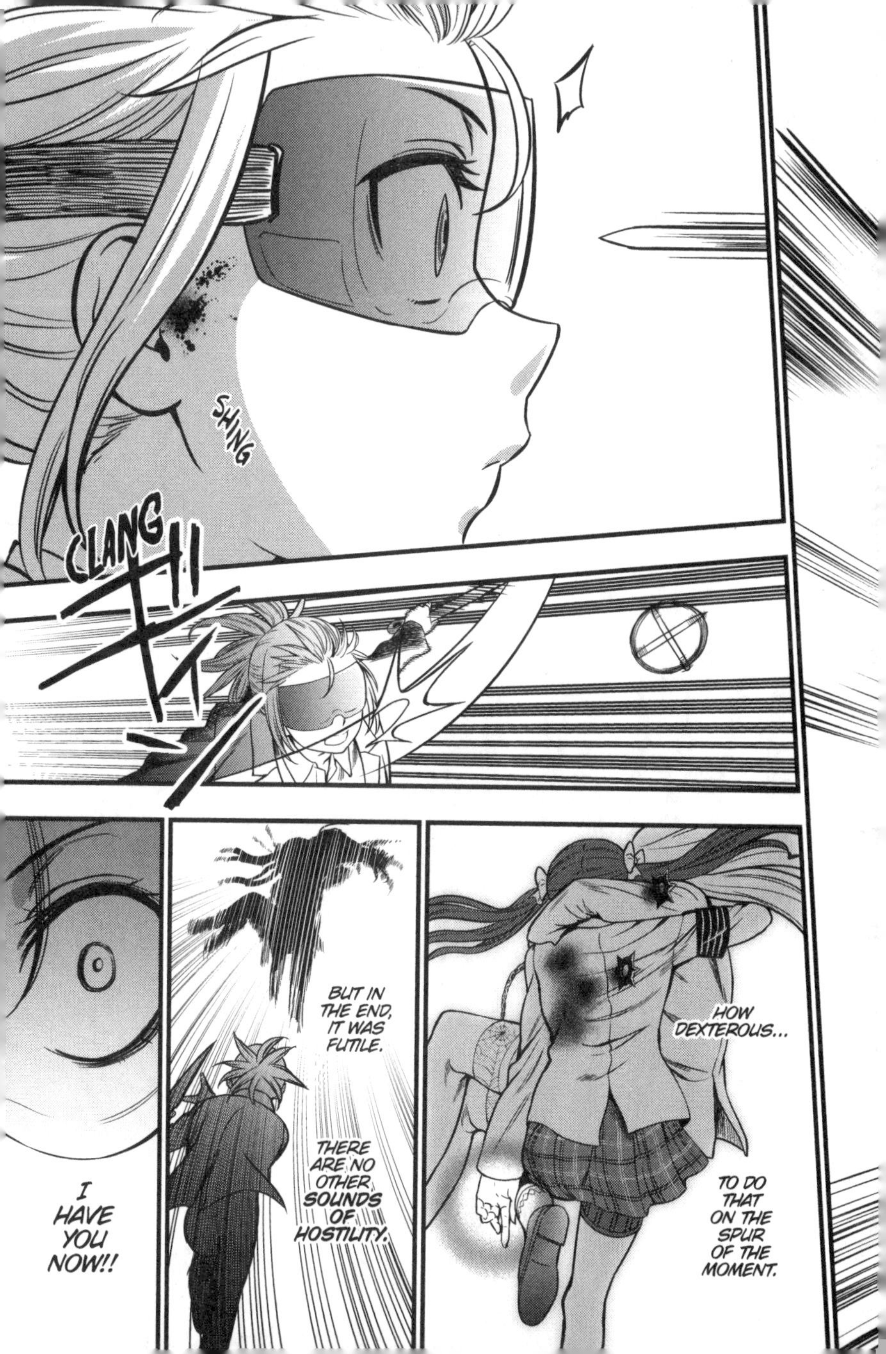
SHING
CLANG
HOW DEXTEROUS...
TO DO THAT ON THE SPUR OF THE MOMENT.
BUT IN THE END, IT WAS FUTILE.
THERE ARE NO OTHER SOUNDS OF HOSTILITY.
I HAVE YOU NOW!!

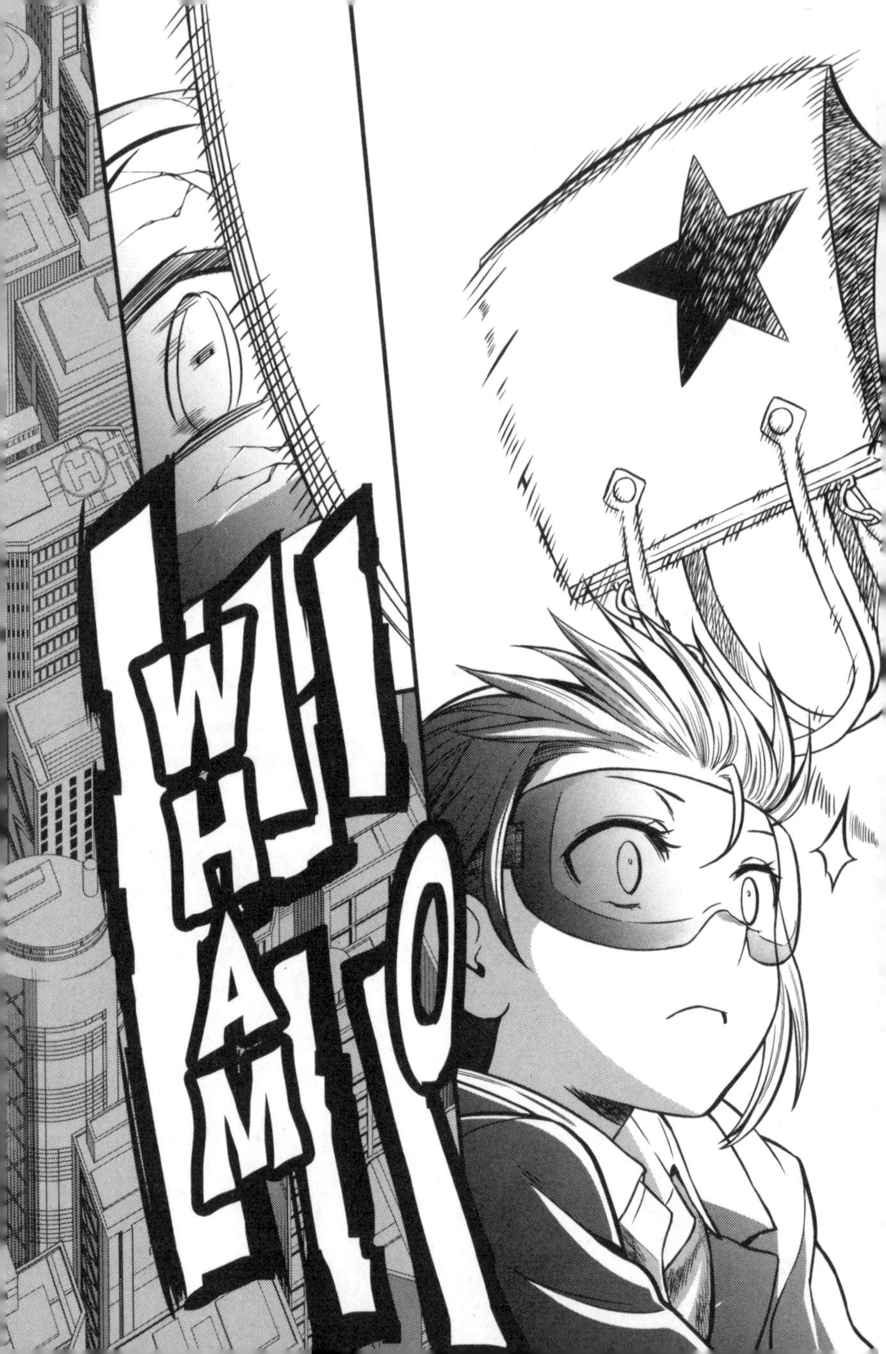
WHAM!

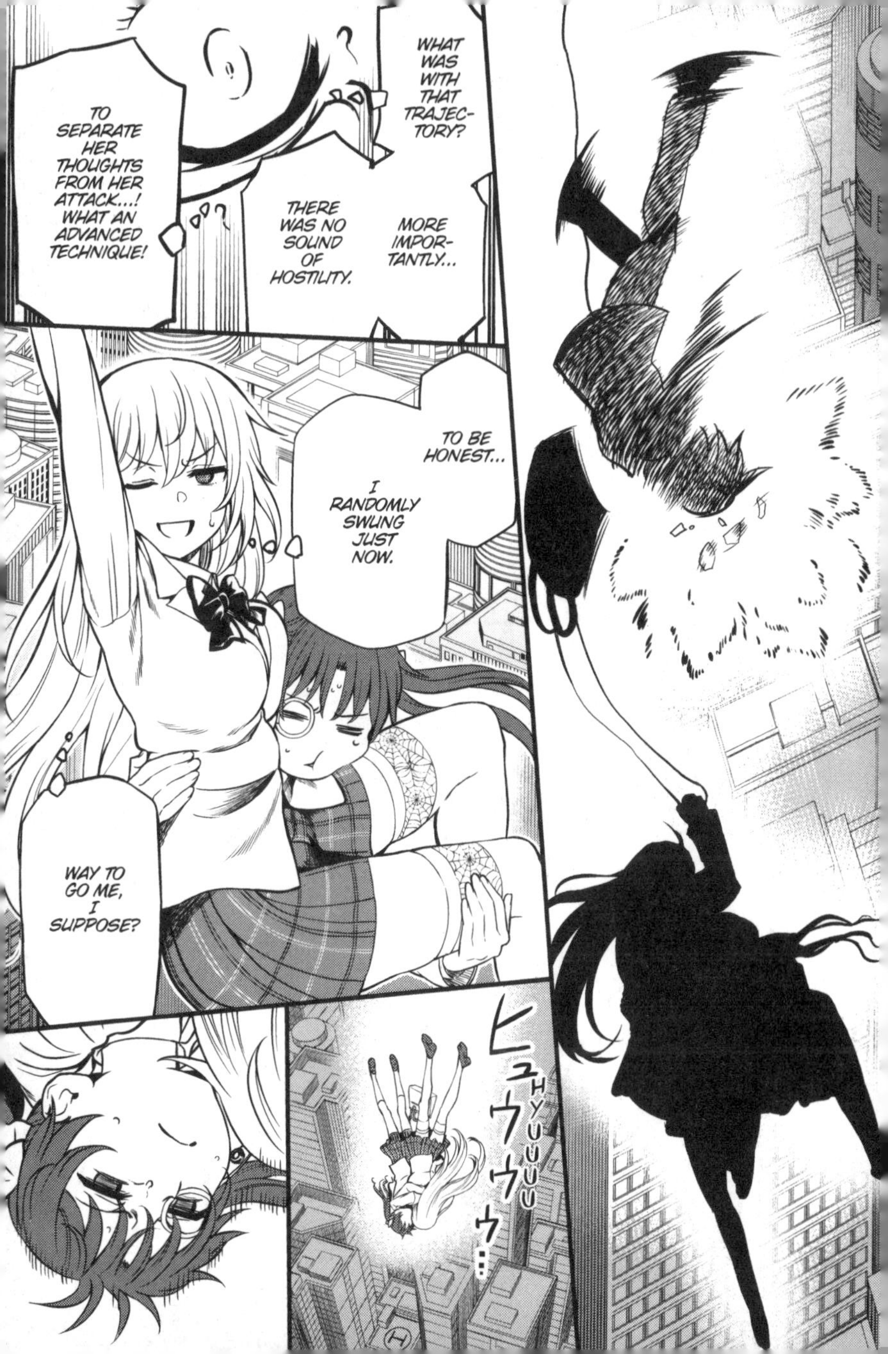
WHAT WAS WITH THAT TRAJECTORY?
MORE IMPORTANTLY...
THERE WAS NO SOUND OF HOSTILITY.
TO SEPARATE HER THOUGHTS FROM HER ATTACK...! WHAT AN ADVANCED TECHNIQUE!
TO BE HONEST...
I RANDOMLY SWUNG JUST NOW.
WAY TO GO ME, I SUPPOSE?
ヒュウウウ HYUUUUU
ウ...

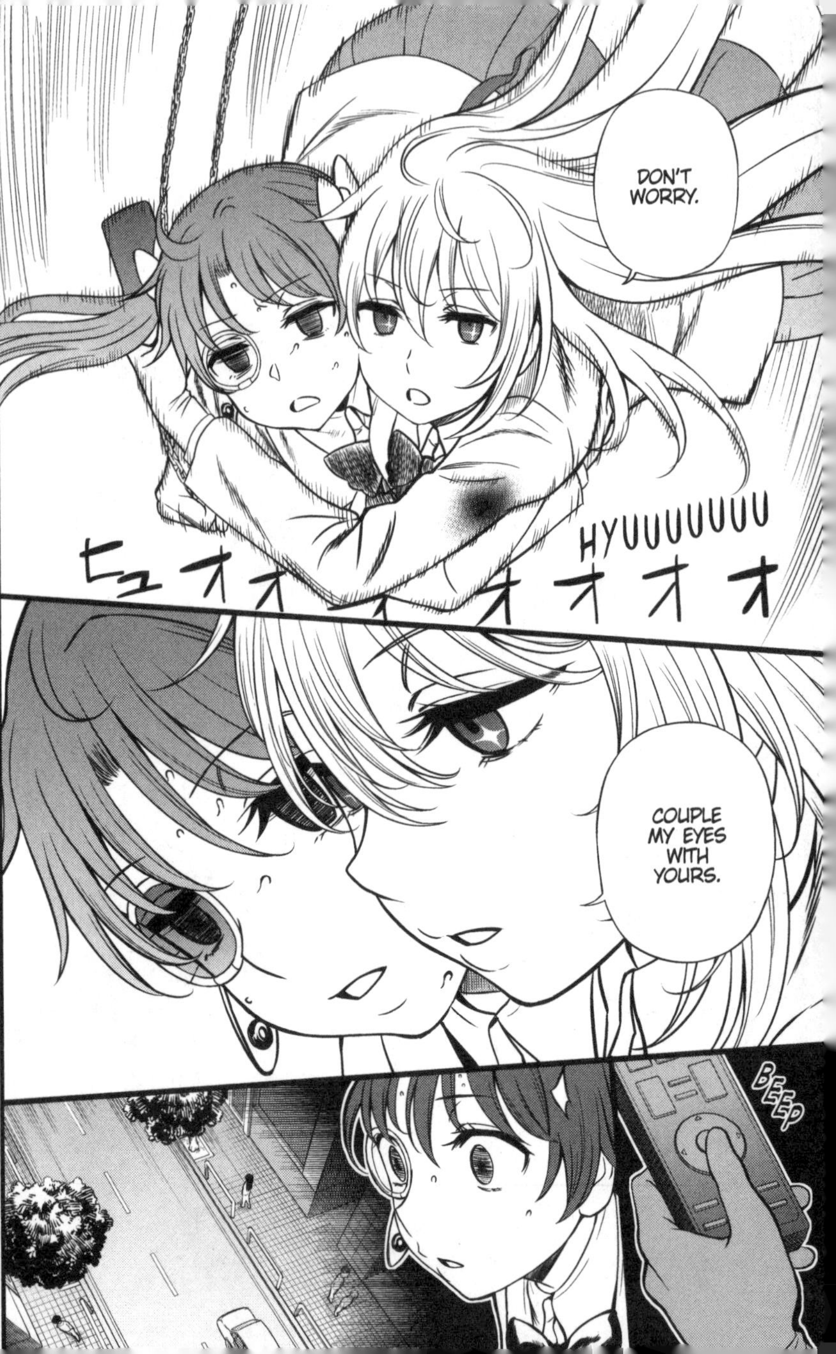
DON'T WORRY.
HYUUUUUUU
ヒュオオオオオオオ
COUPLE MY EYES WITH YOURS.
BEEP

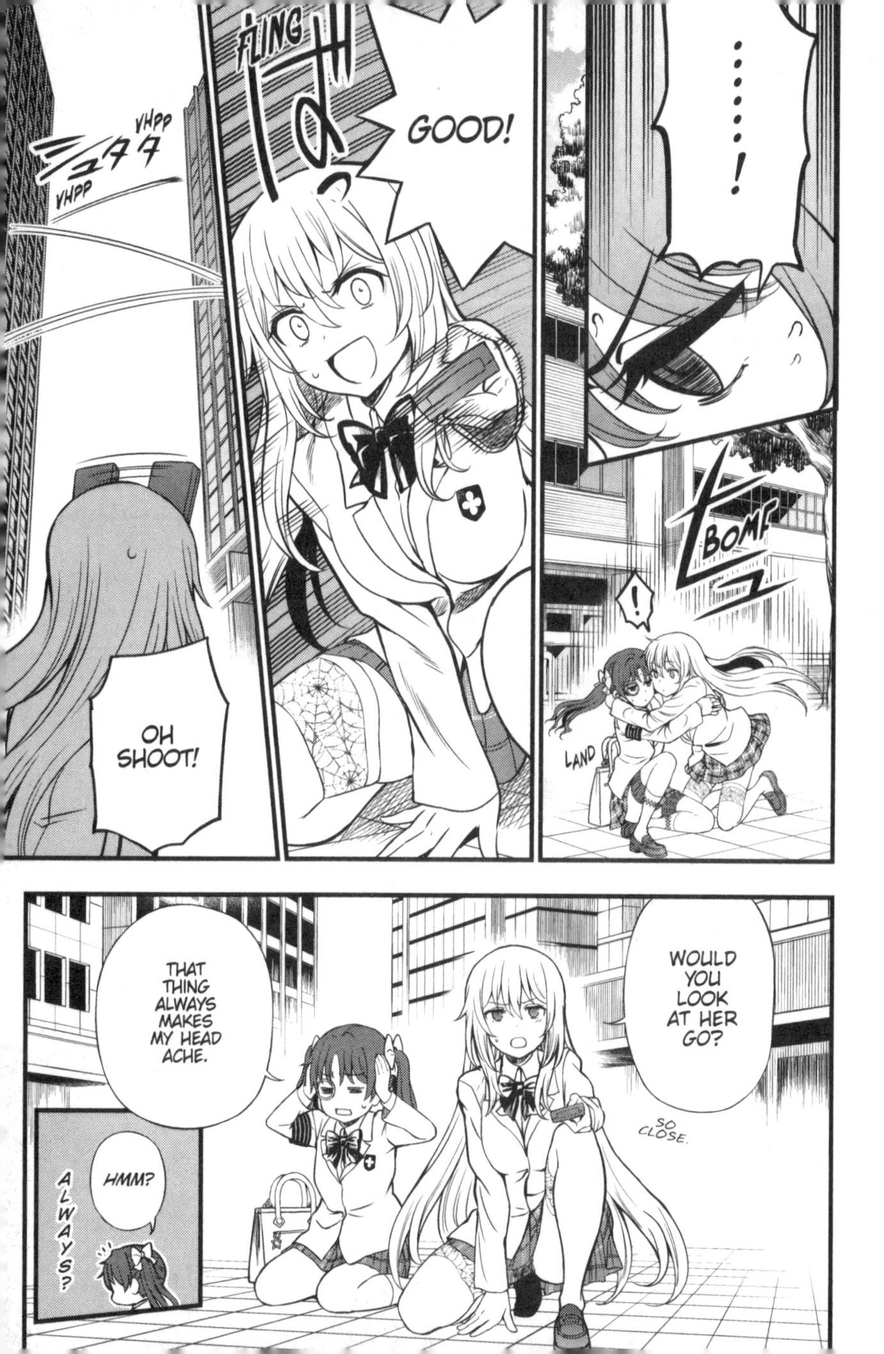
......!
BOMF
!
LAND
FLING
GOOD!
シュタタ
VHPP
VHPP
OH SHOOT!
WOULD YOU LOOK AT HER GO?
SO CLOSE.
THAT THING ALWAYS MAKES MY HEAD ACHE.
HMM?
ALWAYS?

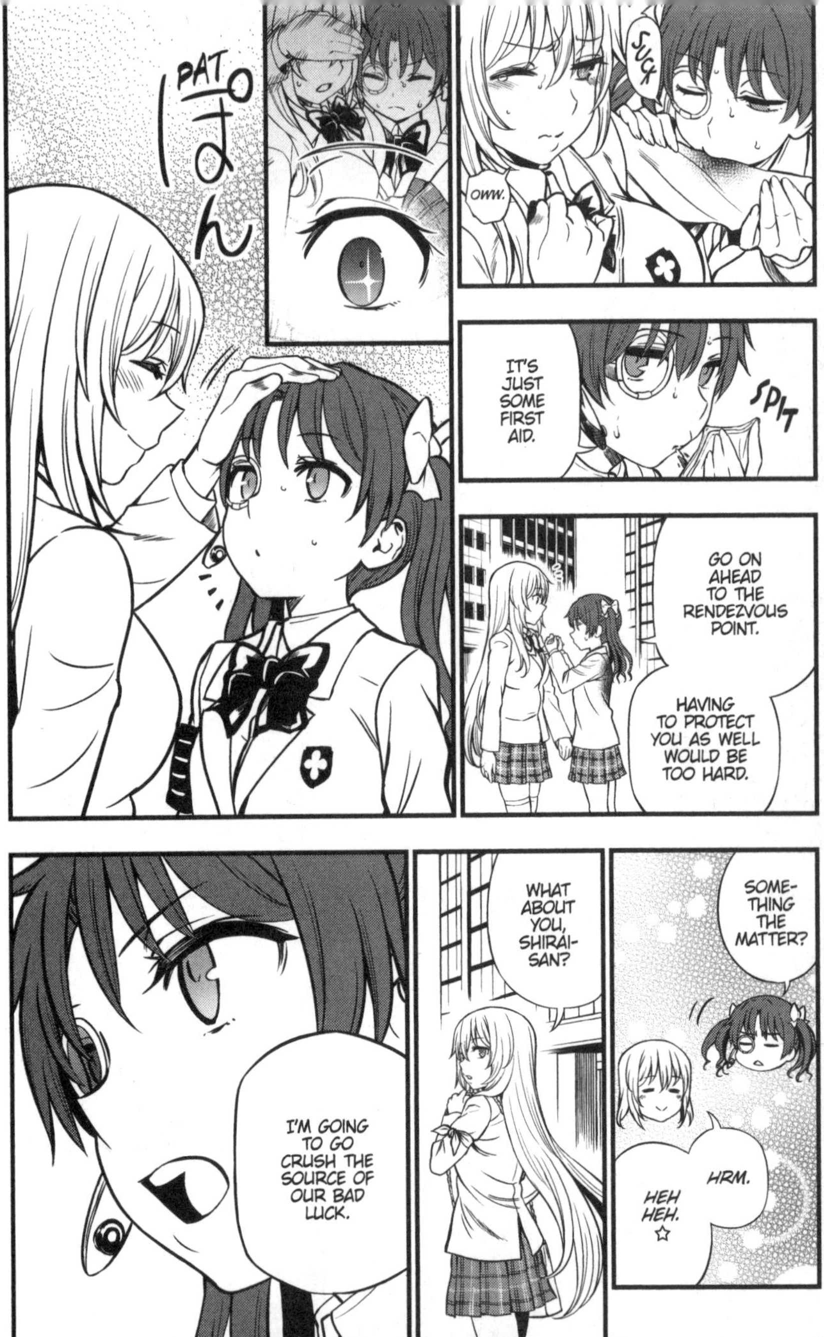
SUCK
OWW.
IT'S JUST SOME FIRST AID.
SPIT
PAT
ぱん
GO ON AHEAD TO THE RENDEZVOUS POINT.
HAVING TO PROTECT YOU AS WELL WOULD BE TOO HARD.
SOME-THING THE MATTER?
HRM.
HEH HEH. ☆
WHAT ABOUT YOU, SHIRAI-SAN?
I'M GOING TO GO CRUSH THE SOURCE OF OUR BAD LUCK.

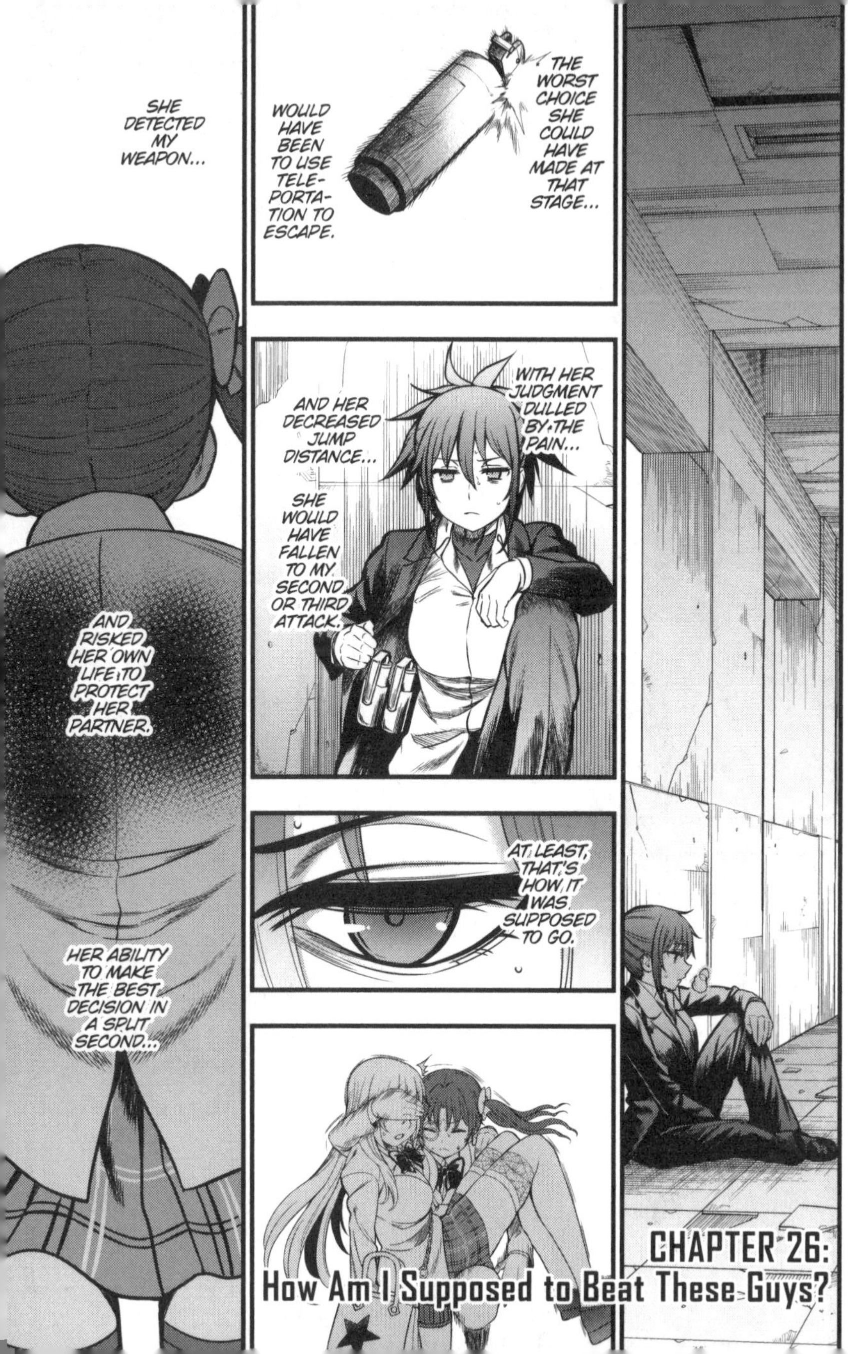
THE WORST CHOICE SHE COULD HAVE MADE AT THAT STAGE...
WOULD HAVE BEEN TO USE TELE-PORTATION TO ESCAPE.
SHE DETECTED MY WEAPON...
WITH HER JUDGMENT DULLED BY THE PAIN...
AND HER DECREASED JUMP DISTANCE...
SHE WOULD HAVE FALLEN TO MY SECOND OR THIRD ATTACK.
AND RISKED HER OWN LIFE TO PROTECT HER PARTNER.
AT LEAST, THAT'S HOW IT WAS SUPPOSED TO GO.
HER ABILITY TO MAKE THE BEST DECISION IN A SPLIT SECOND...
CHAPTER 26:
How Am I Supposed to Beat These Guys?

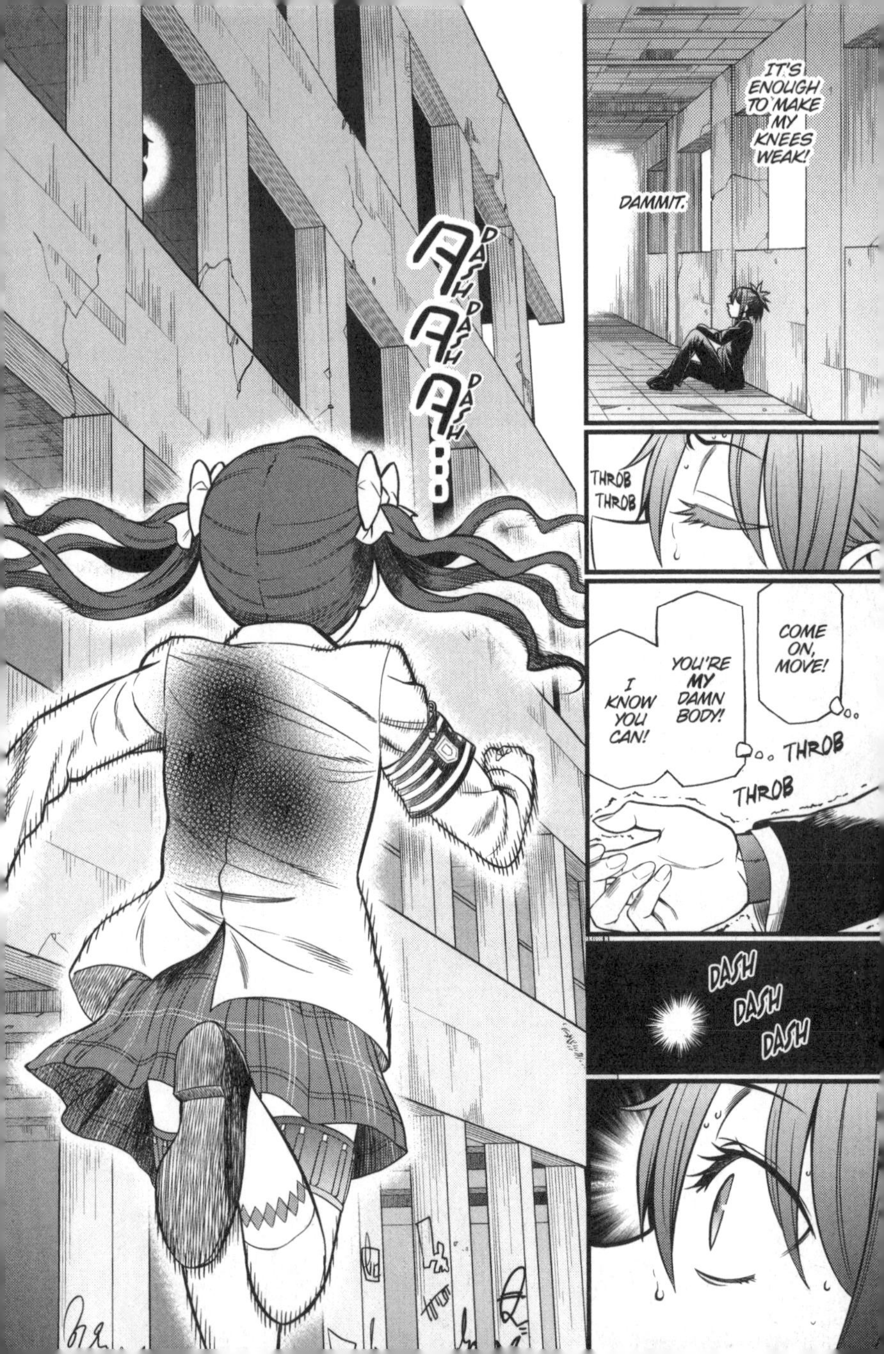
IT'S ENOUGH TO MAKE MY KNEES WEAK!
DAMMIT.
THROB THROB
COME ON, MOVE!
YOU'RE MY DAMN BODY!
I KNOW YOU CAN!
THROB
THROB
DASH
DASH
DASH
AAAH...
DASH DASH DASH DASH

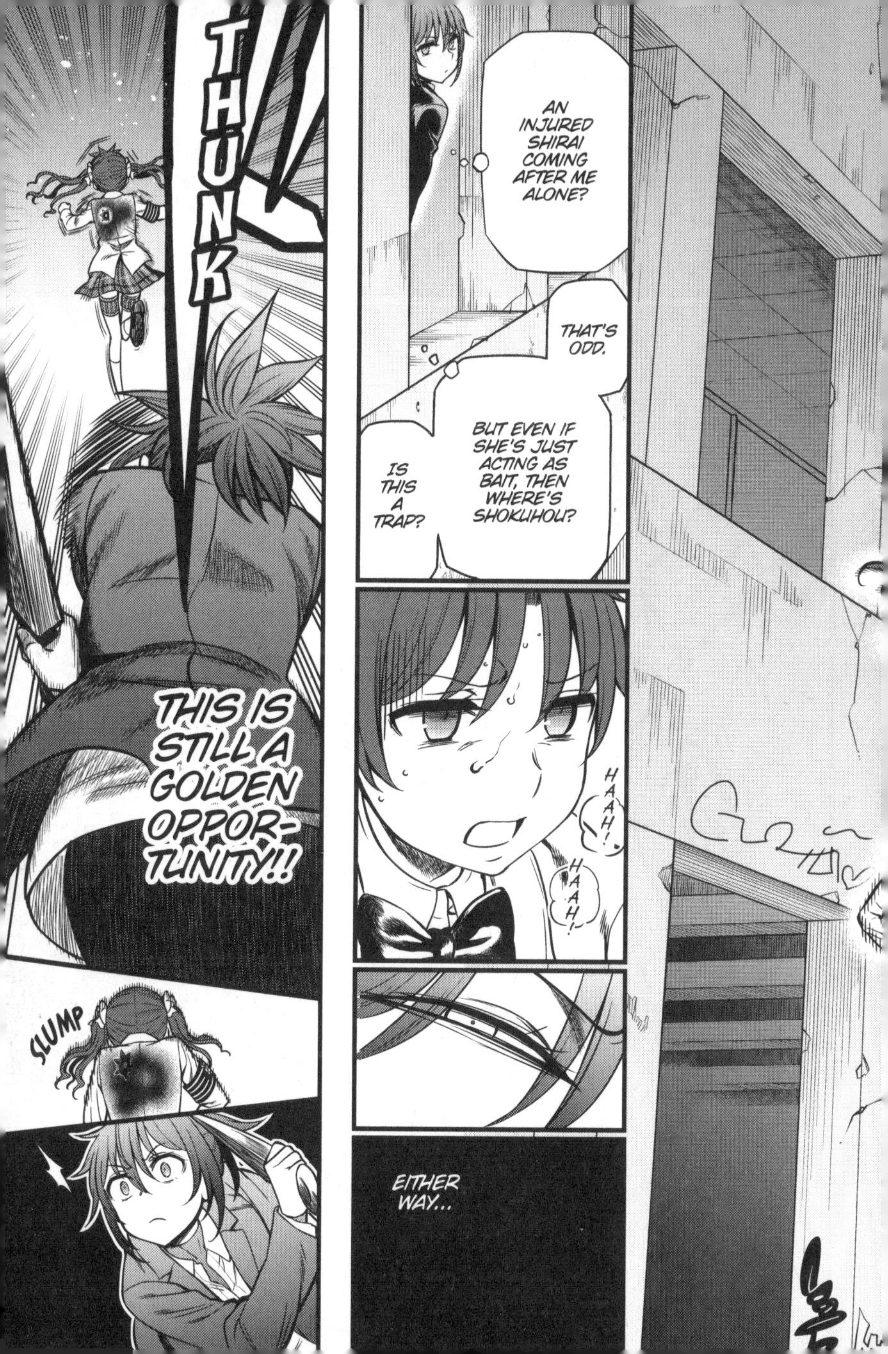
AN INJURED SHIRAI COMING AFTER ME ALONE?
THAT'S ODD.
BUT EVEN IF SHE'S JUST ACTING AS BAIT, THEN WHERE'S SHOKUHOU?
IS THIS A TRAP?
HAAH!
HAAH!
EITHER WAY...
THUNK
THIS IS STILL A GOLDEN OPPORTUNITY!!
SLUMP

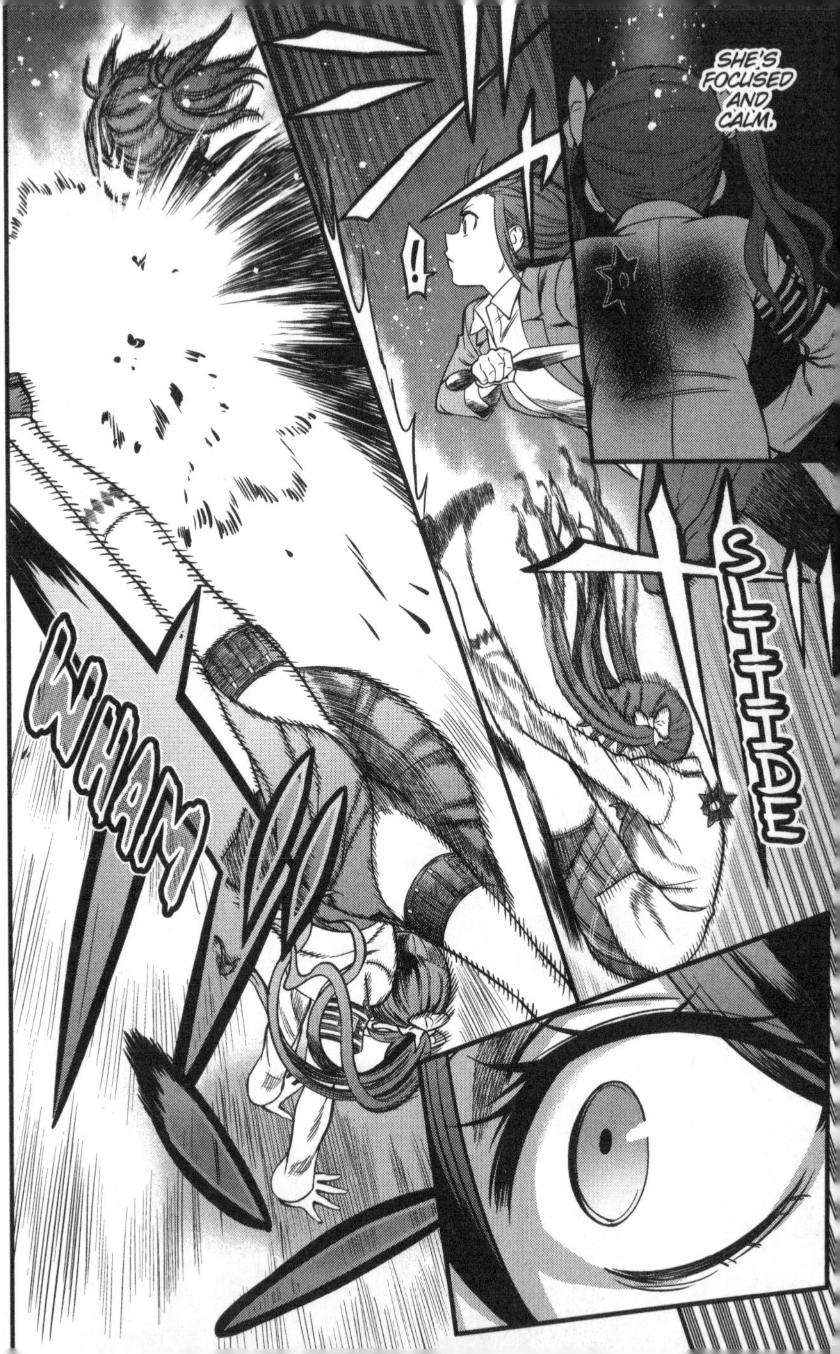
SHE'S FOCUSED AND CALM.
!
SLIIIDE
WHAM

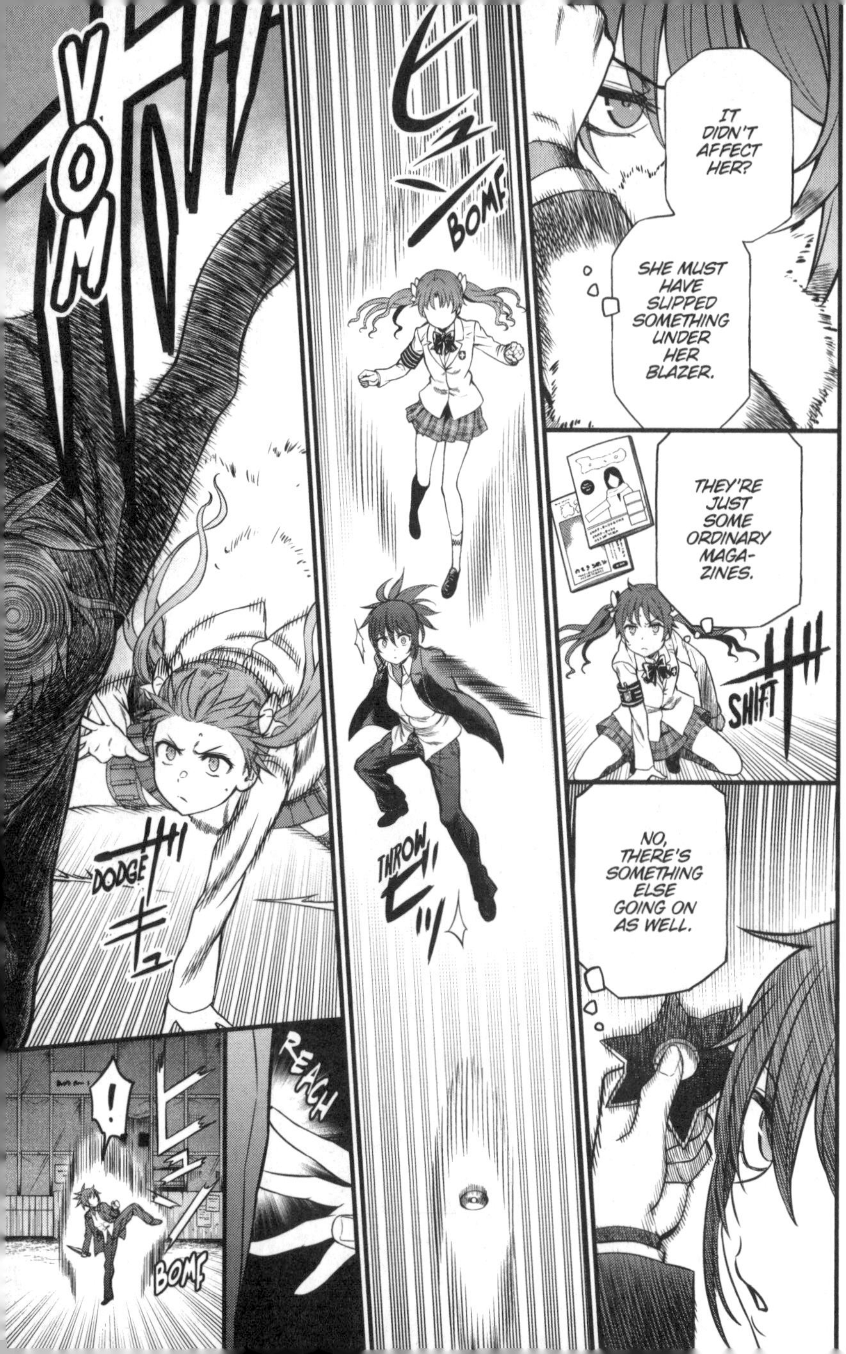
IT DIDN'T AFFECT HER?
SHE MUST HAVE SLIPPED SOMETHING UNDER HER BLAZER.
THEY'RE JUST SOME ORDINARY MAGA-ZINES.
SHIFT
NO, THERE'S SOMETHING ELSE GOING ON AS WELL.
BOMF
THROW
VOM
DODGE
REACH
!
BOMF

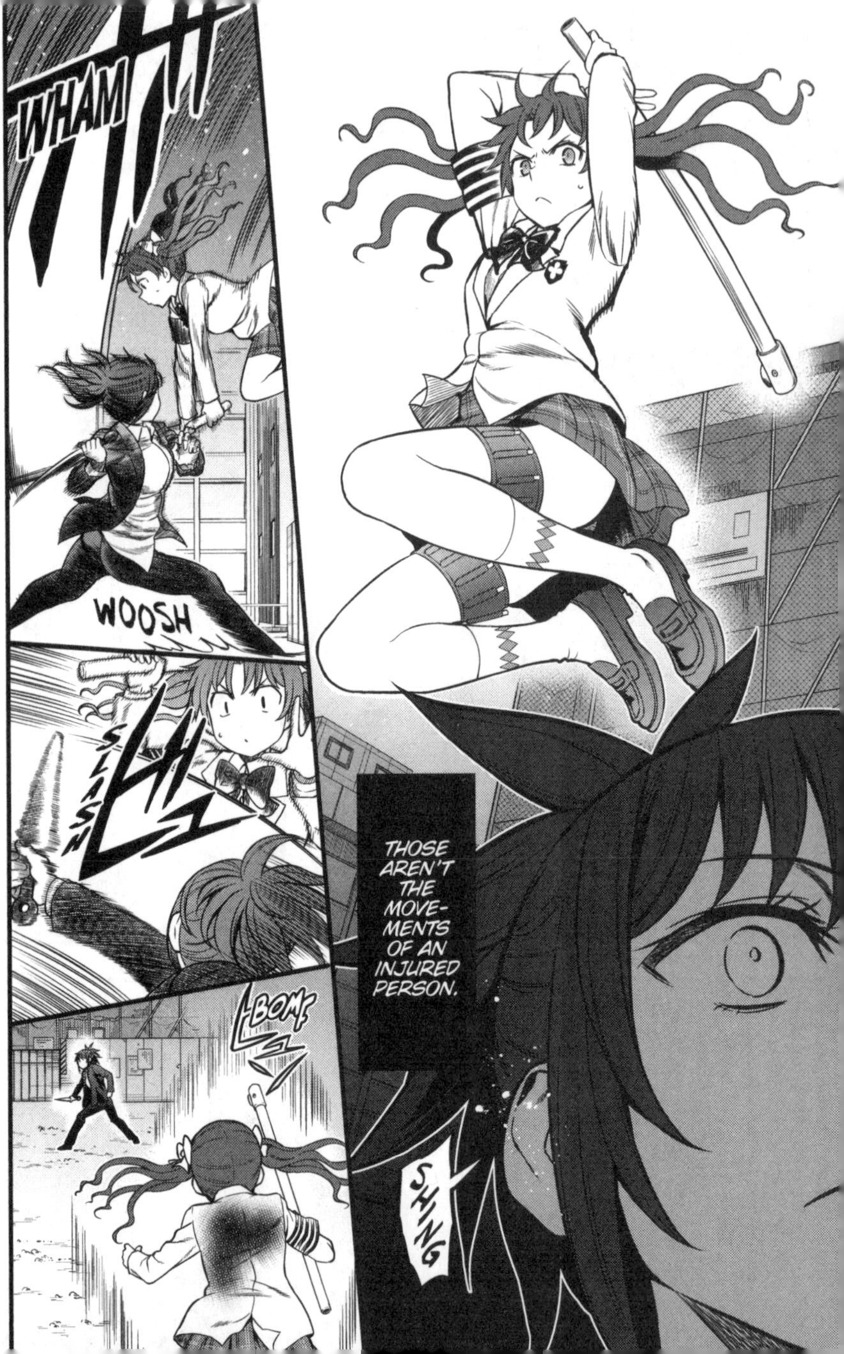
WHAM
WOOSH
SLASH
THOSE AREN'T THE MOVE-MENTS OF AN INJURED PERSON.
BOM
SHING

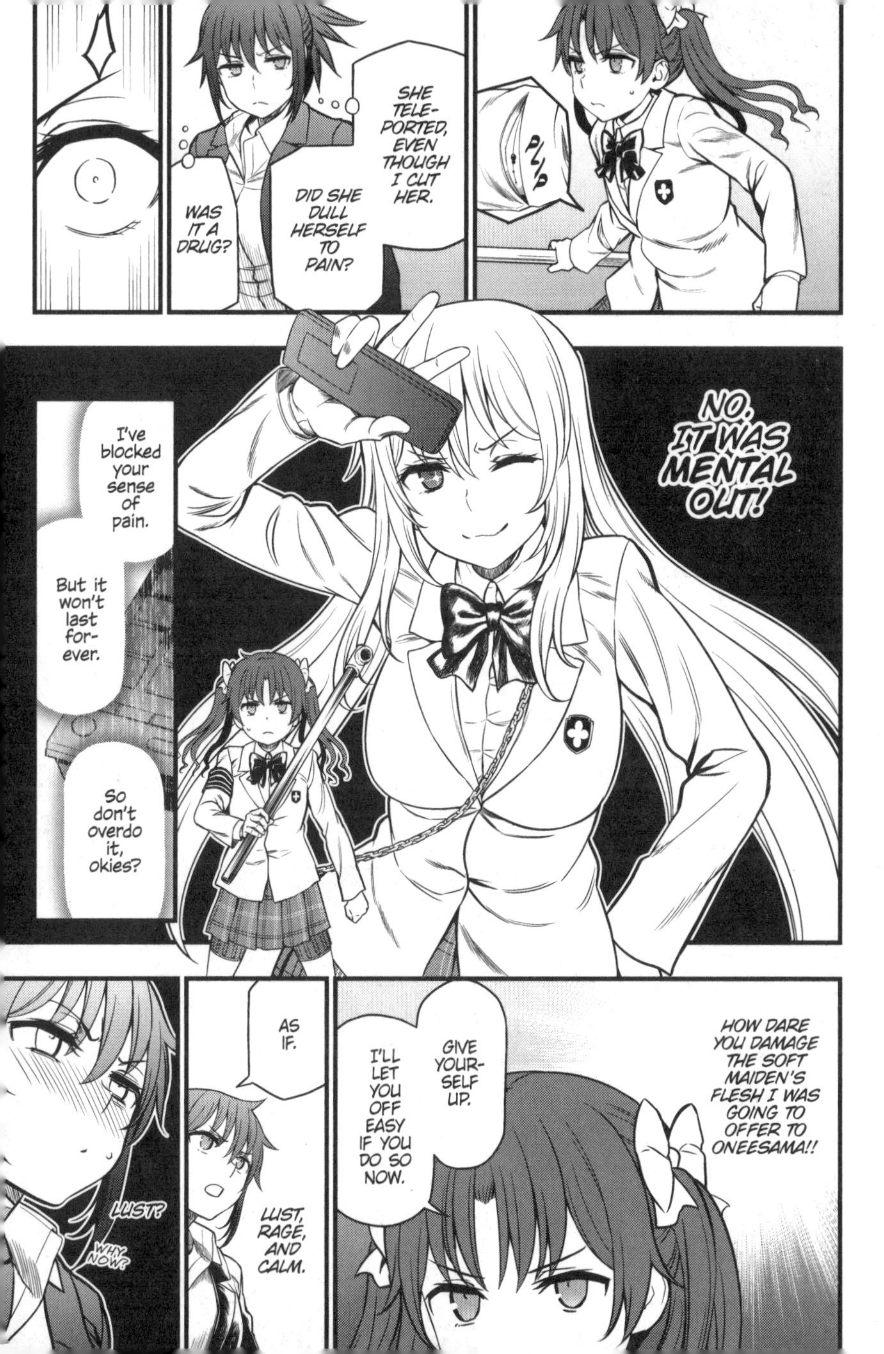

SHE TELE-PORTED, EVEN THOUGH I CUT HER.
DID SHE DULL HERSELF TO PAIN?
WAS IT A DRUG?
NO. IT WAS MENTAL OUT!
I've blocked your sense of pain.
But it won't last forever.
So don't overdo it, okies?
HOW DARE YOU DAMAGE THE SOFT MAIDEN'S FLESH I WAS GOING TO OFFER TO ONEESAMA!!
GIVE YOURSELF UP.
I'LL LET YOU OFF EASY IF YOU DO SO NOW.
AS IF.
LUST, RAGE, AND CALM.
LUST?
WHY NOW?

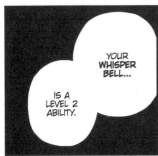

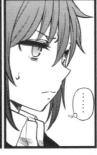

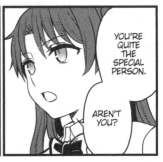

YOU'RE QUITE THE SPECIAL PERSON.
AREN'T YOU?
......
YOUR WHISPER BELL...
IS A LEVEL 2 ABILITY.
HOWEVER, GIVEN YOUR ADVANCED LEVEL OF EXPERTISE AND YOUR SKILLED APPLICATION OF YOUR ABILITY...
YOU WERE DEEMED A LEVEL 3 EQUIVALENT...
AND ACCEPTED BY TOKIWADAI AS A TECHNICAL EXCHANGE STUDENT.
THAT'S WHY YOU'RE AFFILIATED WITH A DIFFERENT MIDDLE SCHOOL.
THAT'S YOU, ISN'T IT?
THAT'S RIGHT.
THANKS TO YOUR PITY.
A SORRY LOSER MIXED IN AMONG...
YOU GENIUSES.
......
IF YOU'RE A SPECIAL CASE AMONG SPECIAL CASES...
THEN ALL THE MORE SO.

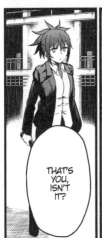

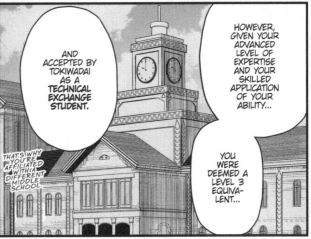

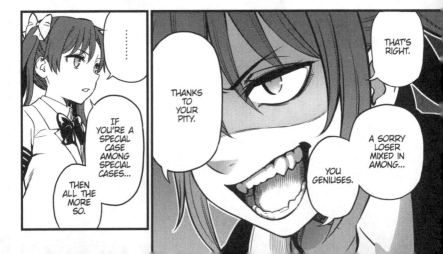

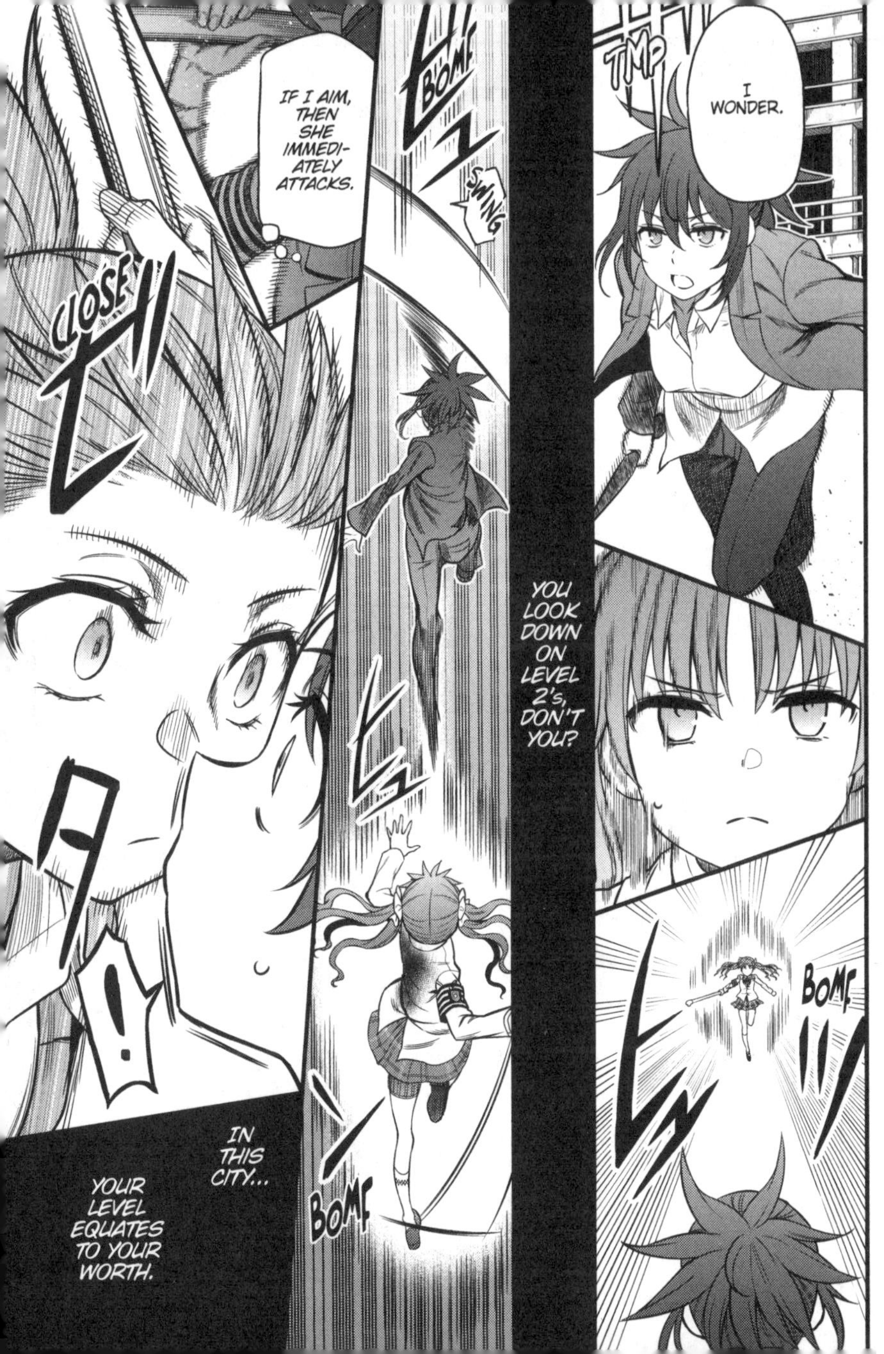
TMP
I WONDER.
YOU LOOK DOWN ON LEVEL 2's, DON'T YOU?
BOMF
BOMF
SWING
IF I AIM, THEN SHE IMMEDIATELY ATTACKS.
BOMF
CLOSE
IN THIS CITY...
YOUR LEVEL EQUATES TO YOUR WORTH.

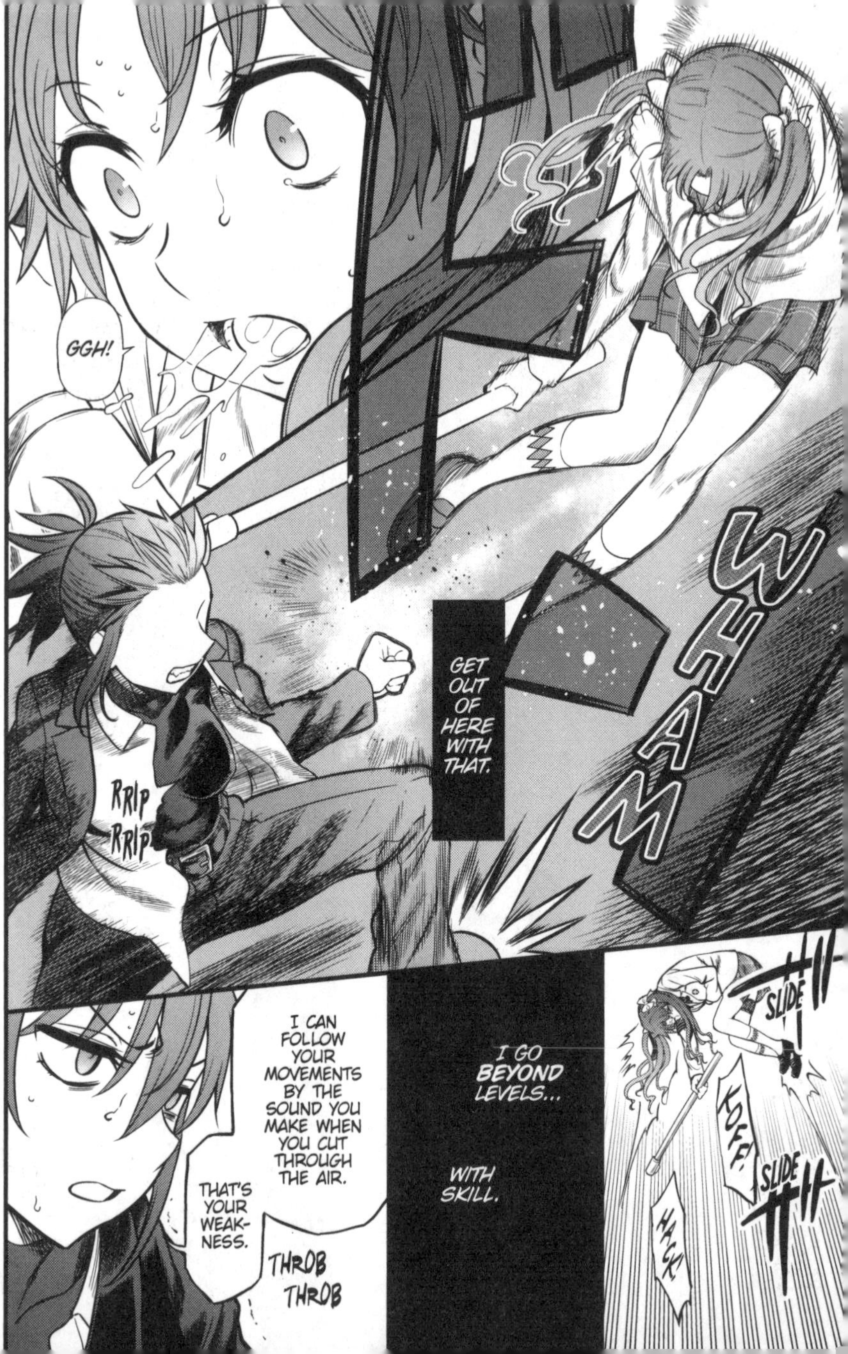
GGH!
WHAM
GET OUT OF HERE WITH THAT.
RRIP RRIP
SLIDE
KOFF!
SLIDE
HACK!
I GO BEYOND LEVELS...
WITH SKILL.
I CAN FOLLOW YOUR MOVEMENTS BY THE SOUND YOU MAKE WHEN YOU CUT THROUGH THE AIR.
THAT'S YOUR WEAK-NESS.
THROB THROB

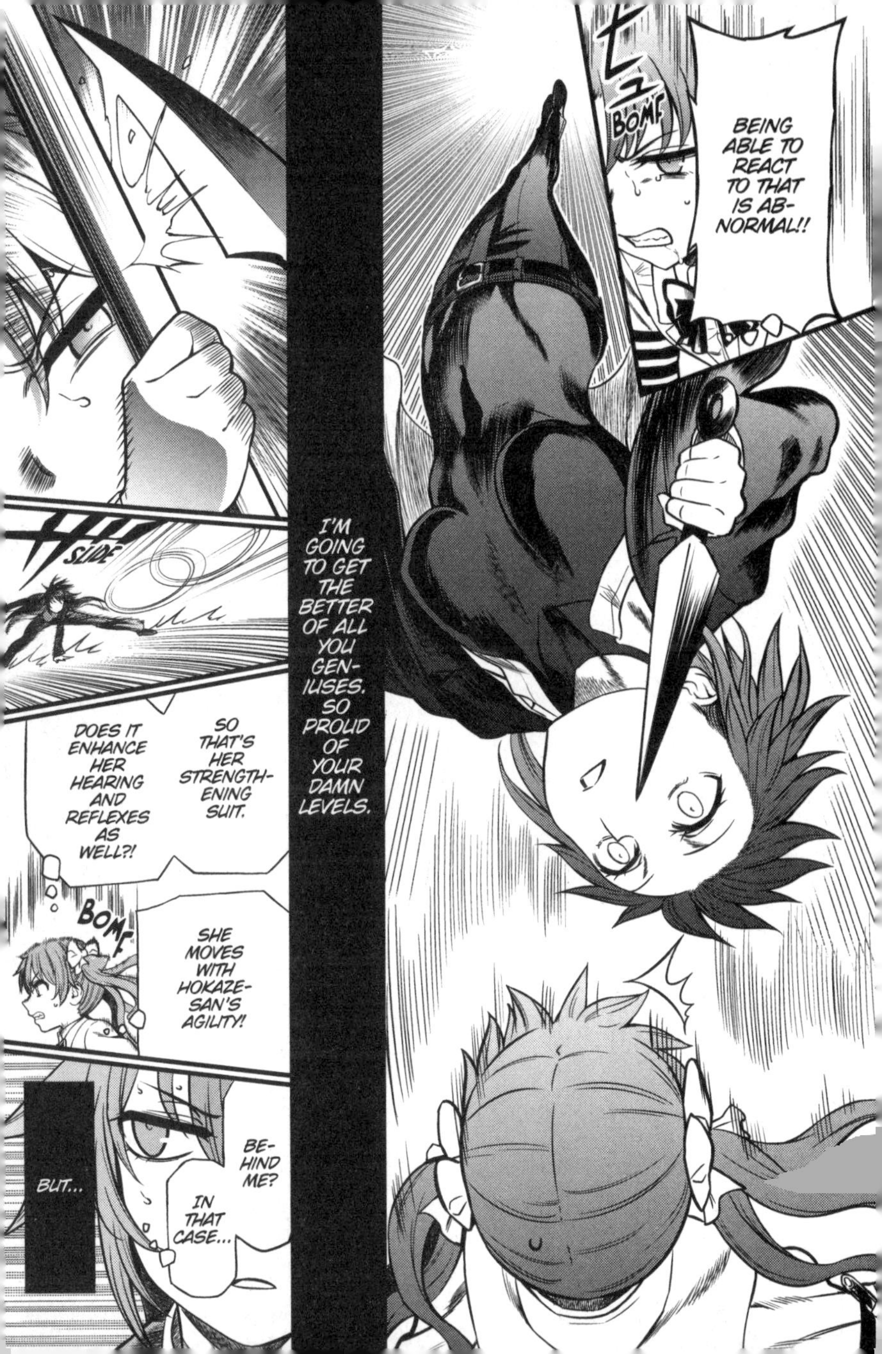
BOMF
BEING ABLE TO REACT TO THAT IS AB-NORMAL!!
I'M GOING TO GET THE BETTER OF ALL YOU GEN-IUSES. SO PROUD OF YOUR DAMN LEVELS.
SLIDE
SO THAT'S HER STRENGTH-ENING SUIT.
DOES IT ENHANCE HER HEARING AND REFLEXES AS WELL?!
BOMF
SHE MOVES WITH HOKAZE-SAN'S AGILITY!
BE-HIND ME?
IN THAT CASE...
BUT...

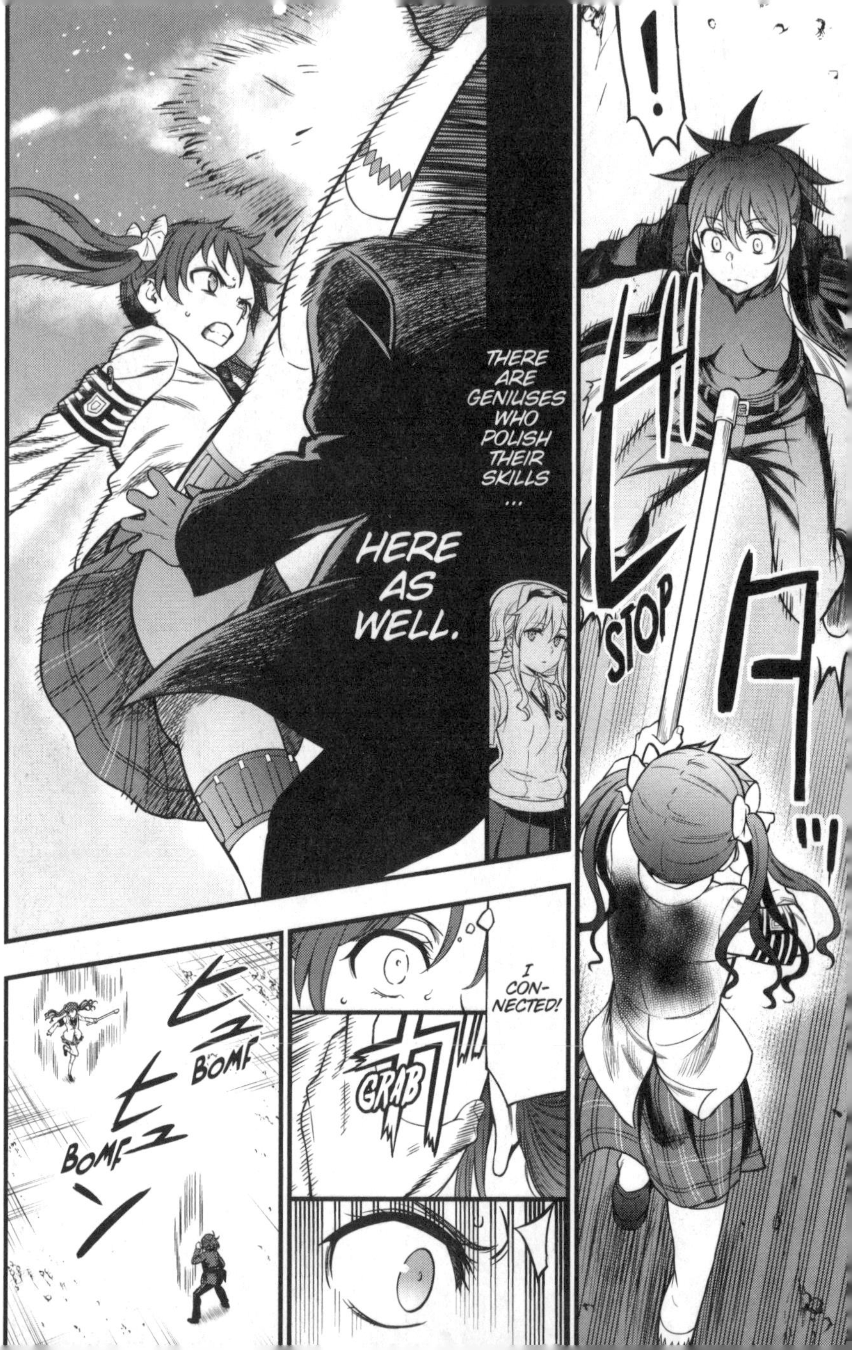
!
STOP
THERE ARE GENIUSES WHO POLISH THEIR SKILLS...
HERE AS WELL.
I CON-NECTED!
GRAB
BOMF
BOMF

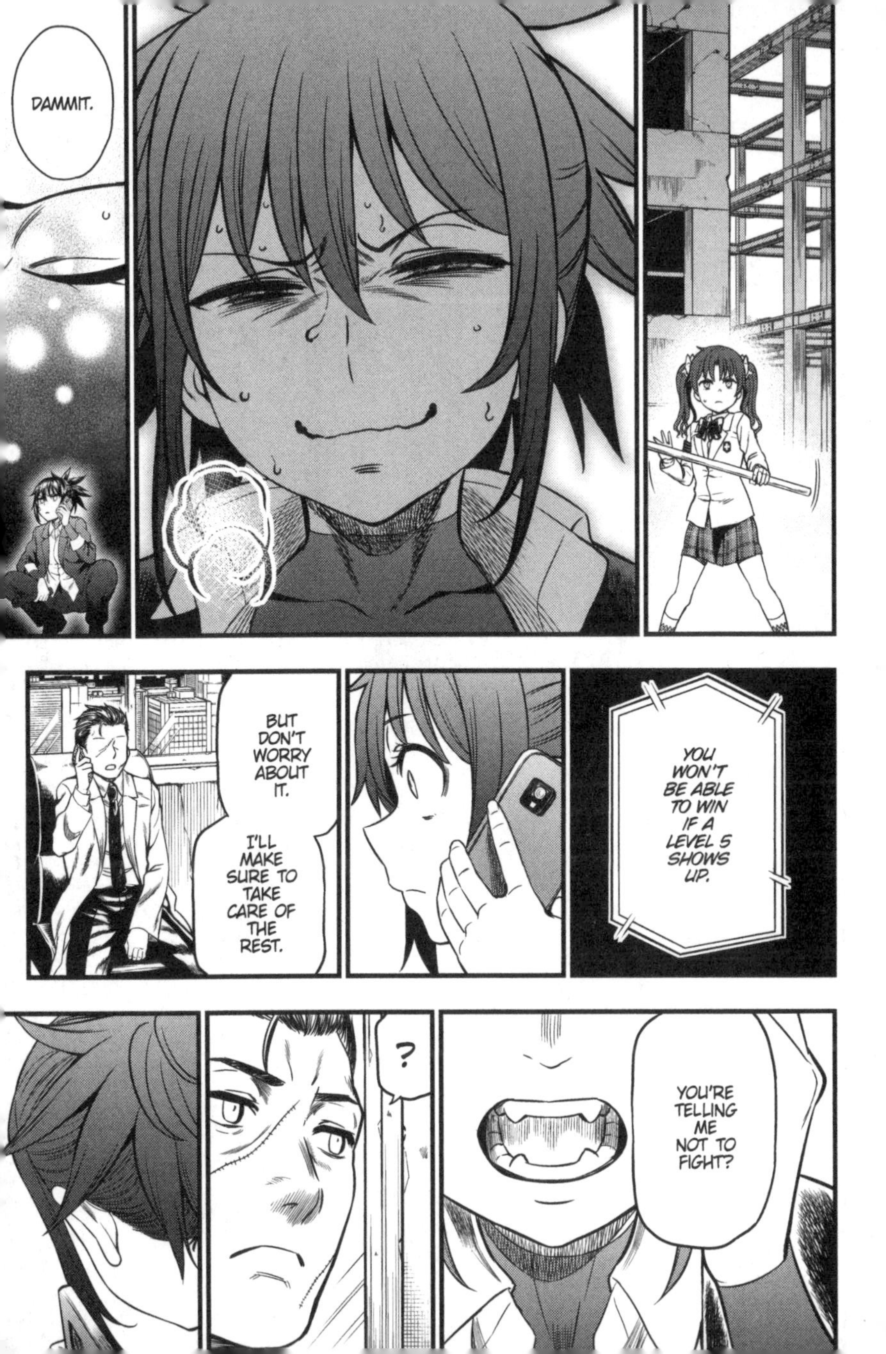
DAMMIT.
YOU WON'T BE ABLE TO WIN IF A LEVEL 5 SHOWS UP.
BUT DON'T WORRY ABOUT IT.
I'LL MAKE SURE TO TAKE CARE OF THE REST.
YOU'RE TELLING ME NOT TO FIGHT?
?

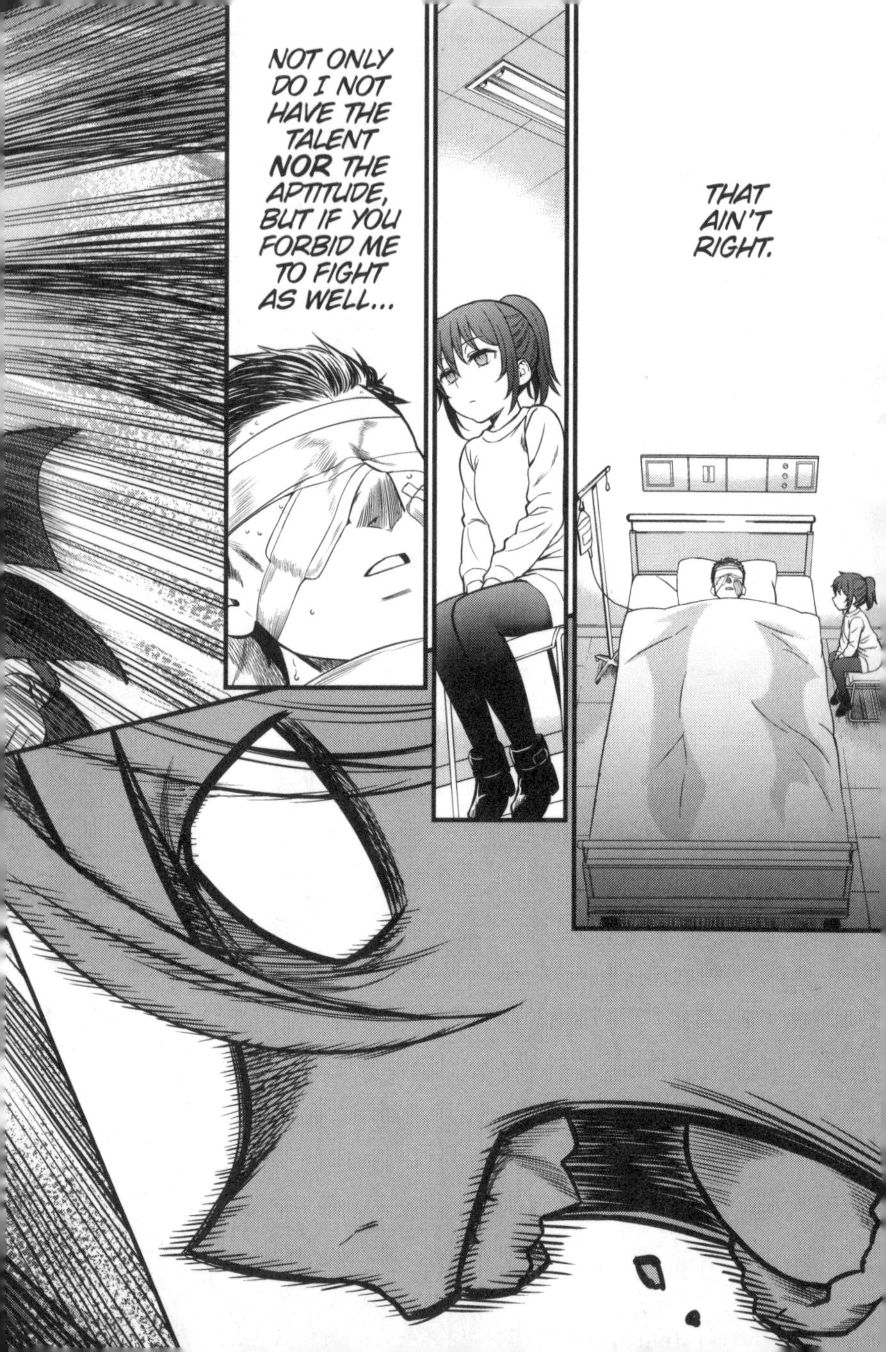
THAT AIN'T RIGHT.
NOT ONLY DO I NOT HAVE THE TALENT NOR THE APTITUDE, BUT IF YOU FORBID ME TO FIGHT AS WELL...

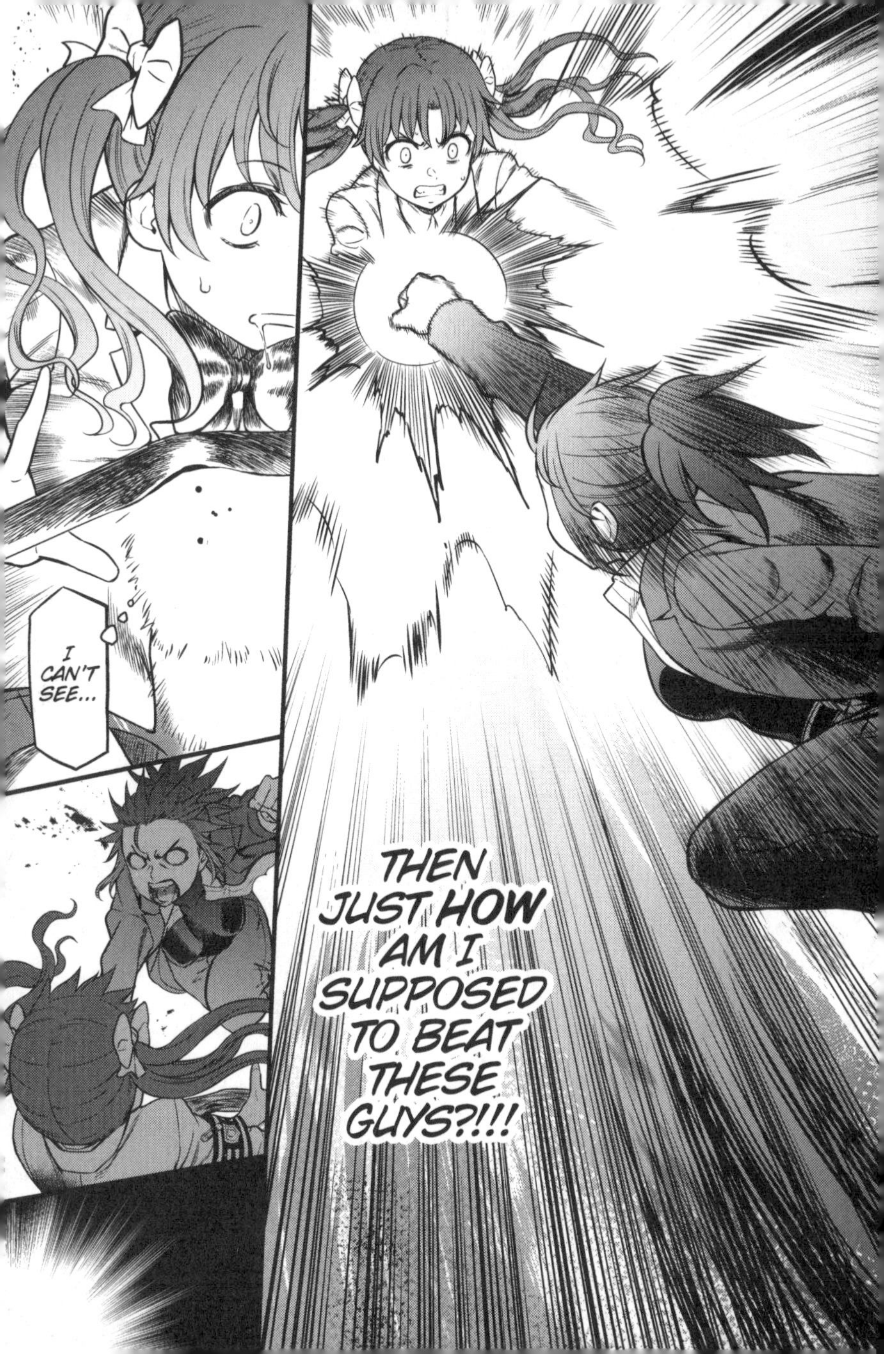
I CAN'T SEE...
THEN JUST HOW AM I SUPPOSED TO BEAT THESE GUYS?!!!

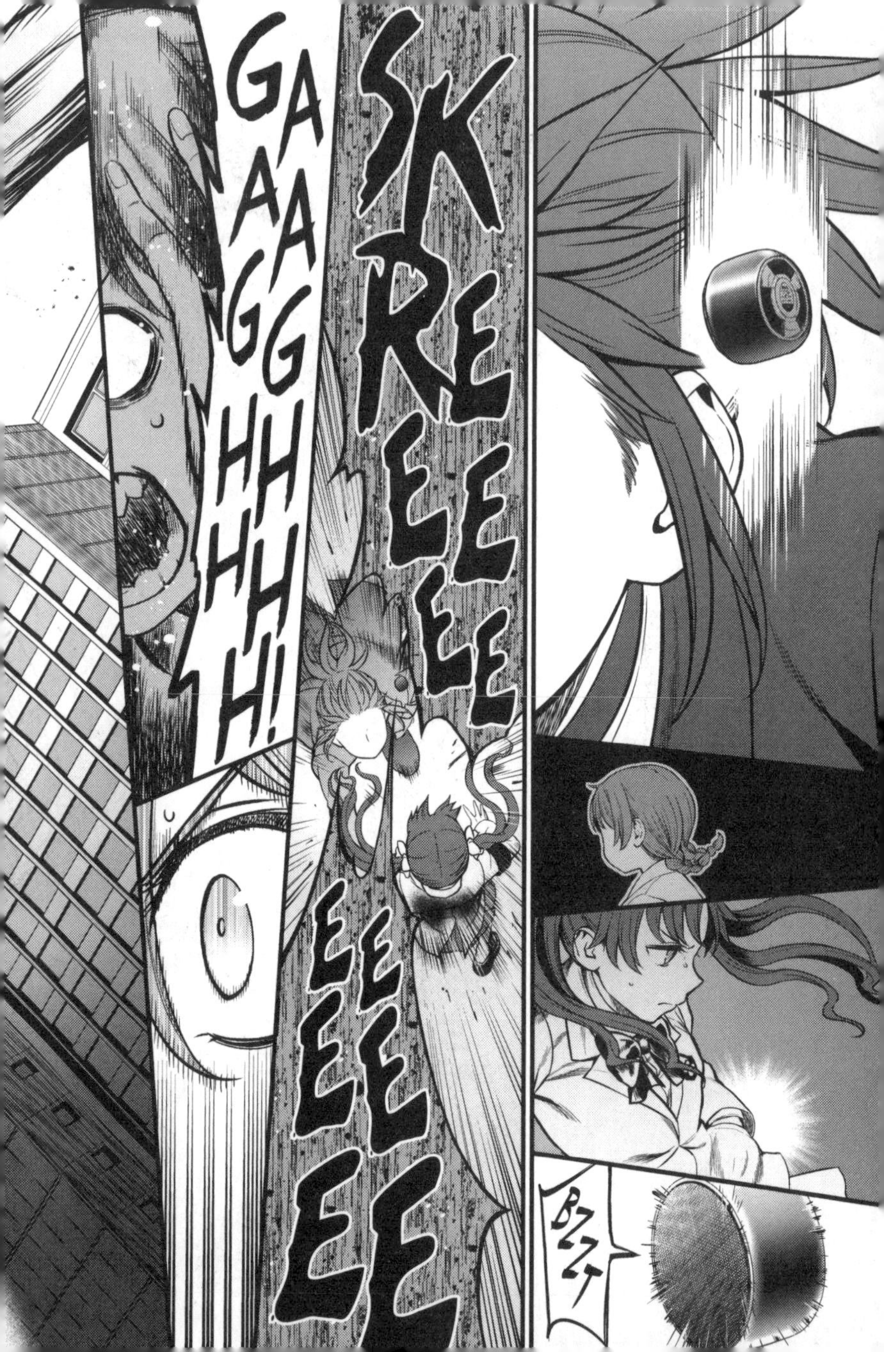
SKREEEEEEEEE
GAAGGHHHHHH!
BZZT

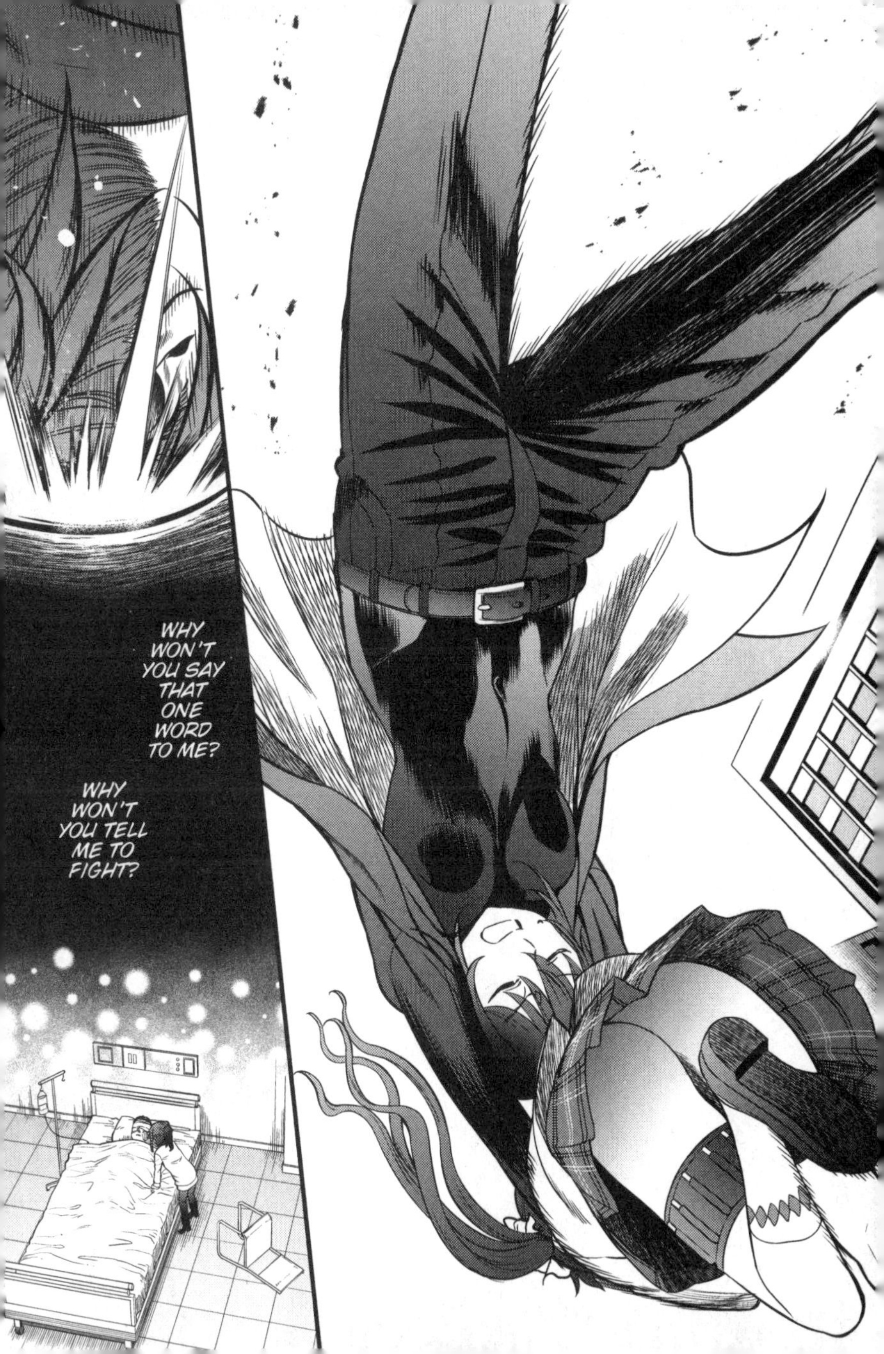
WHY WON'T YOU SAY THAT ONE WORD TO ME?
WHY WON'T YOU TELL ME TO FIGHT?

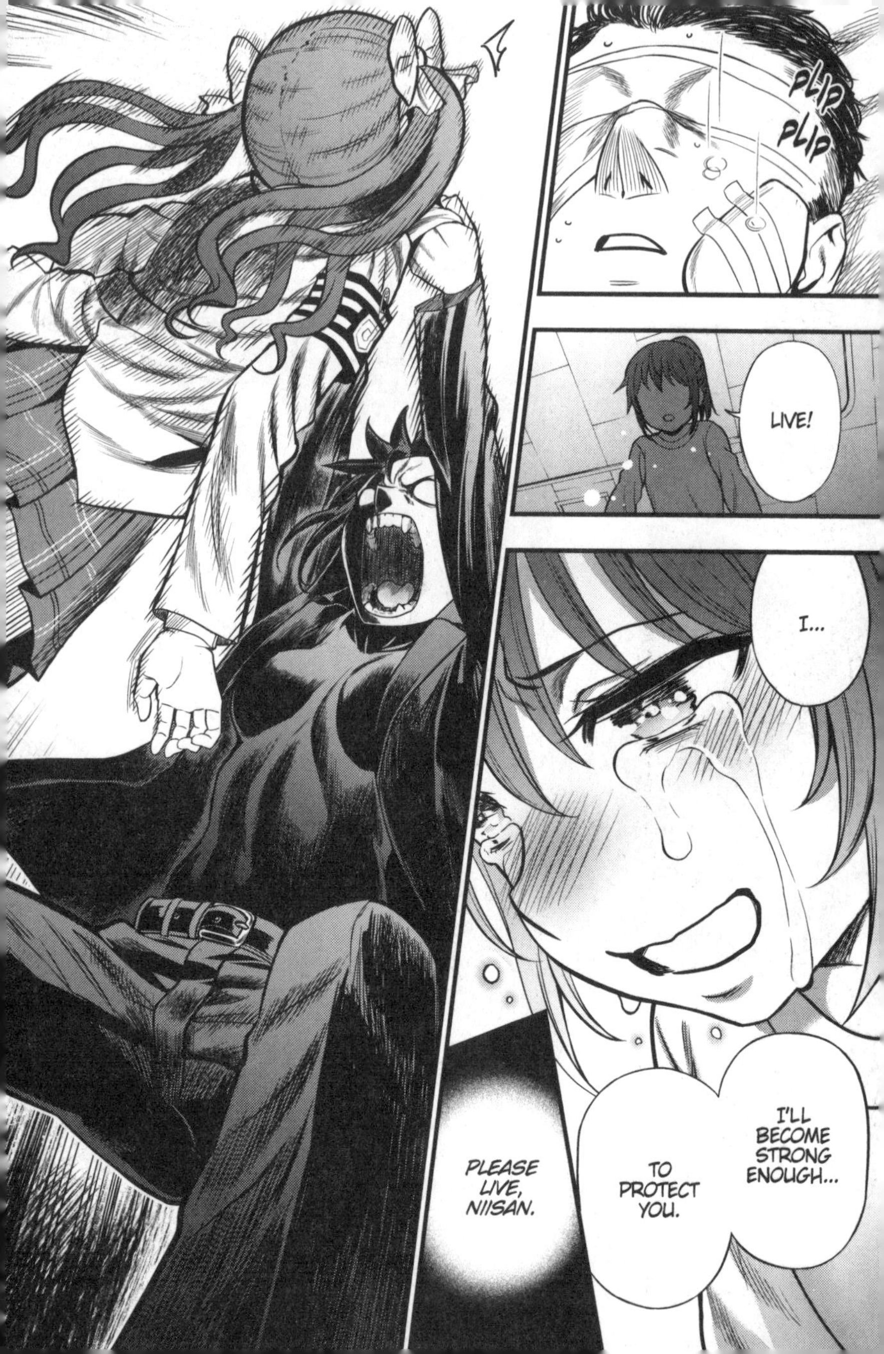
PLIP
PLIP
LIVE!
I...
I'LL BECOME STRONG ENOUGH...
TO PROTECT YOU.
PLEASE LIVE, NIISAN.

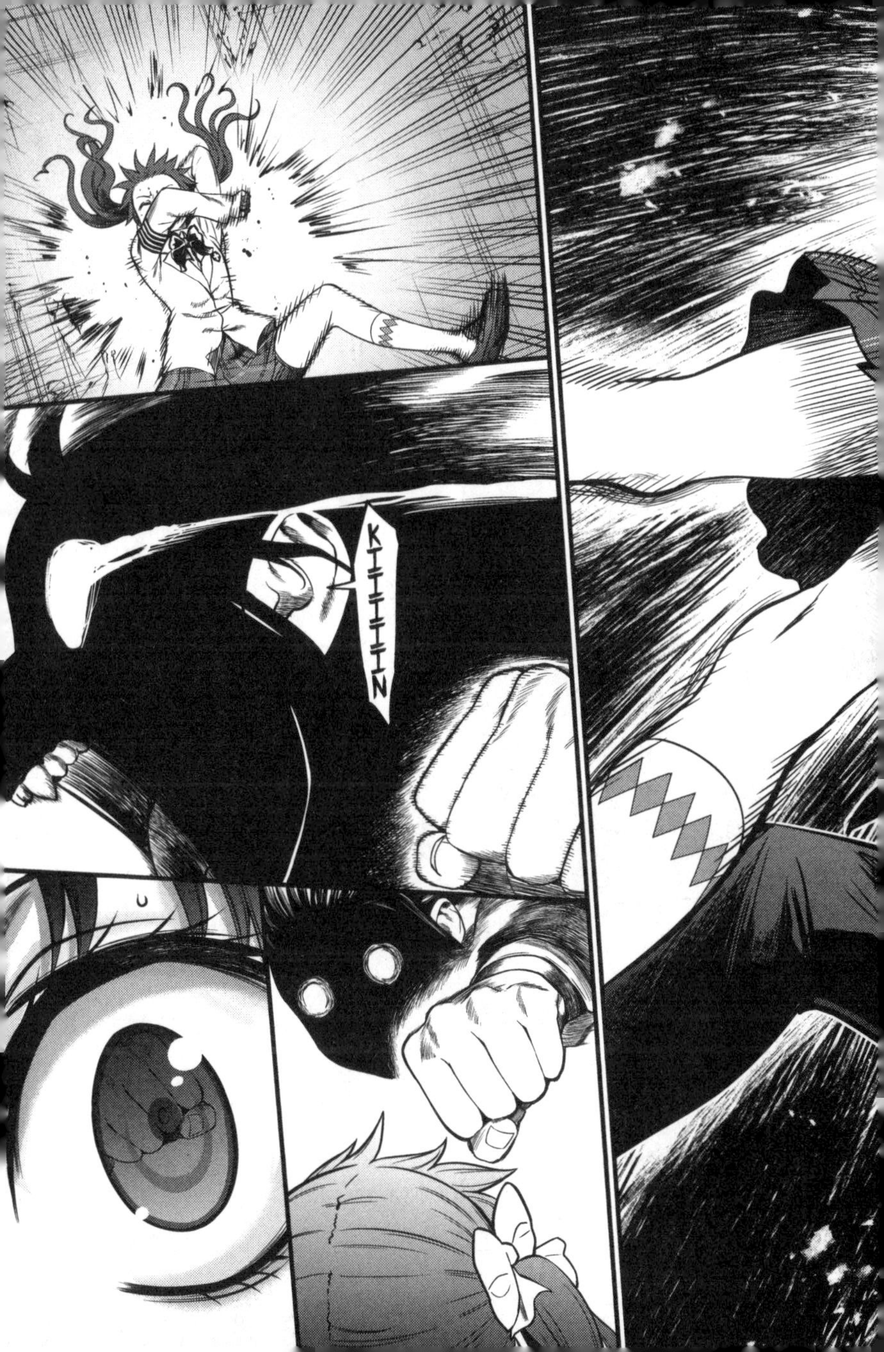
KITTTTIN

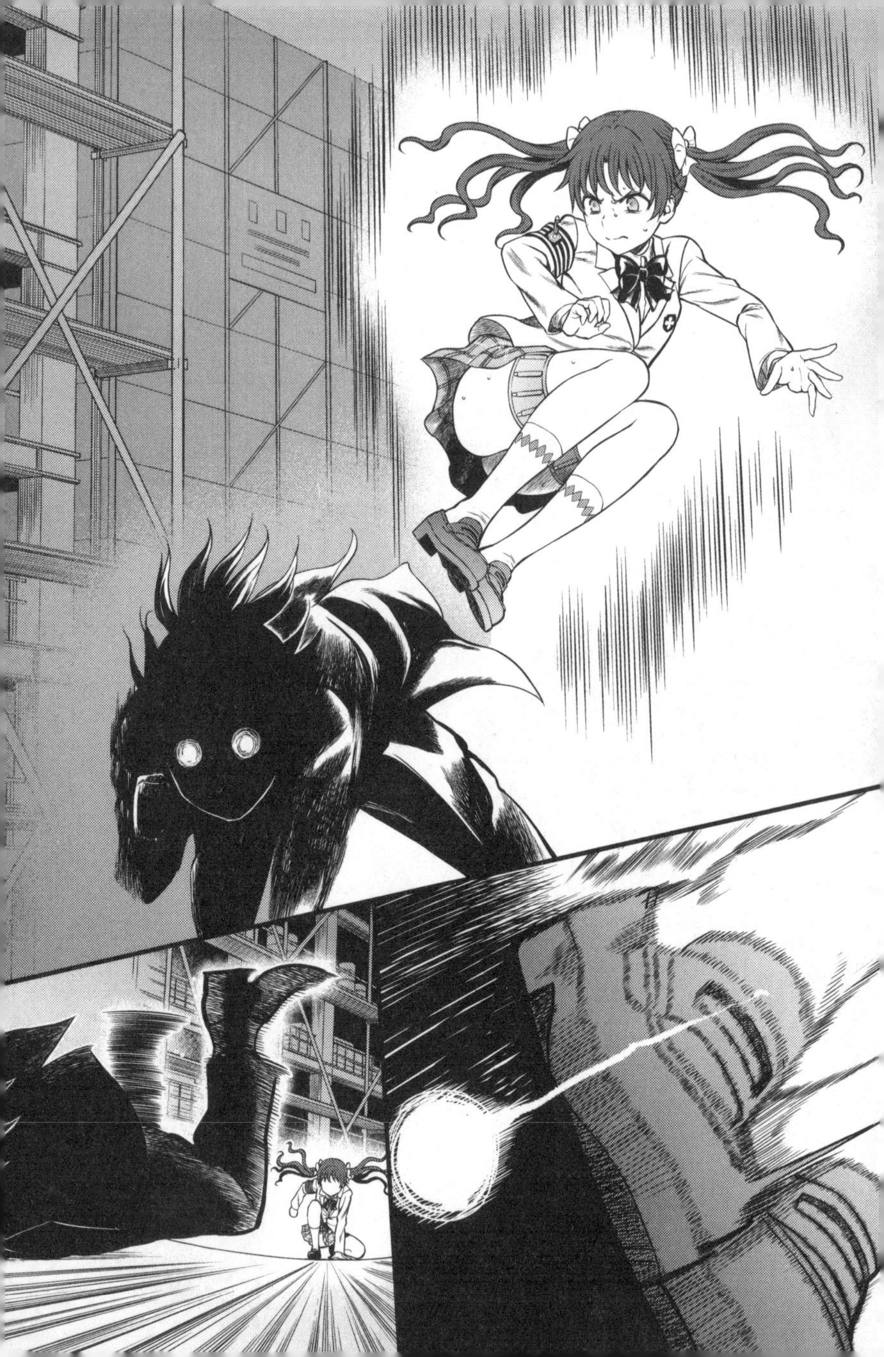

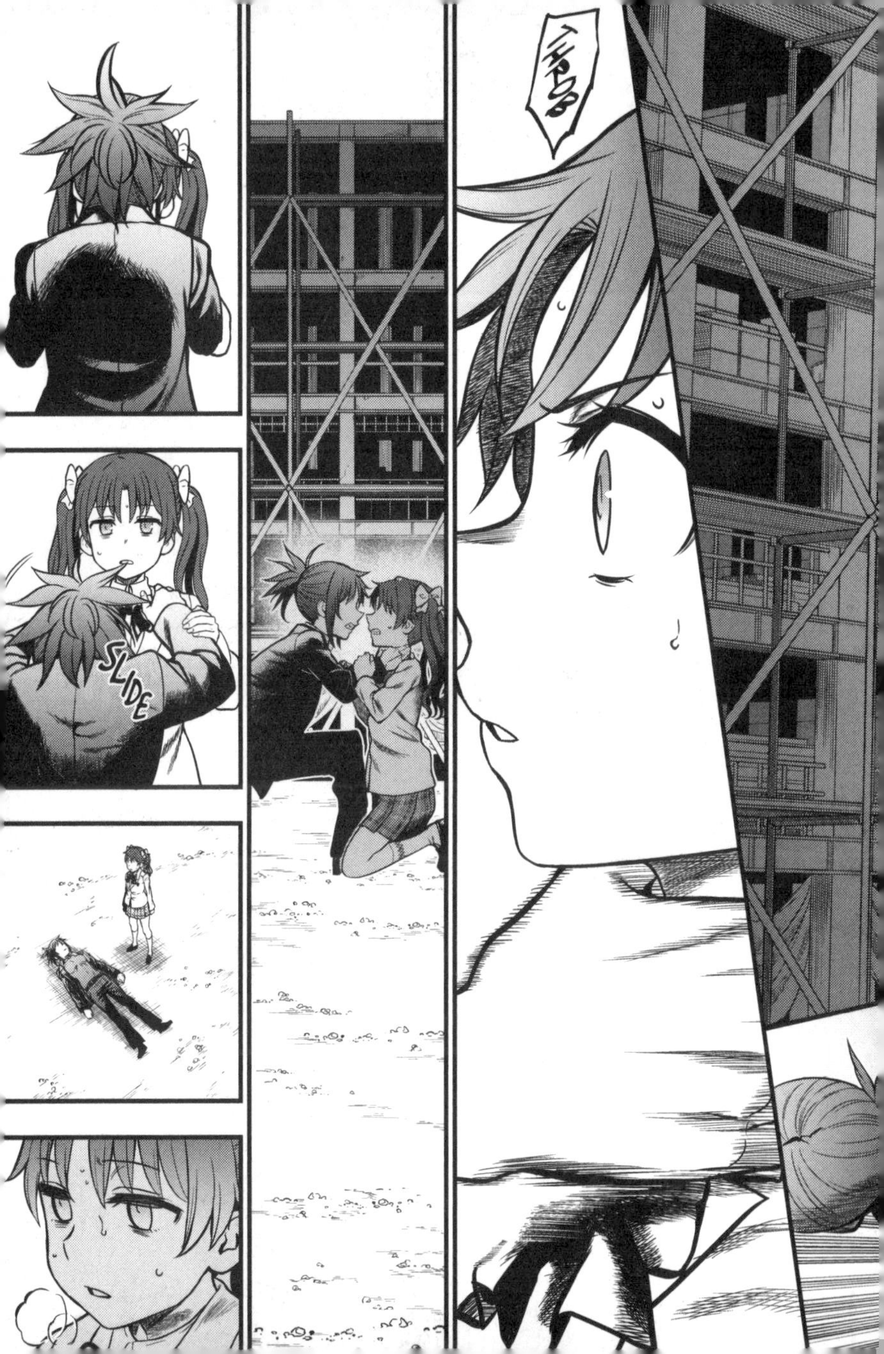
SLIDE

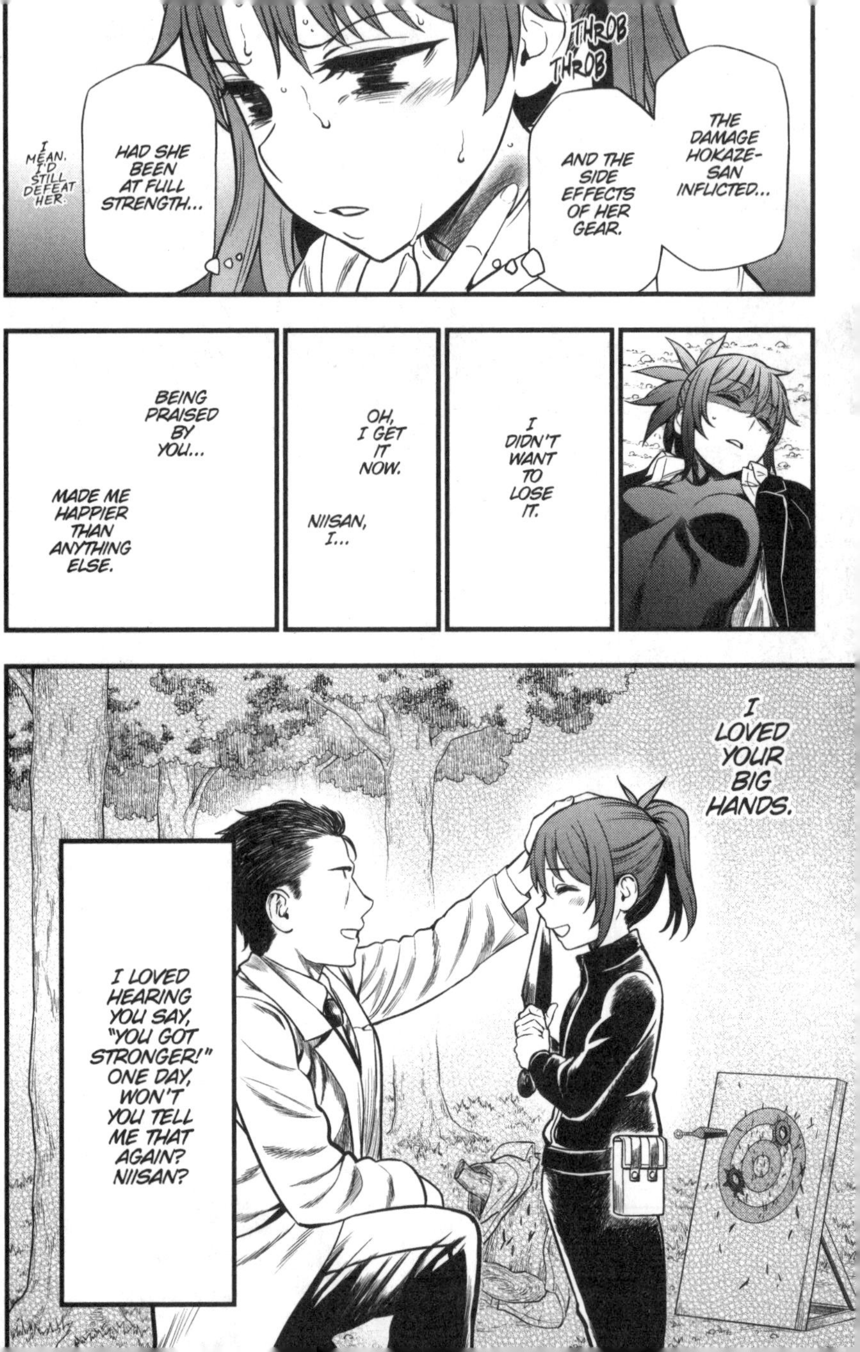
THROB THROB
THE DAMAGE HOKAZE-SAN INFLICTED...
AND THE SIDE EFFECTS OF HER GEAR.
HAD SHE BEEN AT FULL STRENGTH...
I MEAN, I'D STILL DEFEAT HER.
I DIDN'T WANT TO LOSE IT.
OH, I GET IT NOW.
NIISAN, I...
BEING PRAISED BY YOU...
MADE ME HAPPIER THAN ANYTHING ELSE.
I LOVED YOUR BIG HANDS.
I LOVED HEARING YOU SAY, "YOU GOT STRONGER!" ONE DAY, WON'T YOU TELL ME THAT AGAIN? NIISAN?

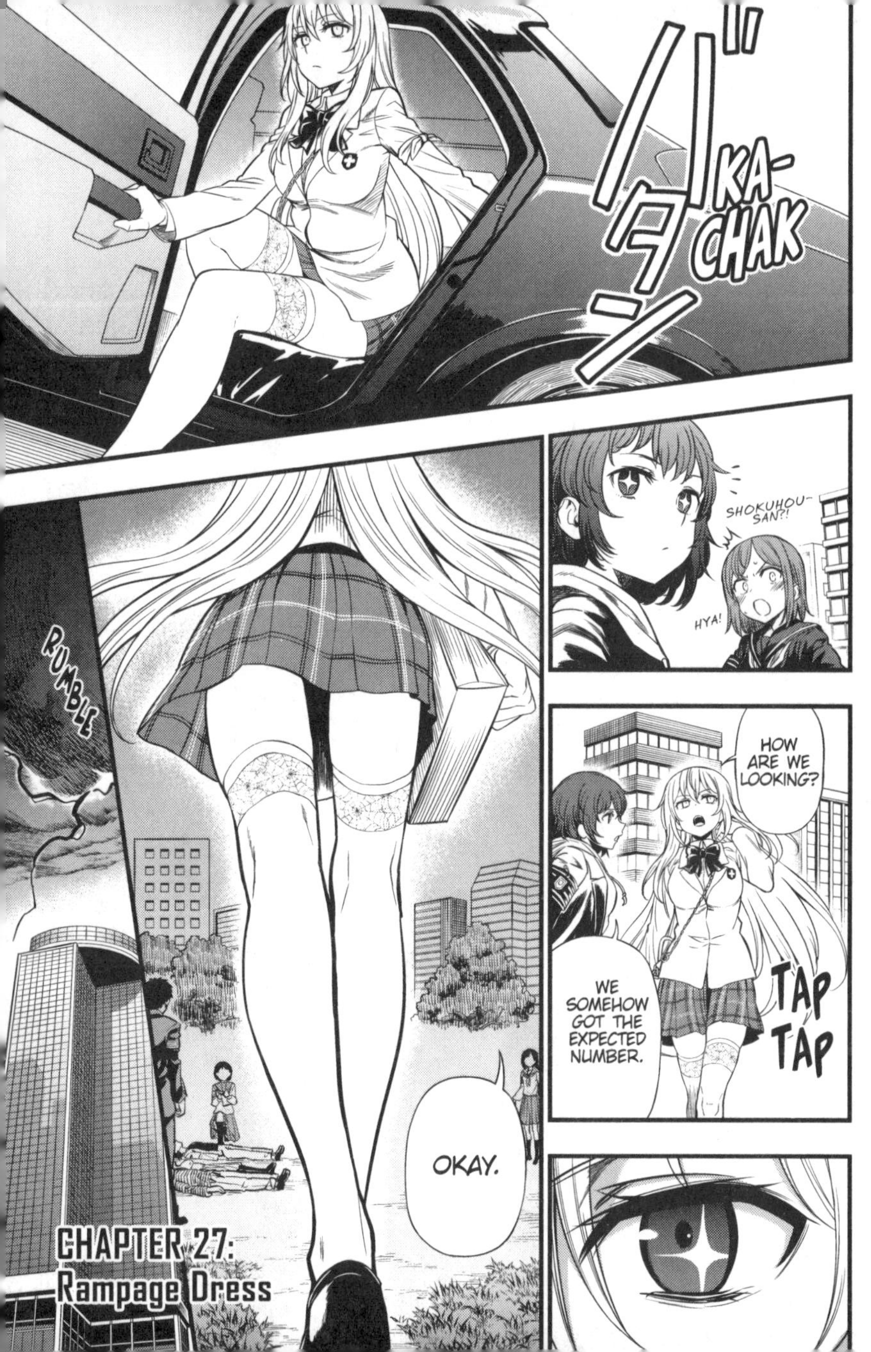
KA-CHAK
SHOKUHOU-SAN?!
HYA!
HOW ARE WE LOOKING?
WE SOMEHOW GOT THE EXPECTED NUMBER.
TAP TAP
RUMBLE
OKAY.
CHAPTER 27:
Rampage Dress

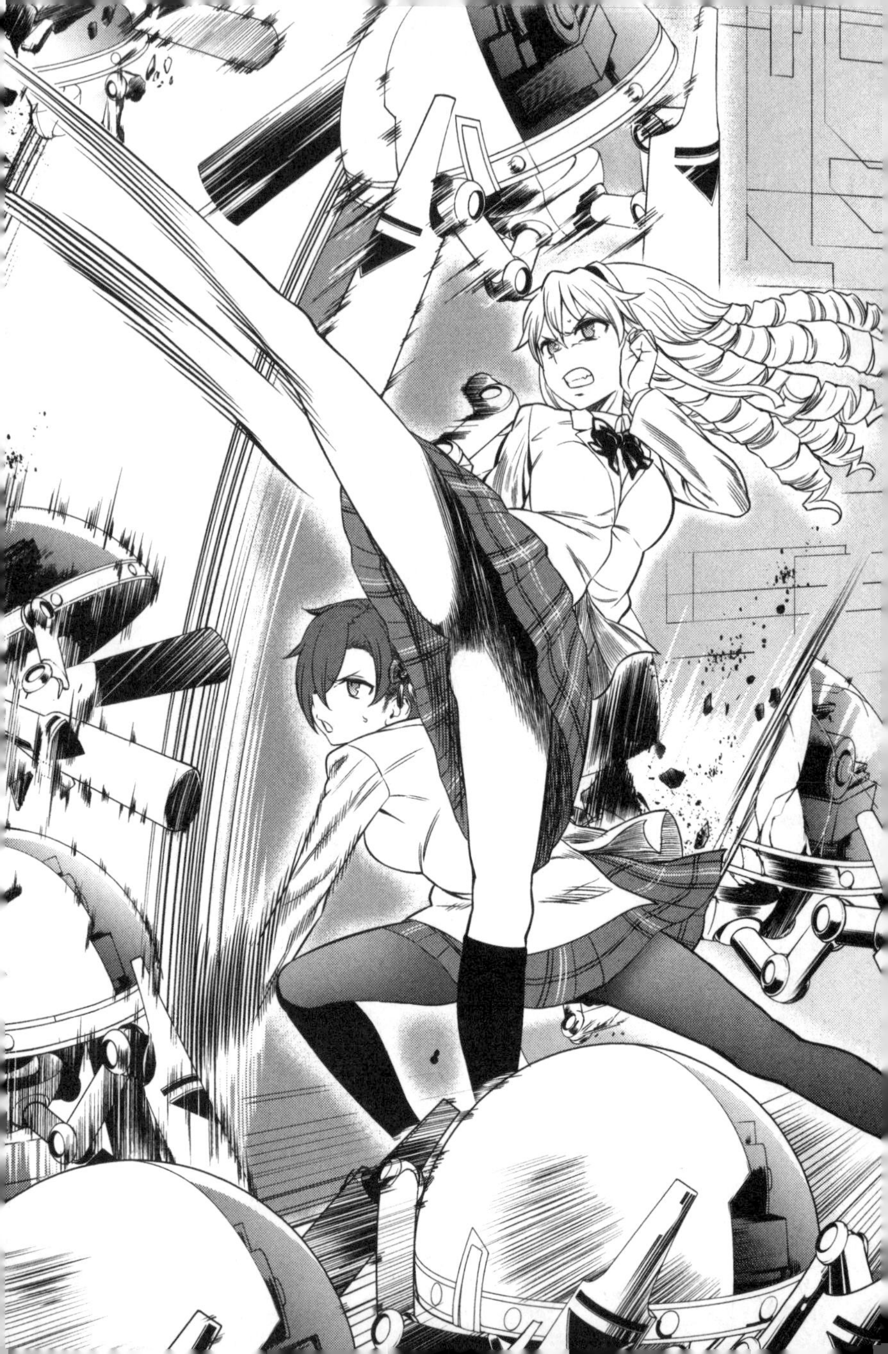

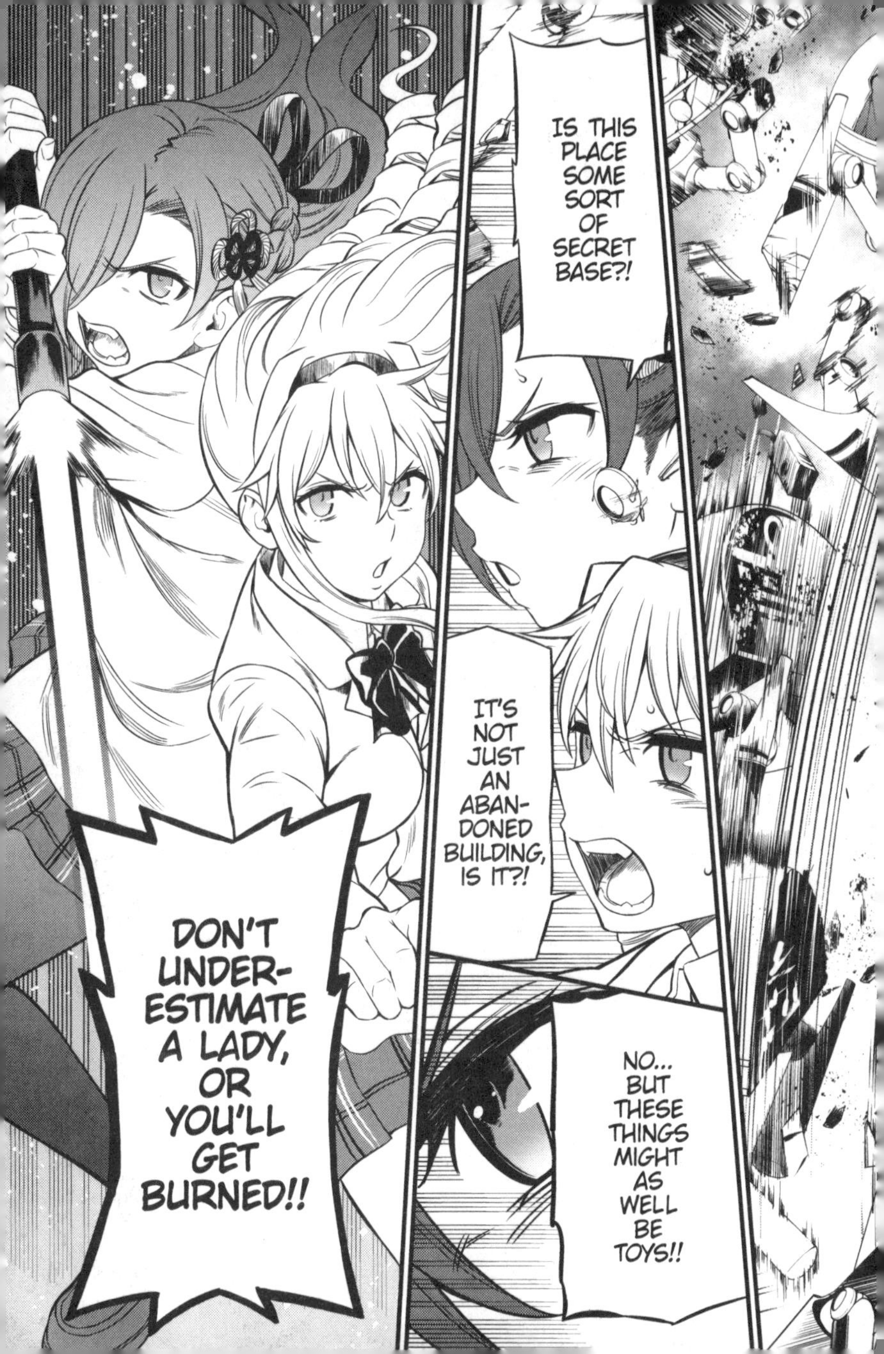
IS THIS PLACE SOME SORT OF SECRET BASE?!
IT'S NOT JUST AN ABAN-DONED BUILDING, IS IT?!
NO... BUT THESE THINGS MIGHT AS WELL BE TOYS!!
DON'T UNDER-ESTIMATE A LADY, OR YOU'LL GET BURNED!!

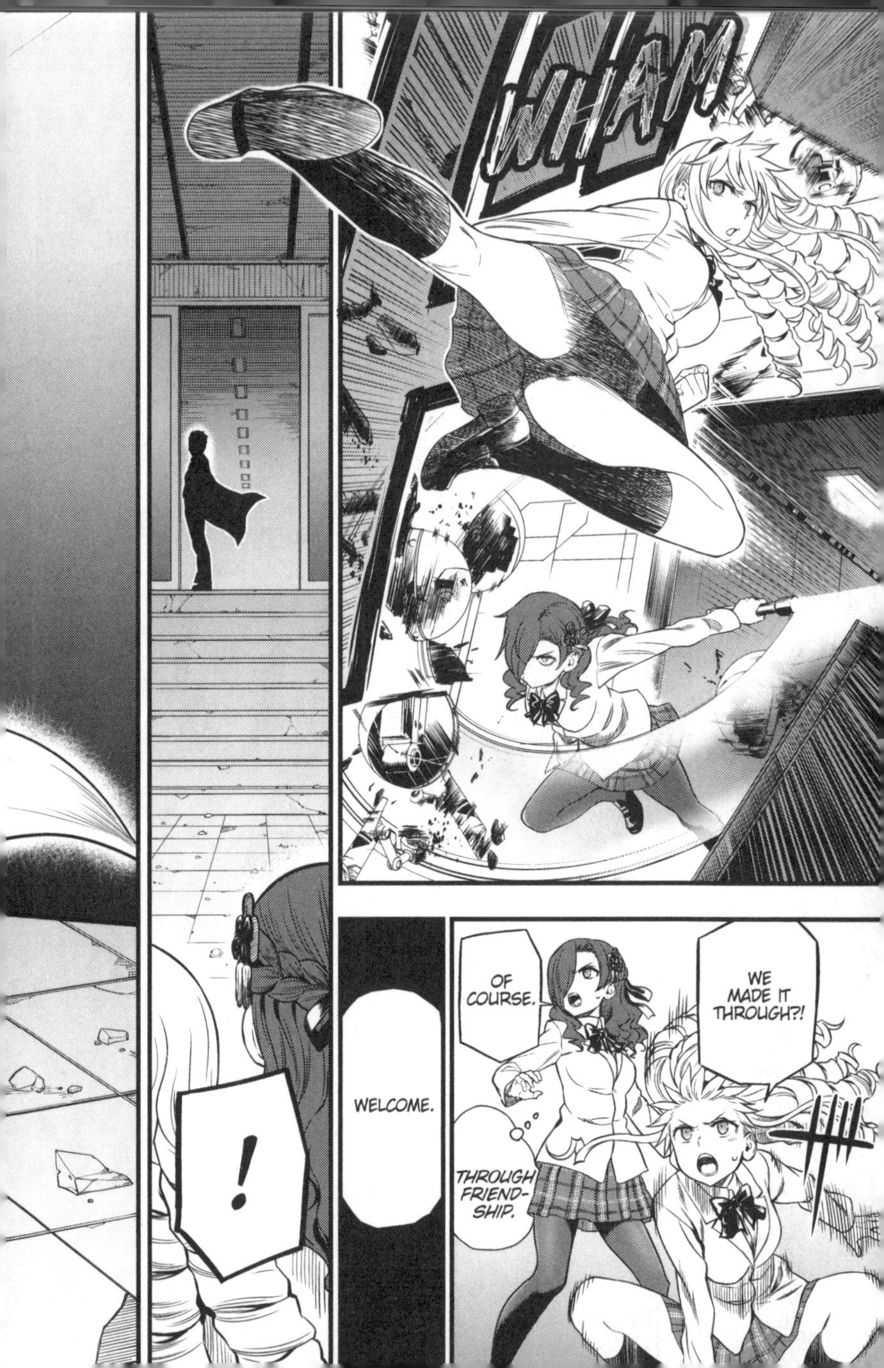
WHAM
WE MADE IT THROUGH?!
OF COURSE.
THROUGH FRIEND-SHIP.
WELCOME.
!

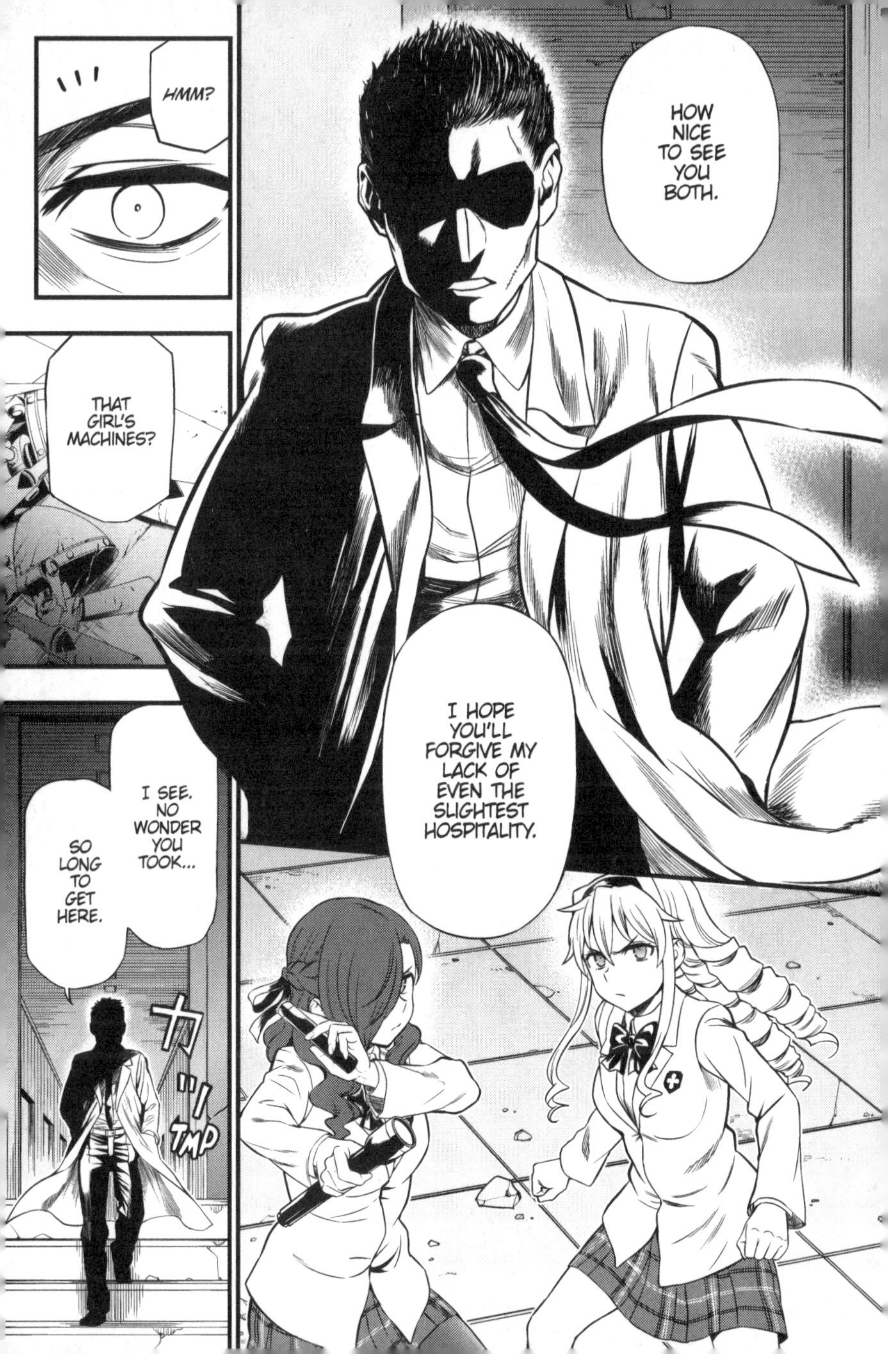

HOW NICE TO SEE YOU BOTH.
I HOPE YOU'LL FORGIVE MY LACK OF EVEN THE SLIGHTEST HOSPITALITY.
HMM?
THAT GIRL'S MACHINES?
I SEE. NO WONDER YOU TOOK...
SO LONG TO GET HERE.
TMP

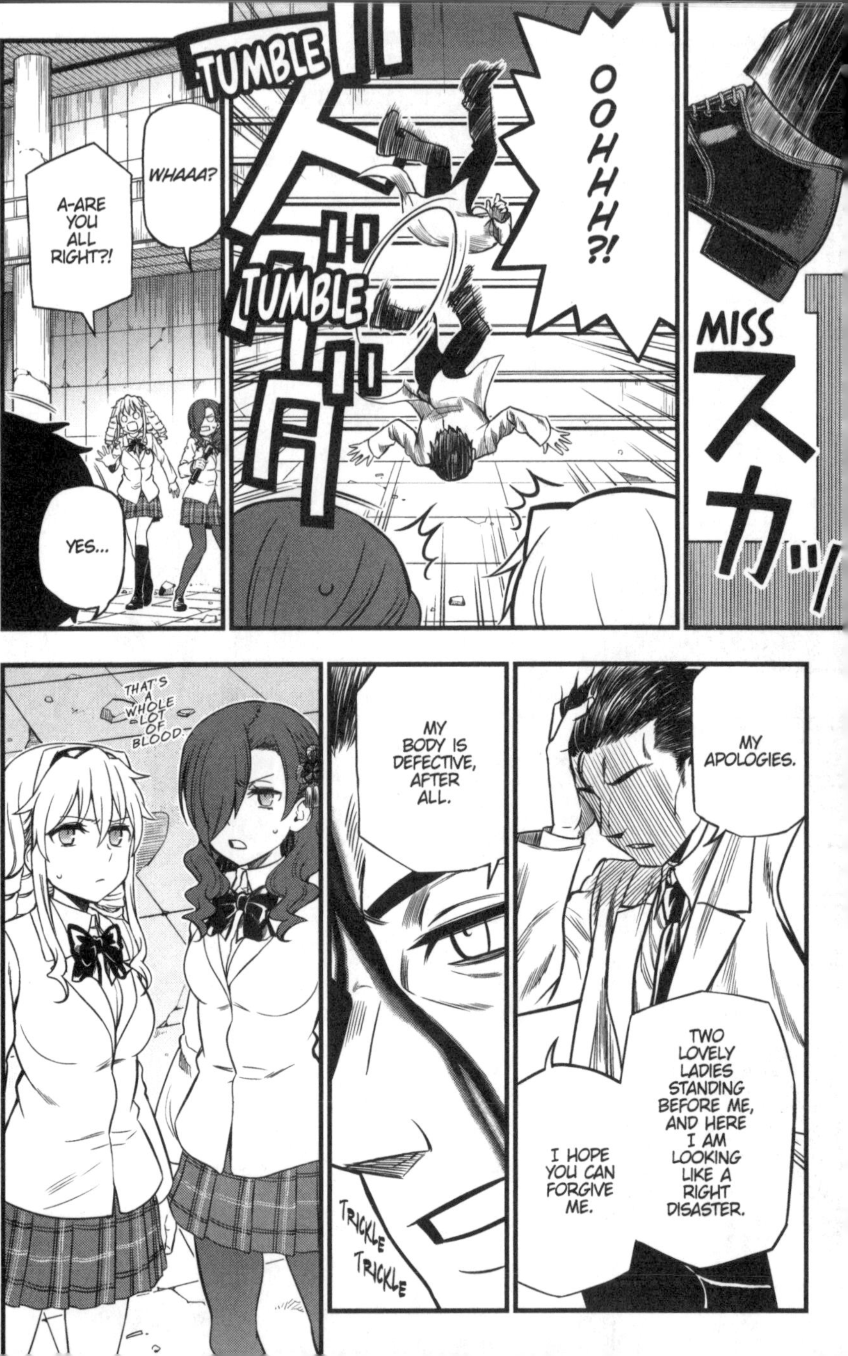
MISS
スカッ
OOHHHH?!
TUMBLE
TUMBLE
WHAAA?
A-ARE YOU ALL RIGHT?!
YES...
MY APOLOGIES.
TWO LOVELY LADIES STANDING BEFORE ME, AND HERE I AM LOOKING LIKE A RIGHT DISASTER.
I HOPE YOU CAN FORGIVE ME.
MY BODY IS DEFECTIVE, AFTER ALL.
TRICKLE TRICKLE
THAT'S A WHOLE LOT OF BLOOD.

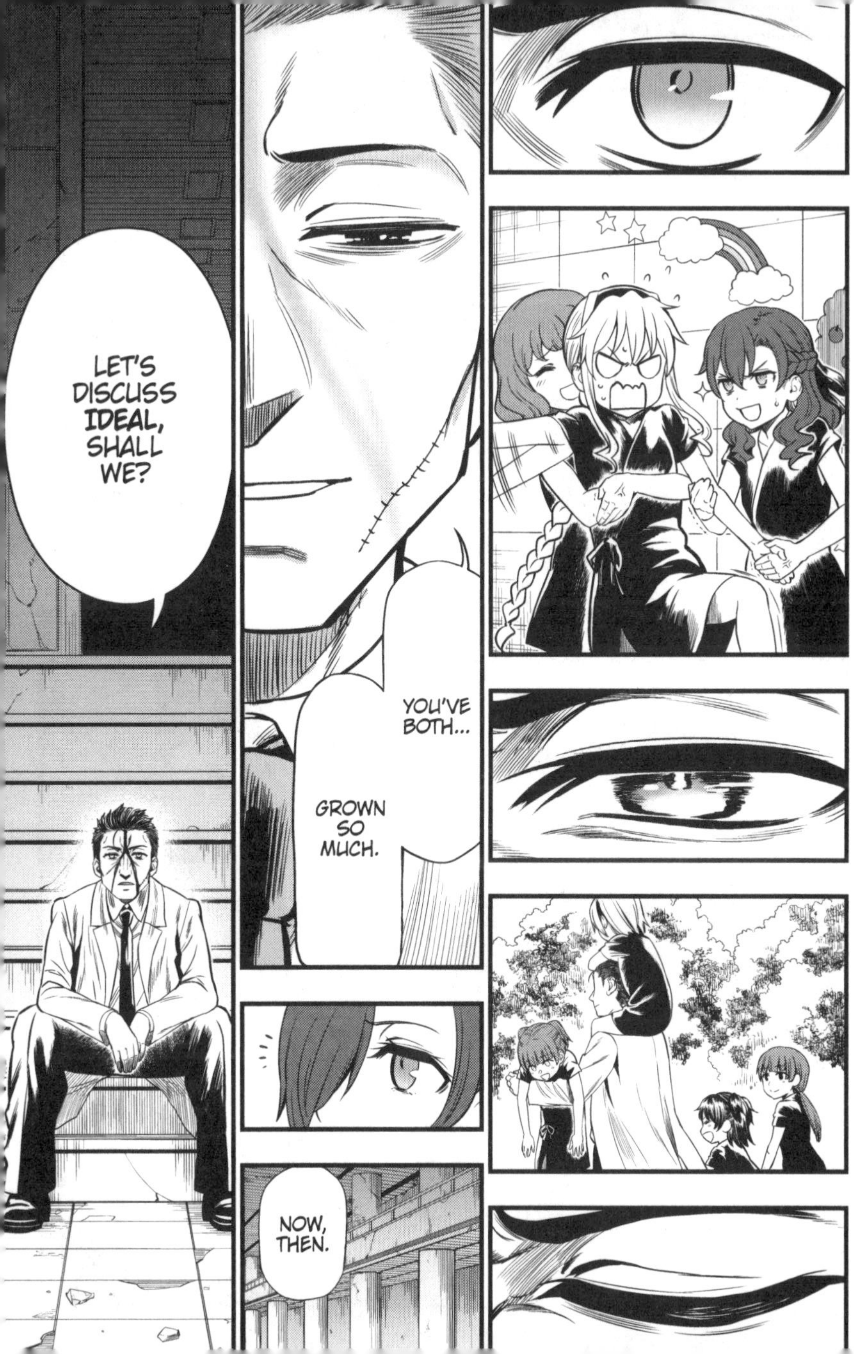

LET'S DISCUSS IDEAL, SHALL WE?
YOU'VE BOTH...
GROWN SO MUCH.
NOW, THEN.

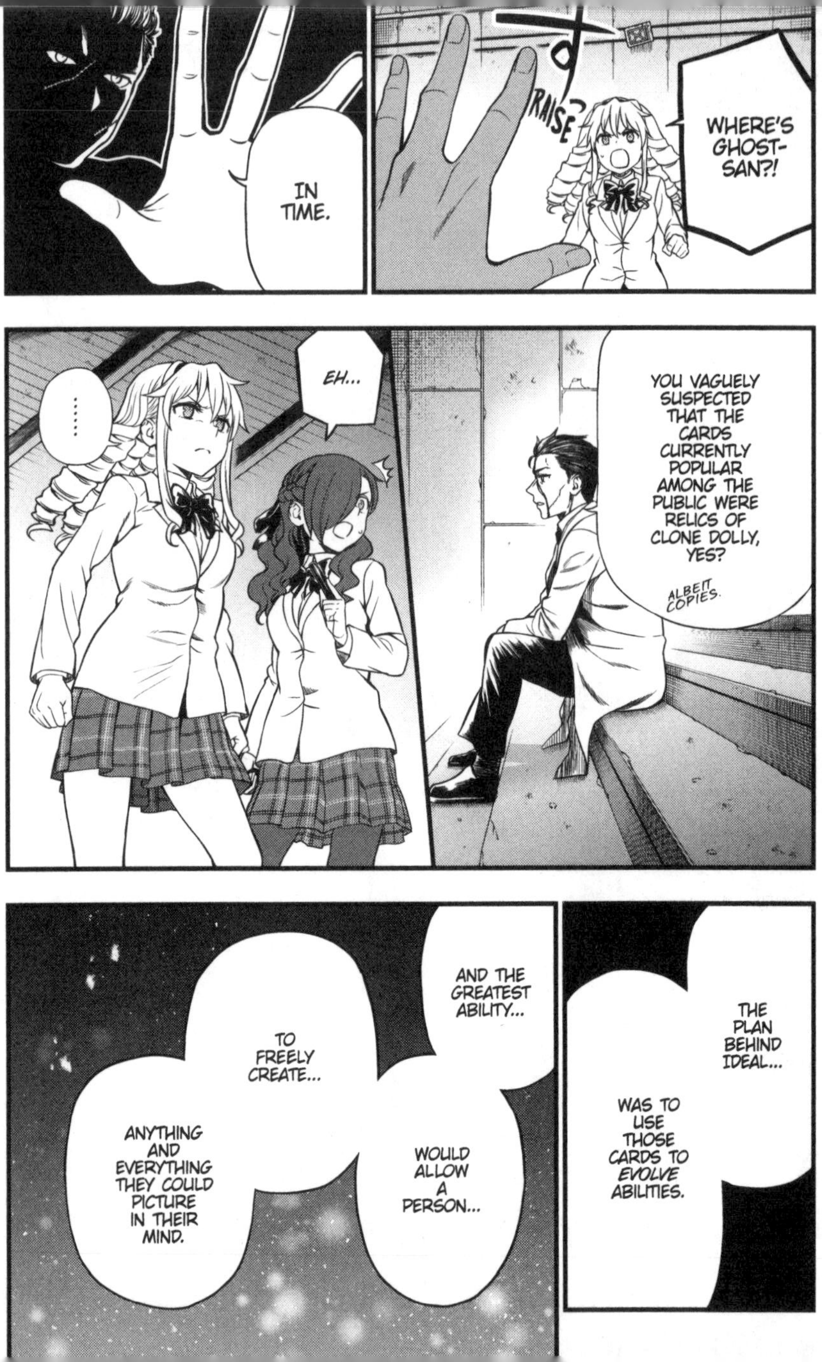
WHERE'S GHOST-SAN?!
RAISE
IN TIME.
YOU VAGUELY SUSPECTED THAT THE CARDS CURRENTLY POPULAR AMONG THE PUBLIC WERE RELICS OF CLONE DOLLY, YES?
ALBEIT COPIES.
EH...
......
THE PLAN BEHIND IDEAL...
WAS TO USE THOSE CARDS TO *EVOLVE* ABILITIES.
AND THE GREATEST ABILITY...
WOULD ALLOW A PERSON...
TO FREELY CREATE...
ANYTHING AND EVERYTHING THEY COULD PICTURE IN THEIR MIND.

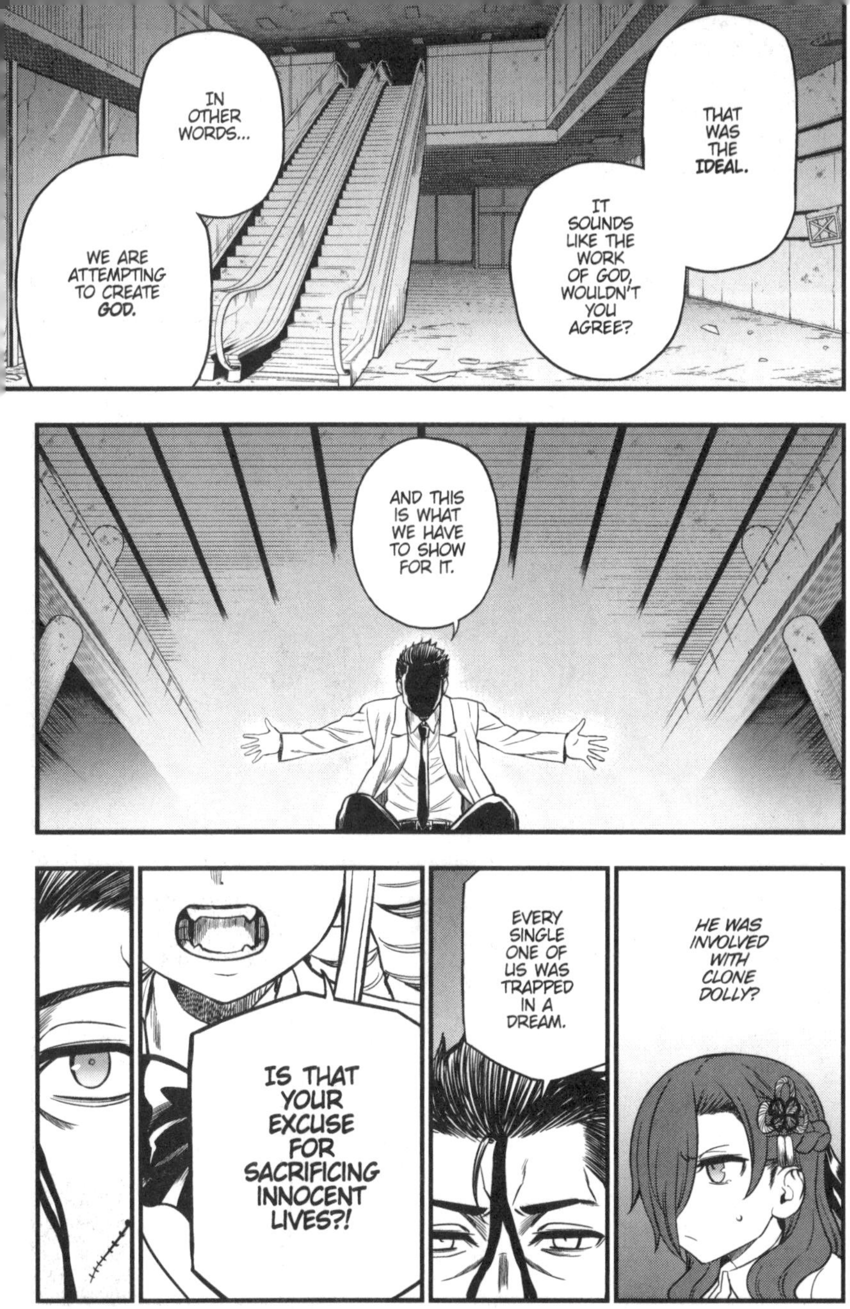
IN OTHER WORDS...
WE ARE ATTEMPTING TO CREATE GOD.
THAT WAS THE IDEAL.
IT SOUNDS LIKE THE WORK OF GOD, WOULDN'T YOU AGREE?
AND THIS IS WHAT WE HAVE TO SHOW FOR IT.
HE WAS INVOLVED WITH CLONE DOLLY?
EVERY SINGLE ONE OF US WAS TRAPPED IN A DREAM.
IS THAT YOUR EXCUSE FOR SACRIFICING INNOCENT LIVES?!

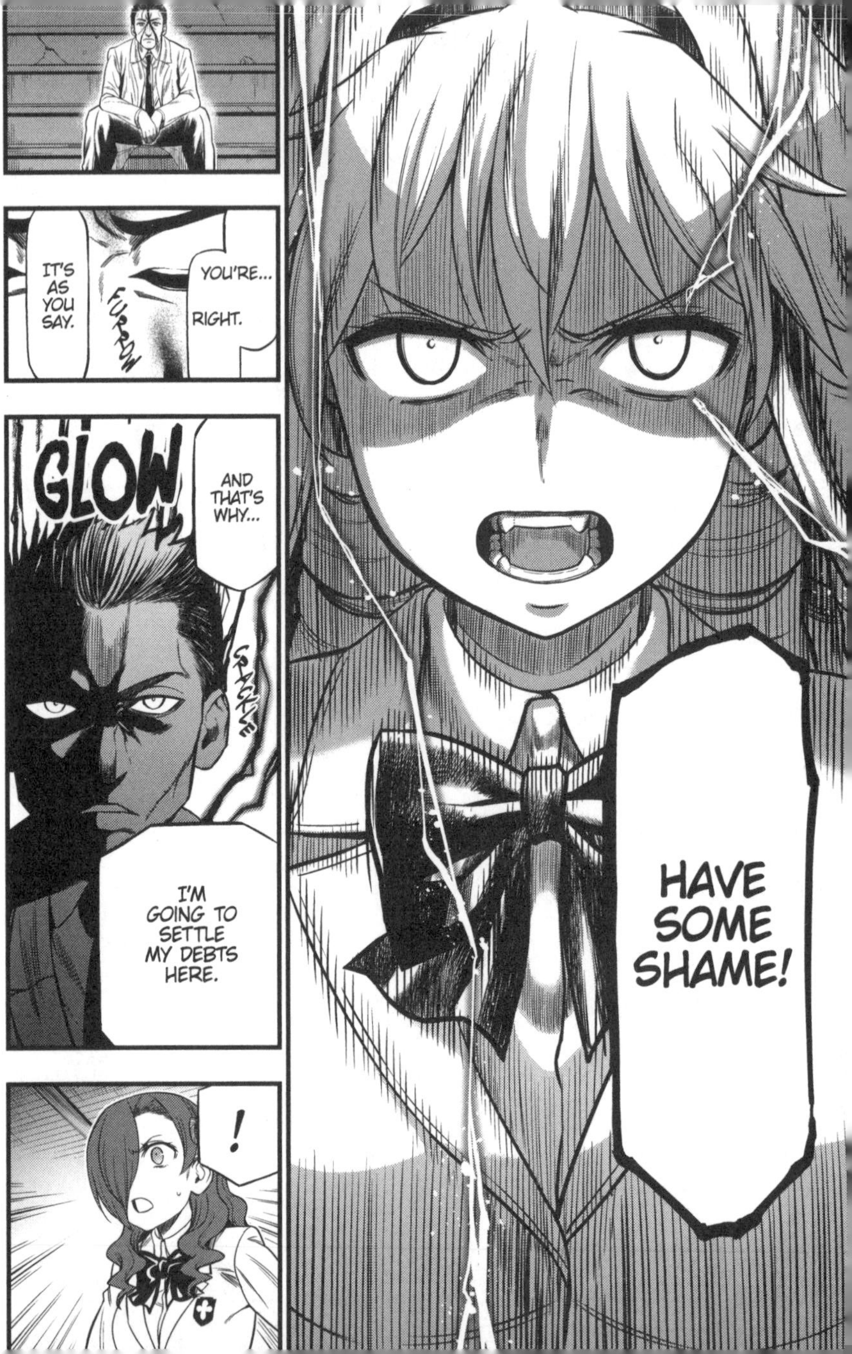
HAVE SOME SHAME!
YOU'RE... RIGHT.
FURROW
IT'S AS YOU SAY.
GLOW
AND THAT'S WHY...
CRACKLE
I'M GOING TO SETTLE MY DEBTS HERE.
!

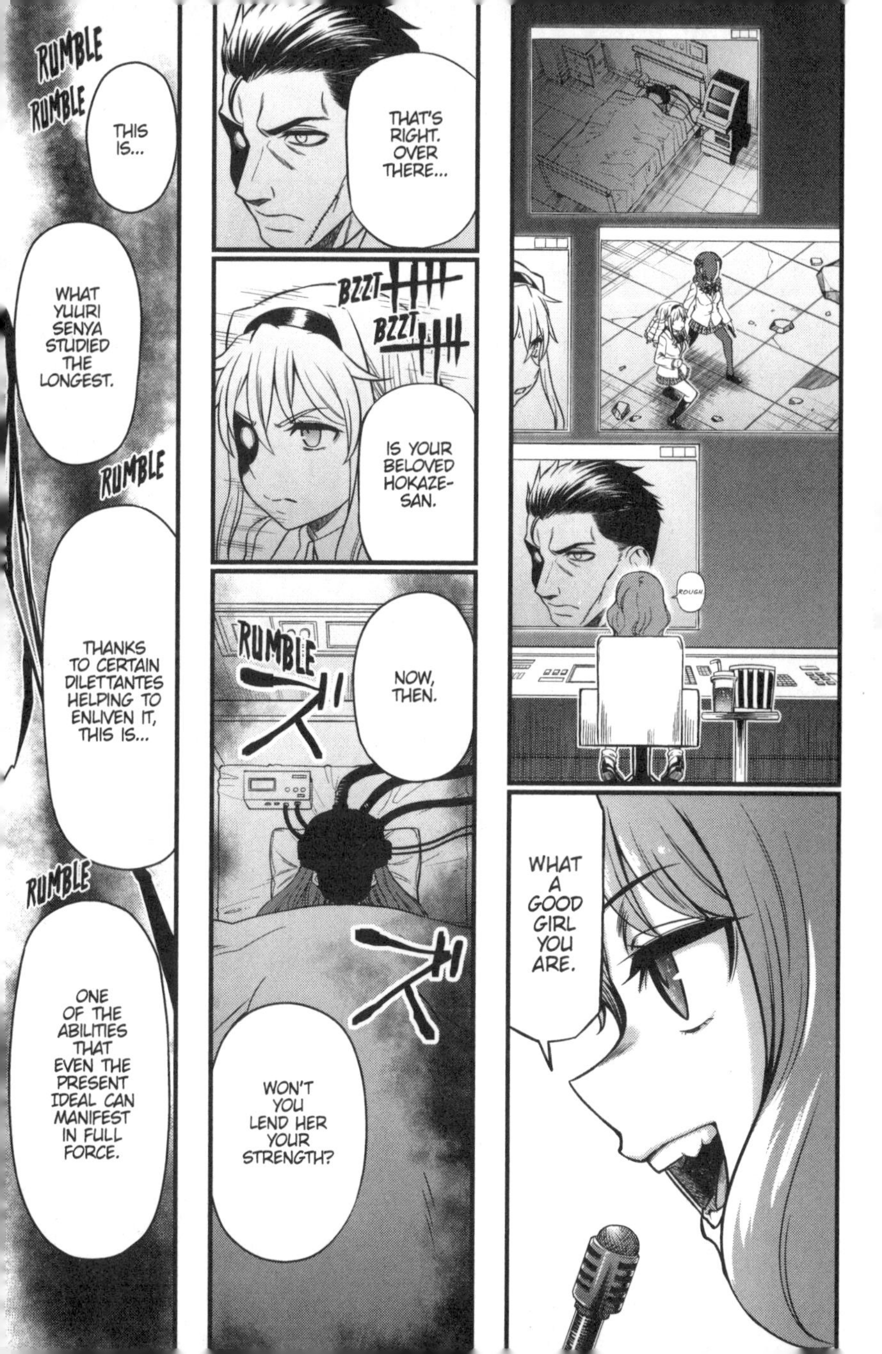
ROUGH
WHAT A GOOD GIRL YOU ARE.
THAT'S RIGHT. OVER THERE...
BZZT
BZZT
IS YOUR BELOVED HOKAZE-SAN.
RUMBLE
NOW, THEN.
WON'T YOU LEND HER YOUR STRENGTH?
RUMBLE
RUMBLE
THIS IS...
WHAT YUURI SENYA STUDIED THE LONGEST.
RUMBLE
THANKS TO CERTAIN DILETTANTES HELPING TO ENLIVEN IT, THIS IS...
RUMBLE
ONE OF THE ABILITIES THAT EVEN THE PRESENT IDEAL CAN MANIFEST IN FULL FORCE.

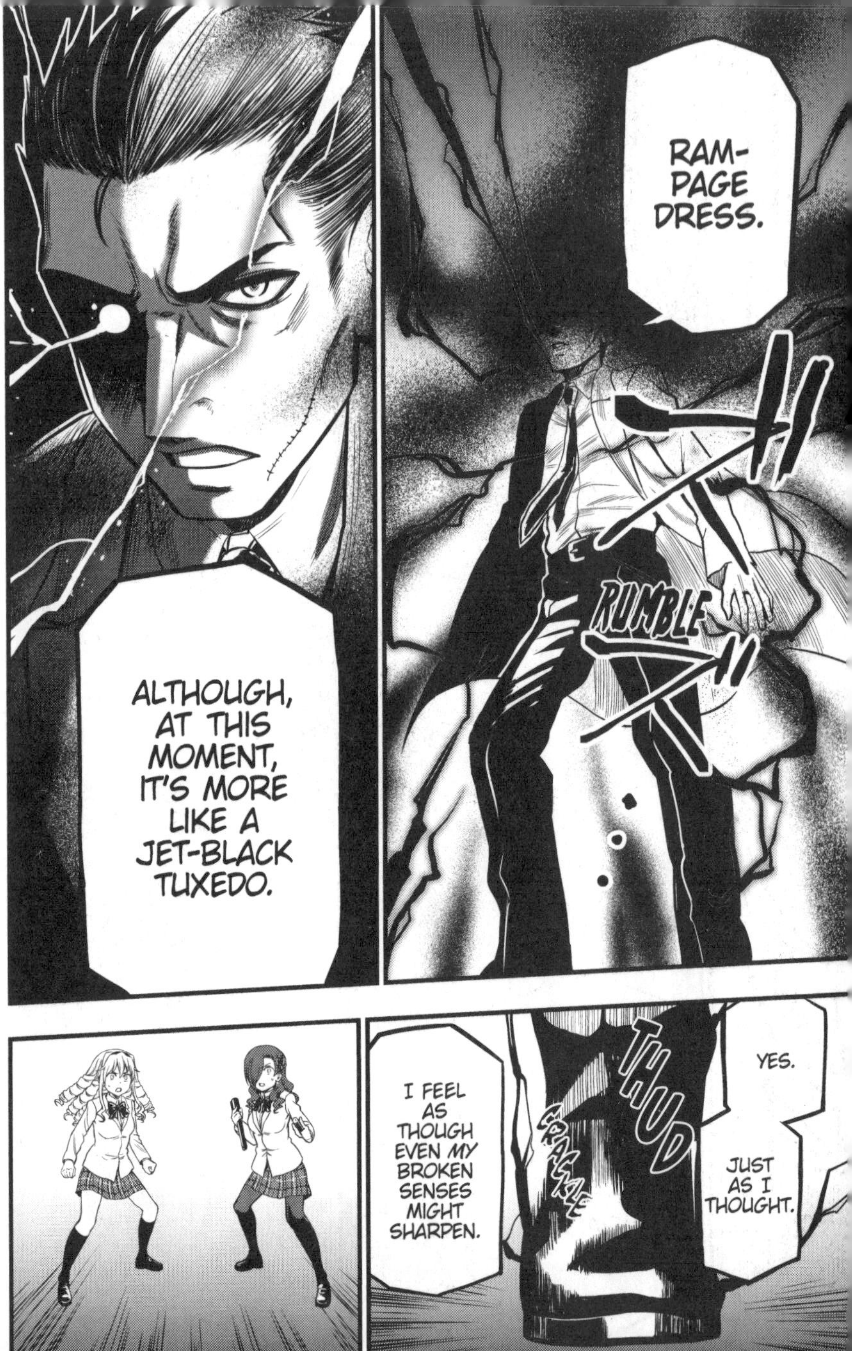
RAM-
PAGE
DRESS.
RUMBLE
ALTHOUGH, AT THIS MOMENT, IT'S MORE LIKE A JET-BLACK TUXEDO.
YES.
JUST AS I THOUGHT.
THUD
CRACKLE
I FEEL AS THOUGH EVEN MY BROKEN SENSES MIGHT SHARPEN.

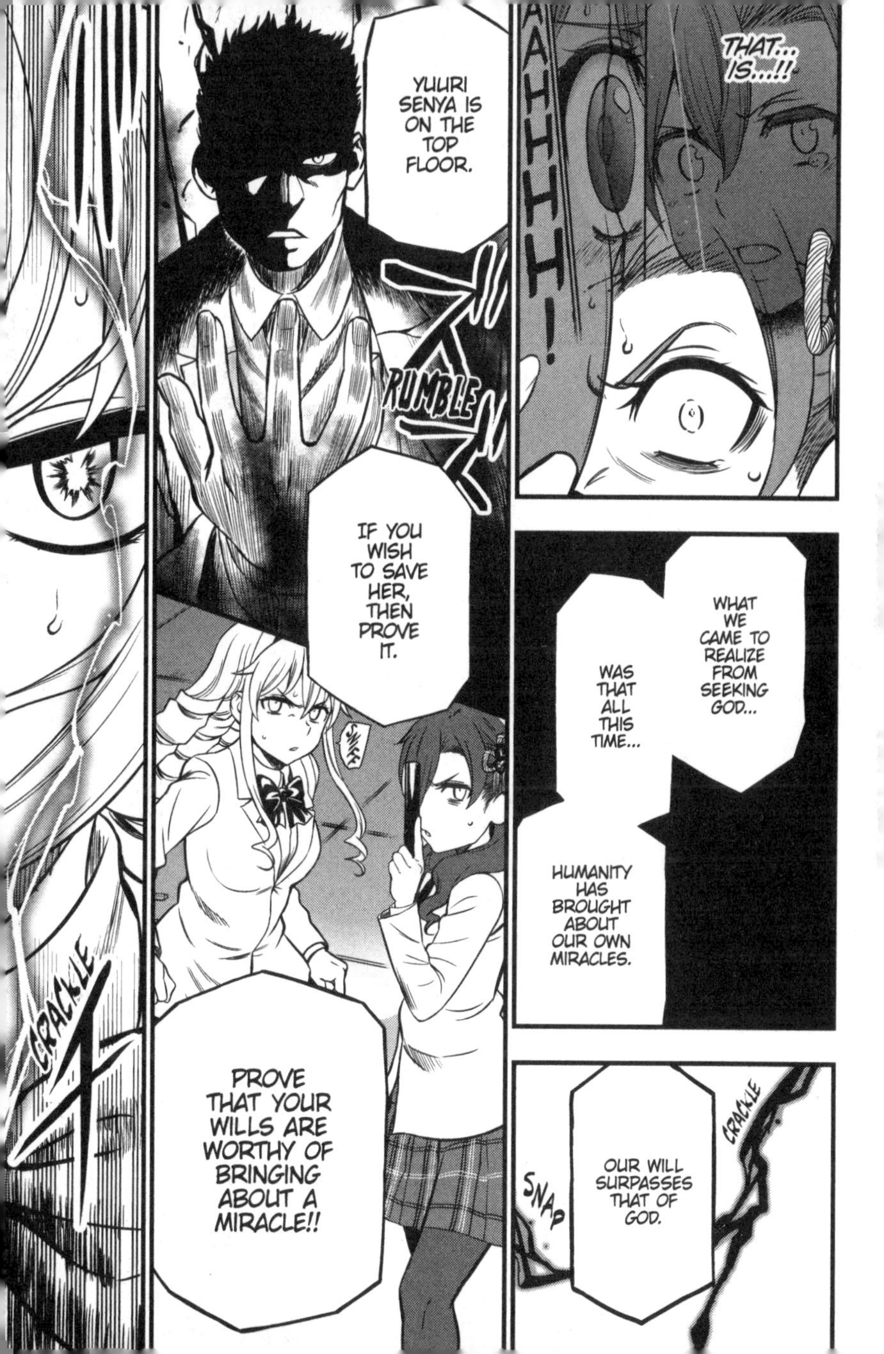
AAHHHH!
THAT... IS...!!
WHAT WE CAME TO REALIZE FROM SEEKING GOD...
WAS THAT ALL THIS TIME...
HUMANITY HAS BROUGHT ABOUT OUR OWN MIRACLES.
CRACKLE
OUR WILL SURPASSES THAT OF GOD.
SNAP
YUURI SENYA IS ON THE TOP FLOOR.
RUMBLE
IF YOU WISH TO SAVE HER, THEN PROVE IT.
SNIFF
PROVE THAT YOUR WILLS ARE WORTHY OF BRINGING ABOUT A MIRACLE!!
CRACKLE

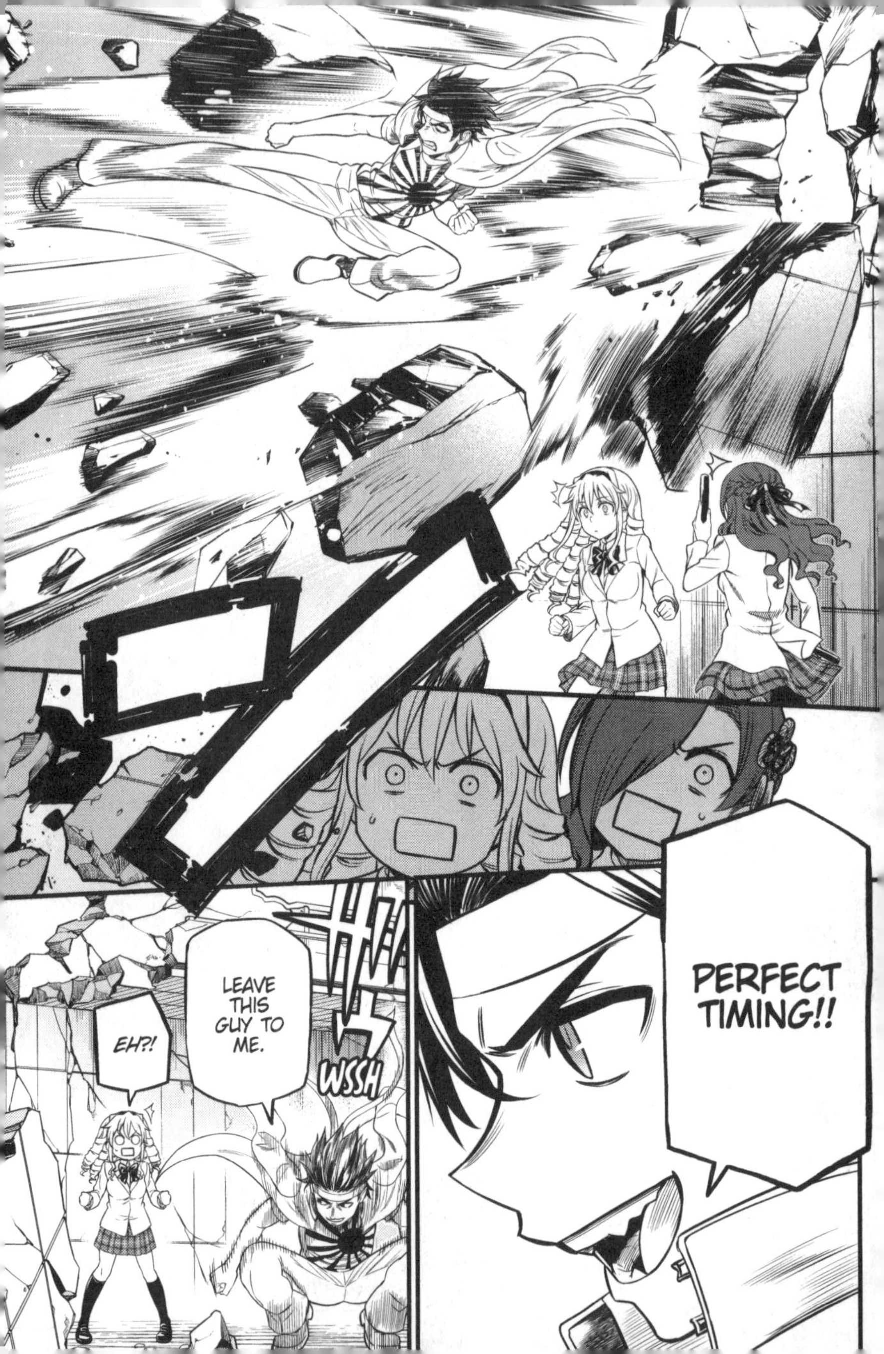
PERFECT TIMING!!
LEAVE THIS GUY TO ME.
WSSH
EH?!

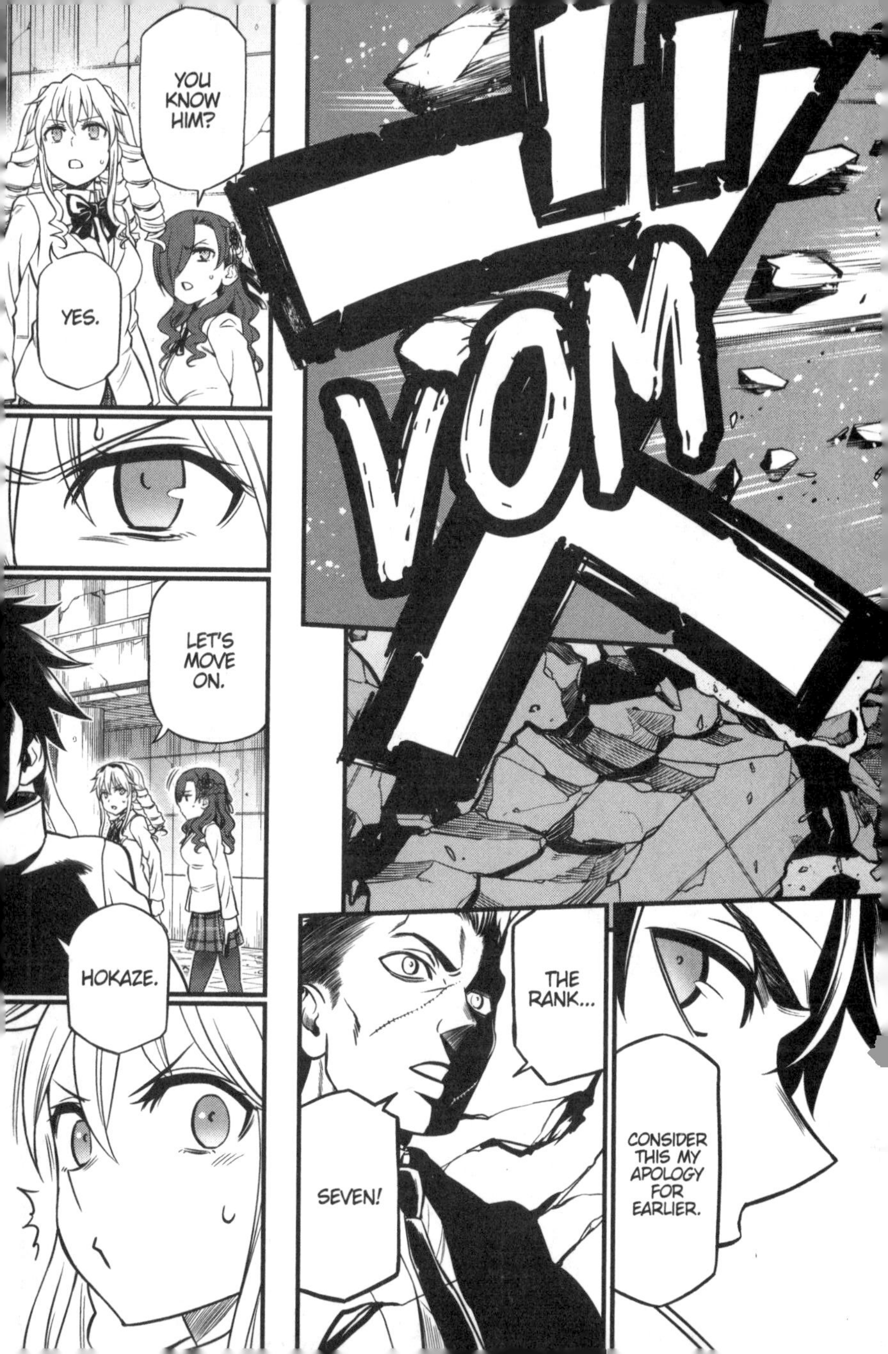
VOM
CONSIDER THIS MY APOLOGY FOR EARLIER.
THE RANK...
SEVEN!
YOU KNOW HIM?
YES.
LET'S MOVE ON.
HOKAZE.

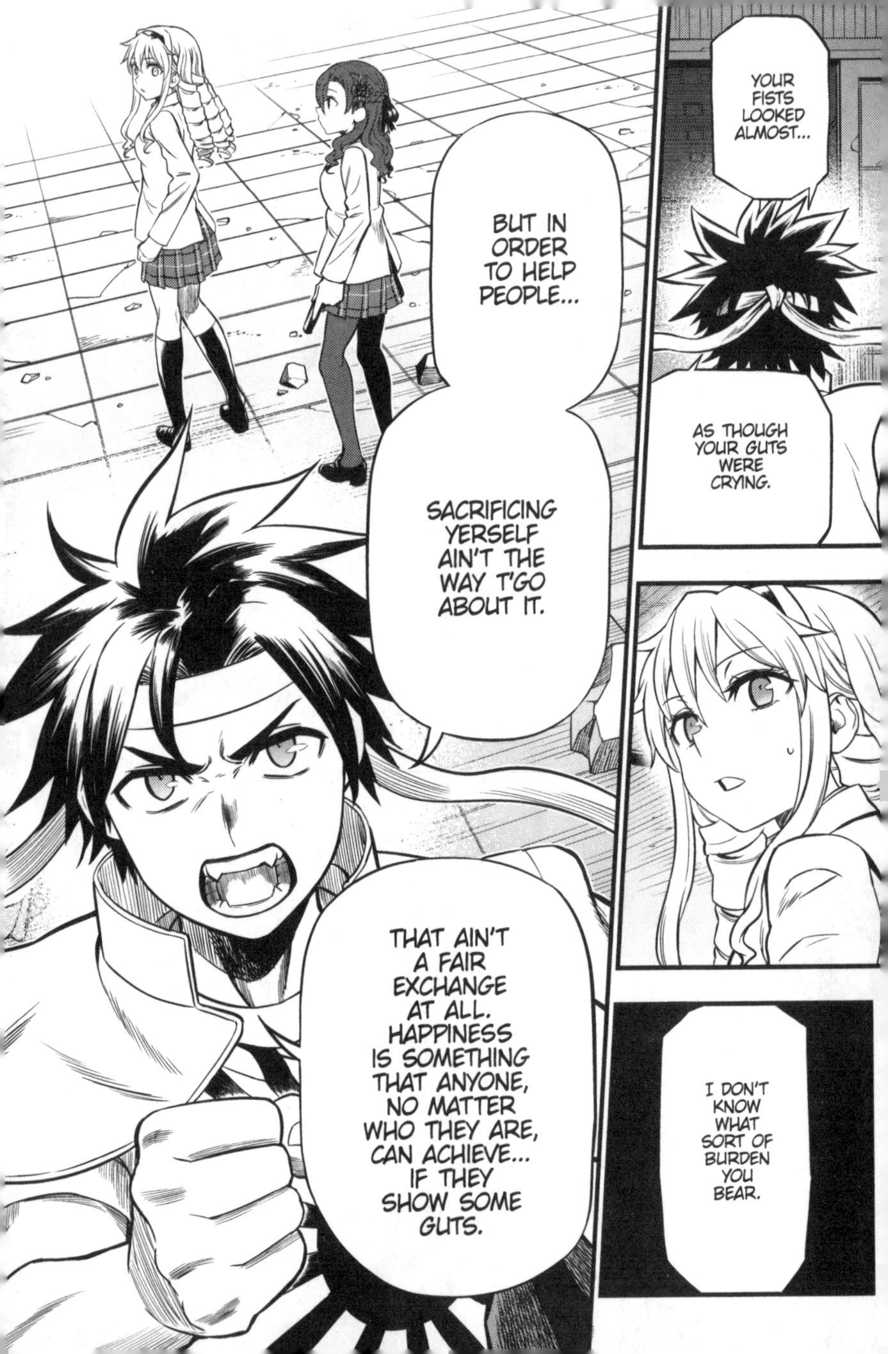
YOUR FISTS LOOKED ALMOST...
AS THOUGH YOUR GUTS WERE CRYING.
I DON'T KNOW WHAT SORT OF BURDEN YOU BEAR.
BUT IN ORDER TO HELP PEOPLE...
SACRIFICING YERSELF AIN'T THE WAY T'GO ABOUT IT.
THAT AIN'T A FAIR EXCHANGE AT ALL. HAPPINESS IS SOMETHING THAT ANYONE, NO MATTER WHO THEY ARE, CAN ACHIEVE... IF THEY SHOW SOME GUTS.

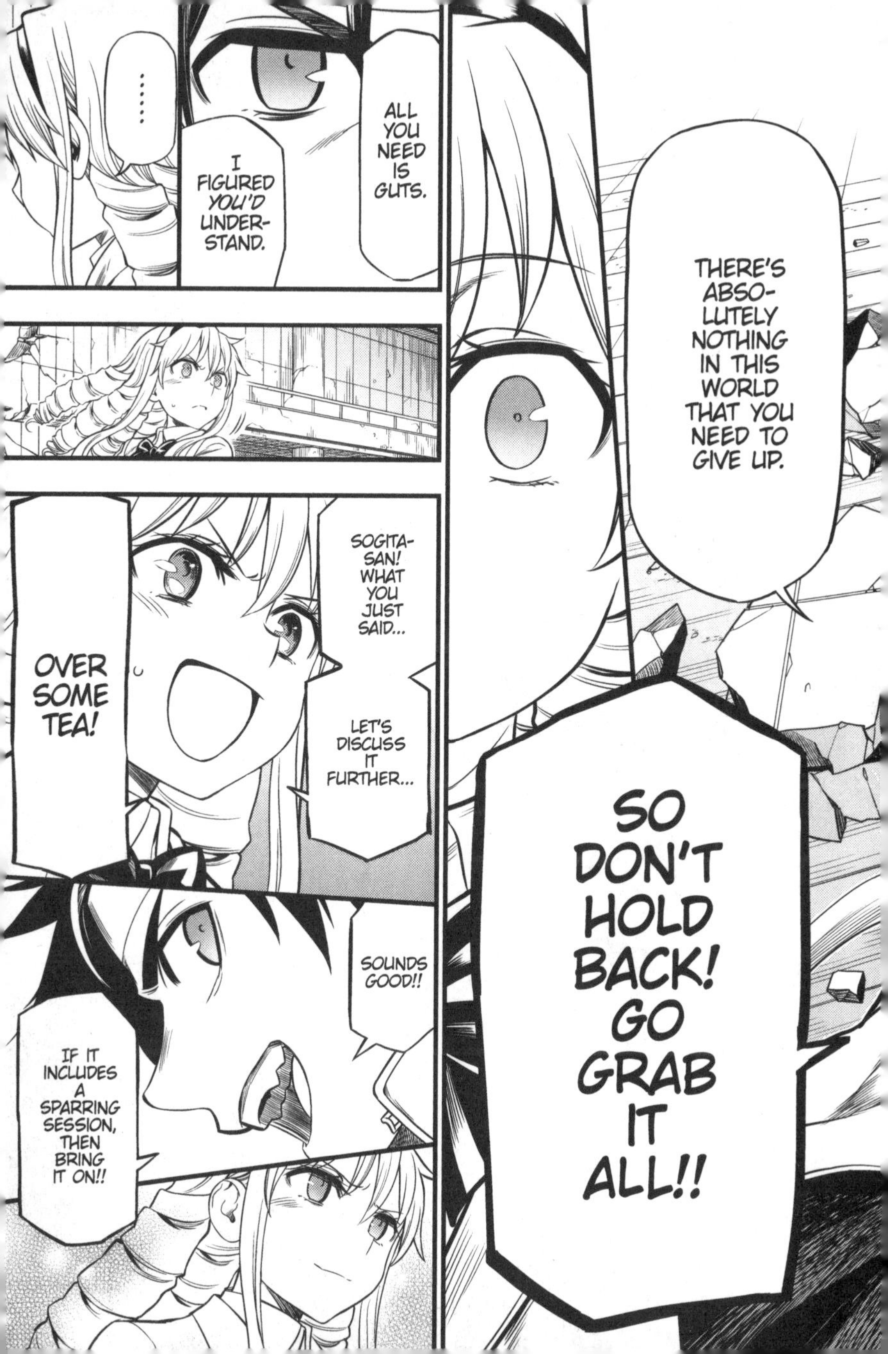
THERE'S ABSO-LUTELY NOTHING IN THIS WORLD THAT YOU NEED TO GIVE UP.
SO DON'T HOLD BACK! GO GRAB IT ALL!!
ALL YOU NEED IS GUTS.
I FIGURED *YOU'D* UNDER-STAND.
......
SOGITA-SAN! WHAT YOU JUST SAID...
LET'S DISCUSS IT FURTHER...
OVER SOME TEA!
SOUNDS GOOD!!
IF IT INCLUDES A SPARRING SESSION, THEN BRING IT ON!!

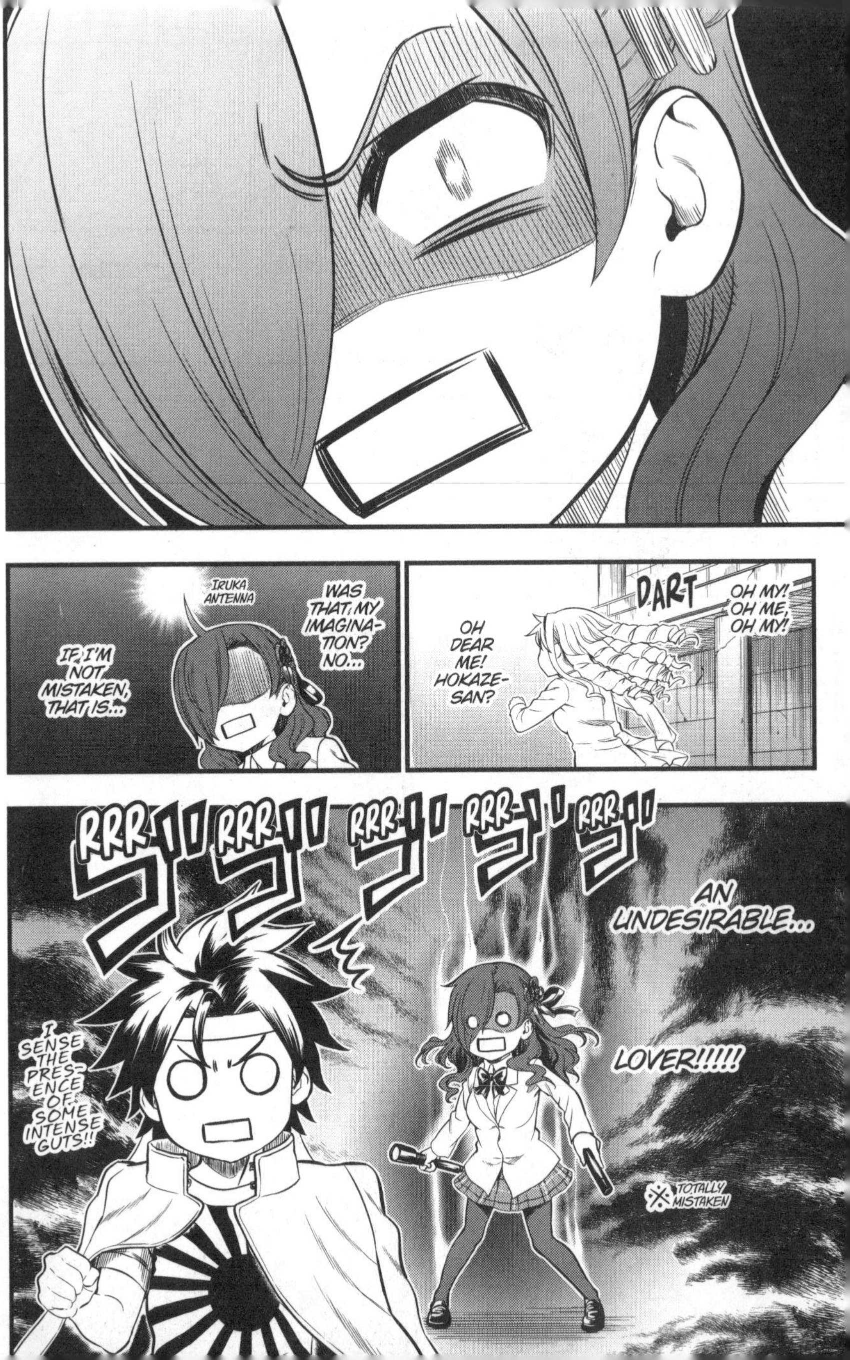
DART
OH MY! OH ME, OH MY!
OH DEAR ME! HOKAZE-SAN?
WAS THAT MY IMAGINATION? NO...
IRUKA ANTENNA
IF I'M NOT MISTAKEN, THAT IS...
RRR RRR RRR RRR RRR
AN UNDESIRABLE...
LOVER!!!!!
I SENSE THE PRESENCE OF SOME INTENSE GUTS!!
※ TOTALLY MISTAKEN

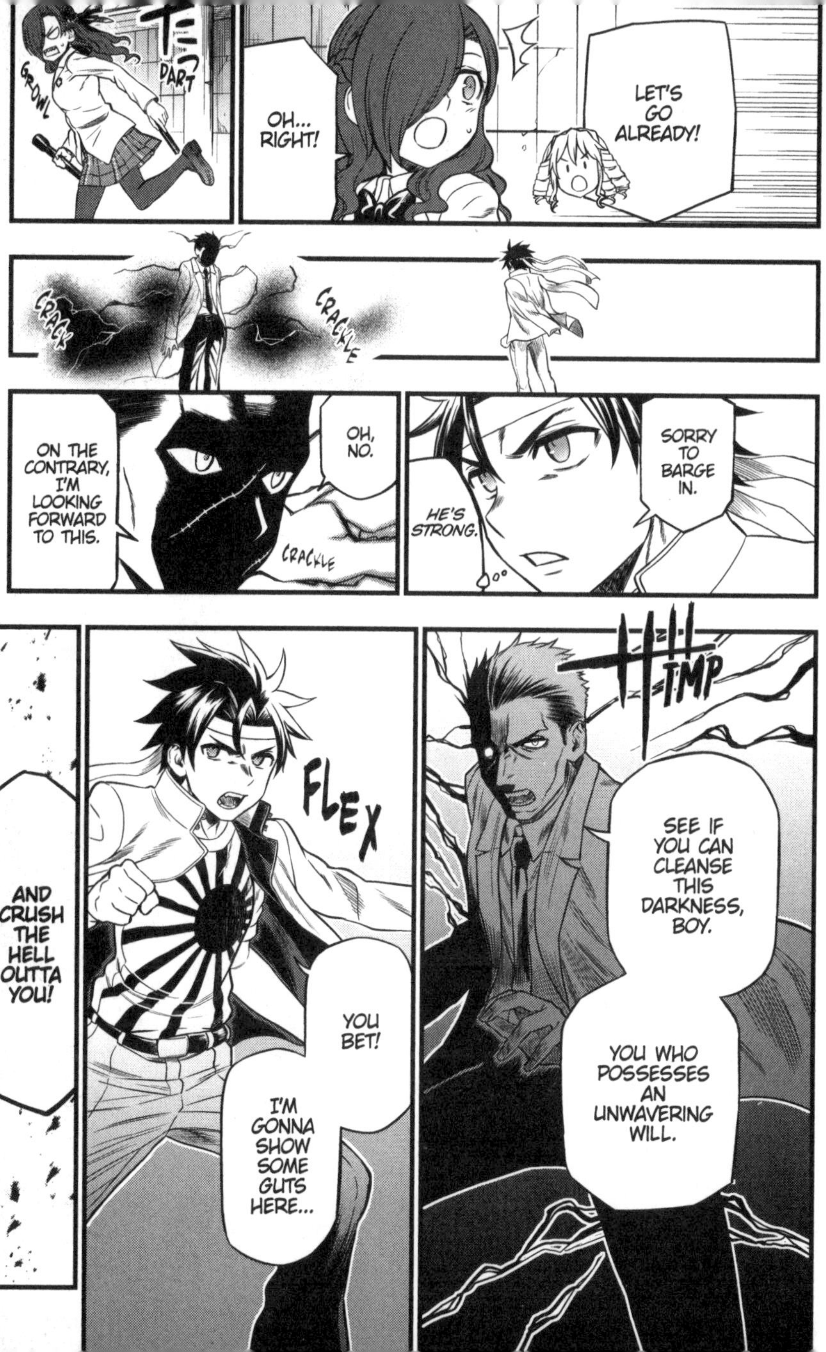
GROWL
DART
OH... RIGHT!
LET'S GO ALREADY!
CRACK
CRACKLE
ON THE CONTRARY, I'M LOOKING FORWARD TO THIS.
OH, NO.
CRACKLE
SORRY TO BARGE IN.
HE'S STRONG.
FLEX
TMP
SEE IF YOU CAN CLEANSE THIS DARKNESS, BOY.
YOU WHO POSSESSES AN UNWAVERING WILL.
YOU BET!
I'M GONNA SHOW SOME GUTS HERE...
AND CRUSH THE HELL OUTTA YOU!

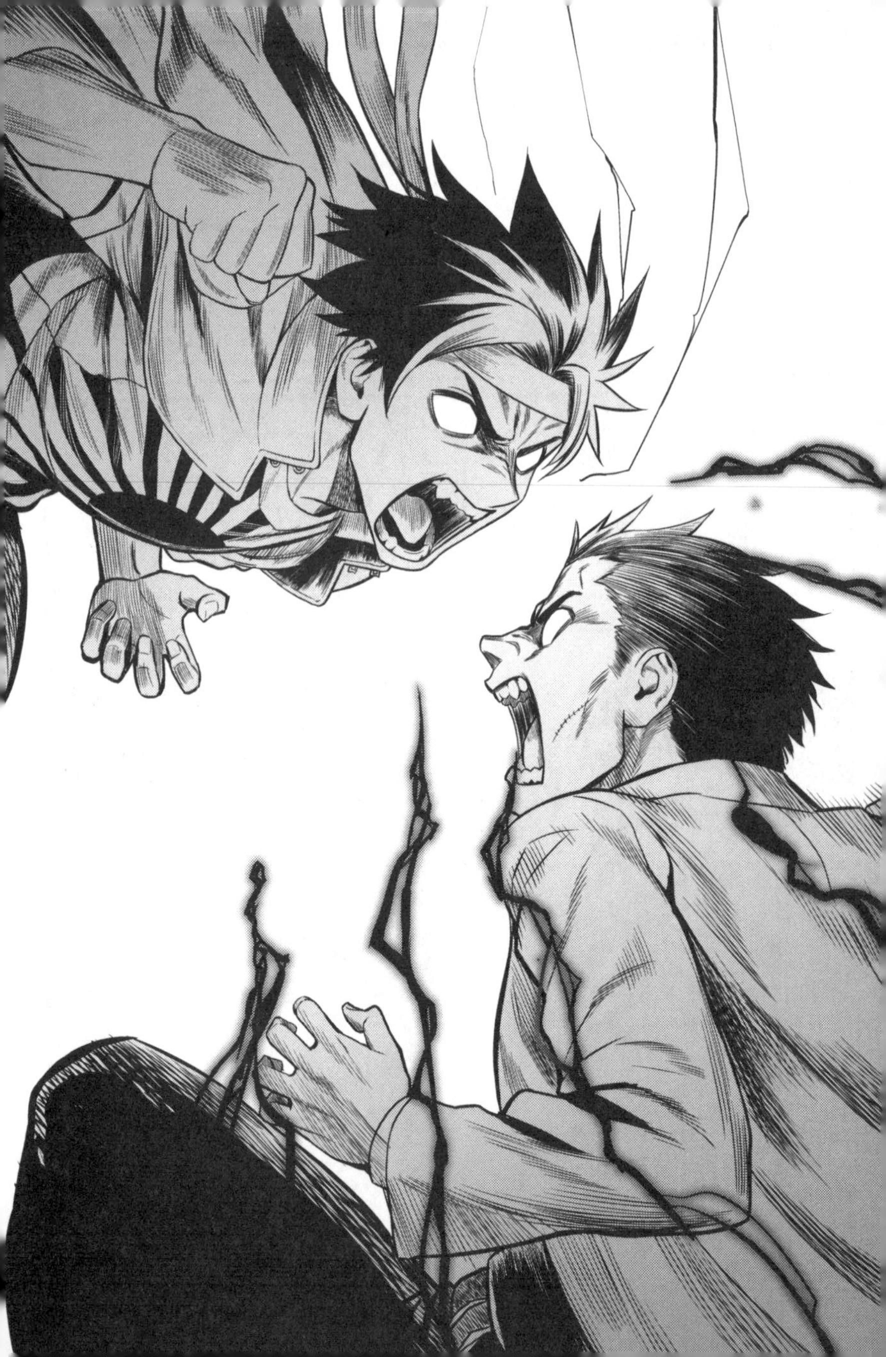

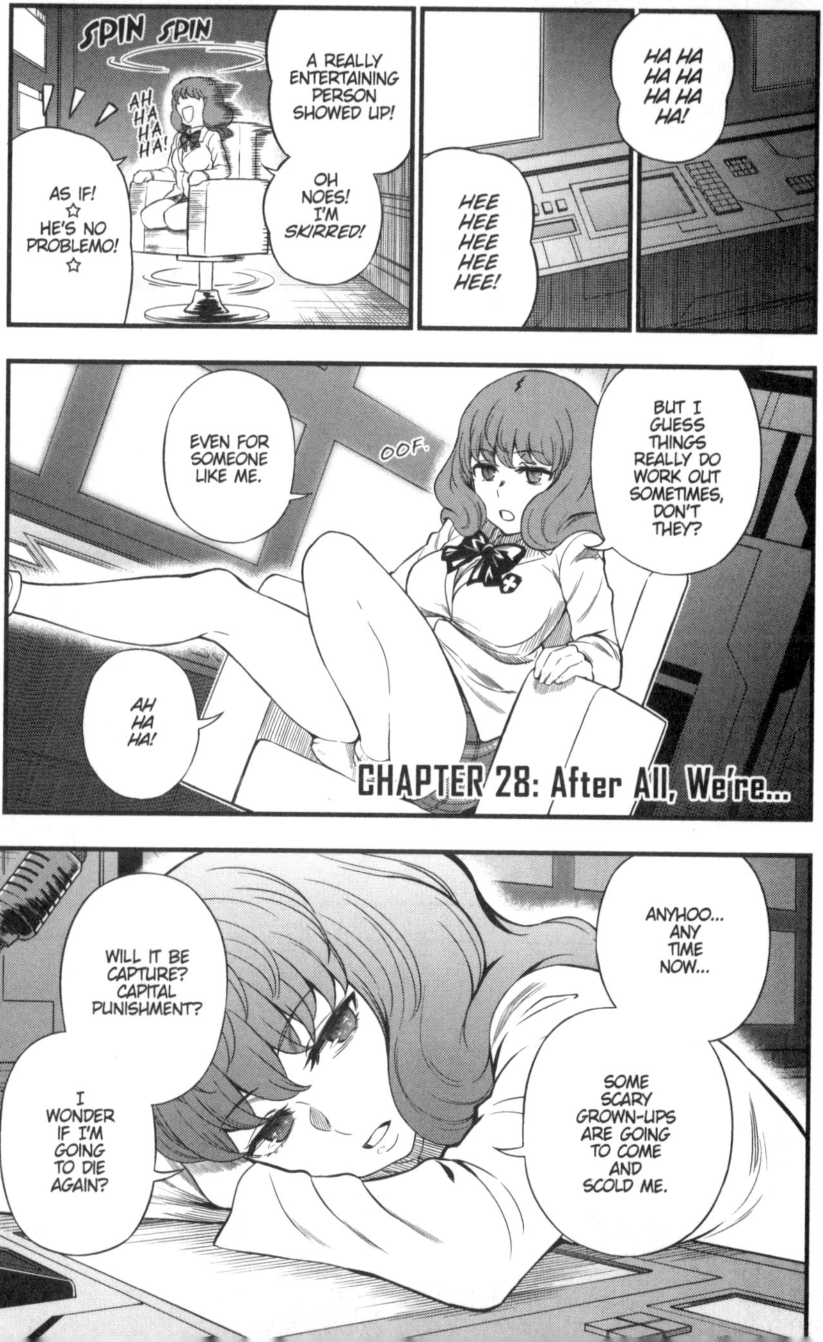
HA HA HA HA HA HA HA!
HEE HEE HEE HEE HEE!
SPIN SPIN
A REALLY ENTERTAINING PERSON SHOWED UP!
AH HA HA HA!
OH NOES! I'M SKIRRED!
AS IF! ☆ HE'S NO PROBLEMO! ☆
BUT I GUESS THINGS REALLY DO WORK OUT SOMETIMES, DON'T THEY?
OOF.
EVEN FOR SOMEONE LIKE ME.
AH HA HA!
CHAPTER 28: After All, We're...
ANYHOO... ANY TIME NOW...
SOME SCARY GROWN-UPS ARE GOING TO COME AND SCOLD ME.
WILL IT BE CAPTURE? CAPITAL PUNISHMENT?
I WONDER IF I'M GOING TO DIE AGAIN?

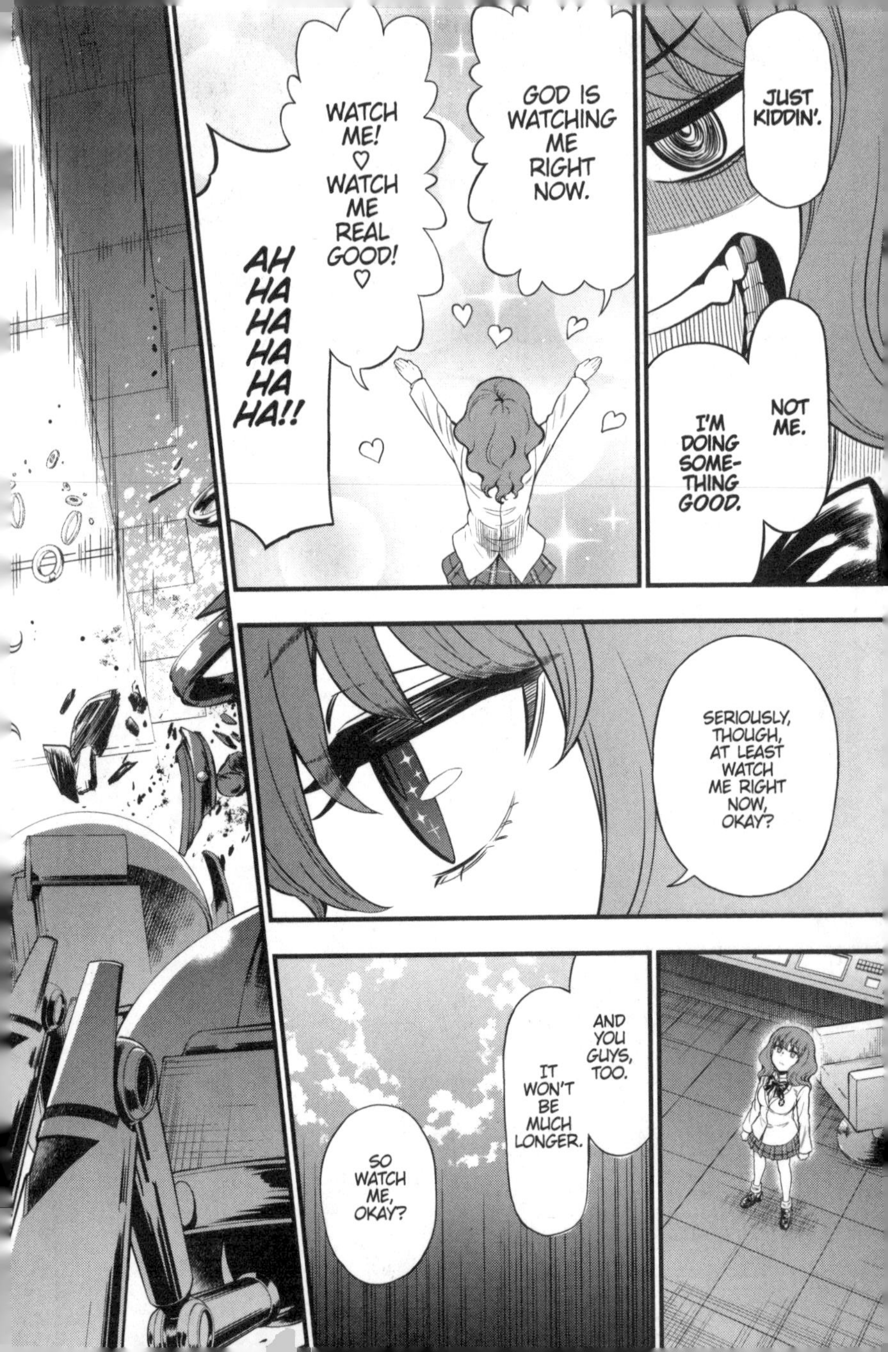
JUST KIDDIN'.
NOT ME.
I'M DOING SOMETHING GOOD.
GOD IS WATCHING ME RIGHT NOW.
WATCH ME! ♡ WATCH ME REAL GOOD! ♡
AH HA HA HA HA HA!!
SERIOUSLY, THOUGH, AT LEAST WATCH ME RIGHT NOW, OKAY?
AND YOU GUYS, TOO.
IT WON'T BE MUCH LONGER.
SO WATCH ME, OKAY?

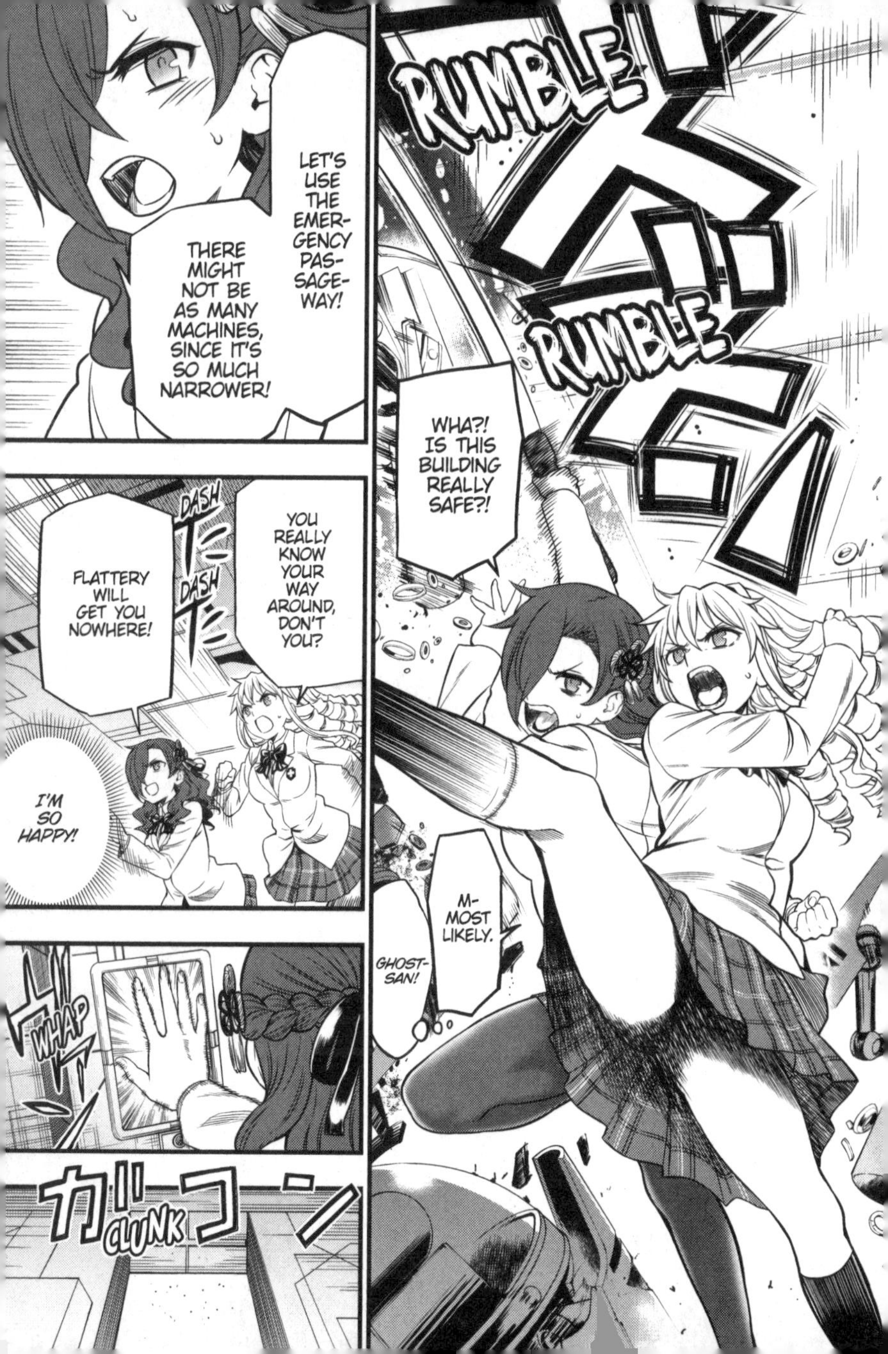
RUMBLE
RUMBLE
WHA?! IS THIS BUILDING REALLY SAFE?!
M-MOST LIKELY.
GHOST-SAN!
LET'S USE THE EMERGENCY PAS-SAGE-WAY!
THERE MIGHT NOT BE AS MANY MACHINES, SINCE IT'S SO MUCH NARROWER!
YOU REALLY KNOW YOUR WAY AROUND, DON'T YOU?
DASH
DASH
FLATTERY WILL GET YOU NOWHERE!
I'M SO HAPPY!
WHAP
CLUNK

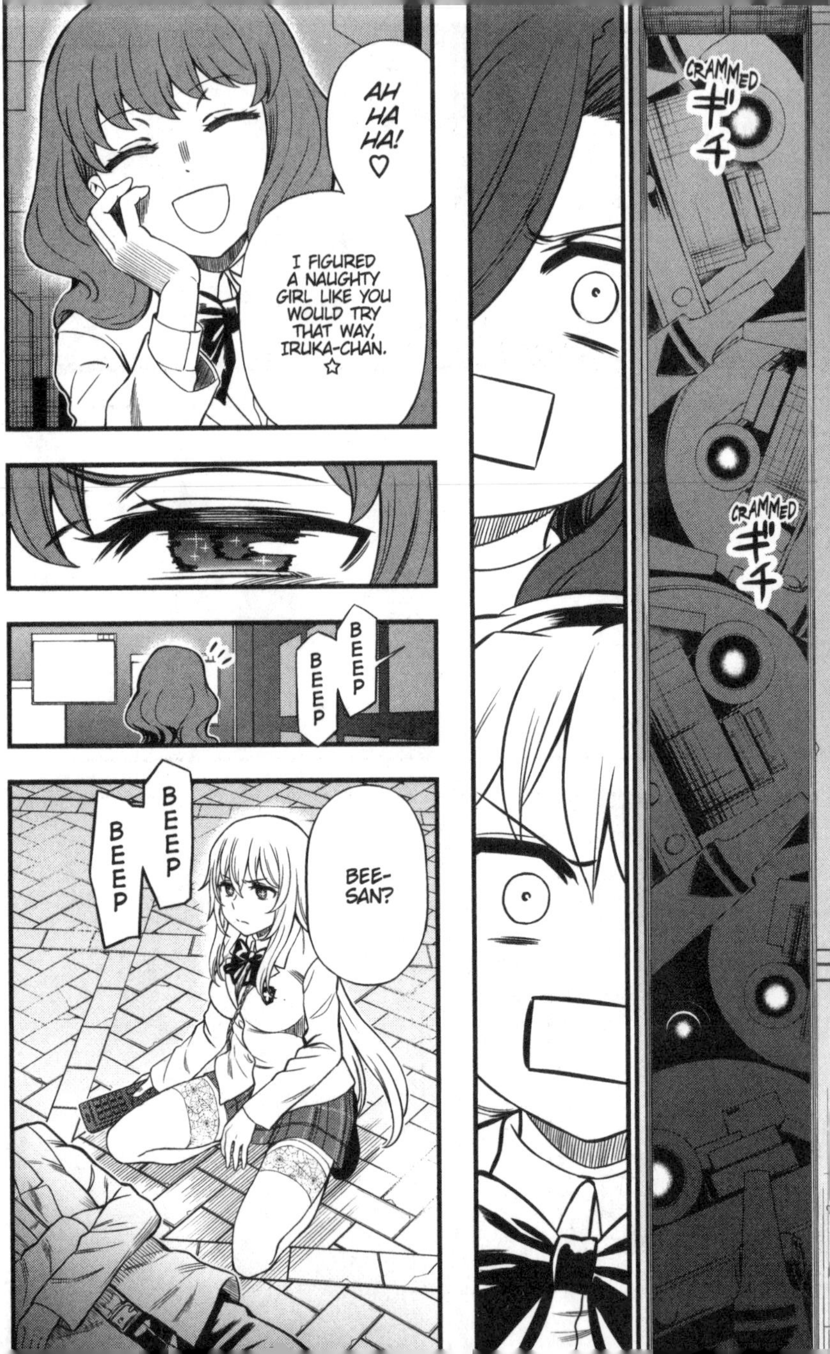
CRAMMED ギチ
CRAMMED ギチ
AH HA HA! ♡
I FIGURED A NAUGHTY GIRL LIKE YOU WOULD TRY THAT WAY, IRUKA-CHAN. ☆
BEEP BEEP
BEEP BEEP
BEE-SAN?

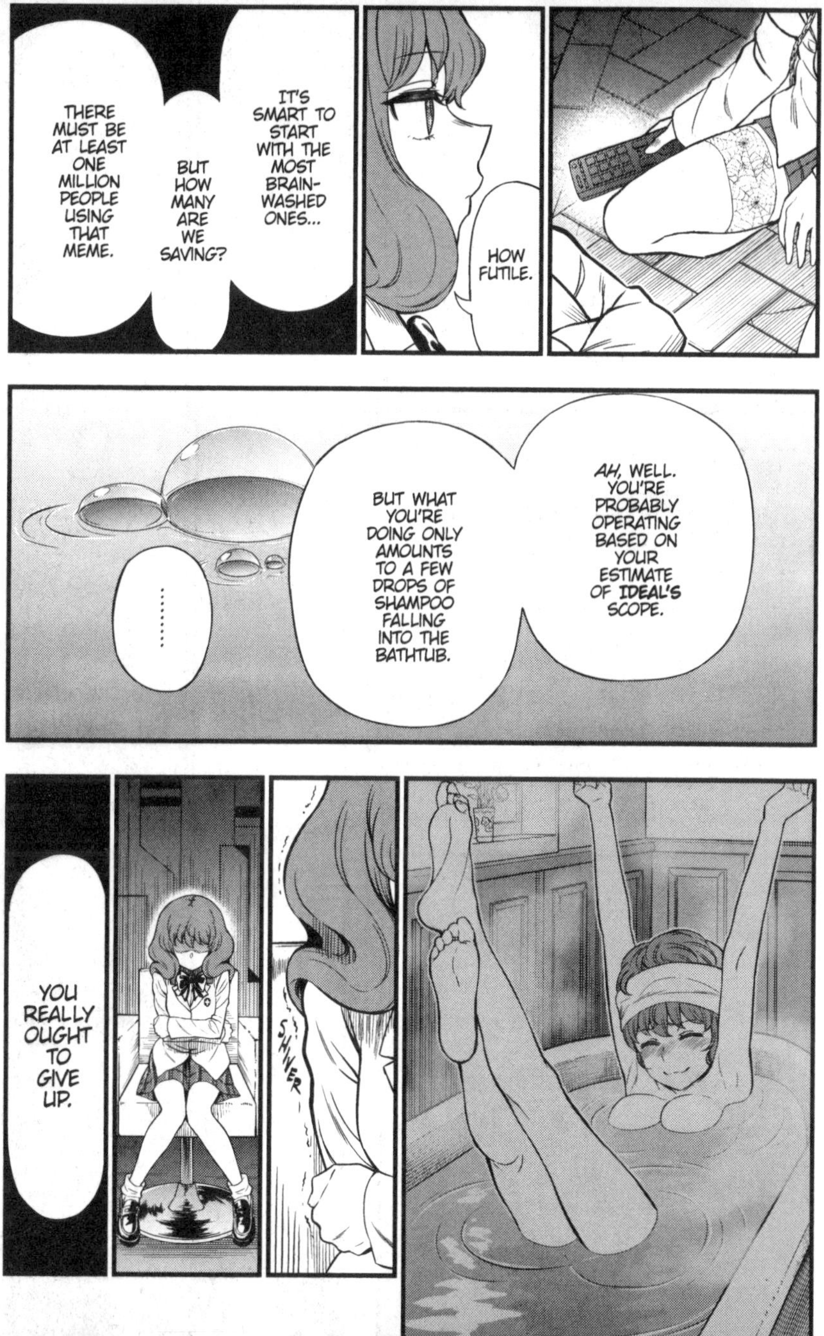

HOW FUTILE.
IT'S SMART TO START WITH THE MOST BRAIN-WASHED ONES...
BUT HOW MANY ARE WE SAVING?
THERE MUST BE AT LEAST ONE MILLION PEOPLE USING THAT MEME.
AH, WELL. YOU'RE PROBABLY OPERATING BASED ON YOUR ESTIMATE OF **IDEAL'S** SCOPE.
BUT WHAT YOU'RE DOING ONLY AMOUNTS TO A FEW DROPS OF SHAMPOO FALLING INTO THE BATHTUB.
....
SHIVER
YOU REALLY OUGHT TO GIVE UP.

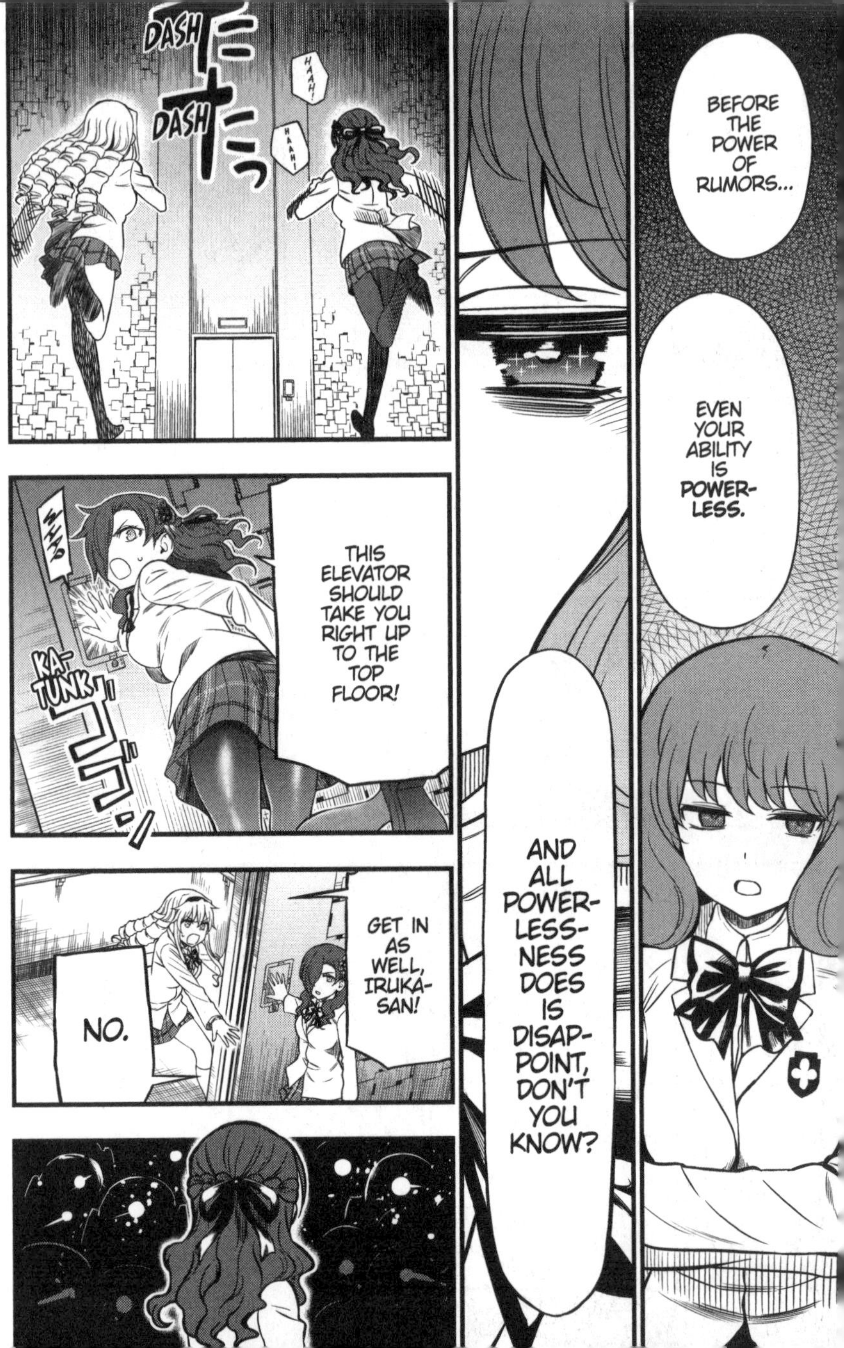
BEFORE THE POWER OF RUMORS...
EVEN YOUR ABILITY IS POWER-LESS.
AND ALL POWER-LESS-NESS DOES IS DISAP-POINT, DON'T YOU KNOW?
DASH
DASH
HAAH!
HAAH!
THIS ELEVATOR SHOULD TAKE YOU RIGHT UP TO THE TOP FLOOR!
KA-TUNK
GET IN AS WELL, IRUKA-SAN!
NO.

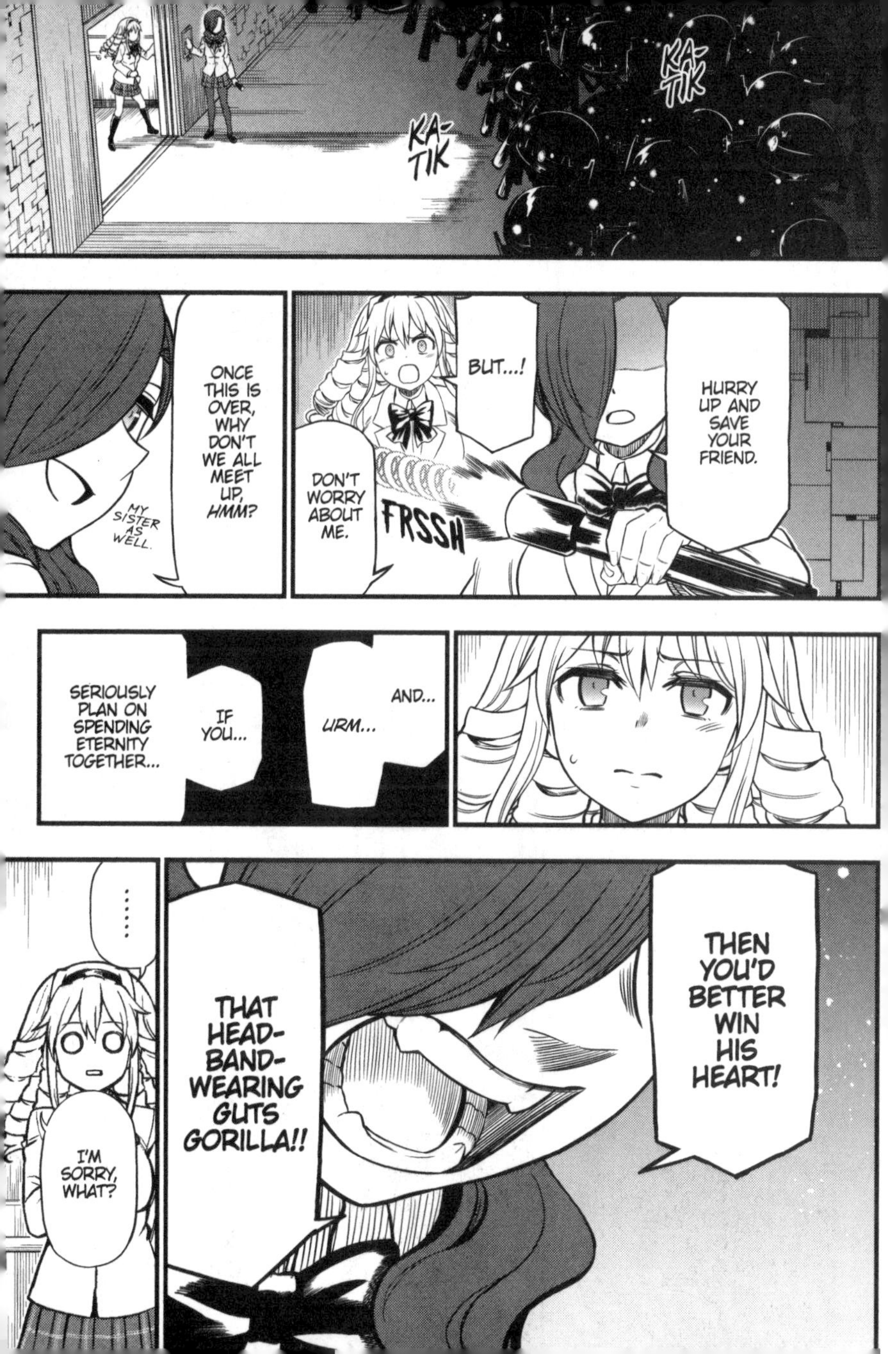
KA-TIK
KA-TIK
HURRY UP AND SAVE YOUR FRIEND.
BUT...!
DON'T WORRY ABOUT ME.
FRSSH
ONCE THIS IS OVER, WHY DON'T WE ALL MEET UP, HMM?
MY SISTER AS WELL.
AND...
URM...
IF YOU...
SERIOUSLY PLAN ON SPENDING ETERNITY TOGETHER...
THEN YOU'D BETTER WIN HIS HEART!
THAT HEAD-BAND-WEARING GUTS GORILLA!!
......
I'M SORRY, WHAT?

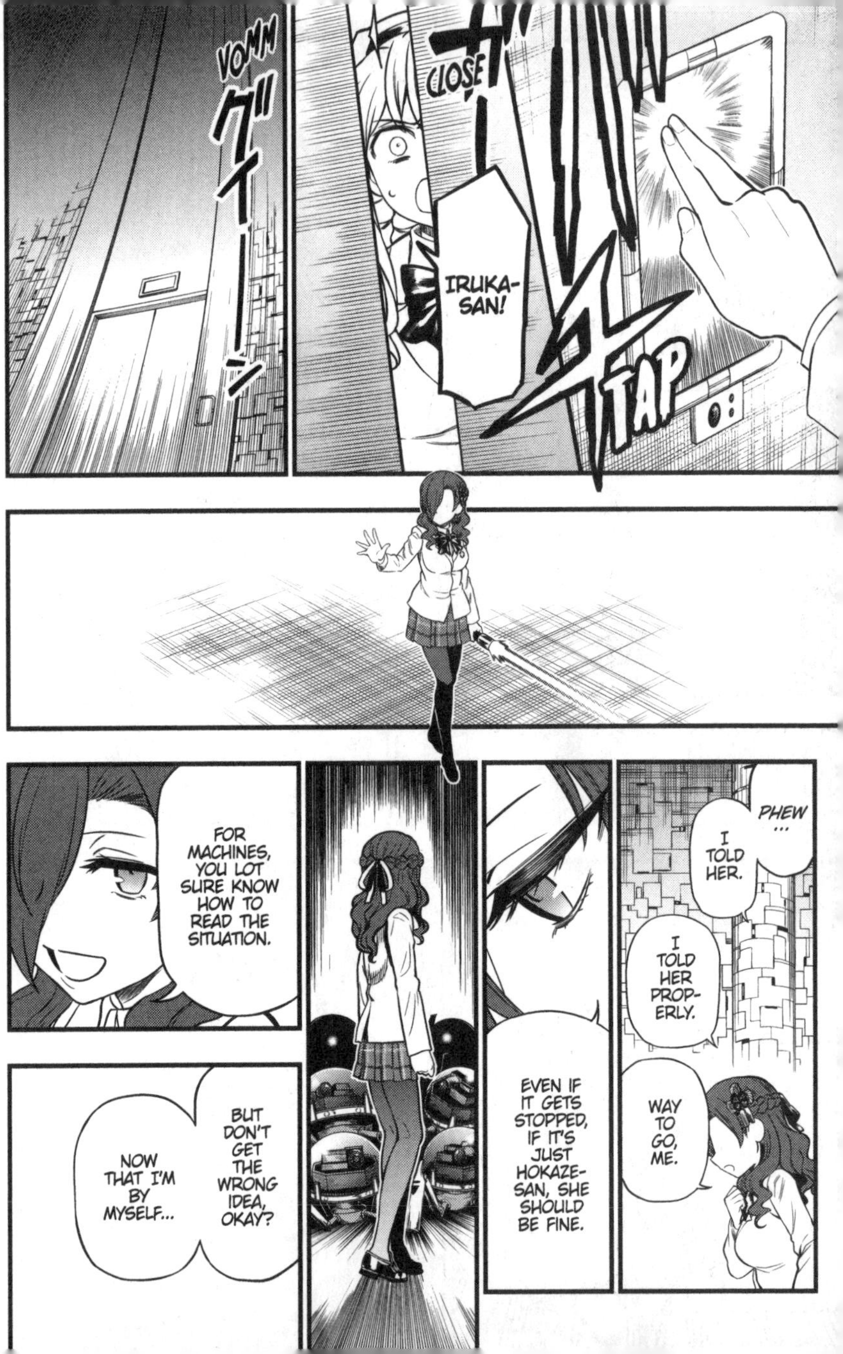
CLOSE
IRUKA-SAN!
TAP
VOMM
PHEW...
I TOLD HER.
I TOLD HER PROPERLY.
WAY TO GO, ME.
EVEN IF IT GETS STOPPED, IF IT'S JUST HOKAZE-SAN, SHE SHOULD BE FINE.
FOR MACHINES, YOU LOT SURE KNOW HOW TO READ THE SITUATION.
BUT DON'T GET THE WRONG IDEA, OKAY?
NOW THAT I'M BY MYSELF...

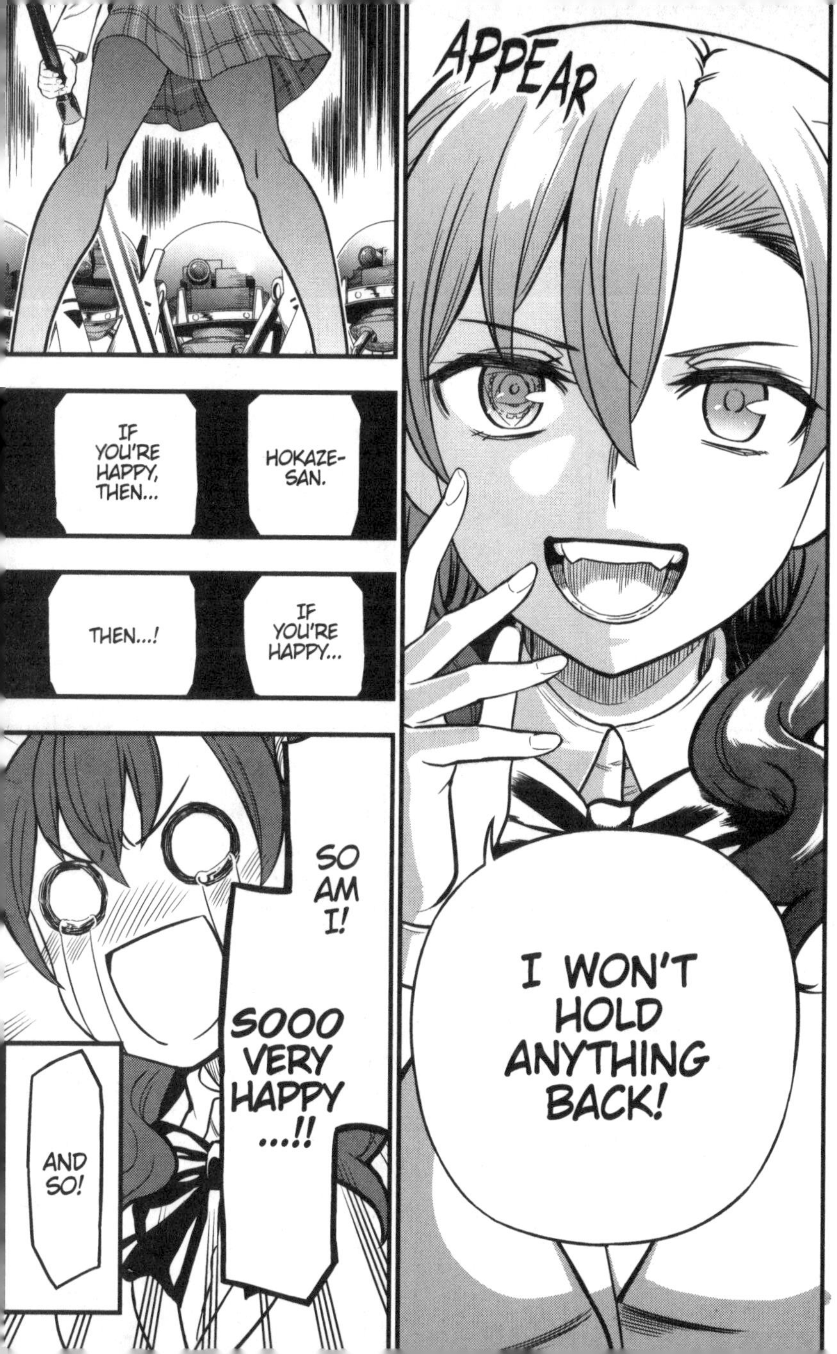
APPEAR
I WON'T HOLD ANYTHING BACK!
HOKAZE-SAN.
IF YOU'RE HAPPY, THEN...
IF YOU'RE HAPPY...
THEN...!
SO AM I!
SOOO VERY HAPPY ...!!
AND SO!

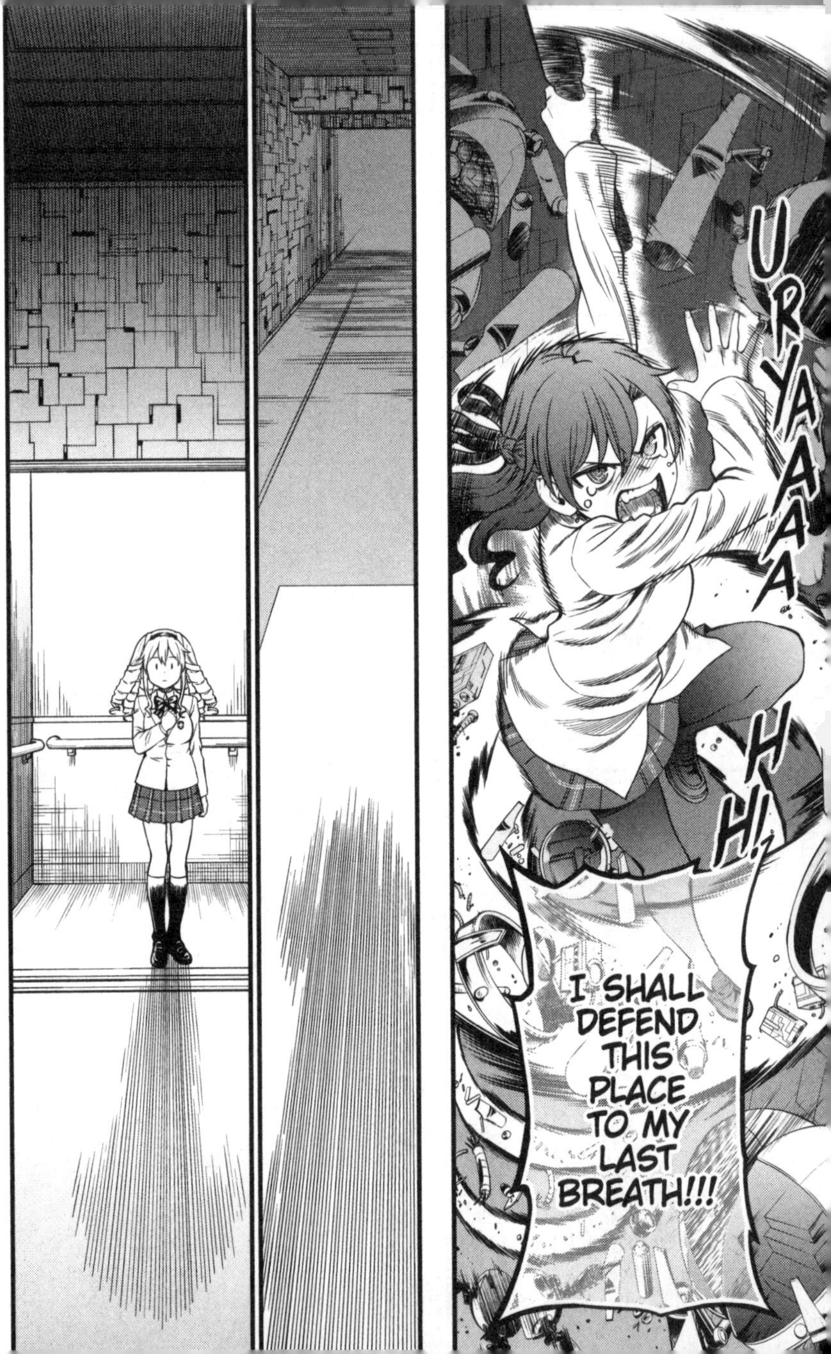
URYAAAAHHH!
I SHALL DEFEND THIS PLACE TO MY LAST BREATH!!!

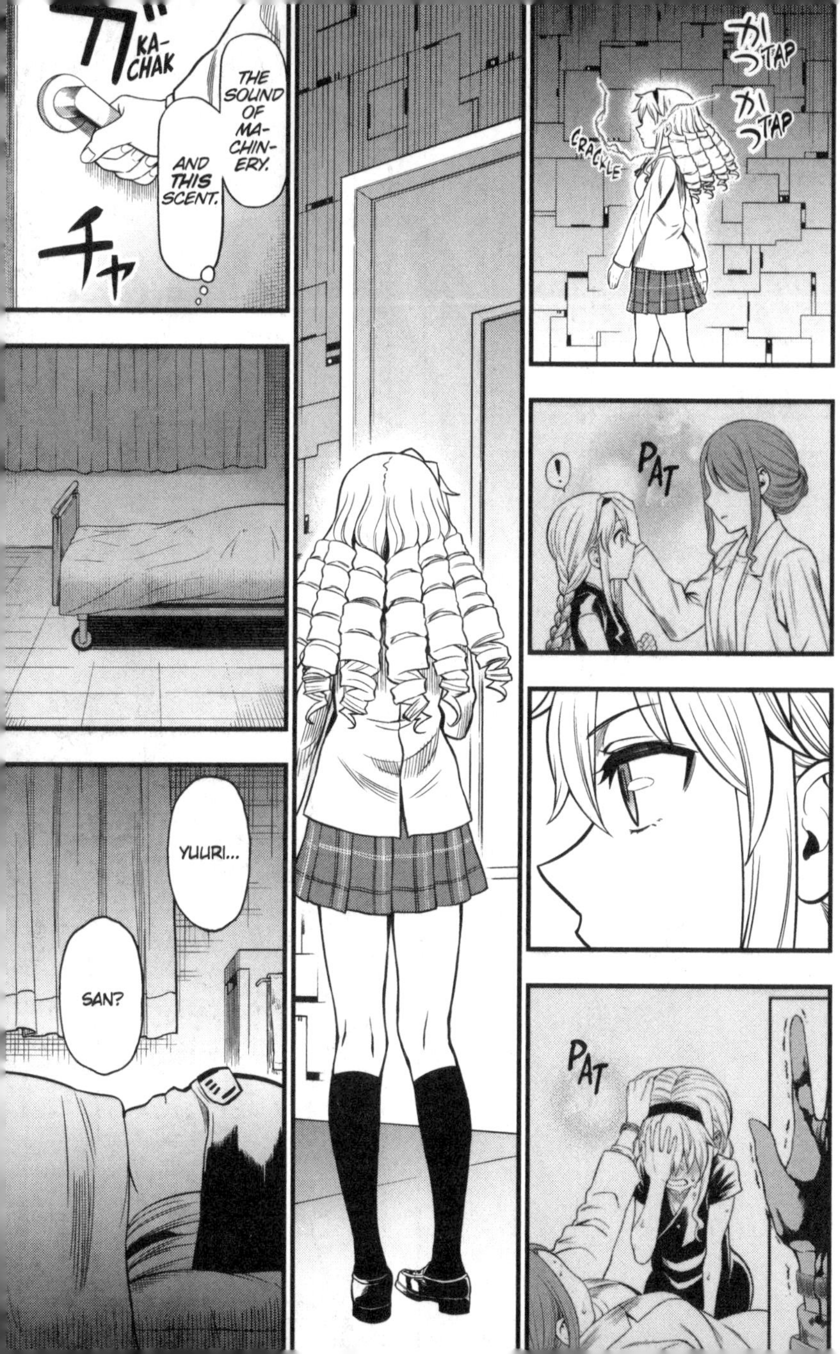
カッ TAP
カッ TAP
CRACKLE
PAT
!
PAT
ガチャ KA-CHAK
THE SOUND OF MA-CHIN-ERY.
AND THIS SCENT.
YUURI...
SAN?

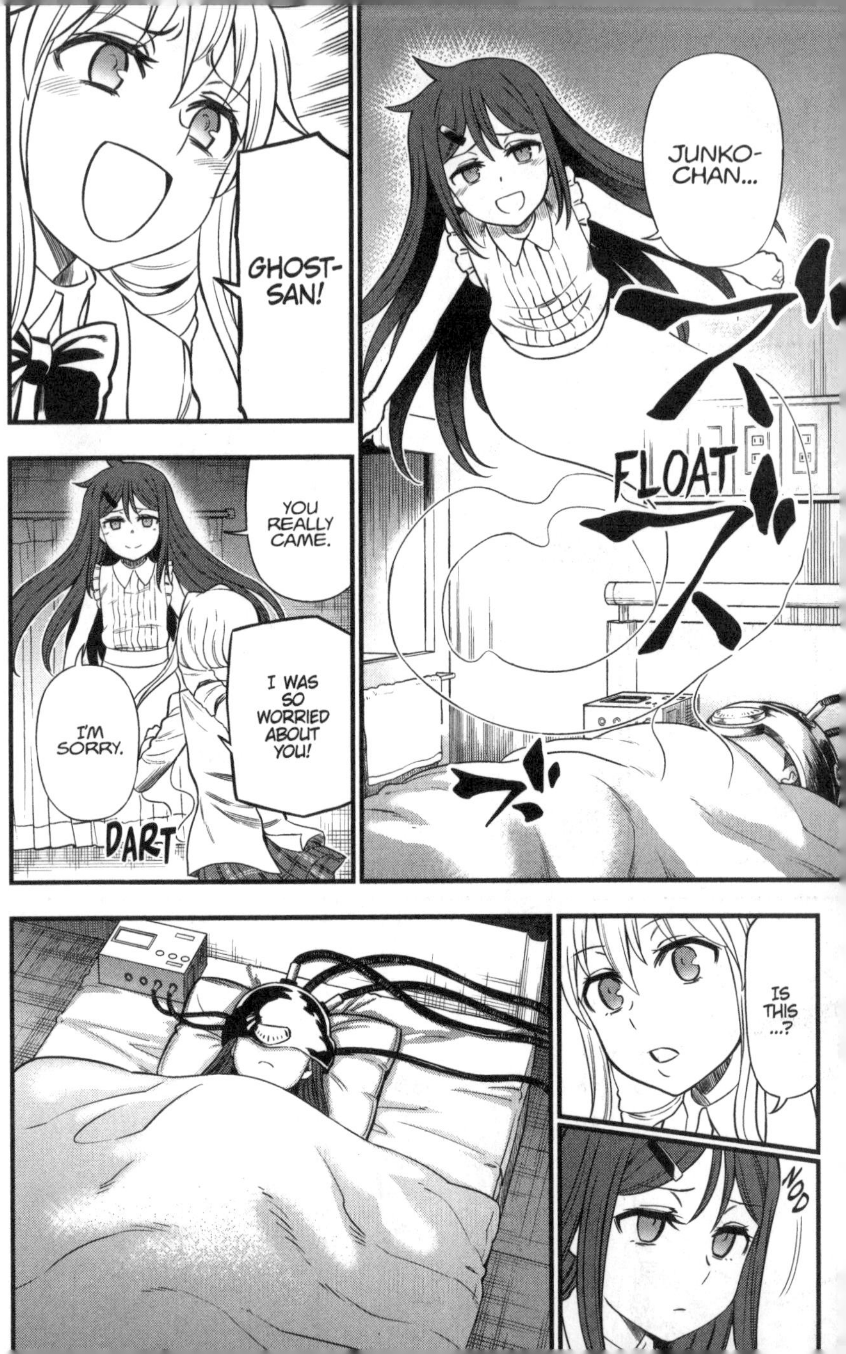
JUNKO-CHAN...
FLOAT
GHOST-SAN!
YOU REALLY CAME.
I WAS SO WORRIED ABOUT YOU!
I'M SORRY.
DART
IS THIS ...?
NOD

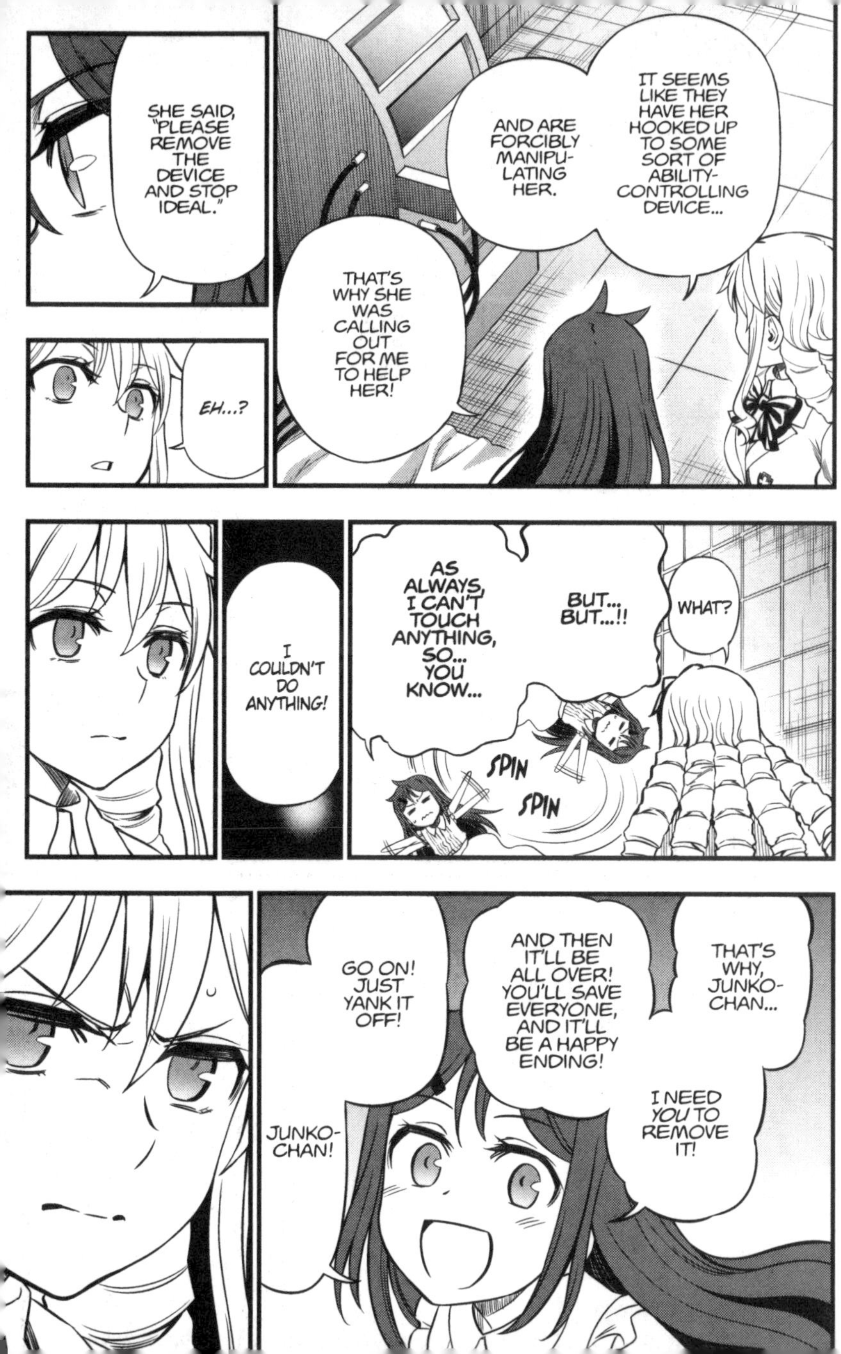
IT SEEMS LIKE THEY HAVE HER HOOKED UP TO SOME SORT OF ABILITY-CONTROLLING DEVICE...
AND ARE FORCIBLY MANIPULATING HER.
THAT'S WHY SHE WAS CALLING OUT FOR ME TO HELP HER!
SHE SAID, "PLEASE REMOVE THE DEVICE AND STOP IDEAL."
EH...?
WHAT?
BUT... BUT...!!
AS ALWAYS, I CAN'T TOUCH ANYTHING, SO... YOU KNOW...
SPIN
SPIN
I COULDN'T DO ANYTHING!
THAT'S WHY, JUNKO-CHAN...
I NEED *YOU* TO REMOVE IT!
AND THEN IT'LL BE ALL OVER! YOU'LL SAVE EVERYONE, AND IT'LL BE A HAPPY ENDING!
GO ON! JUST YANK IT OFF!
JUNKO-CHAN!

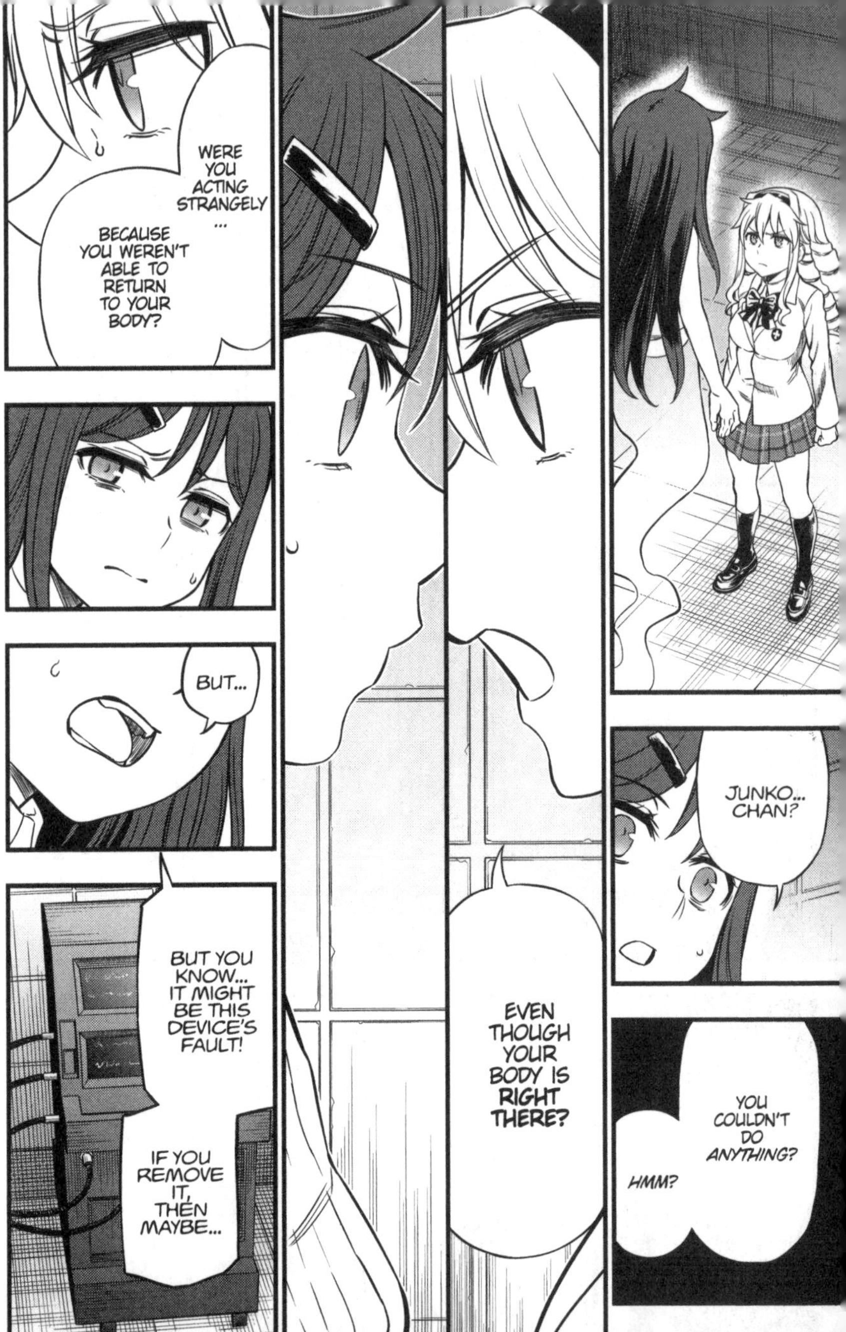
JUNKO... CHAN?
YOU COULDN'T DO ANYTHING?
HMM?
EVEN THOUGH YOUR BODY IS **RIGHT THERE?**
WERE YOU ACTING STRANGELY ...
BECAUSE YOU WEREN'T ABLE TO RETURN TO YOUR BODY?
BUT...
BUT YOU KNOW... IT MIGHT BE THIS DEVICE'S FAULT!
IF YOU REMOVE IT, THEN MAYBE...

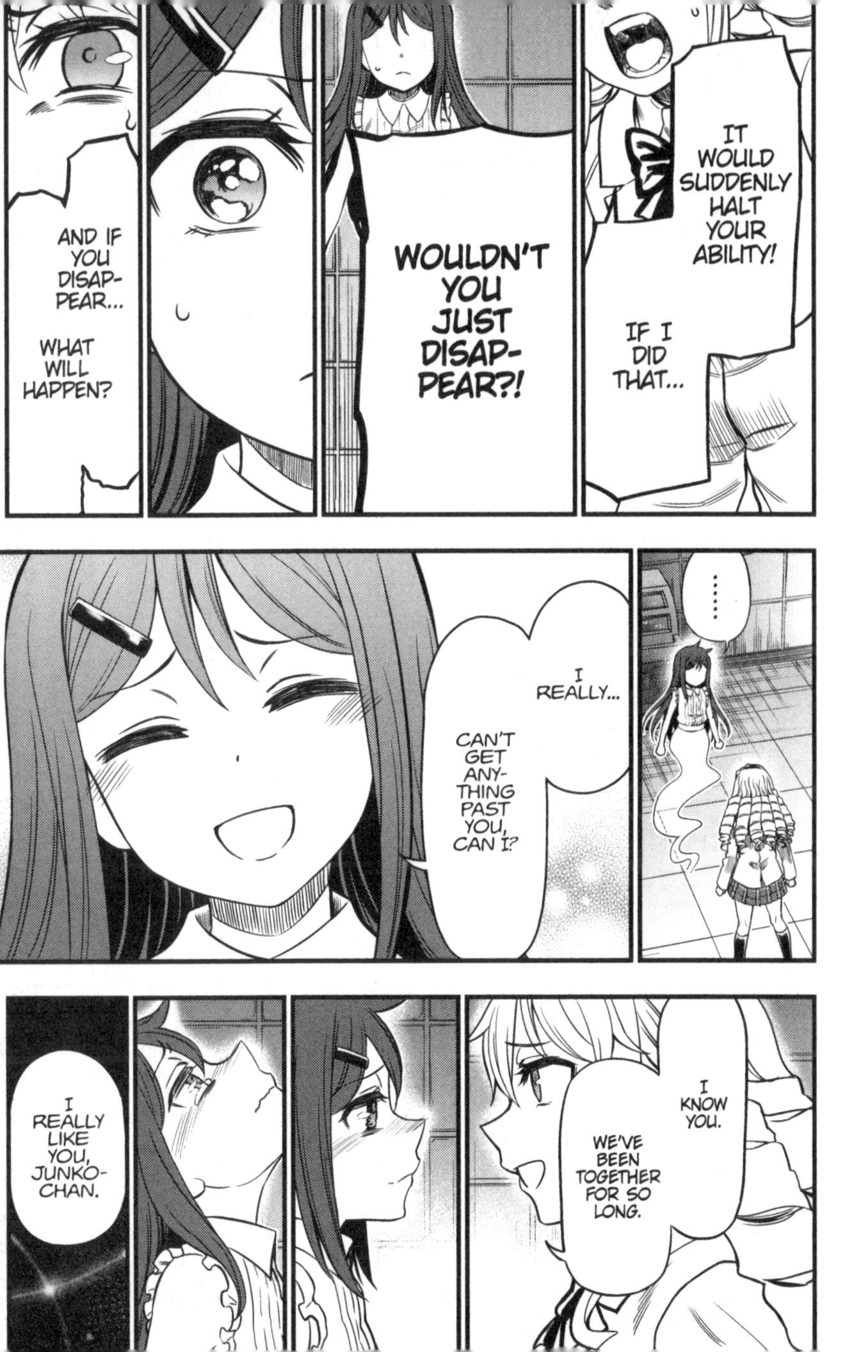
IT WOULD SUDDENLY HALT YOUR ABILITY!
IF I DID THAT...
WOULDN'T YOU JUST DISAP-PEAR?!
AND IF YOU DISAP-PEAR...
WHAT WILL HAPPEN?
......
I REALLY...
CAN'T GET ANY-THING PAST YOU, CAN I?
I KNOW YOU.
WE'VE BEEN TOGETHER FOR SO LONG.
I REALLY LIKE YOU, JUNKO-CHAN.

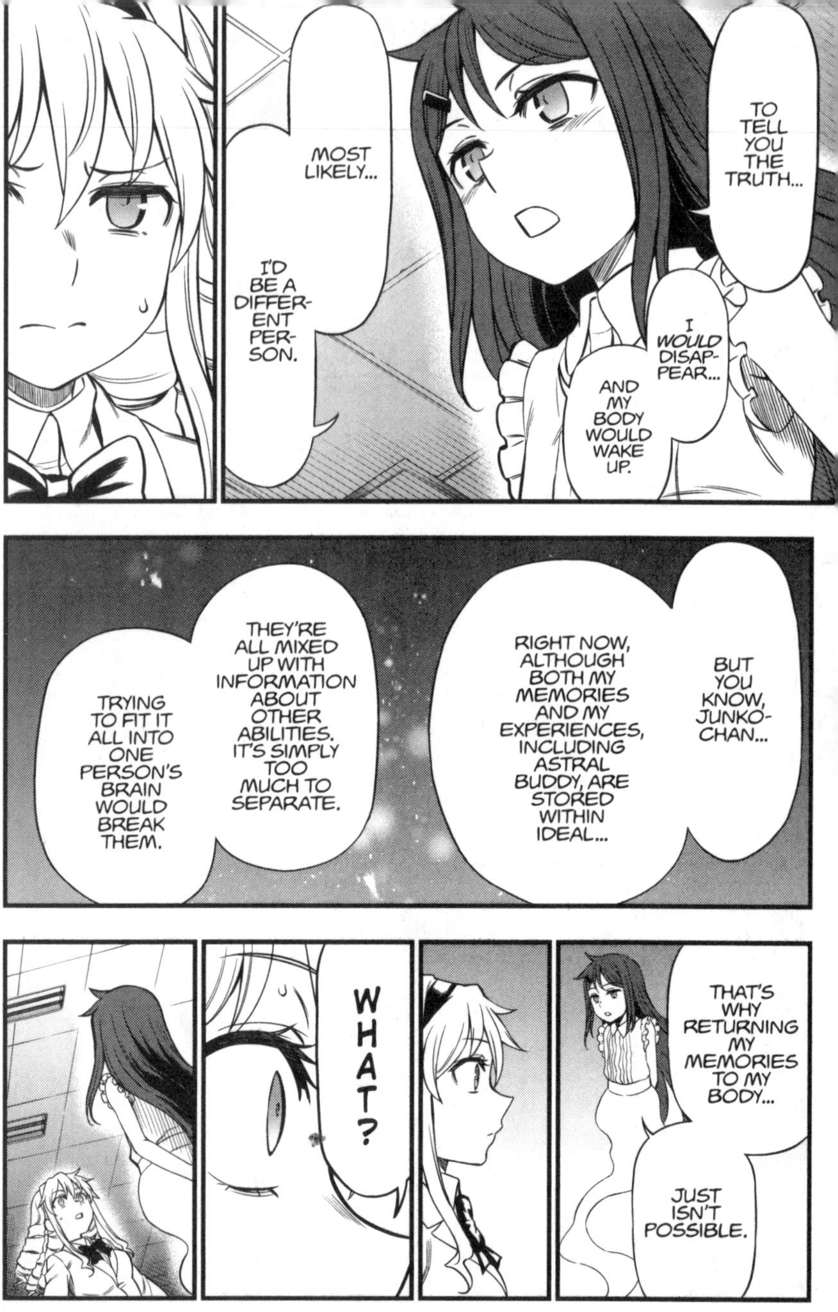
TO TELL YOU THE TRUTH...
I WOULD DISAPPEAR...
AND MY BODY WOULD WAKE UP.
MOST LIKELY...
I'D BE A DIFFERENT PERSON.
BUT YOU KNOW, JUNKO-CHAN...
RIGHT NOW, ALTHOUGH BOTH MY MEMORIES AND MY EXPERIENCES, INCLUDING ASTRAL BUDDY, ARE STORED WITHIN IDEAL...
THEY'RE ALL MIXED UP WITH INFORMATION ABOUT OTHER ABILITIES. IT'S SIMPLY TOO MUCH TO SEPARATE.
TRYING TO FIT IT ALL INTO ONE PERSON'S BRAIN WOULD BREAK THEM.
THAT'S WHY RETURNING MY MEMORIES TO MY BODY...
JUST ISN'T POSSIBLE.
WHAT?

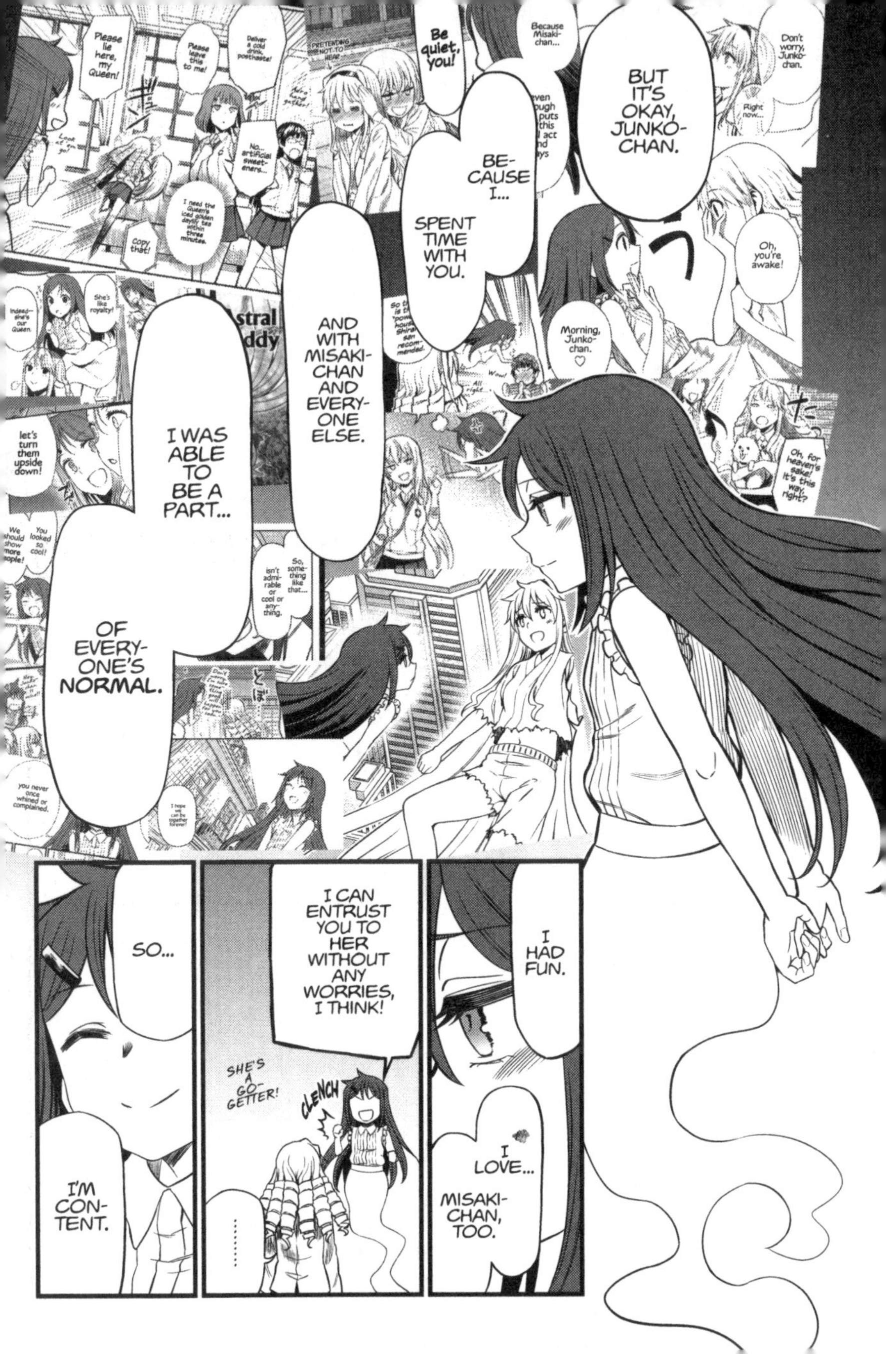

Don't worry, Junko-chan.
Right now...
BUT IT'S OKAY, JUNKO-CHAN.
Because Misaki-chan...
Be quiet, you!
PRETENDING NOT TO HEAR
Deliver a cold drink, posthaste!
Please leave this to me!
Please lie here, my Queen!
Look at 'er go!
No... artificial sweeteners...
I need the Queen's iced golden dew tea within three minutes.
Copy that!
BECAUSE I... SPENT TIME WITH YOU.
Oh, you're awake!
Morning, Junko-chan. ♡
AND WITH MISAKI-CHAN AND EVERYONE ELSE.
Wow!
All right...
She's like royalty!
Indeed—she's our Queen.
I WAS ABLE TO BE A PART... OF EVERYONE'S NORMAL.
Oh, for heaven's sake! It's this way, right?
let's turn them upside down!
You looked so cool!
So, something like that...
isn't admirable or cool or anything.
you never once whined or complained.
I hope we can be together forever!
I HAD FUN.
I LOVE... MISAKI-CHAN, TOO.
I CAN ENTRUST YOU TO HER WITHOUT ANY WORRIES, I THINK!
SHE'S A GO-GETTER!
CLENCH
......
SO...
I'M CONTENT.

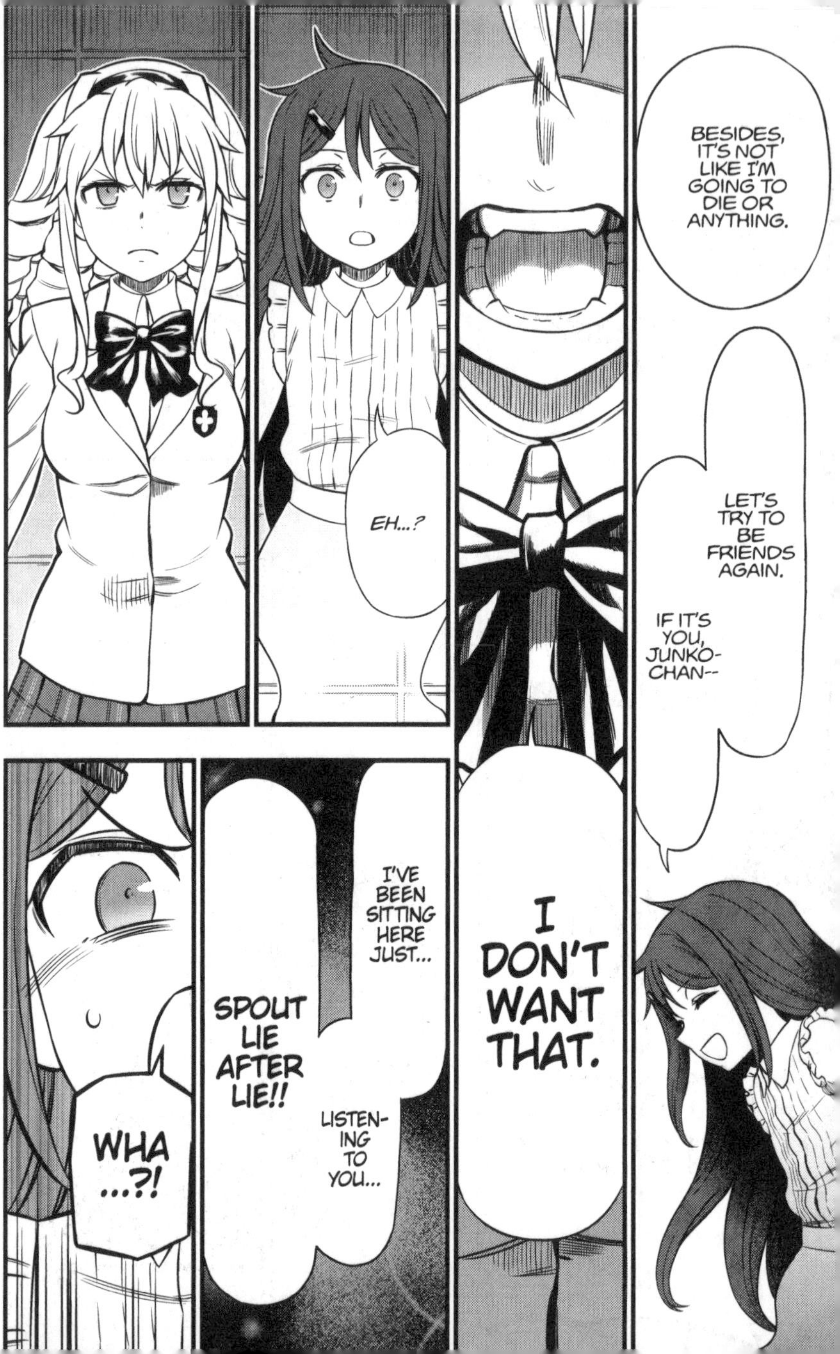
BESIDES, IT'S NOT LIKE I'M GOING TO DIE OR ANYTHING.
LET'S TRY TO BE FRIENDS AGAIN.
IF IT'S YOU, JUNKO-CHAN--
EH...?
I DON'T WANT THAT.
I'VE BEEN SITTING HERE JUST...
LISTENING TO YOU...
SPOUT LIE AFTER LIE!!
WHA ...?!

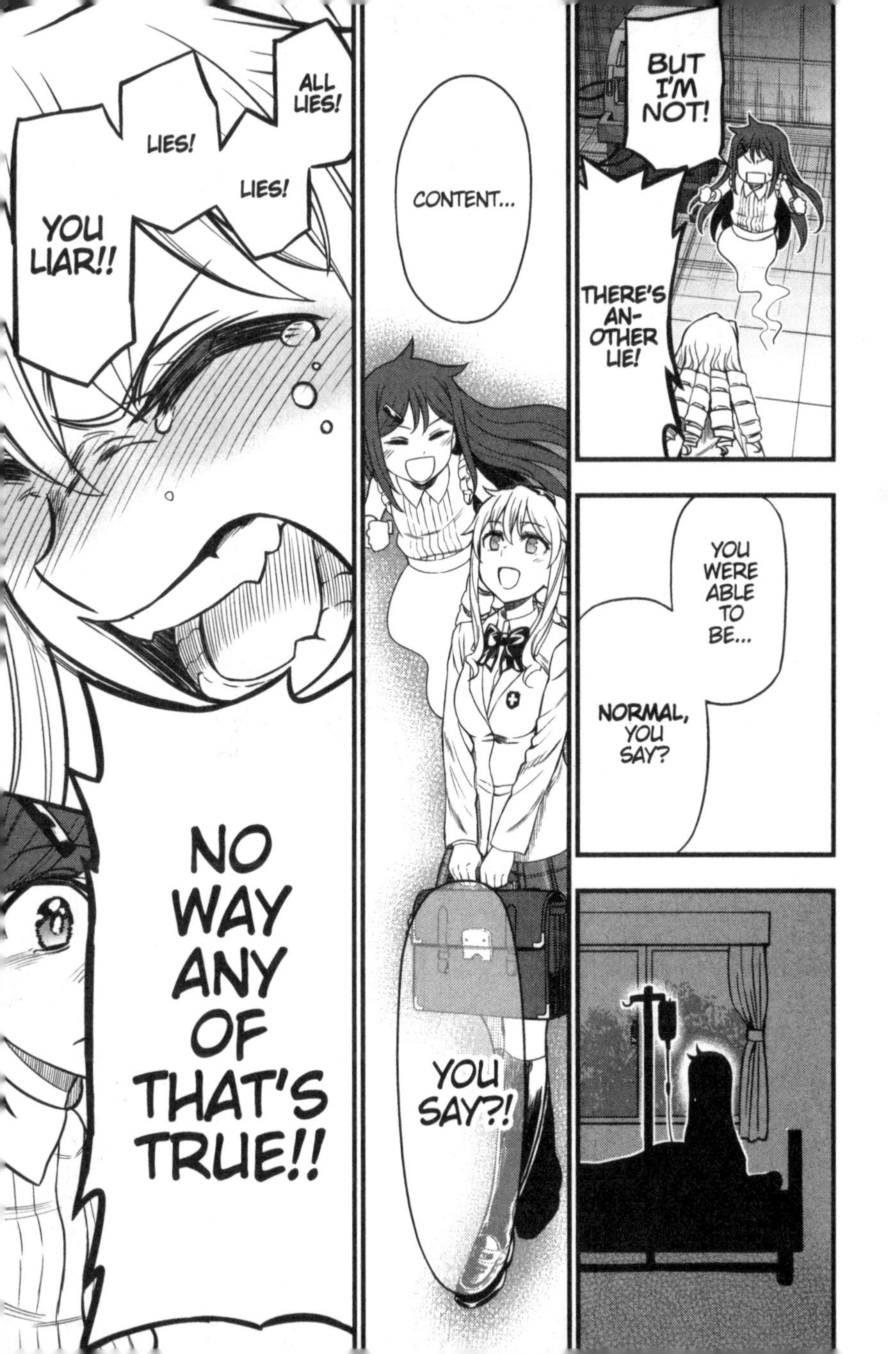
BUT I'M NOT!
THERE'S AN-OTHER LIE!
YOU WERE ABLE TO BE...
NORMAL, YOU SAY?
CONTENT...
YOU SAY?!
ALL LIES!
LIES!
LIES!
YOU LIAR!!
NO WAY ANY OF THAT'S TRUE!!

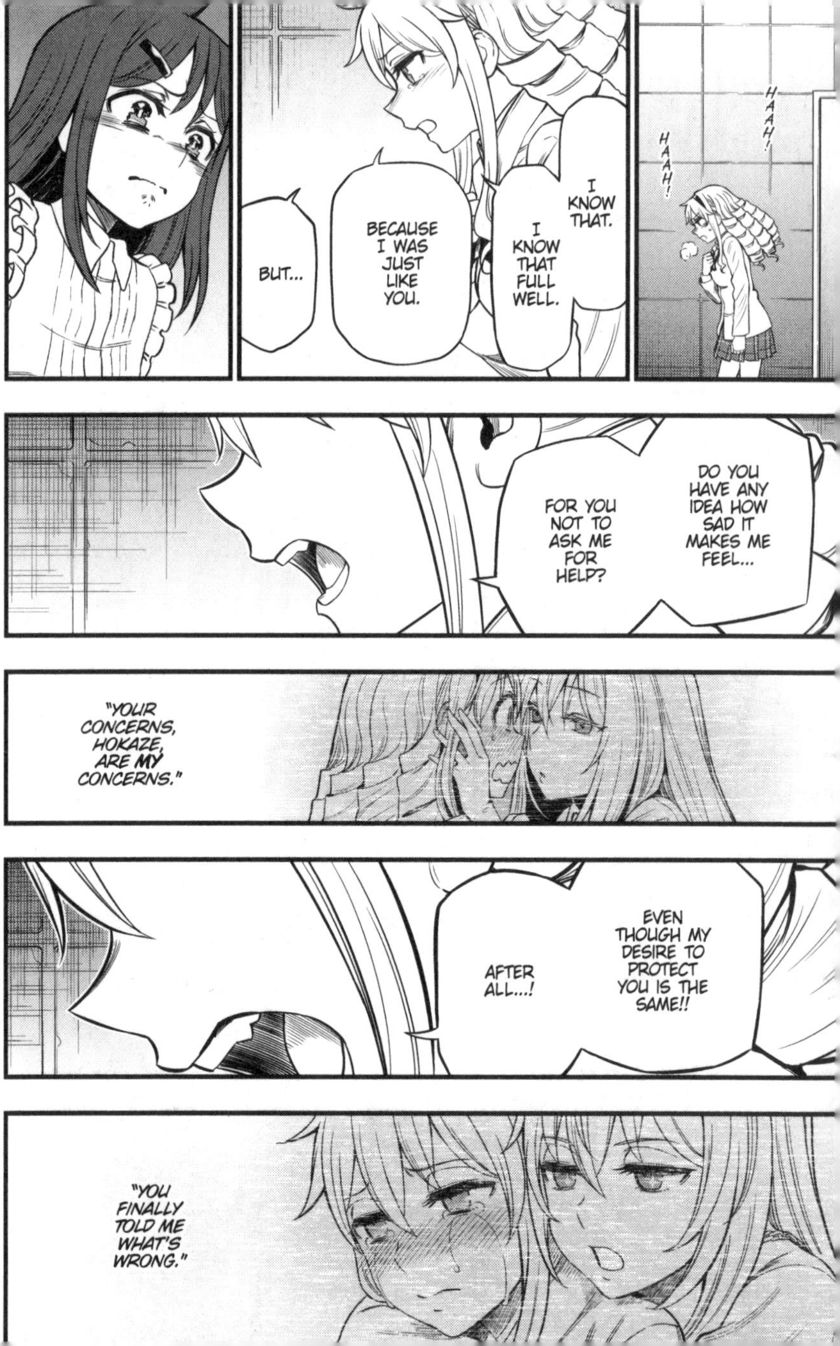
HAAAH!
HAAH!
I KNOW THAT.
I KNOW THAT FULL WELL.
BECAUSE I WAS JUST LIKE YOU.
BUT...
DO YOU HAVE ANY IDEA HOW SAD IT MAKES ME FEEL...
FOR YOU NOT TO ASK ME FOR HELP?
"YOUR CONCERNS, HOKAZE, ARE *MY* CONCERNS."
EVEN THOUGH MY DESIRE TO PROTECT YOU IS THE SAME!!
AFTER ALL...!
"YOU FINALLY TOLD ME WHAT'S WRONG."

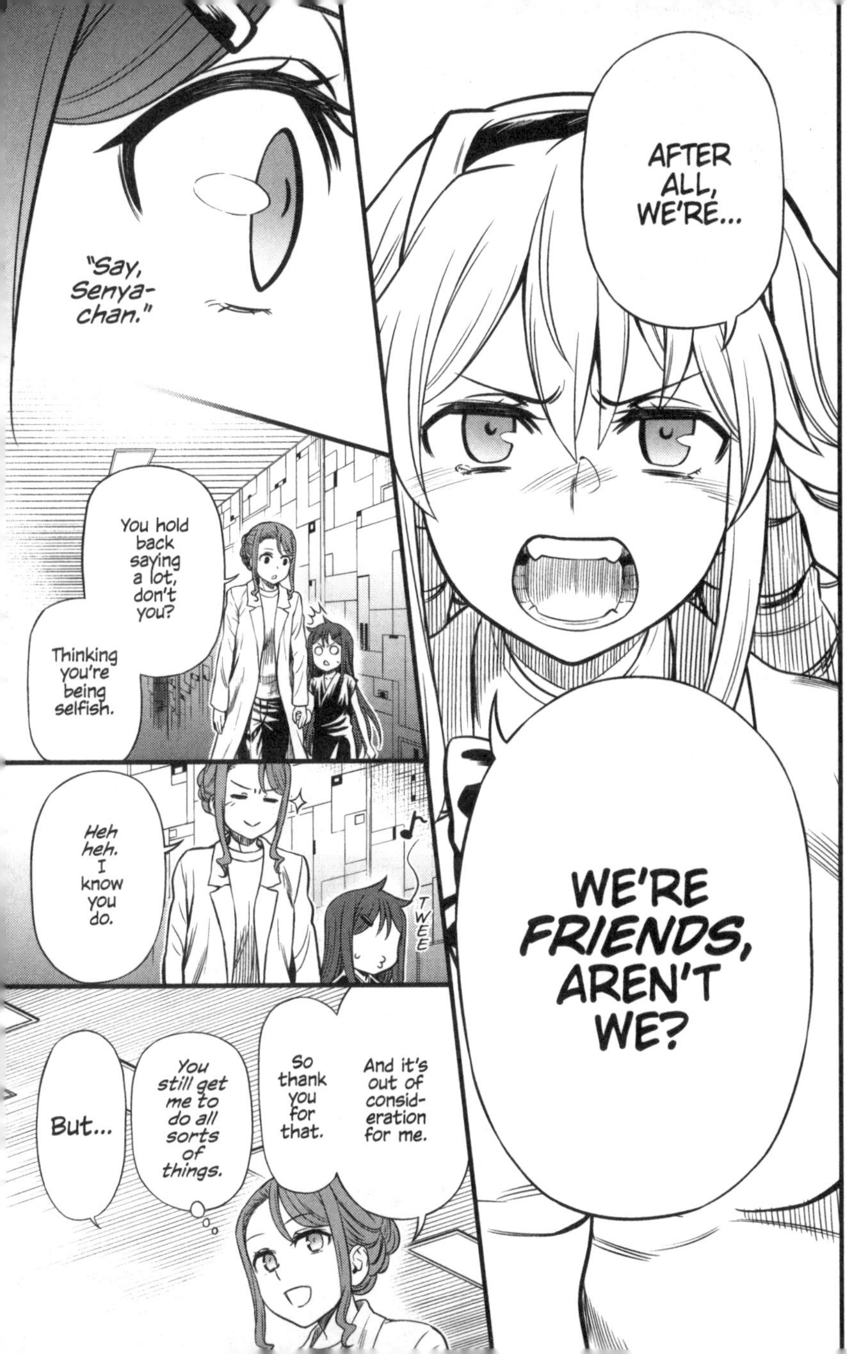
AFTER ALL, WE'RE...
WE'RE FRIENDS, AREN'T WE?
"Say, Senya-chan."
You hold back saying a lot, don't you?
Thinking you're being selfish.
Heh heh. I know you do.
TWEE
And it's out of consideration for me.
So thank you for that.
You still get me to do all sorts of things.
But...

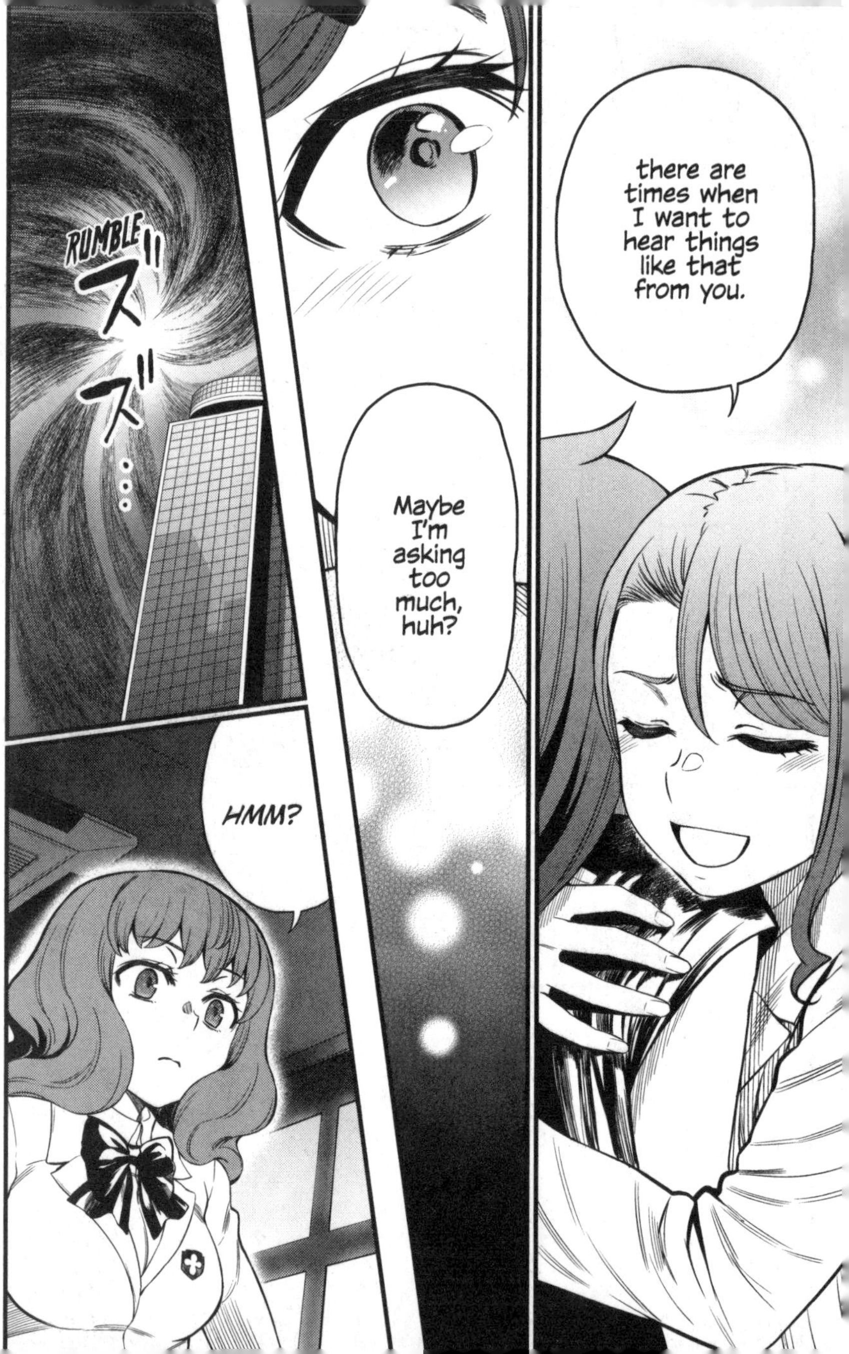
there are times when I want to hear things like that from you.
Maybe I'm asking too much, huh?
RUMBLE
ズズズ…
HMM?

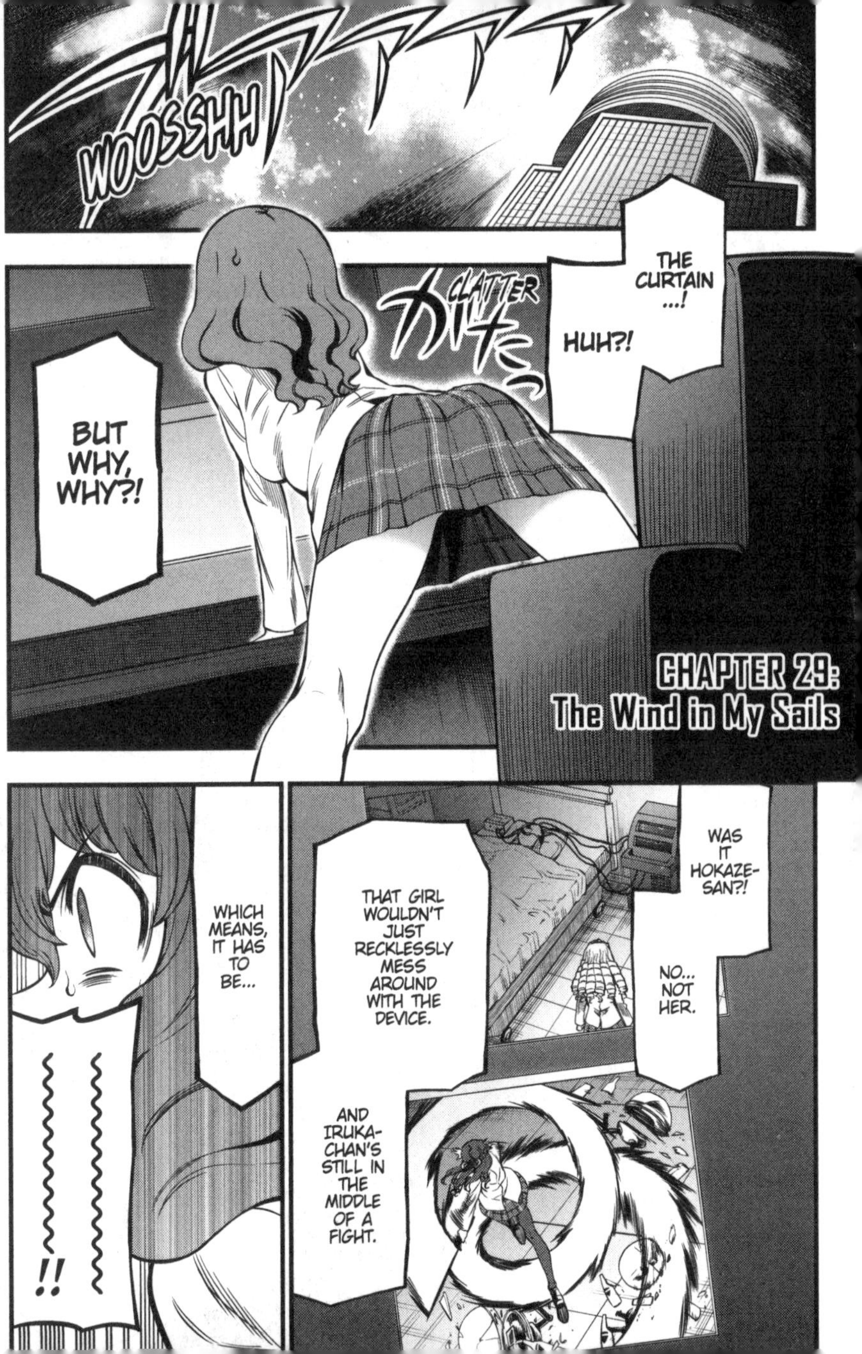
WOOSSHH
THE CURTAIN ...!
HUH?!
CLATTER
BUT WHY, WHY?!
CHAPTER 29: The Wind in My Sails
WAS IT HOKAZE-SAN?!
NO... NOT HER.
THAT GIRL WOULDN'T JUST RECKLESSLY MESS AROUND WITH THE DEVICE.
AND IRUKA-CHAN'S STILL IN THE MIDDLE OF A FIGHT.
WHICH MEANS, IT HAS TO BE...
!!

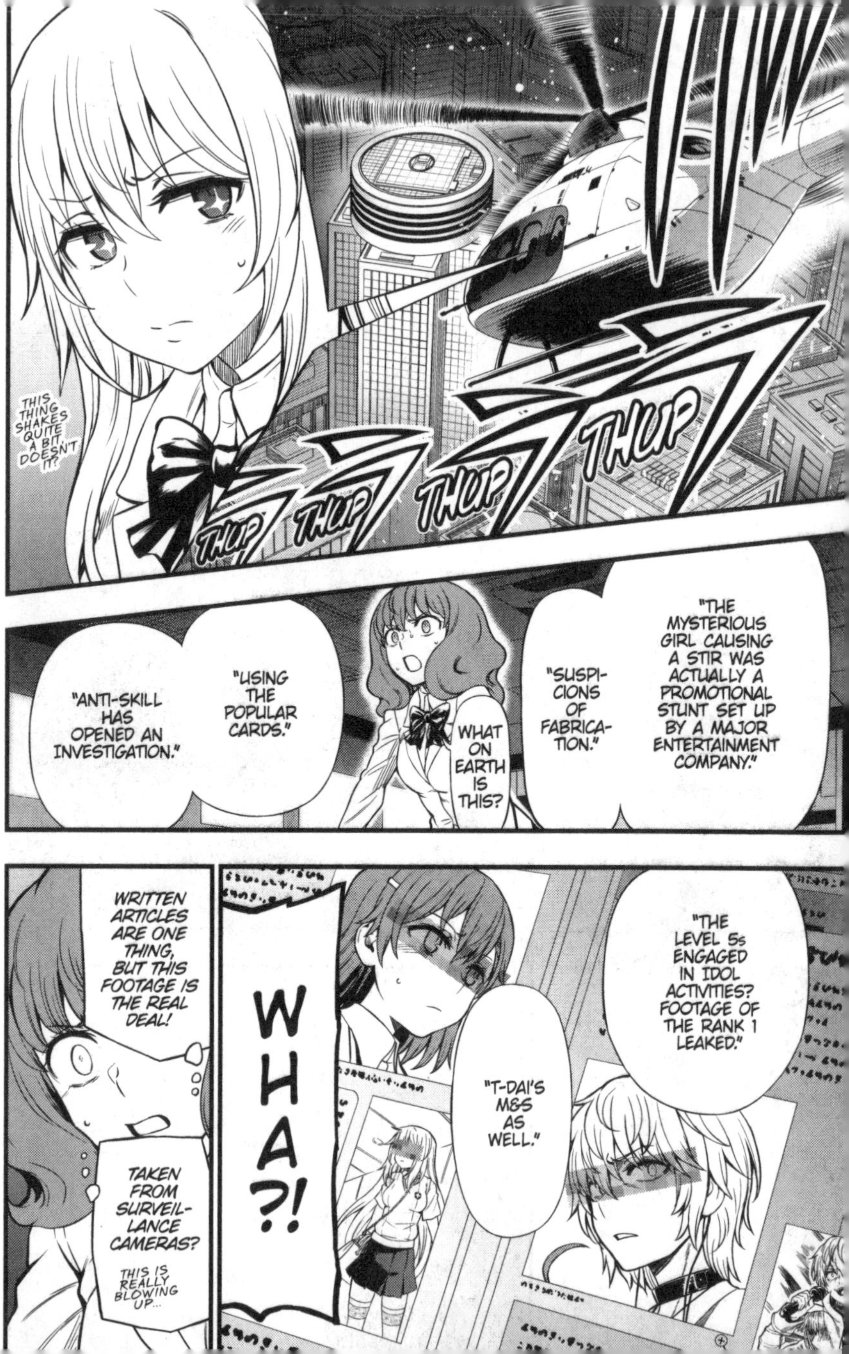
THUP THUP THUP THUP
THIS THING SHAKES QUITE A BIT DOESN'T IT?
"THE MYSTERIOUS GIRL CAUSING A STIR WAS ACTUALLY A PROMOTIONAL STUNT SET UP BY A MAJOR ENTERTAINMENT COMPANY."
"SUSPICIONS OF FABRICATION."
WHAT ON EARTH IS THIS?
"USING THE POPULAR CARDS."
"ANTI-SKILL HAS OPENED AN INVESTIGATION."
"THE LEVEL 5s ENGAGED IN IDOL ACTIVITIES? FOOTAGE OF THE RANK 1 LEAKED."
"T-DAI'S M&S AS WELL."
WHA?!
WRITTEN ARTICLES ARE ONE THING, BUT THIS FOOTAGE IS THE REAL DEAL!
TAKEN FROM SURVEILLANCE CAMERAS?
THIS IS REALLY BLOWING UP...

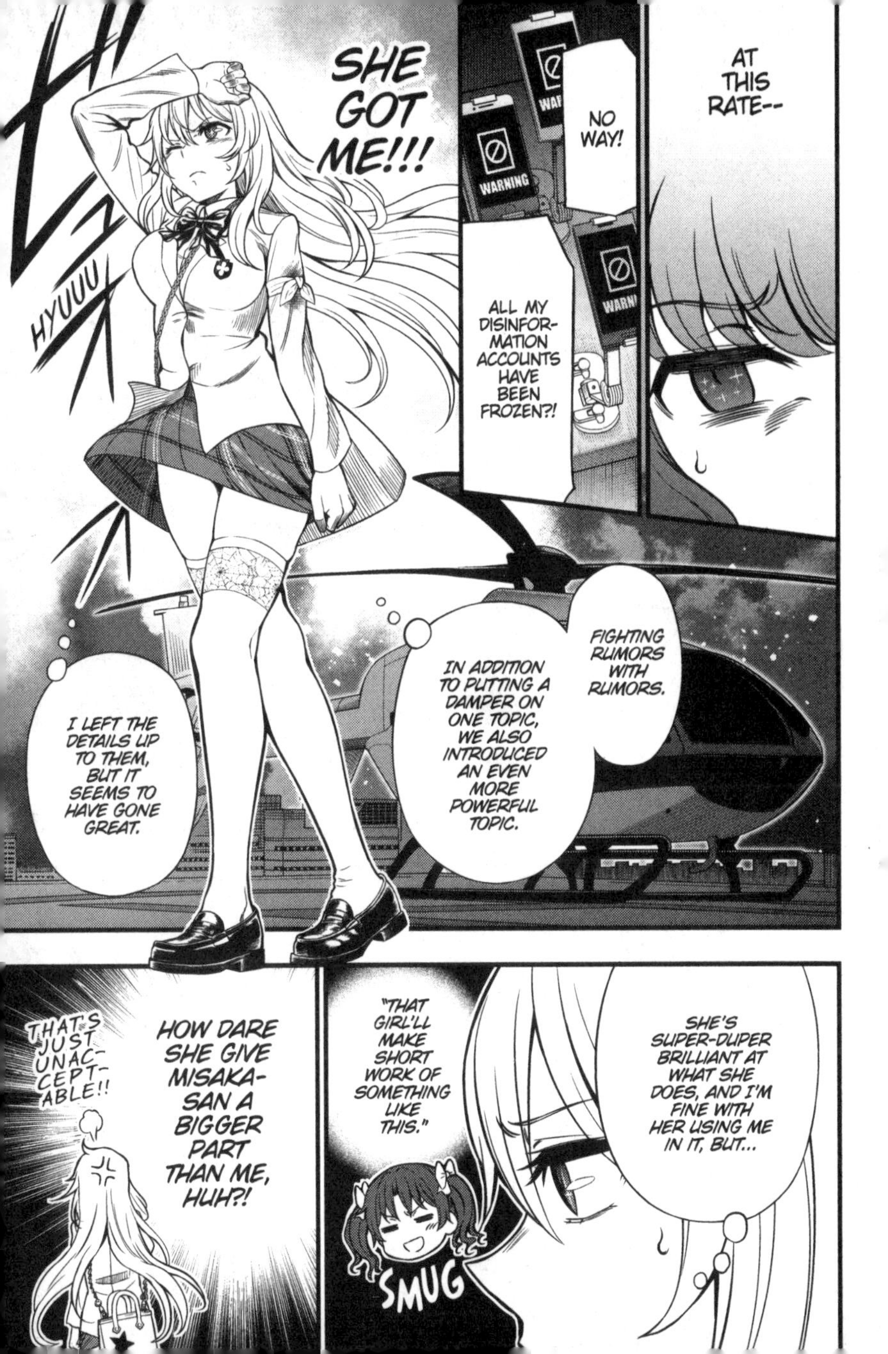
AT THIS RATE--
NO WAY!
ALL MY DISINFORMATION ACCOUNTS HAVE BEEN FROZEN?!
WARNING
WARNING
WARNING
SHE GOT ME!!!
HYUUU
FIGHTING RUMORS WITH RUMORS.
IN ADDITION TO PUTTING A DAMPER ON ONE TOPIC, WE ALSO INTRODUCED AN EVEN MORE POWERFUL TOPIC.
I LEFT THE DETAILS UP TO THEM, BUT IT SEEMS TO HAVE GONE GREAT.
SHE'S SUPER-DUPER BRILLIANT AT WHAT SHE DOES, AND I'M FINE WITH HER USING ME IN IT, BUT...
"THAT GIRL'LL MAKE SHORT WORK OF SOMETHING LIKE THIS."
SMUG
HOW DARE SHE GIVE MISAKA-SAN A BIGGER PART THAN ME, HUH?!
THAT'S JUST UNACCEPTABLE!!

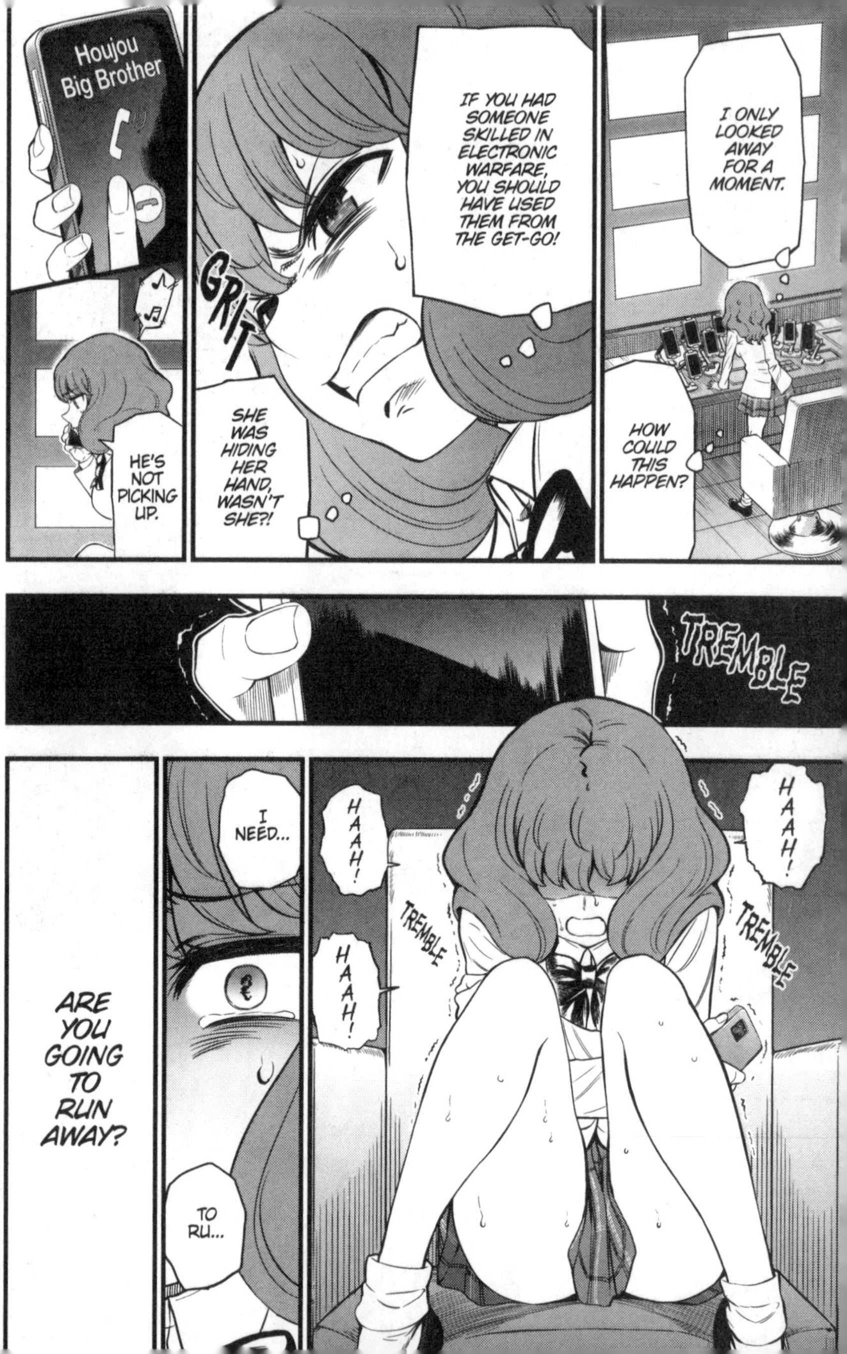
I ONLY LOOKED AWAY FOR A MOMENT.
HOW COULD THIS HAPPEN?
IF YOU HAD SOMEONE SKILLED IN ELECTRONIC WARFARE, YOU SHOULD HAVE USED THEM FROM THE GET-GO!
GRIT
SHE WAS HIDING HER HAND, WASN'T SHE?!
Houjou Big Brother
HE'S NOT PICKING UP.
TREMBLE
HAAAH!
TREMBLE
TREMBLE
HAAAH!
HAAAH!
I NEED...
TO RU...
ARE YOU GOING TO RUN AWAY?

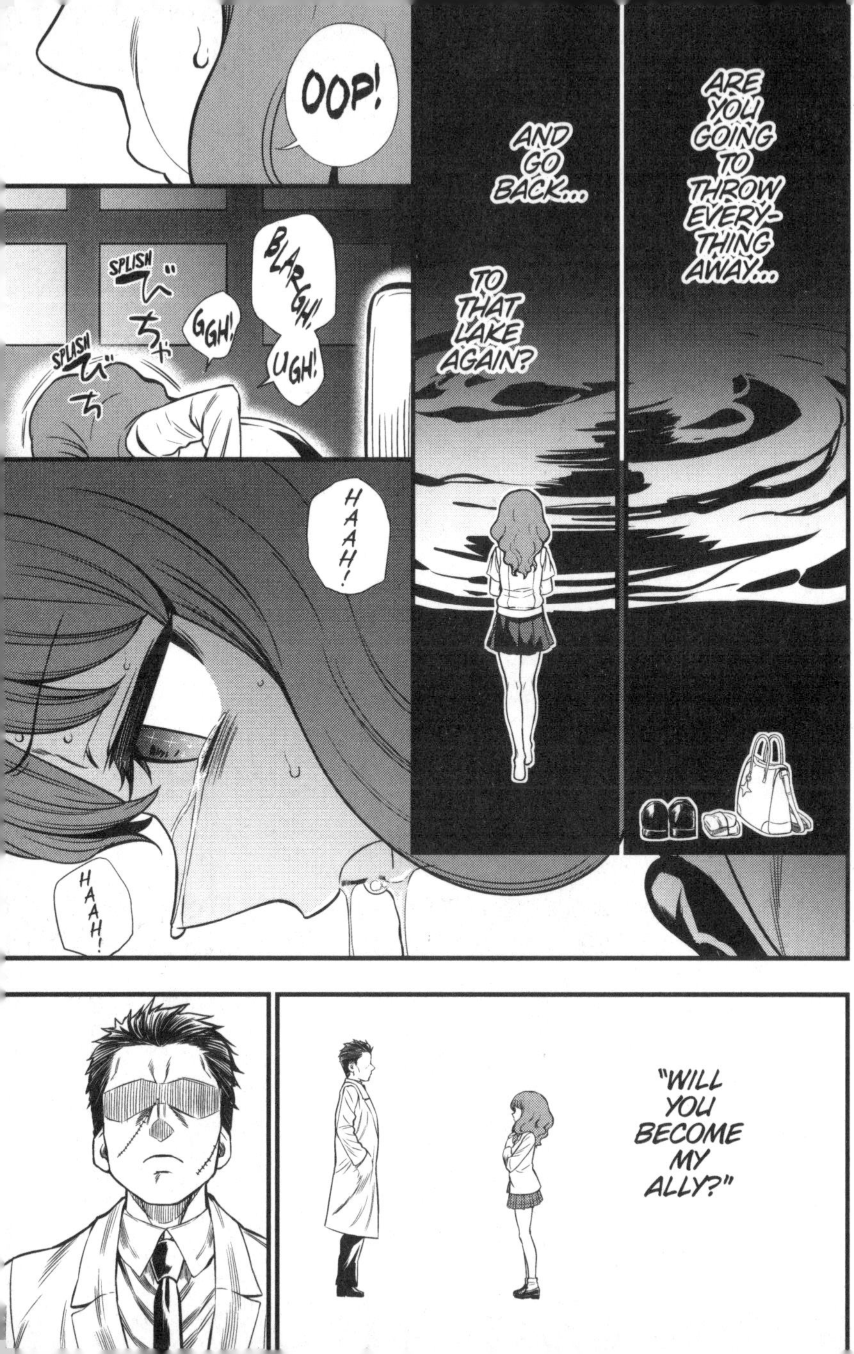
ARE YOU GOING TO THROW EVERY-THING AWAY...
AND GO BACK...
TO THAT LAKE AGAIN?
OOP!
BLARGH!
UGH!
GGH!
SPLISH びちゃ
SPLASH びち
HAAAH!
HAAAH!
"WILL YOU BECOME MY ALLY?"

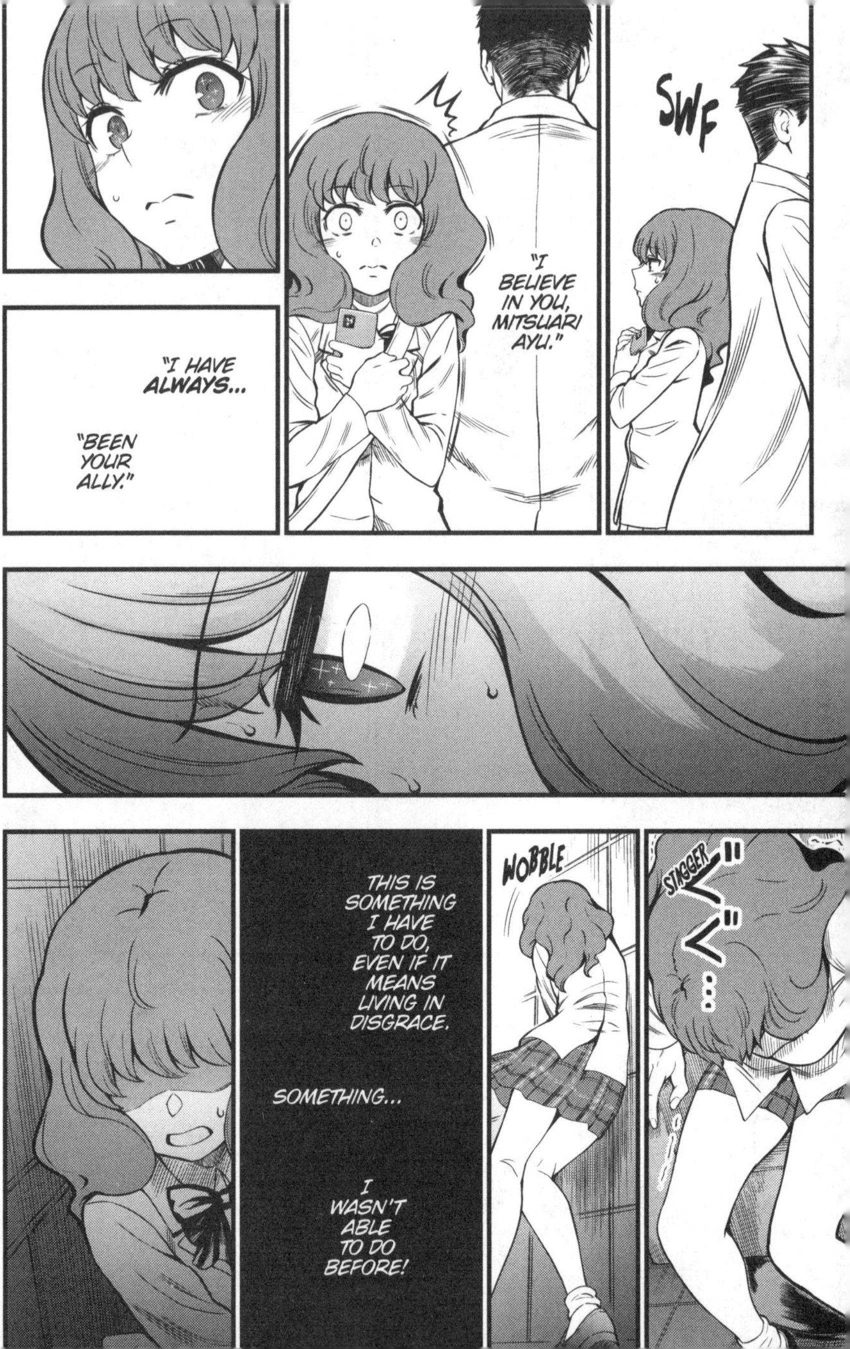
SWF
"I BELIEVE IN YOU, MITSUARI AYU."
"I HAVE ALWAYS...
"BEEN YOUR ALLY."
STAGGER
WOBBLE
THIS IS SOMETHING I HAVE TO DO, EVEN IF IT MEANS LIVING IN DISGRACE.
SOMETHING...
I WASN'T ABLE TO DO BEFORE!

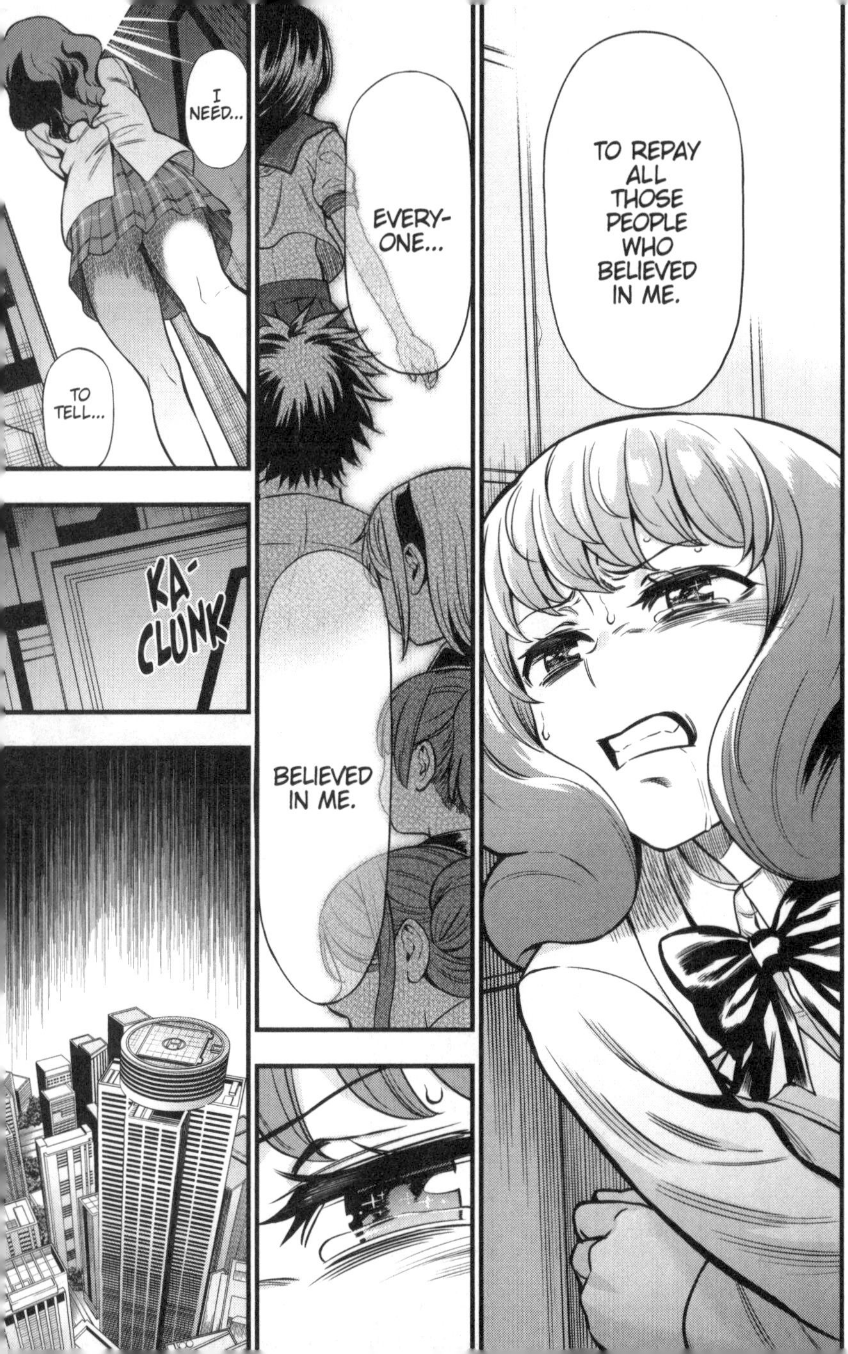
TO REPAY ALL THOSE PEOPLE WHO BELIEVED IN ME.
EVERY-ONE...
BELIEVED IN ME.
I NEED...
TO TELL...
KA-CLUNK

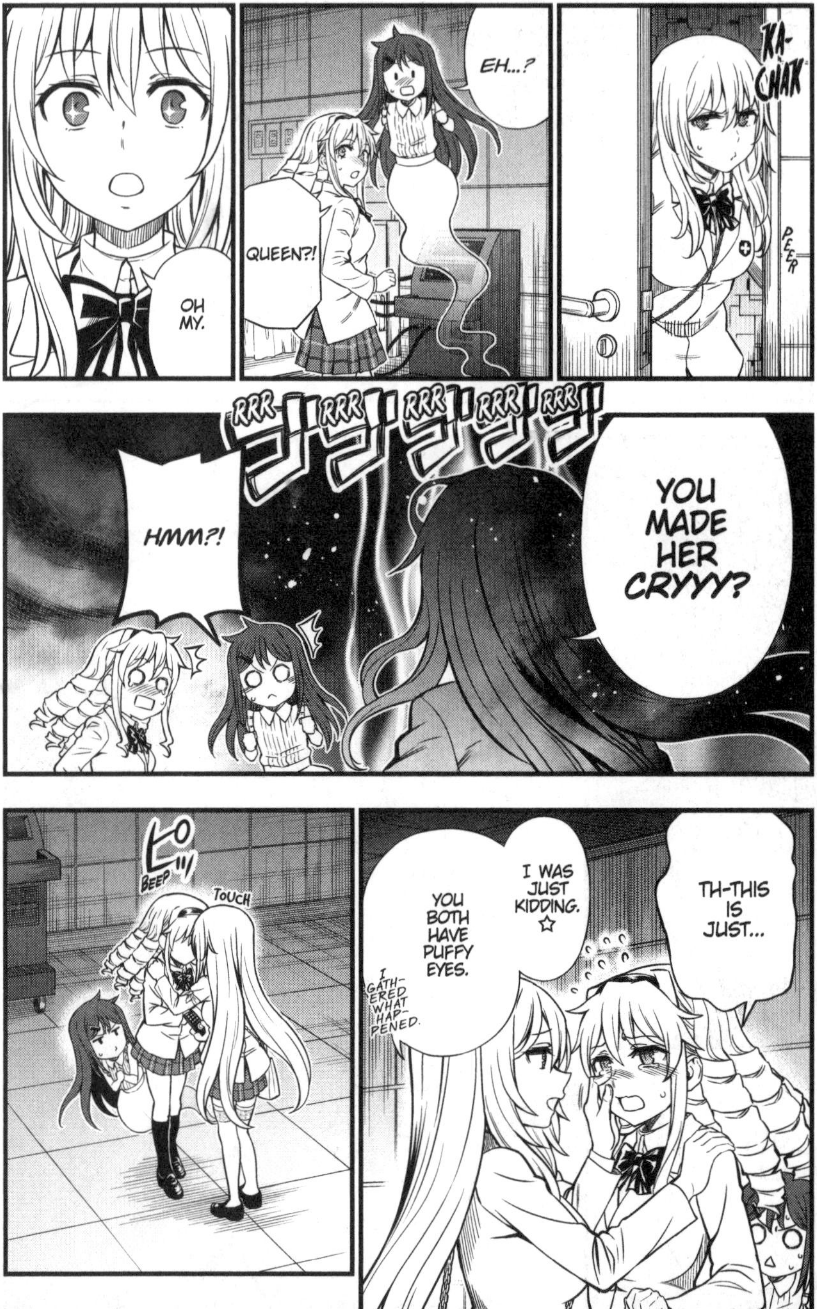
KA-CHAK
PEER
EH...?
QUEEN?!
OH MY.
RRR RRR RRR RRR RRR
YOU MADE HER CRYYY?
HMM?!
TH-THIS IS JUST...
I WAS JUST KIDDING. ☆
YOU BOTH HAVE PUFFY EYES.
I GATHERED WHAT HAPPENED.
BEEP
TOUCH

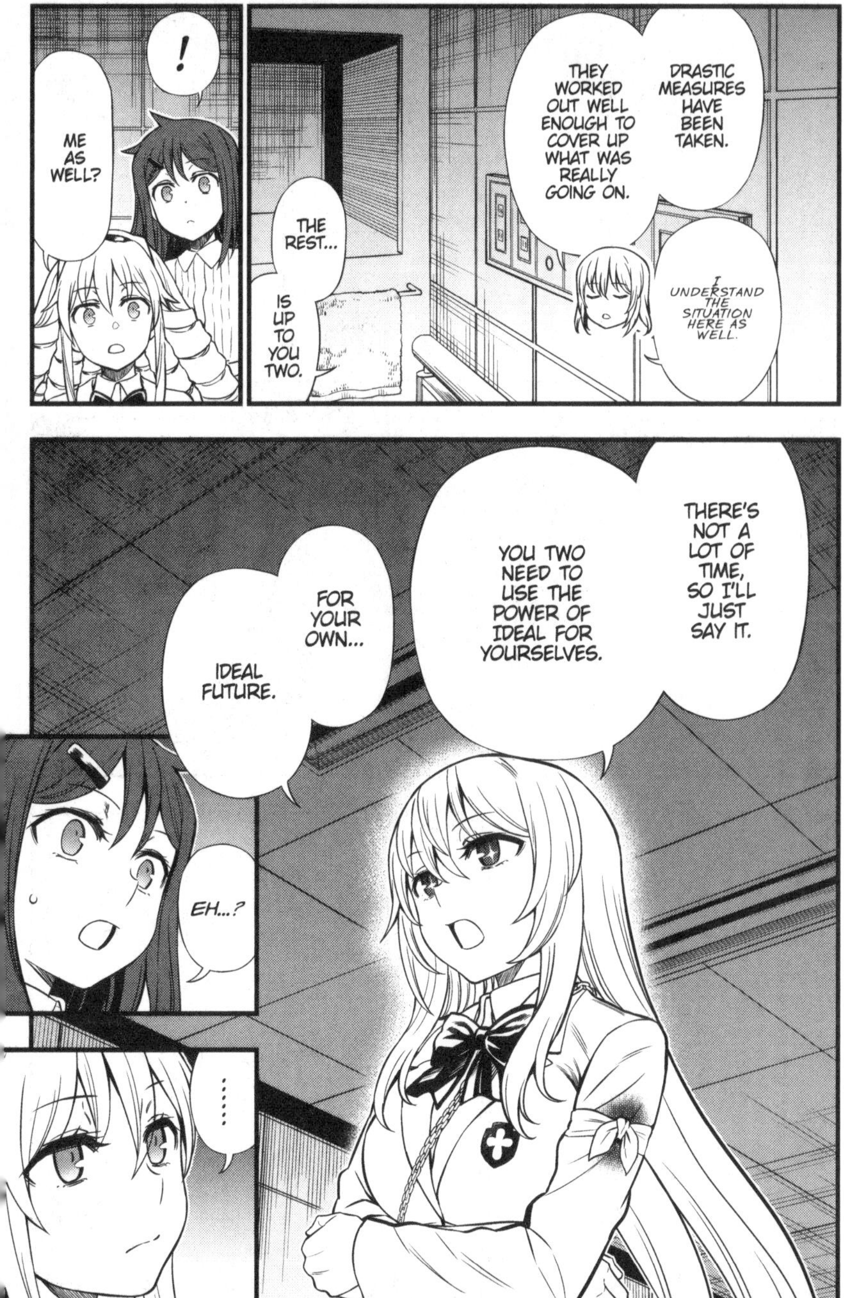
DRASTIC MEASURES HAVE BEEN TAKEN.
THEY WORKED OUT WELL ENOUGH TO COVER UP WHAT WAS REALLY GOING ON.
I UNDERSTAND THE SITUATION HERE AS WELL.
THE REST...
IS UP TO YOU TWO.
!
ME AS WELL?
THERE'S NOT A LOT OF TIME, SO I'LL JUST SAY IT.
YOU TWO NEED TO USE THE POWER OF IDEAL FOR YOURSELVES.
FOR YOUR OWN...
IDEAL FUTURE.
EH...?
......

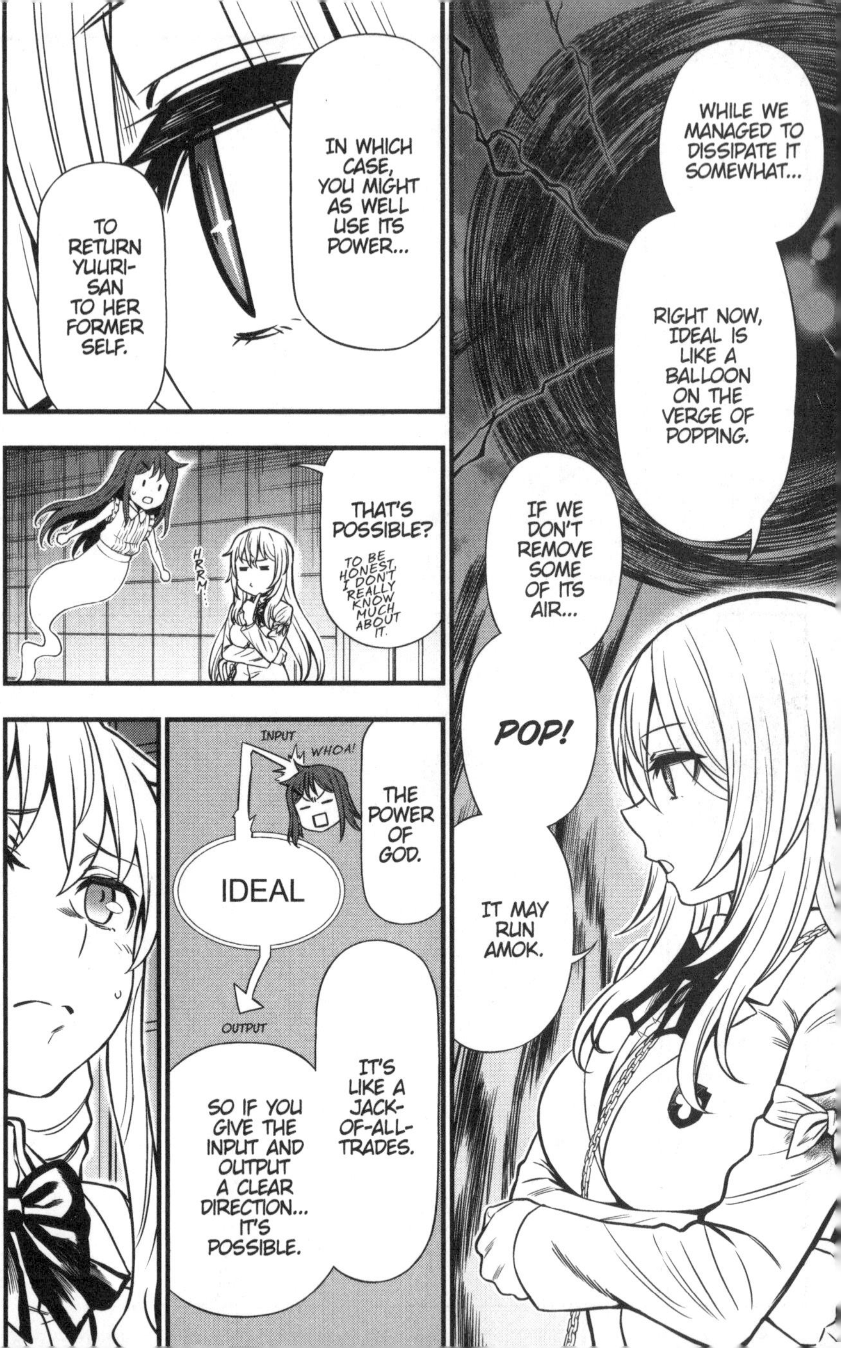
WHILE WE MANAGED TO DISSIPATE IT SOMEWHAT...
RIGHT NOW, IDEAL IS LIKE A BALLOON ON THE VERGE OF POPPING.
IF WE DON'T REMOVE SOME OF ITS AIR...
POP!
IT MAY RUN AMOK.
IN WHICH CASE, YOU MIGHT AS WELL USE ITS POWER...
TO RETURN YUURI-SAN TO HER FORMER SELF.
THAT'S POSSIBLE?
HRRM...
TO BE HONEST, I DON'T REALLY KNOW MUCH ABOUT IT.
THE POWER OF GOD.
INPUT
WHOA!
IDEAL
OUTPUT
IT'S LIKE A JACK-OF-ALL-TRADES.
SO IF YOU GIVE THE INPUT AND OUTPUT A CLEAR DIRECTION... IT'S POSSIBLE.

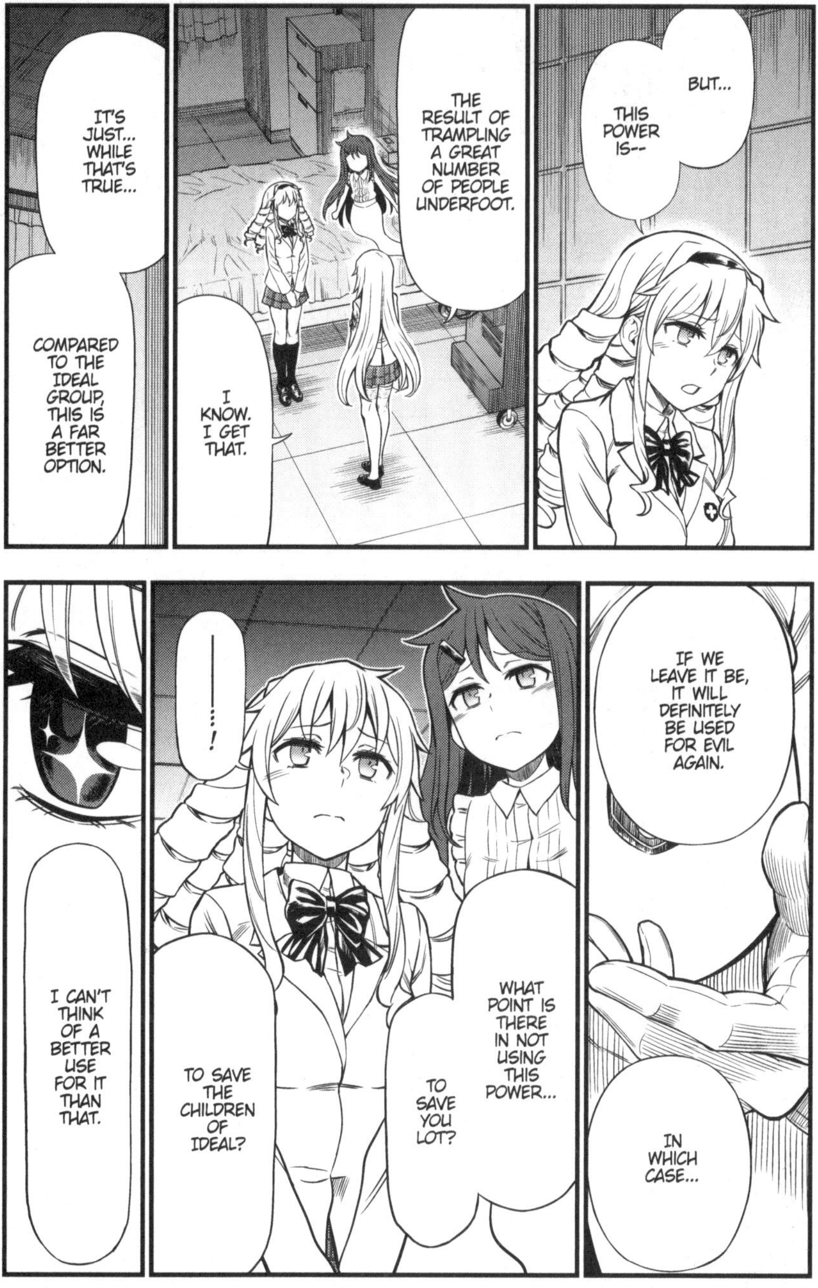
BUT...
THIS POWER IS--
THE RESULT OF TRAMPLING A GREAT NUMBER OF PEOPLE UNDERFOOT.
I KNOW. I GET THAT.
IT'S JUST... WHILE THAT'S TRUE...
COMPARED TO THE IDEAL GROUP, THIS IS A FAR BETTER OPTION.
IF WE LEAVE IT BE, IT WILL DEFINITELY BE USED FOR EVIL AGAIN.
IN WHICH CASE...
WHAT POINT IS THERE IN NOT USING THIS POWER...
TO SAVE YOU LOT?
TO SAVE THE CHILDREN OF IDEAL?
---...!
I CAN'T THINK OF A BETTER USE FOR IT THAN THAT.

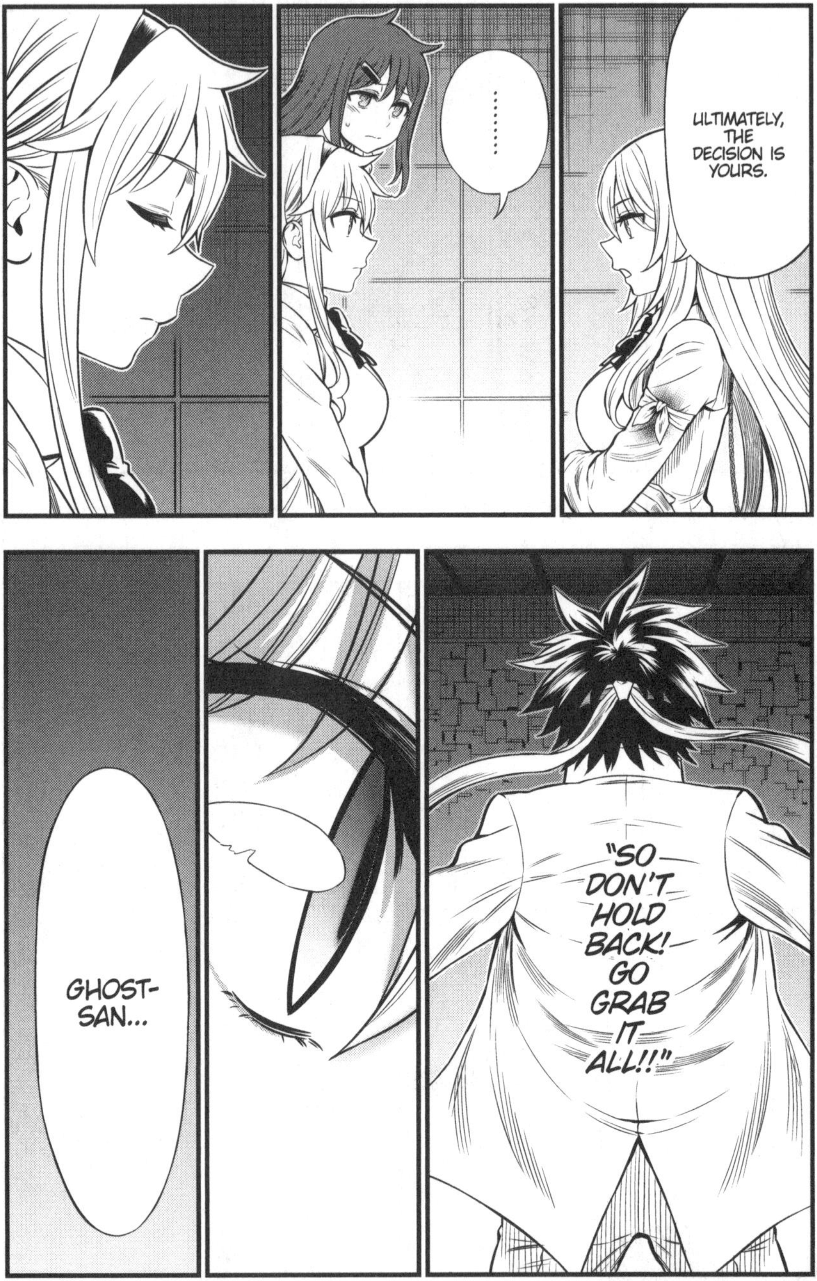
ULTIMATELY, THE DECISION IS YOURS.
......
"SO DON'T HOLD BACK! GO GRAB IT ALL!!"
GHOST-SAN...

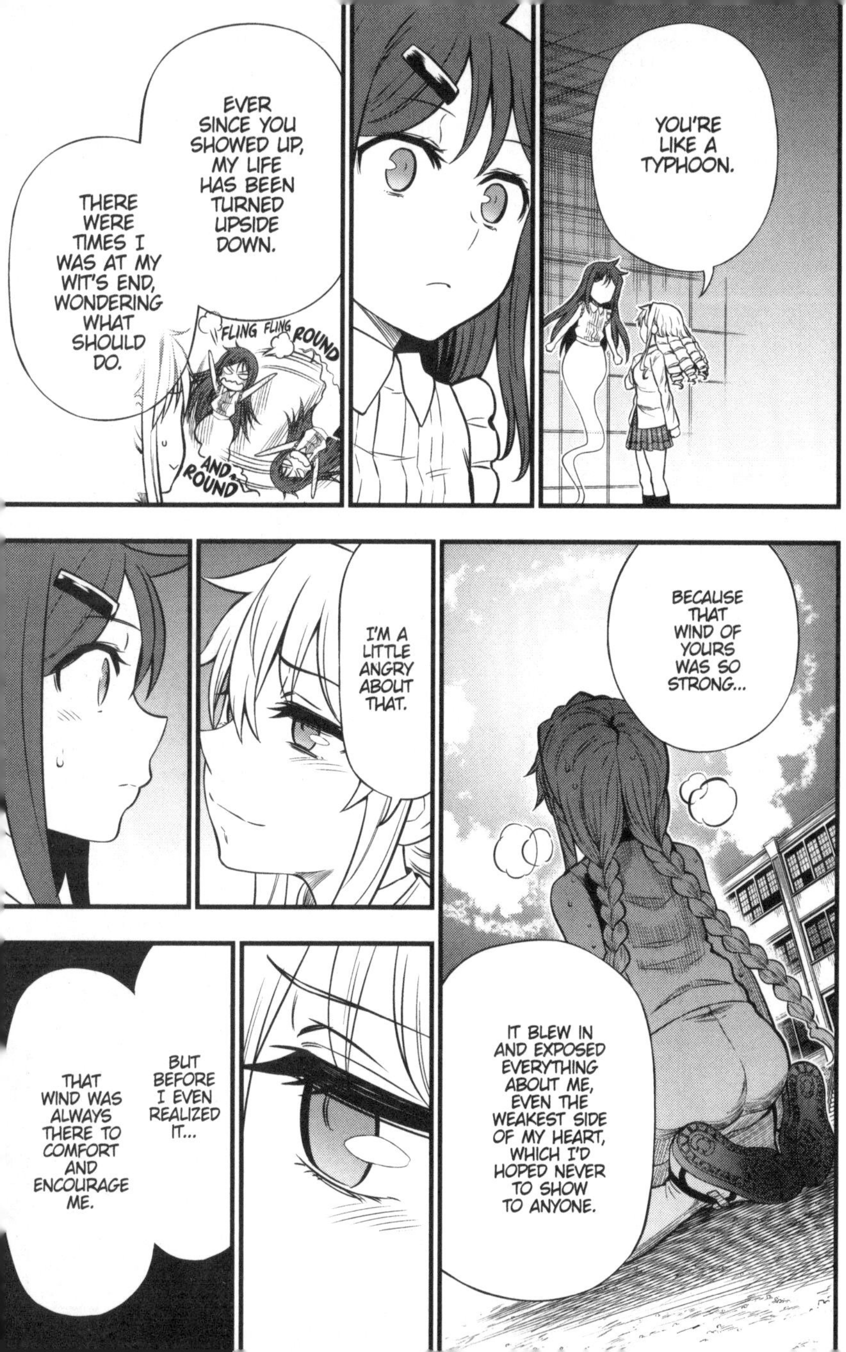
YOU'RE LIKE A TYPHOON.
EVER SINCE YOU SHOWED UP, MY LIFE HAS BEEN TURNED UPSIDE DOWN.
THERE WERE TIMES I WAS AT MY WIT'S END, WONDERING WHAT SHOULD DO.
FLING FLING
ROUND AND ROUND
BECAUSE THAT WIND OF YOURS WAS SO STRONG...
IT BLEW IN AND EXPOSED EVERYTHING ABOUT ME, EVEN THE WEAKEST SIDE OF MY HEART, WHICH I'D HOPED NEVER TO SHOW TO ANYONE.
I'M A LITTLE ANGRY ABOUT THAT.
BUT BEFORE I EVEN REALIZED IT...
THAT WIND WAS ALWAYS THERE TO COMFORT AND ENCOURAGE ME.

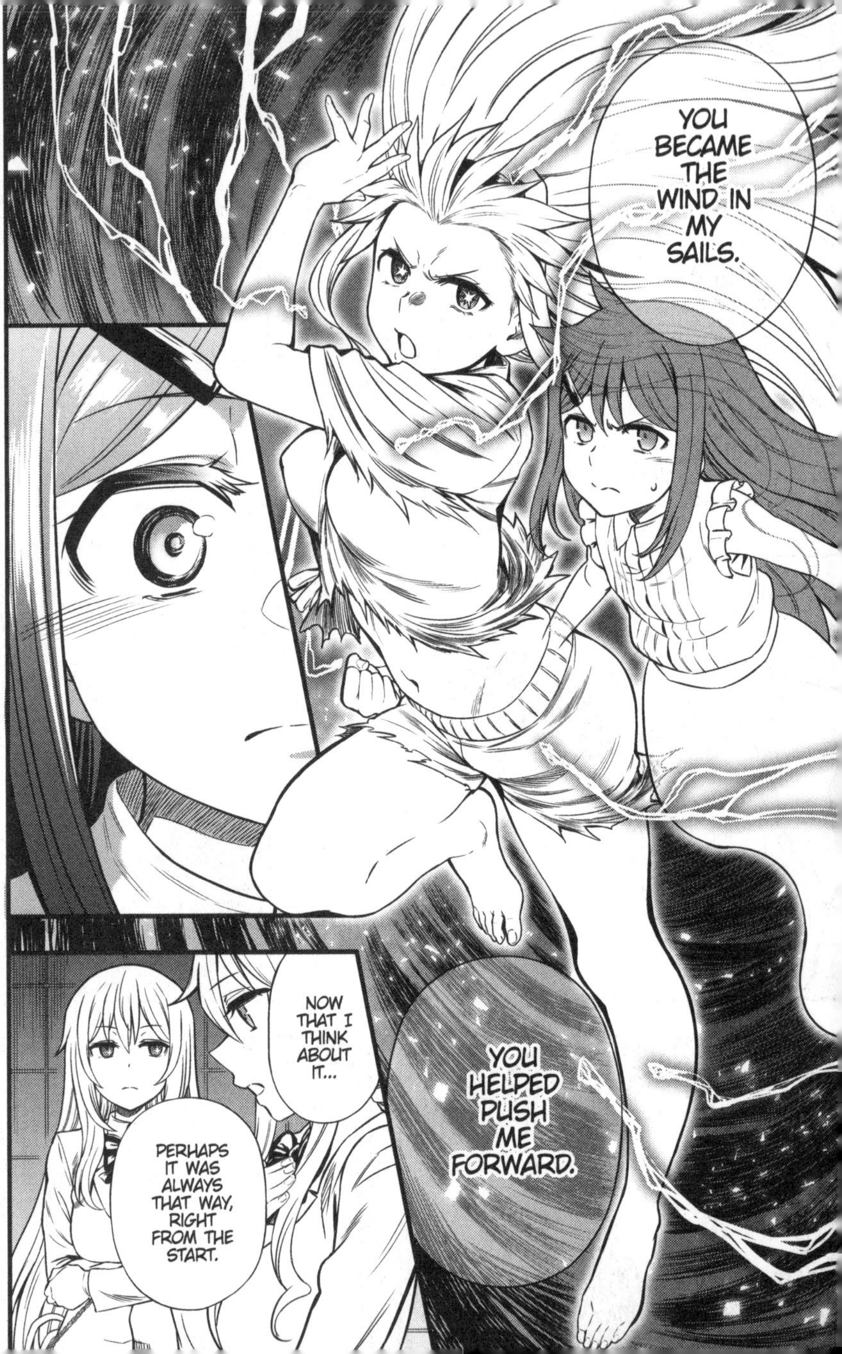
YOU BECAME THE WIND IN MY SAILS.
YOU HELPED PUSH ME FORWARD.
NOW THAT I THINK ABOUT IT...
PERHAPS IT WAS ALWAYS THAT WAY, RIGHT FROM THE START.

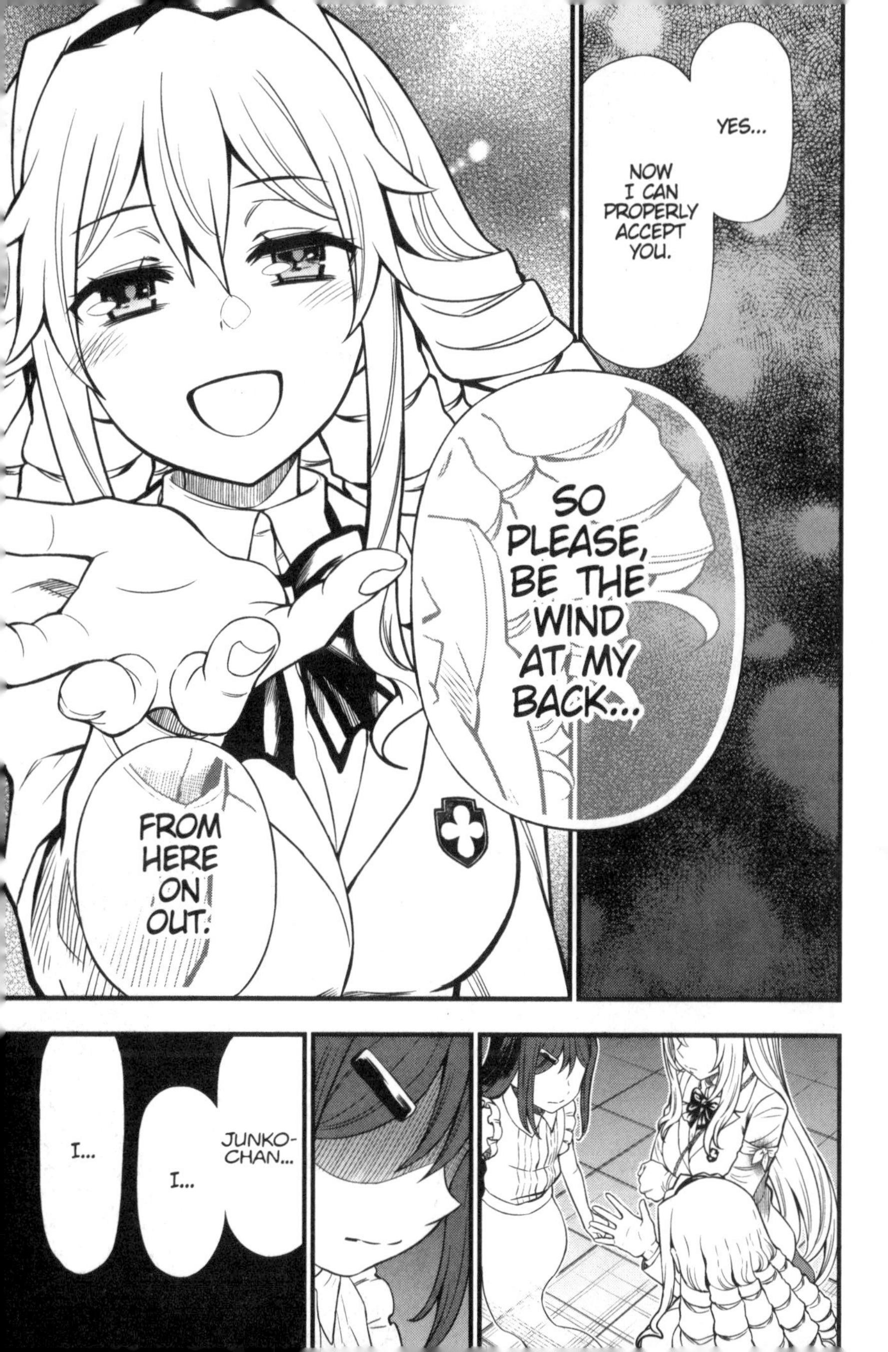
YES...
NOW I CAN PROPERLY ACCEPT YOU.
SO PLEASE, BE THE WIND AT MY BACK...
FROM HERE ON OUT.
JUNKO-CHAN...
I...
I...

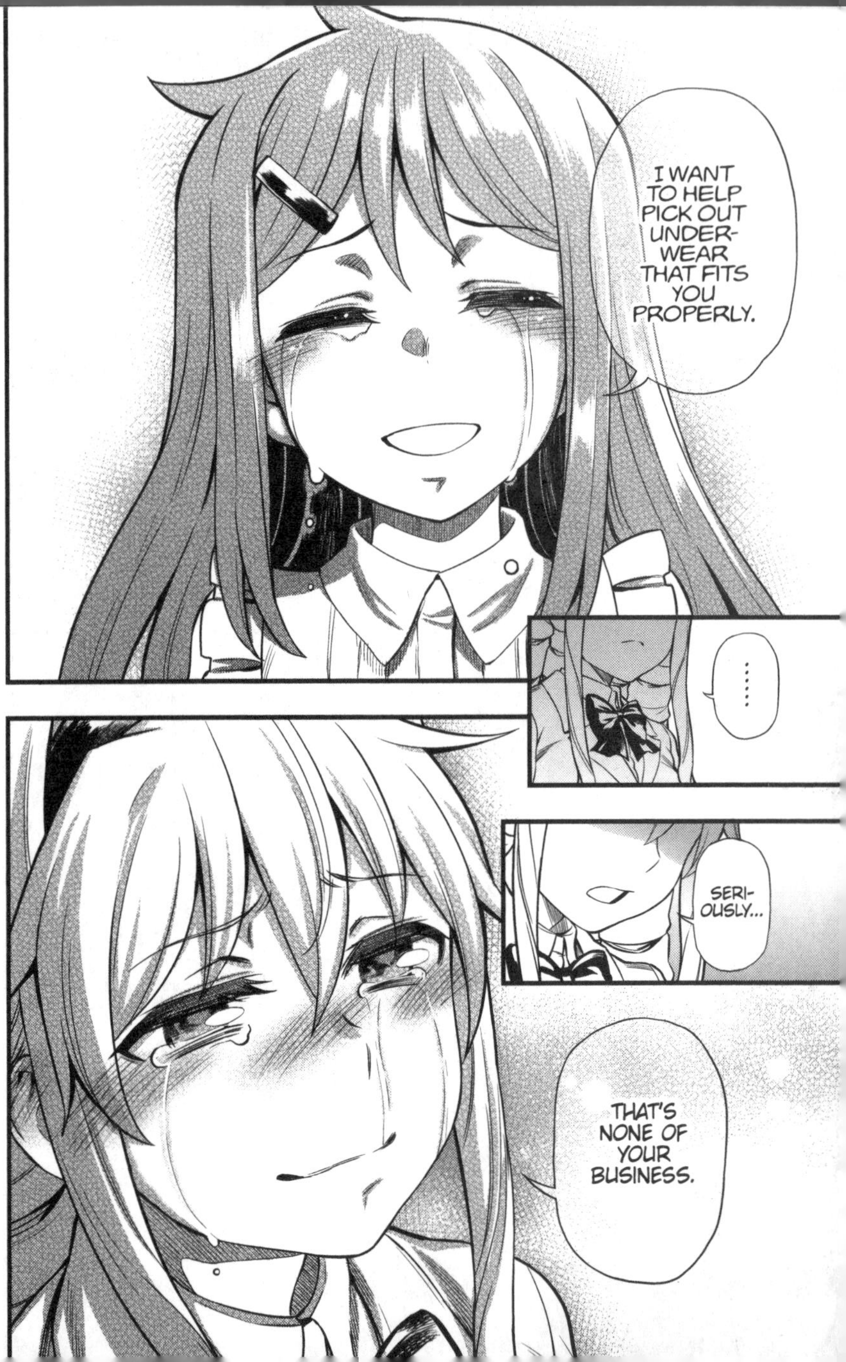
I WANT TO HELP PICK OUT UNDER-WEAR THAT FITS YOU PROPERLY.
......
SERI-OUSLY...
THAT'S NONE OF YOUR BUSINESS.

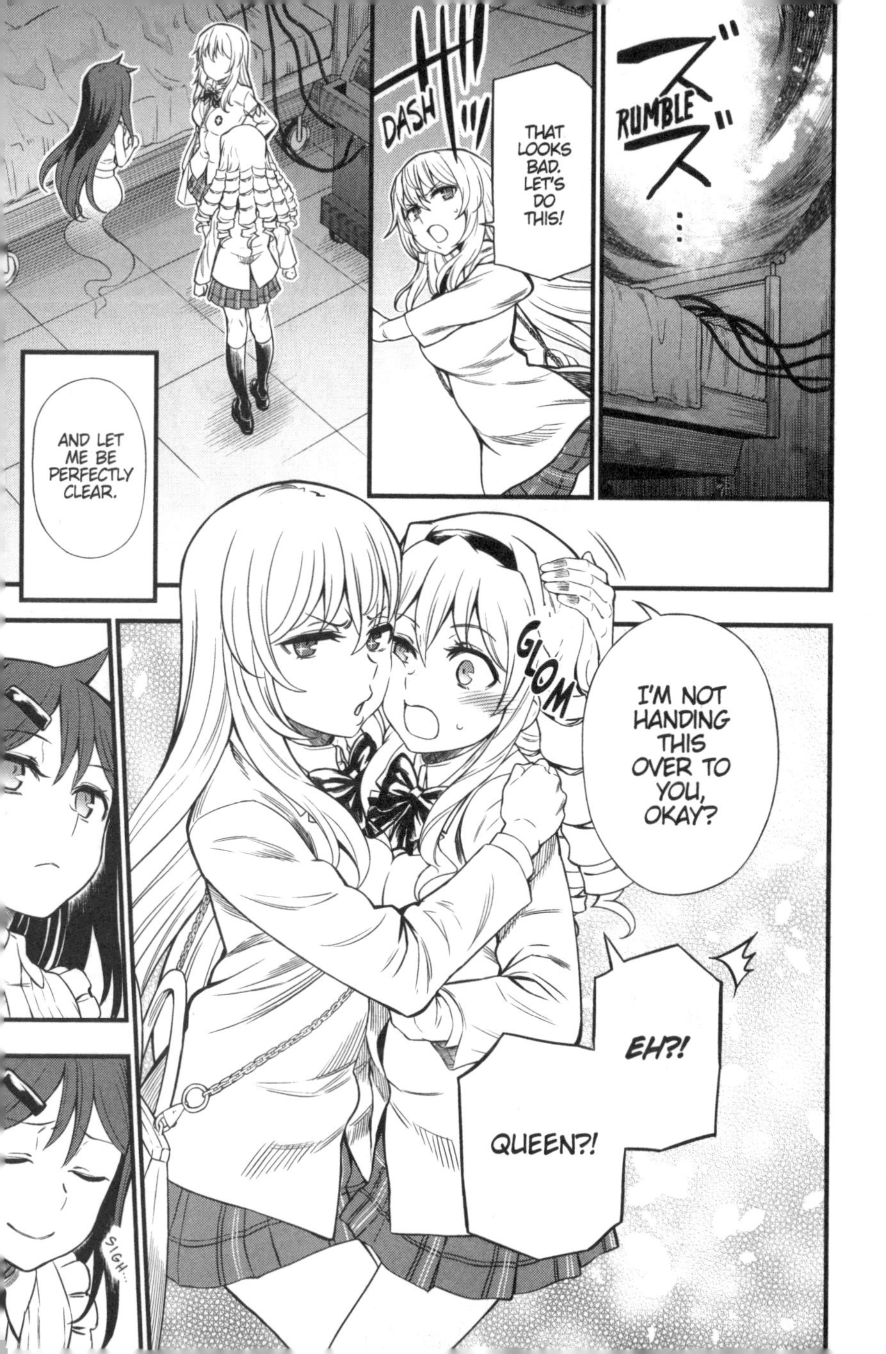
RUMBLE
DASH
THAT LOOKS BAD. LET'S DO THIS!
AND LET ME BE PERFECTLY CLEAR.
GLOM
I'M NOT HANDING THIS OVER TO YOU, OKAY?
EH?!
QUEEN?!
SIGH...

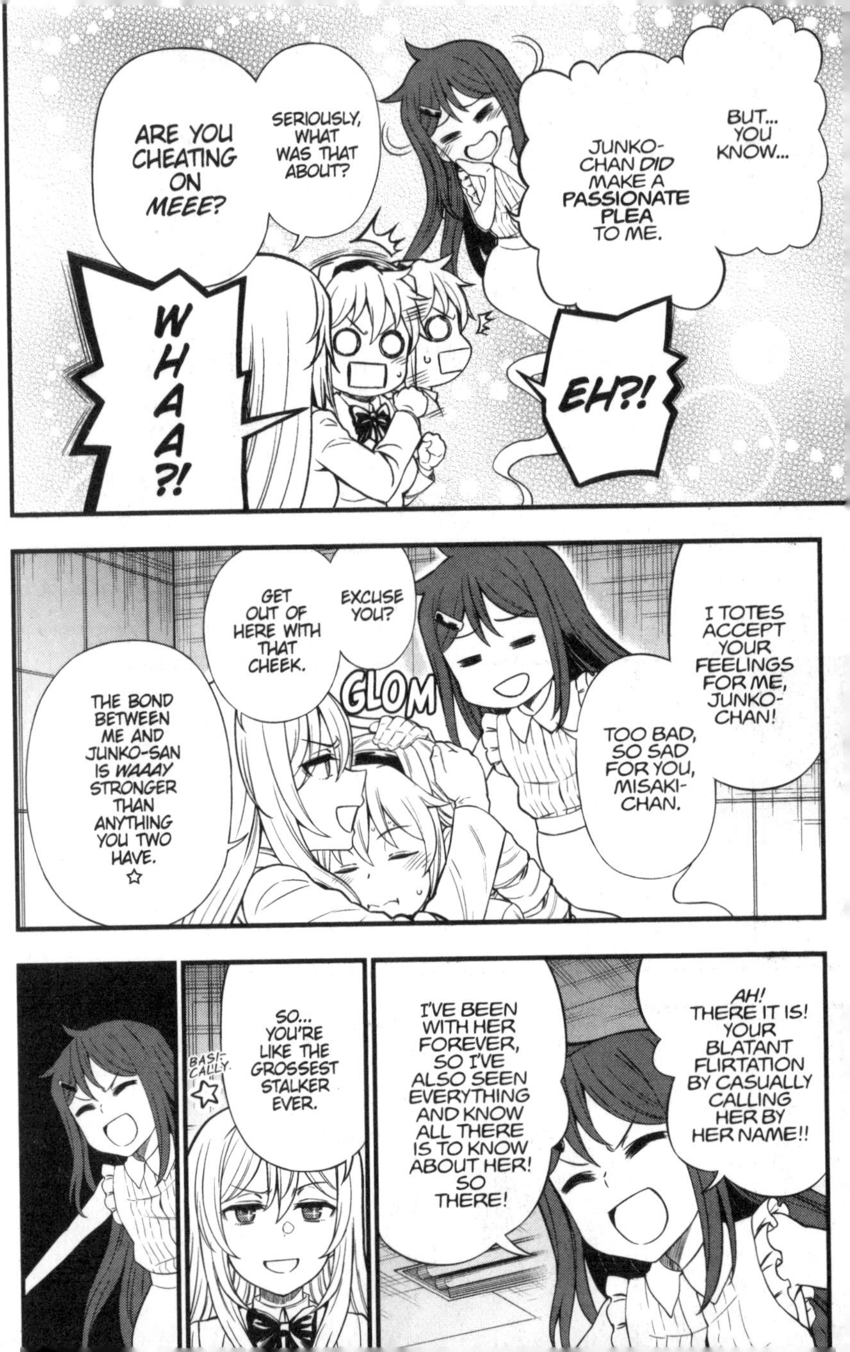
BUT... YOU KNOW...
JUNKO-CHAN *DID* MAKE A **PASSIONATE PLEA** TO ME.
EH?!
SERIOUSLY, WHAT WAS THAT ABOUT?
ARE YOU CHEATING ON *MEEE?*
WHAAA?!
I TOTES ACCEPT YOUR FEELINGS FOR ME, JUNKO-CHAN!
TOO BAD, SO SAD FOR YOU, MISAKI-CHAN.
EXCUSE YOU?
GET OUT OF HERE WITH THAT CHEEK.
GLOM
THE BOND BETWEEN ME AND JUNKO-SAN IS *WAAAY* STRONGER THAN ANYTHING YOU TWO HAVE. ☆
AH! THERE IT IS! YOUR BLATANT FLIRTATION BY CASUALLY CALLING HER BY HER NAME!!
I'VE BEEN WITH HER FOREVER, SO I'VE ALSO SEEN EVERYTHING AND KNOW ALL THERE IS TO KNOW ABOUT HER! SO THERE!
SO... YOU'RE LIKE THE GROSSEST STALKER EVER.
BASICALLY. ☆

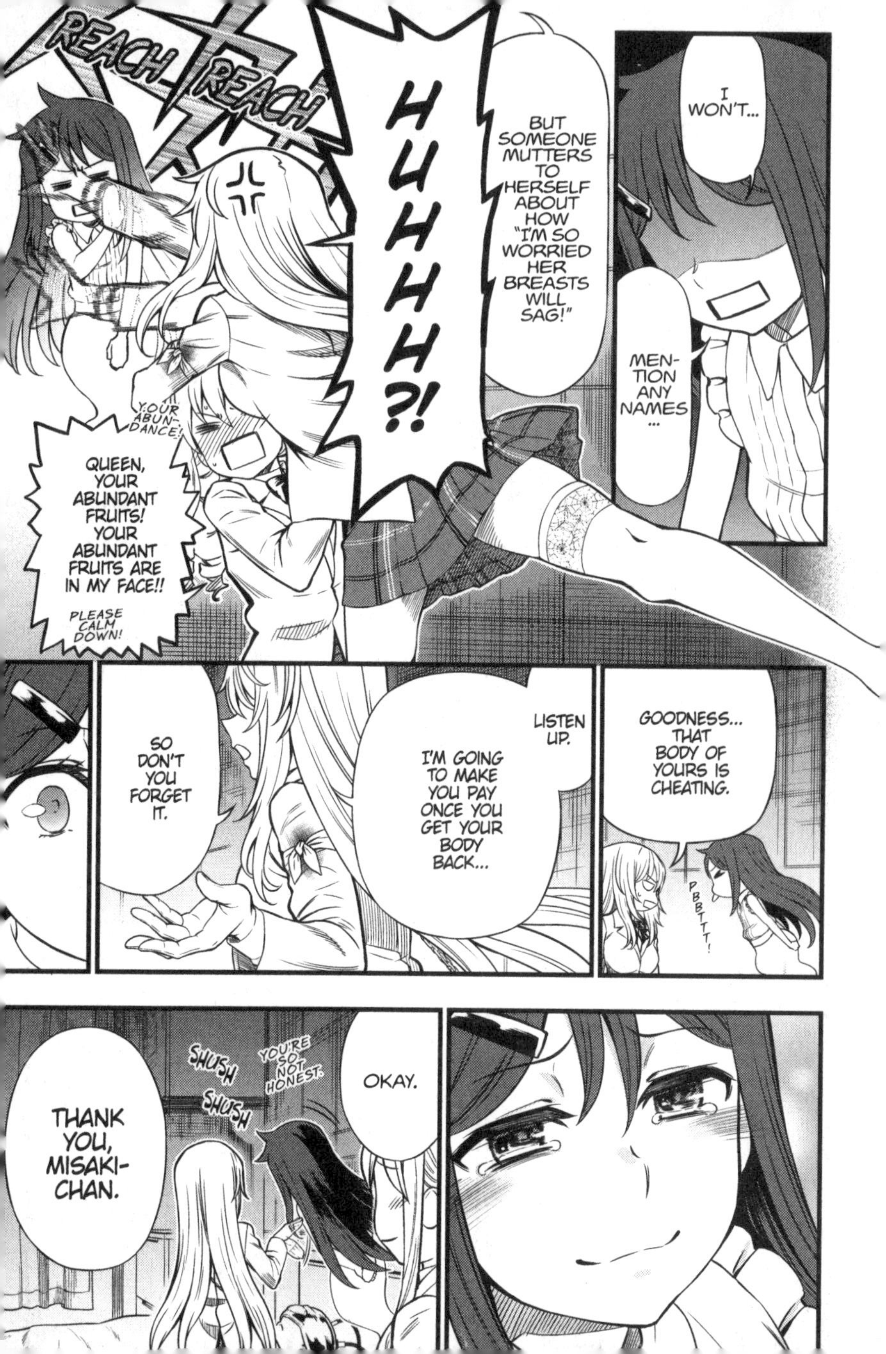
I WON'T...
MEN-TION ANY NAMES...
BUT SOMEONE MUTTERS TO HERSELF ABOUT HOW "I'M SO WORRIED HER BREASTS WILL SAG!"
HUHHHH?!
REACH REACH
QUEEN, YOUR ABUNDANT FRUITS! YOUR ABUNDANT FRUITS ARE IN MY FACE!!
YOUR ABUN-DANCE!
PLEASE CALM DOWN!
GOODNESS... THAT BODY OF YOURS IS CHEATING.
PBBTTT!
LISTEN UP.
I'M GOING TO MAKE YOU PAY ONCE YOU GET YOUR BODY BACK...
SO DON'T YOU FORGET IT.
OKAY.
YOU'RE SO NOT HONEST.
SHUSH
SHUSH
THANK YOU, MISAKI-CHAN.

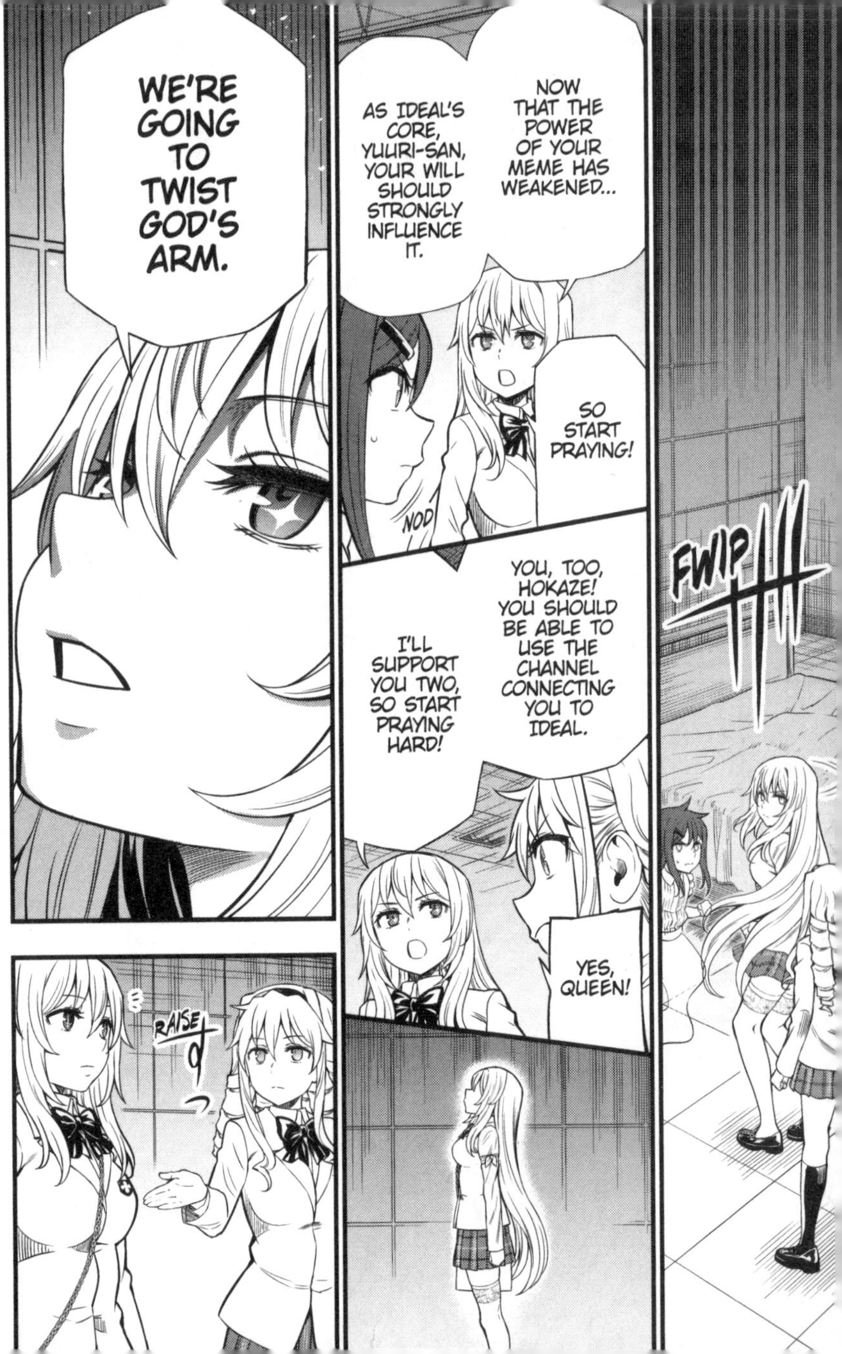
FWIP
NOW THAT THE POWER OF YOUR MEME HAS WEAKENED...
AS IDEAL'S CORE, YUURI-SAN, YOUR WILL SHOULD STRONGLY INFLUENCE IT.
SO START PRAYING!
NOD
YOU, TOO, HOKAZE! YOU SHOULD BE ABLE TO USE THE CHANNEL CONNECTING YOU TO IDEAL.
I'LL SUPPORT YOU TWO, SO START PRAYING HARD!
YES, QUEEN!
WE'RE GOING TO TWIST GOD'S ARM.
RAISE

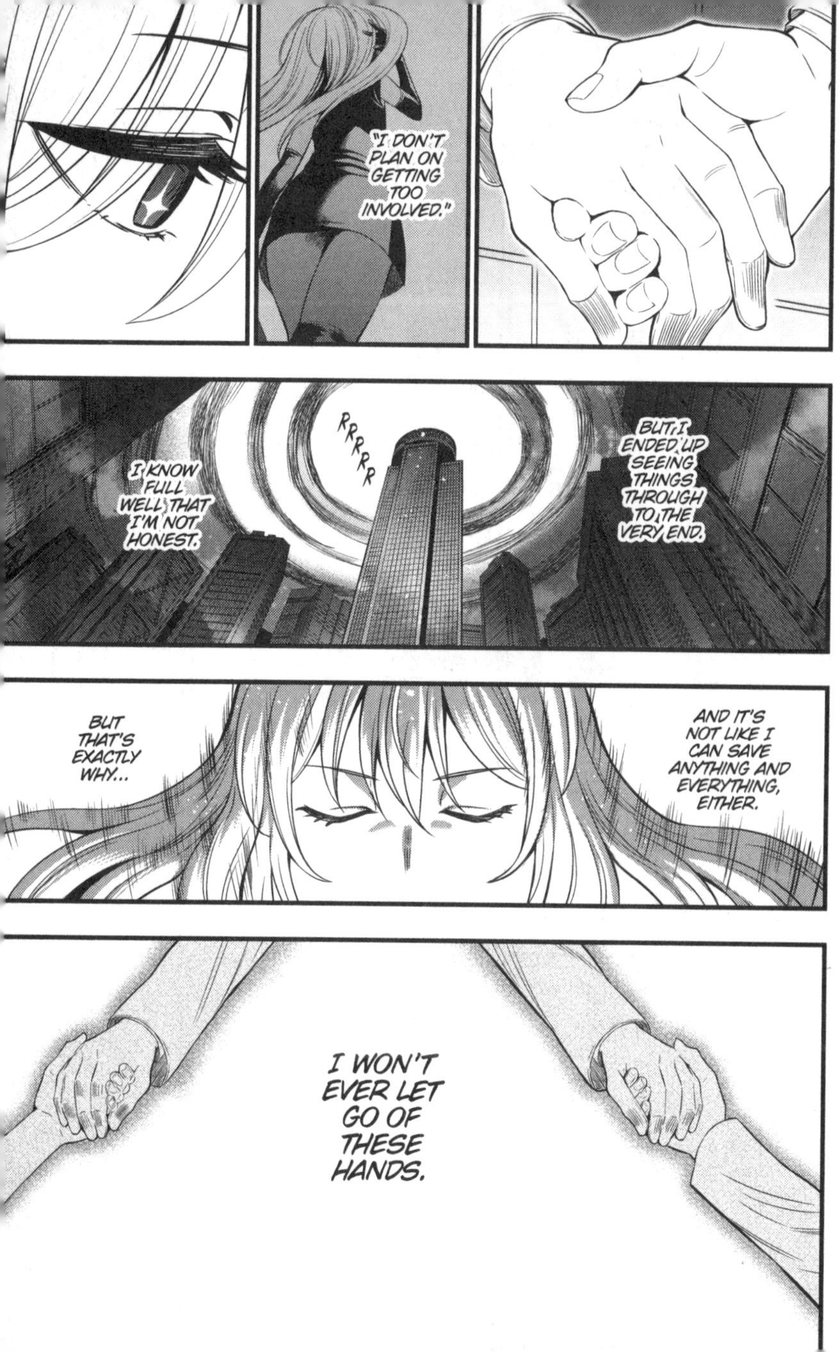
"I DON'T PLAN ON GETTING TOO INVOLVED."
BUT I ENDED UP SEEING THINGS THROUGH TO THE VERY END.
RRRRR
I KNOW FULL WELL THAT I'M NOT HONEST.
AND IT'S NOT LIKE I CAN SAVE ANYTHING AND EVERYTHING, EITHER.
BUT THAT'S EXACTLY WHY...
I WON'T EVER LET GO OF THESE HANDS.

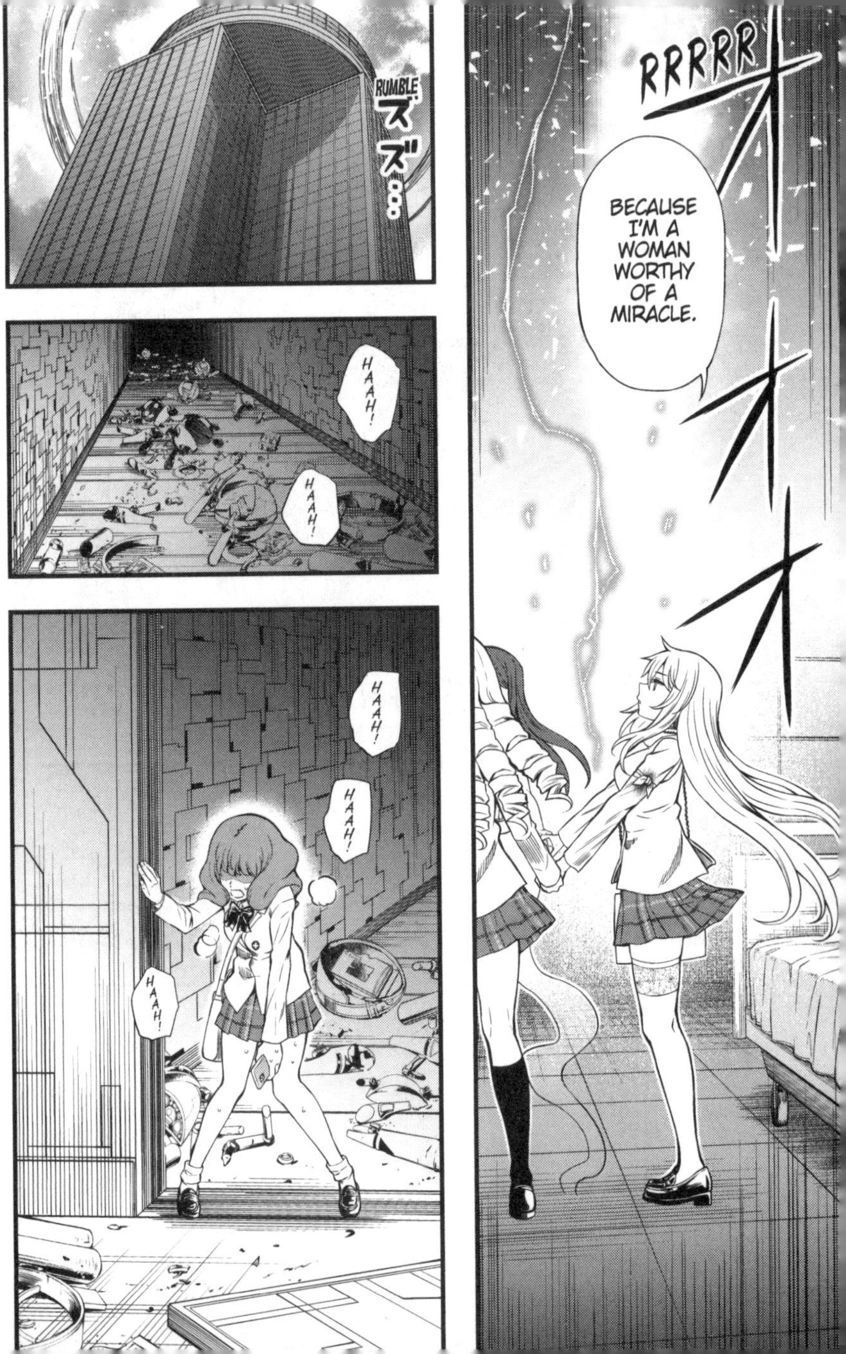
RRRRR
BECAUSE I'M A WOMAN WORTHY OF A MIRACLE.
RUMBLE
ズズ…
HAAH!
HAAH!
HAAH!
HAAH!
HAAH!

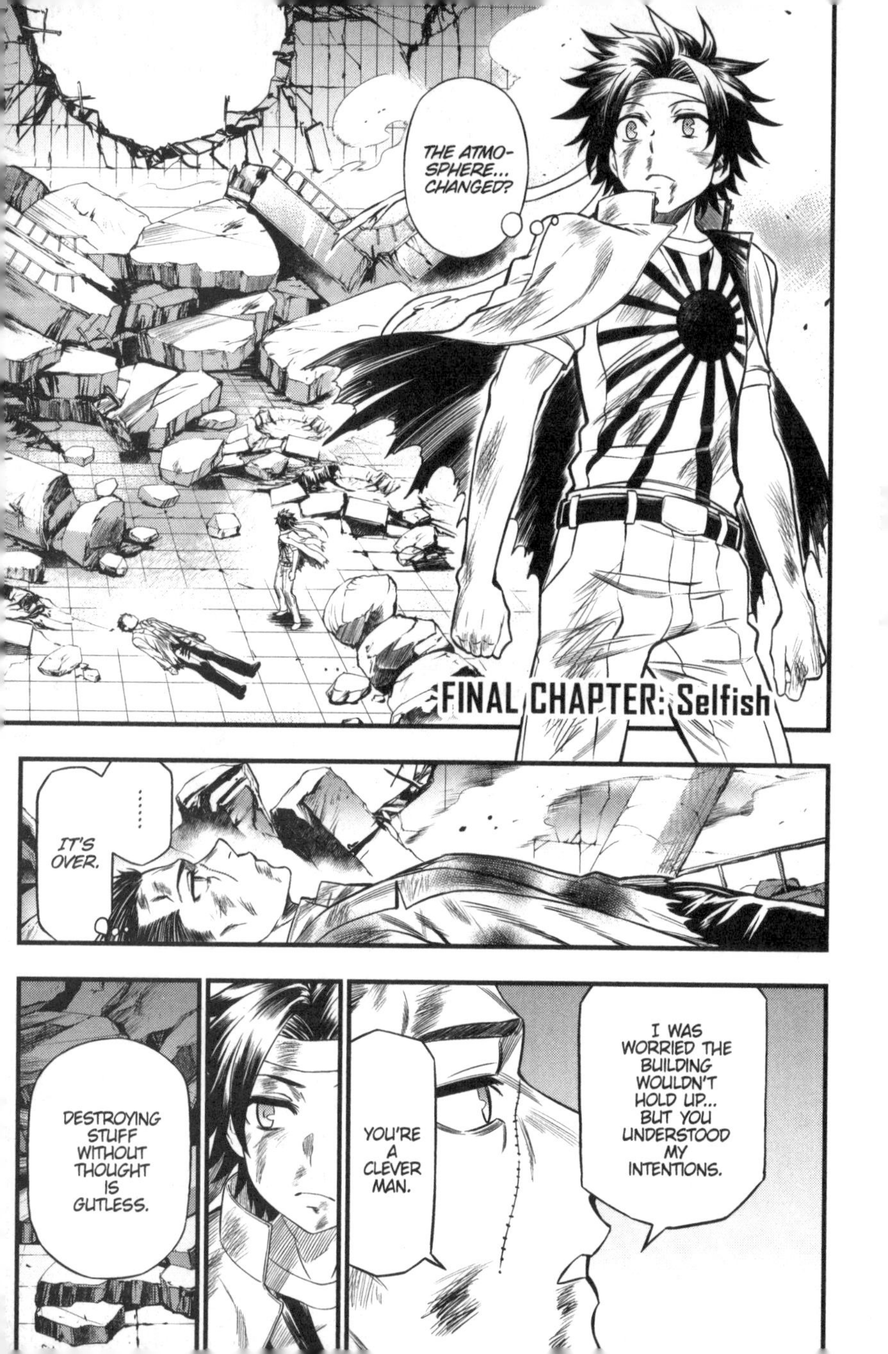
THE ATMO-SPHERE... CHANGED?
FINAL CHAPTER: Selfish
......
IT'S OVER.
I WAS WORRIED THE BUILDING WOULDN'T HOLD UP... BUT YOU UNDERSTOOD MY INTENTIONS.
YOU'RE A CLEVER MAN.
DESTROYING STUFF WITHOUT THOUGHT IS GUTLESS.

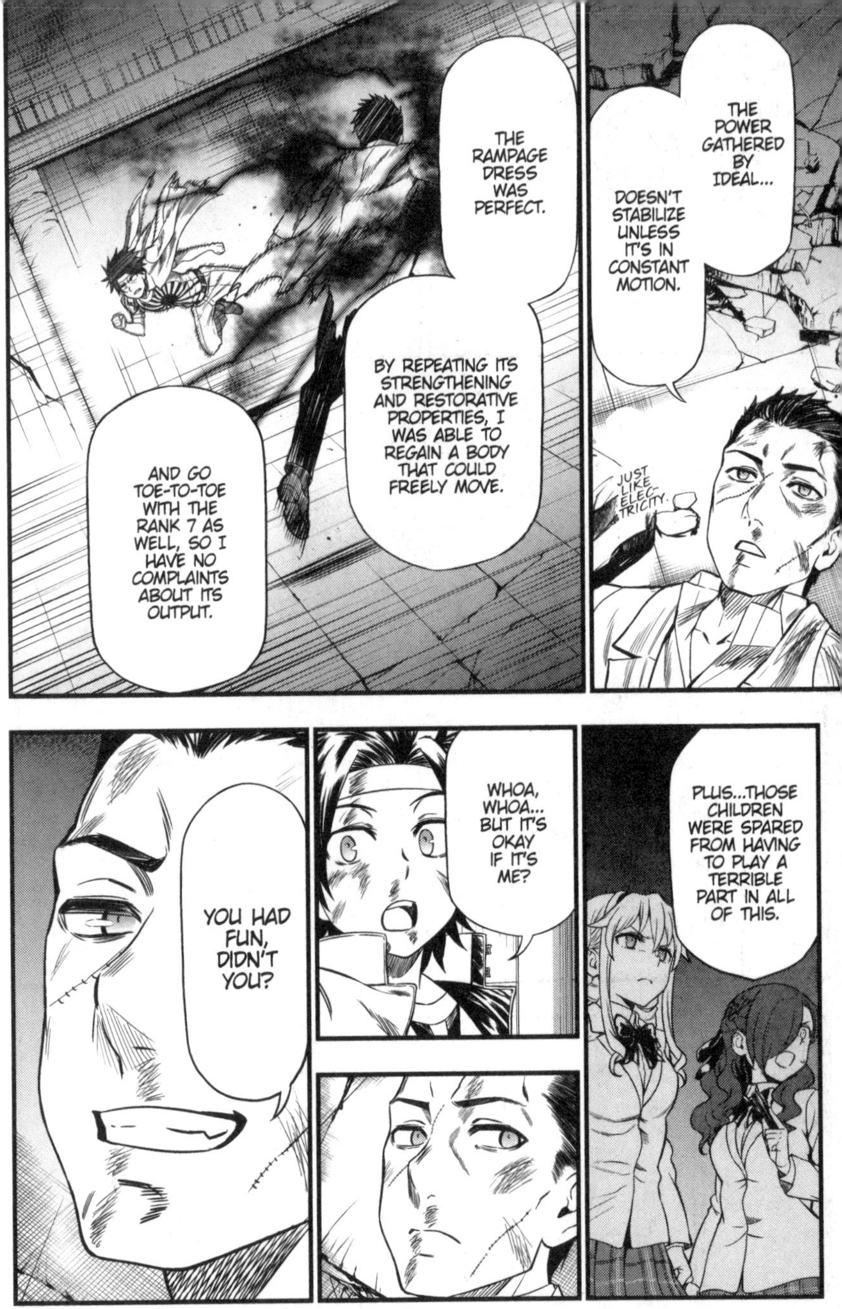
THE POWER GATHERED BY IDEAL...
DOESN'T STABILIZE UNLESS IT'S IN CONSTANT MOTION.
JUST LIKE ELECTRICITY.
THE RAMPAGE DRESS WAS PERFECT.
BY REPEATING ITS STRENGTHENING AND RESTORATIVE PROPERTIES, I WAS ABLE TO REGAIN A BODY THAT COULD FREELY MOVE.
AND GO TOE-TO-TOE WITH THE RANK 7 AS WELL, SO I HAVE NO COMPLAINTS ABOUT ITS OUTPUT.
PLUS...THOSE CHILDREN WERE SPARED FROM HAVING TO PLAY A TERRIBLE PART IN ALL OF THIS.
WHOA, WHOA... BUT IT'S OKAY IF IT'S ME?
YOU HAD FUN, DIDN'T YOU?

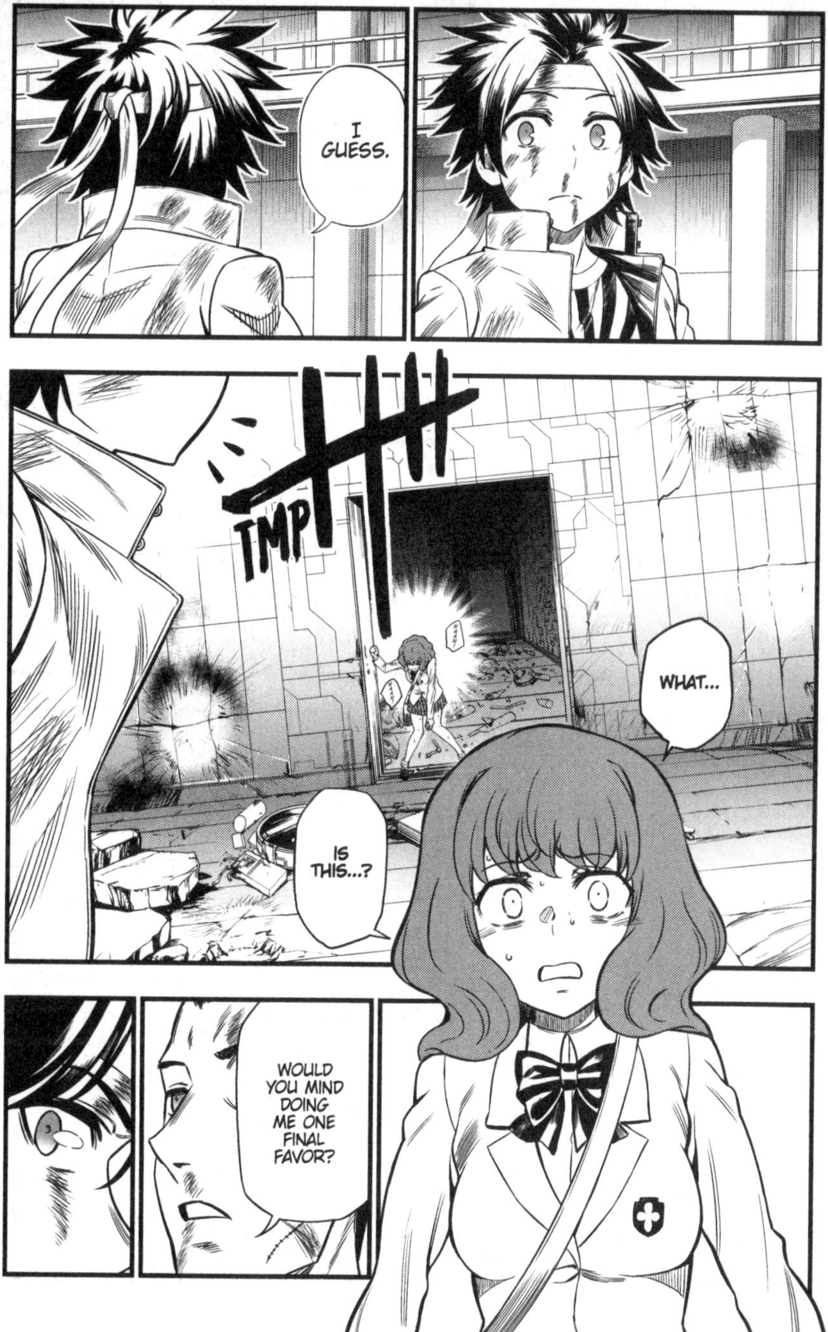
I GUESS.
TMP
WHAT...
IS THIS...?
WOULD YOU MIND DOING ME ONE FINAL FAVOR?

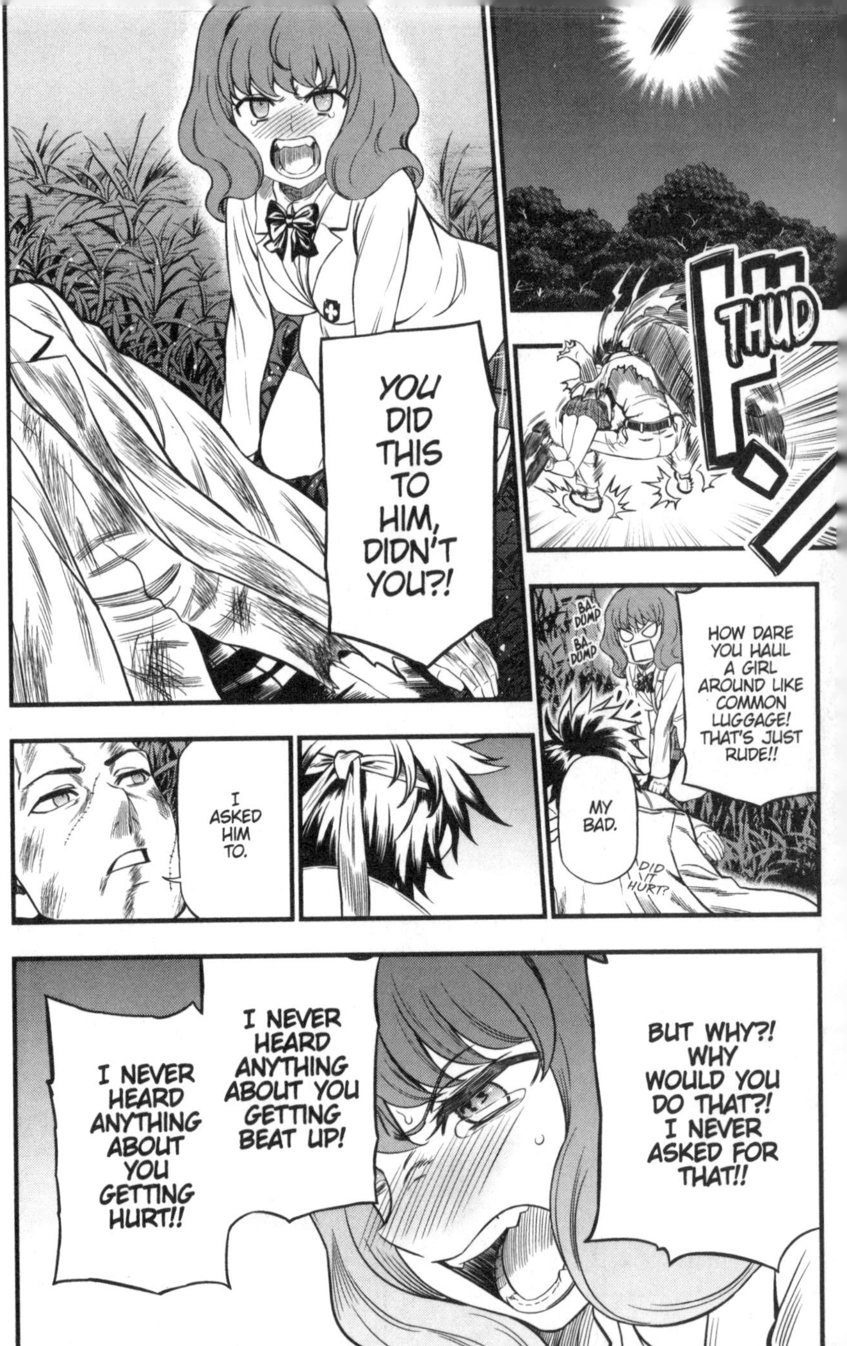
THUD
BA-DUMP BA-DUMP
HOW DARE YOU HAUL A GIRL AROUND LIKE COMMON LUGGAGE! THAT'S JUST RUDE!!
DID IT HURT?
MY BAD.
YOU DID THIS TO HIM, DIDN'T YOU?!
I ASKED HIM TO.
BUT WHY?! WHY WOULD YOU DO THAT?! I NEVER ASKED FOR THAT!!
I NEVER HEARD ANYTHING ABOUT YOU GETTING BEAT UP!
I NEVER HEARD ANYTHING ABOUT YOU GETTING HURT!!

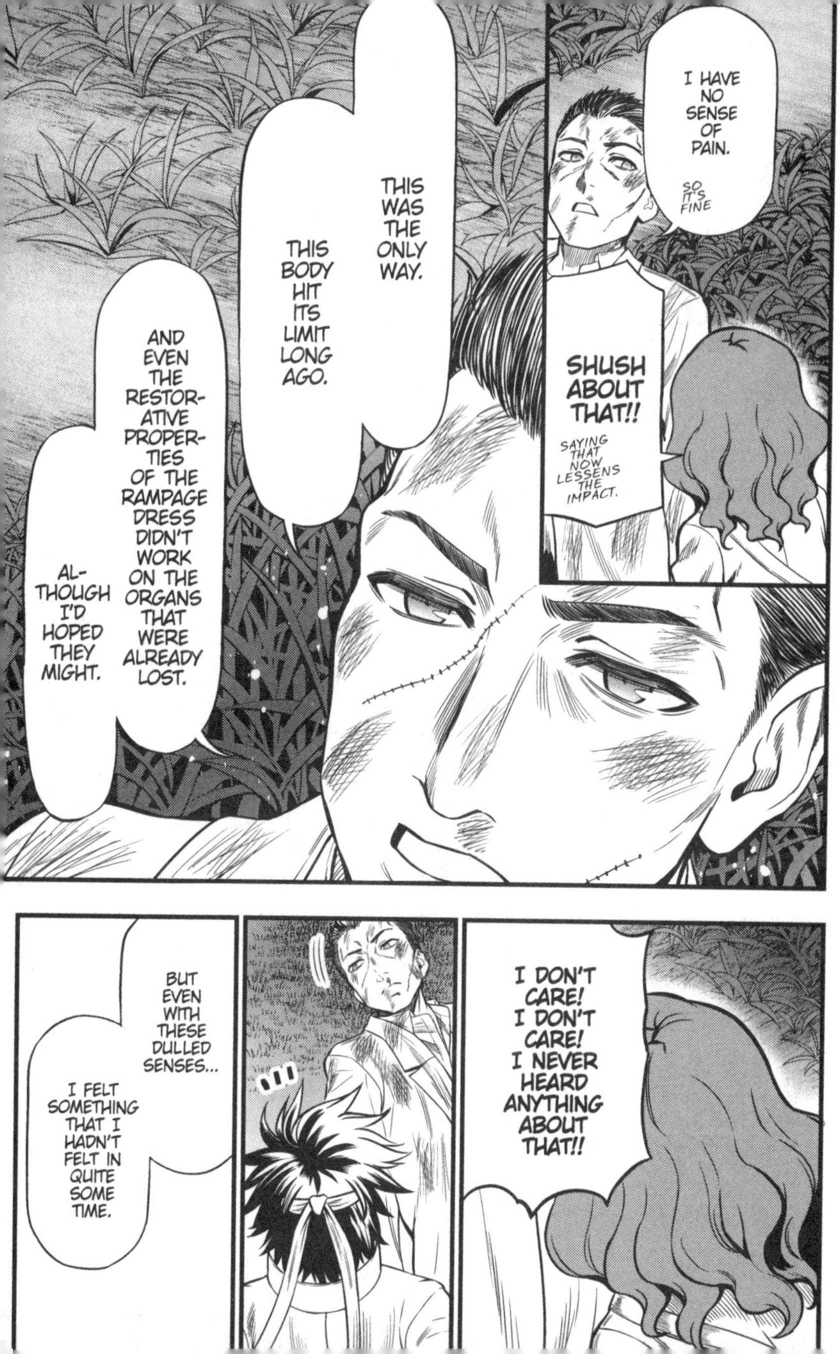
I HAVE NO SENSE OF PAIN.
SO IT'S FINE
SHUSH ABOUT THAT!!
SAYING THAT NOW LESSENS THE IMPACT.
THIS WAS THE ONLY WAY.
THIS BODY HIT ITS LIMIT LONG AGO.
AND EVEN THE RESTORATIVE PROPERTIES OF THE RAMPAGE DRESS DIDN'T WORK ON THE ORGANS THAT WERE ALREADY LOST.
ALTHOUGH I'D HOPED THEY MIGHT.
I DON'T CARE! I DON'T CARE! I NEVER HEARD ANYTHING ABOUT THAT!!
BUT EVEN WITH THESE DULLED SENSES...
I FELT SOMETHING THAT I HADN'T FELT IN QUITE SOME TIME.

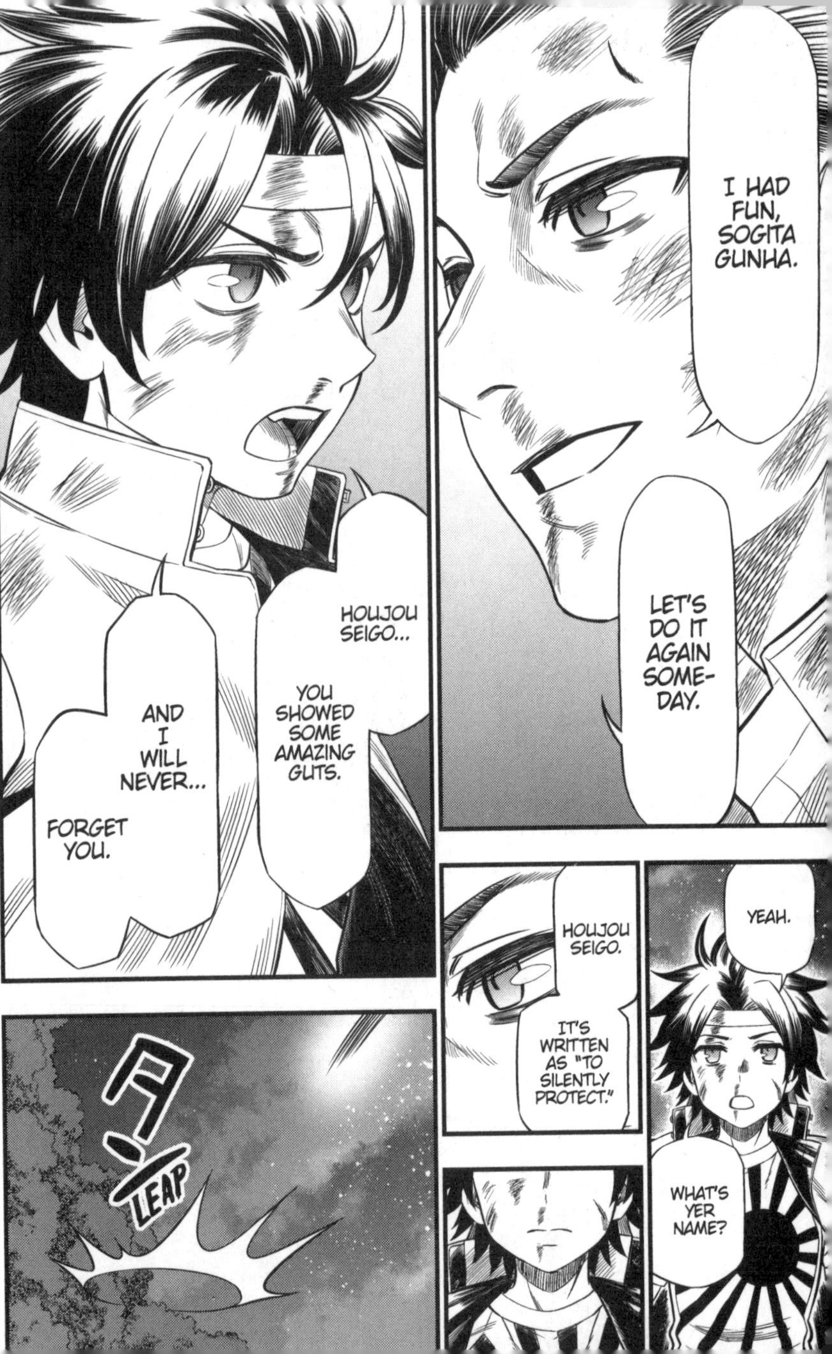
I HAD FUN, SOGITA GUNHA.
LET'S DO IT AGAIN SOME-DAY.
HOUJOU SEIGO...
YOU SHOWED SOME AMAZING GUTS.
AND I WILL NEVER...
FORGET YOU.
YEAH.
WHAT'S YER NAME?
HOUJOU SEIGO.
IT'S WRITTEN AS "TO SILENTLY PROTECT."
タン
LEAP

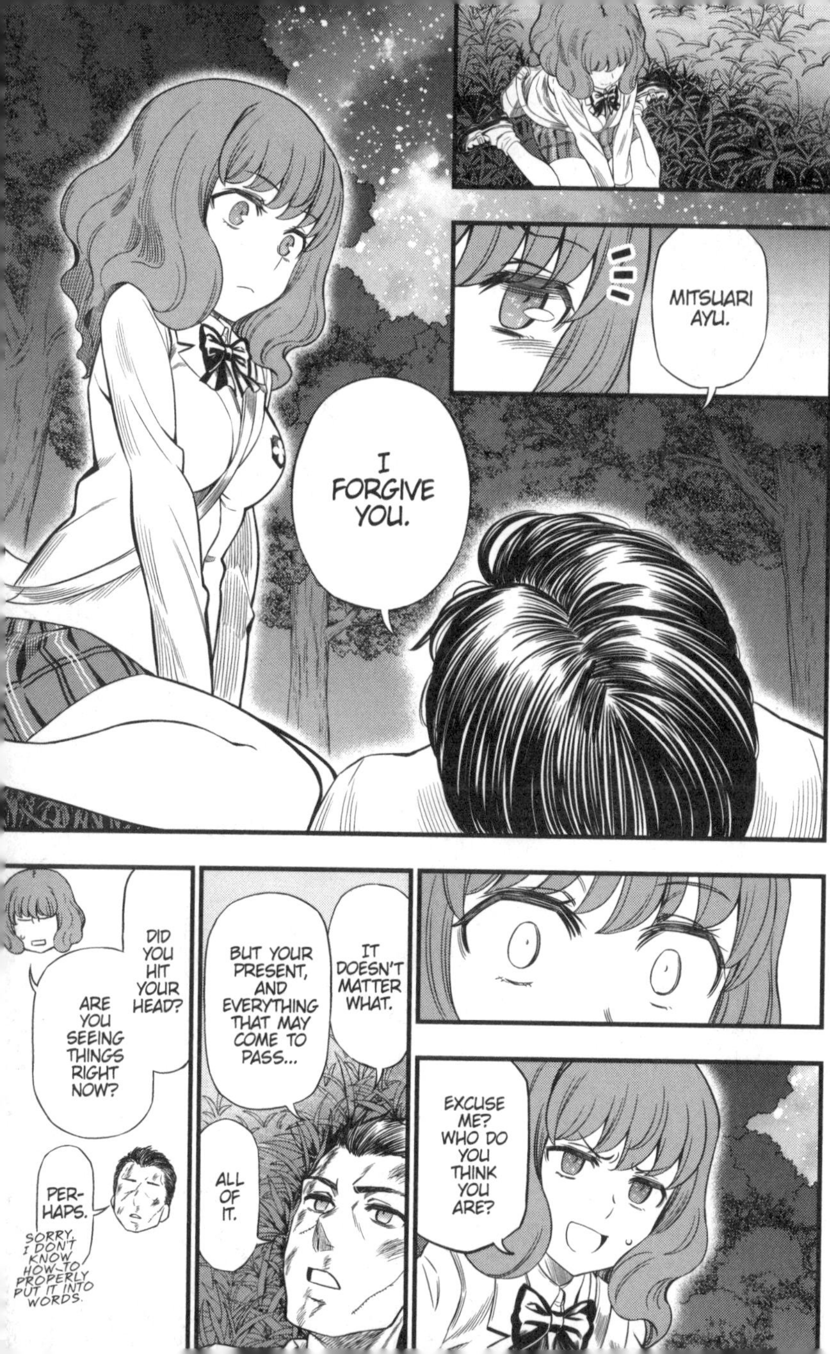
MITSUARI AYU.
I FORGIVE YOU.
EXCUSE ME? WHO DO YOU THINK YOU ARE?
IT DOESN'T MATTER WHAT.
BUT YOUR PRESENT, AND EVERYTHING THAT MAY COME TO PASS...
ALL OF IT.
DID YOU HIT YOUR HEAD?
ARE YOU SEEING THINGS RIGHT NOW?
PER-HAPS.
SORRY, I DON'T KNOW HOW TO PROPERLY PUT IT INTO WORDS.

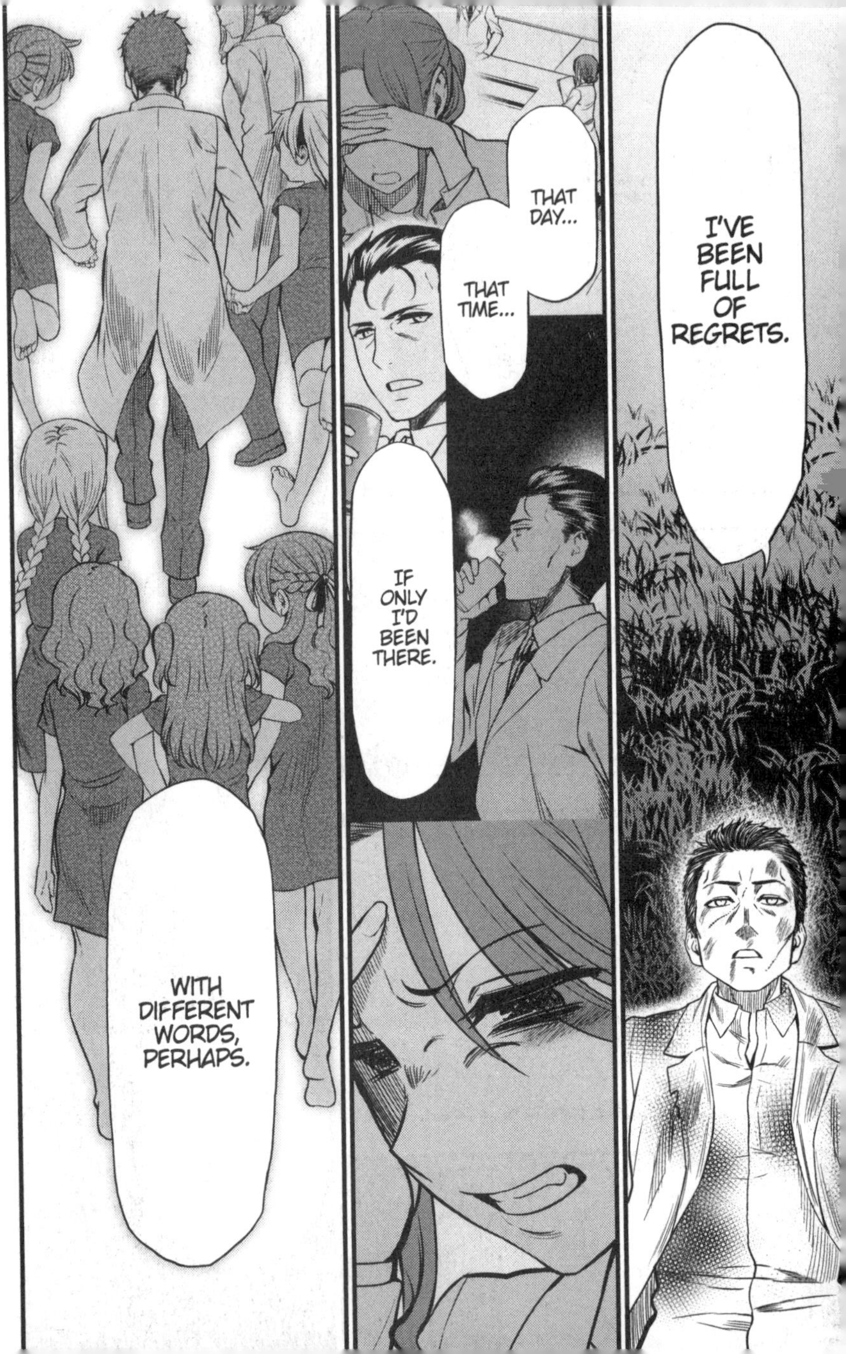
I'VE BEEN FULL OF REGRETS.
THAT DAY...
THAT TIME...
IF ONLY I'D BEEN THERE.
WITH DIFFERENT WORDS, PERHAPS.

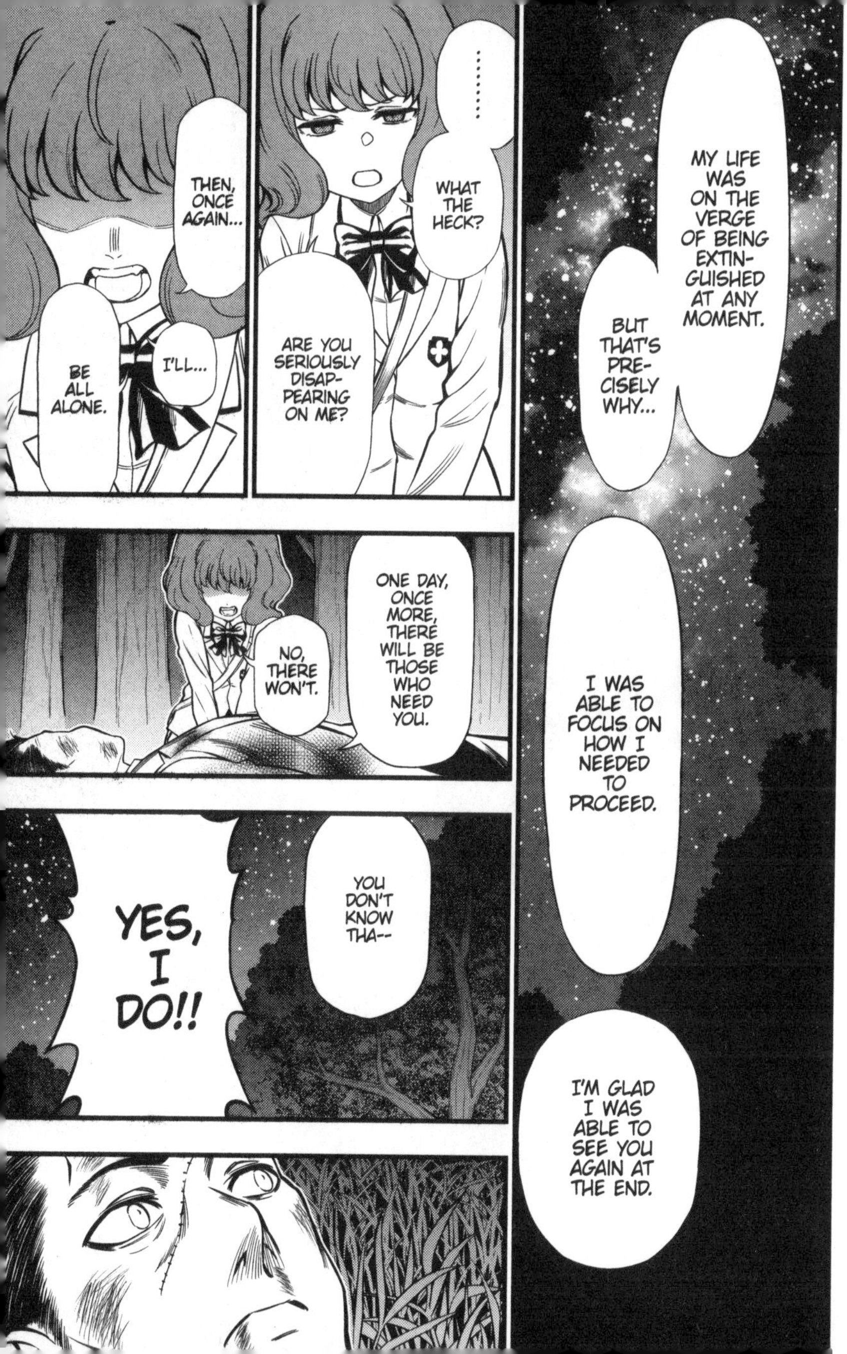
MY LIFE WAS ON THE VERGE OF BEING EXTIN-GUISHED AT ANY MOMENT.
BUT THAT'S PRE-CISELY WHY...
I WAS ABLE TO FOCUS ON HOW I NEEDED TO PROCEED.
I'M GLAD I WAS ABLE TO SEE YOU AGAIN AT THE END.
......
WHAT THE HECK?
ARE YOU SERIOUSLY DISAP-PEARING ON ME?
THEN, ONCE AGAIN...
I'LL...
BE ALL ALONE.
ONE DAY, ONCE MORE, THERE WILL BE THOSE WHO NEED YOU.
NO, THERE WON'T.
YOU DON'T KNOW THA--
YES, I DO!!

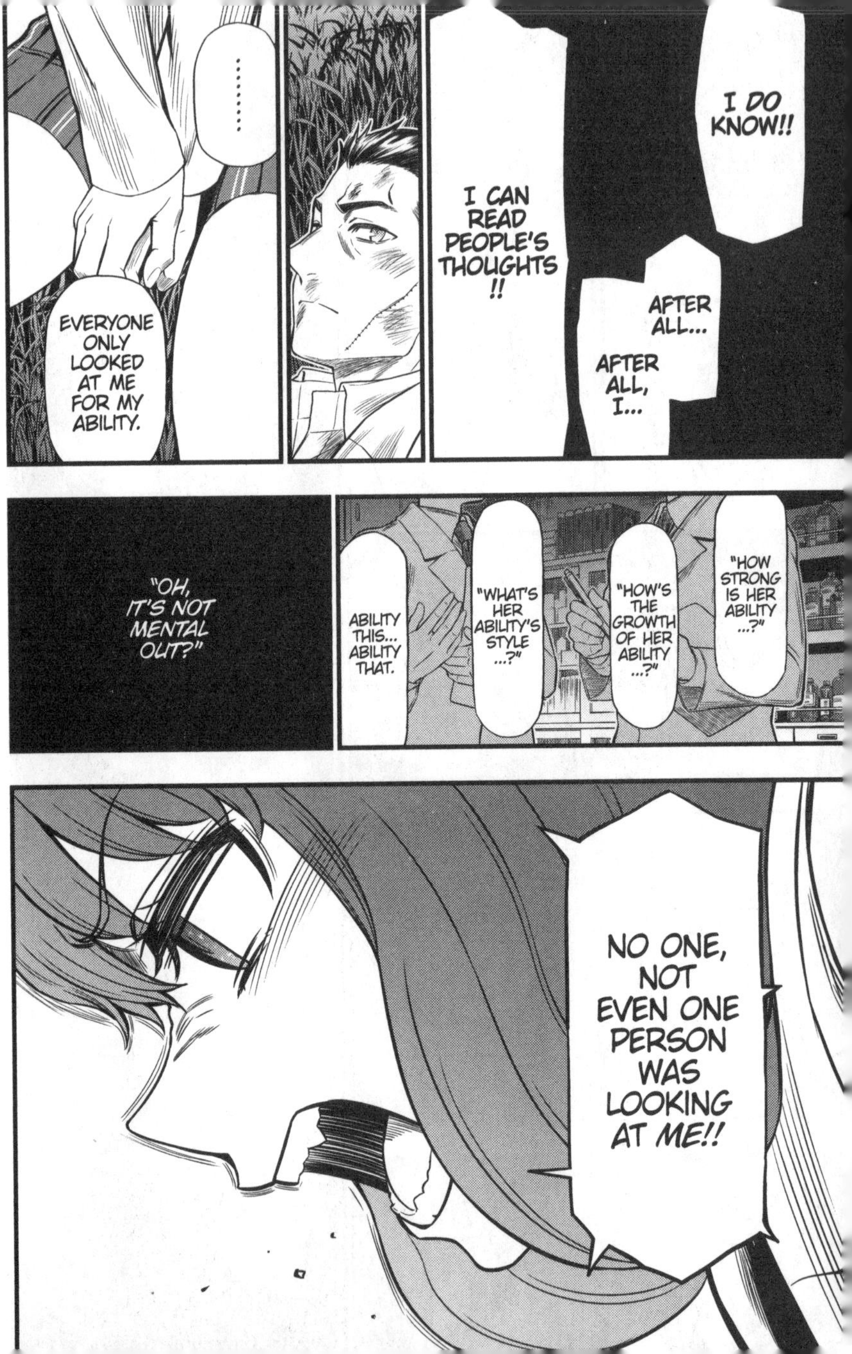

I DO KNOW!!
AFTER ALL...
AFTER ALL, I...
I CAN READ PEOPLE'S THOUGHTS!!
......
EVERYONE ONLY LOOKED AT ME FOR MY ABILITY.
"HOW STRONG IS HER ABILITY...?"
"HOW'S THE GROWTH OF HER ABILITY...?"
"WHAT'S HER ABILITY'S STYLE...?"
ABILITY THIS... ABILITY THAT.
"OH, IT'S NOT MENTAL OUT?"
NO ONE, NOT EVEN ONE PERSON WAS LOOKING AT ME!!

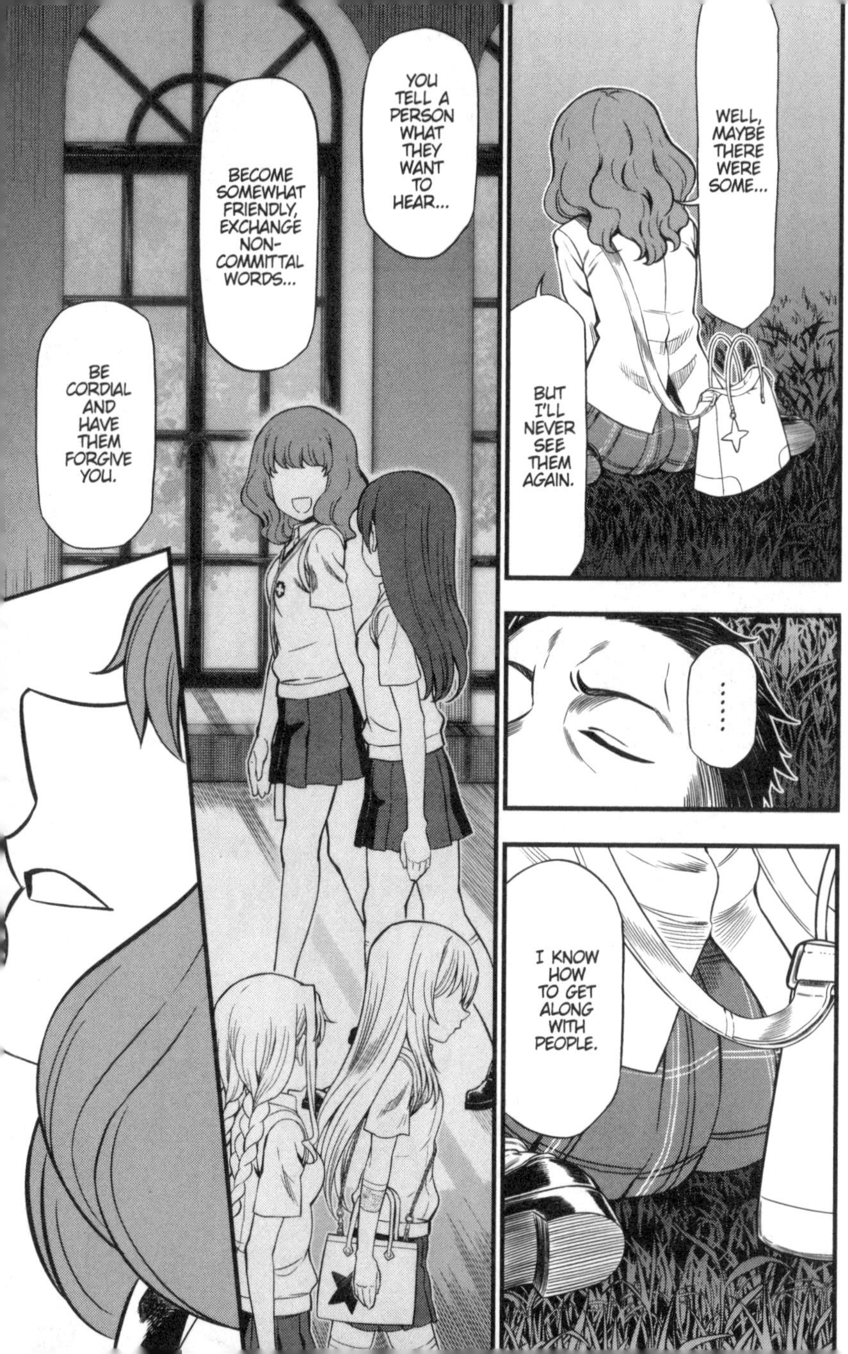
WELL, MAYBE THERE WERE SOME...
BUT I'LL NEVER SEE THEM AGAIN.
......
I KNOW HOW TO GET ALONG WITH PEOPLE.
YOU TELL A PERSON WHAT THEY WANT TO HEAR...
BECOME SOMEWHAT FRIENDLY, EXCHANGE NON-COMMITTAL WORDS...
BE CORDIAL AND HAVE THEM FORGIVE YOU.

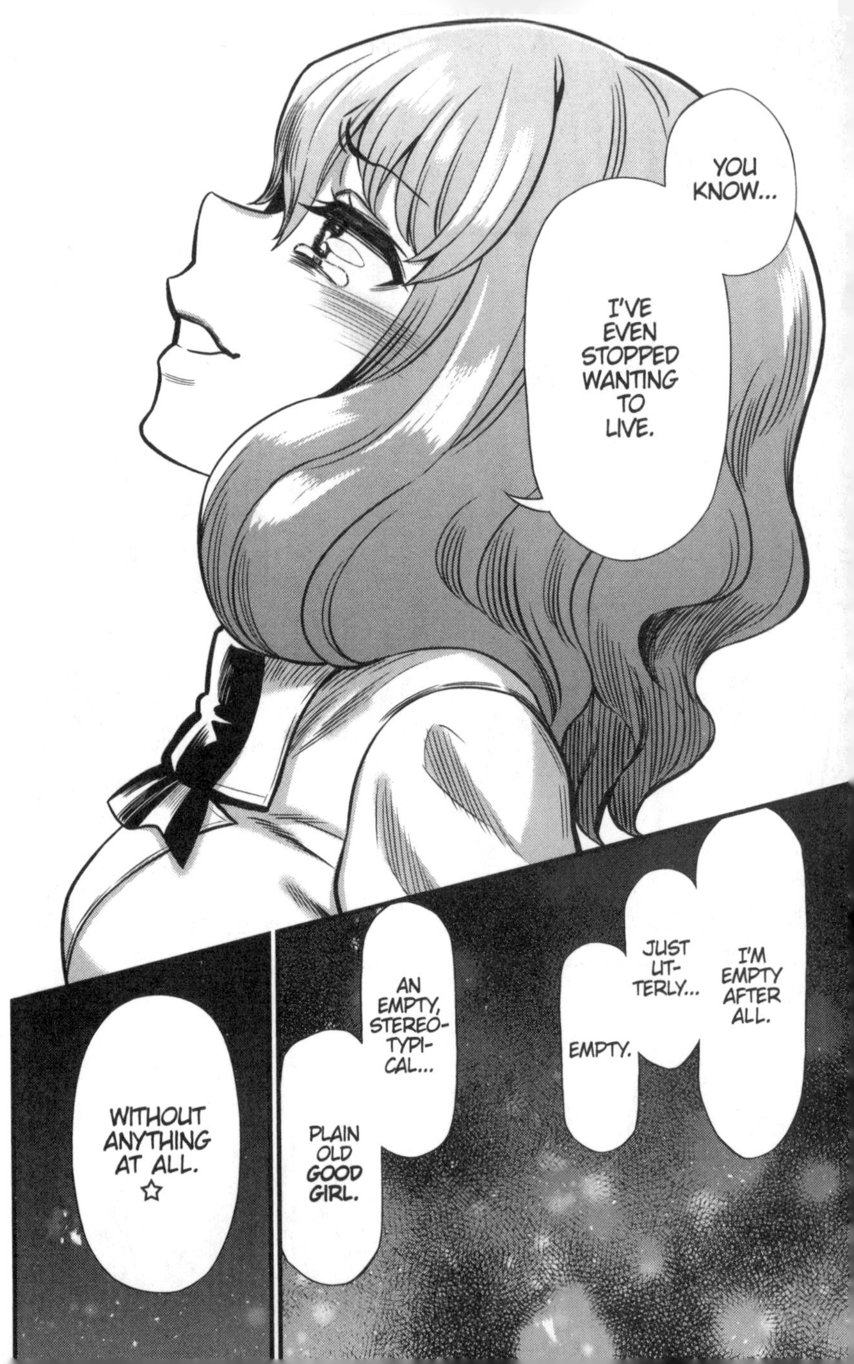
YOU KNOW...
I'VE EVEN STOPPED WANTING TO LIVE.
I'M EMPTY AFTER ALL.
JUST UT-TERLY...
EMPTY.
AN EMPTY, STEREO-TYPI-CAL...
PLAIN OLD GOOD GIRL.
WITHOUT ANYTHING AT ALL. ☆

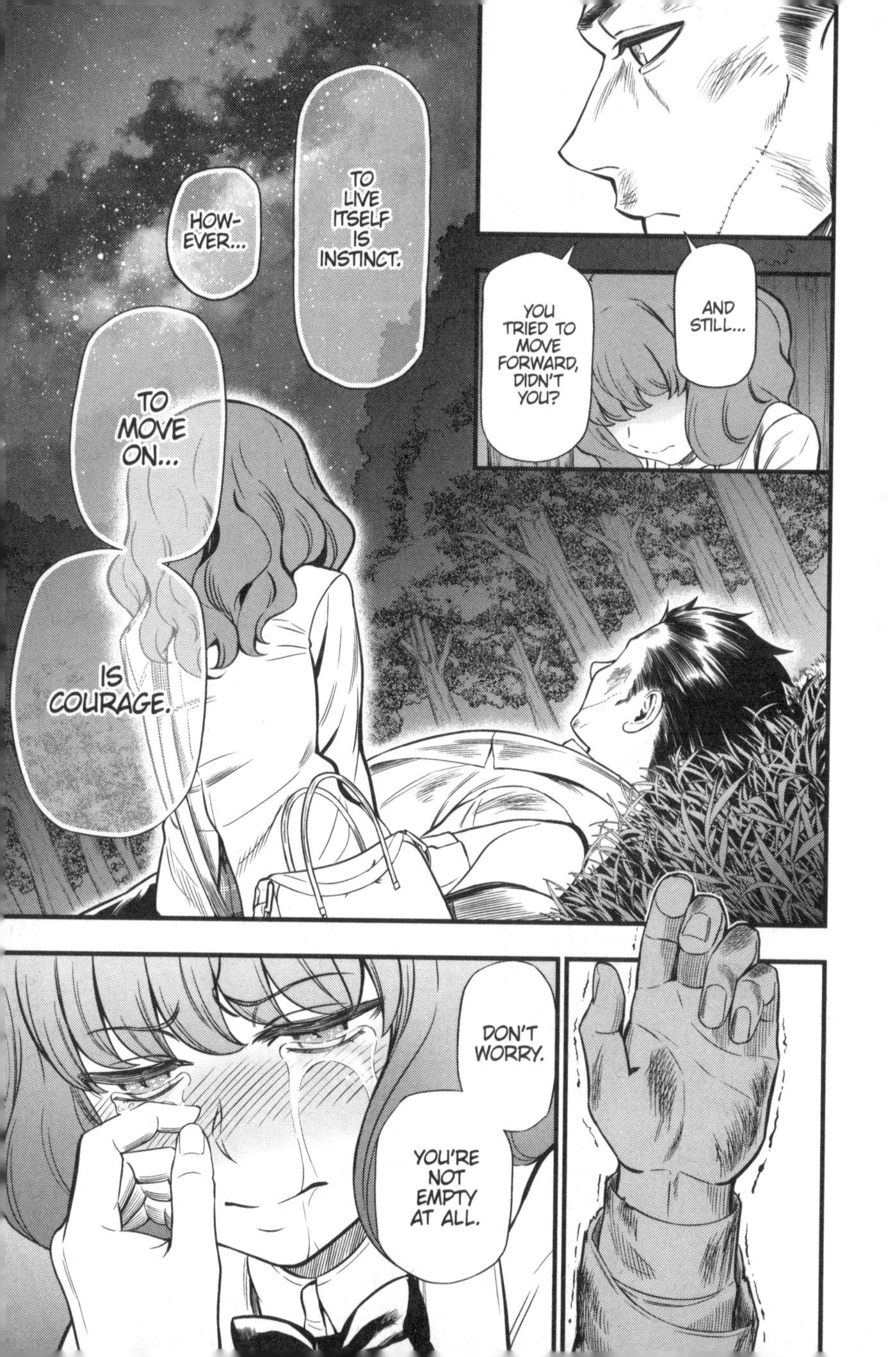
AND STILL...
YOU TRIED TO MOVE FORWARD, DIDN'T YOU?
TO LIVE ITSELF IS INSTINCT.
HOW-EVER...
TO MOVE ON...
IS COURAGE.
DON'T WORRY.
YOU'RE NOT EMPTY AT ALL.

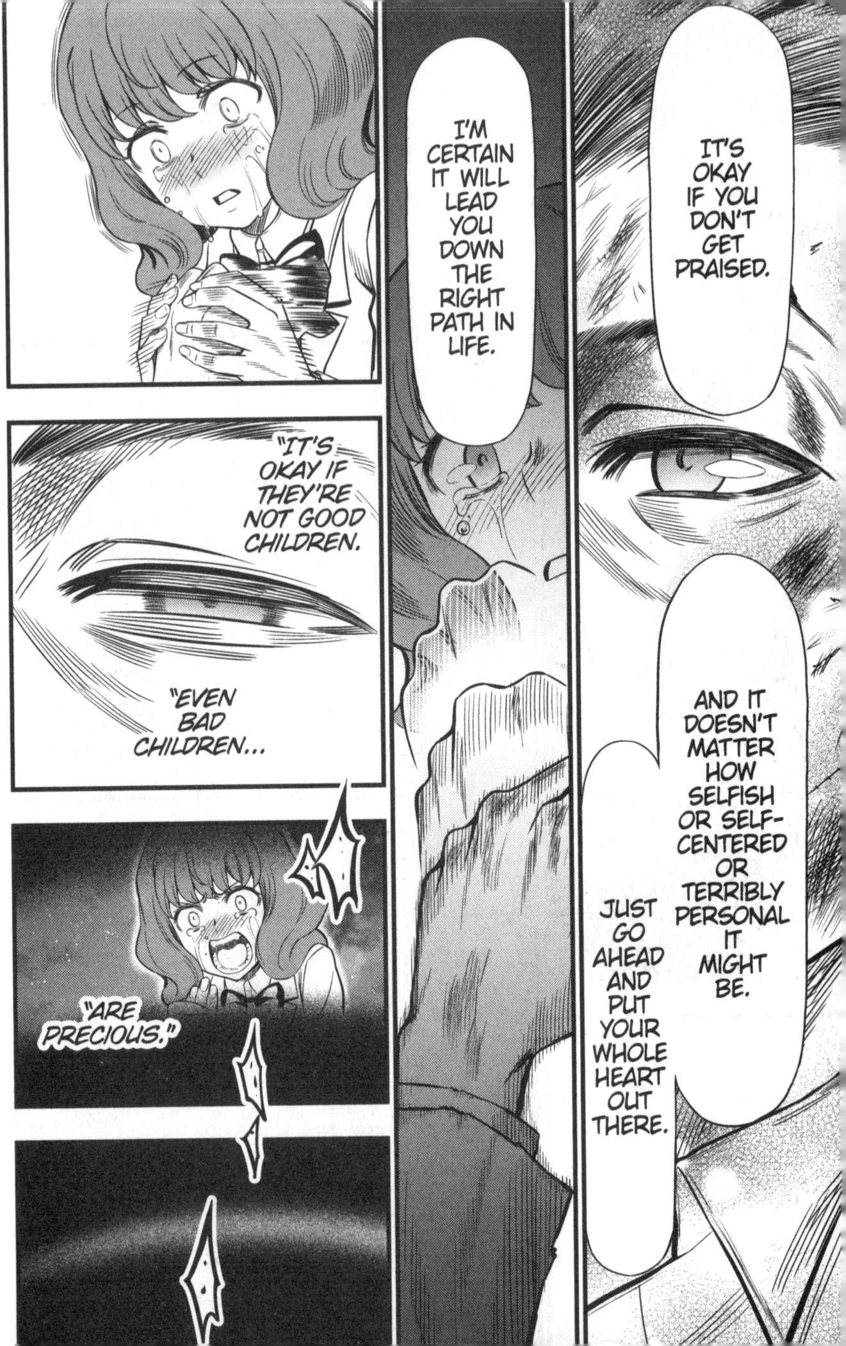
IT'S OKAY IF YOU DON'T GET PRAISED.
I'M CERTAIN IT WILL LEAD YOU DOWN THE RIGHT PATH IN LIFE.
AND IT DOESN'T MATTER HOW SELFISH OR SELF-CENTERED OR TERRIBLY PERSONAL IT MIGHT BE.
JUST GO AHEAD AND PUT YOUR WHOLE HEART OUT THERE.
"IT'S OKAY IF THEY'RE NOT GOOD CHILDREN.
"EVEN BAD CHILDREN...
"ARE PRECIOUS."

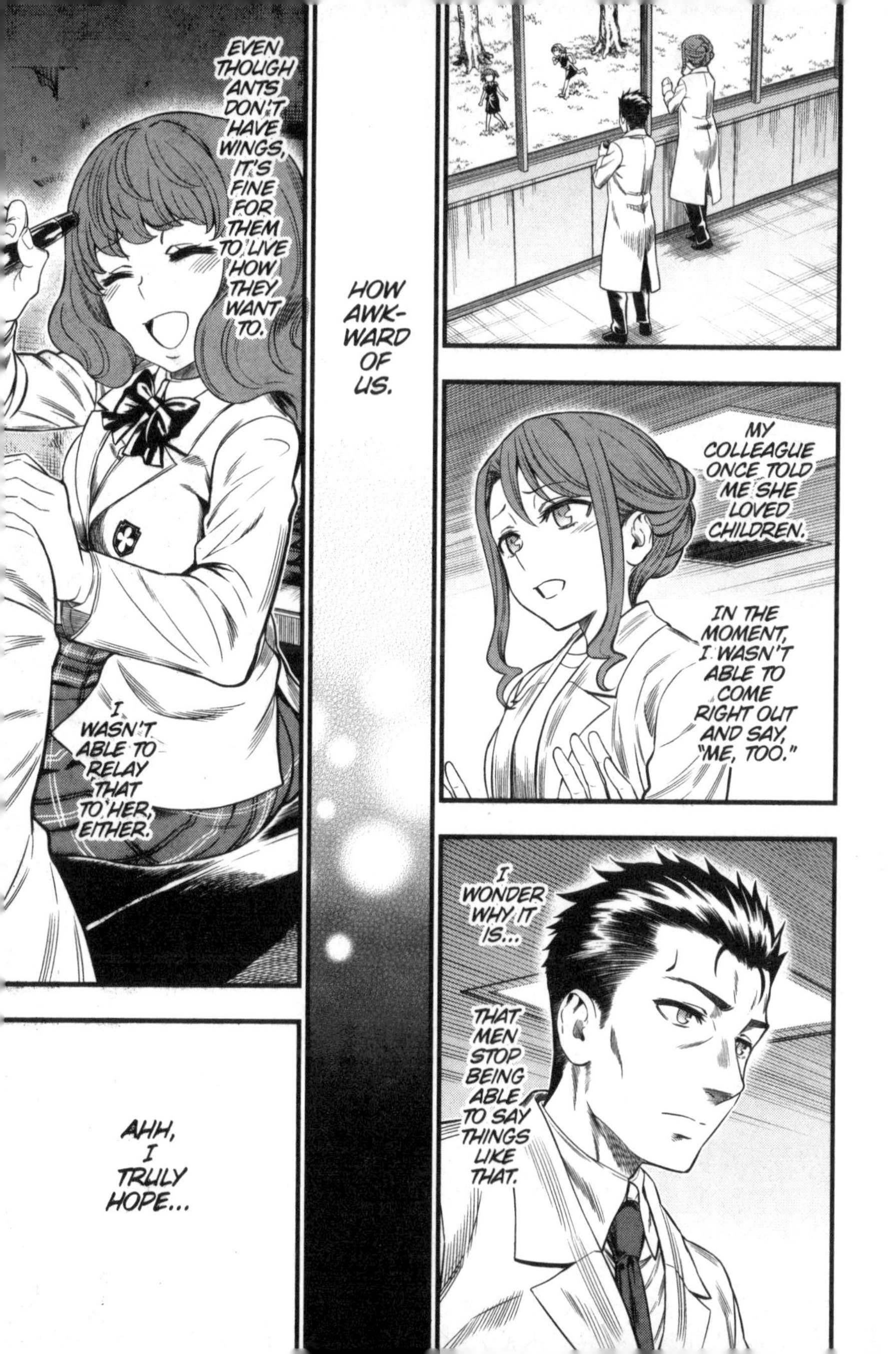
MY COLLEAGUE ONCE TOLD ME SHE LOVED CHILDREN.
IN THE MOMENT, I WASN'T ABLE TO COME RIGHT OUT AND SAY, "ME, TOO."
I WONDER WHY IT IS...
THAT MEN STOP BEING ABLE TO SAY THINGS LIKE THAT.
HOW AWK-WARD OF US.
EVEN THOUGH ANTS DON'T HAVE WINGS, IT'S FINE FOR THEM TO LIVE HOW THEY WANT TO.
I WASN'T ABLE TO RELAY THAT TO HER, EITHER.
AHH, I TRULY HOPE...

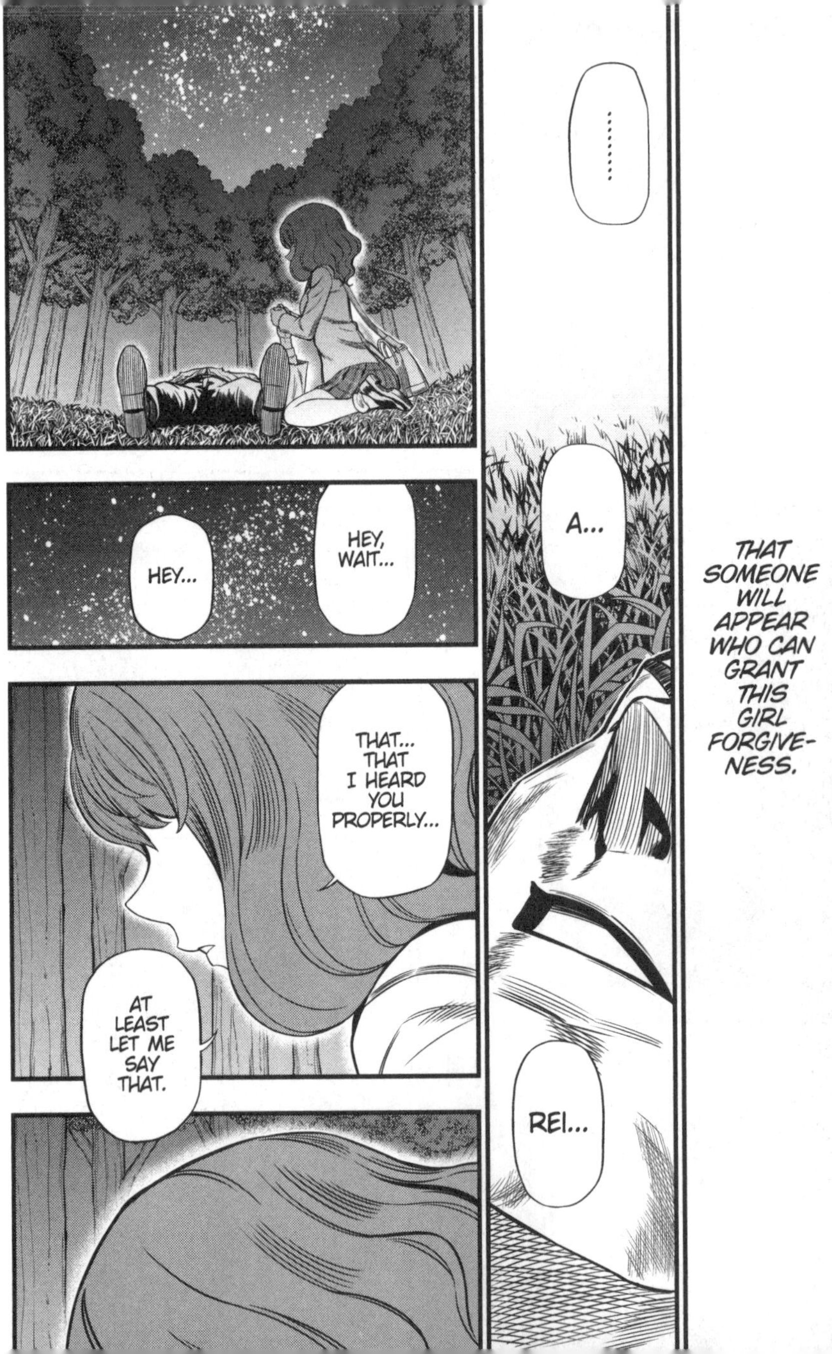
……
A…
REI…
THAT SOMEONE WILL APPEAR WHO CAN GRANT THIS GIRL FORGIVE-NESS.
HEY, WAIT…
HEY…
THAT… THAT I HEARD YOU PROPERLY…
AT LEAST LET ME SAY THAT.

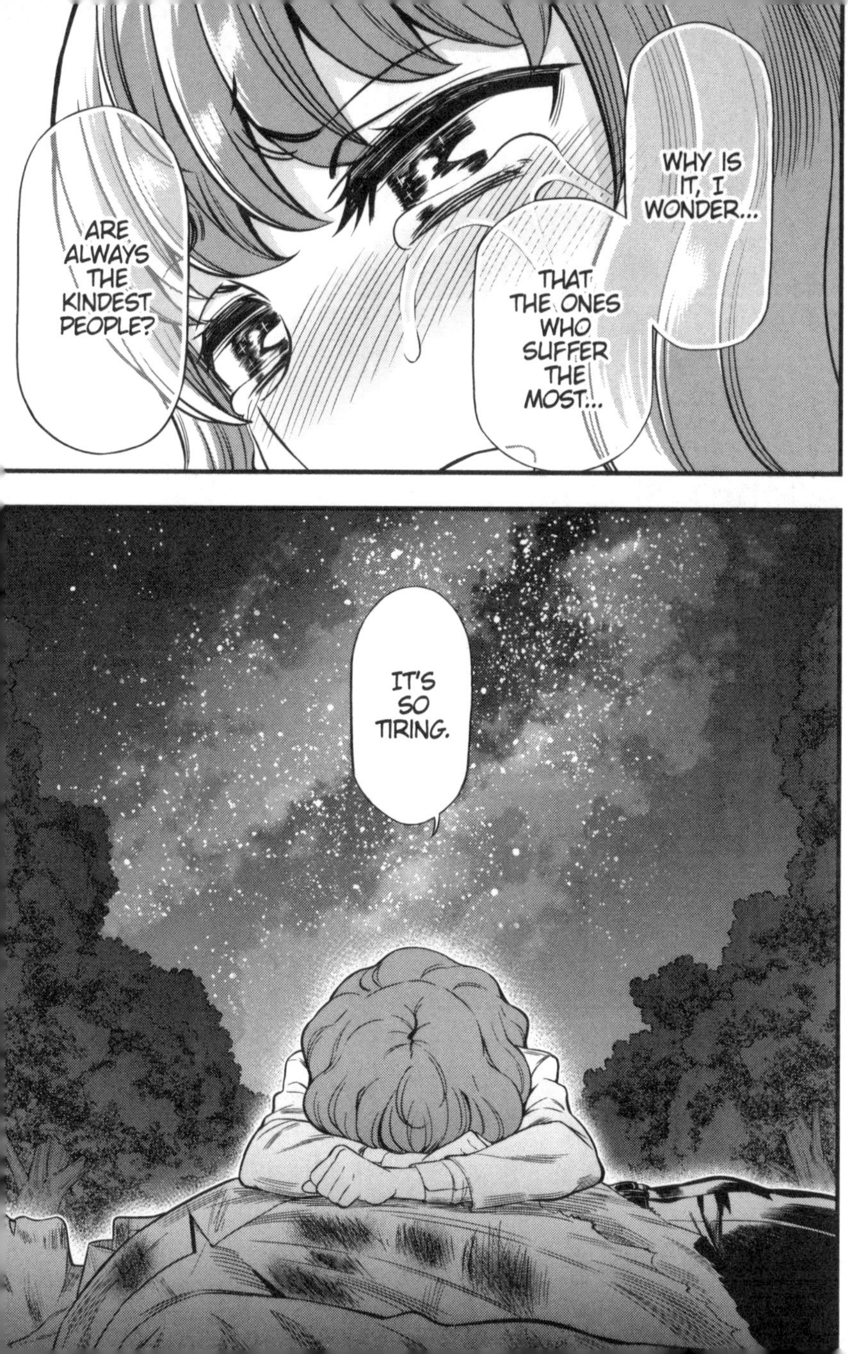
WHY IS IT, I WONDER...
THAT THE ONES WHO SUFFER THE MOST...
ARE ALWAYS THE KINDEST PEOPLE?
IT'S SO TIRING.

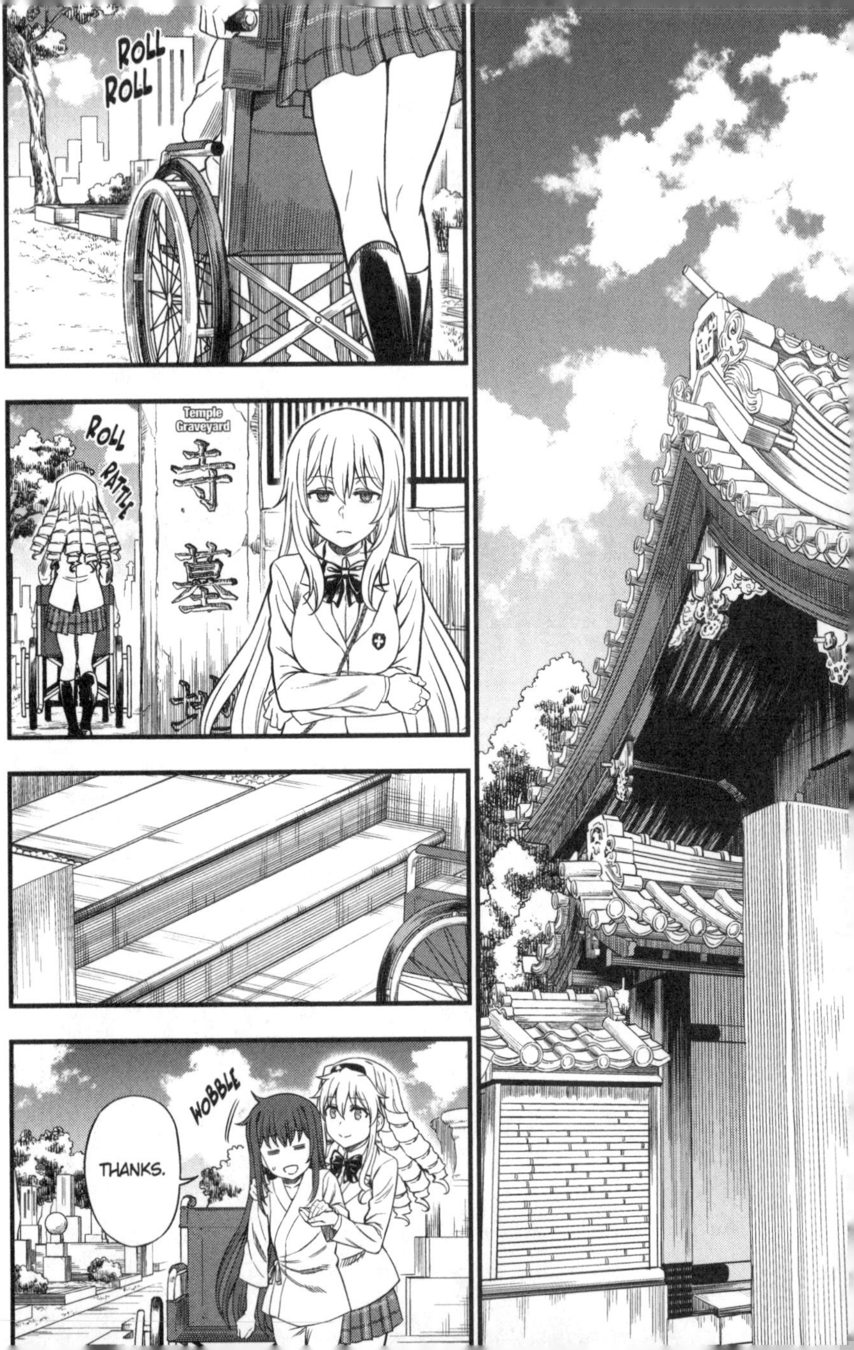
ROLL ROLL
Temple Graveyard
寺墓
ROLL RATTLE
WOBBLE
THANKS.

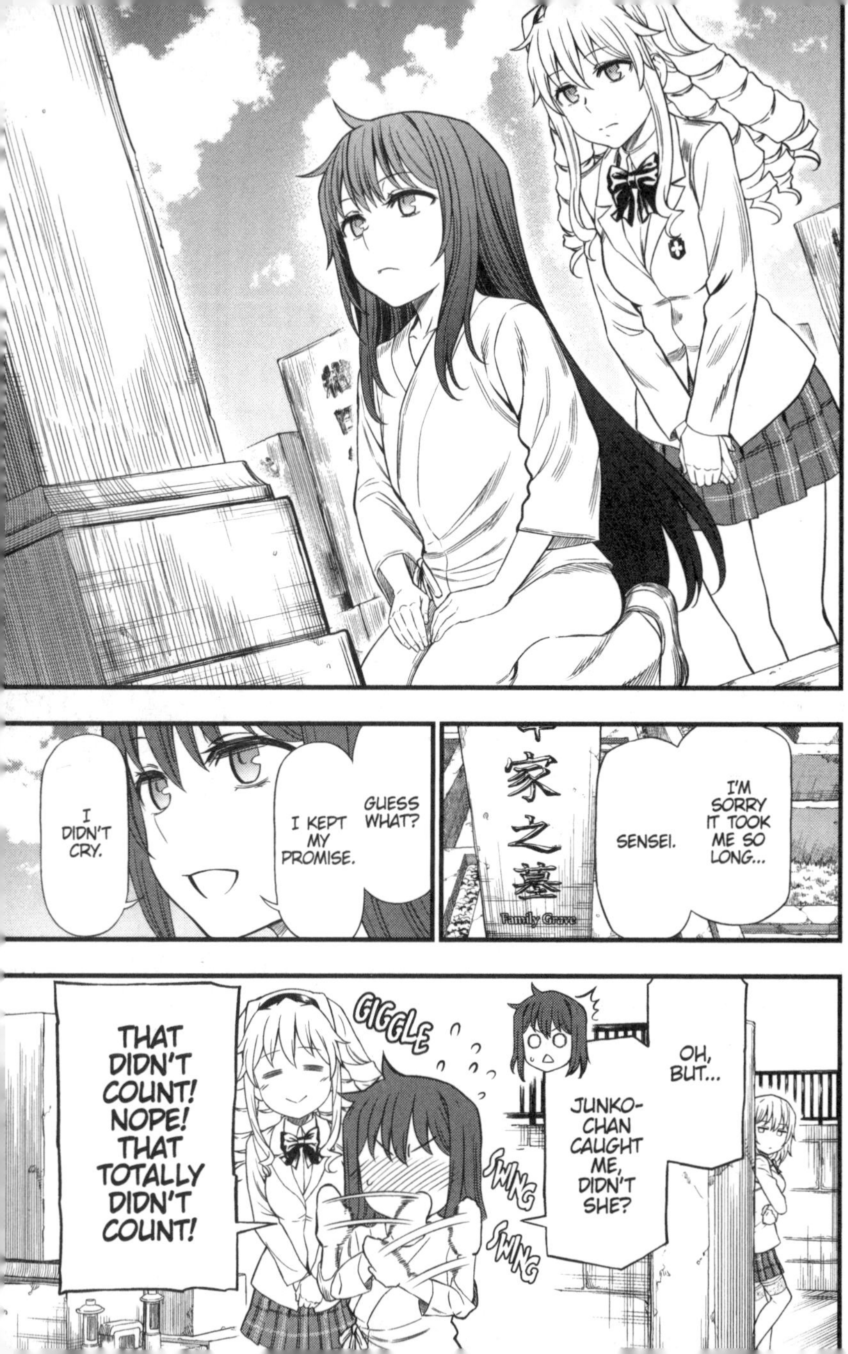
I'M SORRY IT TOOK ME SO LONG...
SENSEI.
家之墓
Family Grave
GUESS WHAT?
I KEPT MY PROMISE.
I DIDN'T CRY.
OH, BUT...
JUNKO-CHAN CAUGHT ME, DIDN'T SHE?
SWING
SWING
GIGGLE
THAT DIDN'T COUNT! NOPE! THAT TOTALLY DIDN'T COUNT!

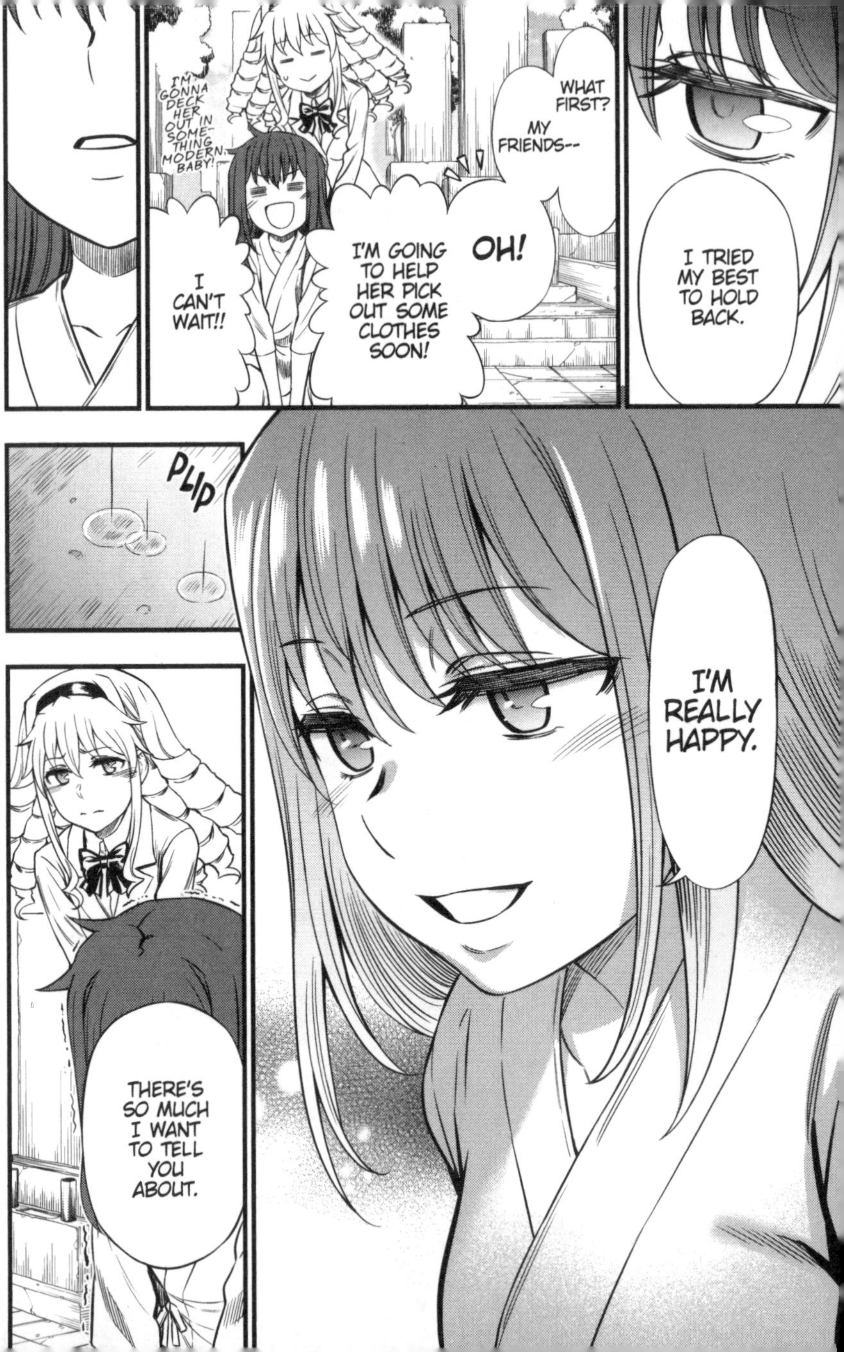
I TRIED MY BEST TO HOLD BACK.
WHAT FIRST? MY FRIENDS--
OH!
I'M GOING TO HELP HER PICK OUT SOME CLOTHES SOON!
I'M GONNA DECK HER OUT IN SOMETHING MODERN, BABY!
I CAN'T WAIT!!
I'M REALLY HAPPY.
PLIP
THERE'S SO MUCH I WANT TO TELL YOU ABOUT.

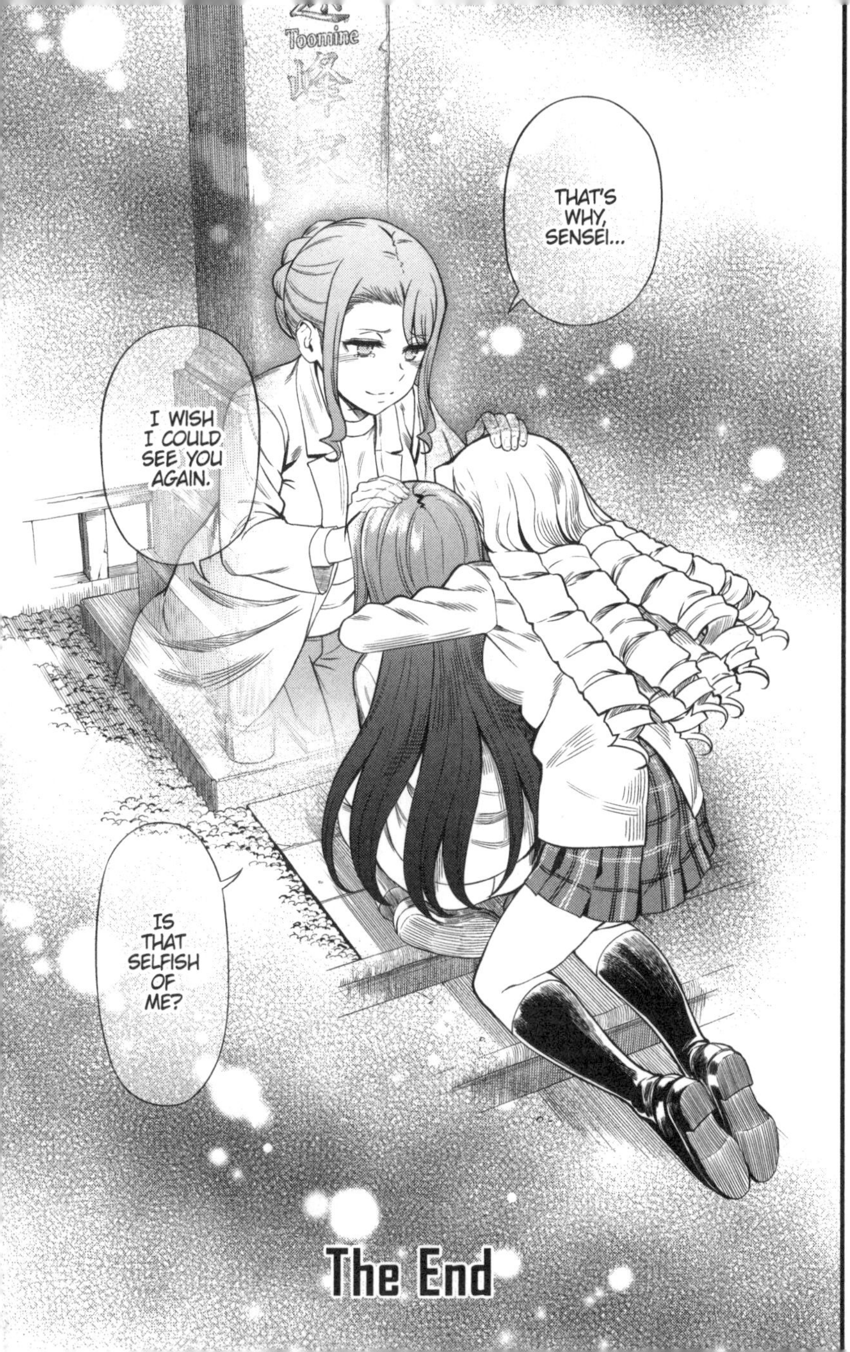
Toomine
THAT'S WHY, SENSEI...
I WISH I COULD SEE YOU AGAIN.
IS THAT SELFISH OF ME?
The End

A CERTAIN SCIENTIFIC RAILGUN
Astral*Buddy

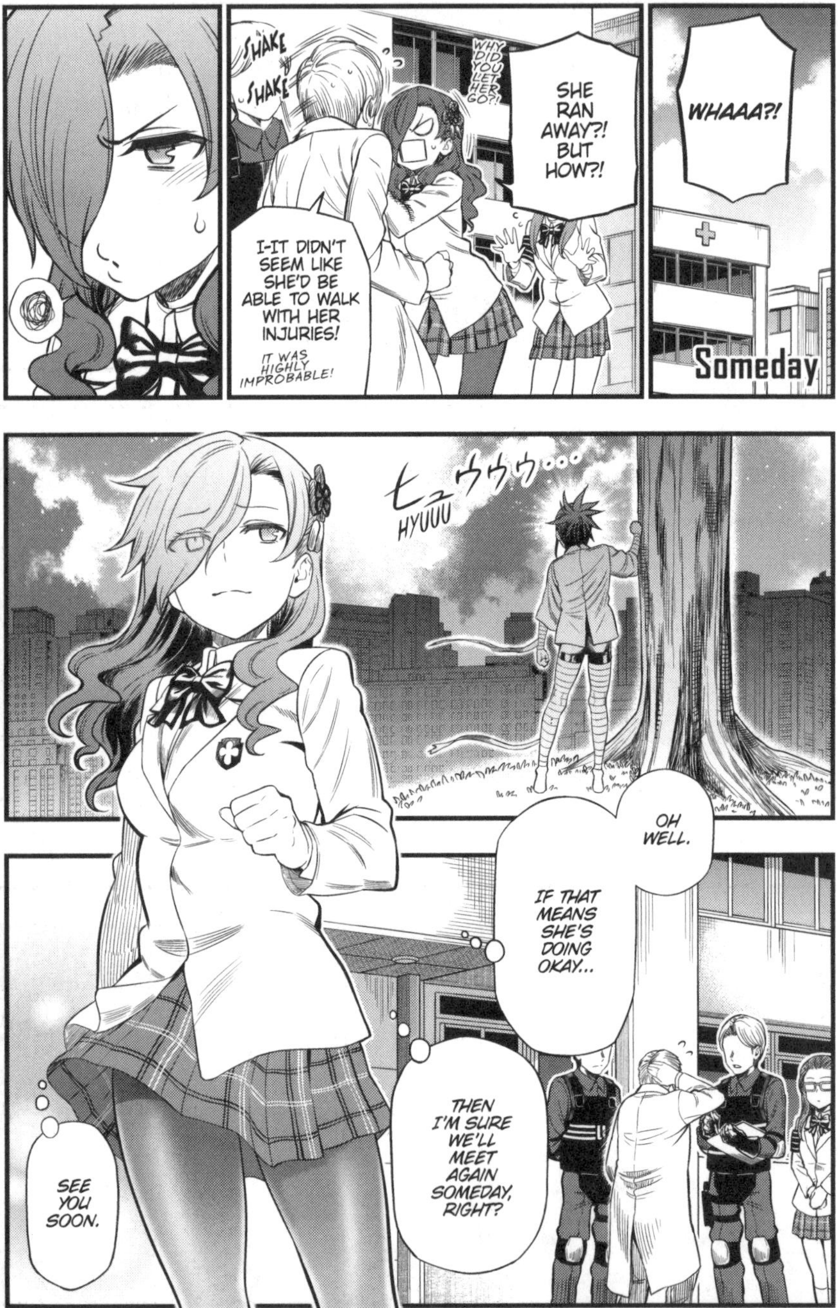
Someday
WHAAA?!
SHE RAN AWAY?! BUT HOW?!
WHY DID YOU LET HER GO?!
SHAKE SHAKE
I-IT DIDN'T SEEM LIKE SHE'D BE ABLE TO WALK WITH HER INJURIES!
IT WAS HIGHLY IMPROBABLE!
ヒュウウウ…
HYUUU
OH WELL.
IF THAT MEANS SHE'S DOING OKAY...
THEN I'M SURE WE'LL MEET AGAIN SOMEDAY, RIGHT?
SEE YOU SOON.

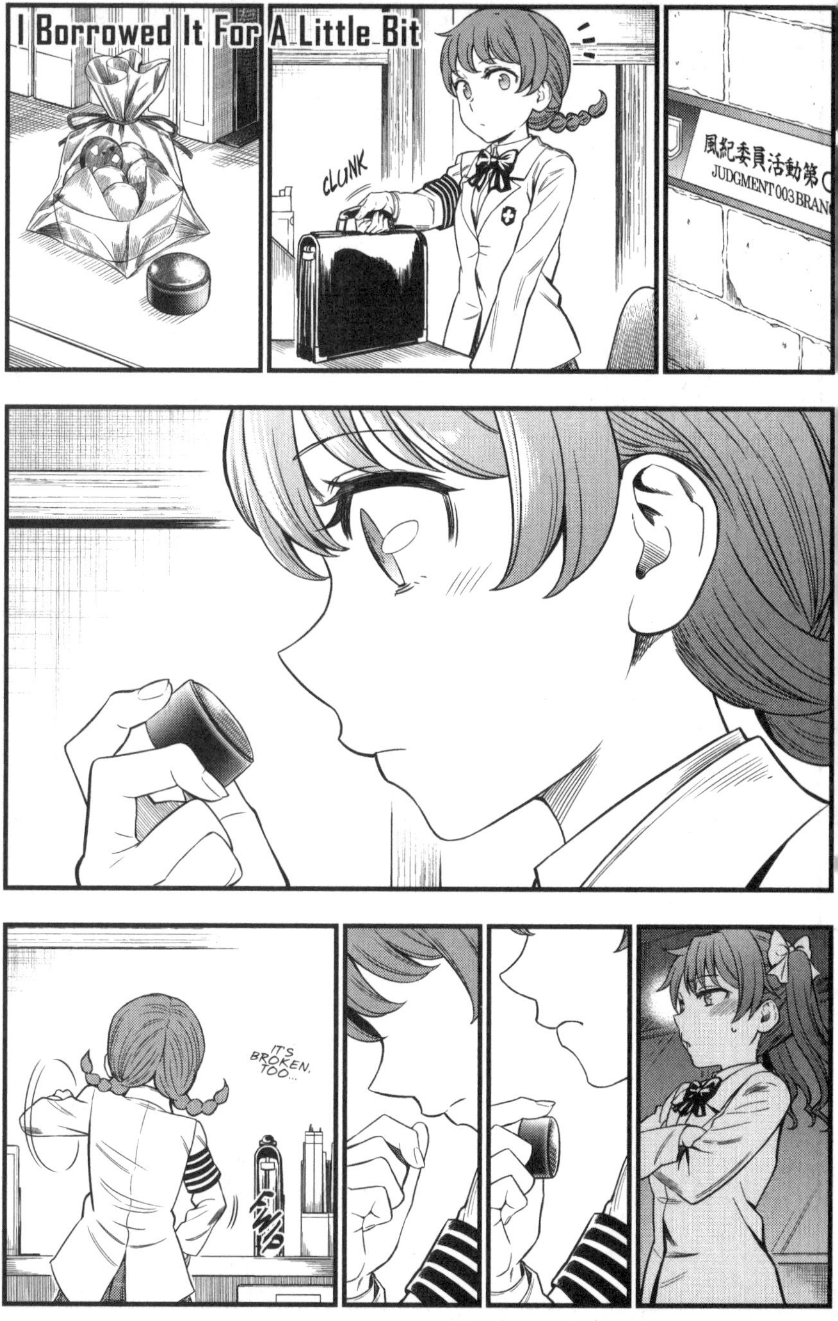
I Borrowed It For A Little Bit
CLUNK
風紀委員活動第
JUDGMENT 003 BRAN
IT'S BROKEN, TOO...
FWIP

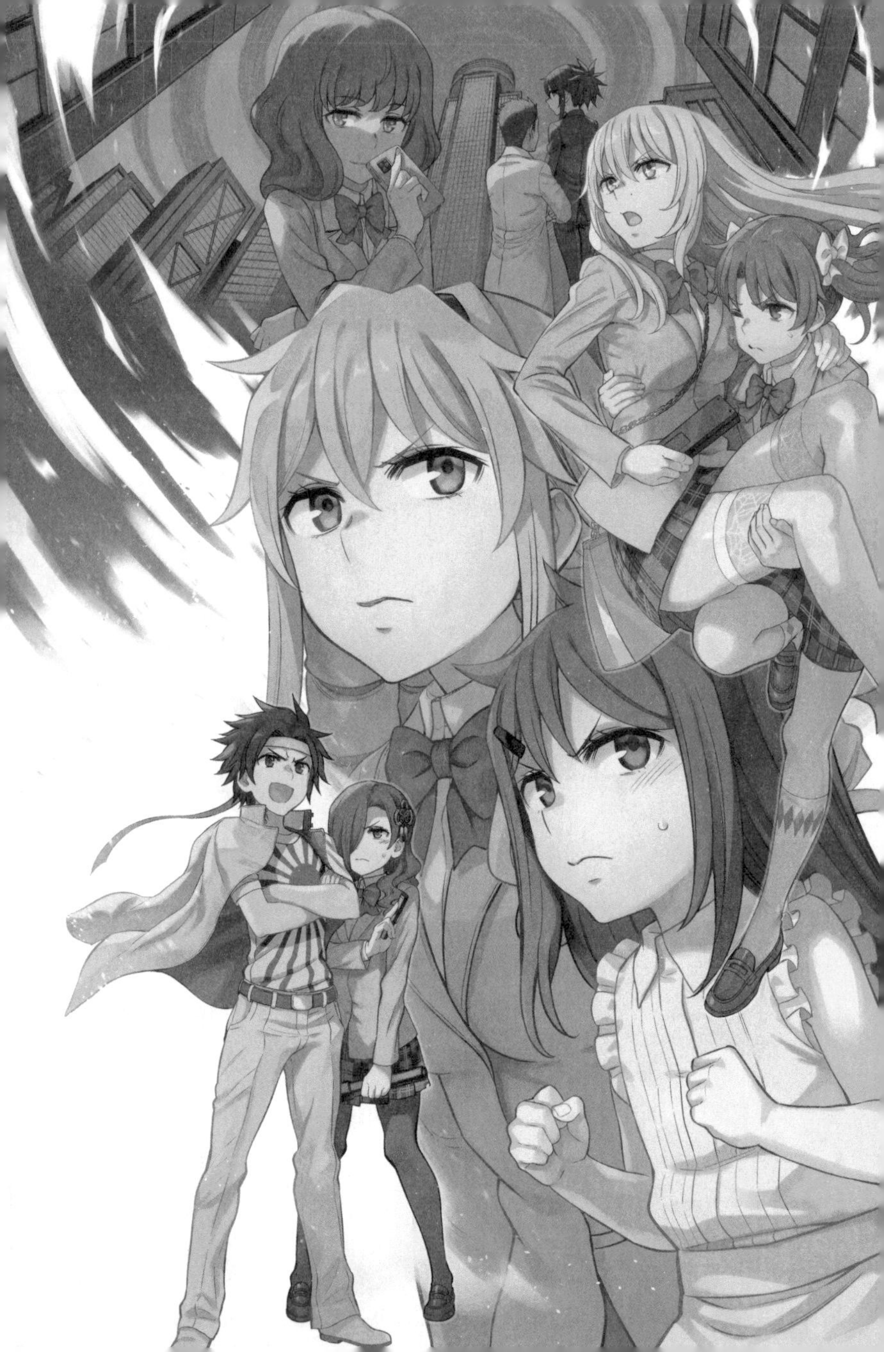

A CERTAIN SCIENTIFIC RAILGUN

Astral*Buddy

A CERTAIN
SCIENTIFIC RAILGUN

Astral ☀ Buddy